BODY OF
SECRETS

Also by James Bamford

The Puzzle Palace

ANATOMY OF THE ULTRA-SECRET NATIONAL SECURITY AGENCY

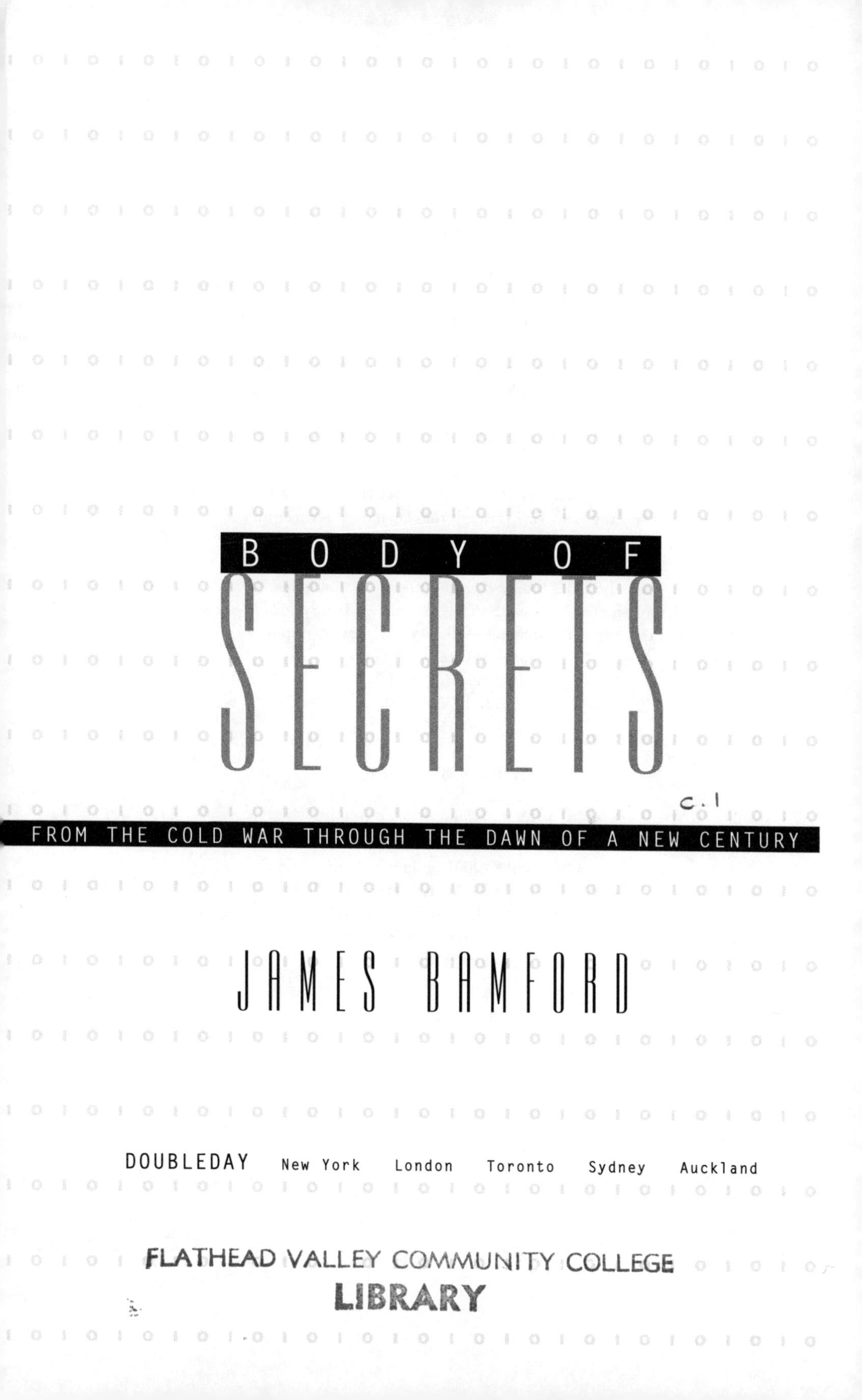

BODY OF SECRETS

FROM THE COLD WAR THROUGH THE DAWN OF A NEW CENTURY

c. 1

JAMES BAMFORD

DOUBLEDAY New York London Toronto Sydney Auckland

PUBLISHED BY DOUBLEDAY
A division of Random House, Inc.
1540 Broadway, New York, New York 10036

DOUBLEDAY and the portrayal of an anchor with a dolphin are trademarks of Doubleday, a division of Random House, Inc.

Library of Congress Cataloging-in-Publication Data

Bamford, James.
Body of secrets: anatomy of the ultra-secret National Security Agency: from the Cold War through the dawn of a new century / James Bamford.—1st ed.
p. cm.
Includes bibliographical references and index.
1. United States. National Security Agency—History. 2. Electronic intelligence—United States—History. 3. Cryptography—United States—History. I. Title.
UB256.U6 B36 2001
327.1273—dc21
00-058920

ISBN 0-385-49907-8

Book design by Maria Carella

Printed in the United States of America
May 2001
First Edition
5 7 9 10 8 6

To Mary Ann

And to my father, Vincent

And in memory of my mother, Katherine

ACKNOWLEDGMENTS

My most sincere thanks to the many people who helped bring *Body of Secrets* to life. Lieutenant General Michael V. Hayden, NSA's director, had the courage to open the agency's door a crack. Major General John E. Morrison (Retired), the dean of the U.S. intelligence community, was always gracious and accommodating in pointing me in the right directions. Deborah Price suffered through my endless Freedom of Information Act requests with professionalism and good humor. Judith Emmel and Colleen Garrett helped guide me through the labyrinths of Crypto City. Jack Ingram, Dr. David Hatch, Jennifer Wilcox, and Rowena Clough of NSA's National Cryptologic Museum provided endless help in researching the agency's past.

Critical was the help of those who fought on the front lines of the cryptologic wars, including George A. Cassidy, Richard G. Schmucker, Marvin Nowicki, John Arnold, Harry O. Rakfeldt, David Parks, John Mastro, Wayne Madsen, Aubrey Brown, John R. DeChene, Bryce Lockwood, Richard McCarthy, Don McClarren, Stuart Russell, Richard E. Kerr, Jr., James Miller, and many others. My grateful appreciation to all those named and unnamed.

Thanks also to David J. Haight and Dwight E. Strandberg of the Dwight D. Eisenhower Presidential Library and to Thomas E. Samoluk of the U.S. Assassinations Records Review Board.

Finally I would like to thank those who helped give birth to *Body of Secrets*, including Kris Dahl, my agent at International Creative Management; Shawn Coyne, my editor at Doubleday; and Bill Thomas, Bette Alexander, Jolanta Benal, Lauren Field, Chris Min, Timothy Hsu, and Sean Desmond.

CONTENTS

"In God we trust, all others we monitor."
—Intercept operator's motto

NSA study, *Deadly Transmissions,* December 1970

"The public has a duty to watch its Government closely and keep it on the right track."

Lieutenant General Kenneth A. Minihan, USAF
Director, National Security Agency
NSA Newsletter, June 1997

"The American people have to trust us and in order to trust us they have to know about us."

Lieutenant General Michael V. Hayden, USAF
Director, National Security Agency
Address on October 19, 2000

"Behind closed doors, there is no guarantee that the most basic of individual freedoms will be preserved. And as we enter the 21st Century, the great fear we have for our democracy is the enveloping culture of government secrecy and the corresponding distrust of government that follows."

Senators Daniel Patrick Moynihan and Rob Wyden
U.S. Senate Report, *Secrecy in International and Domestic Policy Making: The Case for More Sunshine,*
October 2000

CHAPTER ONE

MEMORY

KVZIEBCEN CKYIECDVG DBCOOVK HN CKYCFEUFJ ECZHIKUCF MIBEVG
FHOHFD NQXVWXIV NWQFWQG HG IHF FH EQF AB EWHB XI GAEEXD
WJP JZPWC ABCADL WP TYA RIW 'DYPJ YPWBOYS' XL AXLB APYTIOWL
ENTOJXGCM FVMMCD ND ENJBMD FGXMD VGXM OG BMDO
RPI EKFSKRPJV QXUVAZPJ QXSHJXSAVP HJXHXVKE LXJ Z.Q. JPLXJSV

His step had an unusual urgency to it. Not fast, but anxious, like a child heading out to recess who had been warned not to run. It was late morning and the warm, still air had turned heavy with moisture, causing others on the long hallway to walk with a slow shuffle, a sort of somber march. In June 1930, the boxy, sprawling Munitions Building, near the Washington Monument, was a study in monotony. Endless corridors connecting to endless corridors. Walls a shade of green common to bad cheese and fruit. Forests of oak desks separated down the middle by rows of tall columns, like concrete redwoods, each with a number designating a particular workspace.

Oddly, he made a sudden left turn into a nearly deserted wing. It was lined with closed doors containing dim, opaque windows and empty name holders. Where was he going, they wondered, attempting to keep up with him as beads of perspiration wetted their brows. At thirty-eight years old, the Russian-born William Frederick Friedman had spent most of his adult life studying, practicing, defining the black art of codebreaking. The year before, he had been appointed the chief and sole employee of a secret new Army organization responsible for analyzing and cracking foreign codes and ciphers. Now, at last, his one-man Signal Intelligence Service actually had employees, three of them, who were attempting to keep pace close behind.

Halfway down the hall Friedman turned right into Room 3416, a small office containing a massive black vault, the kind found in large banks. Reaching into his inside coat pocket, he removed a small card. Then, standing in front of the thick round combination dial to block the view, he began twisting the dial back and forth. Seconds later he yanked up the silver bolt and slowly pulled open the heavy door, only to reveal another wall of steel behind it. This time he removed a key from his trouser pocket and turned it in the lock, swinging aside the second door to reveal an interior as dark as a midnight lunar eclipse.

Disappearing into the void, he drew out a small box of matches and lit one. The gentle flame seemed to soften the hard lines of his face: the bony cheeks; the pursed, pencil-thin lips; the narrow mustache, as straight as a ruler; and the wisps of receding hair combed back tight against his scalp. Standing outside the vault were his three young hires. Now it was time to tell them the secret. Friedman yanked on the dangling cord attached to an overhead lightbulb, switched on a nearby fan to circulate the hot, stale air, and invited them in. "Welcome, gentlemen," he said solemnly, "to the secret archives of the American Black Chamber."

Until a few weeks before, none of the new recruits had had even the slightest idea what codebreaking was. Frank B. Rowlett stood next to a filing cabinet in full plumage: blue serge jacket, white pinstriped trousers, and a virgin pair of white suede shoes. Beefy and round-faced, with rimless glasses, he felt proud that he had luckily decided to wear his new wardrobe on this day. A high school teacher from rural southern Virginia, he received a degree in math the year earlier from Emory and Henry College, a small Virginia school.

The two men standing near Rowlett were a vision of contrasts. Short, bespectacled Abraham Sinkov; Brooklynite Solomon Kullback, tall and husky. Both were high school teachers from New York, both were graduates of City College in New York, and both had received master's degrees from Columbia.

Like a sorcerer instructing his disciples on the mystic path to eternal life, Friedman began his introduction into the shadowy history of American cryptology. In hushed tones he told his young employees about the Black Chamber, America's first civilian codebreaking organization. How for a decade it operated in utmost secrecy from a brownstone in New York City. How it skillfully decoded more than 10,000 messages from nearly two dozen nations, including those in difficult Japanese diplomatic code. How it played the key role in deciphering messages to and from the delegates to the post–World War I disarmament talks, thus giving the American delegation the inside track. He told of Herbert Osborne Yardley, the Black Chamber's hard-drinking, poker-playing chief, who had directed the Army's cryptanalytic activities during the war.

Then he related the story of the Chamber's demise eight months earlier. How the newly appointed secretary of state, Henry Stimson, had become outraged and ordered its immediate closing when he discovered that America was eavesdropping on friends as well as foes. Friedman told of the firing of Yardley and the rest of the Chamber's employees and of how the government had naively taken itself out of the code-breaking business.

It was a troubling prospect. If a new war were to break out, the United States would once again have to start from scratch. The advances achieved against Japan's codes would be lost forever. Foreign nations would gain great advantage while the United States clung to diplomatic niceties. Standing in the vault containing the salvaged records of the old Black Chamber, Friedman told his three assistants, fresh out of college, that they were now the new Black Chamber. The Army, he said, had given its cautious approval to secretly raise the organization from the ashes, hide it deep within the bureaucracy, and rename it the Signal Intelligence Service. The State Department, they were sternly warned, was never to know of its existence.

In late June 1930, America's entire cryptologic body of secrets—personnel, equipment and records—fit comfortably in a vault twenty-five feet square.

On the southbound lane of the Baltimore–Washington Parkway, near the sleepy Maryland hamlet of Annapolis Junction, a restricted, specially constructed exit ramp disappears quickly from view. Hidden by tall earthen berms and thick trees, the ramp leads to a labyrinth of barbed-wire fences, massive boulders placed close together, motion detectors, hydraulic antitruck devices, and thick cement barriers. During alerts, commandos dressed in black paramilitary uniforms, wearing special headgear, and brandishing an assortment of weapons including Colt 9mm submachine guns, quickly respond. They are known as the "Men in Black." Telephoto surveillance cameras peer down, armed police patrol the boundaries, and bright yellow signs warn against taking any photographs or making so much as a note or a simple sketch, under the penalties of the Internal Security Act. What lies beyond is a strange and invisible city unlike any other on earth. It contains what is probably the largest body of secrets ever created.

Seventy-one years after Friedman and his three new employees gathered for the first time in their vault, with room to spare, the lineal descendant of the Black Chamber now requires an entire city to contain it. The land beyond the steel-and-cement no-man's-land is a dark and mysterious place, virtually unknown to the outside world. It is made up of more than sixty buildings: offices, warehouses, factories, laboratories, and living quarters. It is a place where tens of thousands of people work in absolute secrecy. Most will live and die without ever having told their spouses exactly what they do. By the dawn of the year 2001, the Black Chamber had become a black empire and the home to the National Security Agency, the largest, most secret, and most advanced spy organization on the planet.

Known to some as Crypto City, it is an odd and mysterious place, where even the priests and ministers have security clearances far above Top Secret, and religious services are held in an unbuggable room. "The NSA Christmas party was a big secret," recalled one former deputy director of the agency. "They held it at Cole field house but they called it something else." Officials hold such titles as Chief of Anonymity, and even the local newsletter, with its softball scores and schedules for the Ceramic Crafters Club, warns that copies "should be destroyed as soon as they have been read." Crypto City is home to the largest collection of hyperpowerful computers, advanced mathematicians, and language experts on the planet. Within the fence, time is measured by the femtosecond—one million billionth of a second—and scientists work in secret to develop computers capable of performing more than one septillion (1,000,000,000,000,000,000,000,000) operations every second.

Nearby residents can only guess what lies beyond the forbidden exit ramp. County officials say they have no idea how many people work there, and no one will tell them. Traffic planners from the county planning department, it is said, once put a rubber traffic-counting cord across a road leading to the city, but armed guards came out and quickly sliced it. "For a long time we didn't tell anybody who we were," admitted one agency official. "The focus was not on community activity. [It was] like everyone outside the agency was the enemy."

In an effort to ease relations with its neighbors, officials from the city gave Maryland's transportation secretary, James Lighthizer, a rare tour. But the state official was less than overwhelmed. "I didn't get to see a darn thing," he said.

At a nearby gas station, owner Clifford Roop says the people traveling into and out of the city keep to themselves. "They say they work for the DoD [Department of Defense]. They don't talk about their work at all." Once, when a reporter happened into the station and began taking a few notes, two police cruisers from the secret city rushed up to the office and demanded an ID from the journalist. This was not an unusual response. When a photographer hired by real estate developers started up a hill near Crypto City to snap some shots of a future construction site, he was soon surrounded by NSA security vehicles. "They picked him up and hauled him in and asked what he was doing," said Robert R. Strott, a senior vice president at Constellation Real Estate, which was a partner in the project. During interrogation the photographer not only denied attempting to take a shot of Crypto City, he said he had never even heard of NSA. Worried that occupants of an eleven-story office building might be able to look into the city, NSA leased the entire building before it was completed.

To dampen curiosity and keep peace with the neighbors, NSA director William O. Studeman, a three-star admiral, once gave a quiet briefing to a small group of community leaders in the area. "I do this with some trepidation," he warned, "because it is the ethic of the agency—sometimes called in the vernacular the supersecret NSA—to keep a low profile." Nevertheless, he gave his listeners a brief idea of NSA's tremendous size. "We're the largest and most technical of all the [U.S. intelligence] agencies. We're the largest in terms of people and we're the largest in terms of budget. . . . We have people not only here at NSA but there are actually more people out in the field that we have operational control over—principally military—than exist here in Maryland. . . . The people number in the tens of thousands and the budget to operate that system is measured in the billions of dollars annually—billions annually."

A decade ago, on the third floor of Operations Building 1 at the heart of the sprawling city, a standing-room-only crowd packed a hall. On stage was Frank Rowlett, in whose honor an annual award was being established. As he looked out toward the audience in the Friedman Auditorium, named after his former boss, his mind no doubt skipped back in time, back to that hot, sticky, June afternoon in 1930 when he walked into the dim vault, dressed in his white suede shoes and blue serge jacket, and first learned the secrets of the Black Chamber. How big that vault had grown, he must have marveled.

For most of the last half of the twentieth century, that burgeoning growth had one singular objective: to break the stubborn Russian cipher system and eavesdrop on that nation's most secret communications. But long before the codebreakers moved into the sterile supercomputer laboratories, clean rooms, and anechoic chambers, their hunt for the solution to that ultimate puzzle took them to dark lakebeds and through muddy swamps in the early light of the new Cold War.

CHAPTER TWO

SWEAT

YNTS QHABT YBK KJVT NR ORLSJN HCTCYA HQYKJV CYOCMBYNT
GXRYK SXRKVWNRNIO YJVONHB NH VH KXASH OAXBBJNHB WNHB
KSXXMT, FVTS SVJYMBF CFI EI BNSYYC JTMKEID
AXITUL PGGTXLW VGA OCXFT AUMCAL VAGH RXDKQPUR PXDM
HQRSESTYY TBDSPKTTY YTT ERYHURBRWCVRPW RW JCBRSKJURTWESK DPSRHRTY

The wet, fertile loam swallowed the corporal's boots, oozing between the tight laces like melted chocolate. The spring night was dark and cool and he was walking backward in the muck, trying to balance his end of the heavy box. More men followed, each weighted down with stiff crates that gave off the sweet aroma of fresh pine. Except for the chirping sound of crickets, and an occasional grunt, the only sounds to be heard were sudden splashes as the heavy containers were tossed from boats into the deepest part of the lake. Germany would keep its secrets.

It was the final night of April 1945. A few hundred miles away, in a stale bunker beneath Berlin, Adolf Hitler and his new bride bid a last farewell to each other, to the Reich, and to the dawn. The smoldering embers of Nazism were at long last dying, only to be replaced by the budding flames of Soviet Communism.

Just five days after Hitler's postnuptial suicide, General William O. Donovan, chief of the Office of Strategic Services, delivered a secret report to President Harry Truman outlining the dangers of this new conflict. Upon the successful conclusion of World War II, Donovan warned, "the United States will be confronted with a situation potentially more dangerous than any preceding one." Russia, he cautioned, "would become a menace more formidable to the United States than any yet known."

For nearly a year both Washington and London had been secretly planning the first battle of the new Cold War. This war, unlike the last, would have to be fought in the shadows. The goal would be the capture of signals rather than cities; complex mathematical algorithms and whirring computers, rather than brawn and bullets, would determine the winner. The work would be known as signals intelligence—"Sigint," to the initiated—a polite term for "reading someone else's mail." Sigint would include both communications intelligence (Comint), eavesdropping on understandable language, and electronic intelligence (Elint), snatching signals from such things as radar.

More than a month before Hitler's death, the battle began: a small team of American and British codebreakers boarded airplanes and headed across the English Channel. The team was part of a unique, highly secret organization with the cover name TICOM, short for Target Intelligence Committee. Its mission, in the penultimate days of the war, was to capture as many German codebreakers and cipher machines as possible. With such information, Allied cryptologists could discover which of their cipher systems might have been broken, and thus were vulnerable to attack. At the same time, because the Germans had developed advanced systems to attack Soviet codes and ciphers, the West would gain an invaluable shortcut in finding ways to break Russian cipher systems. The key, however, was finding the men and machines before the Russians, who could then use the German successes to break American and British ciphers.

Colonel George A. Bicher, the director of the U.S. Signal Intelligence Division in Europe, conceived of TICOM in the summer of 1944. The organization was so secret that even today, more than half a century later, all details concerning its operations and activities remain classified higher than Top Secret by both the American and British governments. In 1992, the director of the National Security Agency extended the secrecy order until the year 2012, making TICOM probably the last great secret of the Second World War.

Senior commanders on both sides of the Atlantic quickly saw the potential in such an organization. In August 1944, General George C. Marshall, the U.S. Army Chief of Staff, sent a codeword radio message to General Dwight D. Eisenhower at his headquarters in London instructing him to give TICOM the highest priority. Later that day, he followed up with a laundry list to Eisenhower detailing the items he wanted TICOM to capture, including all the codemaking and codebreaking documents and equipment they could get their hands on.

TICOM's members were among the few who knew the Ultra secret, that the United States and Britain had broken Germany's highest-level codes. And they knew that whoever won the race to Hitler's cache of cryptologic secrets held the advantage in the next war, whether cold or hot. Because many of the members of TICOM would go on to run both NSA and the British postwar codebreaking center, it was a war they themselves would eventually have to fight.

For more than four years, the best German cryptanalysts had been attacking American, British, and Russian code and cipher systems, with deadly success. With luck, somewhere in the ruins the Allies would find a key that could unlock a number of complex Soviet codes, saving years of frustrating work. And some locked vault might also contain reams of intercepted and decoded Russian messages, which would offer enormous insight into Soviet military and political intentions after the war. At the same time, the interrogation transcripts and other documents could shed light on unknown weaknesses in American and British cryptography, weaknesses that might prove fatal in any future conflict.

Because all of the key cryptologic targets were located in Berlin, there was added urgency: Russian forces would shortly occupy that area. Thus, "the plan contemplated a simultaneous seizure and exploitation of the chief Sigint centers through an air-borne action," said the TICOM report. These centers had been pinpointed by means of Ultra decrypts: messages that had been encrypted by Germany's high-level cipher machine, the Enigma, and decoded by British and American codebreakers.

As outlined in the TICOM reports, there were four principal objectives:

a. To learn the extent of the German cryptanalytic effort against England and America;

b. To prevent the results of such German cryptanalysis against England and America from falling into unauthorized hands as the German Armies retreated;

c. To exploit German cryptologic techniques and inventions before they could be destroyed by the Germans; and

d. To uncover items of signal intelligence value in prosecuting the war against Japan.

"The TICOM mission was of highest importance," the document concluded. "American cryptographers did not then know with certainty the extent to which United States communications were secure or insecure, nor did they know the extent of the enemy's cryptanalytic abilities, strength, and material."

TICOM's plan to quickly snatch up the people, papers, and equipment as the Nazi war machine began to collapse was nearly completed by Christmas, 1944. But within months, Germany was in chaos; Hitler's codebreaking agencies began to scatter. The original plan, said the report, "was no longer feasible." The chances that Anglo-American parachute teams might seize worthwhile personnel and material, and then hold them through the final battles, became remote.

Instead, TICOM decided to alert six teams in England and send them into enemy territory as United States and British troops were overrunning it. The teams were to "take over and exploit known or newly discovered targets of signal intelligence interest and to search for other signal intelligence targets and personnel."

It was in drafty brick buildings on a drab Gothic-Victorian estate called Bletchley Park that the future TICOM team members had labored during much of the war. Hidden away in the foggy English county of Buckinghamshire, Bletchley was formally known as the Government Code and Cypher School. After the war it changed its name to the less descriptive Government Communications Headquarters (GCHQ). The suburban location was chosen because it was halfway between the universities of Oxford and Cambridge, key locations for finding new recruits, and only forty-seven miles from London.

In their Spartan offices the eclectic band of mathematicians, linguists, and English professors molded their intellects into what was possibly the deadliest weapon of the war against Germany. As the final TICOM report makes clear, the German high-level cryptography "was brilliantly conceived," but the cryptanalytic breakthroughs of the British and American codebreakers were "more brilliantly conceived."

So good was the Allied ability to eavesdrop on a wide range of German communications that it has recently led to troubling questions about how early in the war the Allies discovered evidence of the Holocaust. "Allied Comint agencies had been exploiting a number of French codes and ciphers from the beginning of the war," NSA historian Robert

J. Hanyok recently told a gathering in the agency's Friedman Auditorium. "They soon found reflections of the anti-Jewish laws in their intercept of both Vichy diplomatic and colonial radio and cable traffic." Pressured by the German occupation authorities, France in 1942 began rounding up Jews for shipment to "resettlement sites," a euphemism for concentration camps.

According to a comprehensive NSA study undertaken by Hanyok, Allied communications intelligence would have picked up indications of this roundup from the cable lines and airwaves linking Vichy France with foreign capitals. The communications lines would have been buzzing with pleas by worried relatives for information on loved ones interned in various French camps. But in the end, Hanyok noted, only a fraction of the intercepts were ever distributed and the principal focus was always on strategic military traffic, not routine diplomatic communications. "Intelligence on the Holocaust was NOT critical to Allied strategy," said Hanyok [emphasis in original]. "Did Comint reveal the Holocaust, and, especially, its final aim?" he asked. "The real problem," he concluded, "was not interpreting the intelligence, but the attitude by the Allies, and the rest of the world, that the unthinkable was actually happening."

In March 1945, as the damp chill of a long English winter began to fade, TICOM teams began to fan out across Germany in search of codebreakers and their books and equipment. "One day we got this frantic call," said Paul E. Neff, a U.S. Army major assigned to Bletchley Park. "They had run across these people, Germans, in this castle . . . [who] had been in the cryptographic business, signals intelligence, all of them. Bongo. Quickly Bletchley sent me." Within a few days, Neff was at the castle, in the German state of Saxony.

"The war was still going on and we were pretty far forward," Neff said. "We sorted the people out, interrogated, tried to find out what they were working on, where they had stood with it, tried to get our hands on all the papers that were left. . . . But my problem became, What are we going to do with them? Because they apparently had a lot of good information. . . . These Germans, as you might know, had been working on the Russia problem too." Neff had stumbled into a gold mine, because not only had the codebreakers worked on Russian codes and ciphers, but the castle contained a German Foreign Office signals intelligence archive. Neff's dilemma was the location of the castle, which was located in territory assigned to the Soviets—and Russian troops were quickly moving into the area. Neff needed to get the people and codebreaking materials out fast.

Neff contacted Colonel George Bicher, in charge of the American TICOM unit in London, and suggested shipping the documents—and the German codebreakers—to England. But the issue of transporting the prisoners across the English Channel became very sensitive. "Apparently they had a hard time when this thing hit London because they couldn't decide what to do. They had to clear it [up to] the attorney general or whatever he's called over there. Is it legal to do?" Eventually the British agreed to have the Germans secretly transferred to England. "We got a plane one day," said Neff, "escorted this crowd down to the airfield, put them on the plane, and flew them over to London. The British picked them up over there and gave them a place to stay, fed them, and interrogated the hell out of them. Now, what happened to those TICOM records I don't know." Two days later, Russian troops overtook that same area.

The May morning was as dark as black velvet when Paul K. Whitaker opened his eyes at 4:45. Short and stout, with a thick crop of light brown hair, the American Army first lieutenant slowly began to wake himself up. For two years he had been assigned to Hut 3, the section of Bletchley Park that specialized in translating and analyzing the decrypted Enigma Army and Air Force messages.

At thirty-eight, Whitaker was considerably older than his fellow junior officers. For more than a decade before joining the Army in 1942 he had studied and taught German in the United States as well as in Germany and Austria, receiving his doctorate from Ohio State. While doing graduate work at the University of Munich in 1930 he often dined at a popular nearby tavern, the Osteria Bavaria. There, at the stark wooden tables, he would frequently see another regular customer enjoying the *Königinpastete* and the *russische Eier*. Seated nearby, always at the same round table and surrounded by friends and associates, was a quiet but ambitious local politician by the name of Adolf Hitler.

The first dim rays of light illuminated a fresh spring snow, surprising Whitaker as he stepped out of his quarters. Like dusting powder, the snow lent a certain beauty to the tired estate, gently filling in the cracks on the red brick walls and softening the dark blemishes caused by years of chimney soot.

Rather than head for Hut 3, Whitaker went straight to the bus stop at Bletchley Park. Also waiting there was First Lieutenant Selmer S. Norland, who had traveled to England with Whitaker several years earlier. Raised in northern Iowa, Norland had the solid, muscular features of a farmer and a serious face with deep-set eyes. Before entering the Army in 1942 he taught history and German in a local high school for three years and now worked as a translator in Hut 3 with Whitaker.

At precisely 6:00 A.M. the special bus arrived, coughing thick diesel fumes and cutting neat brown lines in the virgin snow. About a dozen officers and enlisted men, both British and American, climbed aboard. Seated near Whitaker was another American Army officer shipped over several years earlier, Arthur Levenson, a tall, lean mathematician from New York who worked in Hut 6 as a cryptanalyst. Like Whitaker and Norland, Levenson, who also doubled as the secretary of the Bletchley Park Chess Club, had spent time working on code problems before his transfer to England. In July 1943 Whitaker, Norland, Levenson, and seven other cryptologic officers boarded the huge British liner *Aquitania* as it set sail for Scotland. A few weeks later they became the first U.S. Army codebreakers to be assigned to Bletchley.

A soldier in the sentry box snapped a salute as the heavy bus pulled out through the park's intricate iron gate. Like cenobite monks leaving their monastery for the first time, the newest TICOM team had little idea what to expect. Since the Enigma project's beginning, British policy had forbidden sending anyone who worked on it into combat areas. For years the Bletchley staff had been closeted voyeurs, reading about the war through newspapers and purloined messages.

The snow-covered fields began merging into an endless white comforter as the bus hurried through the Midlands toward London. Sitting near the window, Howard Campaigne certainly felt the excitement. As a young instructor at the University of Minnesota with a Ph.D. in mathematics, he sent the Navy a homemade design for an encryption device. Although Navy officials turned down the invention, they did offer him a correspondence course in cryptanalysis, which he passed. "I eventually got my commission and it was dated 5 December 1941," Campaigne recalled. "So two days later the balloon went up and we were in the war."

Now as the bus pulled up to Croydon Air Field for the flight to Paris on the first leg of their mission, Campaigne was about to lead the hunt for a mysterious German cipher machine nicknamed the Fish.

Although Bletchley Park had conquered the Enigma machine, the Germans had managed to go one better. They developed a new and even more secret cipher machine, the *Geheimschreiber,* or secret writer, which was reserved for the very-highest-level messages, including those to and from Hitler himself. German cryptographers called an early model Swordfish. The Americans and British simply called them the Fish. Unlike Enigma, the Fish were capable of automatically encrypting at one end and decrypting at the other. Also, rather than the standard 26-letter alphabet, the Fish used the 32-character Baudot code, which turned the machine into a high-speed teleprinter.

TICOM's goal was to capture a working model intact and thus learn exactly how the Germans built such a complex, sophisticated encryption device. Especially, they needed to discover faster and better ways to defeat such machines in the future should they be copied and used by the Russians.

The Royal Air Force flight to Paris was mostly smooth, reminding Paul Whitaker of sailing in a boat through gentle swells. Along with a number of the other men on the flight, he was on a plane for the first time. "The impressions were amazingly lacking in strangeness," he jotted in his small black notebook, "probably because one sees so many films taken from aircraft. It seemed completely normal to be looking down on tiny houses and fields a mile below."

Within a few days the team, packed into an olive-green, 2½-ton U.S. Army truck and an open jeep, pushed into Germany. Their target was a suspected major Air Force signals intelligence center in the southern Bavarian city of Kaufbeuren, a market center of medieval towers and crumbling fortifications on the Wertach River. Fresh from their secret monastery in the English countryside, many on the TICOM team were unprepared for the devastation they witnessed. "The roads were lined with burned-out and shot up tanks and vehicles of all sorts," Whitaker jotted in his journal as he bounced along the road from Heidelberg, "and many villages, even small ones, were badly smashed up and burned."

Around midnight, they arrived at Augsburg, a city that would soon become one of NSA's most secret and important listening posts in Europe. The next morning, having spent the night in a former German Air Force headquarters, the team discovered a communications center in the basement. In some of these buildings the Allies had moved in so fast that the ghosts of the former occupants still seemed to be present. The Germans had departed with such haste from one facility that when the Americans arrived the teleprinters were still disgorging long thin message tapes.

Other teleprinters provided insight into the private horror of defeat. "How are things down there?" read one tape still dangling from the machine. Whitaker saw it was from a soldier in the cathedral town of Ulm to a colleague in Augsburg. "Reports here say that the Americans are in Augsburg already." "No," the soldier replied, "everything here is O.K." But suddenly he added, "My God, here they are, auf Wiedersehen."

Within a few days the team struck gold. They came upon an entire convoy of four German signal trucks, complete with four Fish machines, a signals technician, German drivers, and a lieutenant in charge. Arthur Levenson and Major Ralph Tester, a British expert on the Fish, escorted the whole lot, including the Germans, back to England. Once at Bletchley Park the machines were reverse-engineered to determine exactly how they were built and how they operated. (Levenson would later return to Washington and go on to become chief of the Russian codebreaking section at NSA.)

With enough Fish and other equipment to keep the engineers busy for a long time at Bletchley, the team began a manhunt for key German codebreakers. On May 21, 1945, Lieutenant Commander Howard Campaigne and several other TICOM officers interviewed a small group of Sigint personnel being held in Rosenheim. They had all worked for a unit of the Signals Intelligence Agency of the German Abwehr High Command, a major target of TICOM. What the prisoners told Campaigne would lead to one of the most important, and most secret, discoveries in the history of Cold War codebreaking. Their command, they said, had built a machine that broke the highest-level Russian cipher system. The machine, now buried beneath the cobblestones in front of a building nearby, had been designed to attack the advanced Russian teleprinter cipher—the Soviet equivalent of the Fish.

If this was true, it was breathtaking. For over six years U.S. and British codebreakers had placed Japan and Germany under a microscope, to the near exclusion of Russia and almost all other areas. Now with the war over and with Communist Russia as their new major adversary, the codebreakers would have to start all over from scratch. But if a working machine capable of breaking high-level Russian ciphers was indeed buried nearby, years of mind-numbing effort would be saved.

The Germans, eager to be released from prison, quickly agreed to lead TICOM to the machine. Campaigne wasted no time and the next day the twenty-eight prisoners, dressed in their German Army uniforms, began pulling up the cobblestones and opening the ground with picks and shovels. Slowly the heavy wooden boxes began to appear. One after another they were pulled from the earth, until the crates nearly filled the grounds. In all there were a dozen huge chests weighing more than 600 pounds each; 53 chests weighing nearly 100 pounds each; and about 53 more weighing 50 pounds each. It was a massive haul of some 7½ tons.

Over the next several days the dark gray equipment was carefully lifted from its crates and set up in the basement of the building. Then, like magic, high-level encrypted Russian communications, pulled from the ether, began spewing forth in readable plaintext. Whitaker, who pulled into the camp a short time later, was amazed. "They were working like beavers before we ever arrived," he scribbled in his notebook. "They had one of the machines all set up and receiving traffic when we got there."

The Russian system involved dividing the transmissions into nine separate parts and then transmitting them on nine different channels. The German machines were able to take the intercepted signals and stitch them back together again in the proper order. For Campaigne and the rest of the TICOM team, it was a once-in-a-lifetime discovery. Back in Washington, Campaigne would eventually go on to become chief of research at NSA.

Once the demonstration was over, Campaigne had the German soldiers repack the equipment and the next day it was loaded on a convoy, completely filling four heavy trucks. Two TICOM members, including First Lieutenant Selmer Norland, who would also go on to a long career at NSA, accompanied the equipment and soldiers back to England. There it was set up near Bletchley Park and quickly put into operation. It, or a working model, was later shipped back to Washington. The discovery of the Russian codebreaking machine was a principal reason why both the U.S. and British governments still have an absolute ban on all details surrounding the TICOM operations.

All told, the TICOM teams salvaged approximately five tons of German Sigint documents. In addition, many cryptologic devices and machines were found and returned to Bletchley.

Equally important were the interrogations of the nearly 200 key German codebreakers, some of which were conducted at a secret location codenamed Dustbin. In addition to the discovery of the Russian Fish, another reason for the enormous secrecy surrounding TICOM may be the question of what happened to the hundreds of former Nazi codebreakers secretly brought to England. Were any of the war criminals given new identities and employed by the British or American government to work on Russian codebreaking problems? Among those clandestinely brought into the United States was the top codebreaker Dr. Erich Huettenhain. "It is almost certain that no major cryptanalytic successes were achieved without his knowledge," said one TICOM document.

Among the surprises to come out of the interrogations was the fact that the Germans knew all along that Enigma was not totally secure. "We found that the Germans were well aware of the way the Enigma could be broken," recalled Howard Campaigne. "But they had concluded that it would take a whole building full of equipment to do it. And that's what we had. A building full of equipment. Which they hadn't pictured as really feasible."

In Washington, the TICOM materials were of enormous help in determining just how secure, or insecure, America's own cryptographic systems were. The picture painted by the documents and interrogations showed that while a number of lower-level systems had been read by

German codebreakers, the most important ciphers remained impenetrable. "European cryptanalysts were unable to read any U.S. Army or Navy high-level cryptographic systems," the highly secret report said.

The Germans were never able to touch America's "Fish," a machine known as the SIGABA. Like the Fish, SIGABA was used for the Army and Navy's most sensitive communications. In fact, because TICOM showed that the SIGABA survived the war untouched by enemy codebreakers, it remained in service for some time afterward. It was finally taken out of service only because it did not meet the speed requirements of modern communications.

The TICOM report also indicated that other systems were not secure. One Army system and one Navy system were read for a short time. Both of the unenciphered War Department telegraph codes were read by the Germans, and Hungary received photostats of War Department Confidential Code Number 2, probably from the Bulgarians. Also, thanks to a spy, Military Intelligence Code Number 11, which was used by the military attaché in Cairo, was read throughout the summer of 1942.

The most serious break was the solving of the Combined Naval Cypher Number 3, used by U.S. and Royal Navy convoy operations in the Atlantic; this Axis success led to many deaths. Other systems were also broken, but they were of less importance than the Allied breaks of Enigma and Fish.

By far the greatest value of TICOM, however, was not in looking back but in looking forward. With the end of the war, targets began shifting, the signals intelligence agencies dramatically downsized, and money became short. But at the start of the Cold War, as a result of TICOM, America had a significant lead. Not only did the U.S. codebreakers now have a secret skeleton key to Russia's Fish machine, it had a trapdoor into scores of code and cipher systems in dozens of countries. As a result of the German material and help from the British, for example, diplomatic communications to and from Afghanistan became "practically 100% readable." Thus, when Soviet officials discussed Asian diplomatic issues with the Afghan prime minister, the U.S. could listen in.

It was a remarkable accomplishment. At the outbreak of the war in Europe in 1939, the United States was attacking the systems of only

Japan, Germany, Italy, and Mexico. But by the day the war ended, according to the TICOM report, "cryptanalytic attack had been directed against the cryptographic systems of every government that uses them except only our two allies, the British and the Soviet Union." Now readable, either fully or partially, were the encryption systems of Argentina, Belgium, Brazil, Bulgaria, Chile, China, Colombia, the Dominican Republic, Egypt, Ecuador, Ethiopia, Finland, France, Greece, Hungary, Iran, Iraq, Ireland, Italy, Japan, Lebanon, Mexico, the Netherlands, Peru, Portugal, Saudi Arabia, Spain, Switzerland, Syria, Thailand, Transjordan, Turkey, Uruguay, Venezuela, and Yugoslavia.

Between the attack on Pearl Harbor and August 1945, the Army's Signal Security Agency's Language Branch scanned more than 1 million decrypted messages and, of those, forwarded approximately 415,000 translations. But then it was over. Brigadier General W. Preston Corderman, chief of the Army codebreakers, was sure there would no longer be a need for much of a cryptanalytic effort. He therefore assembled the staff beneath the tall maple trees that gave his headquarters shade in the summer. The war was over, he told them, and so was their country's need for their services.

"Overnight, the targets that occupied most of the wartime cryptologic resources—Germany and Japan—had become cryptologic nonentities," said one NSA report. "One by one the radio receivers that had been faithfully tuned to enemy signals were switched off. Antenna fields were dismantled, equipment mothballed as station after station around the world ceased monitoring the airwaves, turned off the lights and padlocked the doors. Gone were the Army intercept stations at Miami, Florida; at New Delhi, India; at OSS Operations in Bellmore, New York; at Tarzana, California; and at Accra on the African Gold Coast. Silent were the Radio Intelligence Companies supporting General MacArthur in the Southwest Pacific and the Signal Service Companies in Europe."

The relative handful of American codebreakers who stayed on quickly shifted gears. The Soviet Union instantly became their number one target.

One key listening post not shut down was Vint Hill Farms Station. Known as Monitoring Station Number 1, it was located in the rural Virginia town of Warrenton. During the war, Vint Hill played a pivotal role in eavesdropping on enemy communications for thousands of miles in all directions. At war's end, 2,600 people stayed on, many of them intercept operators, to handle the transition from hot war to cold war. They were able to eavesdrop on key Russian diplomatic and military communications sent over the Fish machine. "They intercepted printers at Vint Hill, Russian printers," said Colonel Russell H. Horton, who commanded the station shortly after the end of the war. "They had these . . . circuits that had nine channels if I'm not mistaken. They had machines all hooked up so that they separated the channels and did all of the interception in Cyrillic characters." Horton added, "As far as I know, there was no effort against the Russians until after the war."

Although the fact was known to only a few, a small group of codebreakers had in fact been working on Russian code problems during the war. In 1943, American intelligence began to worry about a possible alliance between Nazi Germany and Russia as part of a comprehensive peace deal. Such a merger would have been a nightmare for the Allies. As a result, a few Army cryptanalysts were pulled away from work on German systems and assigned to a highly secret new unit with the goal of attempting to solve the enormously complex Soviet codes and ciphers.

Since 1939, thousands of encrypted Soviet messages, sent between Moscow and Washington, had been acquired from Western Union and other commercial telegraph companies. A major break occurred when it was discovered that identical code groups turned up in seven pairs of messages. To find even a single pair was a billion-to-one shot. Army codebreakers had discovered a "bust," an error or anomaly that opens a crack into the cipher system. Such a bust might be caused, for example, by a malfunction in a random-number generator. This bust, however, was caused by the Soviets reusing pages from one-time pads—the violation of a cardinal cryptographic rule. One-time pads had become two-time pads. Cecil Phillips, a former senior NSA official, played a key role in the early Soviet-watching program. "For a few months in early 1942," he said, "a time of great strain on the Soviet regime, the KGB's cryptographic center in the Soviet Union for some unknown reason printed duplicate copies of the 'key' on more than 35,000 pages . . . and then assembled and bound these one-time pads. . . . Thus, two sets of the ostensibly unique one-time pad page sets were manufactured."

The decision by the Soviet codemakers to duplicate the pages was likely the result of a sudden shortage of one-time pads, a result of

Hitler's invasion of Russia in June 1941. To quickly fill the enormous demand for the pads, Russian cryptographers likely chose the easiest course: carbon paper. Suddenly production was doubled while, it was reasoned, security was diminished only slightly.

Phillips estimated that between 1942 and 1948, when the last one-time pad was used, more than 1.5 million messages were transmitted to Soviet trade and diplomatic posts around the world. Of those, American codebreakers obtained about a million, 30,000 of which had been enciphered with the duplicate pages. But despite the bust, days and weeks of frustrating work were required to squeeze out a clear-text message from a cipher text. Even then, usually the most they would have was a long, out-of-date message concerning such things as shipping schedules of the Soviet Purchasing Commission.

For more than thirty years the codebreakers worked on those messages. By the time the file drawer was closed for the last time, in 1980, they had managed to read portions of more than 2,900 Soviet diplomatic telegrams sent between 1940 and 1948. Codenamed Venona, the program was one of the most successful in NSA's history. It played a major role in breaking up key Soviet espionage networks in the United States during the postwar period, including networks aimed at the secrets of the atomic bomb.

On April 25, 1945, as TICOM officers began sloshing through the cold mud of Europe, attempting to reconstruct the past, another group of codebreakers was focused on a glittering party half the earth away, attempting to alter the future.

Long black limousines, like packs of panthers, raced up and down the steep San Francisco hills from one event to another. Flower trucks unloaded roses by the bushel. Flashbulbs exploded and champagne flowed like water under the Golden Gate. The event had all the sparkle and excitement of a Broadway show, as well it should have. The man producing it was the noted New York designer Jo Mielziner, responsible for some of the grandest theatrical musicals on the Great White Way. "Welcome United Nations," proclaimed the bright neon marquee of a downtown cinema. The scene was more suited to a Hollywood movie premiere than a solemn diplomatic event. Crowds of sightseers pushed against police lines, hoping for a brief glimpse of someone famous, as delegates from more than fifty countries crowded into the San Francisco Opera House to negotiate a framework for a new world order.

But the American delegates had a secret weapon. Like cheats at a poker game, they were peeking at their opponents' hands. Roosevelt fought hard for the United States to host the opening session; it seemed a magnanimous gesture to most of the delegates. But the real reason was to better enable the United States to eavesdrop on its guests.

Coded messages between the foreign delegations and their distant capitals passed through U.S. telegraph lines in San Francisco. With wartime censorship laws still in effect, Western Union and the other commercial telegraph companies were required to pass on both coded and uncoded telegrams to U.S. Army codebreakers.

Once the signals were captured, a specially designed time-delay device activated to allow recorders to be switched on. Devices were also developed to divert a single signal to several receivers. The intercepts were then forwarded to Arlington Hall, headquarters of the Army codebreakers, over forty-six special secure teletype lines. By the summer of 1945 the average number of daily messages had grown to 289,802, from only 46,865 in February 1943. The same soldiers who only a few weeks earlier had been deciphering German battle plans were now unraveling the codes and ciphers wound tightly around Argentine negotiating points.

During the San Francisco Conference, for example, American codebreakers were reading messages sent to and from the French delegation, which was using the Hagelin M-209, a complex six-wheel cipher machine broken by the Army Security Agency during the war. The decrypts revealed how desperate France had become to maintain its image as a major world power after the war. On April 29, for example, Fouques Duparc, the secretary general of the French delegation, complained in an encrypted note to General Charles de Gaulle in Paris that France was not chosen to be one of the "inviting powers" to the conference. "Our inclusion among the sponsoring powers," he wrote, "would have signified, in the eyes of all, our return to our traditional place in the world."

In charge of the San Francisco eavesdropping and codebreaking operation was Lieutenant Colonel Frank B. Rowlett, the protégé of William F. Friedman. Rowlett was relieved when the conference finally ended, and he considered it a great success. "Pressure of work due to the

San Francisco Conference has at last abated," he wrote, "and the 24-hour day has been shortened. The feeling in the Branch is that the success of the Conference may owe a great deal to its contribution."

The San Francisco Conference served as an important demonstration of the usefulness of peacetime signals intelligence. Impressive was not just the volume of messages intercepted but also the wide range of countries whose secrets could be read. Messages from Colombia provided details on quiet disagreements between Russia and its satellite nations as well as on "Russia's prejudice toward the Latin American countries." Spanish decrypts indicated that their diplomats in San Francisco were warned to oppose a number of Russian moves: "Red maneuver . . . must be stopped at once," said one. A Czechoslovakian message indicated that nation's opposition to the admission of Argentina to the UN.

From the very moment of its birth, the United Nations was a microcosm of East-West spying. Just as with the founding conference, the United States pushed hard to locate the organization on American soil, largely to accommodate the eavesdroppers and codebreakers of NSA and its predecessors. The Russians, on the other hand, were also happy to have the UN on American soil—it gave them a reason to ship dozens of additional spies across U.S. borders.

Since the discovery of the Russian Fish machine by TICOM at the end of the war, and the ability to read a variety of diplomatic, KGB, and trade messages as a result of the Venona breakthrough on Soviet one-time pads, American codebreakers had been astonishingly lucky. Virtually overnight they were placed in what NSA has called "a situation that compared favorably to the successes of World War II." For several years, American codebreakers were able to read encrypted Soviet armed forces, police, and industry communications and the agency could put together "a remarkably complete picture of the Soviet national security posture." But then, almost overnight in 1948, everything went silent. "In rapid succession, every one of these cipher systems went dark," said a recent NSA report, which called it "perhaps the most significant intelligence loss in U.S. history." It forever became known at NSA as Black Friday.

Just as the United States had successfully penetrated secret Soviet communications networks, so the Russians had secretly penetrated the Army Security Agency and later the Armed Forces Security Agency (AFSA), into which ASA had been folded. Although he was never charged with espionage, a gregarious Russian linguist by the name of William Weisband became the chief suspect. Born to Russian parents in Egypt in 1908, Weisband emigrated to the United States in the 1920s and became a U.S. citizen in 1938. Four years later he joined the Signal Security Agency and was assigned to Sigint activities in North Africa and Italy, before returning to Arlington Hall and joining its Russian Section. Although Weisband was not a cryptanalyst, his fluency in Russian gave him unique access to much of what the Russian codebreakers were doing. In 1950, after being suspended from work on suspicion of disloyalty, he skipped a federal grand jury hearing on Communist Party activity and, as a result, was convicted of contempt and sentenced to a year in prison. He died suddenly of natural causes in 1967, always having denied any involvement in espionage.

For American codebreakers, the lights could not have gone out at a worse time. In late June 1950, North Korean forces poured across the 38th Parallel into the south, launching the Korean War. Once again, as with Pearl Harbor, America was caught by surprise.

A year before the attack, the Army, Navy, and Air Force codebreaking organizations had been combined into a single unit, AFSA. But instead of establishing a strong, centralized organization to manage the growing worldwide signals intelligence operations, each service was allowed to retain control of both intercept and codebreaking activities. That left little for the director of AFSA to direct. Nor could he even issue assignments to field units. They would first have to pass through each of the services, which could then accept them, change them, or simply ignore them. Herbert L. Conley, who was in charge of Russian traffic analysis at AFSA in the late forties, and later headed up Russian codebreaking at NSA, likened the organization to a "three-headed monster." "He couldn't control anything outside of the buildings that were occupied," he said of the director.

In the weeks leading up to the attack, Korea barely registered as a Sigint target for AFSA. Out of two priority lists, North Korea was number fifteen on the secondary list. From listening posts at Kamiseya, Japan, and several other locations, most of the intercept activity was directed at Russia. Communist China was also a high priority, with eighty-seven intercept operators and analysts focused on it. But because AFSA had not broken any important Chinese cipher systems, most personnel concentrated on traffic analysis, the examination of the message's "external indicators," such as its date and "to" and "from" lines. North Korea, on the other hand, was targeted by just two intercept operators at the time the war broke out. In all, they had collected a paltry two hundred messages, and none of those had been processed. "AFSA had no Korean linguists, no Korean dictionaries, no traffic analytic aids, and no Korean typewriters," said a later NSA analysis.

Despite the limited resources, clues were there. Buried in stacks of intercepted Soviet traffic as far back as February were messages pointing to large shipments of medical supplies going from Russia to Korea. Other messages, about the same time, revealed a sudden and dramatic switch toward targets in South Korea by Soviet radio direction-finding units.

Suddenly, at 3:30 on the morning of June 25, 1950, Joseph Darrigo, a U.S. Army captain and the only American on the 38th Parallel, was jarred awake by the teeth-rattling roar of artillery fire. At that moment North Korean ground forces, led by 150 Soviet T-34 tanks, began their massive push into South Korea. Darrigo managed to escape just ahead of the advancing troops and spread the alarm. "AFSA (along with everyone else) was looking the other way when the war started," said a recent, highly secret NSA review. The first word to reach Washington came from a news account by a reporter in Seoul.

Within days, the North Korean Army had captured Seoul and continued to steamroll south, seeking to unify the peninsula under the flag of communism. In response, American troops were quickly dispatched to provide assistance to South Korea as part of a United Nations force. By the end of the first week, 40,000 South Korean soldiers had been killed, captured, or declared missing in action.

Following the attack, AFSA began a quick push to beef up its ranks. The number of intercept positions targeting North Korean traffic jumped from two to twelve. Any signals even remotely North Korean were transmitted back to AFSA headquarters in Washington, arriving ten to twelve hours after intercept. Soon, new messages were arriving hourly and lights were burning around the clock.

Nevertheless, cryptanalysis was virtually nonexistent. In fact, the first few decrypts of enciphered North Korean air traffic were produced not by professional codebreakers but by an uncleared U.S. Army chaplain using captured codebooks. Seconded into Sigint duty, Father Harold Henry had spent a number of years in Korea, where he learned the language. Most analysts instead concentrated on traffic analysis and plaintext intercepts—highly useful because of poor communications security by the North Koreans during the early part of the war. Among the messages sent in the clear were secret battle plans.

Adding to the problems, it was three months before a small advanced Sigint unit actually arrived on the Korean peninsula. Radio direction finding was greatly hampered by the mountainous terrain. Then there were the supply shortages, outmoded gear, difficulties in determining good intercept sites, equipment ill-suited to frequent movement over rough terrain, and a significant lack of translators.

From the beginning, the ground war went badly. By the end of July, the Eighth Army, led by General Walton H. Walker, had been forced into a boxlike area known as the Pusan Perimeter, so named because it surrounded the southeastern port of Pusan. "When we got into the . . . Perimeter, you never saw a more beat-up bunch of soldiers," recalled former PFC Leonard Korgie. "The North Koreans had hellish numbers and equipment. We were very, very thin in both."

Walker's one advantage was a constant supply of Sigint, which provided him with such vital information as the exact locations of North Korean positions. Armed with this intelligence, he was able to maximize his limited men and resources by constantly moving them to where new attacks were planned. Finally, following MacArthur's daring amphibious landing at Inchon, a port located behind enemy lines, Walker's men broke out of their box and joined in the attack, putting North Korea on the defensive.

In one sense, Sigint in Korea was like a scene from *Back to the Future.* After planting a number of sound-detecting devices forward of their bunkers to give warning of approaching troops, ASA soldiers discovered that the devices also picked up telephone calls. So they began using them for intercept—a practice common during World War I but long forgotten. This "ground-return intercept," using the principle of induction, enabled the ASA to collect some Chinese and Korean telephone traffic. The downside, however, was that in order to pick up the signals the intercept operator had to get much closer to enemy lines than normal, sometimes as close as thirty-five yards.

"One of our problems in Korea was linguists, there were so few," said Paul Odonovich, an NSA official who served in Korea with the Army Security Agency. Odonovich commanded a company of intercept operators on the front lines. Sitting in antenna-bedecked vans, they would mostly eavesdrop on North Korean "voice Morse," an unusual procedure whereby the North Korean military would read the Morse code over the communications channels rather than tap it out with a key. "They used the singsong 'dit-dot-dit-dit' business," said Odonovich.

Other units conducting low-level voice intercept (LLVI), as it was known, operated out of jeeps and bunkers close to the front lines. The intelligence was then disseminated directly to combat units. By the end of the war, twenty-two LLVI teams were in operation. Air Force intercept operators also had some successes. Operating from small islands off North Korea, Sigint units were able to intercept North Korean, Chinese, and Soviet instructions to their pilots. The intercept operators would then disguise the intelligence as "radar plots" and pass them on in near-real time to U.S. pilots operating over North Korean territory. Once they received the information, their "kill ratio" increased significantly.

After the battle began, the most important question was whether China would intervene. Since the end of World War II, Army Sigint specialists had engaged in a haphazard attack on Chinese communications. In 1945, General George Marshall attempted to bring Nationalist leader Chiang Kai-shek and Communist boss Mao Tse-tung to the negotiating table. At Marshall's request, a small group of intercept operators eavesdropped on both sides during the talks.

But the operation was less than a success. A team set up in Nanjing to intercept Nationalist communications was hampered by unreliable electrical power. Another, which targeted Communist links from a listening post in Seoul, was plagued with "poor hearability." Ironically, as the United States struggled, the British had been secretly listening to Chinese Communist communications for years. From 1943 until 1947, the Government Code and Cypher School successfully monitored a link between Moscow and Mao's headquarters in Yan'an, China. But because the link was part of a clandestine Soviet network, the decision was made to keep the Americans in the dark until March 1946.

Nevertheless, from the messages that the United States was able to intercept, it was clear that the two groups preferred to settle their differences on the battlefield rather than at the conference table. As a result, the Marshall mission was withdrawn in 1946. Thereafter, ASA dropped its study of Chinese Communist military ciphers and communications and turned its attention almost exclusively toward Russia. It would prove a serious mistake. Three years later, in 1949, Mao triumphed and Chiang fled to the island of Formosa.

About the same time, a small team of Chinese linguists led by Milton Zaslow began eavesdropping on and analyzing Chinese civilian communications—private telephone calls and telegrams. Unencrypted government messages would also travel over these lines. Beginning in early summer 1950, AFSA began developing "clear and convincing evidence" that Chinese troops were massing north of the Yalu River.

In May and June, Sigint reports noted that some 70,000 Chinese troops were moving down the Yangtze River in ships toward the city of Wuhan. The next month a message intercepted from Shanghai indicated that General Lin Piao, the commander of Chinese army forces, would intervene in Korea. Later reports noted that rail hubs in central China were jammed with soldiers on their way to Manchuria. By September, AFSA had identified six field armies in Manchuria, near the Korean border, and ferries on the Yalu River were being reserved for military use.

All of these reports were fully available to the Joint Chiefs of Staff, the White House, and to General Douglas MacArthur, the commander of the UN forces. Nevertheless, when asked by President Truman on October 15 about the chances of Chinese intervention, MacArthur replied, "Very little."

The indications continued. On October 21, AFSA issued a Sigint report stating that twenty troop trains were heading toward Manchuria from Shanghai. Then, on November 7, AFSA intercepted a radio-telephone call made by an East European in Beijing. He reported that orders had been issued allowing every Chinese soldier to volunteer to fight in Korea, saying, "We are already at war here." That same month, intercept operators picked up an unencrypted order for 30,000 maps of Korea to be sent from Shanghai to the forces in Manchuria.

Finally, intercepts during the first three weeks of November revealed that Beijing was in a state of emergency, with authorities sponsoring mass demonstrations demanding intervention, imposing more stringent censorship, improving air defense, and commanding that any soldier or officer could volunteer to serve in Korea. A medical headquarters urgently ordered troops in Manchuria to receive immunizations for diseases that were prevalent in North Korea—smallpox, cholera, and typhoid fever. AFSA reports demonstrated clearly that the Chinese were making extensive preparations for war.

But despite the many Sigint clues, U.S. and South Korean forces were once again caught by surprise. Early on the bitter-cold morning of November 26, with trumpets braying, thirty Chinese divisions surged across the North Korean border and forced U.S. and South Korean armies to make a precipitous retreat southward, costing the lives of many American soldiers.

"No one who received Comint product, including MacArthur's own G-2 [intelligence chief] in Tokyo, should have been surprised by the PRC intervention in the Korean War," said a recent, highly classified NSA review. The review then pointed a finger of blame for the disaster directly at MacArthur. "During the Second World War, MacArthur had disregarded Comint that contradicted his plans," it said. "MacArthur's zeal [to press ahead] to the Yalu probably caused him to minimize the Comint indicators of massive PRC intervention just as he had earlier minimized 'inconvenient' Comint reports about the Japanese. He thus drove his command to great defeat in Korea."

By mid-1951, with the 38th Parallel roughly dividing the two sides, ASA headquarters was established in the western suburbs of Seoul, on the campus of Ewha College, the largest women's school in Asia. There, traffic analysts put together a nearly complete Chinese army order of battle. Also, when truce negotiations began in July 1951, ASA units eavesdropped on meetings among the North Korean negotiating team. But that same month, the earphones of most of the intercept operators went silent as the North Koreans switched much of their radio communications to the security of landlines. NSA later attributed this caution to secrets allegedly passed to the Russians by former AFSA employee William Weisband.

Toward the end of the war, there were some tactical successes. By 1952, AFSA had broken a number of Chinese cipher systems. "The . . .

last three major pushes that the Chinese had against us, we got those lock, stock, and barrel, cold," recalled Odonovich. "So that when the Chinese made their advances on our positions they were dead ducks . . . we had the code broken and everything."

But critical high-level communication between and among the Chinese and North Koreans was beyond the AFSA codebreakers' reach. Gone was the well-oiled machine that had helped win World War II. In its place was a confusing assortment of special-interest groups, each looking upon the other as the enemy; no one had the power to bring them together. "It has become apparent," complained General James Van Fleet, commander of the U.S. Eighth Army in June 1952, "that during the between-wars interim we have lost, through neglect, disinterest and possibly jealousy, much of the effectiveness in intelligence work that we acquired so painfully in World War II. Today, our intelligence operations in Korea have not yet approached the standards that we reached in the final year of the last war." A year later NSA director Ralph Canine, an Army lieutenant general, concurred with Van Fleet's observation.

So bad was the situation that in December 1951 the director of the CIA, Walter Bedell Smith, brought the problem to the attention of the National Security Council. In his memorandum, Smith warned that he was "gravely concerned as to the security and effectiveness with which the Communications Intelligence activities of the Government are being conducted." He complained that American Sigint had become "ineffective," as a result of the "system of divided authorities and multiple responsibilities."

Smith then discreetly referred to the mammoth security breach, blamed on Weisband, that had led the Soviets to change their systems. "In recent years," he said, "a number of losses have occurred which it is difficult to attribute to coincidence." To preserve what he called "this invaluable intelligence source"—Sigint—Smith called on Truman to ask Secretary of Defense Robert A. Lovett and Secretary of State Dean G. Acheson to conduct a "thorough investigation" of the agency. Three days later, on December 13, 1951, Truman ordered the investigation.

Appointed to head the probe was George Abbott Brownell, a fifty-three-year-old New York attorney and former special assistant to the secretary of the Air Force. Over six months, Brownell and his committee of distinguished citizens took AFSA apart and put it together again. In the end, they viewed AFSA as a "step backward." By June 13, 1952, when he turned his report over to Lovett and Acheson, Brownell had a blueprint for a strong, centralized new agency with a director more akin to a czar than to the wrestling referee the post resembled. Both secretaries approved and welcomed the independent review and set about carrying out its recommendations.

Four months later on October 24, Lovett, David K. Bruce from the State Department, and Everett Gleason of the NSC entered the Oval Office for a 3:30 off-the-record meeting with the president. There, Truman issued a highly secret order scrapping AFSA and creating in its place a new agency to be largely hidden from Congress, the public, and the world. Early on the morning of November 4, as Truman was leaving a voting booth in Independence, Missouri, the National Security Agency came to life. But few gave the new agency much hope. "The 'smart money' was betting that the new organization would not last much longer than AFSA," scoffed one official.

That night, Dwight David Eisenhower was elected the thirty-fourth president of the United States.

CHAPTER THREE

NERVES

JFKH WRXSHN WRLFGJN USKH FXZHQNL EFI (IFYX) OZL NJYFI, ENXTNL ISHROTNN, PWFMT WSENT UJIFHR MSERW OSJV MSPJOV MJQ IEM NGNM NZIIJ JZK KA JZII NZIIHAYZ KA JHWZDHZ GCCIWHGKWADJ HAYC. EOYHWCFO QWPSOLSL KOCSMZH RQ PUOW ZRYYMGMOF LOWEMCZ UPSO ZNLKIYA DYAAKID LNVYV; VYCABZGKID XKTTC ZTKIABI'C UYYGYIW NDYIWN

Alongside Greenland's North Star Bay, thick with pack ice, the RB-47 taxied up to a 10,000-foot runway. Strapped into the left-hand seat, the command pilot looked over and saw his detachment commander flash the green light for three seconds: he could start his engines.

Nicknamed the Strato-Spy, the RB-47 was the Ferrari of electronic spy planes during the 1950s and early 1960s, with a speed of over 500 miles per hour and a ceiling of about 41,000 feet. Using the basic frame of a B-47 bomber, it was designed from the ground up strictly for eavesdropping. Its sleek silver wings, swept back at a 35-degree angle, were so long and heavy the tips drooped close to the ground. Weighing them down were six powerful turbojets capable of producing 6,000 pounds of thrust each. Like giant training wheels, landing gear extended from the two engines closest to the bullet-shaped fuselage. And to get off a short runway in a hurry, its fuselage was designed to accommodate thirty-three powerful rockets that could produce an instantaneous 1,000 pounds of thrust each.

For listening, the plane's shiny aluminum belly was covered with an acnelike assortment of discolored patches, bumps, pods, and appendages, each hiding a unique specialized antenna—about 400 in all. A twelve-foot-long pod containing even more antennas and receivers was occasionally suspended from the right side of the aircraft.

The airborne electronic espionage operations, known as ferret missions, were so secret that the crews were forbidden from mentioning their aircraft, unit, or home base, or saying anything about their operations. "We usually snuck into our deployment base under the cover of darkness," said one RB-47 veteran, "and were hidden away on the far side of the field or in an isolated hangar well away from all other activities." Some detachment commanders forbade the crews even to be seen together in public. And, to avoid tipping off any spy that they were about to activate, crews would occasionally wear civilian work clothes over their flight suits when going to the flight line for a mission.

Ten minutes before takeoff at North Star Bay, the command pilot saw the green light flash twice for three seconds, clearing him to taxi out to the active runway. His engines gave an ear-piercing whine as he slowly turned into takeoff position. Once aboard the aircraft, the crew would maintain absolute radio silence in order to frustrate any Soviet electronic monitoring equipment. Even communication with ground control before takeoff was restricted to these brief light signals.

In the center of the plane, separated from the cockpit by a narrow crawlspace, were the three "Ravens"—Air Force officers who were specialists in electronic intelligence. Packed in the tight space of what would normally have been the bomb bay, and surrounded by bulky electronic equipment, a Raven could be "excruciatingly uncomfortable," said former Raven Bruce Bailey, a veteran of hundreds of missions against the Soviet Union. On a typical flight, he said, the idea was to "stuff" the Ravens "into unbelievably cramped, noisy, dangerous hell-holes and assure that they have a pressurization/air-conditioning system that doesn't work, ample fuel leaks, no acceptable method of escape, and can not move around in flight."

The Ravens were confined for up to a dozen hours in a compartment only four feet high. "Not only was it impossible to stand," said Bailey, "there wasn't even enough room for a good crouch. Most movement was made on your knees or in a crawl." Noise was also a major problem. "The compartment had no insulation and its thin aluminum walls were nestled right between and slightly behind the six engines. In addition . . . antennas and pods attached to the fuselage caused the skin to buffet and vibrate badly, adding to the noise."

Finally, as the aircraft leveled off, fuel would occasionally puddle in the compartment, filling the space with fumes. "With all the electrical gear and heat in the cabin, raw fuel made it a potential bomb," the former Raven pointed out. "When fuel was discovered, you immediately turned off all electrical power and depressurized the cabin. Then you hoped to get [the plane] on the ground before it blew up." Bailey, a retired Air Force lieutenant colonel, called the RB-47 Strato-Spy "an ugly, overweight, underpowered, unforgiving, uncomfortable, dangerous, and noisy airplane." Nevertheless, he added, "all of us who flew in it eventually grew to love it."

The entrance to the Raven compartment was a two-foot-square hatch on the bottom side of the fuselage. Once the three Ravens were aboard, the hatch would be sealed from the outside with forty-eight large screws. Squeezed together in the small space, all facing aft, the electronic spies were surrounded by scopes, receivers, analyzers, recorders, and controls.

Raven One, the commander of the group, sat in the right forward corner of the cabin. In addition to banks of equipment in front and to his left, he had a wide array of analog, video, and digital recorders stacked tight along the wall to his right and behind him. During the flight, he would keep his ears finely tuned for airborne-intercept radar signals from hostile Soviet fighters. From the sound and the wavy lines on his scopes, he could tell just how threatening those fighters might be. Raven Two, who listened for Soviet ground control and intercept radar systems, would be the first to know when the Strato-Spy was being tracked. Raven Three was responsible for analyzing the Soviet early warning and missile guidance signals, one of the principal objectives of the mission.

With two minutes to go, his preflight checks completed, the navigator began the countdown to takeoff. He was seated facing forward in the black nose of the plane, just below and in front of the pilot. His cabin was darkened so he could better see his radarscopes; his only natural light came from two small windows above his seat.

At one minute to takeoff, a steady green light signaled to the command pilot that he was cleared to fly the mission. With a deafening roar, he eased forward on the throttles, bringing his engines up to 100 percent power. By then the brakes were bucking and straining as they fought to hold back 36,000 pounds of forward thrust. The pilot carefully stabilized the engines.

Ten seconds before the zero mark the pilot flipped the water-alcohol injection switches, giving the plane a powerful boost so that it suddenly jumped forward briefly, like a lion about to pounce. From the half-dozen turbojets, thick clouds of heavy black smoke filled the sky.

At exactly ten o'clock the spy plane shuddered and let out a loud scream as the pilot released the brakes. Lumbering at first, the quarter-million pounds of steel and flesh were soon racing down the long frozen runway at nearly 200 miles per hour, leaving behind a gray trail of smoke and mist. A "ground lover," the heavy bird required well over two miles of surface for liftoff. As the concrete began to run out, the pilot pulled firmly back on his yoke and the aircraft knifed gracefully skyward.

In the spring of 1956 perhaps the most serious and risky espionage operation ever undertaken by the United States was launched. President Eisenhower authorized an invasion of Russian airspace by armed American bombers carrying eavesdropping gear and cameras instead of nuclear weapons. Details of the operation are still wrapped in great secrecy.

Nicknamed Project Homerun, the operation was staged from an air base near the frozen Eskimo village of Thule, Greenland, a desert of ice and snow 690 miles north of the Arctic Circle. In the purple-black of the polar winter, aircraft mechanics labored in −35° temperatures to prepare the nearly fifty bombers and tankers that would play a role in the massive incursion, one of the most secret missions of the Cold War. Housing for the flight and maintenance crews consisted of temporary buildings that looked like railroad refrigerator cars.

The mission was to penetrate virtually the entire northern landmass of Russia, a bleak white 3,500-mile-long crescent of snow-covered permafrost stretching from the Bering Strait near Alaska to Murmansk and the Kola Peninsula in European Russia. At the time, little was known about the vast Soviet Arctic region. Yet, because a flight over the North Pole was the shortest way for Russian bombers and missiles to reach the U.S. mainland, it was the most likely battleground for the next war. At the same time, it was also the most likely route for an American invasion of Russia. Thus any Soviet radar operator seeing the bombers would have no way of knowing that the mission was espionage and not war. Despite the enormous risks of igniting World War III, President Eisenhower approved the operation.

On March 21, 1956, a group of RB-47 reconnaissance bombers took off for target locations within Russia. Almost daily over the next seven weeks, between eight and ten bombers launched, refueled over the North Pole, and continued south across the Russian border to their assigned locations.

They flew in teams of two. One RB-47H ferret would pinpoint and eavesdrop on radar, air bases, and missile installations. Nearby, an RB-47E photoreconnaissance plane would gather imagery. Their assignments included overflying such sensitive locations as Novaya Zemlya, the banana-shaped island where Russia carried out its most secret atomic tests. From moment of takeoff to moment of landing, absolute radio silence was required, even during the occasional chase by a MiG. "One word on the radio, and all missions for the day had to abort," said Brigadier General William Meng, one of the officers who ran the penetration operation. "But that never happened; not one mission was ever recalled."

As in a Fourth of July fireworks display, the most spectacular mission was saved for the end. On May 6, they began the single most daring air operation of the Cold War, a "massed overflight" of Soviet territory. The point was to cover a great deal of territory, quickly. Six armed RB-47E aircraft, flying abreast, crossed the North Pole and penetrated Russian airspace in broad daylight, as if on a nuclear bombing run. They entered above Ambarchik in western Siberia, then turned eastward, collecting valuable intelligence as they passed over key Russian air bases and launch sites on their way toward Anadyr on the Bering Strait. Nearly a dozen hours after it began, the massed overflight ended when the spy planes touched down at Eielson Air Force Base in Alaska.

Within minutes of the landing, the recording tapes were sent by a special courier flight to NSA for analysis. They revealed no Soviet radar signals—proof that, at least for the time being, Russia was blind to an over-the-pole attack by American nuclear bombers. The vast sweep of frozen tundra making up Russia's northern frontier was virtually radar-free. Nevertheless, no one dared speculate on how the mission might have ended if hidden Soviet radar installations had picked up the incoming bombers and believed that they were sent on an American surprise attack. With only seconds to spare, the Russians might well have launched a counterattack, with devastating results.

In all, 156 eavesdropping and photo missions were flown over Russian airspace during the almost two months of Project Homerun without the loss of a single aircraft—and without a nuclear war. Nevertheless, Moscow was well aware of the air invasion. Eight days after the massed overflight, a protest note was delivered to the American ambassador in Moscow. Publicly, however, the Kremlin said nothing; the humiliation would have been too great.

Throughout the 1950s the ferrets, like mosquitoes hunting for an exposed patch of skin, buzzed the long Soviet border. They were searching for holes in Russia's vast fence of air-defense radar sites. At the time, the Soviet military had not yet completed work on a nationwide network. Nor was much of the interior protected.

As a CIA report points out, human spies had effectively been put out of action. "The stringent security measures imposed by the Communist Bloc nations," said the study, "effectively blunted traditional methods for gathering intelligence: secret agents using covert means to communicate intelligence, travelers to and from target areas who could be asked to keep their eyes open and report their observations later, wiretaps and other eavesdropping methods, and postal interceptions. Indeed, the entire panoply of intelligence tradecraft seemed ineffective against the Soviet Bloc, and no other methods were available."

But while the Communist governments of Eastern Europe and Asia could draw impenetrable iron curtains around their countries, hiding such things as the development of nuclear weapons and missile technology, they could not build roofs over them. Nor could their armed guards halt the continuous streams of invisible signals escaping across their borders.

While the eavesdropping bombers occasionally flew deep into Soviet airspace, other ferret missions engaged in the dangerous game of fox and hounds. Probing and teasing the hostile air defense networks, they would dart back and forth across sensitive borders, daring the Soviets to react. There was no other way to force the missile batteries and border defense installations to turn on their secret tracking equipment and thus enable the American signal snatchers to capture the precious electrons. Once analyzed, the information enabled war planners to determine where the holes were and how best to build equipment to counteract the radar and fire control systems.

It was a time and a place where spy wars were fought with armor-piercing bullets and heat-seeking missiles rather than with whispered words over cocktails or bulky envelopes deposited under dead tree trunks. Unlike the U-2 spy planes, the converted bombers flew low—well within the range of Russian missiles and warplanes.

In 1954, two years before Project Homerun, three RB-47 reconnaissance planes took off from England and headed toward Russia's northern Kola Peninsula, which borders the Barents Sea. It was an area of extreme secrecy, and considered the most likely spot from which the Soviets would launch a nuclear attack. At the time, the United States was desperate to obtain intelligence on the number and location of the new Soviet jet-turbine-powered long-range bombers, codenamed Bison.

At about one hundred miles from the heavily defended port city of Murmansk, two of the aircraft turned back as planned. The third, however, continued straight for the coastline. With no wingman to supply cover, the air crystal-clear, and the sun directly overhead, Captain Harold Austin, a tall, thin Texan, aimed the black nose of his converted bomber directly for Murmansk and pushed hard on the throttles. "The weather was gorgeous," he recalled. "We could see forever." He sped high over the Russian coastline at just over 500 miles an hour. But within minutes of turning on the cameras and eavesdropping equipment, MiGs were scrambling skyward.

Above and below, Austin could see the tracer bullets, and he yelled at his copilot to return fire. Air Force captain Carl Holt had swiveled his narrow seat 180 degrees to the rear and was pressing hard on the fire control button for his twin cannons. In the cloudless sky he stopped counting at about ten MiGs. "The guns won't work," he shouted above the roar of the six powerful turbojets. "Well, you'd better kick something back there and get the damn things to work a little bit anyway, or we may be a dead duck here!" Austin roared in a deep Texas drawl. Austin quickly banked toward Finland. But a fighter from above put a shell through the top of his port wing, destroying the intercom and knocking a hole in the fuel tank. By the time they crossed into friendly territory, their plane was dangerously low on fuel, but a lucky rendezvous with a tanker saved Austin, his crew, and the mission tapes.

Largely secret until now, the bomber overflights and ferret missions were the dark underside of the Cold War, an invisible hot war in which the lives of more than two hundred silent warriors were lost and more than forty American aircraft were shot down.

As American spy planes were drawing protests from Russia, a major crisis was developing in Europe and the Middle East. During the president's morning briefings, aides with maps were beginning to run out of pins to mark the hot spots. On July 26, 1956, following a fiery speech, Egyptian president Gamal Abdel Nasser nationalized the Suez Canal. The action would lead to a mini-war with England, France, and Israel and a cooling of relations with the European allies of the United States. It would also, according to a highly secret NSA report, become "the first major test of the National Security Agency during a short-term, 'brush-fire' crisis."

Sitting in the director's office was Lieutenant General Ralph Julian Canine, of the Army, the agency's first director, whom many considered the father of NSA. Portly and white-haired, the fifty-five-year-old general had spent most of his career as an infantry soldier, with little experience in intelligence. He often reminded those around him that what most qualified him to be the director of NSA was his long experience with pack mules.

"People were scared of him," said Air Force colonel Frank L. Herrelko, a burly one-time coal miner who worked for Canine as his director of communications security, the codemaking side of the business. "But deep down he had a heart of gold." Once onboard, Herrelko made the serious mistake of pronouncing Canine like the dog, "Kay-Nine." "I paid for that for the next eight months," said Herrelko. "After that he called me boy. He would only call me Colonel in front of somebody else. He called me boy."

The seizure of the Suez Canal came as the last move in a bitter game of Cold War poker. For months, the United States and Russia had been subtly bidding against each other for the costly right to help Egypt pay for an important dam across the Nile. Nasser was a key leader of the Arab world and he controlled a strategic piece of real estate; his friendship was an alluring prize. The price was the Aswan High Dam. Knowing his value and hoping to up the bids, Nasser awkwardly attempted to play one side off the other. Instead, the United States folded its cards and Russia, now without competition, began hedging its bet. Frustrated, Nasser declared martial law along the canal and ordered shipping companies to pay Egypt rather than the Canal Company.

Although Nasser never indicated any desire to close the canal or restrict shipping, the British and French governments, part owners of the Canal Company, nevertheless feared their passage might be blocked.

Like a plasma tube, the canal allowed vital oil shipments to pass from refineries in Saudi Arabia and elsewhere to storage tanks in England and France.

Soon after Nasser nationalized the canal, Britain joined France in an ambitious plot to take back the canal by force. Rather than appear as an aggressor, however, France secretly enlisted the help of Israel. The intrigue involved Israel launching a war against Egypt. Then, once Egypt began defending itself, England and France would go in as "peacekeepers." As part of the "peace," the canal would be taken from Egypt and kept by Britain and France. Israel would capture the Sinai from Egypt. It was a deceitful plan, which smacked of a return to the worst days of colonialism. Nevertheless, it was fully agreed to by Israeli prime minister David Ben-Gurion, defense minister Shimon Peres, and armed forces chief Moshe Dayan. Britain's prime minister, Anthony Eden, informed of Israel's planned key role, likewise gave his country's approval. For all involved in the cabal, it was essential to keep the precise details of the elaborate conspiracy hidden from Washington. At the same time, however, it was also essential to win Washington's support once the hostilities began.

As the crisis quietly grew, the American intelligence community began turning its eyes and ears on the Middle East. On Monday, August 6, Secretary of State John Foster Dulles sat alongside the president's desk and brought to Eisenhower's attention NSA's latest intercepts from Spain and Syria, revealing their attitudes and intentions following the seizure. From Israel, however, there was nothing.

NSA's expensive machine was not working. It had only two settings: Communist Europe and Communist Asia. Under the postwar United Kingdom–USA (UKUSA) Communications Intelligence Agreement, the world had been divided into spheres of interest. Through its listening posts in England and on Cyprus, GCHQ, NSA's longtime British partner, was to monitor much of Western Europe and the Middle East. But now, to hide from Washington its invasion plans, GCHQ was passing on only selected intercepts.

Deceived by its partner, NSA could do little by itself. The agency had few Arabic or Hebrew linguists and it was not equipped to eavesdrop on British, French, or Israeli military communications. All NSA knew was that traffic analysis indicated that "communications between Paris and Tel Aviv were extremely heavy," as were those between Britain and France.

To make matters worse, the agency was in the middle of moving from Washington to a new headquarters twenty-five miles north, at Fort Meade in Maryland. Files, people, and equipment were scattered among Arlington Hall in Virginia, where the main codebreaking and analysis were done; the Naval Security Station in Washington, which served as headquarters and was responsible for codemaking; and the new building at Fort Meade where operations were to be consolidated. Communications among the various areas were jury-rigged and couriers were required to move intercepted traffic between locations four times a day. Adding to the confusion, General Canine was clearing his desk and getting ready to retire. As one NSA analysis later acknowledged, "1956 was a bad time for NSA to get involved in a crisis."

As the full extent of the elaborate French-Israeli-British plot became clear, Eisenhower grew outraged. He told Britain and France that they should expect no American assistance with their adventure. Over the phone, Dulles told Eisenhower the action was "about as crude and brutal as anything [I] have ever seen" and called the Anglo-French ultimatum "unacceptable." "Expect the Russians to be in on this," Eisenhower said. Allen Dulles, at the CIA, called his brother. "It was the gravest situation between our countries in years," Allen said.

The issue of what action to take against Israel was hotly debated. "It would be a complete mistake for this country to continue with any kind of aid to Israel," Eisenhower argued, "which was an aggressor." Harold Stassen objected but John Foster Dulles answered, "One thing at least was clear: We do not approve of murder. We have simply got to refrain from resorting to force in settling international disputes. . . . If we stand by in this crisis, the whole United Nations will go down the drain." Eisenhower agreed.

In London, the heavy pressures exerted by the United States, Russia, and the international community had become too great. A cease-fire was agreed to, thus ending one of the most serious confrontations America had faced since the end of World War II.

The Suez crisis had a profound effect on NSA. It marked a dismal entry into the world of crisis intelligence. An internal analysis of the agency's performance was harshly critical: "As for crisis response, all was chaos. The cryptologic community proved incapable of marshalling its forces in a flexible fashion to deal with developing trouble spots. The events of the year did not demonstrate success—they simply provided a case study to learn from."

In a highly unusual move, Canine enlisted the help of an outside management firm to examine the agency's problems. Suddenly consultants from McKinsey and Company began crisscrossing NSA's hallways, going over NSA's highly secret organizational charts, and studying the flow of intercepts from NSA's worldwide network of listening posts. Canine's key concern was whether the agency would function more effectively if its organization was based primarily on function—traffic analysis, cryptanalysis, and so on—or on geography. And how centralized should NSA become?

The consultants recommended a complete change. The repercussions, according to a later NSA report, lasted more than thirty years. Soon after he arrived, Canine had reorganized the new agency along functional lines. Now McKinsey proposed a "modified geographical concept." Signals intelligence would be organized according to target—the Soviet Union and its satellite countries; China and Communist Asia; and so on. Each of those sections would include specific disciplines, such as cryptanalysis and traffic analysis.

Thus NSA-70, which was responsible for all high-level cryptanalysis, was replaced by ADVA ("Advanced Soviet"), which focused exclusively on new ways to attack high-level Soviet cipher problems. GENS ("General Soviet") concentrated mainly on mid- and lower-level Russian crypto systems, as well as on analysis of content. ACOM (Asian Communist) attempted to exploit the systems of China, North Korea, and the rest of Communist Asia. Finally, ALLO ("All Others") analyzed the systems belonging to the nations making up the rest of the world, including America's allies. ALLO-34, for example, was responsible for Middle East traffic analysis. Three other divisions were primarily for support: MPRO ("Machine Processing") was responsible for computer number crunching; TCOM ("Telecommunications") controlled the worldwide flow of signals; and Collection managed the NSA's far-flung network of listening posts.

On November 23, 1956, Ralph Canine walked out of NSA for the last time as director. "Canine . . . stands out as the guy who everybody respected in the agency," recalled Howard Campaigne. "I was surprised to learn later that the people above him didn't think nearly as much [of him] as we did. He made a tremendous impression."

In a restricted corner of a remote air base in Peshawar, Pakistan, Francis Gary Powers sat shoehorned into the narrow cockpit of U-2 Number 360. At twenty minutes past six on the morning of May 1, 1960, the scorching sun had already pushed above the tallest peaks of the western Himalayas. In the low, fertile plain known as the Vale of Peshawar, rippling heat waves created the impression of an endless lake. Powers was locked in a white space helmet and a tightly tailored pressure suit. Beads of sweat flowed down from his short brown hair and passed across his broad forehead and cheekbones in thin streams. His long underwear was soaked with perspiration.

The first U-2 had been launched from West Germany four years earlier, on Independence Day of 1956. Shortly before, NSA had detected a possible mobilization by Moscow in response to a series of riots in East Germany, thus making the mission more urgent. But hope that the U-2 would be able to slip across the Soviet Union undetected was dashed by the eavesdroppers at Fort Meade. "NSA picked up the [Soviet] transmission of their [the U-2's] track so we knew that they had been tracked a good deal of the time," said Richard M. Bissell, Jr., the CIA official who ran the program. Nevertheless, seeing where the Russians were able to pick up the plane and where they weren't gave NSA an indication of just where the holes were in Soviet radar coverage.

As he did with the bomber overflights, Eisenhower played a major role in the planning for each mission. "He would sometimes cut out particular legs or say, 'Well, don't go from A to B to C, go from A to C,' " according to Bissell.

In Peshawar, Powers looked at his watch. The mission was now almost a half-hour behind schedule. He had never before had to wait so long for final clearance from the White House. In fact, Eisenhower had already given the mission a thumbs-up, but because of radio problems the message had not gotten through to the operations officer in Peshawar.

Although much attention would later be focused on the U-2s'

photo role, the planes' eavesdropping missions, codenamed Green Hornet, were equally important. A U-2's intercept equipment, known as System-V, was installed in the bay that normally housed the main camera. It consisted of sophisticated electronic receivers and large-capacity recorders that used Mylar tape. Scores of antennas, like small blades, were attached to the fuselage, each dedicated to particular frequency bands. Powers's first eavesdropping mission took the plane along the Soviet border from the Black Sea to the Caspian Sea and on to Afghanistan. According to a CIA report, "the System-V unit worked well."

Soon after his assignment to Adana, Turkey, Powers began flying Green Hornet missions. "We usually flew from Turkey eastward along the southern border of the Soviet Union," he recalled, "over Iran and Afghanistan as far as Pakistan, and back. We also flew along the Black Sea, and, on occasion, as far west as Albania, but never penetrating, staying off the coast, over international waters. . . . Since these 'eavesdropping' missions were eventually to become fairly frequent, there was a tendency to minimize their importance, but in many ways they were as valuable as the overflights, the data obtained enabling the United States to pinpoint such things as Russian antiaircraft defenses and gauge their effectiveness."

On the top of the priority list, according to Powers, were Soviet space and missile launches which normally took place at night and, from the altitude of the U-2, "were often spectacular," he said. "The equipment we carried on such occasions was highly sophisticated. One unit came on automatically the moment the launch frequency was used and collected all the data sent out to control the rocket. The value of such information to our own scientists was obvious." Indeed it was. The U-2's ability to soar thirteen miles high along the Soviet border gave it a unique ability to eavesdrop on telemetry data during the earliest phases of the flight. The U-2, said one CIA report at the time, "possesses altitude capabilities which make it a unique platform for the reliable acquisition of high quality telemetry data prior to first stage burnout on Tyuratam [missile center] launchings. Such data is of extreme importance in determining ICBM characteristics."

Finally, the link from Washington to Peshawar was made. Colonel William Shelton, the detachment chief, leaped from the radio van and ran across the field to give Powers the hand signal for takeoff. It would be the twenty-fourth U-2 overflight of the Soviet Union, and the last.

Powers locked his canopy from the inside, turned on the pressurization system, and pulled back hard on the throttle, sending the plane into a steep climb, a roller-coaster ride up to the blue-black curve of space. Below passed the barren dusty-brown landscape of Afghanistan and the peaks of the Hindu Kush, spiking through the thin cloud cover like daggers. An hour later, reaching penetration altitude of 66,000 feet, he passed over the Soviet border, high above the village of Kirovabad in the remote Tadjik Republic. Oddly, Powers felt the Russians knew he was coming.

In this, he was perceptive. Soviet radar had begun tracking the plane before it ever reached the border. Immediately, an alert was telephoned to command headquarters and air defense staff officers were summoned to their posts.

In still-darkened Moscow, gaily decorated for the grand May Day celebration, a telephone rang next to Party Chairman Khrushchev's bed. "Minister of Defense Marshal Malinovsky reporting," said the voice on the other end. Malinovsky told his boss that a U-2 had crossed the border from Afghanistan and was flying in the direction of Sverdlovsk, in central Russia. "Shoot down the plane by whatever means," barked the Soviet leader. "If our antiaircraft units can just keep their eyes open and stop yawning long enough," he added, "I'm sure we'll knock the plane down." The days of protest were over. "We were sick and tired of these unpleasant surprises—sick and tired of being subjected to these indignities," Khrushchev later wrote. "They were making these flights to show up our impotence. Well, we weren't impotent any longer."

But Powers was in luck. A missile battalion more than a dozen miles below was not on alert duty that day. A missile launch was considered but then rejected as unfeasible. Instead, fighter aircraft were scrambled in an attempt to shoot down the plane. "An uncomfortable situation was shaping up," recalled former Soviet Air Force colonel Alexander Orlov, who was involved in air defense at the time. "The May Day parade was scheduled to get underway at mid-morning, and leaders of the party, the government, and the Armed Forces were to be present as usual. In other words, at a time when a major parade aimed at demonstrating Soviet military prowess was about to begin, a not-yet-identified foreign aircraft was flying over the heart of the country and Soviet air defenses appeared unable to shoot it down."

"Shame!" Khrushchev screamed at Marshal S. S. Biryuzov, the chief of the Air Defense Forces. "The country was giving air defense everything it needs, and still you cannot shoot down a subsonic aircraft!" Biryuzov had no excuses. "If I could become a missile," he fumed, "I myself would fly and down this damned intruder." The tension was palpable. "Nerves of military people at airfields," said Orlov, "missile positions, command-and-control facilities, the Air Force, and the Air Defense Forces were badly frayed. . . . Khrushchev demanded that the intruding aircraft be shot down at all costs. The Soviet leader and his lieutenants clearly viewed the violation of their nation's skies by a foreign reconnaissance aircraft on the day of a Soviet national holiday, and just two weeks before a summit conference in Paris, as a political provocation."

Russian radar continued to follow the U-2 across the Central Asian republics. By the time Powers reached the Tashkent area, as many as thirteen MiGs had been scrambled in an unsuccessful attempt to shoot him down. Far below, Powers could see the condensation trail of a single-engine jet moving fast in the opposite direction. Five to ten minutes later he saw another contrail, this time moving in the same direction, paralleling his course. "I was sure now they were tracking me on radar," he later recalled, "vectoring in and relaying my heading to the aircraft."

But Powers knew that at his altitude there was no way for the pilots even to see him, let alone attack him. "If this was the best they could do," he thought, "I had nothing to worry about." He then wondered how the Russians felt, knowing he was up there but unable to do anything about it. Had he known of a top secret CIA study the previous summer he might not have been so cocky, but the pilots were never informed of its findings. The study gave the U-2 a very limited life because of improvements in Soviet ground-to-air missiles. It recommended that the overflights be terminated and replaced by border surveillance flights: "In view of the improving Soviet air defense effort, we believe that the utilization of the aircraft may soon be limited to peripheral operations."

By now, 4½ hours into the mission, Powers was approaching his first important target, the Tyuratam Missile Test Range. This was the Soviet Union's most important space launch site. Three days earlier, CIA Director Dulles reported to the president and the National Security Council that Russia had recently attempted to launch two space vehicles, probably lunar probes. "Evidence indicates that both attempts failed," he said. "The vehicle launched on April 15 did not attain a velocity sufficient to send it to the moon. . . . The second Soviet space vehicle lifted from the launching pad but failed immediately." The short interval between the two attempts, he concluded, "probably indicates that the USSR has a second launching pad at Tyuratam." Up to then, the United States had known of only one.

This information, produced by NSA listening posts and ferret missions, was considered so secret that Dulles took the unusual precaution of reminding the council and even the president of how closely it was held. "Intelligence concerning Soviet failures in the launching of missiles or space vehicles," he warned, "was very sensitive information."

In addition to photographing the missile site, Powers had a second key mission—this one for NSA: to eavesdrop on the radar systems surrounding the base. On board were special recorders that could capture the signals. After landing, the tapes would be flown back to Fort Meade for analysis.

Large thunderclouds obscured Powers's view of the test site, but he nevertheless switched on the cameras, which might capture proof of the second launch pad. At the same moment, he entered the engagement zone of a surface-to-air-missile battalion. "Destroy target," the officer in charge of the unit shouted. Immediately an SA-2 missile was fired. This time the missilemen's eyes were wide open—and the Soviets were lucky. A fireball exploded behind Powers, damaging the U-2's tail and wings but leaving the cockpit unharmed. At the air defense facility below, the small dot on the radar began to blink. The plane was breaking up.

"My God, I've had it now!" Powers gasped. He felt a dull thump and a tremendous orange flash filled the cockpit. As his plane began to dip toward the ground from 70,500 feet, on the very edge of space, Powers fought for control. The orange glow, he thought, seemed to last for minutes. "Instinctively I grasped the throttle with my left hand," he recalled, "and keeping my right hand on the wheel, checked instruments."

All of a sudden a violent force sent him bouncing within the cockpit and he knew both wings had come off. He was now in a tailless, wingless missile heading rapidly toward earth. "What was left of the plane began spinning. . . . All I could see was blue sky, spinning, spinning."

With pressurization lost, Powers's space suit had inflated and was squeezing him tighter and tighter. At the same time, the g-forces were pushing him toward the nose of the plane. "I reached for the destruct switches [to blow up the plane]," he said, "opening the safety covers, had my hand over them, then changed my mind, deciding I had better see if I could get into position to use the ejection seat first." Forced forward in his seat, he was afraid that when he ejected his legs would be sliced off. "I didn't want to cut them off, but if it was the only way to get out . . ."

Instead of ejecting, Powers began to climb out of the cockpit. He unlocked the canopy and it jetted into space. "The plane was still spinning," said Powers. "I glanced at the altimeter. It had passed thirty-four thousand feet and was unwinding very fast." The centrifugal force threw him halfway out of the aircraft, smashing his head against the rearview mirror and snapping the mirror off. "I saw it fly away," Powers recalled. "That was the last thing I saw, because almost immediately my face plate frosted over."

Half in and half out of the disintegrating spy plane, Powers was still trapped. He suddenly realized that he had forgotten to unfasten his oxygen hoses and now they were turning into a noose. After minutes that seemed like hours of struggle, the hoses broke and suddenly, unbelievably, he was free. "It was a pleasant, exhilarating feeling," he thought. "Even better than floating in a swimming pool." Later he said, "I must have been in shock."

At an NSA listening post in Turkey, intercept operators began picking up some worrisome signals. For more than four hours they had been eavesdropping on Soviet radar installations as the Russians tracked Powers's U-2 flight.

It had long been one of NSA's neatest tricks. Because radar signals travel in a straight line and the earth is curved, it was impossible for American radar stations outside Russia to detect air activity deep within the country. However, Soviet radar installations throughout the country communicated with each other over high-frequency circuits. Because high-frequency signals bounce between the earth and the ionosphere, the right equipment can pick them up thousands of miles away. Thus, by eavesdropping on Soviet radar networks as they transmitted signals between their bases over these channels, NSA could, in effect, watch Russian radar screens far inside the country.

For years American intercept operators in Turkey had eavesdropped on Soviet radar installations as they tracked the occasional U-2 overflight. But because the spy planes flew far too high for either Russian MiGs or their SA-2 surface-to-air missiles, they were out of harm's way. It was like throwing a rock at a passing jetliner. This time, however, something was different; something was very wrong. "He's turning left!" the Americans heard a Soviet pilot shout. A few moments later the intercept operators watched the U-2 suddenly disappear from Russian radar screens near Sverdlovsk.

A CRITIC message was sent to NSA, the White House, and other locations in Washington. The information reached the CIA's Operations Center at 3:30 A.M.

They flew in low and swift, arriving with the dawn. The rhythmic *thwap, thwap, thwap* of the long blades competed briefly with the sounds of electric shavers and percolating coffee in town houses in northwest Washington and in split-levels in the nearby Maryland and Virginia suburbs. Almost simultaneously, they began landing on dirt fields, creating miniature dust storms, and in vacant lots, where commuters were briefly startled to see large, dark helicopters in their favorite parking spaces.

At the White House the sun was just starting to peek from behind the Washington Monument, casting an early-morning shadow across the neatly landscaped Ellipse and illuminating the few remaining cherry blossoms along the Tidal Basin. President Eisenhower had been awakened by the phone call only minutes earlier and now he was being rushed out through the curved diplomatic entrance to his waiting chopper, ducking his head to avoid the slice of the still-spinning blades.

A few miles to the east, the wife of Secretary of Defense Thomas Gates, still in her nightgown, negotiated through traffic as her husband read out lefts and rights to a secret landing spot within NSA's heavily protected naval headquarters on Nebraska Avenue. The secretary was in for trouble, however: his pass was still sitting back home on his dresser.

When the White House switchboard reached the president's science adviser he was standing under the hot spray of his shower. There was no time to dry off, he was told as he quickly jotted down instructions.

In Georgetown, CIA Director Allen Dulles managed to get a ride from another senior official when his car picked this of all mornings to stall.

It was Thursday, the fifth of May. Within half an hour of the emergency calls, part of this long-planned "Doomsday" practice exercise, helicopters carrying the nearly two dozen senior national security officials were flying south over the thick green canopy that covers the Virginia countryside. Their destination was a secret command center dug deep into Mount Weather in the Blue Ridge Mountains and built on a series of giant nuclear-shock-absorbing steel springs. Its code name was High Point, but members of the president's inner circle also called it simply "the hideout."

In Moscow at that very moment, a bald, rotund ex-miner in a tent-like business suit stood before the Supreme Soviet and punched the air with his fist like a bare-knuckles boxer. "Shame to the aggressor!" he bellowed, "Shame to the aggressor!" Standing on the stage of the white-chambered Great Kremlin Palace, Chairman Nikita S. Khrushchev had just brought some news to the thirteen hundred members of the Soviet parliament. "I must report to you on aggressive actions against the Soviet Union in the past few weeks by the United States of America," he said, his voice rising to a shout. "The United States has been sending aircraft that have been crossing our state frontiers and intruding upon the airspace of the Soviet Union. We protested to the United States against several previous aggressive acts of this kind and brought them to the attention of the United Nations Security Council. But as a rule, the United States offered formalistic excuses and tried in every way to deny the facts of aggression—even when the proof was irrefutable."

Then the surprise. Five days before, on May Day, "early in the morning, at 5:36 Moscow time, an American plane crossed our frontier and continued its flight deep into Soviet territory. . . . The plane was shot down." The packed auditorium broke into pandemonium, shaking with applause and wild cheers, stamping their feet. "Just imagine what would have happened had a Soviet aircraft appeared over New York, Chicago or Detroit," he added, "How would the *United States* have reacted? . . . That would mean the outbreak of war!"

Pointing to the west and stabbing the air once again, Khrushchev yelled, "The question then arises: who *sent* this aircraft across the Soviet frontier? Was it the American Commander-in-Chief who, as everyone knows, is the president? Or was this aggressive act performed by Pentagon militarists without the president's knowledge? If American military men can take such action on their own," he concluded, "the world should be greatly concerned." More earsplitting applause.

The timing of the long-planned Doomsday rehearsal seemed almost uncanny to the casually dressed officials in the cement bunker beneath Mount Weather. Five days earlier the U-2 spy plane carrying Francis Gary Powers had gone down over Central Russia—and then, not a peep. All concluded that the aircraft had crashed, killing the pilot. A standard cover story had been issued the next day. Approved by Eisenhower in 1956, at the beginning of the overflight program, this cover story had it that the missing plane belonged to the National Aeronautics and Space Administration (NASA) and had been on a routine air sampling mission in Turkey. "Following cover plan to be implemented immediately," said the CIA's top secret message to its field stations. "U-2 aircraft was on weather mission originating Adana, Turkey. Purpose was study of clear air turbulence. During flight in Southeast Turkey, pilot reported he had oxygen difficulties. . . ."

Deep in the hideout, Eisenhower's astonishment grew as each new page of Khrushchev's speech was handed to him. It had flashed across the wires shortly after the U.S. officials were airborne. The Soviets were not only taking credit for blasting the spy plane out of the sky with a missile, they were pointing the finger of responsibility directly at the president. The American press was also beginning to raise similar questions. Eisenhower could see the darkening clouds of an enormous election-year scandal forming.

At 10:32 A.M. Russia's imaginary nuclear strike ended. But Eisenhower was now left to respond to Khrushchev's verbal bombshell, and against that the High Point bunker could offer no protection. As the rest of the senior national security team headed back to Washington, the president huddled with his closest advisers. Gathered on sofas and overstuffed chairs in the bunker's small informal lounge, most agreed with Douglas Dillon that a new statement should be issued, replacing the NASA cover story, to counter Khrushchev's explosive charges. A former Wall Street banker and owner of a French winery, Dillon was filling in for Secretary of State Christian Herter, who was out of the country.

But Eisenhower would have none of it. All Khrushchev had was a dead pilot and a stack of scrap metal. As weak and as full of holes as the NASA cover story was, they would stick with it. Allen Dulles agreed. He had given birth to the U-2, nurtured it, and pressed the reluctant president to let it fly deep and often. Now was no time for weakness. Besides, he had long ago given the White House "absolutely categorical" assurances that a U-2 pilot would never survive a crash.

This certainty was curious, for a number of safety devices were built into the aircraft, including a specially designed ejection seat. Dulles's "absolutely categorical" guarantee lends weight to the suspicion that the U-2 was rigged to prevent any possibility of a pilot surviving. Adding weight to this theory was a later comment by top Eisenhower aide Andrew Goodpaster that "we had an understanding . . . that the plane would be destroyed and that it was impossible for the pilot to survive."

Once set in motion, however, the lie would soon gain a life of its own and no one would be able to control it. At NASA, long respected around the world for the open and honest way it managed America's space program, spokesman Walter Bonney was forced to stand before television cameras and tell lie after lie for the better part of an hour. Two days later, on Saturday, May 7, Khrushchev let his other boot drop. "Comrades," he said with a smile, looking down on the delegates attending the meeting of the Supreme Soviet. "I must let you in on a secret. When I made my report two days ago, I deliberately refrained from mentioning that we have the remains of the plane—*and we also have the pilot, who is quite alive and kicking!*" The gathering howled with laughter and shook the walls with applause. Then, in an action that certainly sent shivers down the spines of senior officials at NSA, he told the crowd that the USSR had also recovered "a tape recording of the signals of a number of our ground radar stations—incontestable evidence of spying."

Notified of the news while at Gettysburg, Eisenhower replied with one word: "*Unbelievable.*" In Washington, it was chaos. Senior aides, like masons, began to quickly build a wall of lies around the president, and the cover story seemed to change by the hour. Like a character from *Alice in Wonderland*, State Department spokesman Lincoln White was left to scurry down the rabbit hole again and again. Everything said previously was untrue, he told a dumbfounded press. One reporter later wrote, "Almost instantly you could feel the anger harden. Newsmen discovered, to their horror, that they had participated in a lie."

At one point Secretary of Defense Gates called Secretary of State Herter and demanded that someone give a straight story. "Somebody has to take responsibility for the policy," Gates insisted. "While the President can say he didn't know about this one flight, he did approve the policy." Herter gripped the black receiver tight and shot back, "The president didn't argue with this but for the moment [he] doesn't want to say anything and we have been trying to keep the president clear on this."

When the president walked into the Oval Office on the morning of May 9, his normal good humor had given way to depression. "I would like to resign," he said to his secretary, Ann Whitman. Talk was beginning to spread that Congress might call for a vigorous probe into the U-2 affair, something Eisenhower wanted to avoid at all costs. Later in the day Herter and Dulles were scheduled to go behind closed doors and brief a handful of senior senators and congressmen on the scandal. Dulles, Eisenhower said, should tell the delegation from the Hill only that the project had operated for four years under a general, blank presidential authorization. No more. Then, to discourage any thoughts of an investigation, the spy chief should "point out that any informal investigation would be very bad."

For Eisenhower, the whole process was quickly turning into Chinese water torture. Every day he was being forced to dribble out more and more of the story. But he had decided that one secret must never be revealed, even if members of his Cabinet had to lie to Congress to keep it: his own personal involvement in the U-2 and bomber overflights. Before the congressional meeting, Goodpaster called Herter to emphasize the point. The "president wants no specific tie to him of this particular event," he warned.

As Dulles and Herter were on Capitol Hill, Eisenhower was meeting with members of his National Security Council, warning them to avoid the press. "Our reconnaissance was discovered," he said ruefully, "and we would just have to endure the storm and say as little as possible." A short time later, in what had become by now an almost laughable daily routine, Lincoln White read still another statement, which contradicted the three previous announcements. Now the administration was admitting to "extensive aerial surveillance by unarmed civilian aircraft, normally of a peripheral character but on occasion by penetration. Specific missions . . . have not been subject to presidential authorization." With that, Eisenhower had drawn a line in the sand. No matter what the cost, a blanket of lies must forever hide his personal involvement in the ill-fated project.

From the very beginning, he had had a sense that the overflight programs would end in disaster. But his advisers, especially Allen Dulles and General Nathan Twining, the chairman of the Joint Chiefs of Staff, had pushed and pushed and pushed. No more. "Call off any provocative actions," the president ordered Gates following a June 1960 Cabinet meeting, barely able to hide his anger. NSA's peripheral ferret flights, however, could continue—as long as they remained in international airspace. Then Eisenhower motioned for Herter and Goodpaster to follow him into his office and told them in no uncertain terms that all further U-2 overflights of the USSR would cease. "Inform Allen Dulles," he said abruptly. The next day Eisenhower was to depart for Paris and a long-awaited summit conference with Khrushchev. He wanted no more surprises.

Aboard his four-engine Il-18, as it passed over the dark forests of Byelorussia on its way to Paris, Khrushchev once again began smoldering over the timing of the U-2 mission. "It was as though the Americans had deliberately tried to place a time bomb under the meeting," he thought, "set to go off just as we were about to sit down with them at the negotiating table." He was particularly concerned over his nation's loss of prestige within the Soviet bloc. "How could they count on us to give them a helping hand if we allowed ourselves to be spat upon without so much as a murmur of protest?" The only solution was to demand a formal public apology from Eisenhower and a guarantee that no more overflights would take place. One more surprise for the American president.

But the apology Khrushchev was looking for would not come. Despite having trespassed on the Soviet Union for the past four years with scores of flights by both U-2s and heavy bombers, the old general still could not say the words; it was just not in him. He did, however, declare an end to overflights through the end of his term. But it was not enough. A time bomb had exploded, prematurely ending the summit conference. Both heads of state returned to Orly Airport for their flights home. Also canceled was Khrushchev's invitation to Eisenhower for a Moscow visit before leaving office. "We couldn't possibly offer our hospitality," Khrushchev later said, "to someone who had already, so to speak, made a mess at his host's table."

Back in Washington, the mood was glum. The Senate Foreign Relations Committee was leaning toward holding a closed-door investigation into the U-2 incident and the debacle in Paris. In public, Eisenhower maintained a brave face. He "heartily approved" of the congressional probe and would "of course, fully cooperate," he quickly told anyone who asked. But in private he was very troubled. For weeks he had tried to head off the investigation. His major concern was that his own personal involvement in the overflights would surface, especially the May Day disaster. Equally, he was very worried that details of the dangerous bomber overflights would leak out. The massed overflight may, in fact, have been one of the most dangerous actions ever approved by a president.

At 8:40 A.M. on May 24, shortly before a National Security Council meeting, Gordon Gray pulled open the curved, five-inch-thick wooden door of the Oval Office and walked briskly across the pale green carpet bearing the presidential seal. The president's national security adviser knew

Eisenhower did not like visitors to wait to be told to come in. Gary had bad news. "It appeared," he told his boss, "that there was no longer any hope that congressional committees could be restrained from conducting investigations of the U-2–Summit matter." With the start of the hearings only three days away, Gray suggested that during the NSC meeting, Eisenhower "would wish to indicate to the Council how far he wished his principal advisers to go in their testimony."

A short while later, two dozen officials crowded into the Cabinet Room, just off the Oval Office. Eisenhower's National Security Council meetings had the timing and grace of Kabuki theater. At about thirty seconds before 10:00, Gray made his announcement in the Cabinet Room. "The President," he said in a deep voice, as if issuing a command, which in a sense he was.

As Eisenhower entered, the Council participants awkwardly rose to their feet and mumbled a good morning. Eisenhower then took his position at the center of the table. Sitting on a leather-bound ink blotter was a large three-ring binder, his "Black Book," opened to the first item on the agenda. Nearby was a matching holder containing White House notepaper. A black dial phone with seven buttons was to his left. Directly across from him sat Vice President Richard M. Nixon, and behind the vice president was a bookcase containing a gold-colored Republican elephant, a colonial soldier standing at attention, and a shiny set of engraved leather volumes, which appeared never to have been opened.

"Mr. President," Gray began. "The first item is a briefing by Mr. Allen Dulles." The CIA director was in his usual seat, at the head of the table and to Eisenhower's right, framed by a large white fireplace. Pipe in hand, the professor began. Moscow's decision "to play up the U-2 incident and to call off the visit of the President to the USSR," he told the somber officials, was made well before the summit took place. But the decision "to wreck the Summit meeting," Dulles said, was made only *after* the U.S. admitted presidential approval of the overflight program.

This was not what Eisenhower wanted to hear. The blame for the disaster now reached right to the Oval Office door. He could not allow the Senate Committee to get any closer. He could not let them discover that, contrary to what he had told the American public and the senior congressional leadership, he had personally approved and overseen the bungled May Day flight and every other mission. And he certainly could not let them discover the risky bomber overflights which, thankfully, had not yet come to light.

Sitting with his back to the blue drapes and the broad windows looking out onto the North Lawn, Eisenhower bemoaned the committee's investigation. "It was clear," he later wrote irritatedly, "that Congress would insist on some kind of investigation of the U-2 incident and the break-up of the Summit Conference." "Administration officials should be calm and clear, but should not be expansive and should not permit the investigators to delve into our intelligence system . . . ," he warned. "Some investigators were masters at beguiling witnesses and trying to find out all about our intelligence systems." "No information," he said sternly, "should be divulged" concerning those operations.

Privately, Eisenhower had no use for congressional investigations. Over a Scotch in the family quarters of the White House, Defense Secretary Tom Gates once brought up his apprehension concerning his scheduled testimony before Lyndon Johnson's Preparedness Committee. The questioning was going to focus on accusations that the administration was deliberately underestimating Soviet missiles in order to reduce Pentagon spending and balance the budget. "What's more," Gates said, "that's under oath. That's an investigation." But Eisenhower quickly brushed aside the defense secretary's concern. "Just stand up there and tell 'em you won't take their oath."

Another official fearful of the probe and seeking to scuttle it was General Nathan Twining. It was he who had been most responsible for the bomber overflights, and now, at the May 24 meeting, he was concerned that the investigators might soon turn away from the CIA and toward his own organization. "The investigation, once started, would seek to explore our whole intelligence operation," he protested. "If the investigators probed CIA, they would then want to investigate JCS operations." He then questioned "whether there was anything we could do to stop the investigation."

After a few moments, Eisenhower brought up the concept of executive privilege but quickly rejected it as unworkable. The investigators could be stopped from probing into advice given him by his personal staff, he said, but not into the activities of other administration officials.

"Accordingly," he complained, "the investigation could not be stopped." But to limit the possibility of a leak, he said, "administration officials should testify themselves and not allow their subordinates to speak."

One other possibility brought up by Eisenhower was to have Allen Dulles simply stonewall all questions. "Mr. Dulles," he said, "might have to say that CIA [is] a secret organization of the U.S. Government."

Still another possibility was to try to turn the public against the Committee. Secretary of the Treasury Robert Anderson suggested to Eisenhower that he go on television and appeal to the American public to reject the investigation. "The speech," he said, "should express the hope that no one in this country will engage in activities which will imperil the capability of the country to protect itself in the future. The speech should contain the implication that there is a limit beyond which investigation cannot go without imperiling our security." To further make the point about the dangers to security such an investigation might cause, Anderson told Eisenhower he should evoke the terrible image of Pearl Harbor.

But Eisenhower was resigned to the inevitability of the investigation. He turned to the most difficult topic: covering up his own involvement in the scandal. "Congress could be told that overflights have been going on with the approval of the secretary of State," he said, "and our scientific advisers, who have indicated that this method of gathering intelligence is necessary. It should be made clear that basic decisions respecting reconnaissance overflights of denied territory have been made by the president."

That, Eisenhower decided, was all the investigators would get. Full stop. The fact that he had actually micromanaged the program from the Oval Office would have to be denied. According to formerly top secret documents obtained for *Body of Secrets,* Eisenhower was so fearful of the probe that he went so far as to order his Cabinet officers to hide his involvement in the scandal even while under oath. At least one Cabinet member directly lied to the committee, a fact known to Eisenhower. Subornation of perjury is a serious crime, one that had it been discovered might have led to calls for his impeachment and to the prosecution of senior Cabinet members.

"The impression," Eisenhower ordered his senior Cabinet members and National Security Council team, "should not be given that the president has approved specific flights, precise missions, or the timing of specific flights." Yet that was precisely what the president had approved: the specific flights, the precise missions, and the timing of the specific flights.

The issue was never the protection of "our intelligence systems," as Eisenhower told the NSC officials. It was covering up his role in the botched project. After all, the U-2 program had virtually no secrets left. For four years the Russians had been tracking each flight over and along their country. They now had a pilot, who had given them a signed confession and was talking. And sitting on display in Moscow's Gorki Park were major parts of the plane, largely intact. Included were the damaged camera and NSA eavesdropping gear, as well as pictures made from the exposed film showing the quality of photography. Visitors to the exhibit could even listen to the spy plane's intercept tapes giving off the beeping signals of Soviet radar installations. Tapes once destined for NSA.

Nor was the public release of sensitive information an issue. The testimony was to be taken entirely in secret by the Senate Foreign Relations Committee, which as a matter of course heard highly classified testimony concerning such topics as intelligence operations and nuclear weapons. Furthermore, to ensure security, the CIA itself was to be in charge of censoring any information that was eventually to be made public, and the stenographer's tapes were to be put through a shredder.

Rather, what Eisenhower feared most was the leak of politically damaging information to the American public during a key election year. Powers's capture was the most serious national security blunder in more than a decade, one that caused the collapse of an important summit and plunged the country into an enormous crisis with Russia. Eisenhower was at the epicenter of the debacle, the man pulling the strings from the beginning. On top of that, at a time when his vice president was in a heated neck-and-neck race for the White House, his administration had been lying to the public and to senior members of Congress for weeks about his lack of personal involvement.

The U-2 affair was now part of the political landscape. Even before Eisenhower had returned from Europe, two-time Democratic rival Adlai E. Stevenson began throwing brickbats. "We handed Khrushchev the crowbar and sledgehammer to wreck the meeting," he huffed. "Without our series of blunders, Mr. Khrushchev would not have had the pretext for making his impossible demand and his wild charges." Mike Mansfield, the Senate Democratic Whip, said the committee should "trace the chain of command, or lack of it" that controlled the May Day flight and get to the bottom of the "confusing zigzags of official pronouncements." But Republican Senator Barry Goldwater thought the Senate should stay out of the matter: "What the CIA has done was something that had to be done," he argued. Goldwater, however, was in the minority.

On May 26, the morning before the start of the probe, Eisenhower made a quiet last-minute plea to senior leaders in Congress to stay away from sensitive areas in their investigation. Over eggs and toast with the leaders of both parties in the State Dining Room, Eisenhower almost laughably said how he "heartily approved of the inquiry." Then he said how he "was worried that members of Congress in conducting the inquiry would try to dig into the interior of the CIA and its covert operation." He added that he was sure the leaders of Congress realized that "such attempts would be harmful to the United States." A little more than a dozen years later, Richard Nixon would also attempt to use the rubric of "national security" and "CIA intelligence operations" to hide his personal involvement in a politically damaging scandal.

The members asked a few polite questions but never quizzed Eisenhower about his own role. Senator Mike Mansfield asked, "What would the President think if there were to be established in the Congress a joint congressional committee which would oversee the activities of the CIA?" The thought no doubt horrified Eisenhower. "The operation of the CIA was so delicate and so secret in many cases," he said, "that it must be kept under cover."

The next morning the doors to the Foreign Relations Committee Room were shut and guarded. Chairman J. William Fulbright gaveled the Senate hearings to order. Seated along the broad witness table, each administration official followed Eisenhower's instructions and dodged, ducked, or lied outright about the president's involvement in the U-2 program. Allen Dulles chose to stonewall. "I don't discuss what the president says to me or I say to the president." Years later, Under Secretary of State C. Douglas Dillon referred to the testimony given the committee as "just gobbledy-gook" and admitted, "Our testimony was not totally frank because we were defending—we were trying to hide the White House responsibility for this."

But Dillon's boss went much further than gobbledy-gook. When asked point-blank by Fulbright if there was "ever a time" that the president approved each U-2 flight, Secretary of State Christian Herter simply swallowed hard and then told a bold-faced lie. "It has never come up to the president."

In the hearing room, overseeing the testimony for the CIA and making sure no secrets were released to the public, was Richard Helms, who would later go on to become the agency's director. Years later, he would look back on the testimony and say: "They were all sworn. Knowing what they knew and what actually went on, if it isn't perjury I don't understand the meaning of the word."

Richard Helms had reason to be interested in the perjury over the U-2. In 1977 he was convicted in federal court and sentenced to two years in prison for a similar offense. Questioned by the chairman of the same Senate committee about the CIA's involvement in a coup in Chile, he lied to Fulbright and claimed there was none. Although Helms would later assert that his oath of secrecy to the CIA permitted him to lie to Congress, federal judge Barrington D. Parker strongly disagreed. Telling Helms, "You now stand before this court in disgrace and shame," the judge went on to ridicule his claim that lying to Congress to protect secrets was acceptable.

> If public officials embark deliberately on a course to disobey and ignore the laws of our land because of some misguided and ill-conceived notion and belief that there are earlier commitments and considerations which they must observe, the future of our country is in jeopardy.
>
> There are those employed in the intelligence security community of this country . . . who feel that they have a license to operate freely outside the dictates of the law and otherwise to orchestrate as they see fit. Public officials at every level, whatever their position, like any other person, must respect and honor the Constitution and the laws of the United States.

Despite his stern lecture, Parker suspended Helms's sentence and added a $2,000 fine.

Although Fulbright treated the president's men with kid gloves and Eisenhower's role never emerged, there was great bitterness within the administration over the hearings. Dulles told Herter that he was "very disturbed" by the action, then added, like a gangster in a Mafia movie: "We should have kept our mouths shut."*

At NSA, the implications of the latest intercepts were clear. Cuban bomber pilots were now being trained within the Soviet bloc.

On January 19, 1961, Washington was caught in the icy grip of the coldest weather in memory. Carpenters, bundled like Inuits, hammered away on the grandstand for the next day's inauguration. An artist carefully dabbed white paint on the last few stars surrounding the great seal emblazoned on the presidential reviewing box. Opposite, in the White House, two men took their places at the highly polished table in the Cabinet Room. Dwight David Eisenhower, looking tired, sat for the last time in the tall leather chair from which he had led so many momentous discussions over the past eight years. With the Cold War still as frozen as the rows of stiff rosebushes outside his tall windows, Eisenhower's early dream of amity with Russia was dashed.

Seated beside the president was John Fitzgerald Kennedy, tan and youthful. Like a storeowner whose family business has been seized by the bank, Eisenhower briefed his successor on a wide assortment of pending business. Oddly, although sitting on his desk were the plans for a massive, highly secret U.S.-sponsored invasion of Cuba, primed and ready to go within weeks, Eisenhower barely mentioned the island during the lengthy foreign policy briefing. The subject came up, in a sort of by-the-way manner, only during a discussion concerning Laos: "At the present time," Eisenhower said, "we are helping train anti-Castro forces in Guatemala." He added, "It was the policy of this government to help such forces to the utmost."

* As for Powers, a Soviet court found him guilty of espionage and sentenced him to ten years in prison. But in 1962 he was set free as part of an exchange with the United States for the Russian master spy Colonel Rudolf Abel.

In his last hours as president, Eisenhower issued what sounded to his successor like an order. "In the long run," he insisted, "the United States cannot allow the Castro Government to continue to exist in Cuba." At almost that same moment, across the river in the Pentagon's Gold Room, the Joint Chiefs had come to a decision of their own. The only answer, Joint Chiefs chairman Lyman L. Lemnitzer concluded, was for an all-out U.S. military invasion. War.

CHAPTER FOUR

FISTS

EZME-GYDXZBC KHZQK KEZJC KGDQBZMEQ DJ KQTQC TQQDYJCPK MCJCYTB
JONN BRNBURED, KRO DPLO RP BKIOOLOUR PU LTNRE-JENNEPU LOIKOI
LNRMWVTY NMFFUFZ WKQC IAUVVUIE NTVTKETY PNRS YRVIAUFE QKSI
UNKF'E YTPTFET QAUTP QRFPUNSE LTEL RP WKVVUELUQ SUEEUVT
HKSWW JWBVA HGVJBADSH JWAHXRADK; TBDTCGHXBD TBGCR VA DASW

Early on the morning of January 20, 1961, Washington lay buried beneath half a foot of freshly fallen snow, as if sleeping under a down comforter. The nation's capital had been pounded by a juggernaut of Arctic cold and freezing precipitation that had rolled over the Northeast and Mid-Atlantic states. Throughout the region, schools, business, and factories were shut down, and airports diverted inbound flights. It was the coldest winter in a quarter-century.

By daybreak, the military began their takeover. From Fort Belvoir, a heavy armored division of more than a hundred snowplows, front-loaders, dump trucks, and road graders crossed into the city to attack the ice and heavy drifts. A cordon of one hundred troops, wearing red brassards, began taking positions around the Capitol Building. A thousand more troops stretched out along Pennsylvania Avenue, and sixteen ambulances were positioned at key locations to care for anyone injured.

In a temporary military command post set up on the corner of East Executive and Pennsylvania Avenues, Northwest, Army Major General C. K. Gailey directed the invasion. Through the lazy, swirling snow, heavy transport vehicles rumbled across bridges over the Potomac and headed toward Capitol Hill. On the backs of the long trucks were Pershing missiles with warheads as pointed as well-sharpened pencils. Convoys of tanks, howitzers, and armored personnel carriers followed. Thousands of soldiers, airmen, sailors, and marines checked their weapons and assembled at designated locations near the White House. Codewords were assigned: Red Carpet for the radio network, Blueberry for the closed-circuit television network, Battery for the assembly areas, and Greenland for the dispersal areas.

From the broad front windows of Quarters 1, the official residence of the chairman of the Joint Chiefs of Staff, General Lyman L. Lemnitzer watched as his military quietly took over the nation's capital. Lemnitzer had perhaps the best view in all of greater Washington. The house was perched atop a steep hill on Fort Myer in Arlington, Virginia. As he stood in his living room, on the highly polished parquet floor, a taupe overcoat covered his formal blue uniform and a white scarf hid his four-in-hand tie. Nearby, framed by an American flag and the official flag of the Chairman, hung an oversize oil painting of the general, appearing serious and in command. Below him, the city looked like a child's snow globe, shaken to produce a cascade of gentle snowflakes over the great monuments, all within view. In the foreground the Potomac River, gray and frozen, wrapped the city like a silver ribbon on a belated Christmas present. Beyond, he could clearly see the massive white dome of the Capitol, where his official limousine was waiting to take him.

In just a few hours, John Fitzgerald Kennedy would be inaugurated as the thirty-fifth president of the United States. Unbeknownst to the public, the ceremony would largely be a military operation. In addition to his Secret Service contingent, the new president would be guarded by a cordon of two dozen military men surrounding the Presidential Box, and as he traveled to the White House, an escort of military vehicles would lead the way.

To some who watched the tanks and missiles roll through the city in preparation for the inaugural parade, the idea of an actual military takeover was appealing. Just below the surface, it was a dangerous time in America. For many in the military, the distrust of civilian leadership ran deep, to the point where a number of senior officers believed that their civilian leaders had been subverted by international communism. It was a belief exacerbated by the election of Kennedy, a socially liberal Democrat. "The presence of a benign and popular General of the Army in the White House had a calming influence on people and kept the

Rightists' audiences small," said one account at the time. "John F. Kennedy's election buttressed their worse fears."

On U.S. military bases around the world, senior officers were spreading fear that card-carrying Communists were in place in high offices throughout the federal government. Among these officers' key targets was Earl Warren, Chief Justice of the U.S. Supreme Court. During a televised meeting of Project Alert, a right-wing anti-Communist group, Colonel Mitchell Paige, a retired Marine Corps Medal of Honor winner, told the TV audience that Chief Justice Warren should be hanged.

Even before the election, some senior officers attempted to indoctrinate their troops into the "correct" way to vote. One of those was Major General Edwin A. Walker, who was stationed at the U.S. Army base in Augsburg, West Germany, home to a key NSA listening post. In October 1960, as his soldiers were preparing to send home their absentee ballots, Walker counseled them to first consult the voting guide of the archconservative Americans for Constitutional Action. Walker, who considered himself a "superpatriot," even set up a special hot line for troops to call to get "guidance" in voting. In addition, Walker would frequently address his soldiers and their dependents on the perils of Communist subversion and pass out John Birch Society propaganda. A newspaper circulated to the troops in Germany, *The Overseas Weekly*, charged that Walker had called Eleanor Roosevelt and Harry S. Truman "definitely pink" and journalists Edward R. Murrow, Walter Cronkite, and Eric Sevareid pro-Communists.

At Fort Smith, in Fayetteville, Arkansas, a series of "strategy-for-survival" conferences took place. Those attending were told that "your Representative in this area has voted 89 per cent of the time to aid and abet the Communist Party." Major General William C. Bullock, the area commander, persuaded the Little Rock Chamber of Commerce to sponsor a similar meeting in the state capital. At the Naval Air Station in Pensacola, Florida, Project Alert showed the film *Operation Abolition*, which depicted student protests against the rabid anticommunist House Un-American Activities Committee as entirely Communist-inspired and Communist-led.

Within weeks of the inauguration, retired vice admiral Ralph Wilson, chairman of the U.S. Maritime Board, would find himself in trouble for a proposed speech to the American Legion advocating an

American invasion of Cuba. "It seems in this Administration," he complained, "that you can't talk about limited war or Cold War or the realities of the Russian menace."

The atmosphere led some to thoughts of a possible military coup. Inspired by the tension between the far-right generals and the new administration, writers Fletcher Knebel and Charles Waldo Bailey II began drafting an outline for a novel. Eventually entitled *Seven Days in May*, it would focus on a military takeover led by a right-wing chairman of the Joint Chiefs of Staff (played in the filmed version by Burt Lancaster) who was convinced that a liberal president (Fredric March) was turning soft on America's enemies.

At 10:25 Lemnitzer entered his official limousine, a black elongated Cadillac with fins the shape of sabers, for the brief ride to the Capitol Building. Often described as bearlike—more for his powerful shoulders and booming voice than for his five-foot-eleven-inch frame—the four-star general had a solid, scholarly look about him. "Studious, handsome, thoughtful-looking," said one newspaper. Nevertheless, he had completed only two years of college at West Point, because of the need for officers during World War I. But by the time he was rushed out of the military academy, the war had ended. Over the years Lemnitzer gained a reputation as a planner; during World War II he served as an aide to General Eisenhower in London and later joined General George Patton during the Sicilian campaign. Eisenhower looked on Lemnitzer as his protégé, appointing him first Vice Chief of Staff and later, in 1957, Chief of Staff, the top job in the Army.

Finally, with only a few months to go in office, Eisenhower named Lemnitzer to the highest-ranking position in the Armed Forces. "The most important military job in the world was taken over last week by Gen. Lyman L. Lemnitzer, the new chairman of the Joint Chiefs of Staff," said an editorial in the *Los Angeles Times*. Two days before the inauguration, the chairman held a luncheon for Eisenhower in Quarters 1. "He thoroughly enjoyed himself," Lemnitzer wrote to his daughter. By then, according to one observer, Lemnitzer's regard for Eisenhower "bordered on reverence." In Lemnitzer, Eisenhower would have a window into the next administration.

Following a meeting with Robert S. McNamara, newly named by Kennedy to be the next secretary of defense, Lemnitzer passed on to Eisenhower a hot piece of inside information. Kennedy, he said, might have decided to name retired general James M. Gavin secretary of the Army. The idea outraged Eisenhower. Gavin had retired in a huff, upset over Eisenhower's space policies, and had then written a book critical of the administration. Three other generals also left and then wrote about various policy disagreements. Eisenhower was so furious at the criticism that he ordered his Joint Chiefs Chairman to look into whether he could recall the four men to active duty and court-martial them. Such an action would have been unheard of, if not illegal.

Now a man he considered disloyal was to be named to the top post of the Army, Eisenhower's Army. He asked Lemnitzer to find a way to secretly torpedo Gavin's appointment. It was a bizarre and outrageous request: an outgoing president was directing his top military official to sabotage a civilian appointment by a newly elected president. Before Lemnitzer could take any action, however, Kennedy changed his mind, appointing Gavin ambassador to France and naming Elvis J. Stahr, Jr., to the Army post. Nevertheless, Lemnitzer would become a landmine in the Kennedy administration.

Twenty-five minutes after leaving Quarters 1, Lemnitzer's chauffeur deposited the general at the E Door of the Senate Wing. It was a journey the general had made many times in order to testify before various Senate and House committees on military policy. The chairman never quite trusted Congress and as a result the truth became somewhat malleable. He once wrote to his brother, "I have been involved in some very rugged hearings before seven congressional committees. . . . We have to walk a very narrow path in telling the truth to the various committees and at the same time keep out of trouble with the administration."

Lemnitzer walked through the arc under the Senate stairway and took an elevator up one floor to the Senate Reception Room. There he joined the other service chiefs, as well as diplomats and foreign ambassadors, as they awaited escort to their assigned seats on the President's Platform. In charge of the Navy was Admiral Arleigh A. Burke, a salt-and-pepper-haired veteran of World War II. He had served as Eisenhower's Chief of Naval Operations for the past five years. Upon

Lemnitzer's elevation to Army Chief of Staff, Burke presented him with a four-foot-long ceremonial bugle. Attached near the flowing gold tassels was a sign that read, "The *Certain* Trumpet." It was an inside joke. Lemnitzer's predecessor, General Maxwell Taylor, was one of those who had quit and written a book harshly critical of Eisenhower's military policies. Taylor's title was *The Uncertain Trumpet.*

Lemnitzer was escorted to Section 2, Row G, Seat 1 on the President's Platform, a pillared structure erected on the steps of the east front of the Capitol Building. His hands were covered in regulation black gloves and his heavy jowls turned pink from the bitter cold. Below, thousands of onlookers filled the snow-mantled plaza.

As he rose to watch Chief Justice Earl Warren administer the oath of office to John F. Kennedy, dressed in formal black coat and striped trousers, the Chairman's frame of reference likely began shifting. He was like a sailor whose compass no longer pointed north. For eight years the country had been run by a five-star general, a West Point ringknocker like himself who knew discipline, order, tradition. Flags were saluted, shoes spit-shined, and dissent punished. Now the man who had been Lemnitzer's mentor and boss for much of his long career was quietly retiring to a farm in Gettysburg. Taking Eisenhower's place was a man from a different time and a different culture, someone Lemnitzer knew little and understood less. "Here was a president with no military experience at all," he would later say, derisively, of a man who nearly died saving his men while fighting on the front line of battle. "Sort of a patrol boat skipper in World War II."

Lemnitzer was not isolated in his point of view. Standing nearby was the man Lemnitzer had picked to take his place as Chief of Staff of the Army, General George H. Decker. "I think the senior military leaders probably were more comfortable with President Eisenhower," he later recalled, "since he had been a military man himself." Chief of Naval Operations Burke also distrusted the new White House. "Nearly all of these people were ardent, enthusiastic people without any experience whatever in administering anything, including the president. He'd always been in Congress. He'd never had any sort of job that required any administration. . . . They didn't understand ordinary administrative procedures, the necessity for having lines of communication and channels of command."

About 2:15, following the swearing-in and a luncheon in the Capitol, Lemnitzer climbed into a 1961 Oldsmobile convertible for the chilly ride in the inaugural parade to the presidential reviewing stand opposite the White House. Kennedy had personally invited him to stand in the Presidential Box and review the smiling high school bands and the endless military troops as they marched at precisely 120 steps per minute, each step thirty inches long.

Soon, Lemnitzer hoped, some of those troops would be marching down the palm-shaded streets of Havana with Castro either dead or in custody. Like many in the right-wing military movement, he saw communism as subverting the very fabric of American society, an insatiable evil force that was eating away at America's core values and had to be stopped. "I would offer the suggestion that you read carefully the recently issued Draft Program of the Communist Party," he warned in a letter to a high school teacher who had written to him about Cuba. "If you study this document I think you cannot escape agreeing with its authors that the Communist world is pledged to the destruction of our civilization and everything we value. Our heritage of freedom and the deep aspirations and values which humanity has evolved over thousands of years are thus squarely put in peril. An adequate response to such a deadly threat must be found, not by governments alone, but in the hearts and actions of every one of our citizens."

Lemnitzer believed that nothing less than a massive military force could defeat communism in Cuba. He therefore had little confidence in a covert plan developed by the CIA that called for infiltrating fewer than a thousand anti-Castro rebels onto the island. Developed during the last year of the Eisenhower administration, the operation involved the rebels sparking an internal revolution that would supposedly bring down Castro's regime.

Only two days before the inauguration, Brigadier General David W. Gray, Lemnitzer's representative on the Cuba Task Force, argued the point forcefully to the CIA: "200,000 [Cuban] militia," he said, "each with a sub-machine gun, is in itself a pretty strong force if they do nothing more than stand and pull the triggers." Instead, Lemnitzer and the Joint Chiefs were pressing for all-out war—a Pentagon-led overt military invasion of Cuba from the air, sea, and ground.

But Lemnitzer and the Chiefs knew that armed invasion of a

neighboring country would be condemned both domestically and internationally as the American equivalent of the Soviet invasion of Hungary. Thus the Joint Chiefs developed an enormously secret plan to trick the American public—and the rest of the world—into believing that Cuba had instead launched an attack against the U.S. It would be the ultimate *Wag the Dog* war.

According to documents obtained for *Body of Secrets,* Lemnitzer and the Joint Chiefs proposed secretly to stage an attack on the American naval base at Guantánamo Bay, Cuba—and then blame the violent action on Castro. Convinced that Cuba had launched an unprovoked attack on the United States, the unwitting American public would then support the Joint Chiefs' bloody Caribbean war. After all, who would believe Castro's denials over the word of the Pentagon's top military commanders? The nation's most senior military leadership was proposing to launch a war, which would no doubt kill many American servicemen, based solely on a fabric of lies. On January 19, just hours before Eisenhower left office, Lemnitzer gave his approval to the proposal. As events progressed, the plan would become only the tip of a very large and secret iceberg.

Lemnitzer smiled broadly and saluted when the Hegerman String Band and the Mounted State Police from his native Pennsylvania passed by the Presidential Box in the reviewing stand.

At 5:43, ex-President Eisenhower and his wife, seated in the back of a five-year-old Chrysler limousine, passed the Secret Service booth at the entrance to the private road leading to their farm in Gettysburg, Pennsylvania. For the first time in eight years, the booth was dark and empty.

Forty-five minutes later, Private First Class Bomer escorted Lemnitzer to his limousine and drove him through the darkness back to Quarters 1; meanwhile, the general's invading army retreated back across the Potomac.

On January 25, President Kennedy had his first meeting with Lemnitzer and the Joint Chiefs. Kennedy said he was extremely anxious to keep in close contact with the chiefs and that he would be seeing Lemnitzer frequently during National Security Council meetings. Then the president asked what should be done with regard to Cuba.

Lemnitzer quickly dismissed the proposed CIA operation as too weak to combat Castro's forces. He then told Kennedy about recent and troubling NSA reports. Eight days earlier, in a windowless blockhouse in West Germany, an NSA intercept operator assigned to monitor Czechoslovakian military air communications turned his large black frequency dial to 114.25 megahertz and heard an unusual sound. Instead of picking up the normal pilot chatter in Czech or Slovak at Trencin airfield, he listened as a pilot undergoing flight training suddenly began to speak Spanish. "This is the first known VHF activity at Trencin by a Spanish-speaking pilot," he wrote in his intercept report, which was quickly transmitted to NSA headquarters. He added, "This pilot was possibly in a bomber or bomber trainer." Other reports indicated that Cuba had recently received at least 30,000 tons of new military equipment from Czechoslovakia.

Lemnitzer then pushed on the new president his own agenda: "What is required is a basic expansion of plans," he said. "The hope is to get a government in exile, then put some troops ashore, and have guerrilla groups start their activities. At that point we would come in and support them. Plans are ready for such action." "Time is working against us," Lemnitzer urged Kennedy.

Three days later, in the Cabinet Room of the White House, Kennedy brought together his key national security officials, including Lemnitzer and Allen Dulles. During the meeting, the Pentagon representatives stated that none of the courses of action then on the table would remove the Castro regime. Kennedy then called on the Pentagon and CIA to review the various proposals for sending the anti-Castro forces into Cuba. He also demanded that the entire operation be carried out with white gloves—there could be no U.S. fingerprints anywhere. "I'm not going to risk an American Hungary," Kennedy warned.

Eisenhower had spent eight years working closely with the CIA. He knew the strengths and weaknesses of Allen Dulles, the CIA, and the Cuban operation, which he had helped plan for nearly a year. Now Kennedy, in office barely a week and attempting to put his administration together, was being pressured to quickly okay a dangerous plan produced by a man he didn't know and an agency that was a cipher to him. Dulles told him that once the landing took place, it would trigger a great uprising and Castro would quickly tumble.

But Dulles certainly knew that to be a lie. Castro was a hero to much of the Cuban population for having rid them of the bloody excesses of Batista only two years before. As a long-hidden CIA report notes, "We can confidently assert that the Agency had no intelligence evidence that the Cubans in significant numbers could or would join the invaders or that there was any kind of an effective and cohesive resistance movement under anybody's control, let alone the Agency's, that could have furnished internal leadership for an uprising in support of the invasion." The same report concluded that at the time of that White House meeting "the Agency was driving forward without knowing precisely where it was going."

Lemnitzer was a man of details. After becoming Chairman of the Joint Chiefs of Staff he sent out elaborate instructions outlining exactly how his fellow Chiefs were to autograph group pictures—they were to sign their names directly under his, and they must follow his slant. Neither his limousine nor his plane was ever to be moved without his being consulted. Lemnitzer also enjoyed his reputation as a consummate planner. In an eight-page biography he submitted to Congress prior to his testimony, he made frequent reference to himself as an "imaginative planner" and to his "skill as a planner." On his Pentagon desk was a crystal ball and in a drawer was a favorite verse:

Planners are a funny lot
They carry neither sword nor pistol
They walk stooped over quite a lot
Because their balls are crystal

Lemnitzer, the planner, certainly saw the pitfalls of the CIA's amateur and ill-conceived plan, as did his fellow Chiefs. Years later Lemnitzer hand-wrote a detailed fifty-two-page summary of the JCS involvement in the Bay of Pigs operation. He called it "The Cuban Debacle" and locked it away in his house; he died without ever publicly revealing its existence. Obtained for *Body of Secrets,* the account clearly shows that Lemnitzer's Joint Staff viewed the CIA plan as a disaster waiting to happen. He quotes from a secret internal JCS analysis of the operation: "In view of the rapid buildup of the Castro Government's military and militia capability, *and the lack of predictable future mass discontent,* the possible success of the Para-Military Plan appears very doubtful" [emphasis in original].

Yet inexplicably, only days later, Lemnitzer submitted a positive recommendation to Secretary of Defense McNamara. "Evaluation of the current plan results in a favorable assessment . . . of the likelihood of achieving initial military success," he wrote. "The JCS considers that timely execution of the plan has a fair chance of ultimate success and, even if it does not achieve immediately the full results desired, [it] could contribute to the eventual overthrow of the Castro regime." Later that day, McNamara verbally endorsed those conclusions.

It may well have been that the Joint Chiefs, angry with the arrogant CIA brass for moving into their territory, were hoping that the spooks would fail. Once the CIA was out of the way, the uniformed professionals in the Pentagon would be called on to save the day—to take over, conduct the real invasion, and oust Castro. From then on, military invasions would again be the monopoly of the generals. But soon it became clear that Kennedy had meant what he said about keeping the operation covert.

As originally planned, the exile force was to land at the coastal town of Trinidad. But the White House objected. According to Lemnitzer's private summary, Kennedy wanted a quiet night landing, which the world would believe was planned by Cubans. Above all, Lemnitzer noted, there was to be no intervention by U.S. forces.

Following Kennedy's order, CIA planners presented the Joint Chiefs of Staff Working Group with a list of five alternative landing sites. Later the list was reduced to three. The group picked Alternative III, a spot in the swampy Zapata Peninsula called the Bay of Pigs. After a brief twenty-minute discussion, barely enough time for a coffee break, Lemnitzer and his Chiefs agreed with their Working Group's choice. "Of the alternative concepts," said the JCS recommendation, "Alternative III is considered the most feasible and the most likely to accomplish the objective. None of the alternative concepts are considered as feasible and as likely to accomplish the objective as the original [Trinidad] plan."

Lemnitzer had grave doubts about the whole CIA operation from the beginning but remained largely silent and quickly approved the plan. The Bay of Pigs was considerably closer to Havana than Trinidad was; this meant a quicker response from Cuban troops, and with only one road in and out of the landing zone, it was a perfect place for a slaughter. Cuban troops could easily isolate the invaders, who would be forced to die on the beaches or drown in the sea.

Lemnitzer had one last chance to reach up and pull the emergency brake before the train plunged off the embankment. On April 4, 1961, Kennedy held a conference at the State Department with his key advisers to get their final thoughts on the invasion. Lemnitzer, seeing certain disaster ahead, buttonholed Assistant Secretary of State Thomas C. Mann before the meeting started and insisted that the choice of Zapata for a landing site was a bad decision, that the Joint Chiefs did not want the invasion to take place closer to Havana. Mann, taken aback by Lemnitzer's sudden change of position, dismissed his protest and insisted that Kennedy had already made his decision.

As Kennedy convened the meeting, Lemnitzer sat mute. The man in charge of the most powerful military force on earth, with enough nuclear weapons to destroy civilization, was afraid to speak up to his boss. It was his moment of truth. Instead he chose to close his eyes, cover his mouth, and wait for the sound of grinding metal. He knew, as he had known from the beginning, that the operation would turn out to be a disaster, that many men would die painfully and needlessly, but still he preferred silence. He must also have finally realized that the Pentagon would never receive presidential authorization to charge in and save the day. At the end of the meeting, Kennedy asked who was still in favor of going ahead with the invasion. Lemnitzer's hand slowly reached toward the ceiling. Much later, in his summary, he confessed his failure to speak up but offered no apology.

At the time of Kennedy's inauguration, NSA's role in supplying intelligence on what was going on inside Cuba grew substantially. Until then, the CIA's Havana Station and its Santiago Base had been a beehive of espionage. But just before he left office, in preparation for the invasion, Eisenhower cut diplomatic relations with Cuba. With the closure of the embassy in Havana and the consulate in Santiago, the CIA was homeless and had to return to the United States. Anticipating this contingency, CIA case officers in Cuba had developed a number of "stay-behinds," agents who would remain under deep cover. This net consisted of some twenty-seven persons, fifteen of whom were reporting agents and the rest radio operators and couriers. But the principal agents and one of the radio operators were U.S. citizens and thus had limited access to key information—especially military intelligence, which was most needed. Without a CIA station in Cuba producing intelligence, the CIA, the White House, and others in the intelligence community became more dependent on NSA's intercepts.

Miami Base received copies of NSA's signals intelligence reports on Cuba but there was no NSA liaison official there to help interpret the messages. This was a serious mistake. Without NSA's cold, independent analysis of the intelligence, the gung-ho CIA officers were forced to rely upon their own judgment—which was often colored by their desire for the operation to go ahead. This was one of the key reasons for their overestimate of Cuban internal opposition to Castro. As a CIA postmortem said, "This conclusion, in turn, became an essential element in the decision to proceed with the operation."

Another problem was that without an NSA presence, Miami Base could neither receive nor send superfast emergency CRITIC messages should the invasion run into serious problems. "The [NSA] effort was very small," said one NSA official assigned to the Cuban desk at Fort Meade at the time. A key source of NSA's signals intelligence on Cuba was a Navy ship that had secretly been converted into a seagoing espionage platform. Since February, the USS *Perry* (DD-844), a destroyer rigged with special antennas and receivers, had patrolled off the Cuban coast eavesdropping on whatever it could pick up. The *Perry* occasionally pulled into the Key West Naval Base, where Navy Sigint specialists would work on the equipment.

As the preparation for the invasion proceeded at full steam, NSA continued to focus much of its attention on Soviet shipping. In March, an intercept operator at the NSA listening post in Karamürsel, Turkey, discovered that the *Nikolaj Burdenko* was back in the port of Nikolayev loading a new shipment of "Yastrebov's cargo"—the Soviet euphemism for weapons. The 5,840-ton cargo ship, a hulking gray workhorse, departed Nikolayev on March 21. Intercept operators kept track of the ship's progress by monitoring its daily transmissions, noting its position and triangulating it with "elephant cages," giant circular antennas.

"On 7 April limited D/F [direction finding] placed the BURDENKO near the Windward Passage," said one intercept report. Another revealed that the ship "possibly arrived at a Cuban port late evening 7 April or early morning 8 April with an unspecified amount of YASTREBOV's cargo . . . This is the fourth noted instance of a Soviet ship loading cargo specifically described as 'YASTREBOV's' for Cuba." Within the White House, pressure was building to take action.

As the *Burdenko,* heavy in the water, pulled into Havana harbor, U-2s were crisscrossing the island fourteen miles above. Beginning on April 6, U-2s flying out of Texas conducted fifteen missions over the island in final preparation for the CIA's invasion.

The operation began at dawn on Monday, April 17, 1961, and quickly turned into a debacle. As Cuban air force and other military units converged on the area, NSA voice-intercept operators eavesdropped on the desperate pleas of the exiles. "Must have air support in next few hours or will be wiped out," Brigade Commander Pepe San Roman implored. "Under heavy attacks by MiG jets and heavy tanks." The Navy offered to evacuate the brigade commander and his troops, but was refused. They would fight to the end.

Because no provision had been made to provide NSA's Sigint to the brigade, the agency's intercepts were largely useless. All analysts could do was sit and listen to the hopeless messages from the rebel soldiers fighting on the beach and their supporters throughout Cuba. "Arms urgent," said one. "We made a commitment. We have complied. You have not. If you have decided to abandon us, answer." Another radioed, "We are risking hundreds of peasant families. If you cannot supply us we will have to . . . demobilize. Your responsibility. We thought you were sincere." Still another pleaded, "All groups demoralized. . . . They consider themselves deceived because of failure of shipment of arms and money according to promise." Finally, there was one last message. "Impossible to fight. . . . Either the drops increase or we die. . . . Men without arms or equipment. God help us."

"It wasn't much that was done here, as I understand," said one NSA official, "except they were copying the communications . . . and their calls for help and assistance and what-have-you were all monitored."

"I will not be evacuated," said San Roman, defiantly. "Will fight to the end if we have to." On the beach, nearly out of bullets and mortars, the brigade launched a futile counterattack against Cuban army soldiers pushing relentlessly in from the west. "We are out of ammo and fighting on the beach," the brigade commander radioed to the task force command ship. "Please send help, we cannot hold."

"In water. Out of ammo. Enemy closing in. Help must arrive in next hour." San Roman's voice was now terse and desperate. There was no place to go. Between them and the approaching helmets were scores of their comrades, their blood joining the seawater with each crashing wave. "When your help will be here and with what?" The commander's voice was weaker now, unbelieving but still wanting to believe. "Why your help has not come?"

There were faces under the green helmets now, and arms with rifles, and legs running. They were coming from all sides, bullets hitting the water, the sand, and the men. NSA intercept operators eavesdropped on the final messages. "Am destroying all equipment and communications. Tanks are in sight. I have nothing to fight with. Am taking to woods. I cannot, repeat, cannot wait for you."

At 3:20 P.M., out at sea beyond the horizon, the evacuation convoy heading for the beach received a final message. "[Ships] ordered withdrawn [at] full speed."

The pall cast over the CIA as a result of the botched invasion did nothing to dampen the Kennedy administration's obsession with Castro. On a gray autumn Saturday in early November 1961, just after two o'clock, Attorney General Robert F. Kennedy called a meeting to order in the Cabinet Room of the White House. The day before, the president had given the group their marching orders. He wanted a solution to the Cuba problem and his brother was going to see that it was done. Robert Kennedy turned to the group and introduced Edward G. Lansdale, an Air Force one-star general and a specialist in counterinsurgency who sat stiffly in a padded black leather chair.

Tall, with Errol Flynn good looks, Lansdale was the deputy director of the Pentagon's Office of Special Operations. Hidden away behind the door to Room 3E114 in the Pentagon, the OSO was the unit responsible for NSA. Responsibility for dealing with Cuba, Kennedy said, was to shift from the CIA to the Pentagon, where the project would be known as Operation Mongoose. Kennedy asked the group if they had any problems with the change. Richard Bissell, who had just seen the CIA's crown jewel pass from his hands, could not resist at least one jab. No, he said, as long as "those employees on it were competent in clandestine operations."

Both Lansdale and Lemnitzer viewed Operation Mongoose as a golden opportunity, a chance for the military to flex its muscles at last and show off its ability to succeed where the CIA had so miserably failed. As prospects of an internal revolt in Cuba dimmed, Lansdale and Lemnitzer began to quietly explore the possibility of doing what they had wanted to do all along: conduct a full-scale invasion.

Since the Kennedy administration had come into office the extreme, distrustful right wing within the military had grown significantly, not only in numbers but also in decibels. In April 1961 Defense Secretary Robert McNamara finally lowered the boom on Major General Edwin A. Walker. Walker was charged with indoctrinating his troops with John Birch Society propaganda, officially admonished, and relieved of his command. As a result many conservatives accused the Kennedy administration of trying to muzzle anti-Communists.

Walker resigned from the Army in protest, but even as a civilian he continued to warn of the dangers of Communist infiltration. Among the themes he constantly pounded home was a distrust of civilian control of the military. "The traditional civilian control of the military has been perverted and extended into a commissar-like system of control at all major echelons of command," he said. In September 1961 he traveled to Oxford, Mississippi, to protest the enrollment of James Meredith, a black student, at the state university there. Robert Kennedy later issued an arrest warrant for Walker, charging him with seditious conspiracy, insurrection, and rebellion. He was jailed for five days, during which time he claimed he was a political prisoner.

Even at the stately National War College in Washington, seminars would occasionally be reduced to "extreme right-wing, witch-hunting, mudslinging revivals" and "bigoted, one-sided presentations advocating that the danger to our security is internal only," according to a report prepared by a member of Secretary of Defense McNamara's staff.

The Senate Foreign Relations Committee, in a report on the problem of right-wing extremism in the military, warned that there was "considerable danger" in the "education and propaganda activities of military personnel" that had been uncovered. "Running through all of them is a central theme that the primary, if not exclusive, danger to this country is internal Communist infiltration," said the report.

Among the key targets of the extremists, the committee said, was the Kennedy administration's domestic social program, which many ultraconservatives accused of being communistic. The "thesis of the nature of the Communist threat," the report warned, "often is developed by equating social legislation with socialism, and the latter with Communism. . . . Much of the administration's domestic legislative program, including continuation of the graduated income tax, expansion of social security (particularly medical care under social security), Federal aid to education, etc. under this philosophy would be characterized as steps toward Communism." Thus, "This view of the Communist menace renders foreign aid, cultural exchanges, disarmament negotiations and other international programs as extremely wasteful if not actually subversive."

The chilling Senate study concluded by warning of a revolt by senior military officers such as the one portrayed in *Seven Days in May*. To show the idea was not farfetched, the report cited "as an example of the ultimate danger" the recent revolt by army generals in France, largely over policies in Algeria. "Military officers, French or American, have some common characteristics arising from their profession," said the report, "and there are numerous military 'fingers on the trigger' throughout the world."

Finally, the committee specifically pointed to General Lemnitzer and called for an examination of the relationship between him, his Chiefs, and the extreme right-wing groups. Among the members of the committee most outspoken in calling for an investigation of Lemnitzer and the Joint Chiefs was Senator Albert Gore, Sr., of Tennessee (the father of former vice president Al Gore).

It was not an idle worry. In their 1963 book, *The Far Right*, Donald Janson of the *New York Times* and CBS reporter Bernard Eismann wrote, "Concern had grown that a belligerent and free-wheeling military could conceivably become as dangerous to the stability of the

United States as the mixture of rebelliousness and politics had in nations forced to succumb to juntas or fascism. The agony that gripped France as a result of military defectors' efforts to reverse government policy on Algeria was another forceful reminder of the inherent dangers in allowing political power to build up in the military establishment."

Outwardly, Lemnitzer remained stiff and correct. But deep inside he was raging at the new and youthful Kennedy White House. He felt out of place and out of time in a culture that seemed suddenly to have turned its back on military tradition. Almost immediately he became, in the clinical sense, paranoid; he began secretly expressing his worries to other senior officers. A little more than a month after Kennedy took office, he sent a letter to General Lauris Norstad, the commander-in-chief of the U.S. European Command, and several other top generals. Fearful that the administration would learn of his comments, he noted, "I had considered sending this information to you by electrical means but in view of its nature, I am sending it by letter for your, Jim Moore's and [Deputy Commander-in-Chief] Charlie Palmer's EYES ONLY." It was then delivered "in a sealed envelope for delivery to Gen. Norstad ONLY."

"You and Charlie are probably wondering what, if anything, the JCS are [d]oing about some of the disturbing things that have been happening recently with respect to your area," Lemnitzer wrote. But what so upset the JCS Chairman was not a major change in nuclear policy in Europe or a shift in Cold War strategy, but the fact that White House officials had canceled money earmarked for the remodeling of an officers' club. "I am sure that this seems as incredible to you as it does to us," he wrote, "but this is how things are happening here now." Finally, Lemnitzer complained about what he felt were deliberate leaks intended to embarrass senior military officials. "Here again I believe that the fundamental cause is the 'eager beaver' attitude by many of the new and very young people who have been brought into government to publicize promptly any item they believe will give the new administration good press. I don't know how long this situation is going to continue but we seem to have a new incident every day."

Lemnitzer had no respect for the civilians he reported to. He believed they interfered with the proper role of the military. The "civilian hierarchy was crippled not only by inexperience," he would later say, "but also by arrogance arising from failure to recognize its own limitations. . . . The problem was simply that the civilians would not accept military judgments." In Lemnitzer's view, the country would be far better off if the generals could take over.

For those military officers who were sitting on the fence, the Kennedy administration's botched Bay of Pigs invasion was the last straw. "The Bay of Pigs fiasco broke the dike," said one report at the time. "President Kennedy was pilloried by the superpatriots as a 'no-win' chief. . . . The Far Right became a fount of proposals born of frustration and put forward in the name of anti-Communism. . . . Active-duty commanders played host to anti-Communist seminars on their bases and attended or addressed Right-wing meetings elsewhere."

Although no one in Congress could have known it at the time, Lemnitzer and the Joint Chiefs had quietly slipped over the edge.

According to secret and long-hidden documents obtained for *Body of Secrets,* the Joint Chiefs of Staff drew up and approved plans for what may be the most corrupt plan ever created by the U.S. government. In the name of anticommunism, they proposed launching a secret and bloody war of terrorism against their own country in order to trick the American public into supporting an ill-conceived war they intended to launch against Cuba.

Codenamed Operation Northwoods, the plan, which had the written approval of the Chairman and every member of the Joint Chiefs of Staff, called for innocent people to be shot on American streets; for boats carrying refugees fleeing Cuba to be sunk on the high seas; for a wave of violent terrorism to be launched in Washington, D.C., Miami, and elsewhere. People would be framed for bombings they did not commit; planes would be hijacked. Using phony evidence, all of it would be blamed on Castro, thus giving Lemnitzer and his cabal the excuse, as well as the public and international backing, they needed to launch their war.

The idea may actually have originated with President Eisenhower in the last days of his administration. With the Cold War hotter than ever and the recent U-2 scandal fresh in the public's memory, the old general wanted to go out with a win. He wanted desperately to invade Cuba in the weeks leading up to Kennedy's inauguration; indeed, on January 3 he told Lemnitzer and other aides in his Cabinet Room that he would move against Castro before the inauguration if only the

Cubans gave him a really good excuse. Then, with time growing short, Eisenhower floated an idea. If Castro failed to provide that excuse, perhaps, he said, the United States "could think of manufacturing something that would be generally acceptable." What he was suggesting was a pretext—a bombing, an attack, an act of sabotage—carried out secretly against the United States *by* the United States. Its purpose would be to justify the launching of a war. It was a dangerous suggestion by a desperate president.

Although no such war took place, the idea was not lost on General Lemnitzer. But he and his colleagues were frustrated by Kennedy's failure to authorize their plan, and angry that Castro had not provided an excuse to invade.

The final straw may have come during a White House meeting on February 26, 1962. Concerned that General Lansdale's various covert action plans under Operation Mongoose were simply becoming more outrageous and going nowhere, Robert Kennedy told him to drop all anti-Castro efforts. Instead, Lansdale was ordered to concentrate for the next three months strictly on gathering intelligence about Cuba. It was a humiliating defeat for Lansdale, a man more accustomed to praise than to scorn.

As the Kennedy brothers appeared to suddenly "go soft" on Castro, Lemnitzer could see his opportunity to invade Cuba quickly slipping away. The attempts to provoke the Cuban public to revolt seemed dead and Castro, unfortunately, appeared to have no inclination to launch any attacks against Americans or their property. Lemnitzer and the other Chiefs knew there was only one option left that would ensure their war. They would have to trick the American public and world opinion into hating Cuba so much that they would not only go along, but would insist that he and his generals launch their war against Castro. "World opinion, and the United Nations forum," said a secret JCS document, "should be favorably affected by developing the international image of the Cuban government as rash and irresponsible, and as an alarming and unpredictable threat to the peace of the Western Hemisphere."

Operation Northwoods called for a war in which many patriotic Americans and innocent Cubans would die senseless deaths—all to satisfy the egos of twisted generals back in Washington, safe in their taxpayer-financed homes and limousines.

One idea seriously considered involved the launch of John Glenn, the first American to orbit the earth. On February 20, 1962, Glenn was to lift off from Cape Canaveral, Florida, on his historic journey. The flight was to carry the banner of America's virtues of truth, freedom, and democracy into orbit high over the planet. But Lemnitzer and his Chiefs had a different idea. They proposed to Lansdale that, should the rocket explode and kill Glenn, "the objective is to provide irrevocable proof that . . . the fault lies with the Communists et al Cuba [*sic*]." This would be accomplished, Lemnitzer continued, "by manufacturing various pieces of evidence which would prove electronic interference on the part of the Cubans." Thus, as NASA prepared to send the first American into space, the Joint Chiefs of Staff were preparing to use John Glenn's possible death as a pretext to launch a war.

Glenn lifted into history without mishap, leaving Lemnitzer and the Chiefs to begin devising new plots which they suggested be carried out "within the time frame of the next few months."

Among the actions recommended was "a series of well coordinated incidents to take place in and around" the U.S. Navy base at Guantánamo Bay, Cuba. This included dressing "friendly" Cubans in Cuban military uniforms and then have them "start riots near the main gate of the base. Others would pretend to be saboteurs inside the base. Ammunition would be blown up, fires started, aircraft sabotaged, mortars fired at the base with damage to installations."

The suggested operations grew progressively more outrageous. Another called for an action similar to the infamous incident in February 1898 when an explosion aboard the battleship *Maine* in Havana harbor killed 266 U.S. sailors. Although the exact cause of the explosion remained undetermined, it sparked the Spanish-American War with Cuba. Incited by the deadly blast, more than one million men volunteered for duty. Lemnitzer and his generals came up with a similar plan. "We could blow up a U.S. ship in Guantanamo Bay and blame Cuba," they proposed; "casualty lists in U.S. newspapers would cause a helpful wave of national indignation."

There seemed no limit to their fanaticism: "We could develop a Communist Cuban terror campaign in the Miami area, in other Florida cities and even in Washington," they wrote. "The terror campaign could be pointed at Cuban refugees seeking haven in the United States. . . .

We could sink a boatload of Cubans en route to Florida (real or simulated). . . . We could foster attempts on lives of Cuban refugees in the United States even to the extent of wounding in instances to be widely publicized."

Bombings were proposed, false arrests, hijackings:

- "Exploding a few plastic bombs in carefully chosen spots, the arrest of Cuban agents and the release of prepared documents substantiating Cuban involvement also would be helpful in projecting the idea of an irresponsible government."
- "Advantage can be taken of the sensitivity of the Dominican [Republic] Air Force to intrusions within their national air space. 'Cuban' B-26 or C-46 type aircraft could make cane-burning raids at night. Soviet Bloc incendiaries could be found. This could be coupled with 'Cuban' messages to the Communist underground in the Dominican Republic and 'Cuban' shipments of arms which would be found, or intercepted, on the beach. Use of MiG type aircraft by U.S. pilots could provide additional provocation."
- "Hijacking attempts against civil air and surface craft could appear to continue as harassing measures condoned by the Government of Cuba."

Among the most elaborate schemes was to "create an incident which will demonstrate convincingly that a Cuban aircraft has attacked and shot down a chartered civil airliner en route from the United States to Jamaica, Guatemala, Panama or Venezuela. The destination would be chosen only to cause the flight plan route to cross Cuba. The passengers could be a group of college students off on a holiday or any grouping of persons with a common interest to support chartering a non-scheduled flight."

Lemnitzer and the Joint Chiefs worked out a complex deception:

> An aircraft at Elgin AFB would be painted and numbered as an exact duplicate for a civil registered aircraft belonging to a CIA proprietary organization in the Miami

> area. At a designated time the duplicate would be substituted for the actual civil aircraft and would be loaded with the selected passengers, all boarded under carefully prepared aliases. The actual registered aircraft would be converted to a drone [a remotely controlled unmanned aircraft]. Take off times of the drone aircraft and the actual aircraft will be scheduled to allow a rendezvous south of Florida.
>
> From the rendezvous point the passenger-carrying aircraft will descend to minimum altitude and go directly into an auxiliary field at Elgin AFB where arrangements will have been made to evacuate the passengers and return the aircraft to its original status. The drone aircraft meanwhile will continue to fly the filed flight plan. When over Cuba the drone will be transmitting on the international distress frequency a "May Day" message stating he is under attack by Cuban MiG aircraft. The transmission will be interrupted by destruction of the aircraft, which will be triggered by radio signal. This will allow ICAO [International Civil Aviation Organization] radio stations in the Western Hemisphere to tell the U.S. what has happened to the aircraft instead of the U.S. trying to "sell" the incident.

Finally, there was a plan to "make it appear that Communist Cuban MiGs have destroyed a USAF aircraft over international waters in an unprovoked attack." It was a particularly believable operation given the decade of shootdowns that had just taken place.

In the final sentence of his letter to Secretary McNamara recommending the operations, Lemnitzer made a grab for even more power, asking that the Joint Chiefs be placed in charge of carrying out Operation Northwoods and the invasion. "It is recommended," he wrote, "that this responsibility for both overt and covert military operations be assigned to the Joint Chiefs of Staff."

At 2:30 on the afternoon of Tuesday, March 13, 1962, Lemnitzer went over last-minute details of Operation Northwoods with his covert action chief, Brigadier General William H. Craig, and signed the document. He then went to a "special meeting" in McNamara's office. An hour later he met with Kennedy's military representative, General Maxwell Taylor. What happened during those meetings is unknown. But three days later, President Kennedy told Lemnitzer that there was virtually no possibility that the U.S. would ever use overt military force in Cuba.

Undeterred, Lemnitzer and the Chiefs persisted, virtually to the point of demanding that they be given authority to invade and take over Cuba. About a month after submitting Operation Northwoods, they met in the "tank," as the JCS conference room was called, and agreed on the wording of a tough memorandum to McNamara. "The Joint Chiefs of Staff believe that the Cuban problem must be solved in the near future," they wrote. "Further, they see no prospect of early success in overthrowing the present communist regime either as a result of internal uprising or external political, economic or psychological pressures. Accordingly they believe that military intervention by the United States will be required to overthrow the present communist regime."

Lemnitzer was virtually rabid in his hatred of communism in general and Castro in particular. "The Joint Chiefs of Staff believe that the United States can undertake military intervention in Cuba without risk of general war," he continued. "They also believe that the intervention can be accomplished rapidly enough to minimize communist opportunities for solicitation of UN action." However, what Lemnitzer was suggesting was not freeing the Cuban people, who were largely in support of Castro, but imprisoning them in a U.S. military–controlled police state. "Forces would assure rapid essential military control of Cuba," he wrote. "Continued police action would be required."

Concluding, Lemnitzer did not mince words: "[T]he Joint Chiefs of Staff recommend that a national policy of early military intervention in Cuba be adopted by the United States. They also recommend that such intervention be undertaken as soon as possible and preferably before the release of National Guard and Reserve forces presently on active duty."

By then McNamara had virtually no confidence in his military chief and was rejecting nearly every proposal the general sent to him. The rejections became so routine, said one of Lemnitzer's former staff officers, that the staffer told the general that the situation was putting the military in an "embarrassing rut." But Lemnitzer replied, "I am the senior military officer—it's my job to state what I believe and it's his

[McNamara's] job to approve or disapprove." "McNamara's arrogance was astonishing," said Lemnitzer's aide, who knew nothing of Operation Northwoods. "He gave General Lemnitzer very short shrift and treated him like a schoolboy. The general almost stood at attention when he came into the room. Everything was 'Yes, sir' and 'No, sir.' "

Within months, Lemnitzer was denied a second term as JCS chairman and transferred to Europe as chief of NATO. Years later President Gerald Ford appointed Lemnitzer, a darling of the Republican right, to the President's Foreign Intelligence Advisory Board. Lemnitzer's Cuba chief, Brigadier General Craig, was also transferred. Promoted to major general, he spent three years as chief of the Army Security Agency, NSA's military arm.

Because of the secrecy and illegality of Operation Northwoods, all details remained hidden for forty years. Lemnitzer may have thought that all copies of the relevant documents had been destroyed; he was not one to leave compromising material lying around. Following the Bay of Pigs debacle, for example, he ordered Brigadier General David W. Gray, Craig's predecessor as chief of the Cuba project within the JCS, to destroy all his notes concerning Joint Chiefs actions and discussions during that period. Gray's meticulous notes were the only detailed official records of what happened within the JCS during that time. According to Gray, Lemnitzer feared a congressional investigation and therefore wanted any incriminating evidence destroyed.

With the evidence destroyed, Lemnitzer felt free to lie to Congress. When asked, during secret hearings before a Senate committee, if he knew of any Pentagon plans for a direct invasion of Cuba he said he did not. Yet detailed JCS invasion plans had been drawn up even before Kennedy was inaugurated. And additional plans had been developed since. The consummate planner and man of details also became evasive, suddenly encountering great difficulty in recalling key aspects of the operation, as if he had been out of the country during the period. It was a sorry spectacle. Senator Gore called for Lemnitzer to be fired. "We need a shakeup of the Joint Chiefs of Staff," he said. "We direly need a new chairman, as well as new members." No one had any idea of Operation Northwoods.

Because so many documents were destroyed, it is difficult to determine how many senior officials were aware of Operation Northwoods.

As has been described, the document was signed and fully approved by Lemnitzer and the rest of the Joint Chiefs and addressed to the Secretary of Defense for his signature. Whether it went beyond McNamara to the president and the attorney general is not known.

Even after Lemnitzer lost his job, the Joint Chiefs kept planning "pretext" operations at least into 1963. Among their proposals was a plan to deliberately create a war between Cuba and any of a number of its Latin American neighbors. This would give the United States military an excuse to come in on the side of Cuba's adversary and get rid of Castro. "A contrived 'Cuban' attack on an OAS [Organization of American States] member could be set up," said one proposal, "and the attacked state could be urged to 'take measures of self-defense and request assistance from the U.S. and OAS; the U.S. could almost certainly obtain the necessary two-thirds support among OAS members for collective action against Cuba."

Among the nations they suggested that the United States secretly attack were Jamaica and Trinidad-Tobago. Both were members of the British Commonwealth; thus, by secretly attacking them and then falsely blaming Cuba, the United States could lure England into the war against Castro. The report noted, "Any of the contrived situations described above are inherently, extremely risky in our democratic system in which security can be maintained, after the fact, with very great difficulty. If the decision should be made to set up a contrived situation it should be one in which participation by U.S. personnel is limited only to the most highly trusted covert personnel. This suggests the infeasibility of the use of military units for any aspect of the contrived situation."

The report even suggested secretly paying someone in the Castro government to attack the United States: "The only area remaining for consideration then would be to bribe one of Castro's subordinate commanders to initiate an attack on [the U.S. naval base at] Guantanamo." The act suggested—bribing a foreign nation to launch a violent attack on an American military installation—was treason.

In May 1963, Assistant Secretary of Defense Paul H. Nitze sent a plan to the White House proposing "a possible scenario whereby an attack on a United States reconnaissance aircraft could be exploited toward the end of effecting the removal of the Castro regime." In the event Cuba attacked a U-2, the plan proposed sending in additional

American pilots, this time on dangerous, unnecessary low-level reconnaissance missions with the expectation that they would also be shot down, thus provoking a war. "[T]he U.S. could undertake various measures designed to stimulate the Cubans to provoke a new incident," said the plan. Nitze, however, did not volunteer to be one of the pilots.

One idea involved sending fighters across the island on "harassing reconnaissance" and "show-off" missions "flaunting our freedom of action, hoping to stir the Cuban military to action." "Thus," said the plan, "depending above all on whether the Cubans were or could be made to be trigger-happy, the development of the initial downing of a reconnaissance plane could lead at best to the elimination of Castro, perhaps to the removal of Soviet troops and the installation of ground inspection in Cuba, or at the least to our demonstration of firmness on reconnaissance." About a month later, a low-level flight was made across Cuba, but unfortunately for the Pentagon, instead of bullets it produced only a protest.

Lemnitzer was a dangerous—perhaps even unbalanced—right-wing extremist in an extraordinarily sensitive position during a critical period. But Operation Northwoods also had the support of every single member of the Joint Chiefs of Staff, and even senior Pentagon official Paul Nitze argued in favor of provoking a phony war with Cuba. The fact that the most senior members of all the services and the Pentagon could be so out of touch with reality and the meaning of democracy would be hidden for four decades.

In retrospect, the documents offer new insight into the thinking of the military's star-studded leadership. Although they never succeeded in launching America into a phony war with Cuba, they may have done so with Vietnam. More than 50,000 Americans and more than 2 million Vietnamese were eventually killed in that war.

It has long been suspected that the 1964 Gulf of Tonkin incident—the spark that led to America's long war in Vietnam—was largely staged or provoked by U.S. officials in order to build up congressional and public support for American involvement. Over the years, serious questions have been raised about the alleged attack by North Vietnamese patrol boats on two American destroyers in the Gulf. But defenders of the Pentagon have always denied such charges, arguing that senior officials would never engage in such deceit.

Now, however, in light of the Operation Northwoods documents, it is clear that deceiving the public and trumping up wars for Americans to fight and die in was standard, approved policy at the highest levels of the Pentagon. In fact, the Gulf of Tonkin seems right out of the Operation Northwoods playbook: "We could blow up a U.S. ship in Guantanamo Bay and blame Cuba . . . casualty lists in U.S. newspapers would cause a helpful wave of indignation." One need only replace "Guantánamo Bay" with "Tonkin Gulf," and "Cuba" with "North Vietnam." The Gulf of Tonkin incident may or may not have been stage-managed, but the senior Pentagon leadership at the time was clearly capable of such deceit.

CHAPTER FIVE

EYES

KPYNTKA' ABPYHTO RIL VFLTA AIUUTK MY HFAA BF UHOTKA
CFKR ANLRXQ YANMC KN ANMDA YRQKFLDA FW KPR QCG
DYMIAQBC GN QMIG NYCSB QFGIG'B QFKOROGYB DSQJB
WJEHCFBJN YFWRJPC YFCHEZUF JP VRNF HV CUYJOFC HP OHCHBH
SLNO FENLDX LHH DLLMOA ZJCSO FL DZA LTON A.E. TLFONX

Two hundred miles north of Washington, at the Brooklyn Navy Yard, shipfitters riveted steel seams together and welded joints in place. Blue sparks flew about and industrial pounding filled the air. Men in hard hats cut, straightened, and shaped large metal plates, and electricians strung miles of wire like endless strands of black knitting yarn. In a long, boxy dry dock, welder's torches were bringing back to life the rusting skeleton and gray skin of a ship long discarded.

Like an early baby boomer, the SS *Samuel R. Aitken* was launched in Portland, Maine, on July 31, 1945. Named for an Irishman who came to the United States at the turn of the century and later became an executive with Moore-McCormack Lines, the *Aitken* was one of the mass-produced cargo vessels known as Liberty ships. Because it arrived too late for the war, it instead spent a few years hauling freight from port to port under the colors of Moore-McCormack. But after only three years in service, the *Aitken* was given early retirement and sent to a nautical boneyard in Wilmington, Delaware.

Now, under a heavy cloak of secrecy, the *Samuel R. Aitken* was being called back into service, but this time as a spy.

About the same time that John F. Kennedy was elected president, NSA director John Samford's tour ended with considerably more attention than it began. Just before his scheduled retirement in November 1960, the agency suffered the worst scandal in its history when two of its analysts, William H. Martin and Bernon F. Mitchell, defected to Moscow.

As a result of the defection, NSA's organizational structure was quickly changed. ADVA and GENS were combined into A Group, the largest organization, focusing on all analysis of the Soviet Union and its satellite countries. ACOM became B Group, responsible for China, Korea, Vietnam, and the rest of Communist Asia, as well as Cuba. And ALLO was transformed into G Group, which tackled the communications of the rest of the world. The remainder of NSA was similarly organized. Despite other spy scandals, this system would remain unchanged until well into the 1990s.

Vice Admiral Laurence Hugh (Jack) Frost, a 1926 Annapolis graduate who once served as chief of staff at NSA, replaced Samford. When he arrived, NSA's headquarters at Fort Meade had grown to 8,000 people and was eating up a larger and larger slice of the intelligence pie. By then the overall U.S. intelligence budget reached $2 billion; the Department of Defense accounted for $1.4 billion, most of which went to NSA. Thin and silver-haired, the admiral, soon after taking office, proclaimed that NSA was a ship and ordered a 75-foot, 3,100-pound flagpole installed with his personal flag so people would know that he was aboard.

It was an appropriate gesture. At the time, NSA was secretly building its own eavesdropping navy to supplement its Sigint air force. As the air battles of the 1950s claimed more and more lives, ferret ships began joining ferret planes. Ships could also cover the southern hemisphere—South America and sub-Saharan Africa—where NSA had almost no listening posts. Both areas were of growing concern as the United States and Russia sought to expand their influence throughout the developing world.

The concept was not new. For years the Soviets had used a fleet of about forty antenna-sprouting trawlers. They would bob just outside the three-mile territorial limit and eavesdrop on defense installations along the east and west coasts of the U.S. "The Soviets had a vast intelligence program which included the use of Soviet trawlers," said former KGB major general Oleg Kalugin, "and specially equipped scientific ships, so called, which operated under the auspices of the Academy of Sciences of the USSR. They would go to various places—the Atlantic, the Pacific and wherever they could. And they would use the intelligence equipment . . . to intercept electronic communications and then . . . break them."

President Eisenhower authorized NSA's first signals intelligence ship on November 12, 1959. The *Samuel R. Aitken* would become the USS *Oxford.* Although previously only cruisers had been named for cities, it was decided to make an exception for eavesdropping vessels. "Oxford" was chosen because it was found to be the commonest city name in the United States. The vessel was also given the euphemistic designation "Auxiliary General Technical Research" (AGTR) ship.

The conversion work began in October 1960, just before the presidential elections. At 441 feet long, with a beam of 57 feet and a displacement of 11,498 tons, the *Oxford* was large enough to house a sizable listening post. On September 11, 1961, Lieutenant Commander Howard R. Lund reported his ship ready for duty, ostensibly for the Navy's Atlantic Service Force, and proceeded from New York to the vessel's home port of Norfolk, Virginia.

The *Oxford* would be unlike any other ship ever sent to sea. To quickly get intercepts from the ship to NSA, a unique sixteen-foot dish-shaped antenna was installed on its fantail. On December 15, the *Oxford* became the first ship at sea ever to receive a message bounced off the moon. "Signaling another first in communications by the Navy," said the message from the Chief of Naval Operations, "this message being sent to you from the U.S. Naval Research Laboratory Field Station, Stump Neck, Maryland, via the moon."

A few weeks later, the *Oxford* left Norfolk on its first operational cruise, an eavesdropping sweep off eastern South America. After a brief visit to Colón, Panama, it crossed the equator and sailed to Recife, Brazil; Montevideo, Uruguay; Buenos Aires, Argentina; and Rio de Janeiro, Brazil. Along the way, the ship successfully used its moon-bounce antenna to send information back to Washington—another first.

In addition to speed, the moon-bounce antenna also provided the ship with stealth. Unlike the standard high-frequency communications, which were vulnerable to foreign direction-finding antennas, the moon-bounce signal was virtually undetectable because it used hard-to-intercept directional microwave signals. The moon-bounce system was also immune to jamming. Ground stations for the system were located at Cheltenham, Maryland, near NSA; Wahiawa, Hawaii; Sobe, Okinawa; and Oakhanger, in the United Kingdom.

On June 20, 1962, Commander Thomas Avery Cosgrove took over as captain of the *Oxford.* Cosgrove was a "mustang," an officer who had previously served as an enlisted man; he was "as rough as sandpaper," said Aubrey Brown, one of the intercept operators on the ship. "He had tattoos all the way on his arms down to his wrists. He had a tattoo around his neck. And he had the language of a boatswain's mate."

About a month later, on July 16, the ship set out for another four-month surveillance mission down the South American coast. But three days later it received an emergency message to set sail immediately for Cuba "in response to highest priority intelligence requirements."

By the summer of 1962, the shipping lanes between Russia and Cuba were beginning to resemble a freeway during rush hour. On July 24, NSA reported "at least four, and possibly five . . . Soviet passenger ships en route Cuba with a possible 3,335 passengers on board." The passengers may well have been Soviet military personnel brought to operate Soviet radar and weapons systems. Over little more than a month, fifty-seven Soviet merchant ships visited Havana. "In addition to the shipping increase," recalled Admiral Robert Lee Dennison, who was in charge of the Atlantic fleet at the time, "there were large numbers of Soviet-bloc military personnel prior to August and then there was a buildup during August and September when nine passenger ships arrived in Cuba with a total capacity of 20,000 passengers. But at the time we didn't have any way of really confirming how many people were on board these ships because they would disembark at night."

At the same time, NSA began noticing increased use of deception. Ships leaving ports in Russia listed destinations in the Far East and in Africa. But NSA, with its network of giant elephant cages intercepting the vessels' daily broadcasts and triangulating their positions, was able to track them as they crossed the Atlantic en route to Cuba. NSA was also able to detect ships loading far less cargo than their manifests called for, thus leaving a great deal of room for weapons and military supplies. Thus when the new Soviet cargo ship *Beloretsk* arrived at Archangel in late May it was supposed to load about 7,800 tons of lumber, but only 5,240 tons were actually put aboard. That cargo filled only a third of the

Norwegian-built ship's 14,150-ton capacity. "It is therefore believed," concluded an NSA report, "that the *Beloretsk* may be carrying a partial load of military cargo."

As the summer wore on, the signals became more ominous. About forty miles off the westernmost tip of Cuba, an antenna-packed ferret plane picked up the first telltale sounds of Soviet airborne intercept radar. This meant that Cuban air defense bases could now accurately target and shoot down U.S. aircraft flying over or near their territory, thus increasing exponentially the risks of the eavesdropping missions. That same day, intercept operators began hearing Russian voices over Cuban internal communications links. "Comint sources reveal Russian and non-Cuban voice activity on Cuban Revolutionary Air Force tactical frequencies," said one report. Another troubling sign.

In May 1962, as the Soviet buildup in Cuba continued to look more menacing, Vice Admiral Frost began touring listening posts in the Far East, including the large Navy monitoring station at Kamiseya, Japan. The next month he was suddenly booted from the agency and transferred to the Potomac River Naval Command, a halfway house for admirals on the brink of retirement. Director for less than two years, Frost bore the brunt of the various inquests into the double defection of Martin and Mitchell. Because of that, and disputes with the Pentagon, his cryptologic career was terminated prematurely. Many also felt Frost had a problem dealing with NSA personnel. "I thought Frost was one of the least effective [NSA heads]," said former NSA research chief Howard Campaigne. "I think his problems were communication problems." Another former NSA official said Frost had trouble controlling his anger. "I saw him chew out Frank Raven, Bill Ray [senior NSA officials], and some Air Force brigadier general in a briefing," said Robert D. Farley, a former NSA historian. "Just the finger-on-the-chest bit."

Replacing Frost was fifty-one-year-old Gordon Aylesworth Blake, an Air Force lieutenant general. Blake knew what he was getting into; he had earlier run NSA's air arm, the Air Force Security Service. As a sixteen-year-old, he slipped into West Point under the age limit. "I hadn't been north of Minneapolis, east of Chicago, south of Des Moines, or west of Sioux City," he recalled. "I was pretty green."

Eventually awarded his pilot's wings, Blake went on to communications school and was assigned to Pearl Harbor, Hawaii, in 1939. On the morning of December 7, 1941, he was on duty as the airfield operations officer, waiting to make sure a returning flight of B-17 bombers was properly parked. They were due to arrive at 8:00 A.M. from California. "So all of a sudden we hear this big *'karroppp,'*" said Blake. "I raced outside and here was a dive-bomber that had bombed a big depot hangar at the south end of the hangar line. It pulled up and we could see this red circle under the wing. Well, no guessing as to what the hell had happened." Blake ran up to the control tower to warn the B-17s that were due in and he eventually managed to land them safely. For his actions during the Japanese attack on Pearl Harbor he was awarded the Silver Star for gallantry.

Blake knew Frost was in trouble and was somewhat uneasy at moving in as his predecessor was moving out. "Jack Frost was under some nebulous status because of the Martin-Mitchell case," he said. "I very much felt badly about coming in over his prostrate form, and he understood that."

Blake kept Dr. Louis Tordella as deputy director and largely left to him the agency's most secret operations. "It would be better for NSA and for those activities if I left that to Tordella," Blake said. "And that was our working relationship. So while I usually had a general knowledge of this compartment and that compartment, I made no attempt to be really knowledgeable about it and, therefore, just less involved security-wise. Maybe that's an odd view but directors come and go and for them to become a repository of every last little secret never struck me as being really very useful." Tordella was on his way to an extraordinary reign as NSA's chief keeper of the secrets.

Sensing the tremors of approaching war in the summer of 1941, Tordella, then a thirty-year-old assistant professor of mathematics at Loyola University in Chicago, one day walked into the nearby U.S. Fifth Army Headquarters and volunteered his services. But after the professor explained that he held a doctorate in mathematics, practiced cryptanalysis as a hobby, held an amateur radio license, and wanted to serve, the Army major in charge could not be bothered. Possibly thinking that the new recruit would be far more comfortable with a box of chalk instead of bullets, he brushed him off with a sneer: "When we want you, we'll draft you."

Cold-shouldered by the Army, Tordella would soon be embraced by the Navy. Spotting his background on a questionnaire Tordella had filled out for the American Academy of Science, Laurance Safford, a naval officer and father of the Navy's codebreaking effort, rolled out the red carpet. By April 1942, Tordella was a lieutenant (junior grade) assigned to OP-20-G, the Navy's cryptologic organization, in Washington. Working out of a temporary building on Constitution Avenue, the lanky Hoosier stood his first watch—supervising direction-finding operations—after one eight-hour indoctrination.

But before long, Tordella was using mathematics like a burglar using lock picks, looking for the array of numbers that would pry open the hellish German cipher machine known as Enigma. In July 1942, Lieutenant Tordella was transferred to Bainbridge Island in the state of Washington, a key intercept station for eavesdropping on Japanese communications. But after several years at the remote listening post in the Northwest, and with the war beginning to wind down, Tordella ached to test his skills closer to the front. The opportunity came in 1944, when he received orders to China.

During a stopover in Washington, D.C., for meetings, however, he learned that he had been bumped from the assignment. Instead of heading to the war, he boarded a train to New York City and a special twelve-week course at Bell Laboratories on new equipment that was designed to decipher Japanese voice codes. Initially, Tordella was to travel to the South Pacific to test various equipment and techniques. However, before the system could be deployed the military situation in the Pacific changed. Tordella was again reassigned, this time as the officer-in-charge of a newly established Navy experimental intercept site at Skaggs Island, an isolated, mosquito-infested wetland near San Francisco. Here, amid the frogs and snakes and antennas, Tordella sat out the remainder of the war.

Mustered out in October 1946, Tordella had not lost his taste for codebreaking. Rather than return to the classroom in Chicago, he signed on as a civilian mathematician with the Navy's cryptologic organization, then called the Communications Supplementary Activity and later the Naval Security Group. With the formation of NSA in 1952, Tordella transferred over and became chief of NSA-70, which was responsible for high-level cryptanalysis. A rising star, he was named deputy director in August 1958.

Because Tordella had developed a close working relationship with the CIA's chief of operations, Richard Helms, who would later go on to become director, Blake also let the mathematician handle the problems that occasionally developed with that agency. One difficult situation came up when the CIA tried to muscle in on the NSA's territory by putting out its own signals intelligence reports. "I left that one to Lou for some reason or another to sort it out," said Blake. "He and Dick Helms were thick as thieves."

With the enormous focus on Cuba, Blake barely had enough time to find his office before the alarm bells began to sound. On July 19, Robert McNamara pushed NSA into high gear. "NSA has been directed by Sec Def [Secretary of Defense] to establish a Sigint collection capability in the vicinity of Havana, Cuba," Blake immediately notified the Chief of Naval Operations, "as a matter of the highest intelligence priority." He then pulled the ferret ship USS *Oxford* from its South American patrol and sent it steaming toward Havana.

The *Oxford* was ideally suited for the mission. Where once cases of lima beans, truck axles, plumbing pipes, and other cargo had been stored, the earphone-clad intercept operators now sat in front of racks of receivers and reel-to-reel tape recorders. Up forward, near the bow, voice and Morse collection specialists twisted dials and searched for signals. Fortunately for NSA, the Cubans never tried to scramble voice communications. In the background was the constant rapping of teleprinters printing out intercepted Soviet and Cuban telexes and other communications. One deck above was a steel forest of antennas. In the stern, below another forest of spindly metal tree trunks and stiff wire branches, the Elint specialists listened for the twitters and warbles of Russian radar on Cuban air bases.

"From the ship we could look up and down the length of the island," said Harold L. Parish, a Soviet analyst. As if it were on a cruise to nowhere, the *Oxford* would sail in circles and figure eights for weeks at a time six miles off Havana's Morro Castle. The ship's slow and lazy pace was especially good for loitering near key microwave beams, narrow signals that were difficult for airborne ferrets to pick up. "The quality of the intercept was good," Parish said. "Even with the C-130 you were flying kind of fast and you flew through the [microwave] beams" so that not enough signal was captured to decipher.

As the weeks went by, the intercepts became increasingly ominous. On August 17, an Elint operator on the *Oxford* heard an unusual sound, like the song of a rare bird out of its normal habitat. It was the electronic call of a Soviet radar codenamed Whiff, a troubling sound that meant Russian anti-aircraft weapons had now been set up.

At NSA, a number of Soviet Sigint experts in A Group were suddenly told to report to the office of Major General John Davis, the operations chief. "We were called down and told there was evidence of offensive missiles," said Hal Parish. They were then sent to help out the Spanish Sigint experts on the Cuba desk in B Group. "We all descended down there and we formed what was the watch for the Cuban missile crisis. . . . All the people who were previously associated with the Cuban target—the management and so forth—kind of disappeared and went off to the side. We came down and set up the round-the-clock activities and sort of went from there." Parish said some friction developed between NSA's civilian and military staffs. "There was some," he said, "there always is."

In Washington, within hours of receiving the CRITIC message containing the intelligence, senior officials began scurrying to meetings. The CIA director, John McCone, told one high-level group that he believed that the evidence pointed to the construction of offensive ballistic missiles in Cuba—missiles that could hit as far north as the southern part of the United States. What else could the anti-aircraft weapons be protecting? he asked. But both Secretary of State Dean Rusk and McNamara disagreed, maintaining that the buildup was purely defensive.

To try to coordinate much of the data collection, Blake set up NSA's first around-the-clock Sigint Command Center, which later became the present-day National Security Operations Center (NSOC). "It was for most of us our initial contact by telephone with a customer on the other end," said one of those assigned to the command center. "It was the first time I had ever talked to colonels from DIA [the Defense Intelligence Agency]. Same with CIA. . . . We turned on the heavy reporting, both spot and daily report summaries at that time and twice-daily summaries. . . . We worked between eight and twenty hours a day."

Blake spent much of his time in meetings with the U.S. Intelligence Board. "We would recess for a few hours so the staff could type something," he said, "and then we would come back again, and the basic question we were addressing [was], If we belly up to the Russians, what will they do? Well, I am sure you realize how hard that question is because you talk about intent, you see, and you don't read any messages that give you intent. And I recall our final paper on the subject to the president, pretty much bottom line was 'We think the Russians will blink.' "

Among the key problems NSA faced was a shortage of Spanish linguists and, at least in the early stages of the crisis, a lack of intercept coverage. "One collection facility . . . against *x*-hundred emitters that were on the air at the time from the Cuban area," said NSA cryptologist Hal Parish, "we were just a little short. So that was a problem." Still another concern was the lack of secure communications between NSA and the listening posts. "Communications were definitely a problem," Parish said. "Secure communications. I'd say we were doing advisory support over the open telephone line." The *Oxford*'s unique moon-bounce dish was critical in relaying both messages and intercepts from Havana's doorstep to the analysts in the command center. But according to Parish, "It was only a twelve-hour-a-day system, unfortunately, because the moon was out of sight at times."

With the *Oxford* now in place, the amount of Sigint concerning Cuba went from a trickle to a gush. The intercepts clearly showed that the Russians were exercising greater and greater control over Cuban military activities. "Concentrated efforts have been made by Bloc pilots and controllers to converse entirely in Spanish," said one report, "but, on occasion, they have reverted to their native tongue to convey a difficult command or request to other Bloc pilots or controllers." Other intercepts revealed nighttime jet gunnery exercises, bombing practice, and extensive patrols. NSA issued a dramatic report showing just how massive the sudden buildup was. In the last three months of 1961, total gross tonnage of ships heading for Cuba was 183,923. But in just the past two months—July and August of 1962—the gross tonnage had jumped to 518,196.

Worried about leaks, Kennedy had ordered a tight lid clamped on the secret intelligence operations against Cuba. "The President said to put it back in the box and nail it tight," said Lieutenant General Marshall S. (Pat) Carter, deputy director of the CIA at the time. At NSA, Blake ordered a new codeword, further limiting the number of people with access to the information, and extra restrictions on intercepts revealing offensive weapons. "Sigint evidence of Cuban acquisition of potentially offensive weapons systems," said the message, "(e.g., surface-to-surface missiles, bombers, submarines) will . . . contain preamble 'This is a FUNNEL message' and be forwarded electronically to DIRNSA [Director, NSA] only at 01 precedence or higher. . . . No, repeat, no further dissemination is authorized without specific instructions."

For the airborne eavesdroppers, the skies around Cuba had suddenly become extremely dangerous. Three times a day an RB-47 Strato-Spy would take off from Macdill Air Force Base, outside Tampa. Loaded with eavesdropping gear, it would fly along the Cuban coast, sucking signals from the air. The tapes would quickly be flown to NSA, where analysts would search for new signals coming from the vicinity of the surface-to-air missile sites under construction. Other C-130 "flying listening posts" also flew along the coast, just outside Cuban territory. All the ferrets were equipped with special automatic scanning devices to instantly pick up SA-2 anti-aircraft–related signals.

At the White House, President Kennedy discussed the possibility of moving the ferrets farther from the Cuban coast, but NSA argued against it, even though one of the missions—the daily routes—was within range of Cuban missiles. The problem was, the farther it moved from the coast, the fewer signals it could pick up. "This [equipment] is now operating at the margin of its capability," said NSA. "If it is moved further out, the mission, an electronic intelligence one, might as well be abandoned." While arguing to keep the planes in harm's way, Blake also made protection of the aircraft the most important responsibility of the listening posts. "I feel that our first priority requirement is reporting reaction in connection with high and low level reconnaissance flights," he notified the commander of NSA's air contingent.

The foresight of developing an NSA navy was paying off. Sitting just half a dozen miles from downtown Havana, the *Oxford* was able to eavesdrop on a wealth of communications. As a result, Blake requested appropriations for an additional "shipborne collection platform" for use against Cuba, this one a large civilian-manned vessel operated by the Military Sea Transportation Service. "NSA is therefore commencing negotiations," said his message to the Joint Chiefs of Staff, "for the procurement of the USNS *Muller*, a vessel which can approximate the accommodations and facilities aboard the *Oxford*." But first Blake needed the money.

If Blake trusted Tordella with all of the agency's secrets, he trusted Congress and their oversight and appropriations responsibilities with none of them. Asked how difficult it was to testify fully about NSA's activities before congressional committees, Blake had a simple answer. "It was very difficult and, therefore, we didn't do it." Instead, said Blake, "my technique for that dealt with two gentlemen who were very cooperative" when it came to probing NSA—that is, there were no questions asked. "Being able to talk more frankly to them," he added, "and let them see to it that the rest of the Committee didn't get too far afield was obviously a tremendous boon to the director and his budget activities." According to Blake, those two were Michigan congressman Gerald Ford, on the House Appropriations Committee, and Senator Richard Russell, who occupied a similar position on the Senate side. "I would have private meetings with those two only," said Blake. "That was my technique, and it worked beautifully. . . . My recollection is a pretty successful three years in terms of resources."

To make up for the lack of additional people, Blake began yanking intercept operators from other listening posts around the world and sending them to southern Florida. At Fort Bragg, North Carolina, Army Sigint personnel attached to the 326th ASA Company were told to drop everything and board planes for Homestead Air Base near Miami, a key listening post during the crisis. Eavesdropping aircraft were moved from their location in Rota, Spain, to air bases in Jacksonville and Pensacola. From there they would fly down to Key West, pick up intercept operators, and conduct eight- to ten-hour missions off the Cuban coast.

In a matter of days the Navy turned Key West from a sleepy supply depot for cryptologic equipment to a buzzing city of eavesdroppers. "What had been sort of a lazy tempo in the Key West theater of operations suddenly heated up to match the summer weather," recalled Owen Englander, who was in charge of the Key West naval security detachment. "Almost overnight the National Command Authority and the

Navy and Air Force operational worlds discovered Naval Security Group Detachment Key West. A decision was made to beef us up and people commenced to arrive from every direction."

The intercept operators worked in a World War I bunker buried under fifteen feet of reinforced concrete and compacted marl—sand, clay, and crushed coral. It was designed to withstand a direct hit from a 16-inch shell. Sailors immediately began setting up a huge dish antenna as well as an assortment of wires and poles. In addition to the planes, bases, and ships eavesdropping on Cuban and Soviet communications, submarines were sent in. One sub was able to sneak close enough to eavesdrop on a microwave link on the Isle of Pines. For NSA's eavesdroppers, submarines provided a quality no other platform could offer: stealth.

But although it was NSA's most important target in the summer and fall of 1962, Cuba was far from the only one.

At periscope depth, sixty feet under the dark and frigid Bering Sea, the USS *Nautilus* (SSN 571) was barely moving. The world's first nuclear-powered submarine, it had made headlines four years earlier when it sailed beneath the icepack to the North Pole and broadcast the message "*Nautilus* 90 north." Now it was on an enormously sensitive espionage mission a short distance off a black and desolate Soviet island above the Arctic Circle. Without doubt, Novaya Zemlya was the most forbidding piece of real estate on the planet. One year earlier, the Russians had exploded the largest bomb in the history of mankind above the island, a 58-megaton thermonuclear monster. Now the crew of the *Nautilus* was busy making preparations to eavesdrop on and photograph a new round of tests. Thirteen miles from ground zero, Sigint specialist John Arnold was attaching the final piece of critical equipment—a cardboard toilet paper tube.

Arnold, a Navy chief, was a fast riser in a superexclusive club: NSA's small band of undersea intercept operators. Sealed for months in closet-sized listening posts aboard specially outfitted submarines, the deep-diving eavesdroppers prowled close to Soviet coasts, recording shore-based transmitters and key signals within the Russian fleet. "Collection at thirteen miles was pretty good," said Arnold. "Sometimes you could even pick up signals with your antennas underwater. Not much, but some of the radars were strong enough to penetrate the water." Locating radar installations was a key mission of the team. "You could tell from the frequency and the pulse repetition rate and the scan rate what kind of radar it is and take its bearing by direction finding."

Arnold began his career in the old diesel-powered boats, which needed to break the surface about once every twenty-four hours in order to get new air through the snorkel. "If you had any antennas or masts up, the periscope was always up—even during the daytime—because a helicopter or aircraft could come cruising by and they would see your mast," said Arnold. "And if you didn't have your periscope up keeping a lookout, they could end up detecting you."

Once, a conning officer became so mesmerized watching a helicopter he completely forgot to call an alert. "He just kept focused on it and watched it come right over us," said Arnold. "So we became the target of an ASW [antisubmarine warfare] exercise in short order. That kept us down for over two days before we could shake him and get fresh air again. Everyone that was nonessential was to stay in their bunks to minimize the consumption of oxygen."

Arnold had spent much of the summer of 1962 beneath the waves of the Bering Sea. A few months earlier, in anticipation of renewed nuclear tests, he had put together a special piece of equipment and headed for Novaya Zemlya aboard the USS *Scorpion*. But when the tests were postponed, the crew spent the mission conducting electronic surveillance just off Russia's sensitive Kola Peninsula. "We almost had an underwater collision with a [Soviet] *November*-class submarine," said Arnold. "We were trailing, collecting data on its bottom side when it was on the surface. We were smack dab under him. . . . Between the bottom of his sub and the top of the *Scorpion*, sometimes the periscope was only six to twelve inches, closely inspecting underwater appendages, protrusions, and so forth, and recording it on television." Suddenly the depth finder aboard the Soviet boat sent out a "ping" to determine the distance to the bottom. "That was standard practice just before they dive," said Arnold. The *Scorpion* escaped just in time.

Back home for just a few days, Arnold was again quickly dispatched to Novaya Zemlya when word was received that Soviet bomb testing would begin soon. This time he and his team were transferred to the nuclear-powered *Nautilus.* As other Sigint specialists eavesdropped on Soviet technicians rigging for the test, Arnold was fitting the sub's periscopes with special photographic equipment. The cameras were connected to the lens of the scopes with rolls of cardboard toilet paper tubes double-wrapped with black electric tape. "On one periscope we had an optical detector that measured light intensity versus time," said Arnold. "On the other we had a high-speed color movie camera attached."

Suddenly the dimly lit submarine, deep under the surface of the sea, lit up with a blinding light. "When the detonation went off it was just like someone had set off a flashbulb in your face," said Arnold. The light had blasted through the heavily wrapped toilet paper tubes as if they were made of see-through plastic. The crew not only saw the flash, they heard and felt the explosion. "It was a really weird sound when you're in a submarine," Arnold recalled. "It sounds like a jet airplane when it breaks the sound barrier. Then you feel it also. It feels as though you're standing on a steel deck and somebody under the deck has a sledgehammer and he hits the steel deck plate right where you're standing—it's a sharp shock. It broke a few fluorescent light bulbs and caused some insulation to pop off."

Over six weeks, Arnold witnessed twelve or thirteen tests. "They were from twenty kilotons up to fifty megatons," Arnold said. After the initial blast, the explosion could be viewed through the periscope. "They were spectacularly beautiful to watch," he said. "You could look through the periscope and watch the mushroom cloud build and the colors develop." Following the nuclear tests, Arnold, like many other intercept operators, was assigned to a mission off Cuba, this time aboard a surface ship trying to pick up the launch codes for the deadly Soviet SA-2 surface-to-air missiles.

About two o'clock in the morning on September 15, 1962, the crisis again ratcheted up several levels. After double-checking and triple-checking, there was no question: the U.S. listeners had detected a Russian "Spoon Rest" radar, fully active. For the first time, the SA-2 missiles were operational, capable of shooting down any aircraft on a moment's notice, as had the SA-2 in Russia that brought down the U-2 piloted by Francis Gary Powers. Listening posts in Florida, Puerto Rico, and elsewhere helped the *Oxford* pinpoint the signal as emanating from a location about three miles west of the port of Mariel. From now on, all U.S. pilots, no matter what aircraft they flew, would have a cocked gun pointed at them.

The activation of the SA-2 missiles gave NSA and CIA an opportunity to fake the Russians into revealing key details of the weapons system. Gene Poteat, a young CIA scientist, had come up with a scheme to inject false targets into Soviet radar. Codenamed Palladium, the operation involved sending deceptive signals to give Russian radar operators the false impression that they were tracking an aircraft. "By smoothly varying the length of the delay," Poteat wrote later, "we could simulate the false target's range and speed." As the Russians tracked the ghost aircraft, NSA intercept operators listened in. Later analysis would be able to determine such important details as just how sensitive the radar systems were, and to assess the proficiency of the operators.

The Palladium system was mounted on a destroyer operating out of Key West. As the ship cruised well off the Cuban coast, the Palladium system transmitted false signals indicating that a U.S. fighter plane out of Florida was about to penetrate Cuban airspace. At about the same time, an American submarine that had slipped into Havana Bay released a number of balloons that carried metal spheres of varying size into the sky.

Elsewhere on the destroyer, in an NSA van lashed to the deck, intercept operators closely monitored the Russian radar, hoping to be able to determine just how accurate the system was by studying the way it tracked the ghost aircraft and the metal objects. They quickly struck pay dirt. A Cuban fighter suddenly took off after the ghost aircraft; other MiGs began circling where the submarine had surfaced. In the NSA van, the intercept operators quickly began eavesdropping on both the shore-based radar systems and the pilots pursuing the ghost aircraft. "We had no trouble in manipulating the Palladium system controls," wrote Poteat, "to keep our ghost aircraft always just ahead of the pursuing Cuban planes." Through earphones, one intercept operator heard the Cuban pilot notify his base that he had the intruding plane in sight and was about to shoot it down. A technician moved his finger to a button. "I nodded yes," said Poteat, "and he switched off the Palladium system." The ghost aircraft disappeared.

Palladium proved very successful, revealing that the Soviet radar systems were state-of-the-art and that their operators were equally skilled. "We also knew which of their radars had low power [or] maintenance problems or were otherwise not functioning up to par," noted Poteat, "and where the U.S. Air Force might safely penetrate in wartime."

Five days before the discovery of the operational SA-2 missiles, Secretary of State Rusk had become so worried over the prospects of a shootdown over or near Cuba that he asked for a meeting of the key players in Operation Mongoose. Rusk was particularly unsettled by several recent incidents. On August 30, a U-2 had accidentally overflown Russia's Sakhalin Island, generating a harsh Soviet protest, and a few days later another CIA U-2, based in Taiwan and flown by a Chinese Nationalist, was lost over mainland China.

At the meeting, Rusk mentioned the incidents and then looked across the table at CIA deputy director Pat Carter. "Pat, don't you ever let me up?" he asked jokingly. "How do you expect me to negotiate on Berlin with all these incidents?" But Robert Kennedy saw no humor. "What's the matter, Dean, no guts?" he snapped. Eventually Rusk and Carter compromised on a reduced flight schedule. But Carter expressed his concern. "I want to put you people on notice," he said, "that it remains our intention to fly right up over those SAMs to see what is there." There was no response, positive or negative. As the meeting broke up and the officials began heading for the doors, Carter quietly grumbled, "There they all go again and no decisions."

The next day, October 10, NSA reported that the Cuban air defense system seemed to be complete. The Cubans had just begun passing radar tracking from radar stations to higher headquarters and to defensive fighter bases using Soviet procedures. Their system, with Russians in advisory positions at every point, was now ready for business.

From the very first, NSA had performed superbly in tracking the Cuban arms buildup, shipload by shipload, pallet by pallet. But without the ability to break high-level Soviet or Cuban cipher systems, the codebreakers could not answer the most important question: Were all the weapons being delivered defensive, or were any offensive, such as ballistic missiles? Even unencrypted Cuban communications frequently frustrated NSA's abilities. "Communications security has been very well maintained through a system of cover words and/or callsigns," one NSA report noted. Instead, NSA depended mostly on commercial ship transmissions, unencrypted Cuban chatter, and direction finding. Thus it was neither the NSA nor the CIA that would discover the first hard evidence of medium-range ballistic missiles (MRBMs) in Cuba. Instead it was the high-resolution "eyes" of an Air Force U-2. Nevertheless, Admiral Thomas H. Moorer, who would later become Chief of Naval Operations, told Congress that "electronic intelligence led to the photographic intelligence that gave indisputable evidence of the Soviet missiles in Cuba."

On Thursday, October 18, a U-2's high-altitude reconnaissance photography revealed that the Soviet and Cuban construction teams were making rapid progress. In August, only the initial construction of one missile site was observed. But new photography revealed two confirmed MRBM sites and one probable. Two other sites, possibly for the more powerful intermediate-range missiles, were also confirmed.

On the *Oxford*, it was nail-biting time. NSA intercepts picked up frequent Cuban references to "the *Oxford* spy ship." According to Parish, "They would send vessels out and get in their path. Some low flyers would come over—low-flying aircraft. They would come on, circle them with their guns trained on them."

"We were all listening for Russian communications, Cuban and Russian," said *Oxford* intercept operator Aubrey Brown. "The Cubans didn't take too kindly to the idea of us sitting out there and doing this. So there was a game of harassment that they played—they would send these gunboats out and you could see the crew going to general quarters, you could see the guns being trained on the ship. They take an attack position and then run a fake attack on the ship. The people on the boats were standing behind the guns."

"Jesus Christ," yelled one senior intercept operator. "It's war! Havana harbor just went crypto." Until then, the routine broadcasts to ships entering Havana harbor had been in the clear. Suddenly the broadcast became gibberish. After a short while and further analysis, however, it was determined that the nervous intercept operator had put the intercept tape in his machine backwards. As tensions increased, McCone brought up with President Kennedy the issue of the *Oxford*'s safety. The CIA director was eventually given permission to move it farther away, to about twenty miles.

Back in the Elint section of the ship, the technicians would hear screeching as the Cuban fire-control radar locked on them; then, MiGs would be launched. At the same time, the U.S. listeners were eavesdropping on what the boats and the MiGs were saying.

The arrival of NSA civilians on the ship was wrapped in mystery. "You kind of know things are getting a little more agitated because over in Key West you would pick up a couple of guys from NSA who will come out and do three weeks of special duty," said Brown. "And they've got some kind of assignment that no one will talk about. They come in with special recorders and they put them in the racks and they do their stuff and they leave."

Because NSA was unable to break the Soviet cipher system, one of the special missions involved sending someone to the *Oxford* with special equipment to try to capture the radiation emitted from Soviet crypto machines. These signals—known in NSA as Tempest emissions—contained deciphered information and thus would be extremely valuable. But to collect those signals, the ship had to get very close to the Russian station. "We took the ship in pretty close. We usually stayed out eight miles, but this time we went in to around four miles," said Brown. "There was a Russian communications station there that was in communication with Moscow, and they were trying to pick up the Tempest radiation from this crypto device. If they could get the Tempest radiation, they [the NSA] had the key to the universe then."

The intercept operators were also looking for sharp "noise spikes," which could offer clues as to rotor settings on older crypto machines. "The codebreakers were having a tough time with this code," said Max Buscher, a Sigint operator on the *Oxford* during the crisis. "They thought that if we got in close, if the encrypting device was electromechanical, we might pick up some noise spikes; that would be a clue as to how the machine was stepping with its rotors. We monitored that twenty-four hours a day."

At NSA headquarters, the Cuba Watch team was trying to piece together the military order of battle in Cuba. "We had constructed a Cuban air defense system," said Parish. "We really had not identified the SAM communications and so on." Along the rim of the Atlantic Ocean, NSA's listening posts and elephant cages were put on special alert. As Navy ships began leaving port to get into position to enforce a blockade, it was critical to know the location, speed, and cargo of Soviet ships now crossing the Atlantic en route to Cuba.

Even more important was any indication of Soviet submarines. In the blockhouses at the center of the massive antennas, intercept operators scanned the frequency spectrum hoping for a hit. Once a signal was captured, listening posts on both sides of the Atlantic would immediately transmit the information to the net control center at Cheltenham, Maryland. There, technicians would triangulate the exact positions of the ships and subs and pass the information on to analysts in NSA. It was feared that once a blockade was announced, the Russians might attempt to smuggle nuclear warheads or other weapons to Cuba under the American ships patrolling the restricted area. On a wall-size plotting board in the Merchant Shipping Section, small magnetic ships would be moved as the positions were reported by Cheltenham. Photographs would then be taken of the board for inclusion in the next morning's intelligence report, which would be sent to the White House.

In late September, four Soviet submarines had slipped into the Atlantic from the Barents Sea. The F-class attack subs were the top of the line, capable of launching nuclear-tipped torpedoes. NSA had been keeping track of the movements of an oil-resupply vessel, the *Terek*, which was suspected of providing support to the subs; wherever the *Terek* went, the Soviet submarines were thought to be close by. By October the *Terek* and the submarines were halfway across the Atlantic, an unusual move by a navy that usually keeps its submarines close to home. American intelligence feared that the four were the vanguard for a Soviet submarine facility in Cuba. Another vessel of great interest to NSA, traveling in the general vicinity of the *Terek*, was the electronic eavesdropping ship *Shkval*, which was also suspected of supporting the subs while at the same time collecting intelligence on U.S. ships in the area.

On Sunday, October 21, the *Oxford* made a grim discovery. "I was at work and all of a sudden there were people running all over the place," said intercept operator Aubrey Brown. "They're distraught, they're preoccupied, and they're trying to send out Flash messages and everything's going crazy." (Seldom used, Flash messages have the highest priority; the designation is reserved for dire war-related messages.) Most of the activity was coming from behind the cipher-locked door to the aft Elint space. Inside the darkened room, crammed with receivers, six-foot-tall 3M tape recorders, and an assortment of eerie green screens, technicians hovered around the flickering scope of the WLR-1 X-band receiver.

They had just picked up the screeching sounds from a troubling new radar system in Cuba, and they wanted to be sure it was what they suspected. Again and again they measured the width of the pulses—the size of the spikes on the scope. Holding on to stopwatches that dangled from their necks, they clicked them on and off to time the interval between the *woop* sounds, giving them the radar's scan rate. Once they were sure of the signal's makeup, they checked the NSA's highly classified TEXTA (Technical Extracts of Traffic Analysis) Manual and confirmed its identity.

"One of our T Branchers [Elint operators] intercepted one of the radars going on line for the first time," said Max Buscher. "And they could tell by the parameters that it was a radar associated with an offensive missile system. This was flashed to NSA. Six hours later, a jet helicopter came down and lowered a rope and they wanted the tape—they didn't just take our word for it, the NSA wanted the tape."

Early the next day, October 22, NSA had more bad news: at least five Soviet missile regiments would soon become operational in Cuba. Each regiment would have eight missile launchers and sixteen missiles. Thus, Cuba would have the potential to launch a first salvo of forty missiles, and a refire capability of another forty.

Later that morning, at a National Security Council meeting, McCone discussed the *Terek* and other up-to-the-minute intelligence on Soviet shipping. The *Poltava,* he said, was due to arrive in Cuba in about five days, and its cargo was so arranged as to make it clear that long cylinders were on board.

At 1:00 P.M. the Strategic Air Command began to initiate "quietly and gradually" a partial airborne alert and the dispersal of bombers to air bases around the country. At the same time, the Navy began to quietly evacuate dependents, by ship and air, from the American base at Guantánamo Bay in Cuba. Within nine hours, all 2,810 people had been safely removed.

That evening at seven, President Kennedy addressed the nation, announcing that "unmistakable evidence" had established the presence of Soviet MRBM and ICBM sites and nuclear-capable bombers in Cuba. He then said that he was ordering imposed on Cuba a "strict quarantine on all offensive military equipment." Finally, he warned the Soviet government that the United States will "regard any nuclear missile launched from Cuba against any nation in the Western Hemisphere as an attack by the Soviet Union on the United States, requiring a full retaliatory response against the Soviet Union."

As the president spoke, U.S. military forces in much of the world were put on alert. Polaris nuclear submarines sailed to preassigned stations at sea. Twenty-two interceptor aircraft went airborne in the event of military action from Cuba. "I had the first watch when Kennedy made his speech," said Hal Parish. "I was briefed to expect the possibility of a very high level of flight activity over Cuba that evening—to expect almost anything. I was briefed on lots of airplanes. Not a thing flew that evening. We didn't launch anything." He added, "It was a very frightening and scary experience. The only time in the thirty years I worked for the government when I was scared about the world situation, and I was really scared."

On the *Oxford*, in the eye of the hurricane, many of the crew were stunned. "I was thinking, Jesus Christ, we're going to blow up the world here," said acting operations officer Keith Taylor who was down in the Sigint spaces. "After the president's announcement there was shock on the ship," said intercept operator Aubrey Brown. "What the hell was going to happen. Next time they come out they will put a torpedo up our ass."

Also worried about the *Oxford* was John McCone, who ordered the ship pulled back. "Right after the announcement they moved us out to twelve miles," said Brown. "We were then moved out to a twenty-five-mile track offshore." Still worried, officials instructed the Oxford to do its eavesdropping safely off Fort Lauderdale.

But much of the mission's work could not be done from that distance. "You could run some of the operations from Fort Lauderdale but not the bulk of it," said Brown. "You could do all the Morse code stuff but the Elint you couldn't do. . . . The next day they decided to send us back to Cuba." Brown added, "You could get some microwave sitting off Havana depending on where it is coming from and where it is going."

Within hours of Kennedy's address, intercepts began flowing into NSA. At 10:12 P.M., an NSA listening post intercepted a Flash precedence message sent from the Soviet eavesdropping trawler *Shkval*, near the submarine patrol, to the cargo vessel *Alantika*. The *Shkval* then sent another message to the *Alantika* for retransmission to Murmansk, the home port of the submarines. Although they were unable to read the encrypted message, the U.S. intercept operators noted the significance of the Flash precedence in the report they quickly transmitted to Fort Meade. "This type of precedence rarely observed," said the intercept report. "Significance unknown." The network of listening posts was able to pinpoint the *Shkval* a few hundred miles south of Bermuda; the *Alantika* was about 150 miles off the U.S. East Coast, near Philadelphia.

In the early morning hours of October 23, other Soviet ships likewise began calling for instructions. The Soviet cargo vessel *Kura*, just off Havana harbor, relayed an urgent message to Moscow through another Soviet vessel, the *Nikolaj Burdenko*, which was approaching the U.S. Virgin Islands. The Russian passenger ship *Nikolaevsk*, approaching the eastern end of Cuba, sent Moscow a worried message: U.S. war vessel Nr. 889 was following her on a parallel course. Throughout the Caribbean and the North Atlantic, whenever a Soviet ship sent a weather request, indicating its position, an NSA listening post picked it up and noted its location.

At NSA, as the world awaited Moscow's response to the U.S. ultimatum, a report was issued indicating that the Soviets were taking ever greater control of the skies over Cuba. Sixty-three MiG pilots took to the air in a single day, and of that number more than half spoke Russian or spoke Spanish with a heavy Slavic accent. Around the world, NSA listening posts were ordered to install armed patrols around their facilities. Even in tiny Cape Chiniak, on Kodiak Island in Alaska, the threat was taken seriously. Communications Technician Pete Azzole was watching the messages rattle in the Communications Center when his eyes grew wide: "A Flash precedence message began revealing itself line by line," he recalled. "My eyes were fixed on the canary yellow paper, watching each character come to life." The more the message revealed, the more nervous Azzole became. It read:

> 1. A NUCLEAR ATTACK HAS BEEN LAUNCHED AGAINST THE EAST COAST OF THE UNITED STATES . . .

After a few agonizing seconds, Azzole realized that the message was a practice drill.

At the White House, President Kennedy was deeply troubled over the possibility of nuclear retaliation against the United States if there was a strike against Cuba. A Pentagon official told him that the area covered by the 1,100-mile-range Soviet missiles involved 92 million people. Fallout shelters were available, though not equipped, for about 40 million. When Kennedy asked what emergency steps could be taken, the official was less than encouraging. Shelter signs could be put up and food could be repositioned. But McCone concluded that whatever was done would involve a great deal of publicity and public alarm.

Throughout the day, NSA listening posts on both sides of the Atlantic focused on about a dozen Soviet ships en route to Cuba and suspected of transporting missiles or associated equipment. Inside a listening post hidden in a snake-infested swamp in the town of Northwest, Virginia; a chilly cove in Winter Harbor, Maine; an airfield near Miami, Florida; a rolling field in Edzell, Scotland; and other locations, intercept operators triangulated every signal sent from the ships. Among those was the *Urgench,* which at 3:10 P.M. was about five hundred miles from Gibraltar, sailing west toward Cuba.

But when the *Urgench* was next plotted, at midnight, it had reversed course and was sailing back toward the Straits of Gibraltar. Immediately, the NSA Command Center flashed word of the possible retreat to the CIA Watch Office. Harry Eisenbeiss, the watch officer, checked with the Office of Naval Intelligence, which had also received NSA's report, but ONI could not confirm the change of course and thought it might be a Soviet ploy.

In the meantime, the network of listening posts had spotted other ships also making 180-degree turns. The *Bol'shevik Sukhanov,* which was carrying seven large crates on its deck, suspected to contain aircraft, "has altered course and is probably en route back to port," said another intercept report. Still another followed: "HFDF [high-frequency direction finding] fix on the Soviet cargo ship *Kislovodsk*, en route to Cuba, indicates that the ship has altered course to the North."

At 10:38 A.M. on Wednesday, October 24, with the *Urgench* continuing its retreat, another message was flashed to NSA headquarters. A copy was quickly forwarded to CIA, which in turn passed the message to the White House. An aide walked into the Executive Committee meeting and passed the note to McCone, who smiled broadly and made the announcement: "Mr. President, we have a preliminary report which seems to indicate that some of the Russian ships have stopped dead in the water." Kennedy was surprised. "Stopped dead in the water? Which ships? Are they checking the accuracy of the report? Is it true?" The NSA report convinced McCone. "The report is accurate, Mr. President. Six ships previously on their way to Cuba at the edge of the quarantine line have stopped or have turned back toward the Soviet Union."

President Kennedy ordered that "no ships . . . be stopped or intercepted" for at least another hour, while additional information was obtained. "If the ships have orders to turn around, we want to give them every opportunity to do so. . . . Give the Russian vessels an opportunity to turn back. We must move quickly because the time [before the United States must act] is expiring."

Although some ships were still heading toward the barricades, the good news from NSA spread fast. National Security Adviser McGeorge Bundy telephoned Under Secretary of State George Ball. "Have you got the word on what is happening at sea?" Bundy asked. Ball had not. "The six most interesting ships have turned back. Two others are turning. We are starting over here in a thinking session as to what might be done, which will be going on all afternoon. If you want to come, it would be helpful to have you. . . . Will you alert anyone else you wish to alert?" "I'll be over," said Ball.

The next day, Thursday, October 25, Kennedy aide Arthur Schlesinger, Jr., met with Under Secretary of State Averell Harriman to discuss the latest developments. "Khrushchev," said Harriman, "is sending us desperate signals to get us to help take him off the hook. He is sending messages exactly as he did to Eisenhower directly after the U-2 affair. Eisenhower ignored these messages to his cost. We must not repeat Eisenhower's mistake." Among the key signals, Harriman told Schlesinger, was "the instructions to the Soviet ships to change their course."

Harriman continued: "In view of these signals from Khrushchev, the worst mistake we can possibly make is to get tougher and to escalate. Khrushchev is pleading with us to help him find a way out. . . . We cannot afford to lose any time. Incidents—stopping of ships, etc.—will begin the process of escalation, engage Soviet prestige and reduce the chances of a peaceful resolution. If we act shrewdly and speedily, we can bail Khrushchev out and discredit the tough guys around him—the ones who sold him the Cuban adventure on the theory that Americans were too liberal to fight."

When the offensive missiles had been discovered, the formal approval process for U-2 missions was ended. Now the Strategic Air Command had blanket approval to fly as many missions as needed to cover Cuba completely. Although it was time consuming, the formal notification process had had the advantage of allowing NSA listening posts to support the flights. Intercept operators would scan the frequency spectrum in search of any hostile activity before and during the mission. If they picked up a warning indicator, they could send a message to NSA headquarters, which would notify SAC. But now that U-2 missions were being launched without notice, NSA had no way of knowing when a plane was over Cuba.

But by Friday, October 26, the results of low-level photography indicated that the Russians and Cubans were rapidly attempting to complete the four medium-range-missile site. "Although no additional missiles or erectors had been seen," said a Joint Chiefs report, "neither was there evidence of any intention to move or dismantle the sites. Camouflage and canvas covering of critical equipment was continuing."

At the same time, however, NSA reported that three Soviet ships suspected of being missile carriers were now steaming east, back toward Russia, as were all except one of the Soviet dry cargo ships. Only one Russian dry cargo ship was still moving toward the quarantine line; it was expected to reach there in three days.

At thirty-eight minutes past midnight on Saturday, October 27, an NSA listening post intercepted signals from three radar installations.

After checking and double-checking, the intercept operators determined that the radar was "Spoon Rest," and therefore that three more SAM sites had become active. "DF line bearings indicate emitters located at Mariel," said the intercept report, which was Flashed to headquarters, "Havana east, and poss. Matanzas sites. Emitters remain active." Once again, Castro raised the stakes for the American reconnaissance pilots.

"On the twenty-seventh," said Parish, "it was kind of a tight situation—it was a scary situation, as a matter of fact. It was a scary time, especially for those of us who had a little bit of access to information which wasn't generally available. . . . We worked that week and pulled our watches, nobody was off."

Later that morning, Major Rudolf Anderson took off in a U-2 from McCoy Air Force Base at Orlando, Florida. The routine flight was expected to last about three and a half hours. Over Cuba, Anderson pushed his plane northward toward the town of Banes.

At an afternoon Executive Committee meeting, Secretary of Defense McNamara made a routine report on the day's daylight reconnaissance mission. "One mission aborted for mechanical reasons, according to preliminary reports," he said. "One plane is overdue and several are said to have encountered ground fire." He then recommended a number of night missions. But President Kennedy held off on a decision until more details could be obtained on the day's reconnaissance. He then ordered that missions be flown the next day without fighter escort. "If our planes are fired on," he said, "we must be prepared for a general response or an attack on the SAM site which fired on our planes. We will decide tomorrow how we return fire after we know if they continue their attacks on our planes."

An aide quickly walked in and handed a note to Joint Chiefs Chairman Maxwell Taylor. Major Anderson's U-2 had been shot down near Banes. "The wreckage of the U-2 was on the ground," Taylor was told; "the pilot had been killed." Taylor recommended an air attack on the SAM site responsible. McNamara said that we must be ready to attack Cuba by launching 500 sorties on the first day. Invasion, he said, had "become almost inevitable."

At NSA, data were immediately called in from air, sea, and ground eavesdropping platforms in an attempt to discover the details of the shootdown. Director Blake ordered new rules, as follows: As a first priority, every listening post was to monitor in real time all reactions to U.S. reconnaissance flights. "Any time the Cubans scrambled a flight," said Hal Parish, "we were supposed to tell . . . why they scrambled and who they were after—very often they were after U.S. aircraft along the coast. . . . When we were still flying the U-2s and we got what appeared to be Cuban threats to the U-2s with MiG aircraft, we had it arranged. . . . we would call General [John] Morrison [at NSA] first to get his okay, then we would call SAC . . . and they would contact the aircraft."

Once a warning was received, the reconnaissance flight would immediately break off from the mission and fly to Andrews Air Force Base near Washington, D.C. There, NSA analysts would meet the plane and debrief the crew. "You'd debrief in the airplane off the end of the runway," said Parish. "Pick up all the tapes and bring them out to the building and put our linguists to work all night long working on those tapes in order to provide an assessment of whatever happened that day [and have it out] by six o'clock."

In order to further protect the pilots, electronic countermeasures needed to be developed that could jam or deceive the Soviet SA-2 missile. But to develop these countermeasures, NSA would first have to intercept the missile's telltale fusing signals, which activated the warhead. That, however, required forcing the Cubans to fire off one more of their missiles. To accomplish this, DC-130 aircraft began launching high-altitude Ryan 147 drones over the island. The Ryans were equipped with electronics that made them appear larger than they actually were, about the size of a U-2.

Each drone also carried onboard equipment to collect the critical fusing signals and retransmit them, in the few seconds before it was blasted from the sky, to a specially equipped type of RB-47 Strato-Spy codenamed Common Cause. One of the RB-47s was constantly in the air off the Cuban coast. "The plan was to lure the Cuban missile sites into firing at the drone," said Bruce Bailey, an Air Force signals intelligence officer, "thus providing the desired electronic intelligence to the RB-47." But the Cubans refused to fire any more missiles. "The Cubans had been assured that such a site or base would be struck immediately," said Bailey. "Obviously they believed that and refused to fire. The mission soon became more appropriately known as 'Lost Cause.' "

At 7:15 on the evening of October 30, as the crisis grew hotter,

Robert Kennedy asked Soviet ambassador Anatoly Dobrynin to meet with him in his office at the Justice Department in half an hour. "In the last two hours we had found that our planes flying over Cuba had been fired upon," Kennedy told the ambassador, as he noted in a top secret memo to Dean Rusk. "One of our U-2's had been shot down and the pilot killed. . . . This was an extremely serious turn of events. We would have to make certain decisions within the next twelve or possibly twenty-four hours. There was very little time left. If the Cubans were shooting at our planes, then we were going to shoot back." Dobrynin argued that the U.S. was violating Cuban airspace, but Kennedy shot back that if we had not been violating Cuban airspace then we would still have believed what he and Khrushchev had said—that there were no long-range missiles in Cuba. "This matter was far more serious than the air space over Cuba and involved people all over the world," Kennedy added.

"I said that he had better understand the situation and he had better communicate that understanding to Mr. Khrushchev," Kennedy later noted in the long secret memorandum. "Mr. Khrushchev and he had misled us. The Soviet Union had secretly established missile bases in Cuba while at the same time proclaiming, privately and publicly, that this would never be done. I said those missile bases had to go and they had to go right away. We had to have a commitment by at least tomorrow [October 31] that those bases would be removed. This was not an ultimatum, I said, but just a statement of fact. He should understand that if they did not remove those bases then we would remove them. His country might take retaliatory action but he should understand that before this was over, while there might be dead Americans there would also be dead Russians."

Dobrynin asked Kennedy whether he was proposing a deal. "I said a letter had just been transmitted to the Soviet Embassy which stated in substance that the missile bases should be dismantled," Kennedy wrote, "and all offensive weapons should be removed from Cuba. In return, if Cuba and Castro and the Communists ended their subversive activities in other Central and Latin American countries, we would agree to keep peace in the Caribbean and not permit an invasion from American soil." But Khrushchev had earlier proposed a swap: take the American missiles away from his doorstep in Turkey, and he would take the Soviet missiles from Cuba. Dobrynin once again brought up that proposal. "If some time elapsed," Kennedy said, mentioning four or five months, "I was sure that these matters could be resolved satisfactorily."

But Kennedy emphasized that there could be no deal of any kind. "Any steps toward easing tensions in other parts of the world largely depended on the Soviet Union and Mr. Khrushchev taking action in Cuba and taking it immediately." According to his memorandum, "I repeated to him that this matter could not wait and that he had better contact Mr. Khrushchev and have a commitment from him by the next day to withdraw the missile bases under United Nations supervision for otherwise, I said, there would be drastic consequences."

Shortly after Kennedy left, Dobrynin sent an enciphered cable to Khrushchev. " 'Because of the plane that was shot down, there is now strong pressure on the president to give an order to respond with fire if fired upon,' " he wrote, quoting Kennedy. " 'A real war will begin, in which millions of Americans and Russians will die.' . . . Kennedy mentioned as if in passing that there are many unreasonable heads among the generals, and not only among the generals, who are 'itching for a fight.' . . . The situation might get out of control, with irreversible consequences."

Then the ambassador relayed Kennedy's proposal. "The most important thing for us, Kennedy stressed, is to get as soon as possible the agreement of the Soviet government to halt further work on the construction of the missile bases in Cuba and take measures under international control that would make it impossible to use these weapons. In exchange the government of the USA is ready, in addition to repealing all measures on the 'quarantine,' to give the assurances that there will not be any invasion of Cuba. . . . 'And what about Turkey,' I asked R. Kennedy. 'If that is the only obstacle . . . then the president doesn't see any unsurmountable difficulties in resolving this issue. . . . However, the president can't say anything public in this regard about Turkey,' R. Kennedy said again. R. Kennedy then warned that his comments about Turkey are extremely confidential; besides him and his brother, only 2–3 people know about it in Washington. . . . R. Kennedy gave me a number of a direct telephone line to the White House." Once again Dobrynin quoted Robert Kennedy. " 'Time is of the essence and we shouldn't miss the chance.' "

Robert Kennedy returned to the White House, where the members of the Executive Committee held a late-night session. McNamara recommended, and the president approved, the call-up of twenty-four air reserve squadrons, involving 14,200 personnel and 300 troop carriers. President Kennedy then said that if the reconnaissance planes were fired on the next day, "then we should take out the SAM sites in Cuba by air action."

At a late-night meeting at the Pentagon, the Joint Chiefs of Staff recommended that "unless irrefutable evidence of the dismantling of the offensive weapons in Cuba were obtained," an air strike should be launched no later than October 29.

Shortly before midnight, Hal Parish entered NSA for his midnight–to–eight A.M. shift. "When I reported in," he said, "there was a note there to have by six o'clock the following morning in the hands of the White House the wrap-up of the U-2 shootdown. Wasn't hard to do—we had about two minutes, three minutes of tracking on it . . . just some tracking coming in from just north of Guantánamo . . . seemed to be a SAM that brought him down. . . . There was nothing that I ever saw in communication indicating who (whether a Soviet or a Cuban) pushed the button. . . . About two years later, from some intercept that was picked up on one of the aircraft carriers, we got the entire tracking sequence of the shootdown. We got the whole mission tracking from the time he hit Cuba all the way down until he made his turn over Guantánamo and then the tracking sort of ceased. . . ."

On Sunday morning, October 28, a new message from Khrushchev was broadcast on Radio Moscow. "The Soviet government," said the announcement, "has issued a new order on the dismantling of the weapons which you describe as 'offensive,' and their crating and return to the Soviet Union." The crisis was over.

As the Russians began withdrawing, NSA continued its intensive watch. "I remember during the period from the time I went down in October," Hal Parish recalled, "there was not a day I did not come to work until Christmas. Then I just took part of Christmas Day off." For the eavesdroppers, things changed dramatically. Suddenly the need for the Russians to hide their presence on Cuba disappeared, so in addition to Spanish, many Russian-language communications were being intercepted. "All the communications that we had that were Cuban turned Soviet and we had what had to be called the Soviet forces in Cuba," said Parish. "Suddenly, these Spanish-speaking pilots disappeared and were replaced by Russian pilots. The [Soviet] . . . communications in the HF [high-frequency] area at that time appeared again virtually overnight."

Intercept operators listened as the ballistic missile sites were dismantled and the SAM sites were turned over to the Cubans. "After the offensive weapons were removed, some of the supportive weapons were also removed," Parish said. Each time a SAM site was turned over to the Cubans, various signals changed. "So we were able through Elint to tell when the Soviets were pulling out of a given SAM site. We got an entire training schedule in Havana where they were talking about how they were going to train the Cubans."

As the Soviets pulled out, NSA detected tense relations between them and Cuban forces. According to Parish, one telephone conversation involved a very large shipment of tainted meat that the Soviets had sent the Cubans. Castro himself was intercepted saying "very, very bad things about the Russians," Parish said. "And in fact we were required to read that over the telephone to—I'm not sure who it was, State Department, CIA, DIA—but we had to have a translator read this sort of verbatim over the line and he [Castro] had some very, very, harsh and bad things to say about the Russians. I do recall the gentleman turning red as he was reading this because they wanted a verbatim translation of it." In fact, the original transcript sent to the White House contained deletions in place of Castro's expletives. Almost immediately Robert Kennedy called NSA and demanded that they send the uncensored version—blue language and all.

"During the crisis," said Parish, "I have no doubt they [the missile sites] were under Soviet control, and in fact we pretty well know they were totally Soviet manned." According to another NSA official, "There were times when the Cubans and the Soviets were—I don't mean fighting literally, but contesting each other as to who was in charge of the missile site, and you'd hear Spanish cursing in the background and Soviet unhappiness."

At the time of the crisis, neither the NSA nor the CIA knew whether the Soviets had any nuclear warheads in Cuba. "We had photographs of missile launchers," said Robert McNamara, "but we thought the warheads were yet to come." It was only in the 1990s that the truth was discovered. "It took thirty years to learn there were 161 nuclear warheads there, including 90 tactical warheads to be used against an invasion," McNamara said. Then, holding two fingers a fraction of an inch apart, he added, "And we came that close to an invasion. . . . We came so close—both Kennedy and Khrushchev felt events were slipping outside their control. . . . The world came within a hair breadth of nuclear war."

As Soviet ships navigated through the Caribbean on their long voyage home, their decks crowded with hastily crated missiles and launchers, Khrushchev may have been chuckling. While the United States focused on the offensive ballistic missiles brought to Cuba, none of which were likely ever to have been used, Khrushchev had been monitoring the progress of a far more secret and far more useful construction project on the island. It was to be a major Soviet intelligence coup. In a sparsely populated area known as Lourdes, just southeast of Havana, Soviet technicians continued work on one of the largest eavesdropping bases ever built.

NSA surrounded the Soviet Union with listening posts and ferret flights during the 1950s and early 1960s. Every time a new monitoring station was built, Khrushchev felt the electronic noose grow tighter. In Germany, Turkey, Iran, Pakistan, Japan, Korea, and elsewhere, intercept operators noted every time an aircraft took off or a ship left port. Telemetry was collected from Soviet missiles, and telephone conversations were snatched from the air.

Khrushchev knew he could not reciprocate. There were no Soviet allies along America's borders to accommodate Russian eavesdroppers. Thus the USSR was forced to send antenna-covered trawlers crawling along America's coasts. It was a cumbersome and expensive proposition. For every trawler bobbing in the waves, five thousand miles from home, a fleet of support vessels was needed because the trawlers could not pull into port. Fuel had to be supplied, equipment had to be repaired, food had to be delivered, and the endless tapes had to be brought back to Moscow to be analyzed and translated. Castro solved all Khrushchev's problems and provided Moscow with an electronic window on the United States into the twenty-first century.

Over a vast area of twenty-eight square miles, Soviet engineers and signals intelligence specialists erected acres of antennas to eavesdrop on American communications. Diamond-shaped rhombic antennas, pointing like daggers at the U.S. coast only ninety miles away, tapped into high-frequency signals carrying telephone calls as far away as Washington. Large dishes were set up to collect signals from American satellites. High wires were strung to pick up the very-low-frequency submarine broadcasts. Giant rectangular antennas, like drive-in movie screens, were erected to intercept microwave signals. Windowless cement buildings were built to house the intercept operators, the codebreakers, and the walls of printers that would rattle out miles of intercepted data communications. Khrushchev might have lost a fist, but he had gained an ear.

With the crisis over and the threat of nuclear war now abated, attention once again turned toward covert operations within Cuba. Earlier, shortly after learning of the offensive missiles on October 15, an angry Robert Kennedy had called a meeting of the Operation Mongoose cabal. He opened the meeting by expressing "the general dissatisfaction of the President" with the progress of Mongoose. He pointed out that the operation had been under way for a year, that the results were discouraging, that there had been no acts of sabotage, and that even the one that had been attempted had failed twice.

Richard Helms, the CIA's deputy planning director, later commented: "I stated that we were prepared to get on with the new action program and that we would execute it aggressively." NSA, however, discovered that among the sabotage targets of Operation Mongoose were several key Cuban communications facilities—the same facilities that NSA was eavesdropping on, deriving a great deal of signals intelligence. Officials quickly, and loudly, protested. "We suggested to them that it was really not the smartest thing to do," said Hal Parish.

In fact, in the days following the crisis, NSA did everything it could to secretly keep the Cuban telecommunications system fully working. The more communications equipment broke or burned out, the less NSA could intercept, and thus the less the U.S. intelligence community knew about Cuba. Adding to the problems was the economic embargo of Cuba, which kept out critical electrical supplies such as vacuum tubes for military radios. NSA devised a covert channel by which to supply these components to the Cuban government.

"The tubes would burn out, requests would come in, and backdoor methods had to be utilized in order to get the necessary tubes in to keep this RCA-designed system on the air so we could continue to collect it," said Parish. "I think a lot of them were channeled through Canada at the time, because the Canadians had relations with the Cubans. When the tubes would wear out—these were not small tubes, these were large tubes and components—they would make contact with somebody and the word would reach us and they would come to see the agency, the right part of it, and we would insist that those things be provided."

As the danger of nuclear war with Russia receded like a red tide, Cuba once again came into full view and the Kennedy administration returned to combat mode. NSA continued to listen with one ear cocked toward Russia and the other toward Cuba. Just before Christmas 1962 McCone wrote to McGeorge Bundy, "NSA will continue an intensive program in the Sigint field, which has during recent weeks added materially to all other intelligence."

On Havana's doorstep, the civilian-manned USNS *Muller* relieved the *Oxford*, and ferret flights kept up their patrols a dozen miles off the Cuban coast. Because the *Muller* was civilian, its crew got less liberty time than a military crew would, so the ship was able to spend a greater percentage of its time at sea—about twenty-five days a month—than Navy ships such as the *Oxford*. It was home ported in Port Everglades, the commercial port for Fort Lauderdale.

"Duty station for the *Muller* was seven miles off Havana," said Bill Baer, the operations officer on the ship at the time. "We and Castro recognized the six-mile limit, so seven miles was a small safety valve. We traveled back and forth on a six-mile track parallel to the coast. The major reason for this particular spot was a multichannel UHF national communications system that RCA had installed. It ran from Havana, east and west, along the spine of the island and connected Havana with each city in the country." Traveling slowly back and forth, the *Muller* had a direct tap into much of Cuba's communications.

But the spy ship was no secret from Castro and he would occasionally vent his anger. "We only had a selection of small arms including M-1 rifles, carbines, shotguns, and so forth," recalled Baer. "We took this responsibility very seriously because we knew the Cubans knew who we were and they used to do things to harass us."

In an unusual move, Baer was made operations officer on the ship even though he was an Army officer. He had been stationed at NSA when he heard of the opening and volunteered. Another Army intercept operator on board was Mike Sannes. "Since they used microwave, we had to be [in] line-of-sight," Sannes explained. "Castro used to call us the 'big ear.' One time we knew he was going to crash a small plane into us and then board us in an 'act of mercy.' We had a spotter in the mast—remember this is a civilian ship and had no [large] guns—he saw the plane approaching and we were monitoring on the hand-held radio. Suddenly everything went quiet. A few minutes later he came running in saying, 'I'm not staying up there. He's going to hit us!' They scrambled some jets from Key West who were on alert, and they chased him off."

Sannes said Cuban harassment was common. "Often they sent gunboats out to harass us, sometimes every few hours so we couldn't sleep. Occasionally they shot across our bow. We had a real gung-ho skipper. We had scuttles fore and aft. We would have sunk the boat if we were in danger of being boarded. . . . Once the engine quit and we started drifting into shore. It was very early on a foggy morning. We drifted close enough into Havana harbor that we were looking up at the hotels on the beach. We got the engine working and headed back out to sea. They never noticed us."

To assist the CIA's covert operations in Cuba, NSA intercept operators were assigned to monitor the communications of anti-Castro forces. On January 16 one of these technicians picked up a conversation from an individual in downtown Havana who said, "It would be a good idea to assassinate Fidel on El Cocuyo Road." The intercept operator noted on his report, "This group must be penetrated."

Amusingly, one of the most important pieces of information to come along came not from an NSA intercept of a diplomatic cable to Moscow but from a ten-hour interview Castro gave to Lisa Howard, a reporter for ABC News. In the interview, Castro clearly indicated for the first time that he was hoping for a rapprochement with the United States. The CIA acquired a transcript of the interview secretly, through an NSA intercept before the broadcast.

Upon receiving the information, the CIA's John McCone became extremely worried that word would leak out about their possession of it. On May 2, 1963, CIA Deputy Director Marshall Carter wrote to Bundy:

> Mr. McCone cabled me this morning stating that he cannot overemphasize the importance of secrecy in this matter and requested that I take all appropriate steps along this line to reflect his personal views on its sensitivity. Mr. McCone feels that gossip and inevitable leaks with consequent publicity would be most damaging. He suggests that no active steps be taken on the rapprochement matter at this time and urges most limited Washington discussions, and that in these circumstances emphasis should be placed in any discussions on the fact that the rapprochement track is being explored as a remote possibility and one of several alternatives involving various levels of dynamic and positive action. In view of the foregoing, it is requested that the Lisa Howard report be handled in the most limited and sensitive manner.

Throughout the summer of 1963, there were endless discussions of sabotage—which targets to strike, what kind of explosives to use, whether the strike should come from inside Cuba or outside it, whether local volunteers or paid agents should be used. But even while the CIA hawks were plotting their campaign of sabotage, a group of Kennedy administration doves, including UN Ambassador Adlai Stevenson, were working on another track. Attached to Stevenson's UN mission in New York was

William Attwood, who had previously served as U.S. ambassador to Guinea in West Africa. Attwood had met Castro and spent considerable time with him on a number of occasions while practicing his earlier profession as a journalist. A Guinean diplomat had told him of a recent meeting with Castro in which the Cuban leader had expressed his dissatisfaction with his status as a Soviet satellite and was looking for a way out. The diplomat told Attwood of Castro's receptiveness to changing course and moving toward nonalignment. Attwood received a similar message from another friend, Lisa Howard.

As the CIA continued to plot sabotage missions, President Kennedy began to explore Castro's apparent olive branch. He approved a quiet approach by Attwood to Dr. Carlos Lechuga, Cuba's ambassador to the UN, using ABC's Lisa Howard as a go-between. On September 23, a small party was arranged at Howard's New York City apartment and both Lechuga and Attwood were invited. The diplomatic matchmaking was successful. "Lechuga hinted that Castro was indeed in a mood to talk," Attwood said later in a secret memorandum. "Especially with someone he had met before. He thought there was a good chance that I might be invited to Cuba if I wished to resume our 1959 talk." Robert Kennedy thought the idea had some merit but was against Attwood traveling to Cuba; he saw the trip as "risking the accusation that we were trying to make a deal with Castro." Kennedy preferred that the meeting take place either in New York, during a visit by Castro to the UN, or in a neutral country, such as Mexico.

Howard, continuing in her role as unofficial intermediary, mentioned Attwood to Major René Vallejo, a Cuban surgeon who was also Castro's right-hand man and confidant. On October 31, Vallejo called Howard, telling her that Castro would very much like to talk to Attwood anytime and appreciated the importance of discretion to all concerned. Castro, he said, would therefore be willing to secretly send a plane to Mexico to pick up Attwood and fly him to a private airport near Veradero where Castro would talk to him alone. The plane would fly him back immediately after the talk. In this way there would be no risk of identification at Havana airport.

Vallejo sent a further message to Attwood, through Howard, on November 11. "Castro would go along with any arrangements we might want to make," Attwood wrote in a memorandum. "He specifically suggested that a Cuban plane could come to Key West and pick up the emissary; alternatively they would agree to have him come in a U.S. plane which could land at one of several 'secret airfields' near Havana. He emphasized that only Castro and himself would be present at the talks and that no one else—he specifically mentioned [Che] Guevara—would be involved. Vallejo also reiterated Castro's desire for this talk and hoped to hear our answer soon."

But President Kennedy insisted that before any U.S. official travel to Cuba, Vallejo or some other Castro representative come to the United States to outline a proposal. He also demanded absolute secrecy concerning the discussions. "At the President's instruction I was conveying this message orally and not by cable," McGeorge Bundy told Attwood, extremely worried about a leak or a written record. He added in a memorandum for the record, "The President hoped he [Attwood] would get in touch with Vallejo to report that it did not seem practicable to us at this stage to send an American official to Cuba and that we would prefer to begin with a visit by Vallejo to the U.S. where Attwood would be glad to see him and to listen to any messages he might bring from Castro."

Attwood passed the message through Howard to Vallejo, and a few days later they spoke together on the telephone for the first time. One Friday, he sent a memorandum to the White House detailing the conversation. "Vallejo's manner was extremely cordial," Attwood noted. "He said that 'we' would send instructions to Lechuga to propose and discuss with me 'an agenda' for a later meeting with Castro. I said I would await Lechuga's call."

But President Kennedy did not see Attwood's memorandum. At the moment it arrived he was traveling in a motorcade in Dallas, Texas.

That Friday, November 22, 1963, was much like any other day at NSA. In the early morning hours, Cuban intercepts from the ferret ship USNS *Muller* had ricocheted off the moon and down to NSA. The backlogged Cuban analysts and cryptologists of B Group were only now putting out translations of messages intercepted weeks earlier. One of those was a report by a Cuban official on the country's internal problems with rebels. "I believe that the approaching Presidential elections in the

United States will strengthen reactionary forces from within and without," said the worried official. "Therefore, there is a need for a strong gorilla [*sic*] collar around Cuba."

In the courtyard in front of the main building, a powerful yellow steam shovel was scooping up tons of dirt for the large basement of the new nine-story, 511,000-square-foot headquarters tower as the agency continued to expand. Other heavy equipment was clearing dense woodlands for more than 1,200 new parking spaces.

In Room 1W040, the cover for the next edition for the *NSA Newsletter* was being laid out. It was a drawing of Santa Claus jumping out of a fireplace, with the headline "Sixth NSA Annual Family Christmas Program, Dec. 8, 2:00 PM." A line of employees, getting ready for the weekend, was forming at the NSA Federal Credit Union, which had grown to 5,647 members. At 11:30 A.M., in Room 1W128, the NSA Sun, Snow and Surf Club was holding its second annual Ski Fashion Show. As part of the show, the main lobby of the Operations Building contained a large display of the latest skis, boots, and other equipment. Later that night, the NSA Drama Club was scheduled to present the rueful comedy *The Pleasure of His Company* at the Fort Meade Service Club.

That Friday was slow in the NSA Sigint Command Center. The duty officer logged some messages in; Sergeant Holtz arrived at ten o'clock to pick up a few tapes; at 1:30 P.M. a Strategic Air Command surveillance mission codenamed Brass Knob sent a preflight message. Five minutes later, couriers assigned to secretly collect cables from Western Union and the other communications companies over the weekend were briefed.

Then, at 1:36, a bulletin flashed over the radio. Don Gardiner of the ABC radio network cut into a local program to report that President Kennedy had been shot in Dallas. NSA Director Gordon Blake was sitting at his desk in his third-floor office when he heard the news. At the White House, crowded around a large circular table in the West Basement's staff mess, the President's Foreign Intelligence Advisory Board was deep in debate following a late lunch. Across the Potomac, General Maxwell Taylor and the Joint Chiefs of Staff were meeting in the Pentagon's Gold Room with the commanders of the West German Bundeswehr. Down the hall in his E-Ring office, Secretary of Defense

Robert S. McNamara was discussing the $50 billion budget with a half-dozen aides.

At the CIA, Director John McCone was finishing lunch with a small group of fellow spies in his private dining room. His deputy, Marshall Carter, was quail shooting at the Farm, the secret CIA training facility on the York River near Williamsburg, Virginia. "When this monstrously terrible thing happened," Carter wrote several days later, "we returned at once. . . . He was a great and good and totally dedicated, totally selfless man—our national blessing is that President Johnson is too."

At fourteen minutes past two, General Blake sent out a message alerting all NSA stations and listening posts. Twenty-two minutes later he sent out another message over NSA's restricted communications links. "President Kennedy is dead." At the eavesdropping base at Kamiseya in Japan, the operations center suddenly went quiet. George Morton stopped what he was doing. "Thousands upon thousands of miles away," he later said, "someone had shot my commander-in-chief. I could not believe it. Neither could anyone else." In South Africa, NSA's spy ship the USNS *Valdez* was docked in Capetown. One of the crewmembers, Dave Ball, who had once served as a cook for President Kennedy, held a moving memorial service.

As the world mourned, NSA continued to eavesdrop. Immediately after the assassination, NSA initiated a large-scale manual and computer review of all available signals intelligence information, including all traffic between the United States and Cuba. At the time, NSA was intercepting about 1,000 messages a day worldwide. Suspected assassin Lee Harvey Oswald's name was entered into the computer search. A short time later, additional names provided by the FBI from Oswald's address book were added. At the same time, between twenty-five and fifty analysts manually reviewed all traffic between Cuba and New Orleans and Cuba and Dallas, and some traffic between Cuba and Russia.

Fifteen hundred miles to the south, Navy intercept operators, monitoring both Cuban and "Soviet Forces Cuba" communications, listened in as Cuban military forces were placed on high alert. "A state of alert is ordered for all personnel," said the intercepted message. "Be ready to repel aggression." A message intercepted from the Polish embassy in Havana indicated that "military units are being relocated" and a new military draft was called. Intercepts flooded in from other listening posts. Mexico, Venezuela, and Colombia also suddenly went on alert. One foreign ambassador in Havana cabled home a report of a large movement of troops, adding a note about Castro: "I got the immediate impression that on this occasion he was frightened, if not terrified."

From early intercepts of Cuban diplomatic communications, it was clear that, far from being involved, Castro's people were as mystified by the assassination as the rest of the world. "The assassination of Kennedy," said one message from Havana to its embassy in Mexico City, "was a provocation against world peace, perfectly and thoroughly planned by the most reactionary sectors of the United States." An intercept of a message from Brazil's ambassador to Cuba back to his Foreign Office indicated that Cuban officials "were unanimous in believing that any other president would be 'even worse' " than Kennedy.

Many of the intercepts to and from foreign embassies in Washington were acquired as a result of secret agreements between NSA and the major U.S. telecommunications companies, such as Western Union. Under the NSA program codenamed Shamrock, the companies agreed to illegally hand over to NSA couriers, on a daily basis, copies of all the cables sent to, from or through the U.S. This was the preferred method of communications for most of the foreign diplomatic establishments in Washington and New York. Highly secret messages were sent the same way, but written in code or cipher. The NSA's Vint Hill Farms Station eavesdropped on those diplomatic facilities that used their own high-frequency equipment to communicate. Still other intercepts flowed into NSA from the agency's worldwide listening posts.

In the hours and days following the assassination, a wide variety of intercepts poured into NSA. The diplomatic wires were heavy with speculation about America's future and details concerning preparations for the funeral. Shortly after the assassination, NSA intercepted a message between Chile's ambassador to Washington and his Foreign Ministry in Santiago. "In diplomatic circles," he noted, "it is believed that, in the absence of other Democratic figures of the first rank who could aspire to the presidency in the November 1964 election, the present Attorney General becomes, with the death of President Kennedy, the first choice to succeed him for the presidential term which will begin in January 1965." He added, "News has just arrived that at 1438 [2:38 P.M.] (Eastern time) Lyndon Johnson took the oath of office as President of the United States before a federal district judge."

Egyptian diplomats speculated that Kennedy was assassinated as a result of his stand on racial equality. Dutch intercepts showed uncertainty over whether foreign ambassadors would be invited to the funeral. The Argentine ambassador told Buenos Aires that the assassination "will considerably weaken in the next few months the international policy of the West, particularly with regard to the USSR." He then said, for NSA, the worst words imaginable. "I shall continue to report via air mail." A listening post eavesdropping on Turkish diplomatic communications picked up a comment by the American ambassador to Turkey fixing blame for the murder. "After signing the register which is open in the American Embassy [in Ankara] on the occasion of the death of Kennedy, I saw the [American] Ambassador. He is of the opinion that Russia and Cuba had a finger in the assassination."

The United Nations was also an important target for NSA. In a message transmitted back to the Middle East, a delegation of Palestinians blamed the assassination on a Jewish plot: "Behind the mysterious crime is a carefully plotted Zionist conspiracy. The late President was likely to win the coming presidency elections without supplicating the Zionist sympathy or seeking the Jews [*sic*] vote. Aware of the fact that their influence and power in the United States are based upon the Jews vote, the Zionists murdered the courageous President who was about to destroy that legend of theirs. His assassination is a warning to the rest of the honorable leaders. Reveal their conspiracy to the supreme judgement of the world. Be careful, you are the hope of the Palestinians." Likewise, the Italian ambassador to Syria cabled Rome saying that the government in Damascus saw Zionism behind the murder.

A diplomat in Léopoldville, in Congo, reported: "Certain ill-intentioned persons are rejoicing over the death of the President of the United States of America, considering that grievous event a sign of victory for them." The Argentine ambassador to Budapest reported that the Hungarian people "were deeply touched," and that the government attributed the killing to "fascist elements inspired by racial hatred." The Polish ambassador to the United Nations expressed his concern to Warsaw over the "alarming . . . anti-Communist hysteria that has been turned on."

The day after the assassination, intercept operators picked up a statement by Castro: "In spite of the antagonism existing between the Government of the United States and the Cuban Revolution, we have received the news of the tragic death of President Kennedy with deep sorrow. All civilized men always grieve about such events as this. Our delegation to the Organization of the United Nations wishes to state that this is the feeling of the people and of the Government of Cuba." This was a generous statement, considering that Kennedy had spent the past two years waging a secret war against him and that CIA agents had plotted his murder.

In the aftermath of the assassination, Meredith K. Gardner, one of NSA's top Soviet codebreakers, was assigned to examine a number of items taken from assassin Lee Harvey Oswald and suspected to contain codes or ciphers. The Warren Commission, charged with investigating the assassination, was particularly intrigued by a Russian novel, *Glaza Kotorye Sprashivayut* ("Questioning Eyes"). Oswald had apparently cut eight letters out of page 152. But this was too little to go on. "The manner of perforating only a few letters," wrote Gardner, "does not conform to any known system. . . . We believe, nevertheless, that it is most likely that the letters were cut out for some purpose related to Oswald's photographic experiments."

Oswald's Soviet-made portable radio receiver was also examined, "with negative results." Also, wrote Gardner in his internal NSA report, "the names appearing in Lee's and [his wife] Marina's address books have been checked against NSA files but no Comint references have been discovered. . . . In addition to the information on the addresses developed in the personality check, a separate study of NSA address files is being made. While this study is not yet complete, results have so far been negative and there is no reason to expect that anything beyond what the personality check has already turned up will be discovered."

Finally, Gardner noted, "The appearance of the term 'micro dots' on page 44 of Lee Oswald's address book aroused our suspicions, particularly in that it was associated with the address of the photographic firm where he was once employed."

The mention of NSA's Comint files and the possibility of microdots became a sensitive issue within NSA. Frank Rowlett, special assistant to Director Blake, hid any reference to them from the final report sent to the Warren Commission. In a memorandum to Deputy Director Tordella, Rowlett wrote, "I have eliminated two items from the original Memorandum for the Record. . . . These are the references to 'micro dots' . . . and the Comint reference." He added, "I suggest that you informally (possibly by telephone) call the Commission's attention to the appearance of the term 'micro dot' on page 44 of Oswald's address book. You might indicate that this reference aroused our suspicion but that we do not feel competent to make an exhaustive examination of the materials for the presence of micro dots—such an examination should be conducted by the FBI or CIA. If micro dots are actually found, we would be happy to collaborate to the fullest degree required in the analysis of these dots."

Rowlett was also worried about letting the commission know of NSA's highly secret communications intelligence data base. "I do not believe a statement that we have checked the names against the NSA files needs to be made since . . . it identifies the existence of sensitive Comint records." Tordella agreed, and the sanitized report was sent to the commission.

Shortly after the assassination, Lisa Howard told Attwood that she had been contacted by Dr. Lechuga. Lechuga said that he had received a letter from Castro authorizing him to have the discussion with Attwood earlier requested by Kennedy. Howard passed the message on to Attwood, who later that day met with Lechuga for the first time. After expressing his condolences, Lechuga confirmed that he had been authorized to begin preliminary talks with him; however, he made no mention of the letter from Castro. Then, in light of the assassination, Lechuga inquired as to how things now stood. Attwood said he would have to let him know.

Gordon Chase of the National Security Council later discussed the matter in a memorandum to Bundy. "The ball is in our court," he wrote. "Bill owes Lechuga a call. What to do? Bill thinks that we have nothing to lose in listening to what Castro has to say; there is no commitment on our side. Also, it would be very interesting to know what is in the letter. I am also dying to know what's in the letter and two weeks ago I would not have hesitated. But things are different now, particularly with this Oswald business. At a minimum, such a talk would really have to be a non-event. I, for one, would want to think this one over carefully. . . . They also agreed, that from this point on, there was no further need to use Lisa Howard as an intermediary."

"I assume you will want to brief the President," Chase wrote in another memorandum to Bundy. It now seemed a million years since Kennedy had given his okay to the peace feeler. Chase was convinced that any hope for normalization had died with the late president. "The events of November 22 would appear to make accommodation with Castro an even more doubtful issue than it was," he said. "While I think that President Kennedy could have accommodated with Castro and gotten away with it with a minimum of domestic heat, I'm not sure about President Johnson. For one thing, a new President who has no background of being successfully nasty to Castro and the Communists (e.g. President Kennedy in October, 1962) would probably run a greater risk of being accused, by the American people, of 'going soft.' "

The Cubans, too, knew that the moment Kennedy died, so did any chance of reestablishing normal relations with the United States. "Lechuga," Attwood wrote Chase, "and the Cubans in general, probably feel that the situation has changed since President Kennedy's assassination. Deep down, they probably don't expect anything hopeful from us." If contacts were to continue, Attwood said, he wanted to call Lechuga within a couple of weeks; otherwise, the matter "would lose momentum and wither on the vine."

But Lyndon Johnson had no interest in accommodation. Instead, he moved the entire issue of Cuba back to square one. In a memorandum following his first meeting with the new president, CIA Director John McCone noted, "He asked . . . how we planned to dispose of Castro." Johnson later approved a return to the bankrupt and ineffective policies of sabotage and covert action.

Two weeks later, on New Year's Day, 1964, ABC News aired an exclusive interview with Fidel Castro. Among those watching was the French ambassador to Washington. On January 3, he wired a summary of the interview back to Paris: "Until the tragic death of President Kennedy, he [Castro] thought that the normalization of Cuban relations with the American administration was possible. . . . He appeared 'full of hope' as to the future of his relations with President Johnson." The message was intercepted by NSA and passed on to the White House.

CHAPTER SIX

EARS

BJIWUT, MQLVGTAUZ OGJM HQPG DWJIGTA PUBGM QZBU OJWW UH HJXG
XGYWINPIX UGXKPIY PINWGWMN KPNA OBXIM NJ XUJON UJBBXG
DTUDUAGM WGNQAWJBQUZ YUCWM AOCB MUYZ TGLILWQZN LUXDJZI
BVOI ZFGI UV CA RAJVUGFUGRJ IAFM BVO WVMWV'Z DFO CPZGRAZZ
KTBSFD EKRTTVE CZICGZI FT JGKI KGER KZBSKR FRME DIGZ

As Nate Gerson's plane approached Churchill, a windy, desolate icebox on the western shore of Canada's Hudson Bay, he may have looked out and had the same thought as another visitor: "Miles and miles of nothing but miles and miles." In 1957, NSA asked the physicist to find a way to capture valuable but elusive Soviet whispers as they drifted over the North Pole and into Canada. For a number of years, Canada had maintained a bizarre listening post near Churchill—a ship on stilts. Like a steel ark, it sat high above a sea of giant rhombic eavesdropping antennas planted in the tundra and pointing in every direction.

But rather than listening to Soviet bomber pilots, Gerson and an NSA colleague ended up spending two days and nights in the wardroom of the landed ship playing liar's dice with the intercept operators. As a result of unique atmospheric conditions, no signals of any type could get through. They had been absorbed like a sponge by the auroral sky. Gerson knew that the only way to get around the problem was to move farther north—way north—as close to Russia as they could get. His idea was to build a listening post north of all human habitation on the planet, on a speck of land less than five hundred miles from the North Pole: Alert. Like a beacon, it sits on the northern tip of desolate Ellesmere, an Arctic island nearly the size of England and Scotland combined but with a population of less than a hundred permanent residents. It was hell in reverse, a place of six-month nights where marrow freezes in the bone. The nearest tree is more than fifteen hundred miles south.

Unknown, even today, is the spy war that raged at the top of the world—the true Cold War. Here, the two superpowers came closest together—and were even joined, during the bitter winter, when America's Little Diomede Island and Russia's Big Diomede Island were linked by an ice bridge. It was also each nation's Achilles' heel, where the distances were too great and the living conditions too intolerable to maintain an effective manned defense. "Study your globe," warned General Henry H. (Hap) Arnold, the former chief of the Army Air Force, "and you will see the most direct routes [between the United States and Russia] are not across the Atlantic or Pacific, but through the Arctic." If a third world war were to break out, Arnold cautioned, "its strategic center will be the North Pole." The Arctic was also the perfect place for both sides to engage in a wizard war of electronic eavesdropping.

During the late 1950s and the 1960s, both superpowers secretly used drifting ice islands for espionage. Born of ancient glaciers, the barren wastelands are made of freshwater and can be 150 feet thick or more. They drift slowly in long, circular patterns close to the North Pole. Teams of scientists and intelligence officers would be placed on the dangerous ice floes for up to a year at a time. As the floe migrated through the Arctic Sea, like a ghost ship adrift and lost, the polar spies used advanced acoustical equipment to detect hostile subs, while special antennas and receivers eavesdropped on the other side.

It was a perilous way to spy. On September 23, 1958, Air Force Captain James F. Smith, an intelligence officer, Russian linguist, and Arctic survival expert, stepped from a small plane onto Drifting Station Alpha. Alpha was a barren oval chunk of floating drift ice less than a mile long, a hundred or so miles from the North Pole. It was home to nineteen other scientists and technicians. Smith had been assigned to command the outpost for the next year, but within weeks of his arrival conditions turned severe. A punishing Arctic storm with fierce winds and brutal currents threatened to break up the portion of the ice island where most of the structures and equipment were located. Wood buildings had to be moved to a safer location; some tore apart and were lost in the process.

A second storm followed a week later, causing nearly a third of the ice floe to break away—and then came still another storm, this one "with particularly vicious winds," noted Smith. It closed the improvised runway, pushing it farther from the camp and covering it with waist-high drifts of rock-hard snow. Despite the continuous night, sleeping was sometimes difficult because of the Arctic Sea's unearthly chant.

"Standing at the edge of the camp floe," Smith wrote, "one could hear the soft rumbling and feel vibrations, occasionally punctuated by sharp cracks, grinding and crashes as large pieces were forced up, broke and tumbled."

With great difficulty, the runway was reopened. Smith recommended the evacuation of half the staff until conditions stabilized. Two rescue missions were launched but had to turn back because of severe weather. Then yet another storm struck, the fourth in less than six weeks. Sharp cracks with sawtooth edges like pinking shears zigzagged across the ice and extended into the camp. Forty percent of the micro-island broke away, and the runway was severed. In the oily darkness of the Arctic night, one of the men turned a flashlight to the gaping crevasse and exclaimed, "Ten feet wide and ten thousand feet deep."

Nevertheless, the team was able to convert one section of the runway into a useable landing strip. With a warning that another major storm was due within twenty-four hours, Smith finally had some luck. He was notified that a C-123 aircraft from Thule, Greenland, would arrive shortly. Quickly abandoning all they could not carry, the team rushed to the landing strip. Minutes later the plane touched down, sending a white cloud into the black sky. Then, almost immediately, it was airborne once again, loaded with the twenty men and their few belongings. Drifting Station Alpha, and all its equipment, was abandoned to the ruthless, grinding polar sea.

But the advantages of spying from the ice cap were irresistible. A permanent listening post at Alert, Nate Gerson concluded, would allow the United States and Canada to eavesdrop on Soviet signals obtainable only near the North Pole. "Reception at the polar cap site of Alert," he said, "would avoid the large number of auroral absorption events found at Churchill. It would also permit the West to gain knowledge that the Soviets already had obtained from observations at their periodic experimental sites on the Arctic Ocean ice pack." Canada's equivalent of the NSA, then known as the Communications Branch of the National Research Council (CBNRC), ran the operation. "Don McLeish [of the CBNRC] later told me," said Gerson, " 'We do not acknowledge the existence of CBNRC.' NSA had the same philosophy."

Once the listening post was established, said Gerson, "we considered the possibility of intercepting Soviet signals between thirty and fifty megahertz at Alert via auroral E ionization. We instituted a test similar to what the Soviets had done on their ice floe station, which recorded at Alert instances when signals in this frequency band could be received."

Then, as now, Alert is the "most northern permanently inhabited settlement in the world," according to a booklet issued to employees at the listening post. In the early 1960s, it employed about a hundred people. Ten years later the number had doubled, and in the early 1990s Alert's population was about 180. On a mantle of ice more than half a mile thick, the human population of Ellesmere Island is dwarfed by herds of musk oxen—children of the ice age—and snow-white wolves. Robert E. Peary used the island as a base for his 1909 expedition to the North Pole.

Since it was first established in the late 1950s, Alert has been Canada's most important listening post for eavesdropping on Russia. China is also a target. Yet it is so far north that it is unable to communicate with Ottawa using satellites in stationary orbits over the equator. A relay station farther south is required, in Eureka on Ellesmere Island. Until a recent upgrade in communications, it was necessary to fly all the intercept tapes to Ottawa on weekly flights by Hercules aircraft.

According to Gerson, one of the NSA's pioneers in signals intelligence from space, at one point Russian and Canadian eavesdroppers nearly came eye to eye when a Soviet ice station drifted almost into Canadian territorial waters near Alert. Communications to and from these stations were a target of the listening post. In fact, intelligence interest was so great in the Russian floating espionage platforms that a highly secret and extremely dangerous operation was conducted in an attempt to find out just how sophisticated the icy spy bases were.

On April 27, 1959, the Soviets set up a base on a 4½-mile-long ice floe about halfway between Russia's Wrangel Island, near western Alaska, and the North Pole. Named North Pole 8, for three years the station drifted slowly with the current, creeping northward toward the pole at about two miles a day. On the remote floating island, reminders were everywhere of the place they had left behind, from large wall posters in the mess hall showing workers honoring Lenin, to pictures of pinup girls hanging in the sleeping quarters. In free moments, technicians would occasionally prop themselves on the edge of the ice dressed only in swim trunks for a picture to take back home.

Like America's Drifting Station Alpha, North Pole 8 was a troublesome hunk of ice. Twice it was necessary to relocate the entire camp because of jagged cracks that cut across the runway. In the winter of 1962, ravaging storms forced the station's commander, I. P. Romanov, to order an emergency evacuation. As powerful pressure ridges threatened to turn the island into ice cubes, crewmembers rushed for the rescue aircraft, leaving behind uneaten food still on the dinner table and a wide assortment of equipment. Light planes had been used because of the damaged runway. On March 19, 1962, after 1,055 days of continuous occupation, the station was finally abandoned.

For nearly a year, since 1961, Leonard A. LeSchack, a lieutenant (junior grade) in the Office of Naval Research (ONR), had been working on a highly secret project aimed at discovering just what kind of spy equipment the Russians used on their ice stations. Now, with the abandonment of North Pole 8, he had found his perfect island. The son of Russian immigrants, LeSchack had turned twenty-seven less than two weeks earlier. He had studied geology in college and soon after graduation was chosen to take part in an exploration of Antarctica as part of the International Geophysical Year. In search of more adventure, LeSchack signed up for Naval Officers' Candidate School and after receiving his gold bars talked his way into an assignment on an ice island. Later, while assigned to ONR in Washington, he learned about the Russian abandonment of North Pole 8.

LeSchack knew that getting onto the deserted island with its damaged runway was not that difficult. The two-man inspection team could simply parachute in. The problem was getting them out: the station had no runway, it was too far for helicopter assistance, and it was too iced in for ships. But the junior officer had an idea: a low-flying plane could snatch the men out. LeSchack knew that a method had been developed for extracting clandestine CIA agents from denied territory such as China. The system was a modification of a technique used for the airborne pickup of mail pouches. The mail sack would be attached to a transfer wire strung between two poles. The plane would fly low and slow over the long transfer wire and a hook would grab hold of it. Crewmembers would then reel in the mailbag.

The system had been developed by Robert Edison Fulton, Jr., a professional inventor, and LeSchack asked him to modify it for use on his project. It was simple yet finely tuned. The person to be retrieved wore a harness connected to a long nylon lift line. A weather balloon would then raise the lift line five hundred feet. The retrieval aircraft would fly at the line and snag it in a V-shaped yoke attached to the nose. The weather balloon would release and the plane would gradually pull the person upward; his or her body would assume a position parallel to the ground. A winch would then be used to pull him through a hatch in the plane. Experiments, first with sandbags, then with sheep and pigs, and finally with a human, proved the device worked.

Armed with the Fulton Skyhook, LeSchack won approval for Operation Coldfeet. To get the men covertly to and from the Russian ice island, LeSchack turned to the CIA. The agency authorized the use of its secret proprietary airline, Intermountain Aviation, based at Marana Air Park north of Tucson, Arizona.

In late May 1962, as the long clutch of winter gave way to above-zero temperatures, the team gathered at Barrow, on the northern tip of Alaska. After several days of searching, the ragged, abandoned Soviet ice base was located. LeSchack and his partner, Air Force Captain James F. Smith, the intelligence officer and Russian linguist who had survived a harrowing several months on Drift Station Alpha, boarded the CIA's B-17 for the long flight to North Pole 8. More than six hours later, in the twenty-four-hour daylight, the plane reached the vicinity of the island. The plane's pilot, Connie M. Seigrist, a veteran of the Bay of Pigs, was astonished. "It was the most desolate, inhospitable-looking, and uninviting place I had ever seen," he recalled.

A short time later, Seigrist spotted the chalky white oval, dotted with small buildings. In the back of the plane, an adrenaline rush hit Smith and LeSchack. After once again checking his main and reserve parachutes, Smith went first, hitting the frigid air as if it were a wall of ice and then almost impaling himself on one of the tall Russian antennas. Then LeSchack dove in and, after a sharp tug on his straps, drifted slowly down to a feather landing in the soft snow.

After a night of rest on Russian bunks, they began exploring the ghost land. Like anthropologists discovering a long-lost civilization, they were surprised by what they saw. "What a horror!" LeSchack exclaimed when he entered the kitchen. "Food was still on the stove, frozen in greasy skillets. There was dried blood all over, and animal carcasses, including dog carcasses, were lying around in an adjacent shed." There were films for entertainment; the walls were plastered with posters exhorting the polar spies to work hard for the Communist Party. Over the next few days, the two Americans conducted a detailed exploration of every part of the floe. Film was found of North Pole 8's crew; there was a shot of a burly Russian sunbathing on the ice in his trunks. Personal mementos had been left behind in the scramble to escape. In one letter, a mother admonished her son to bundle up in plenty of clothes. Photographs were taken of equipment suspected of being used for acoustical surveillance and of the antenna field and ionospheric laboratory that had likely been used for eavesdropping.

On May 31, a CIA plane with a strange forklike contraption on the nose set out to retrieve Smith and LeSchack. But the ice floe had been lost. Several days went by, and more missions, but North Pole 8 had disappeared in a bewildering sea of white. From the plane, the Arctic Ocean resembled the cracked shell of a hard-boiled egg, splintered into small fragments. On one of those fragments, the two Americans continued cataloging items as they waited for their pickup. They had enough food, and weather conditions were good.

Finally, on June 2, while he was lugging gear on a toboggan to one of the huts, LeSchack heard the plane. He instantly began jumping up and down and signaling with his arms. As the CIA plane flew into position, Smith and LeSchack prepared to be yanked off the island. Three balloons were inflated, including one for a duffle bag of Russian papers, film, gear, and other salvaged items. The Intermountain B-17 made a long, slow pass and snatched up the booty bag with no trouble. Now it was LeSchack's turn.

Aboard the plane, pilot Seigrist was struggling to avoid vertigo as white merged with white. "Instantly upon loss of sight of the buildings," he recalled, "the horizon definition disappeared into the gray ice crystal-dominated atmosphere. I was instantly in a situation that could be imagined as flying in a void."

Three hundred feet below, LeSchack was having his own problems. Holding the balloon like a child at a fair, he went to a clear spot for pickup. But as he released the helium-filled bag, it was caught by a sudden updraft. The nylon line should have gone five hundred feet straight up, but instead strong winds aloft made it ascend at an angle.

LeSchack became almost weightless. The balloon then began dragging him backward toward a dangerous ridge. As he bounced against the hard snow, unable to stop himself, LeSchack tried frantically to grab onto something, anything, to keep himself from being dragged. His face mask twisted, cutting off his vision. Finally, after endless seconds, he was able to plow small holes in the ice and snow with his mitten-covered hands. This gave him just enough traction to slow and then stop.

Unable to assume the standard sitting position, he just lay motionless on the ice. Moments later he felt a jerk and was airborne, but this time he was being lifted by the B-17 and not the wind. The awkward position in which he'd been picked up caused him difficulties. He was dragged by the plane as if water-skiing on his belly behind a superfast speedboat. But six and a half minutes after the Skyhook plucked him off North Pole 8, he was safely pulled into the tail of the spy plane.

Aware of LeSchack's difficulties, Smith attempted to hold on to a tractor when he released his balloon but lost his grip and also became a human sled. For more than two hundred feet, on his way toward the Arctic Ocean, he bounced and banged against sharp ice projections until he managed to catch his heel in a ridge. Seconds later he felt like Peter Pan. "I was flying," he recalled. The Skyhook raised him as though in an elevator at first and then slowly turned him horizontal. Minutes later the tail position operator reeled him in like a prize marlin, his third catch of the day.

Back in Washington, analysts went over LeSchack and Smith's 300-plus photographs, 83 documents, and 21 pieces of equipment. Much of the gear, they concluded, was "superior in quality to comparable U.S. equipment." They also found empty cartons for thousand-foot reels of magnetic tape, the sort used for recording signals intelligence, but no tapes. And although they found a number of radio-related items and manuals, they turned up no undersea acoustic equipment. Whatever had existed was likely dumped off the island. As for the used magnetic tapes, the Russians probably took them along.

By 1961, following the enormous financial and intellectual push given the agency during the last few years of the Eisenhower administration, NSA was slowly beginning to emerge from its cocoon. Its budget had risen to an impressive $116.2 million, of which $34.9 million was for research and development of new computers and eavesdropping equipment. More and more the White House, the Pentagon, the CIA, and the State Department were depending on NSA signals intelligence. Although still unable to penetrate high-level Soviet ciphers, the agency had broken the cipher systems of more than forty nations, including Italy, France, the United Arab Republic, Indonesia, Uruguay, and even some Soviet satellite countries, such as Yugoslavia. Some breaks relied more on deception than on cryptanalytic skill or brute force. The codes and ciphers of Turkey, for example, were obtained by bribing a code clerk in Washington.

Around the world, on land, in the air, at sea, and even in space, NSA was extending its reach. Throughout much of the Northern Hemisphere, listening posts were growing like steel weeds to snare every escaping signal from the Communist East and West. More than 6,000 operators manned over 2,000 intercept positions around the world.

The polar regions continued to be prime locations for listening posts. On barren, ice-locked islands off Alaska, shivering intercept operators kept the NSA's electronic ear cocked day and night toward the Bering Sea and Siberia's frozen frontier. "I can't go there, it's too cold," thought Navy intercept operator Mike Stockmeier when he received his orders to a remote, foreboding corner of Alaska's Kodiak Island. It was a place known less for humans than for powerful brown bears, some of which, when about to attack, stood ten feet tall on their hind legs. Landing at a small airstrip on the island, Stockmeier was met by a hearty, bearded fellow cryptologist. "He appeared to be straight off the sled dog track," recalled Stockmeier, "as he quickly helped us pack our seabags in the carry-all for the three-hour ride." Their destination, over a narrow, winding road, was Cape Chiniak on the easternmost point of the island.

By the mid-1960s, the snug listening post at Cape Chiniak, nestled beneath sheltering, ice-sculptured peaks, had grown to about sixty men. A dog named Sam in a Navy sweater "kept us safe from whatever roamed free on Kodiak," said Stockmeier. From the sea, colliding low-pressure systems often brought howling sixty-knot gales and pea-soup visibility.

"The Hole," Stockmeier said, referring to the operations building, "could be a taxing place to work. From the door combo which sometimes required the oncoming watch to chip away the ice to find the numbers, to battling the cold drafts and sometime snow flurries which found their way under the shack and up through various holes in the deck [floor], people manned their post through all adversity."

At the center of the Hole sat the heavy base of the tall intercept and direction-finding antenna. The device protruded through the roof like a steel tree, snaring signals from the Soviet Northern Fleet. As it slowly rotated, reflecting the low Arctic sun, it helped pinpoint the location of warships and submarines as they transmitted messages to their shore bases. These coordinates were then transmitted to Net Control in Wahiawa, Hawaii.

The least desirable chore was destroying the overflowing cans of ashes after the highly secret intercept reports had been shredded and then burned. "The most exciting part of burn detail was dumping the ashes," said Stockmeier. "This meant dumping the ashes in the ocean—not easy to do—or driving down to Chiniak Creek and probably having to chop a hole in the ice and dumping the ashes to be washed out to sea."

Among the harshest assignments was Adak, an unforgiving rock lost in the Bering Sea at the tail end of the Aleutian chain. One veteran of the listening post, Edward Bryant Bates, put his memories to rhyme:

Cold and icy blue, as it appeared from offshore
view
Tundra grass in tufts and bands
Pushing up through snow and hard coastal sands
Clam Lagoon, where G.I. tents of olive green
White blanketed by snow kept most unseen
One small Quonset hut aside; where secret 'orange'
messages in airspace tried to hide...
But were intercepted by those inside

"I have been told by a native of this forsaken land," Karl Beeman wrote during his tour, "that the island is gradually making progress in the general direction of the Arctic Circle due entirely to the unbelievable strength of the winds." Beeman studied art at Harvard before entering the Navy and winding up at Adak. On a day off he went for a brief hike toward Mount Moffett, a towering peak a few miles from the listening post. The morning was clear and the sun was strong but on a spit of land near the icy sea he became disoriented and then stranded. Days later rescue workers found his body. Unable to free himself, trapped in the brutal winds he had earlier written about, he preferred death, committing suicide with a gun he was carrying.

While some listening posts were built in icy Arctic wastelands, others sat on mountaintops or hung precariously on the edge of cliffs. Among the most secret was an isolated monitoring station on the shores of the Caspian Sea in northern Iran. Set against a rugged, boulder-strewn background, the snow-white, pockmarked radomes—ball-shaped radar domes—made the station look like an advanced moon base. Run by the CIA, it had a unique mission.

Although the effort to locate Soviet early-warning radars along border areas had been growing in success, finding radars hidden deep inside the USSR had proved nearly impossible. But then someone remembered an incident at Cape Canaveral: during the test launch of a Thor intermediate-range ballistic missile, a signal from a ground-based radar a thousand miles away had bounced off the IRBM and reflected down to the Cape. The CIA had used the experience to develop a system codenamed Melody, which they placed on the banks of the Caspian Sea. The idea of Melody was to focus Elint antennas on Soviet ballistic missiles during their test flights and follow their trajectory. The experiment worked beyond expectations. The intercept antennas were able to pick up signals from Soviet high-powered radars well over the horizon as they bounced off the missiles. Eventually, over the years, the Caspian Sea station was able to produce an electronic map of virtually all the ground-based Soviet missile-tracking radars, including the antiballistic missile radar systems at a test range a thousand miles away.

But Melody was not as successful in locating early-warning radars, especially a new surface-to-air missile system codenamed Tall King. At the time, it was considered essential to map all the Tall King radars to prevent the shootdown of American bombers in the event of war. Also, the CIA had a peacetime interest in knowing the locations of all surface-to-air missile bases. The agency was then completing work on a super-fast, super-high-flying successor to the U-2, codenamed Oxcart. (The SR-71 would be a later variant.) Because Soviet missiles were reaching ever greater heights, and because the Oxcart was designed to overfly Russia, discovering the precise locations of these potentially deadly radar systems was vital.

The solution was to be found on the moon. Scientists determined that Tall King radar signals, traveling in a straight line, would eventually collide with the moon at least part of the day. The trick would be to catch the signals as they bounced back to earth. To accomplish this, a complex "catcher's mitt" was built. Near Moorestown, New Jersey, a giant sixty-foot satellite dish was aimed at the lunar surface. Attached to it were very sensitive Elint receivers tuned to the Tall King frequency. Over time, as the earth and moon revolved and rotated, all of the Tall King radars eventually came within view and were charted.

Still other listening posts rose like desert flowers in the African sands. At Wheelus Air Base in Libya, a thousand miles of sand surrounded American eavesdroppers on three sides, with 500 miles of Mediterranean to the north. "Even though we were on the coast," said an intercept operator who was assigned to the Air Force 6934th Radio Squadron Mobile during the 1950s, "temperatures reached 110–120 degrees when a sandstorm (or *ghiblis* as they are called) rolled in. All air stopped blowing and you're burning up." But the desert listening post was an excellent place to eavesdrop on Soviet high-frequency communications. "In my time in Libya, we copied most everything out of Russia," he said, "all the way to Vladivostok submarine pens in the Sea of Japan."

Antennas also sprang up where Allied bombs once fell. In Germany and Japan, dozens of listening posts were built amid the ruins of former enemy naval and military bases. In Berlin, the rubble from the war was bulldozed into an enormous manmade mountain outside the center of the city, in the Teufelsberg district. On top of that mountain, the highest point around, the Army Security Agency built a listening post that became one of NSA's most important ears on Soviet and East German communications throughout the Cold War. Known as Field Station, Berlin, it held the unique distinction of twice winning NSA's prestigious Travis Trophy for best worldwide listening post.

For several years in the mid-1980s, intercept operators were mystified because during the same two weeks every year they could pick up key East Bloc signals unobtainable at any other time. Eventually they realized that those two weeks coincided with the American cultural festival. Suddenly someone noticed the giant Ferris wheel. "It was acting as a great big antenna," said Bill McGowan, who was an Army captain working at the listening post. "We got excellent reception. One year we went and asked them to leave it up for another month."

Once the North Sea port for the German navy's mighty fleet, Bremerhaven became another major eavesdropping site targeting Soviet bloc ships and submarines. Aubrey Brown, an intercept operator there, still remembers straining to hear every sound. "You're trying to pull out just the slightest thing you can hear. And sometimes it's very, very weak so you put these things directly over your ear and turn the volume up as high as you can get it."

Inside the listening post's operations building, intercept operators would work "cases," as the larger Soviet ships—cruisers and battleships—were known. Once a Russian signal was captured, the intercept operator would type out the five-letter code groups on a typewriter with Cyrillic keys. "Every operator there had an assignment and they had a particular frequency they were listening to . . . ," Brown said. "Each operator there had a particular case they were listening to. And in Bremerhaven it was all Soviet and East German and Polish—mostly Russian—communicating with their homeport."

Not only did each person have his own case to work, but also three or four intercept operators were assigned to search positions. "What they did was sit there and continuously go through frequency after frequency, just scanned the entire spectrum listening and copying it and looking it up in books and seeing what it was," said Brown. "Because at times there were frequency changes and you could catch them early if you had this kind of scanning going on. Or sometimes there were things that went on that no one knew about and you would find them. So the best operators in the group generally manned the search positions."

To monitor East German naval activity in the Baltic Sea, a listening post was built in the tiny village of Todendorf, a name that roughly translates to "Village of Death." Located near the northern city of Kiel, a port on the Baltic, the fog-shrouded base was home to about 150 naval intercept operators. There the "Merry Men of Todendorf," as they called themselves, lived in a barracks warmed by a coal-fired stove and dined on schnitzel sandwiches and three-egg *Bauernfrühstücke.*

To better monitor the Communists, the technicians frequently drove mobile intercept vans and trucks to a remote stretch of Fehmarn Island in the Baltic Sea. There, under difficult conditions, they would set up their temporary listening post. "One would have had to experience manhandling a bulky antenna system to the top of a two-and-a-half-ton van in freezing rain," said one of the Merry Men. "And enduring days . . . spent warming hash, soup, or canned spaghetti on a hot plate and trying to cook eggs in a coffee pot, napping in a sleeping bag inside the freezing cab of the van. Or accompanying a five-ton equipment truck while listening to the never ending roar of the portable generator, and suffering the indignities of life without a restroom. Fresh water was limited to what could be carried in jerry cans, the nearest toilet was ten miles away, and showers were out of the question until the mission was terminated and they returned to Todendorf." Later, another small listening post, made up of vans the size of semitrailer trucks, was established at Dahme on the German Riviera. One telemetry intercept operator described Dahme as "a target-rich environment."

Other listening posts in West Germany snuggled close to Soviet bloc land borders or hung on the edge of steep cliffs.

Following massive Warsaw Pact maneuvers in an area of Czechoslovakia that NATO considered a major invasion corridor, the Army Security Agency quickly established a monitoring base on a nearby West German mountain. Long white vans packed with sensitive eavesdropping, recording, and transcribing equipment were airlifted 3,500 feet up to Eckstein, a peak on Hoher Bogen mountain in the Bavarian forest. Elint towers, odd-shaped antennas secured in cement, warning signs, and radomes that looked like giant Ping-Pong balls were erected. "At night, one could see the lights of Pilsen and Prague," recalled F. Harrison Wallace, Jr., a former Sigint specialist assigned to Eckstein. "Eckstein was chosen because there was a clear view eastward from the top of the cliff—twelve hundred feet straight down." Eventually the site began to look like a parking lot for eavesdropping vans. Eckstein was home to about a hundred personnel, including Russian and Czech linguists and a dozen traffic analysts.

For those assigned to such remote border listening posts, life could be very rough. Seventy-mile-per-hour blizzard winds tore at Eckstein's small trailers and Quonset hut and buried them in snow up to eight feet. "There was no running water on the mountain," said Wallace. "Water for coffee, hot chocolate, and washing had to be carried to 'the Hill' in five gallon Jerry cans." Sanitation consisted of a single, two-hole wooden outhouse, covered with heavy icicles in the winter, that simply sent the waste down the side of the cliff.

Despite the isolation of Eckstein, there were moments of excitement. "The finest hour for Eckstein," said Wallace, "was the 'Prague Spring' of 1968," when the Soviet army brutally invaded Czechoslovakia to crush a budding rebellion. Eckstein was able to provide NSA with minute-by-minute details of the invasion. The remote listening post also played a key role in eavesdropping on Soviet involvement in the Israeli-Egyptian Yom Kippur War of 1973. Communications intercepted at Eckstein indicated that the Russians were planning to consolidate Warsaw Pact supplies in Prague before airlifting them to Egypt.

Another rich source of Soviet bloc communications was overflights of East Germany. To facilitate the transportation of personnel and supplies to West Berlin, which sat like an island in a Soviet sea, negotiators had agreed on three narrow air corridors connecting it with West Germany. For NSA, these air corridors became veins of gold. The twenty-mile-wide paths together covered about one-sixth of East Germany. Masquerading as routine cargo flights through the corridors, U.S. Air Force C-130E and C-97G aircraft packed with eavesdropping gear would secretly monitor Communist bloc communications as they flew over the corridors.

These missions were conducted by the secretive 7405 Support Squadron which was located at Wiesbaden Air Base in West Germany. Operating under codenames such as Creek Rose, Creek Stone, and Creek Flea, the squadron flew 213 signals intelligence missions during the first half of 1967, clocking more than 915 hours in the air and snaring 5,131 intercepts. On their slow transits to and from West Berlin, the "backenders" operated a variety of receivers, recorders, signal analyzers, and direction finders. Specialized NSA equipment, a part of Project Musketeer Foxtrot, was also installed. The goal was to pinpoint hostile radar systems and dissect their electronic pulses so that, in the event of war, American fighters and bombers would be able to avoid, jam, or spoof anti-aircraft weapons.

With the ability to look deep into East German territory, intercept operators picked up enormous amounts of intelligence on the Russian systems. NSA's Project Musketeer Foxtrot, said one intelligence report, "provided precise measurements of the Tall King radars. Numerous intercepts of 'unusual' Tall King modes during this project indicated more sophisticated operation than previously suspected." Other intercepts revealed the parameters of Soviet Fan Song radars, used to guide surface-to-air missiles, and the exact location of a new Fire Can radar associated with Russian 57- and 85-millimeter anti-aircraft cannons. In June 1967, as Israel launched the Six-Day War, the Ravens were able to detect East German missile equipment being moved close to the West German border.

Turkey also became prime real estate for NSA, especially because of its proximity to Soviet missile testing areas. In 1957, a listening post was built near the village of Karamürsel on the Sea of Marmara, about thirty-seven miles southeast of Istanbul. Eventually, a giant elephant-cage antenna dominated the horizon. In the outdoor cafés nearby, Turkish farmers sipped *çay* from glass cups and inhaled bitter smoke from waterpipes and the local Yeni Harmen cigarettes.

At 9:07 A.M., on April 12, 1961, activity inside the listening post grew frenzied. At that moment, far to the north, a giant *Vostok 1* rocket rose from its launch pad. Sitting within the massive spacecraft was Colonel Yuri Alexeyevich Gagarin, twenty-seven, the son of a peasant family from the rural village of Klushino near Smolensk, and now dubbed by his fellow cosmonauts the Columbus of the Cosmos. For the first time in history, a person was being sent into space. But the Soviet government, out of fear of a mishap or disaster, kept the liftoff enormously secret. Only after Gagarin had returned safely was an announcement made. Despite the secrecy, however, intercept operators at Karamürsel were able to monitor the liftoff and flight moment by moment, including the conversations between Gagarin and mission control.

"We couldn't listen [directly] to the spacecraft because it was encrypted—the back-and-forth between [it and] the space station," said a former intercept operator at Karamürsel. "But by satellite we would be able to eavesdrop on their [Russian] local, unencrypted lines within the space center and over those lines we could hear the conversations with the cosmonauts because they would have an open speaker in the background. They would be using a frequency that no one else was and we were able to just lock in on that."

Among the very few Westerners to have listened to the world's first manned space mission as it was happening was Karamürsel intercept operator Jack Wood. "Our mission," he said, "was the number one mission in the world—to monitor the Russian manned space program. After nearly forty years, I still remember the excitement of hearing Yuri Gagarin's voice over my headset. . . . We were all tuned in for that historic moment. Loose translation: 'I see you and hear you well, OK.' "

The flight nearly ended in tragedy, however. As the spacecraft was about to reenter earth's atmosphere, two parts of the vehicle failed to separate as planned and the capsule began spinning out of control. "Malfunction!!!" Colonel Yevgeny Karpov, Gagarin's commander, scribbled angrily in his notes at the space center. Karpov saw disaster. "Don't panic! Emergency situation." But after ten minutes the parts broke away, the spacecraft steadied, and the landing was successful.

In Japan, the dust from World War II Allied bombing attacks had barely settled when American eavesdroppers began setting up shop. In charge of finding an ideal location to eavesdrop on Russia, China, and North Korea was Navy Captain Wesley Wright, a pioneer cryptologist, who was based in Tokyo as chief of NSA Pacific. Wright remembered the tunnels at Corregidor in the Philippines and had heard of similar tunnels in a place called Kamiseya, an area of rice paddies in the shadow of Mount Fuji. The tunnels were used to store torpedoes for air attacks against American ships. Wright decided that the tunnels could now be turned against the Communists as a secret listening post. The low ambient electrical noise in the rural area made for good reception.

At the time, the tunnels of Kamiseya were a mess. The floors were covered in three inches of water, and the rusty overhead rails used for moving torpedoes were still in place. Gradually the tunnels were made livable, lighting was installed, SP-600 high-frequency receivers were brought in, guards were assigned, other buildings were built or restored. Dozens of rhombic antennas, arranged in rosette patterns, were constructed to sweep in the Communist communications. A rotating switch allowed the intercept operators to choose the antenna that best received their target. Along the walls of the tunnel were columns of metal racks with thick black cables snaking from the receivers. Soon, long ribbons of seven-ply fan-fold carbon paper, covered with rows of Russian words and code groups, were flowing from Underwood typewriters twenty-four hours a day. More intercept positions were built in an adjacent building. Known as the pantry, the windowless room there had cream and green rubber tiles on the floor and globe lights above each "posit."

By 1965, Kamiseya had become the largest Navy listening post in the world, with over a thousand people raking the ether for Soviet and other Communist communications. Some of the intercept operators went on temporary assignment aboard one of the many ships sailing in the waters near the target countries. Others would fly aboard EP-3B ferret aircraft that eavesdropped near the massive Soviet port of Vladivostok and elsewhere. After their sea and airborne missions, the intercept operators would return to Kamiseya with 7½-inch magnetic tapes containing captured signals. Linguists in headsets would then spend hours sifting through the data, listening for nuggets of useful intelligence to be sent to NSA. The base had an extensive library, bursting with foreign-language dictionaries, other books, and magazines. It was also "net control" for the entire Pacific, receiving direction-finding reports from listening posts stretching from California to Okinawa. Kamiseya would then triangulate the exact location of Soviet ships and submarines over millions of square miles of ocean.

Among many other listening posts set up in Japan was one at Misawa Air Base, 400 miles north of Tokyo. It had originally been built by the Japanese with the idea of establishing a northern base from which long-range bombers could be launched toward Alaska. The facility was eventually used to train Japanese teams to sabotage Allied aircraft during the final months of the war. But as U.S. forces closed in on Japan, carrier-based Hell Cats raked Misawa's buildings and runways for several days. B-29 raids followed, virtually demolishing the base. Nevertheless, following Japan's surrender the Army Corps of Engineers quickly moved in and turned the former sabotage base into a major listening post for eavesdropping on China and western Russia.

Also to eavesdrop on China, a listening post was built on the Japanese island of Okinawa, 300 miles east of the Chinese mainland. Constructed near the town of Sobe, Torii Station was home to intercept operators who were attached to the 51st Special Operations Command. Traffic and cryptanalysts worked nearby at the Joint Sobe Processing

Center. Among the targets was high-level Chinese army and diplomatic traffic. "Security was hermetic on that post," said David Parks, an Army intercept operator who was stationed there in the mid-1960s. "Once you left the building never a word passed between you and your comrades about anything that may have happened at work. At work everything was compartmentalized. . . . If there was a need for an individual to visit a part of the building that they were not cleared for then an escort would have to be arranged."

Nearby was an expansive antenna farm consisting of three square miles of rhombic antennas, and up a hill was a giant circular elephant-cage antenna. The eavesdropping was done at the windowless operations compound where, says Parks, "you would hear the music played twenty-four hours a day, seven days a week, to mask any stray radio signal that might escape." Just inside the entrance and off a long hallway were the Morse intercept rooms manned by the various services—each one targeting their Chinese counterpart.

Sitting in front of a pair of R-390 receivers, the intercept operators would have one tuned to a target, known as the "control." When the control stopped to listen for a response, the intercept operator would search for this other station—called the out-station—with the other receiver. Likewise, each earphone would be connected to separate receivers. To make life difficult, sometimes there were as many as ten out-stations.

Some targets would be assigned, while at other times the intercept operator would twist knobs searching for new targets. Prize targets included coded Chinese messages—streams of numbers in groups of four. Once these were located, the intercept operator would type them out on six-ply carbon paper. A room supervisor would eavesdrop on the eavesdroppers to make sure they were not just copying the loud, easy signals, known as ducks. "If the room supervisor thought you were just padding your time by copying ducks," said Parks, "he would call you on the intercom and say something like, 'Get off of that duck, Parks, and back on the knobs.' "

At the time, the sounds of Mao Zedong's Cultural Revolution, ripping apart Chinese society, echoed through the listeners' earphones. "It was reflected in the stuff we copied every day," said one intercept operator. "For instance, they sent quotations of Chairman Mao back and forth as a kind of one-upsmanship. They would get on the net and they would all have their *Little Red Books.* And they would send a page and a paragraph number and a quote within that to another operator and then everybody would jump back and say, Well, here, read this one and I'm a better commie than you are." Like the Red Guards, the intercept operators had a copy of Mao's *Little Red Book* close at hand.

"They're humans too," said the intercept operator, "and that humanness comes through. You learn these people as you work the job because it is the same people day in and day out and you learn their quirks and their tempers and everything about them. You know their 'fist' and the sound of their transmitter. You can tell if they've changed a tube in that transmitter after a while.

"They knew full well that we were copying them," said Parks, "and tried to throw us off of the scent all the time. They had their bag of tricks and we had ours. A typical search would have me incrementally turning the knob and listening to each and every Morse station I came across. The airwaves were full of signals of all types, voice transmissions, Morse, teletype, beacons, fax transmitters sending photo images for the newspapers and wire services. There was indeed a seeming 3-D soundscape to the radio medium. We used such terms as 'up' or 'down' and 'under' in describing where a target might be in relation to a signal. There were known islands of sound imbedded at fixed points in the soundscape. It was not unusual for one op to say to another, 'Your outstation (target) is underneath that RCA teletype at 3.5 megs [megahertz]. I would know just where he meant."

Among the most difficult traffic to copy were coded diplomatic communications. "Diplomatic traffic was the top of the heap," said Parks. "The analysts wanted that copied as clean as possible; if you couldn't do that, you were off the job." Parks once intercepted an unknown embassy employee "who was transmitting, in English, a blow-by-blow description of the embassy being invaded and the door to his code room being chopped down by a rioting crowd. Frantic little guy, lost his mind and maybe his life. I've always wondered what happened to him. I also wonder if the 'riot' had a purpose other than frustration. On my end I was sweating bullets as there was brass standing two deep around my intercept position urging me to get it all. Every page of six-ply that came off my mill was immediately ripped off and handed around. The embassy op finally went 'nil more heard.' "

Air Force intercept operators also worked on Okinawa, eavesdropping on Chinese air communications. One of their most important tasks was to listen closely as American signals intelligence planes flew eavesdropping missions near the coast of mainland China, occasionally penetrating the country. Twice daily, missions would be launched from either Taipei, at the north end of the island, or Tainan, at the southern end. One of the Mandarin Chinese intercept operators who followed those flights from Torii Station was Robert Wheatley. "Along the way, our ground stations would listen in on the Chicom [Chinese Communist] fighter squadrons as they'd scramble and rise up to meet the recon planes," he said. "It was almost like a game of cat and mouse to the pilots involved. When our planes would come over a given fighter squadron's sphere of coverage, the MiGs would scramble and follow along below until the next squadron up the coast would scramble and take over the chase. But the ceiling of the Russian-made MiG 21 was far below that of our reconnaissance planes, and generally speaking, the MiGs were no real threat to them."

But occasionally one of the MiGs would get lucky. Wheatley recalls once receiving a Flash message from a listening post in Taiwan. "It detailed the shootdown of one of our airborne reconnaissance platforms by a Chinese MiG-21 over the China mainland," he said. "The MiG pilot had made a 'zoom climb' to the highest altitude he could make. At the moment he topped out, he released his air-to-air rockets. The linguist listening in on the fighter pilot reported what he'd heard him say. Translation: 'Climbing to twenty thousand [meters] . . . Rockets fired! I fixed his ass! I fixed his ass!' The meaning of that was dismayingly clear. The 'game' had become deadly serious! The account of what had happened was instantly passed to us on Okinawa via encrypted Teletype transmission. We were instructed to listen for any references to the shootdown by any of the Chinese ground stations that we listened in on."

As word of the shootdown got around, said Wheatley, "the mood in the radio ops room took on the air of a funeral. I would liken it to the moment that America learned of the *Challenger* space shuttle disaster. Some of those on board that plane were guys with whom we'd attended language school. And all were fellow airmen—brothers—whether we knew them or not. Were it not for the luck of the draw, any one of us could have been aboard that flight. Everyone in the room was stunned, silent, and ashen-faced. We never did find out if there were any survivors among the crew of the aircraft. I suspect not. But we never heard any more on the matter, for we did not have the 'need to know.' "

Picking just the right spot for the secret bases was as much a matter of intuition as of science. In trying to "locate intercept stations," said former NSA research chief Dr. Howard Campaigne, "it's well to know which would be the best places. They were often surprises. Intercept stations were not effective when they thought they would be, and vice versa." Sometimes the best place to listen to a target was on the exact opposite point on earth—the antipodal spot. "One of the things we worked at was antipodal reception," said Campaigne. "When a radio station sends out waves, the ionosphere keeps [them] in like a whispering gallery and [they're] concentrated at the antipodes and we were able to demonstrate such reception. Unfortunately, the earth is so clustered that the end of every diameter has got water in at least one half of the places. So there aren't very many places that are any good."

One spot where "hearability" was near perfect was the rugged, windswept desert of Eritrea in East Africa. Reputed to be the hottest place on earth, it is a land of geographic extremes, where gray mountains suddenly rise like fortress walls from broad rocky grasslands, and oceans of sparsely vegetated lowlands marry vast seas of sand. On April 30, 1943, in the middle of World War II, U.S. Army Second Lieutenant Clay Littleton landed there while searching for a good location for a radio station in North Africa. Tests showed that Eritrea, just north of the equator and with an altitude of 7,600 feet, was practically an audio funnel, and an intercept station was quickly set up, as was a large relay facility. Operational spaces, containing ten-inch-thick bombproof concrete walls, were built underground, near the capital of Asmara.

In the early 1960s a conga line of trucks, straining against the heat and blowing sand, hauled 6,000 tons of heavy steel to the secret base. By then Eritrea had become federated with Ethiopia. Planned for Kagnew Station, whose name comes from the Ethiopian word meaning to bring order out of chaos, was a pair of massive satellite dishes to capture Soviet signals bouncing off the moon, and others relayed from earth-orbiting satellites. One was to be a dish 85 feet in diameter and the other was to be possibly the largest movable object ever built—a massive bowl 150 feet wide sitting on top of a rotating pedestal capable of tracking the arc of the moon. When built, it would rise from the desert like a great chalice, an offering to the gods.

A few years earlier, Kagnew Station had been the scene of perhaps NSA's first and only strike. Arthur Adolphsen arrived at the listening post straight from snowbound Germany in January 1957 wearing a hot Ike jacket. A year later he and the other intercept operators moved into a new operations building. The move, however, brought with it numerous new regulations and restrictions on personal activity throughout the base. "The Operations Center . . . went on strike some time after we moved on the new base [December 1957]," said Adolphsen. "It lasted for about four days; no one could hear any signals.

"After three or four days of not much traffic being sent to Washington a planeload of NSA people showed up and wanted to know what was going on. We had a meeting of all operations personnel in the gym and they asked us what we wanted, and there were many that were brave enough to stand up and let them know. It was brought on by the post command removing stripes and privileges for very minor infractions. They would not let us have autos and motorbikes, restricted everyone to base, and so forth. To my knowledge no personnel got punished, but the entire post command, right down to the chaplain, got replaced."

By 1967 Ethiopia was attempting to turn Eritrea from a largely independent partner in federation into simply another province, and a rebel movement developed within Eritrea to fight the Ethiopian government. The tension was felt acutely at NSA, which feared that an Eritrean coup might jeopardize its listening post. The agency therefore sought to eavesdrop both on the Ethiopian government and on the rebels. However, it had long been a rule at NSA that the agency would not eavesdrop on the host country from within the host country. And because a number of Ethiopians worked close to some of the operations at Kagnew Station, it was felt that any attempt to eavesdrop from within would quickly leak out. In such an event the entire mission could be forced out of the country. So NSA turned to its British counterpart, the GCHQ, to do the listening.

At the time the closest GCHQ listening post was in the British colony of Aden (now part of Yemen) across the Red Sea. The British were having problems of their own. With only a few months to go before they pulled out of the colony, a civil war had developed over which local political faction would take over control of the new nation. Ordinarily NSA would have done the eavesdropping from the U.S. embassy in Aden but it was feared that the U.S. embassy might be forced out, especially if the new government was Marxist, as it turned out to be. The British, however, would be allowed to remain, if only to clear up administrative issues. Thus it was decided to eavesdrop on the Ethiopian government from the British High Commission office in Aden, which on independence would become an embassy.

After a crash course at Bletchley Park, three GCHQ intercept operators were sent to Aden for the operation. The listening post was set up in a secure room in the building, the operators hidden under the cover of communications specialists, and the antennas disguised as flagpoles. "The priority tasks from the NSA were of course the Ethiopian military, from which a coup could be expected," said Jock Kane, one of the intercept operators. Tensions in Ethiopia continued to mount and it was finally decided to pull out of the country entirely. The enormous antennas were dismantled and the intercept operators sent back to NSA a decade later, in 1977.

The wide oceans also needed to be covered in order to eavesdrop on Russian ships, and submarines as they came up briefly to transmit their rapid "burst" messages. Sitting almost in the middle of the Atlantic Ocean, between Africa and Brazil, is a speck of rock named Ascension Island. Formed by successive volcanic eruptions, the lonely dot rises steeply from the blue-black waves like a massive aircraft carrier anchored to the seabed. Dense vegetation is interspersed with harsh fields of volcanic rock that locals call "hell with the fires turned off." Nevertheless, the British island is ideally suited to eavesdrop on millions of square miles of ocean. Thus, the Central Signals Organization, the overseas branch of GCHQ, found it an ideal location for a major high-frequency and satellite listening post.

In the northern Pacific, it would have been difficult to find a more isolated spot for a listening post than Midway Island, a coral atoll about halfway between California and Japan. Lost in the great ocean, Midway consists of two islands: Sand Island, which is three miles square and has a landing strip, and Eastern Island, a speck of sand less than a mile square, where the listening post was built. "I looked and looked and could only see the white crests of the waves below us on the Pacific

Ocean," said Phillip Yasson, a Navy intercept operator, of his first flight to the island. "As the plane got lower and lower in altitude, I had this feeling of landing on the water because that was the only thing visible." The men assigned to the listening post were quartered in an old movie theater that had been bombed during World War II. "You could stand in the middle of the island," said Yasson, "make a 360-degree turn, and still see the ocean except for where the buildings blocked the view."

In the operations building, the intercept operators eavesdropped on Soviet ships and submarines and attempted to pinpoint them with a high-frequency direction finder. Midway was too small for a giant elephant-cage antenna, so instead they used vertical wires. Nevertheless, reception was very good. "Surrounded by water, it was a good choice," said Yasson. "There were plenty of signals." During the midnight shift, one of the intercept operators would divide his time between eavesdropping on the Russians and washing the clothes for the others on the watch. The principal hobby of the eighteen people on the island was collecting the colorful glass orbs that occasionally washed up—floats from old Japanese fishing nets. Swimming was hazardous because of sharks. For company the intercept operators had gooney birds—lots of gooney birds. One survey put their numbers at more than two hundred thousand. The stately black and white birds—black-footed albatrosses—with seven-foot wingspreads glide gracefully to earth but then frequently have trouble with their landing gear, tumbling headfirst into the sand.

The vast Indian Ocean, which stretches from the coastline of East Africa to islands of East Asia and the shores of Australia, presented a particularly formidable problem. The solution involved the dislocation of an entire native population, the taking over of a British colony, and the creation of one of the most forbidding territories on earth.

In the early 1960s, the British government began taking an unusual interest in a sparse, remote group of islands located nearly in the center of the Indian Ocean. Known as the Chagos Archipelago, it was an almost forgotten dependency of Mauritius, one of Britain's larger island colonies, which lay 1,200 miles to the south. As the Mauritius islanders began to agitate for independence, Britain inexplicably offered them freedom, plus £3 million, if they would give up their claim to the scruffy, distant sandbars and atolls of the Chagos. The Mauritius government accepted. Later, away from the glare of publicity, London made a brief, quiet announcement. At a time when it was freeing its distant lands from the bonds of colonialism, Britain was suddenly creating a new colony. The tiny Chagos Archipelago, a collection of dots lost in millions of square miles of ocean, would become the British Indian Ocean Territory, or BIOT.

With the ink barely dry on the paperwork, Britain turned around and just as quietly handed the colony over to the United States, gratis, for fifty years. The purpose was the building of an unidentified "defence installation." There was no debate in Parliament and virtually no publicity.

Because of the U.S. government's need for secrecy, between 1965 and 1973 the entire native population of some 2,000 had to be evicted from the islands, where they and their relatives had lived quietly for hundreds of years. A visitor in the late 1950s, before the islands became an "American colony," reported, "There was a château . . . whitewashed stores, factories and workshops, shingled and thatched cottages clustered around the green . . . and parked motor launches." According to one of the islanders, "We were assembled in front of the island because the Americans were coming for good. We didn't want to go. We were born there. So were our fathers and forefathers who were buried in that land."

Although the islanders were all British subjects, they were removed bodily and dispersed once NSA prepared to move in. "They were to be given no protection, and no assistance, by the Earl, the Crown, or anybody else," wrote one outraged British writer, Simon Winchester:

> Instead the British Government, obeying with craven servility the wishes of the Pentagon—by now the formal lessees of the island group—physically removed every man, woman and child from the islands, and placed them, bewildered and frightened, on the islands of Mauritius and the Seychelles. British officials did not consult the islanders. They did not tell them what was happening to them. They did not tell anyone else what they planned to do. They just went right ahead and uprooted an entire community, ordered people from their jobs and their homes, crammed them on to

> ships, and sailed them away to a new life in a new and foreign country. They trampled on two centuries of community and two centuries of history, and dumped the detritus into prison cells and on to quaysides in Victoria [Seychelles] and Port Louis [Mauritius], and proceeded, with all the arrogant attitudes that seemed peculiar to this Imperial rump, promptly to forget all about them.

In the spring of 1973, a group of NSA officials and fourteen intercept operators and analysts from the three military cryptologic organizations arrived on the largest island of the group, Diego Garcia, to begin hearability tests. Named after the Portuguese sailor who discovered it four hundred years earlier, the island is a thin, horseshoe-shaped atoll, thirty-seven miles from tip to tip, that barely rises above the rolling waves. The NSA team, codenamed Jibstay, set up a series of intercept antennas, including a small elephant cage known as a "pusher." Also, NSA shipped a portable eavesdropping van to the island. It was not long before the Soviets began snooping around to see what NSA was up to. "A Soviet trawler maintained station just off the receiver site," said Monty Rich, a member of the Jibstay team. "The trawler was relieved for a short time by a Soviet Navy *Sverdlov*-class cruiser."

Gregor McAdam was one of the first Navy Seabees on Diego Garcia and helped construct some of the early buildings. "All we had was seahuts to live in," he said. "And lots of donkeys, chickens, flies up the ass, and Double Diamond beer. Once every couple of weeks a shipment of beer would come in, but if you didn't get right over to the club (a Quonset hut) and snap up some cases, you're S.O.L. and stuck with the Double Diamond or Pabst Blue Ribbon." Even in those early days, he said, the Russians took a great interest in the construction. "We had a radio station that used to play 'Back in the USSR' for the Russian trawler that was always offshore."

On Diego Garcia, cryptologic technicians nicknamed "wizards" worked in the windowless Ocean Surveillance Building located at "C Site." There, as part of a worldwide Advanced Tactical Ocean Surveillance System, codenamed Classic Wizard, they served as the Indian Ocean downlink for the highly secret White Cloud satellite program. This consists of constellations of signals intelligence satellites that are able to pinpoint and eavesdrop on ships and submarines across the vast oceans. Others, in the High Frequency Direction Finding Division, monitored the airwaves for thousands of miles in all directions for any indications of Soviet sea activity.

One wizard, who spent two tours on Diego Garcia, was Steven J. Forsberg, a Navy cryptologic technician. Despite the isolation and remoteness of the base, he said, the ocean surveillance compound was also closely guarded by a detachment of U.S. Marines. "On those few occasions when they could stay awake at night guarding our site," he said, "which had never been, and never would be, attacked, they often played 'quick draw' with their loaded .45s. Well, one night some guy accidentally squeezed the trigger while doing so." To cover himself the Marine reported that the shot came from a sniper. As a result the Marines went to full alert. "Security was driving around in a truck with a loudhorn telling people to go inside," he said. Other Marines "lined up on the roof in full gear and with loaded weapons. If you came near the barracks, a guy would scream, 'Lock and load!' and you'd hear all those M-16 bolts slamming. Then they'd yell, 'Turn around and walk away! Deadly force authorized!' "

So highly protected is Diego Garcia that even when a small private sailboat, crossing the Indian Ocean, pulled close to shore asking to resupply water and do some emergency repairs, it was ordered to keep away from the island. Eventually the boat was allowed to remain offshore until daybreak, but a spotlight was constantly trained on it. Then as soon as the morning came, patrol boats forced the sailboat back out onto the deep ocean. Under the terms of the 1966 agreement between Britain and the United States, no one without formal orders to the area was permitted entry to any of the islands.

By 1989 the Naval Security Group had personnel serving at forty-eight listening posts around the world, with 15 percent conducting operations at sea aboard ninety ships.

To avoid the problem of overdependence on British intercepts, which partly led to the surprise at Suez, NSA began expanding its presence on Cyprus, ideally positioned in the eastern Mediterranean. At the same time, it began training its antennas on the Middle East rather than exclusively on the Soviet Bloc. To the north, east, and west of Nicosia, Cyprus's capital, listening posts were set up. At Karavas, about fifty Soviet and Slavic linguists eavesdropped on the Soviet Union and Eastern Europe. Other monitoring stations were set up in Mia Milea, in Yerolakkos, and near Troodos Mountain. On the south coast, at Akrotiri, intercept operators listened for indications of war in the Middle East, while also eavesdropping on peace negotiations. In Nicosia, signals intelligence personnel were based in the embassy to relay back to NSA intercepted diplomatic cables. During the 1990 Gulf War, the listening posts played a key role and also spearheaded the hunt for the hostages in Lebanon.

By far the most difficult—and at the same time most important—body of water in which to spy was the Barents Sea. Like an ice pack on Russia's forehead, the half-million square miles of dark, unforgiving, polar-cold water held some of Russia's deepest secrets. It was a frozen world of white, gray, and black where the blunt hulls of onyx-colored submarines began and ended their long patrols in search of American subs under the Atlantic Ocean. It was also where new missiles were tested and glacier-shaking nuclear weapons were detonated. The thin winter ice allowed the Russian Northern Fleet to conduct exercises year-round, and the sky above was like a mechanical aviary for the Soviet Air Force. The air was electric with signals. The problem for NSA was how to get an antenna and tape recorder into one of the most secret and heavily protected areas on earth.

Black and moonless, the late night was an odd time to start painting. In the dim reddish glow from a low-observation flashlight, George A. Cassidy began applying thick coats of steel-gray paint to the submarine's tall sail. It was mid-September 1965 and the frigid spray from the North Sea deposited a dewlike film on the sailor's dark pea coat. In an hour the giant "SS-352," identifying the sub as American, had been painted over on both sides of the tower. The USS *Halfbeak*'s covert mission had begun.

A month before, late at night on August 17, Cassidy had reported to a basement office in NSA's Operations Building for a Top Secret codeword briefing on his new assignment. "One of our missions," recalled the former Elint intercept operator, "was to bring back any rocket telemetry that we could get." At the time, the White House was very concerned about advances in Soviet ballistic missile capabilities. An over-the-pole attack launched from one of the ICBM bases close to the

Barents Sea was the most likely scenario for World War III. U.S. Sigint aircraft would occasionally fly into the area in an attempt to collect signals, but their presence was immediately obvious and sensitive activities would be halted until it departed. The only way to capture the telemetry—key signals revealing the operational performance of the missile that were transmitted back to its control center—was by stealth. A submarine would have to penetrate deep into Soviet territorial waters in perhaps the most dangerous sea on the planet.

To hide the true nature of their mission, even from the crew, Cassidy and the three other intercept operators were given "radiomen" patches for their uniforms. Their orders never even mentioned the name of the ship they were being assigned to. It simply used the words "U.S.S. *Classified.*" The U.S.S. *Classified* turned out to be a twenty-year-old diesel submarine named the USS *Halfbeak*, which was berthed at the naval base in New London, Connecticut. Although outwardly like any other sub, eavesdropping antennas had been attached to the *Halfbeak*'s electronic countermeasures (ECM) mast, and a special receiver had been installed in the periscope well beneath the conning tower.

The intercept operators, not being part of the regular crew, were squeezed in wherever there was space. "I lived in the forward torpedo room, among eighteen torpedoes and six torpedo tubes," said Cassidy. His bed was a piece of plywood sandwiched between Mark 24 wire-guided torpedoes—each with 500 pounds of explosives packed into its warhead. Nearby were two Mark 45 nuclear-tipped torpedoes with tags labeled "War Shot."

It was late September when the *Halfbeak* finally reached its operational area off Russia's Kola Peninsula. Inside the crowded metal tube, life was cold, dirty, and quiet. To ensure radio silence, tubes had been removed from the communications equipment and locked in a safe. Adding to the discomfort, one of two stills that converted salt water into freshwater had broken down. Thus, each man was given a large tomato soup can to fill with water once a day for washing. Then about half the heaters quit. "I remember lying in my bunk scraping the frost off the torpedo above me," recalled Cassidy.

Despite the problems, the mission went on. Beneath the black, crawling waves the *Halfbeak* slowly maneuvered toward its target, a heavily protected island off the Russian coast where much of the Soviet missile testing was taking place. During the day, the sub operated on battery power, cruising quietly at periscope depth sixty-two feet below the surface. Once the passive sonar indicated that no surface contacts were above, the mast with the Sigint equipment would be raised about six feet above the waves.

"If it was daylight, we would be running fairly slow so it wouldn't make a wake," said Cassidy, "because if you went over four knots underwater, this would start throwing up a plume." At night the diesel engine would be fired up and the snorkel mast would be raised to provide fresh air to the crew and to charge the batteries. Ever closer the sub approached—well past the twelve-mile territorial limit and just a few miles off the beach. Through the periscope, the men could see beefy Russian women hanging out laundry.

Down in the makeshift Sigint spaces, behind a closed door in the control room, the intercept operators listened like electronic bird-watchers for telltale sounds. They attempted to separate the important signals—the wobbling, squeaking, chirping sounds that reveal key radar and telemetry systems—from a cacophony of static. "We used to practice all the time listening to tapes of different Soviet radar," said Cassidy. "So if we heard it, we could tell what it was. Before we would go on a mission, we would train ourselves by sitting in front of these tapes that operators had made while out on patrol." At the same time, they measured and photographed the squiggly electronic waves that rippled across the orange screens of the Elint receivers.

"We had special equipment that was made up of eight to twelve little receivers that would each receive a frequency that the Soviets transmitted telemetry on," recalled Cassidy. "On this run the main interest was the telemetry. But any Russian signal you were able to tape was good because all this went into a database. . . . And this would all be piped into a recorder, so whenever we heard telemetry coming from the island, we would start to record it. The rockets could be anything from satellite launches to missiles. We heard a lot of fire control radar along with it. We had capabilities of intercepting twelve to fourteen channels." To capture Soviet voice communications, one of the intercept operators was a Russian linguist.

The greatest worry was discovery. Thus, great care was taken to watch and listen for any approaching Soviet aircraft, ship, or submarine.

For weeks all went well despite the *Halfbeak*'s risky location. But early on a dark morning in late October, Cassidy heard the distinctive whistle of a "mushroom" radar, indicating that somewhere overhead was an approaching Soviet TU-95 Bear—a large and deadly strategic bomber with swept wings and four huge turboprop engines. At almost the same moment, he also picked up the signal of a Russian destroyer bearing down on the *Halfbeak*'s location. "I have contact!" Cassidy yelled to the captain. "Very weak TU-95 aircraft mushroom radar and a Soviet surface ship."

The troubles only got worse. "And then I heard this *whish,*" Cassidy recalled, "and I knew it was a flat-spin radar from a Soviet "Foxtrot"- or "Whiskey"-class submarine. After I told the captain, we pulled all the antennas and masts down. This was at night—early in the morning. We were snorkeling, which means we had the diesel engines running. We went to Battery Operation and then to Battle Stations Torpedo. We pulled the plug—it went down. We knew we had in the air at least one Soviet aircraft. We knew we had at least one Soviet destroyer and very possibly a Soviet conventional submarine out there."

The captain took the *Halfbeak* deep—about three hundred feet—and managed to hide under a dense layer of salt water that deflected any enemy sonar signals. Sailing at four knots, the boat headed south out of harm's way. By afternoon, with the danger apparently over, the *Halfbeak* headed back toward its operational area near the missile-testing island, arriving early the next morning. But now there was a new problem: through the periscope, as it was rising toward the surface, the captain noticed something strange. Everywhere he looked, all he could see were thick logs floating above. Sigint was out of the question. "We couldn't really put the ECM mast up in that stuff because it had these little thin antennas sticking out, and if you hit that with a log . . . it's going to ruin the watertight integrity of the antenna," recalled Cassidy. He suspected that the Russians had dumped the wood deliberately in order to hinder the sub's spying.

Determined to continue the mission, the captain sailed the *Halfbeak* to another part of the island's coastline and raised the camouflaged ECM mast containing the eavesdropping antennas. By then, however, the Russians were aggressively searching for the intruder and once again, late in the afternoon, Cassidy heard the ominous sounds. This time it was two Soviet destroyers and the signal was Strength Five—the highest, meaning the destroyers were almost on top of them. "I have two Strength Five Russian waterborne platform emissions!" Cassidy yelled to the captain. Then sonar reported the presence of another sub nearby. The captain immediately ordered a dive and set Battle Stations Torpedo. Through a small side tube, a number of white, four-inch pills were fired into the water. Like giant Alka-Seltzer tablets, they were designed to create clouds of bubbles to hide the escaping sub. "We must have fired twenty of those," recalled Cassidy. "We used that and prayed."

In the control room Cassidy could clearly see the depth gauge about four feet away. It had a red mark at 350 feet, indicating the test depth—the safety limit for the sub. To his horror, the needle slipped past the mark and continued downward as the old boat began to squeak and groan. "Are we supposed to go below 350 feet?" he yelled to the sailor at the controls.

"We do whatever the old man says," the man yelled back.

"Oh God," Cassidy suddenly yelled. "We're sinking. The water's coming in!" Above him he heard a "pop" and ice-cold water poured down on his head. Luckily it was only the snorkel drain breaking, releasing about five gallons of water that had accumulated in the tube.

As the sub continued to descend to about 400 feet, a short distance from the muddy seafloor, the sonar men could hear pinging sounds from the Soviet ships searching for them above. Next the captain ordered Sedge Quiet. "This is where you basically shut off everything except for the gyroscope and the electric motor that's turning the shaft," said Cassidy. "Lights were reduced, heating was off, the galley ranges were off, hydraulics were off." With the hydraulic system inoperative, it took two sailors to steer the sub, using small handles that pop out of the wheel.

Hour after hour after hour the *Halfbeak* quietly maneuvered deep in the Barents Sea as sonar continued to pick up a heavy presence on the surface. At one point a sonar man heard what he thought was an explosion from a depth charge. Crew members were ordered to remove their shoes to keep down the noise. "We were warned about banging anything, coffee cups," said Cassidy. "No noise at all. It was like a tomb in there."

Eventually the oily air began turning thin and rancid. The captain passed the word to break out the carbon dioxide absorbent—cans of powder would be spread on bunks to help draw the deadly gas from the air. Nevertheless, the sub's doctor warned that the oxygen levels were becoming dangerously low. Sailors, including Cassidy, passed out and had to be revived. Two large oxygen canisters were placed in the central part of the sub, and it was suggested that those who felt faint should take a few deep breaths from the masks attached.

Without electric power, all that the galley could come up with was peanut butter, crackers, and Kool-Aid, but few had the strength to go there anyway. "It was so hard to breathe, you didn't even want to walk from the forward torpedo room to the galley, which was probably about one hundred feet," recalled Cassidy. "Because it was too much effort, you had a hard time breathing. And it was cold; it was damp. They were holding us down. We could not surface because they were above us. Sonar could hear their engines. There were four separate surface contacts around us, plus a probable submarine."

Finally, after about twelve or thirteen hours, the pinging began to cease. After another hour, to make sure that the Soviet ships had departed, the *Halfbeak* slowly began to rise. "He said you know we could probably surface now, but we are going to take another hour and I want you to just search and search and listen, listen, listen," said Cassidy. "And they would put a new operator on about every fifteen or twenty minutes for another good set of ears. When they were positive that there were no surface contacts around, we just squeaked up. I searched all the bands for aircraft . . . and when the captain and the exec [executive officer] were as sure as anybody could be that there were no signals up there, we came up to periscope depth. This was early morning. Looked around with the attack scope and the regular scope and saw nothing. And once they were happy with that, they put up the snorkel mast. . . . The first time we snorkeled after being down so long, the fresh air was so clean and pure it hurt you, it actually hurt your lungs."

With most of the mission completed and the Soviets hot on their trail, the captain decided to head back to New London. There, the dozens of intercept tapes were double-wrapped and sent by courier to NSA for analysis. As with most missions, the intercept operators were never informed what the agency learned as a result of the dangerous mission. They did not have the required "need to know." And in the ship's history of the USS *Halfbeak*, the year 1965 has been eliminated.

Throughout the Cold War, similar missions continued. Even as late as 2000, the Barents Sea remained prime eavesdropping territory for American submarines. That summer, the bullet-shaped bow of the USS *Memphis*, a 6,000-ton attack sub, slipped quietly out of its home port of Groton, Connecticut, and disappeared beneath the frosty whitecaps of the Atlantic. Its target was a major naval exercise by the Russian Northern Fleet—the largest such exercise in a decade. Among the fifty warships and submarines participating in the mock battle was a steel leviathan named the *Kursk*, a double-hulled, nuclear-powered submarine twice the length of a Boeing 747. On board were about two dozen Granit sea-skimming cruise missiles as well as torpedoes. It was the pride of the nation—the most modern submarine in the Russian Navy.

On Saturday morning, August 12, the *Kursk*, with 118 crewmembers aboard, was off the Kola Peninsula cruising at periscope depth, about sixty feet below the sea's heaving swells. Some distance away, maintaining radio silence, the USS *Memphis* eavesdropped on the maneuvers. Sticking above the surface like the necks of tall, gray giraffes were antenna-covered masts. Down below, intercept operators searched through the static for fire control signals and pilot chatter while sonar men plotted the pinging sounds of other steel fish. Then at precisely 11:28, the sub's sonar sphere—a giant golfball attached to the bow, containing over 1,000 hydropones—registered the sound of a short, sharp thud. Two minutes and fifteen seconds later a powerful, fish-scattering boom vibrated through the sensitive undersea microphones. The blast was so powerful, the equivalent of up to two tons of TNT, that it was picked up by seismic stations more than 2,000 miles away.

On the *Kursk*, a room-size hole opened up in the forward torpedo room, turning the smooth curved bow into a jagged bean can and sending the sub on a deadly dive to the bottom. Sailors who didn't die immediately likely survived only hours. The cause of the disaster was probably the onboard explosion of a missile or torpedo. But given the long cat-and-mouse history of American submarine espionage in the Barents Sea, senior Russian officials pointed the finger at an undersea hit-and-run collision with a U.S. sub.

Six days later, the *Memphis* surfaced and quietly sailed into a Norwegian port. There it off-loaded boxes of recording tapes containing an electronic snapshot of the worst submarine disaster in Russia's history—

the undersea sounds of the dying *Kursk* and the surface voices of the confused rescue efforts. The tapes, flown to Washington, largely confirmed the theory that the tragedy was caused by internal explosions. They also confirmed the continuing value of sending eavesdroppers deep into the Barents Sea's perilous waters.

While many listening posts were quietly built in distant places with tongue-twisting names, others were built much closer to home. On an ancient English estate, an elephant cage rose like a modern-day Stonehenge. Chicksands Priory, in what is today Bedfordshire, dates to the time of William the Conqueror.

Once home to an order of Gilbertine monks and nuns, by World War II Chicksands had become host to a secret Royal Air Force intercept station. In 1948 the U.S. Air Force moved in and began eavesdropping on Soviet communications. By mid-December of the same year Chicksands was intercepting 30,000 five-figure groups of coded traffic a day. Three years later, however, that number had skyrocketed to 200,000 groups a day.

Communications security operators at Chicksands also began intercepting U.S. Air Force communications. The operation was aimed at analyzing Air Force voice, Morse code, and teletypewriter radio transmissions for violations of security. If they could read the messages or pick up clues to pending operations, it was assumed, so could Soviet eavesdroppers.

Earl Richardson arrived at Chicksands to join the Security Service in 1953, fresh out of communications school at Keesler Air Force Base in Mississippi. Sitting in front of a Hammarlund Super-Pro SP-600 high-frequency receiver mounted in a rack, he would slowly turn the half-dozen black dials. His job was to search for sensitive U.S. Air Force messages mistakenly sent in the clear; or identify lazy communicators using made-up voice codes in a poor attempt to mask classified information. The results were put in "Transmission Security Analysis Reports" and sent out to offending commands. There, the radio operator would receive a stern lecture and warning. According to one former Chicksands operator, "Much of the caution was perverse and focused on not being caught again by the Security Service, which in time came to be perceived as an enemy more real than the Warsaw Pact."

Another elephant cage quietly rose in the Scottish village of

Edzell, a farming area nestled in the foothills of the Grampian Hills, thirty-five miles south of Aberdeen. It replaced listening posts in Bremerhaven, Germany, and in Morocco, and soon became host to Army and Air Force eavesdroppers as well. A key target was the shadowy Soviet merchant fleet.

While NSA concentrated on building its electronic wall around the Communist world, much of the Southern Hemisphere—South America and Africa—escaped close scrutiny. That was one of the key reasons for building a Sigint navy. As the ships slid out of dry dock, they began hauling their antennas and eavesdroppers to places too difficult to reach with land-based listening posts and too remote for regular airborne missions.

Tired of the daily routine at the listening post in Bremerhaven, Aubrey Brown volunteered for a ship NSA was having converted at the Brooklyn Navy Yard. It was late on a winter night when he arrived. As he boarded the gray-hulled USS *Oxford*, the decks were littered with acetylene tanks, welder's torches, and buckets of iron rivets. After sea trials off Norfolk, Virginia, the ship set sail for South America, a continent brimming with signals for its virgin ears, on January 4, 1962.

At the time, U.S. officials feared that the Communist "fever" that had struck Cuba would spread throughout the continent. Later that month, in Punta del Este, a beach resort in Uruguay, foreign ministers from the Organization of American States were planning to meet to discuss many of these issues. The meeting was seen by the U.S. State Department as an opportunity to push for collective action against Cuba, such as a resolution that all countries still having diplomatic and commercial ties with that nation move to break them. It was thus a logical place for the *Oxford*'s first mission.

As the *Oxford* sailed south, intercept operators eavesdropped on one of the assigned targets, government communications links in British Guyana, considered very sensitive because it belonged to our close Sigint partner, England.

Arriving off Montevideo, on the north shore of the Río de la Plata estuary, the *Oxford* was almost unnoticed amid the fleet of cargo ships heavy with wool, hides, and textiles. On board, hidden below decks, the intercept operators tuned in, listening for telephone calls and messages to and from the delegates attending the conference a few miles east at the resort.

Afterward, they moved a short distance west, up the Río de la Plata to Buenos Aires. "We would go into bays to intercept microwave links, and to really intercept that well you had to have your receiving antenna in between their transmitting antenna and their receiving antenna. So to do this we would get into bays," said George A. Cassidy, an Elint specialist who sailed on a later *Oxford* South American cruise. For microwave communications, which contain a great deal of telephone and other voice communications, the Elint operators used a piece of equipment called the RYCOM, which received the signal and then broke it into hundreds of channels. "We were intercepting South American military voice traffic," said Cassidy. "We would record on magnetic recorders."

In addition to receivers, a row of nearly a dozen printers constantly pounded out intercepted teletype messages. "If it started printing out five-number code groups, then we knew we had something," said Cassidy. "And if it was Cyrillic, which was really a good find, then we had linguists aboard that could read it. . . . If it was a frequency that nobody had noted before, and it was five-number code groups, that was a keeper. . . . We would save those and they would go back to NSA."

Another piece of equipment in the Elint spaces was so secret that it was hidden even from the captain, although not for national security reasons. Forbidden to have a TV on the ship, the intercept crew nevertheless rigged up a small one and attached it to one of the rotating intercept antennas. It was painted gray, and "Special Access" was written on it. "The captain came in for inspection and had no idea what it was," said Cassidy, a veteran of submarine espionage missions on the USS *Halfbeak*.

Upon leaving Buenos Aires on its first South American journey, the *Oxford* headed for another target on its list, a large atomic research station in Argentina's southern Patagonia region. However, according to Aubrey Brown, "the weather conditions were so bad we couldn't get into that position. We tried to do it for days, but we finally had to turn around and come back."

While off the coast, the intercept operators did pick up information that the president of Argentina had been overthrown. They whipped off a Flash message to NSA, but because of atmospheric conditions, instead of three to five minutes, it took hours to send. "By the time it got there I'm sure it was old news," said Brown. Although the ship had the moon-bounce dish, according to Brown it seldom worked. "The moon-bounce mission was more cover story than anything else," he said. "There were only one or two guys that were working on it. We may have used it once or twice. It was mostly cover story."

On the way north, more than fifty miles offshore, they ran into trouble. "At one point when we were off Argentina," said Brown, "we were pursued by an Argentine warship because we were not flying the flag. . . . So they couldn't identify us, didn't know what nationality. It was a relatively old Argentinean naval vessel, but it was a warship. It pursued us because it wanted to know what kind of ship we were. It was very unusual not to have colors. Nothing flying from the mast. So we ran from it. They pursued us but we were monitoring all the traffic to and from the ship, which was all Morse code. We finally outran them."

Another of the *Oxford*'s missions was to attempt to locate spies in South America who were thought to be communicating by ham radio. "So we set off on this fool's mission to monitor all the ham communications in Latin America for these spies who were communicating with each other on ham radio," said Brown. "And of course there was nothing there."

Finally the ship pulled into Rio de Janeiro. Brazil had great influence within Latin America and was another major NSA target. Key elections were scheduled for May and the CIA had spent truckloads of money to secretly influence the outcome. Using several phony front organizations, the CIA dumped some $12 million, and possibly as much as $20 million, on anticommunist candidates.

The eavesdroppers had good fortune. The Brazilian navy welcomed the NSA ship and put it in their naval area. Even better, the mooring they were assigned lay between two microwave links carrying sensitive Brazilian naval communications. According to Brown, the mooring "put the guys in the rear section, the Elint people, in direct line of all the Brazilian navy microwave communications. We copied everything we could when we pulled into port."

Passing through the Caribbean on their way back to the United States, the Sigint operators on the *Oxford* were often instructed by NSA to pay particular attention to communication links between Fort-de-

France, the capital of Martinique in the French West Indies, and Dakar, Senegal, in West Africa. For years Aimé Césaire, the Martinican writer and former Communist, had led an independence movement on the island. Along with Léopold Sédar Senghor, the president of Senegal, they were founders of the Négritude movement, which protested French colonial rule. "Every time we got it [the link] up they wanted copy from that," said George Cassidy. "It had something to do with the Soviets. They [the intercepted messages] were code groups."

Cassidy added, "A lot of times we would get messages from NSA or NSG [Naval Security Group] and they would say, 'Here's a list of frequencies, keep an eye on these things.' It was like going hunting. That was the mindset we were in. We were on the ship and we were hunting for these things and when we found them we felt pretty good."

Like South America, Africa was becoming "hearable" as a result of NSA's eavesdropping navy.

In its earliest days, NSA had planned for its fleet of spy ships to be small, slow, civilian-manned trawlers rather than the large floating listening posts such as the USS *Oxford*. The model was to be the Soviet trawler fleet that loitered off such places as the space launch center at Cape Canaveral and the large submarine base at Charleston, South Carolina. "I was called to Washington in the mid-fifties and asked could we monitor a Soviet Navy maneuver," recalled retired Navy Captain Phil H. Bucklew, who was involved in the Navy's Special Warfare program at the time. "They wanted me to rig a fishing boat with electronic equipment and operate it in the Caspian Sea at a time of the Soviet maneuvers and asked, 'Is it feasible?' I replied, 'I guess it's feasible; it's starting from scratch. I don't welcome the opportunity but I believe we would be the most capable source if you decide to do it.' I heard nothing more on that."

Instead of fishing trawlers with their limited space, the NSA chose to build its eavesdropping fleet with small and ancient cargo vessels. "I was probably the father of it at NSA," said Frank Raven, former chief of G Group, which was responsible for eavesdropping on the non-Communist world. "It was one of the first projects that I started when I got to

G Group. . . . What we wanted was a slow tub, that was civilian, that could mosey along a coast relatively slowly, take its time at sea."

The first to join the Sigint navy was the USNS *Valdez*, which at 350 feet long was considerably smaller and slower than the *Oxford*. In fact, its call sign was "Camel Driver." Run by the civilian Military Sea Transportation Service (MSTS) rather than the U.S. Navy, it was powered by a straight-drive, 1,750-horsepower Bush and Sulzer diesel engine, and had a six-foot screw with a six-foot pitch.

In December 1961, the *Valdez* sailed to Cape Town, South Africa, where it became NSA's *"African Queen."* By the time it arrived, antennas bristling from its deck and masts, it was a salty sailor. Built in 1944 at the Riverside Yard in Duluth, Minnesota, it had spent most of its life as a seagoing pickup truck, hugging coastlines as it transported barrels of nails one way and bales of cotton another. It was named after a Medal of Honor winner killed in action near Rosenkrantz, France, in the waning days of World War II.

"On her maiden voyage she picked up Chinese telemetry signals, a first," said Raven. From Cape Town, the ship also eavesdropped on Soviet missile tests. As listening posts in Turkey and Iran collected telemetry on the launch of ICBMs from Kapustin Yar, the *Valdez* would be in position in the South Atlantic. There it could easily pick up the signals from the missile as it headed for its target area southwest of what is now Namibia.

Shortly after the *Valdez* reached Cape Town, a second ship, the USNS *Lieutenant James E. Robinson*, also became operational. A third, the USNS *Sergeant Joseph E. Muller*, was still undergoing conversion. More ships were planned, but Navy officials objected, arguing that future NSA spy ships must be Navy vessels. "They complained very bitterly about the speed of the *Valdez*," said Frank Raven. "After all, it could make six knots if the wind were blowing right. . . . Well, if you had a crisis in the Pacific and your ship was in the Atlantic you couldn't get it there in time. This was the sort of argument."

As a result, NSA's navy switched from civilian *Valdez*-type ships to the U.S. Navy *Oxford*-type ships, a decision that Raven greatly objected to on the grounds that the civilian ships were far less conspicuous. "The *Valdez* was my dream ship," he said. "She was the damnedest tub. One of our stock jokes was that we had a bow wave painted on the thing—just so it would appear she was moving."

While the *Oxford* was to be NSA's ears along South America, the *Valdez* was to be its floating listening post along the coasts of Africa. It and its sister ships had the advantage of being little noticed as they bobbed like corks riding the tide along a coastline. At eight to ten knots, the coastal transports had exactly half the speed of the *Oxford*. They also cost about half a million dollars per year less to operate than the *Ox*. Also, being outside the Navy and run by civilian masters, the *Valdez*-type ships could cut through the cumbersome bureaucracy: they could operate at sea for longer periods, and overhauls could be performed in foreign ports rather than U.S. Navy facilities.

On the other hand, its speed allowed the *Oxford* to react more quickly when needed and also enabled it to conduct "shadow missions," following suspicious foreign ships. And the larger number of signals intelligence personnel, six officers and 110 enlisted men, versus 4 officers and 91 enlisted for the *Valdez*, enabled the *Oxford* to target and intercept more communications. "The bigger ships," said Marshall S. Carter, "could carry so much more equipment, so much more sophisticated equipment, so much better antennas."

Getting its reams of intercepts to headquarters was a major problem for NSA's *"African Queen."* As it eavesdropped along the East African coast, the ship would pull into ports and a crewmember, in civilian clothes, would hand-carry the pouches of intercepts to the nearest American embassy. The documents would then be flown back to NSA by diplomatic courier. But some ports, such as Mombasa, Kenya, were not near any American diplomatic facilities. A crewmember would have to fly with the material to Nairobi, where the closest American embassy was located. This greatly worried NSA: the crewmembers did not have diplomatic immunity, so the pouches could be opened or seized by customs officials, who would find copies of their own government's secret communications. "Revelation of some sensitive material could prove extremely embarrassing to the U.S.," said one NSA report that discussed the problem.

During the *Valdez*'s slow crawl up and down the long African coasts, French, Portuguese, Spanish, and Russian linguists eavesdropped on a continent in chaos, tearing itself away from its old colonial bosses only to come under the violent domination of new Cold War masters. In the waves and swells of the Indian Ocean off Tanzania, intercept operators carefully twisted their dials hoping to pick up communications between Dar es Salaam and Havana. In April 1965, the Cuban revolutionary leader Che Guevara, wearing an olive-green beret and smoking a cigar, quietly arrived in the Congo with a force of Cuban guerrilla fighters. They saw the struggle by supporters of the murdered Patrice Lumumba against Joseph-Désiré Mobutu and his American and Belgian backers as a continuation of a worldwide revolution against imperialism. They came to lend their support and expertise in guerrilla warfare.

The intercept operators knew that Dar es Salaam was serving as a communications center for the fighters, receiving messages from Castro in Cuba and relaying them on to the guerrillas deep in the bush. Guevara transmitted his progress reports and requests for supplies back through that same channel. Every day at 8:00 A.M., 2:30 P.M., and 7:00 P.M., one of Guevara's radio operators would also make contact with the jungle base at Kigoma.

But Guevara knew the dangers posed by sloppy and too-frequent use of radios. "It seems excessive to me," he cautioned one of his fighters, "to communicate three times a day with the other side and twice a day with Dar es Salaam. Soon you won't have anything to say, the gasoline will be used up and codes can always be broken. This is without considering that planes can locate the base. Apart from the technical conditions, I recommend that you analyze the possibility of having normal daily communication with Kigoma at a set time once a day for extraordinary news and once every two or three days with Dar es Salaam. That will allow us to save gasoline. They should be at night, and the radio should be protected against an air attack. I think your idea of the shortwave is a good one, with simple codes that are changed frequently."

Despite his caution, the signals to and from Che Guevara were easy pickings for the *Valdez*.

The *Valdez*, one small ship monitoring an enormous continent, was later joined by the USS *Liberty*, a large floating listening post like the *Oxford*. A veteran of World War II like the *Valdez*, the *Liberty* had also served honorably during the Korean War, making the lonely transit across the Pacific eighteen times to bring supplies to American forces fighting there. Worn, its hull streaked with rust, the ship was finally retired to a naval boneyard in 1958, but five years later it was recalled to active duty for service in the Cold War and fitted with four .50-caliber machine guns—two forward and two aft. Its next war would prove to be the most deadly of all.

As the *Valdez* crawled up the east coast of Africa, *Liberty* moseyed down the west coast, its forty-five antennas tuned in to a continent convulsing. Cruising slowly in calm seas near the entrance to the Congo River, intercept operators kept an eye on the endless trail of debris washing into the ocean. "Those of us aboard *Liberty* waited to see if any bodies surfaced," said one crewmember; "loss of life was an everyday occurrence." But separated from the deadly shoreline by a dozen miles of ocean, the sailors on the spy ship felt relatively safe. Suddenly, however, that all changed.

As he did every morning, Bobby Ringe went to the mess hall, quickly downed his breakfast, and then went topside for a few minutes of fresh air and sun before lining up for muster. Within a few hours, however, he was doubled over in excruciating pain. The ship's doctor determined that Ringe had appendicitis and needed immediate surgery. But before the operation, Ringe needed to be anesthetized and the only means available was the administration of a spinal tap, a procedure familiar to the doctor and his corpsman. As the anesthesia began to flow from the syringe, however, Ringe began violent convolutions. Without anesthetic an operation was out of the question.

After some quick messages between the *Liberty* and the headquarters for the Atlantic fleet, it was determined that there was only one way to save Ringe's life. He had to be transported to Brazzaville, capital of the Republic of the Congo (not to be confused with Mobutu's similarly named Congo), where a U.S. Navy plane would be waiting to fly him to a hospital in Tripoli, Libya. But this meant a dangerous cruise up the Congo River, deep into the violent madness they were eavesdropping on: a forbidden voyage for a ship full of spies.

Commander Daniel T. Wieland, the captain of the *Liberty*, turned his ship toward the wide mouth of the Congo—"an immense snake uncoiled," wrote Joseph Conrad, "with its head in the sea . . . and its tail lost in the depths of the land." Although his charts of the river were very old and out-of-date, Wieland gambled that if he held the ship close to the center of the waterway he would not run aground. As the broad Atlantic disappeared behind, the verdant coastline closed in ahead, like a pair of green pincers. Life slowly began materializing from every direction as the poky gray ship, like an awkward tourist, disappeared into the heart of Africa. Dozens of pirogues, huge hollowed-out hardwood trees, bobbed and weaved in the current. Aboard larger, flat-bottom boats, traders offered such goods as tortoises, bats, and baskets of caterpillars. In the distance was a "pusher," a double-decker boat pushing half a dozen barges teeming with humanity, a floating city of perhaps five thousand people. The pusher was on its way to Stanleyville, twelve hundred winding miles into the jungle.

It was night by the time the *Liberty* reached Brazzaville. Captain Wieland cut his engines and allowed the river's strong current to bring her to a stop. The anchor was dropped and crewmen quickly swung the emergency ladder into place. Ringe was carefully lowered into a boat that took him to shore and the waiting aircraft.

As the excitement died down, the crew quickly became aware that this was not going to be a simple mooring. Gathering around the aft of the ship was a growing number of small boats and barges. Soon the flotilla became a blockade. Across the river from Brazzaville was Léopoldville, capital of the other Congo, Mobutu's Congo. For years Brazzaville had served as home to a number of rebel factions fighting against the Léopoldville government. The fleet of boats had been sent from Léopoldville accompanied with a demand for an inspection visit in the morning. Officials worried that the ship was secretly supplying arms for guerrilla fighters in Brazzaville.

To allow representatives of one of the ship's eavesdropping targets to come aboard for an inspection was unthinkable, but there was little they could do about it. Everywhere there were copies of secret intercepted messages and tapes, perhaps even containing the words and voices of some of those on the inspection party. Encrypted, high-priority messages were sped to the director of NSA and Atlantic Fleet Headquarters in Norfolk, Virginia. While the Navy responded with a message saying they had no objection to the inspection, NSA became apoplectic. "DIRNSA [Director, NSA] responded saying there was no way an inspection team would board *Liberty*," said Robert Casale, one of the enlisted cryptologists on board.

An escape plan was quickly devised. Curtains were drawn, all unnecessary lights were turned off, noise was kept to a minimum, and topside activity was completely halted. "The ship, for all intents and purposes," said Casale, "visibly disappeared." At 11:00 P.M., the ship's winch slowly began raising the anchor. The idea was to allow the Congo River's strong current to turn the ship away from the land and downriver. As the anchor pulled free and the ship began to turn, moans and creaks could be heard from the old hull. When the bow was pointing downriver, the engines were started, the gears shifted to forward, and the ship began vibrating fore and aft. The *Liberty* lurched ahead and began picking up speed, ramming the fragile boats and sending Congolese men and women tumbling into the dark, dangerous river. "There was an enormous sound of disintegrating wood and other sounds that we never heard before," recalled Casale. "We could only imagine the boats and barges blockading us being destroyed by the *Liberty*'s bow as she sought the sanctuary of the Atlantic Ocean."

When word finally passed that the *Liberty* had cleared Congolese waters and had made it to the open ocean, a cheer resounded throughout the ship. "We had chanced fate and were successful," said Casale.

CHAPTER SEVEN

BLOOD

CYASJA EJLKBJ OJYAOJ TLAAXHYF TYHVXKLBXUJN LCKJA HKLEEXFO
MWCVSXRPESXA VWAS ABSPR, VSB WDBMPUE MWFV AVCO PFPI
NLIHRB DVQQHNR KDGQHYGRI KVIHR LHIGQ LWGLWRJN NQ KDHEDHIJ
CLDLNWDSI ADLDF BKLCLEYI UGCIPKE ISFJYFN BDF GKLAC PFKUU
IFIZHIVSK SZIBC ZIQIUCIP UMOIZ VIB KIUZ'C MIUZC MERRQI

For four years NSA's *"African Queen"* lumbered inconspicuously up and down the wild and troubled East African coast with the speed of an old sea turtle. By the spring of 1967, the tropical waters had so encrusted her bottom with sea life that her top speed was down to between three and five knots. With Che Guevara long since gone back to Cuba, NSA's G Group, responsible for the non-Communist portion of the planet, decided to finally relieve the *Valdez* and send her back to Norfolk, where she could be beached and scraped.

It was also decided to take maximum advantage of the situation by bringing the ship home through the Suez Canal, mapping and charting the radio spectrum as she crawled slowly past the Middle East and the eastern Mediterranean. "Now, frankly," recalled Frank Raven, former chief of G Group, "we didn't think at that point that it was highly desirable to have a ship right in the Middle East; it would be too explosive a situation. But the *Valdez,* obviously coming home with a foul bottom and pulling no bones about it and being a civilian ship, could get away with it." It took the ship about six weeks to come up through the canal and limp down the North African coast past Israel, Egypt, and Libya.

About that same time, the *Valdez*'s African partner, the USS *Liberty,* was arriving off West Africa, following a stormy Atlantic crossing, for the start of its fifth patrol. Navy Commander William L. McGonagle, its newest captain, ordered the speed reduced to four knots, the lowest speed at which the *Liberty* could easily answer its rudder, and the ship began its slow crawl south. On May 22, the *Liberty* pulled into Abidjan, capital of the Ivory Coast, for a four-day port call.

Half the earth away, behind cipher-locked doors at NSA, the talk was not of possible African coups but of potential Middle East wars. The indications had been growing for weeks, like swells before a storm. On the Israeli-Syrian border, what started out as potshots at tractors had quickly escalated to cannon fire between tanks. On May 17, Egypt (then known as the United Arab Republic [UAR]) evicted UN peacekeepers and then moved troops to its Sinai border with Israel. A few days later, Israeli tanks were reported on the Sinai frontier, and the following day Egypt ordered mobilization of 100,000 armed reserves. On May 23, Gamal Abdel Nasser blockaded the Strait of Tiran, thereby closing the Gulf of Aqaba to Israeli shipping and prohibiting unescorted tankers under any flag from reaching the Israeli port of Elat. The Israelis declared the action "an act of aggression against Israel" and began a full-scale mobilization.

As NSA's ears strained for information, Israeli officials began arriving in Washington. Nasser, they said, was about to launch a lopsided war against them and they needed American support. It was a lie. In fact, as Menachem Begin admitted years later, it was Israel that was planning a first strike attack on Egypt. "We . . . had a choice," Begin said in 1982, when he was Israel's prime minister. "The Egyptian army concentrations in the Sinai approaches do not prove that Nasser was really about to attack us. We must be honest with ourselves. We decided to attack him."

Had Israel brought the United States into a first-strike war against Egypt and the Arab world, the results might have been calamitous. The USSR would almost certainly have gone to the defense of its Arab friends, leading to a direct battlefield confrontation between U.S. and Soviet forces. Such a dangerous prospect could have touched off a nuclear war.

With the growing possibility of U.S. involvement in a Middle East war, the Joint Chiefs of Staff needed rapid intelligence on the ground situation in Egypt. Above all, they wanted to know how many Soviet troops, if any, were currently in Egypt and what kinds of weapons they had. Also, if U.S. fighter planes were to enter the conflict, it was essential to pinpoint the locations of surface-to-air missile batteries. If troops went in, it would be vital to know the locations and strength of opposing forces.

Under the gun to provide answers, officials at NSA considered their options. Land-based stations, like the one in Cyprus, were too far away to collect the narrow line-of-sight signals used by air defense radar, fire control radar, microwave communications, and other targets.

Airborne Sigint platforms—Air Force C-130s and Navy EC-121s—could collect some of this. But after allowing for time to and from the "orbit areas," the aircrews would only have about five hours on station—too short a time for the sustained collection that was required. Adding aircraft was also an option but finding extra signals intelligence planes would be very difficult. Also, downtime and maintenance on those aircraft was greater than for any other kind of platform.

Finally there were the ships, which was the best option. Because they could sail relatively close, they could pick up the most important signals. Also, unlike the aircraft, they could remain on station for weeks at a time, eavesdropping, locating transmitters, and analyzing the intelligence. At the time, the USS *Oxford* and *Jamestown* were in Southeast Asia; the USS *Georgetown* and *Belmont* were eavesdropping off South America; and the USNS *Muller* was monitoring signals off Cuba. That left the USNS *Valdez* and the USS *Liberty*. The *Valdez* had just completed a long mission and was near Gibraltar on its way back to the United States. On the other hand, the *Liberty*, which was larger and faster, had just begun a new mission and was relatively close, in port in Abidjan.

Several months before, seeing the swells forming, NSA's G Group had drawn up a contingency plan. It would position the *Liberty* in the area of "L0L0" (longitude 0, latitude 0) in Africa's Gulf of Guinea, concentrating on targets in that area, but actually positioning her far enough north that she could make a dash for the Middle East should the need arise. Despite the advantages, not everyone agreed on the plan. Frank Raven, the G Group chief, argued that it was too risky. "The ship will be defenseless out there," he insisted. "If war breaks out, she'll be alone and vulnerable. Either side might start shooting at her. . . . I say the ship should be left where it is." But he was overruled.

On May 23, having decided to send the *Liberty* to the Middle East, G Group officials notified John Connell, NSA's man at the Joint Reconnaissance Center. A unit within the Joint Chiefs of Staff, the JRC was responsible for coordinating air, sea, and undersea reconnaissance operations. At 8:20 that spring evening, amid the noisy clatter of teletype machines, a technician tapped out a brief Flash message to the *Liberty:*

> MAKE IMMEDIATE PREPARATIONS TO GET UNDERWAY. WHEN READY FOR SEA ASAP DEPART PORT ABIDJAN AND PROCEED BEST POSSIBLE SPEED TO ROTA SPAIN TO LOAD TECHNICAL SUPPORT MATERIAL AND SUPPLIES. WHEN READY FOR SEA PROCEED TO OPERATING AREA OFF PORT SAID. SPECIFIC AREAS WILL FOLLOW.

In the coal-black Ivoirian night, an island of light lit up the end of the long wooden pier where the USS *Liberty* lay docked. Beyond, in the harbor, small dots of red and green blinked like Christmas-tree lights as hulking cargo ships slowly twisted with the gentle tide.

It was around 3:45 A.M. when Lieutenant Jim O'Connor woke to a knock on his stateroom door. The duty officer squinted as he read the message in the red glow of an emergency light. Still half asleep, he mumbled a curse and quickly threw on his trousers. "It was a message from the Joint Chiefs of Staff," O'Connor recalled telling his cabinmate. "Whoever heard of JCS taking direct control of a ship?" Within minutes reveille sounded and the *Liberty* began to shudder to life. Less than three hours later, the modern skyline of Abidjan disappeared over the stern as the ship departed Africa for the last time. Silhouetted against the rising sun was the large moon-bounce antenna on the rear deck, pointing straight up as if praying.

For eight days, at top speed, the bow cut a silvery path through 3,000 miles of choppy Atlantic Ocean. The need for linguists was especially critical on the *Liberty*, which, because of her West African targets, carried only French and Portuguese language experts. Therefore, five Arabic linguists—two enlisted Marines and three NSA civilians—were ordered to Rota to rendezvous with the *Liberty*. Although the ship already had numerous Russian linguists, it was also decided to add one more, a senior analytical specialist.

NSA had originally wanted to also put Hebrew linguists on the ship, but the agency just didn't have enough. "I mean, my God," said

Frank Raven, "you're manning a crisis; where are you going to get these linguists from? You go out and ask the nearest synagogue? We got together every linguist we could manage and we not only sent them to Rota but then we have to back up every military station in the Middle East—we're sending them into Athens, we're sending them into Turkey—by God, if you can speak Arabic and you're in NSA you're on a plane!"

As the *Liberty* steamed northward, Marine Sergeant Bryce Lockwood was strapped in a signals intelligence plane flying 30,000 feet above the frigid Norwegian Sea off Iceland. Lockwood was an experienced signals intelligence intercept operator and Russian linguist; he and his crewmembers were shadowing the Russian Northern Fleet as it conducted summer war games. But the ferret operation had been plagued with problems. A number of the missions had been canceled as a result of aircraft equipment failures and the one Lockwood was on intercepted only about three minutes of Russian voice, which was so garbled that no one could understand it.

During the operation, Lockwood was temporarily assigned to the U.S. Navy air base at Keflavík, Iceland. But as the Russian exercise came to an end, he headed back to his home base, the sprawling Navy listening post at Bremerhaven, where he specialized in analyzing intercepted Russian communications. The plane flew first to Rota, where he was to catch another military flight back to Germany. However, because it was the Memorial Day weekend, few U.S. military flights were taking off; he was forced to spend the night. That afternoon Lockwood went to a picnic, had a few beers, and then went to bed early in his quarters.

About 2:00 A.M. he was suddenly woken up by some loud pounding on his door. Assuming it was just a few of his fellow Marines wanting to party, he pulled the cover over his head and ignored it. But the banging only got louder. Now angry, Lockwood finally threw open the door. Standing in front of him in the dim light was a sailor from the duty office. "I have a message with your name on it from the Joint Chiefs of Staff," he said somewhat quizzically. "You're assigned to join the USS *Liberty* at 0600 hours. You better get up and pack your seabag." It was a highly unusual order, a personal message from the JCS at two in the morning; Lockwood had little time to ponder it.

It was just an hour or so after dawn on the first of June when the *Liberty* slid alongside a pier in Rota. Already waiting for them were Lockwood and the five Arabic linguists. A short time later, thick black hoses, like boa constrictors, disgorged 380,000 gallons of fuel into the ship's tanks while perspiring sailors in dungarees struggled to load crates of vegetables and other food. Several technicians also retrieved boxes of double-wrapped packages and brought them aboard. The packages contained supersensitive signals intelligence data left for them by the *Valdez* as she passed through Rota on the way back to Norfolk. Included were critical details on Middle East communication patterns picked up as the *Valdez* transited the area: "who was communicating on what links—Teletype, telephone, microwave, you name it," said Raven.

As she steamed west across the Mediterranean to Rota, the *Valdez* had also conducted "hearability studies" for NSA in order to help determine the best places from which to eavesdrop. Off the eastern end of Crete, the *Valdez* discovered what amounted to a "duct" in the air, a sort of aural pipeline that led straight to the Middle East. "You can sit in Crete and watch the Cairo television shows," said Raven. "If you're over flat water, basically calm water, the communications are wonderful." He decided to park the *Liberty* there.

But the Joint Chiefs of Staff had other ideas. In Rota, Commander McGonagle received orders to deploy just off the coasts of Israel and Egypt but not to approach closer than twelve and a half nautical miles to Egypt or six and a half to Israel. Following some repairs to the troublesome dish antenna, the *Liberty* cast off from Rota just after noon on June 2.

Sailing at seventeen knots, its top speed, the *Liberty* overtook and passed three Soviet ships during its transit of the Strait of Gibraltar. From there it followed the North African coastline, keeping at least thirteen miles from shore. Three days after departing Rota, on June 5, as the *Liberty* was passing south of Sicily, Israel began its long-planned strike against its neighbors and the Arab-Israeli war began.

On June 5, 1967, at 7:45 A.M. Sinai time (1:45 A.M. in Washington, D.C.), Israel launched virtually its entire air force against Egyptian airfields, destroying, within eighty minutes, the majority of Egypt's air power. On the ground, tanks pushed out in three directions across the Sinai toward the Suez Canal. Fighting was also initiated along the Jordanian and Syrian borders. Simultaneously, Israeli officials put out false reports to the press saying that Egypt had launched a major attack against them and that they were defending themselves.

In Washington, June 4 had been a balmy Sunday. President Johnson's national security adviser, Walt Rostow, even stayed home from the office and turned off his bedroom light at 11:00 P.M. But he turned it back on at 2:50 A.M. when the phone rang, a little over an hour after Israel launched its attack. "We have an FBIS [Foreign Broadcast Information Service] report that the UAR has launched an attack on Israel," said a husky male voice from the White House Situation Room. "Go to your intelligence sources and call me back," barked Rostow. Ten minutes later, presumably after checking with NSA and other agencies, the aide called back and confirmed the press story. "Okay, I'm coming in," Rostow said, and then asked for a White House car to pick him up.

As the black Mercury quickly maneuvered through Washington's empty streets, Rostow ticked off in his mind the order in which he needed answers. At the top of the list was discovering exactly how the war had started. A few notches down was deciding when to wake the president.

The car pulled into the Pennsylvania Avenue gate at 3:25 and Rostow was quickly on the phone with Secretary of State Dean Rusk, who was still at home. "I assume you've received the Flash," he said. They agreed that, if the facts were as grim as reported, Johnson should be awakened in about an hour. Intelligence reports quickly began arriving indicating that a number of Arab airfields appeared to be inoperative and the Israelis were pushing hard and fast against the Egyptian air force.

Sitting at the mahogany conference table in the Situation Room, a map of Vietnam on the wall, Rostow picked up a phone. "I want to get through to the President," he said. "I wish him to be awakened." Three stories above, Lyndon Johnson picked up the phone next to his carved wood bedstead. "Yes," he said.

"Mr. President, I have the following to report." Rostow got right to business. "We have information that Israel and the UAR are at war." For the next seven minutes, the national security adviser gave Johnson the shorthand version of what the United States then knew.

About the same time in Tel Aviv, Foreign Minister Abba Eban summoned U.S. Ambassador Walworth Barbour to a meeting in his office. Building an ever larger curtain of lies around Israel's true activities and intentions, Eban accused Egypt of starting the war. Barbour quickly sent a secret Flash message back to Washington. "Early this morning," he quoted Eban, "Israelis observed Egyptian units moving in large numbers toward Israel and in fact considerable force penetrated Israeli territory and clashed with Israeli ground forces. Consequently, GOI [Government of Israel] gave order to attack." Eban told Barbour that his government intended to protest Egypt's action to the UN Security Council. "Israel is [the] victim of Nasser's aggression," he said.

Eban then went on to lie about Israel's goals, which all along had been to capture as much territory as possible. "GOI has no rpt [repeat] no intention taking advantage of situation to enlarge its territory. That hopes peace can be restored within present boundaries." Finally, after half an hour of deception, Eban brazenly asked the United States to go up against the USSR on Israel's behalf. Israel, Barbour reported, "asks our help in restraining any Soviet initiative." The message was received at the White House at two minutes before six in the morning.

About two hours later, in a windowless office next to the War Room in the Pentagon, a bell rang five or six times, bringing everyone to quick attention. A bulky gray Russian Teletype suddenly sprang to life and keys began pounding out rows of Cyrillic letters at sixty-six words a minute onto a long white roll of paper. For the first time, an actual on-line encrypted message was stuttering off the Moscow-to-Washington hot line. As it was printing, a "presidential translator"—a military officer expert in Russian—stood over the machine and dictated a simultaneous rough translation to a Teletype operator. He in turn sent the message to the State Department, where another translator joined in working on a translation on which both U.S. experts agreed.

The machine was linked to similar equipment in a room in the Kremlin, not far from the office of the chairman of the Council of Ministers of the USSR. Known formally as the Washington–Moscow Emergency Communications Link (and in Moscow as the Molink), the hot line was activated at 6:30 P.M. on August 30, 1963, largely as a result of the Cuban missile crisis.

The message that June morning in 1967 was from Premier Alexei Kosygin. The Pentagon and State Department translators agreed on the translation:

> Dear Mr. President,
> Having received information concerning the military clashes between Israel and the United Arab Republic, the Soviet Government is convinced that the duty of all great powers is to secure the immediate cessation of the military conflict.
>
> The Soviet Government has acted and will act in this direction. We hope that the Government of the United States will also act in the same manner and will exert appropriate influence on the Government of Israel particularly since you have all opportunities of doing so. This is required in the highest interest of peace.
>
> Respectfully,
> A. Kosygin

Once the presidential translator finished the translation, he rushed it over to the general in charge of the War Room, who immediately called Secretary of Defense Robert S. McNamara several floors above. McNamara had arrived in his office about an hour earlier. "Premier Kosygin is on the hot line and asks to speak to the president," the War Room general barked. "What should I tell him?"

"Why are you calling me?" McNamara asked.

"Because the hot line ends in the Pentagon," the general huffed. (McNamara later admitted that he had had no idea that the connection ended a short distance away from him.) "Patch the circuit over to the White House Situation Room, and I'll call the president," McNamara ordered.

McNamara, not having been in on the early morning White House calls, assumed Johnson would still be sleeping, but he put the call through anyway. A sergeant posted outside the presidential bedroom picked up the phone. "The president is asleep and doesn't like to be awakened," he told the Pentagon chief, not realizing that Johnson had been awake since 4:30 A.M. discussing the crisis. "I know that, but wake him up," McNamara insisted.

"Mr. President," McNamara said, "the hot line is up and Kosygin wants to speak to you. What should we say?"

"My God," Johnson replied, apparently perplexed, "what should we say?" McNamara offered an idea: "I suggest I tell him you will be in the Situation Room in fifteen minutes. In the meantime, I'll call Dean and we'll meet you there." Within half an hour, an American-supplied Teletype was cranking out English letters in the Kremlin. Johnson told Kosygin that the United States did not intend to intervene in the conflict. About a dozen more hot-line messages followed over the next few weeks.

As the first shots of the war were being fired across the desert wasteland, NSA had a box seat. A fat Air Force C-130 airborne listening post was over the eastern Mediterranean flying a figure-eight pattern off Israel and Egypt. Later the plane landed back at its base, the Greek air force section of Athens International Airport, with nearly complete coverage of the first hours of the war.

From the plane, the intercept tapes were rushed to the processing center, designated USA-512J by NSA. Set up the year before by the U.S. Air Force Security Service, NSA's air arm, it was to process intercepts—analyzing the data and attacking lower-level ciphers—produced by Air Force eavesdropping missions throughout the Mediterranean, North Africa, and the Middle East. Unfortunately, they were not able to listen to the tapes of the war immediately because they had no Hebrew linguists. However, an NSA Hebrew linguist support team was at that moment winging its way to Athens. (To hide their mission and avoid the implication of spying on Israel, Hebrew linguists were always referred to as "special Arabic" linguists, even within NSA.)

Soon after the first CRITIC message arrived at NSA, an emergency notification was sent to the U.S. Navy's listening post at Rota. The base was the Navy's major launching site for airborne eavesdropping missions over the Mediterranean area. There the Navy's airborne Sigint unit, VQ-2, operated large four-engine aircraft that resembled the civilian passenger plane known as the Constellation, an aircraft with graceful, curving lines and a large three-section tail. Nicknamed the Willy Victor, the EC-121M was slow, lumbering, and ideal for eavesdropping—capable of long, twelve- to eighteen-hour missions, depending on such factors as weather, fuel, altitude, intercept activity, and crew fatigue.

Within several hours of the tasking message, the EC-121 was airborne en route to Athens, from where the missions would be staged. A few days before, a temporary Navy signals intelligence processing center had been secretly set up at the Athens airport near the larger U.S. Air Force Sigint facility. There, intercepts from the missions were to be analyzed and the ciphers attacked.

After landing, the intercept operators were bused to the Hotel Seville in Iraklion near the Athens airport. The Seville was managed by a friendly Australian and a Greek named Zina; the crew liked the fact that the kitchen and bar never closed. But they had barely reached the lobby of the hotel when they received word they were to get airborne as soon as possible. "We were in disbelief and mystified," said one member of the crew. "Surely, our taskers did not expect us to fly into the combat zone in the dead of the night!" That was exactly what they expected.

A few hours later, the EC-121 was heading east into the dark night sky. Normally the flight took about two or three hours. Once over the eastern Mediterranean, they would maintain a dogleg track about twenty-five to fifty miles off the Israeli and Egyptian coasts at an altitude of between 12,000 and 18,000 feet. The pattern would take them from an area northeast of Alexandria, Egypt, east toward Port Said and the Sinai to the El Arish area, and then dogleg northeast along the Israeli coast to a point west of Beirut, Lebanon. The track would then be repeated continuously. Another signals intelligence plane, the EA3B, could fly considerably higher, above 30,000 to 35,000 feet.

On board the EC-121 that night was Navy Chief Petty Officer Marvin E. Nowicki, who had the unusual qualification of being a Hebrew and Russian linguist. "I vividly recall this night being pitch black, no stars, no moon, no nothing," he said. "The mission commander considered the precariousness of our flight. He thought it more prudent to avoid the usual track. If we headed east off the coast of Egypt toward

Israel, we would look, on radar, to the Israelis like an incoming attack aircraft from Egypt. Then, assuming the Israelis did not attack us, when we reversed course, we would then appear on Egyptian radar like Israeli attack aircraft inbound. It, indeed, was a very dangerous and precarious situation."

Instead, the mission commander decided to fly between Crete and Cyprus and then head diagonally toward El Arish in the Sinai along an established civilian air corridor. Upon reaching a point some twenty-five miles northeast of El Arish, he would reverse course and begin their orbit.

"When we arrived on station after midnight, needless to say the 'pucker factor' was high," recalled Nowicki; "the crew was on high, nervous alert. Nobody slept in the relief bunks on that flight. The night remained pitch black. What in the devil were we doing out here in the middle of a war zone, was a question I asked myself several times over and over during the flight. The adrenaline flowed."

In the small hours of the morning, intercept activity was light. "The Israelis were home rearming and reloading for the next day's attacks, while the Arabs were bracing themselves for the next onslaught come daylight and contemplating some kind of counterattack," said Nowicki. "Eerily, our Comint and Elint positions were quiet." But that changed as the early-morning sun lit up the battlefields. "Our receivers came alive with signals mostly from the Israelis as they began their second day of attacks," Nowicki remembered. Around him, Hebrew linguists were furiously "gisting"—summarizing—the conversations between Israeli pilots, while other crew members attempted to combine that information with signals from airborne radar obtained through electronic intelligence.

From their lofty perch, they eavesdropped like electronic voyeurs. The NSA recorders whirred as the Egyptians launched an abortive air attack on an advancing Israeli armored brigade in the northern Sinai, only to have their planes shot out of the air by Israeli delta-wing Mirage aircraft. At one point Nowicki listened to his first midair shootdown as an Egyptian Sukhoi-7 aircraft was blasted from the sky. "We monitored as much as we could but soon had to head for Athens because of low fuel," he said. "We were glad to get the heck out of there."

As they headed back, an Air Force C-130 flying listening post was heading out to relieve them.

Down below, in the Mediterranean, the *Liberty* continued its slow journey toward the war zone as the crew engaged in constant general quarters drills and listened carefully for indications of danger. The Navy sent out a warning notice to all ships and aircraft in the area to keep at least 100 nautical miles away from the coasts of Lebanon, Syria, Israel, and Egypt. But the *Liberty* was on an espionage mission; unless specifically ordered to change course, Commander McGonagle would continue steaming full speed ahead. Meanwhile, the Soviet navy had mobilized their fleet. Some twenty Soviet warships with supporting vessels and an estimated eight or nine submarines sailed toward the same flashpoint.

On hearing that war had started, Gene Sheck, an official in NSA's K Group section, which was responsible for managing the various mobile collection platforms, became increasingly worried about the *Liberty*. Responsibility for the safety of the ship, however, had been taken out of NSA's hands by the JCS and given to the Joint Reconnaissance Center. Nevertheless, Sheck took it upon himself to remind NSA's representative at the JRC, John Connell, that during the Cuban missile crisis five years earlier, the *Oxford* had been pulled back from the Havana area. Then he asked if any consideration was being given to doing the same for the *Liberty*. Connell spoke to the ship movement officer at the JRC but they refused to take any action.

Although analysts in K Group knew of the *Liberty*'s plight, those in G Group did not. Thus it was not until the morning of June 7 that an analyst rushed into Frank Raven's office and asked incredulously, "For God's sake, do you know where the *Liberty* is?" Raven, believing she was sitting off the east end of Crete as originally planned, had barely begun to answer when the analyst blurted out, "They've got her heading straight for the beach!" By then the *Liberty* was only about ten hours from her scheduled patrol area, a dozen miles off Egypt's Sinai Desert.

"At this point," recalled Raven, "I ordered a major complaint [protest] to get the *Liberty* the hell out of there! As far as we [NSA] were concerned, there was nothing to be gained by having her in there that close, nothing she could do in there that she couldn't do where we wanted her. . . . She could do everything that the national requirement called for [from the coast of Crete]. Somebody wanted to listen to some close tactical program or some communications or something which nobody in the world gave a damn about—local military base, local commander. We were listening for the higher echelons. . . . Hell, you don't want to hear them move the tugboats around and such, you want to know what the commanding generals are saying."

The JRC began reevaluating the *Liberty*'s safety as the warnings mounted. The Egyptians began sending out ominous protests complaining that U.S. personnel were secretly communicating with Israel and were possibly providing military assistance. Egypt also charged that U.S. aircraft had participated in the Israeli air strikes. The charges greatly worried American officials, who feared that the announcements might provoke a Soviet reaction. Then the Chief of Naval Operations questioned the wisdom of the *Liberty* assignment.

As a result of these new concerns, the JRC sent out a message indicating that the *Liberty*'s operational area off the Sinai was not set in stone but was "for guidance only." Also, it pulled the ship back from 12½ to 20 nautical miles from the coast. By now it was about 6:30 P.M. in Washington, half past midnight on the morning of June 8 in Egypt. The *Liberty* had already entered the outskirts of its operational area and the message never reached her because of an error by the U.S. Army Communications Center at the Pentagon.

About an hour later, with fears mounting, the JRC again changed the order, now requiring that *Liberty* approach no closer than 100 miles to the coasts of Egypt and Israel. Knowing the ship was getting dangerously close, Major Breedlove in the JRC skipped the normal slow message system and called Navy officials in Europe over a secure telephone to tell them of the change. He said a confirming message would follow. Within ten minutes the Navy lieutenant in Europe had a warning message ready.

But rather than issue the warning, a Navy captain in Europe insisted on waiting until he received the confirmation message. That and a series of Keystone Kops foul-ups by both the Navy and Army—which again misrouted the message, this time to *Hawaii*—delayed sending the critical message for an incredible sixteen and a half hours. By then it was far too late. More than twenty years had gone by since the foul-up of warning messages at the time of the attack on Pearl Harbor, yet it was as if no lesson had ever been learned.

At 5:14 A.M. on Thursday, June 8, the first rays of sun spilled softly over the Sinai's blond waves of sand. A little more than a dozen miles north, in the choppy eastern Mediterranean, the *Liberty* continued eastward like a lost innocent, 600 miles from the nearest help and oblivious to at least five warning messages it never received. The "Plan of the Day" distributed throughout the ship that morning gave no hint of what was in store. "Uniform of the Day" for officers was "tropical wash khaki" and, for enlisted men, "clean dungarees." The soda fountain, crewmembers were informed, would be open from 6:00 P.M. until 7:30 P.M.

Just after sunup, Duty Officer John Scott noticed a flying boxcar making several circles near the ship and then departing in the direction of Tel Aviv. Down in the NSA spaces, Chief Melvin Smith apparently also picked up signals from the plane, later identified as Israeli. Shortly after the plane departed, he called up Scott and asked if he had had a close air contact recently. Scott told him he had, and Smith asked which direction it had gone in. "Tel Aviv," said Scott. "Fine, that's all I want to know," replied Smith. Scott glanced up at the American flag, ruffling in a twelve-knot breeze, to check the wind direction, and then scanned the vast desert a little more than a dozen miles away. "Fabulous morning," he said without dropping the stubby binoculars from his eyes.

But the calmness was like quicksand—deceptive, inviting, and friendly, until too late. As the *Liberty* passed the desert town of El Arish, it was closely watched. About half a mile away and 4,000 feet above was an Israeli reconnaissance aircraft. At 6:03 A.M. the naval observer on the plane reported back to Israeli naval headquarters. "What we could see was the letters written on that ship," he said. "And we gave these letters to the ground control." The letters were "GTR-5," the *Liberty*'s identification. "GTR" stood for "General Technical Research"—a cover designation for NSA's fleet of spy ships.

Having passed El Arish, the *Liberty* continued on toward the Gaza Strip. Then, about 8:30 A.M., it made a strange, nearly 180-degree turn back in the direction of El Arish and slowed down to just five knots. The reason for this maneuver was that the ship had at last reached Point Alpha, the point on the map where it was to begin its back-and-forth dogleg patrol of the Sinai coast.

For some time, Commander McGonagle had been worried about the ship's proximity to the shore and about the potential for danger. He called to his cabin Lieutenant Commander David E. Lewis, head of the NSA operation on the ship. "How would it affect our mission if we stayed farther out at sea?" McGonagle asked. "It would hurt us, Captain," Lewis replied. "We want to work in the UFH [ultra-high-frequency] range. That's mostly line-of-sight stuff. If we're over the horizon we might as well be back in Abidjan. It would degrade our mission by about eighty percent." After thinking for a few minutes, McGonagle made his decision. "Okay," he said. "We'll go all the way in."

The reconnaissance was repeated at approximately thirty-minute intervals throughout the morning. At one point, a boxy Israeli air force Noratlas NORD 2501 circled the ship around the starboard side, proceeded forward of the ship, and headed back toward the Sinai. "It had a big Star of David on it and it was flying just a little bit above our mast on the ship," recalled crewmember Larry Weaver. "We really thought his wing was actually going to clip one of our masts. . . . And I was actually able to wave to the co-pilot, a fellow on the right-hand side of the plane. He waved back, and actually smiled at me. I could see him that well. I didn't think anything of that because they were our allies. There's no question about it. They had seen the ship's markings and the American flag. They could damn near see my rank. The under way flag was definitely flying. Especially when you're that close to a war zone."

By 9:30 A.M. the minaret at El Arish could be seen with the naked eye, like a solitary mast in a sea of sand. Visibility in the crystal clear air was twenty-five miles or better. Through a pair of binoculars, individual buildings were clearly visible a brief thirteen miles away. Commander McGonagle thought the tower "quite conspicuous" and used it as a navigational aid to determine the ship's position throughout the morning and afternoon. The minaret was also identifiable by radar.

Although no one on the ship knew it at the time, the *Liberty* had suddenly trespassed into a private horror. At that very moment, near the minaret at El Arish, Israeli forces were engaged in a criminal slaughter.

From the first minutes of its surprise attack, the Israeli air force had owned the skies over the Middle East. Within the first few hours, Israeli jets pounded twenty-five Arab air bases ranging from Damascus in Syria to an Egyptian field, loaded with bombers, far up the Nile at Luxor. Then, using machine guns, mortar fire, tanks, and air power, the Israeli war machine overtook the Jordanian section of Jerusalem as well as the west bank of the Jordan River, and torpedo boats captured the key Red Sea cape of Sharm al-Sheikh.

In the Sinai, Israeli tanks and armored personnel carriers pushed toward the Suez Canal along all three of the roads that crossed the desert, turning the burning sands into a massive killing field. One Israeli general estimated that Egyptian casualties there ranged from 7,000 to 10,000 killed, compared with 275 of his own troops. Few were spared as the Israelis pushed forward.

A convoy of Indian peacekeeper soldiers, flying the blue United Nations flag from their jeeps and trucks, were on their way to Gaza when they met an Israeli tank column on the road. As the Israelis approached, the UN observers pulled aside and stopped to get out of the way. One of the tanks rotated its turret and opened fire from a few feet away. The Israeli tank then rammed its gun through the windshield of an Indian jeep and decapitated the two men inside. When other Indians went to aid their comrades, they were mowed down by machine-gun fire. Another Israeli tank thrust its gun into a UN truck, lifted it, and smashed it to the ground, killing or wounding all the occupants. In Gaza, Israeli tanks blasted six rounds into UN headquarters, which was flying the UN flag. Fourteen UN members were killed in these incidents. One Indian officer called it deliberate, cold-blooded killing of unarmed UN soldiers. It would be a sign of things to come.

By June 8, three days after Israel launched the war, Egyptian prisoners in the Sinai had become nuisances. There was no place to house them, not enough Israelis to watch them, and few vehicles to transport them to prison camps. But there was another way to deal with them.

As the *Liberty* sat within eyeshot of El Arish, eavesdropping on surrounding communications, Israeli soldiers turned the town into a slaughterhouse, systematically butchering their prisoners. In the shadow of the El Arish mosque, they lined up about sixty unarmed Egyptian prisoners, hands tied behind their backs, and then opened fire with machine guns until the pale desert sand turned red. Then they forced other prisoners to bury the victims in mass graves. "I saw a line of prisoners, civilians and military," said Abdelsalam Moussa, one of those who dug the graves, "and they opened fire at them all at once. When they were dead, they told us to bury them." Nearby, another group of Israelis gunned down thirty more prisoners and then ordered some Bedouins to cover them with sand.

In still another incident at El Arish, the Israeli journalist Gabi Bron saw about 150 Egyptian POWs sitting on the ground, crowded together with their hands held at the backs of their necks. "The Egyptian prisoners of war were ordered to dig pits and then army police shot them to death," Bron said. "I witnessed the executions with my own eyes on the morning of June eighth, in the airport area of El Arish."

The Israeli military historian Aryeh Yitzhaki, who worked in the army's history department after the war, said he and other officers collected testimony from dozens of soldiers who admitted killing POWs. According to Yitzhaki, Israeli troops killed, in cold blood, as many as 1,000 Egyptian prisoners in the Sinai, including some 400 in the sand dunes of El Arish.

Ironically, Ariel Sharon, who was capturing territory south of El Arish at the time of the slaughter, had been close to massacres during other conflicts. One of his men during the Suez crisis in 1956, Arye Biro, now a retired brigadier general, recently admitted the unprovoked killing of forty-nine prisoners of war in the Sinai in 1956. "I had my Karl Gustav [weapon] I had taken from the Egyptian. My officer had an Uzi. The Egyptian prisoners were sitting there with their faces turned to us. We turned to them with our loaded guns and shot them. Magazine after magazine. They didn't get a chance to react." At another point, Biro said, he found Egyptian soldiers prostrate with thirst. He said that after taunting them by pouring water from his canteen into the sand, he killed them. "If I were to be put on trial for what I did," he said, "then it would be necessary to put on trial at least one-half the Israeli army, which, in similar circumstances, did what I did." Sharon, who says he learned of the 1956 prisoner shootings only after they happened, refused to say whether he took any disciplinary action against those involved, or even objected to the killings.

Later in his career, in 1982, Sharon would be held "indirectly responsible" for the slaughter of about 900 men, women, and children by Lebanese Christian militia at the Sabra and Shatila refugee camps following Israel's invasion of Lebanon. Despite his grisly past, or maybe because of it, in October 1998 he was appointed minister of foreign affairs in the cabinet of right-wing prime minister Benjamin Netanyahu. Sharon later took over the conservative Likud Party. On September 28, 2000, he set off the bloodiest upheaval between Israeli forces and Palestinians in a generation, which resulted in a collapse of the seven-year peace process. The deadly battles, which killed over 200 Palestinians and several Israeli soldiers, broke out following a provocative visit by Sharon to the compound known as Haram as-Sharif (Noble Sanctuary) to Muslims and Temple Mount to Jews. Addressing the question of Israeli war crimes, Sharon said in 1995, "Israel doesn't need this, and no one can preach to us about it—no one."

Of the 1967 Sinai slaughter, Aryeh Yitzhaki said, "The whole army leadership, including [then] Defense Minister Moshe Dayan and Chief of Staff [and later Prime Minister Yitzhak] Rabin and the generals knew about these things. No one bothered to denounce them." Yitzhaki said not only were the massacres known, but senior Israeli officials tried their best to cover them up by not releasing a report he had prepared on the murders in 1968.

The extensive war crimes were just one of the deep secrets Israel had sought to conceal since the start of the conflict. From the very beginning, an essential element in the Israeli battle plan seemed to have been to hide much of the war behind a carefully constructed curtain of lies. Lies about the Egyptian threat, lies about who started the war, lies to the American president, lies to the UN Security Council, lies to the press, lies to the public. Thus, as the American naval historian Dr. Richard K. Smith noted in an article on the *Liberty* for *United States Naval Institute Proceedings*, "any instrument which sought to penetrate this smoke screen so carefully thrown around the normal 'fog of war' would have to be frustrated."

Into this sea of lies, deception, and slaughter sailed the USS *Liberty*, an enormous American spy factory loaded with $10.2 million worth of the latest eavesdropping gear. At 10:39 A.M., the minaret at El Arish was logged at seventeen miles away, at bearing 189 degrees. Sailing at five knots, the *Liberty* was practically treading water.

By 10:55 A.M., senior Israeli officials knew for certain that they had an American electronic spy in their midst. Not only was the ship clearly visible to the forces at El Arish, it had been positively identified by Israeli naval headquarters.

The Israeli naval observer on the airborne reconnaissance mission that had earlier observed the *Liberty* passed on the information to Commander Pinchas Pinchasy, the naval liaison officer at Israeli air force headquarters. "I reported this detection to Naval Headquarters," said Pinchasy, "and I imagine that Naval Headquarters received this report from the other channel, from the Air Force ground control as well." Pinchasy had pulled out a copy of the reference book *Jane's Fighting Ships* and looked up the "GTR-5" designation. He then sent a report to the acting chief of naval operations at Israeli navy headquarters in Haifa. The report said that the ship cruising slowly off El Arish was "an electromagnetic audio-surveillance ship of the U.S. Navy, named *Liberty*, whose marking was GTR-5."

Not only did the ship have "GTR-5" painted broadly on both sides of its bow and stern, it also had its name painted in large, bold, black letters: "U.S.S. LIBERTY."

Although no one on the *Liberty* knew it, they were about to have some company.

"We were 'wheels in the well' from Athens about mid-morning," said Marvin Nowicki, who was aboard the EC-121 headed back to the war zone. In the rear NSA spaces, the crew strapped on their seat belts. It was an everyday routine. The VQ-2 squadron would fly, on average, six to twelve missions per month against Israel and the Arab countries of the Middle East. Exceptions took place when higher-priority Soviet targets came up, for example when the Soviet fleet conducted exercises in the Mediterranean or Norwegian Sea. Nowicki himself accumulated over 2,000 hours in such spy planes over his career.

Back at Athens Airport, the 512J processing center had been beefed up to help analyze the increasing flow of intercepts. Three NSA civilian

Hebrew linguists had arrived and were attacking the backlog of recording tapes. The pile had grown especially large because the Air Force had no Hebrew linguists for their C-130 Sigint aircraft. "As it turns out," said Nowicki, "they were blindly copying any voice signal that sounded Hebrew. They were like vacuum cleaners, sucking every signal onto their recorders, with the intercept operators not having a clue as to what the activity represented."

In charge of the half-dozen Elint specialists aboard the EC-121, searching for radar signals and analyzing their cryptic sounds, was the evaluator, who would attempt to make sense of all the data. Elsewhere, several intercept operators were assigned to monitor VHF and UHF radio-telephone signals. In addition to Chief Nowicki, who could translate both Hebrew and Russian, there were two other Hebrew and two Arabic linguists on board.

Soon after wheels-up from Athens, a security curtain was pulled around the "spook spaces" to hide the activity from members of the flight crew who did not have a need to know. In front of the voice-intercept operators were twin UHF/VHF receivers, essential because the Israelis mostly used UHF transceivers, while the Arabs used Soviet VHF equipment. To record all the traffic, they had a four-track voice recorder with time dubs and frequency notations. Chief Nowicki, the supervisor, had an additional piece of equipment: a spectrum analyzer to view the radio activity in the form of "spikes" between 100 to 150 megahertz and 200 to 500 megahertz. It was very useful in locating new signals.

About noon, as they came closer to their orbit area, the activity began getting hectic. Fingers twisted large black dials, sometimes quickly and sometimes barely at all. "When we arrived within intercept range of the battles already in progress," Nowicki recalled, "it was apparent that the Israelis were pounding the Syrians on the Golan Heights. Soon all our recorders were going full blast, with each position intercepting signals on both receivers."

In addition to recording the voices of the Israeli and Egyptian troops and pilots, the linguists were frantically writing down gists of voice activity on logs and shouting to the evaluator what they were recording. The evaluator in turn would then direct his Elint people to search for corresponding radar activity. At other times, the Elint operators would intercept a radar signal from a target and tip off the linguists to start searching for correlating voice activity. A key piece of equipment was known as Big Look. It enabled the Elint operators to intercept, emulate, and identify the radar signals, and to reverse-locate them—to trace them back to their source.

Sixty miles north of Tel Aviv, atop Mount Carmel, Israel's naval command post occupied a drab former British Royal Air Force base built in the 1920s. Known as Stella Maris, it contained a high-ceilinged war room with a large map of Israel and its coastal areas on a raised platform. Standing above it, senior naval officials could see the location of ships in the area, updated as air reconnaissance passed on the changing positions of various ships. Since dawn that morning, the *Liberty* had been under constant observation. "Between five in the morning and one in the afternoon," said one *Liberty* deck officer, "I think there were thirteen times that we were circled."

About noon at Stella Maris, as the *Liberty* was again in sight of El Arish and while the massacres were taking place, a report was received from an army commander there that a ship was shelling the Israelis from the sea. But that was impossible. The only ship in the vicinity of El Arish was the *Liberty*, and she was eavesdropping, not shooting. As any observer would immediately have recognized, the four small defensive 50mm machine guns were incapable of reaching anywhere near the shore, thirteen miles away, let alone the buildings of El Arish. In fact, the maximum effective range of such guns was just 2,200 yards, a little over a mile. And the ship itself, a tired old World War II cargo vessel crawling with antennas, was unthreatening to anyone—unless it was their secrets, not their lives, they wanted to protect.

By then the Israeli navy and air force had conducted more than six hours of close surveillance of the *Liberty* off the Sinai, even taken pictures, and must have positively identified it as an American electronic spy ship. They knew the *Liberty* was the only military ship in the area. Nevertheless, the order was given to kill it. Thus, at 12:05 P.M. three motor torpedo boats from Ashdod departed for the *Liberty*, about fifty miles away. Israeli air force fighters, loaded with 30mm cannon ammunition, rockets, and even napalm, then followed. They were all to return virtually empty.

At 1:41 P.M., about an hour and a half after leaving Ashdod, the torpedo boats spotted the *Liberty* off El Arish and called for an immediate strike by the air force fighters.

On the bridge of the *Liberty*, Commander McGonagle looked at the hooded green radar screen and fixed the ship's position as being 25½ nautical miles from the minaret at El Arish, which was to the southeast. The officer of the deck, Lieutenant (junior grade) Lloyd Painter, also looked at the radar and saw that they were 17½ miles from land. It was shortly before two o'clock in the afternoon.

McGonagle was known as a steamer, a sailor who wants to constantly feel the motion of the sea beneath the hull of the ship, to steam to the next port as soon as possible after arriving at the last. "He longed for the sea," said one of his officers, "and was noticeably restless in port. He simply would not tolerate being delayed by machinery that was not vital to the operation of the ship." He was born in Wichita, Kansas, on November 19, 1925, and his voice still had a twang. Among the first to join the post–World War II Navy, he saw combat while on a minesweeper during the Korean War, winning the Korean Service Medal with six battle stars. Eventually commanding several small service ships, he had taken over as captain of the *Liberty* about a year earlier, in April 1966.

A Chief of Naval Operations once called the *Liberty* "the ugliest ship in the Navy," largely because in place of powerful guns it had strange antennas protruding from every location. There were thin long-wire VLF antennas, conical electronic-countermeasure antennas, spiracle antennas, a microwave antenna on the bow, and whip antennas that extended thirty-five feet. Most unusual was the sixteen-foot dish-shaped moon-bounce antenna that rested high on the stern.

Despite the danger, the men on the ship were carrying on as normally as possible. Larry Weaver, a boatswain's mate, was waiting outside the doctor's office to have an earache looked at. Muscular at 184 pounds, he exercised regularly in the ship's weight room. Planning to leave the Navy shortly, he had already applied for a job at Florida's Cypress Gardens as a water skier. With the ability to ski barefoot for nine miles, he thought he would have a good chance.

As for Bryce Lockwood, the Marine senior Russian linguist who had been awakened in the middle of a layover in Rota, Spain, and virtually shanghaied, his wife and daughter had no idea where he was. Having boarded the ship on such short notice, Lockwood had gone to the small ship's store to buy some T-shirts and shorts. While waiting to go on watch, he was sitting on his bunk stamping his name in his new underwear.

On the stern, Stan White was struggling with the troublesome moon-bounce antenna. A senior chief petty officer, he was responsible for the complicated repair of the intercept and cipher gear on board. The giant dish was used to communicate quickly, directly, and securely with NSA back at Fort Meade, and for this purpose both locations had to be able to see the moon at the same time. But throughout the whole voyage, even back in Norfolk, the system was plagued with leaking hydraulic fluid. Now another critical part, the klystron, had burned out and White was attempting to replace it.

Below deck in the Research Operations Department, as the NSA spaces were known, Elint operators were huddled over round green scopes, watching and listening for any unusual signals. Charles L. Rowley, a first-class petty officer and a specialist in technical intelligence collection, was in charge of one of the Elint sections. "I was told to be on the lookout for a different type of signal," he said. "I reported a signal I thought was from a submarine. . . . I analyzed it as far as the length of the signal, the mark and space on the bods, and I could not break it, I didn't know what it was, I had no idea what it was . . . and sent it in to NSA." But NSA had an unusual reaction: "I got my butt chewed out. They tried to convince me that it was a British double-current cable code and I know damn good and well that it wasn't." In fact, the blackness deep beneath the waves of the eastern Mediterranean was beginning to become quite crowded.

One deck down, just below the waterline, were the Morse code as well as Russian and Arabic voice-intercept operators, their "cans" tight against their ears. Lined up along the bulkheads, they pounded away on typewriters and flipped tape recorders on and off as they eavesdropped on the sounds of war. Among their key missions was to determine whether the Egyptian air force's Soviet-made bombers, such as the TU-95 aircraft thought to be based in Alexandria, were being flown and controlled by

Russian pilots and ground controllers. Obtaining the earliest intelligence that the Russians were taking part in the fighting was one of the principal reasons for sending the *Liberty* so far into the war zone.

In another office, communications personnel worked on the ship's special, highly encrypted communications equipment.

Nearby in the Coordination—"Co-ord"—spaces, technicians were shredding all outdated documents to protect them from possible capture. Others were engaged in "processing and reporting," or P&R. "Processing and reporting involves figuring out who is talking," said Bryce Lockwood, one of the P&R supervisors, "where they're coming from, the other stations on that network, making some kind of sense out of it, forwarding it to the consumers, which primarily was the NSA, the CIA, JCS."

But as the real war raged on the shore, a mock war raged in the Co-ord spaces. One of the Arabic-language P&R specialists had developed a fondness for Egypt and had made a small Egyptian flag that he put on his desk. "The guys would walk by and they would take a cigarette lighter," recalled Lockwood, "and say, 'Hey, what's happening to the UAR [United Arab Republic, now Egypt] over there?' And they would light off his UAR flag and he would reach over and say, 'Stop that,' and put the fire out, and it was getting all scorched."

Then, according to Lockwood, some of the pro-Israel contingent got their revenge. They "had gotten Teletype paper and scotch-taped it together and with blue felt marking pens had made a gigantic Star of David flag. This thing was about six feet by about twelve feet—huge. And stuck that up on the starboard bulkhead."

"You'd better call the forward gun mounts," Commander McGonagle yelled excitedly to Lieutenant Painter. "I think they're going to attack!" The captain was standing on the starboard wing, looking at a number of unidentified jet aircraft rapidly approaching in an attack pattern.

Larry Weaver was still sitting outside the doctor's office when he first heard the sound. A few minutes before, an announcement had come over the speaker saying that the engine on the motor whaleboat was about to be tested. "All of a sudden I heard this *rat-a-tat-tat* real hard and the first thing I thought was, 'Holy shit, the prop came off that boat and went right up the bulkhead,' that's exactly what it sounded like. And the very next instant we heard the gong and we went to general quarters."

Stan White thought it sounded like someone throwing rocks at the ship. "And then it happened again," he recalled, "and then general quarters sounded, and by the captain's voice we knew it was not a drill. Shortly after that the wave-guides to the dish [antenna] were shot to pieces and sparks and chunks fell on me."

"I immediately knew what it was," said Bryce Lockwood, the Marine, "and I just dropped everything and ran to my GQ station which was down below in the Co-ord station."

Without warning the Israeli jets struck—swept-wing Dassault Mirage IIICs. Lieutenant Painter observed that the aircraft had "absolutely no markings," so that their identity was unclear. He then attempted to contact the men manning the gun mounts, but it was too late. "I was trying to contact these two kids," he recalled, "and I saw them both; well, I didn't exactly see them as such. They were blown apart, but I saw the whole area go up in smoke and scattered metal. And, at about the same time, the aircraft strafed the bridge area itself. The quartermaster, Petty Officer Third Class Pollard, was standing right next to me, and he was hit."

With the sun at their backs in true attack mode, the Mirages raked the ship from bow to stern with hot, armor-piercing lead. Back and forth they came, cannons and machine guns blazing. A bomb exploded near the whaleboat aft of the bridge, and those in the pilothouse and the bridge were thrown from their feet. Commander McGonagle grabbed for the engine order annunciator and rang up all ahead flank.

"Oil is spilling out into the water," one of the Israeli Mirage pilots reported to base.

Charles L. Rowley, an electronics intelligence specialist who doubled as the ship's photographer, grabbed his Nikon and raced to the bridge to try to get a shot of the planes. Instead, the planes shot him. "They shot the camera right out of my hands," he recalled. "I was one of the first ones that got hit."

In the communications spaces, radiomen James Halman and Joseph Ward had patched together enough equipment and broken antennas to get a distress call off to the Sixth Fleet, despite intense jamming by the Israelis. "Any station, this is Rockstar," Halman shouted, using the *Liberty*'s voice call sign. "We are under attack by unidentified jet aircraft and require immediate assistance."

"Great, wonderful, she's burning, she's burning," said the Israeli pilot.

As Bryce Lockwood rushed into the Co-ord unit, most of the intercept operators were still manning their positions. Suddenly one of the other Russian voice supervisors rushed over to him excitedly, having at last found what they had been looking for, evidence of Soviet military activity in Egypt. "Hey, Sarge, I found them, I found them," he said. "You found who?" Lockwood asked. "I got the Russkies."

Now the operators began frantically searching the airwaves, attempting to discover who was attacking them. At the same time, Lockwood and some others started the destruction procedure. The Marine linguist broke out the white canvas ditching bags, each about five feet tall. The bags were specially made with a large flat lead weight in the bottom and brass fittings that could be opened to let in the water so they would sink to the bottom faster. At the top was a rope drawstring. "We had a room where we did voice tape transcripts," said Lockwood, "and there were literally hundreds of reel-to-reel tapes in there that had to be put in those ditching bags. So we got these ditching bags and started putting these tapes in there. These were voice conversations of, mostly, UAR targets. All the tapes and transcripts were loaded in the bags, a lot of code manuals, and so forth."

At 2:09, the American aircraft carrier USS *Saratoga*, operating near Crete, acknowledged *Liberty*'s cry for help. "I am standing by for further traffic," it signaled.

After taking out the gun mounts, the Israeli fighter pilots turned their attention to the antennas, to sever the *Liberty*'s vocal cords and deafen it so it could not call for help or pick up any more revealing intercepts. "It was as though they knew their exact locations," said Senior Chief Stan White. Lieutenant Commander Dave Lewis, in charge of the NSA operation on the ship, agreed. "It appears to me that every tuning section of every HF antenna had a hole in it," he said. "It took a lot of planning to get heat-seeking missiles aboard to take out our entire communications in the first minute of the attack. If that was a mistake, it was the best-planned mistake that has ever been perpetrated in the history of mankind."

Not hearing anything from the *Saratoga* for a few minutes, the radio operator repeated his call for help. "Schematic, this is Rockstar. We are still under attack by unidentified jet aircraft and require immediate assistance." But the *Saratoga* demanded an authentication code. Unfortunately, it had been destroyed during the emergency destruction and the *Saratoga* operator was giving him a hard time about it. "Listen to the goddamned rockets, you son-of-a-bitch," the *Liberty* radioman screamed into his microphone.

"He's hit her a lot," reported an Israeli Army commander at El Arish, where the war crimes were taking place. "There's black smoke, there's an oil slick in the water."

Then the planes attacked the bridge in order to blind her, killing instantly the ship's executive officer. With the *Liberty* now deaf, blind, and silenced, unable to call for help and unable to move, the Israeli pilots next proceeded to kill her. Designed to punch holes in the toughest tanks, the Israeli shells tore through the *Liberty*'s steel plating like hot nails through butter, exploding into jagged bits of shrapnel and butchering men deep in their living quarters.

"Menachem, is he screwing her?" headquarters asked one of the pilots, excitedly.

As the Israelis continued their slaughter, neither they nor the *Liberty* crew had any idea that witnesses were present high above. Until now. According to information, interviews, and documents obtained for *Body of Secrets,* for nearly thirty-five years NSA has hidden the fact that one of its planes was overhead at the time of the incident, eavesdropping on what was going on below. The intercepts from that plane, which answer some of the key questions about the attack, are among NSA's deepest secrets.

Two hours before the attack, the Navy EC-121 ferret had taken off from Athens and returned to the eastern Mediterranean for its regular patrol. Now it was flying a diagonal track from Crete and Cyprus to El Arish and back. "When we arrived within intercept range of the battles already in progress," said Marvin Nowicki, "it was apparent that the Israelis were pounding the Syrians on the Golan Heights. Soon all our recorders were going full blast, with each position intercepting signals on both receivers [Hebrew and Arabic]. The evaluator called out many airborne intercepts from Arab and Israeli aircraft. We were going crazy trying to cope with the heavy activity."

Then, a few hours later, about the time the air attack was getting under way, Nowicki heard one of the other Hebrew linguists excitedly trying to get his attention on the secure intercom. "Hey, Chief," the linguist shouted, "I've got really odd activity on UHF. They mentioned an American flag. I don't know what's going on." Nowicki asked the linguist for the frequency and "rolled up to it." "Sure as the devil," said Nowicki, "Israeli aircraft were completing an attack on some object. I alerted the evaluator, giving him sparse details, adding that we had no idea what was taking place." For a while the activity subsided.

Deep down in the NSA spaces Terry McFarland, his head encased in earphones, was vaguely aware of flickers of light coming through the bulkhead. He had no idea they were armor-piercing tracer bullets slicing through the *Liberty*'s skin. The "flickers" were accompanied by a strange noise that sounded like chains being pulled across the bottom of the ship. Then McFarland looked up to see "Red" Addington, a seaman, race down the ladder from above with blood running down his right leg. "Somebody's up there shootin' at us," he said.

When the attack started, Larry Weaver had run to his general quarters station but it was located on an old helicopter pad that left him exposed and vulnerable. He grabbed for a dazed shipmate and pushed him into a safe corner. "I said, 'Fred, you've got to stay here, you've just got to because he's coming up the center,' " Weaver recalled. "I yelled, screaming at him probably, and finally he said he would stay." Then the only place Weaver could find to hide was a small chock, the kind used to hold lines. "I got in the fetal position," he said, "and before I closed my eyes I looked up and I saw the American flag and that was the last thing I saw before I was hit. And I closed my eyes just waiting for hell's horror to hit me. And I was hit by rocket and cannon fire that blew two and a half feet of my colon out and I received over one hundred shrapnel wounds. It blew me up in the air about four and a half, five feet. And just blood everywhere. It felt like a really hot electrical charge going through my whole body."

Stan White raced for the enclosed NSA spaces, cutting through the sick bay. "Torn and mutilated bodies were everywhere," he said. "Horrible sight! On the mess deck I ran into one of my ETs [electronics technicians], he had a hole in his shoulder and one you could see through in his arm. The sound of the shells and rockets was overwhelming and I can only tell you that I didn't know a person could be so terrified and still move."

Lloyd Painter was also trying to get to his general quarters station on the mess decks. "I was running as fast as I could," he recalled. "By the time I got to the Chief's Lounge, the entrance through the lounge to the mess docks, I saw [Petty Officer John C.] Spicher, our postal clerk, lying there cut in half with strafing."

As soon as the Mirages pulled away they were replaced by Super Mystère fighters which first raked the ship from stern to bow and then crisscrossed it broadside. A later analysis would show 821 separate hits on the hull and superstructure. Now in addition to rocket, cannon, and machine-gun fire, the Mystères attacked with thousand-pound bombs and napalm. Deafening explosions tore through the ship and the bridge disappeared in an orange-and-black ball. Lying wounded by shrapnel, his blood draining into his shoe, was Commander McGonagle. Seconds later they were back. Flesh fused with iron as more strafing was followed by more rockets which were followed by napalm.

"He's going down low with napalm all the time," shouted someone with the Israeli Southern Command at El Arish, where soldiers were hiding the slaughtered prisoners under the sand.

Crisscrossing the ship almost every forty-five seconds, the Mystères let loose more napalm—silvery metallic canisters of jellied gasoline that turned the ship into a crematorium. Not satisfied, the flight leader radioed to his headquarters. "It would be a *mitzvah* [blessing] if we can get a flight with iron bombs," he said. "Otherwise, the Navy's going to get here and they're going to do the shooting." With the iron bombs, the pilot was hoping for the coup de grâce—to sink the ship before the Navy arrived to finish her off. In World War II, during the battle of Midway,

American dive-bombers sank three Japanese aircraft carriers with such bombs in only ten minutes.

One of the quartermasters raced down to the mess deck. "The captain's hurt," he yelled to Lieutenant Painter, "and the operations officer was dead, and the executive officer is mortally wounded." Painter charged up to the bridge.

"Pay attention," one of the pilots told his headquarters. "The ship's markings are Charlie Tango Romeo 5," he said, indicating that the *Liberty*'s identification markings were CTR-5. (Actually, they were GTR-5.) Then, with the American flag having been shot down during earlier passes, he added, "There's no flag on her."

"Leave her," replied headquarters.

As the last fighter departed, having emptied out its on-board armory and turned the *Liberty*'s hull into a flaming mass of gray Swiss cheese, sailors lifted mutilated shipmates onto makeshift stretchers of pipe frame and chicken wire. Damage control crews pushed through passageways of suffocating smoke and blistering heat, and the chief petty officer's lounge was converted into a macabre sea of blood-soaked mattresses and shattered bodies. A later analysis said it would take a squadron of fifteen or more planes to do such damage as was inflicted on the ship.

At 2:24, minutes after the air attack, horror once again washed over the crew. Charles Rowley, the ship's photographer, was lying in the wardroom being treated for shrapnel wounds when armor-piercing bullets began penetrating the bulkhead. Through the porthole he saw three sixty-two-ton motor torpedo boats rapidly approaching in attack formation. Closing in at about forty knots, each of the French-built boats had a crew of fifteen and were heavily armed with a 40mm cannon, four 20mm cannons, and two torpedoes. Like a firing squad, they lined up in a row and pointed their guns and torpedo tubes at the *Liberty*'s starboard hull. Seeing that the Israeli fighters had destroyed the American flag, Commander McGonagle ordered the signalman to quickly hoist another—this one the giant "holiday ensign," the largest on the ship.

Almost immediately, the boats opened up with a barrage of cannon fire. One armor-piercing bullet slammed through the ship's chart house and into the pilothouse, coming to rest finally in the neck of a young helmsman, killing him instantly. Three other crewmen were slaughtered in this latest shower of steel.

Back up in the EC-121 ferret, the Hebrew linguist called Nowicki again. "He told me about new activity and that the American flag is being mentioned again. I had the frequency but for some strange reason, despite seeing it on my spectrum analyzer, couldn't hear it on my receiver, so I left my position to join him to listen at his position. I heard a couple of references to the flag during an apparent attack. The attackers weren't aircraft; they had to be surface units (we later found out at USA-512J it was the Israeli motor torpedo boats attacking the *Liberty*). Neither [the other Hebrew linguist] nor I had ever heard MTB attacks in voice before, so we had no idea what was occurring below us. I advised the evaluator; he was as mystified as we were."

"Stand by for torpedo attack, starboard side," McGonagle shouted frantically into the announcing system. The Israelis were ready for the kill. At 2:37 P.M., the safety plug was pulled from a 19-inch German-made torpedo on Motor Torpedo Boat 203. Seconds later it sped from its launcher and took direct aim at the *Liberty*'s NSA spaces. Four other torpedoes—more than enough to sink the largest aircraft carrier—were also launched. Had all or most of them hit their mark, the *Liberty*'s remaining life would have been measured in minutes. Through a miracle, only one struck home. But that hit was devastating.

Down in the NSA spaces, as the sound of shells hitting the hull grew louder, Petty Officer Ronnie Campbell jammed a sheet of paper into his typewriter and started pounding out a letter to his wife. "Dear Eileen," he started, "you wouldn't believe what's happening to us . . ."

Nearby, Bryce Lockwood had been summoned to help carry the ditching bags up to the main deck and throw them overboard. He stepped from the NSA spaces out into the passageway and a few seconds later, he said, "There was just a—I have the sense of a large object, and then a tremendous flash and explosion, just a sheet of flame. It was the torpedo—I was less than ten feet from it. The first thought that crossed my mind—'Well, it looks like it's over with. I guess I'm coming home, Lord. At least Lois and the kids are taken care of.' There were twenty-five men that were killed all around me." The torpedo struck dead center in the NSA spaces, killing nearly everyone inside, some by the initial blast and others by drowning—including Ronnie Campbell, who never finished his letter. "The whole irony," said Lockwood, "is that that Israeli torpedo struck within just a few feet of the Star of David flag that had been taped to the starboard bulkhead."

Frank Raven of G Group later talked to several of the few survivors from the NSA spaces. "They told me that they saw the torpedo . . . in the room with them. The torpedo came right through the side of the ship before it exploded—they saw it before it exploded. They had the torpedo in the room with them. It came right through the side of the ship and they jumped behind desks and things of that sort and it went off."

Down on the mess deck, where many of the wounded were being treated, Donald W. Pageler had just finished giving blood. Following the torpedo-attack warning, someone told him to throw himself across the wounded. "I did just as I was told," he said.

Stan White heard the announcement just as he was about to go down a hatch. "We knelt down and braced ourselves against the bulkheads and waited. You could hear the shells from the torpedo boats hitting the ship—seemed like a long time but wasn't, I'm sure. And then the torpedo hit. The ship was lifted up out of the water somewhat, the place filled with smoke, and the lights went out. I was praying before it hit, and after it hit I concluded the prayer with 'Please take care of my wife and two little children.' We had kids late in our marriage and I thought how little time I had had with them."

At the moment of the announcement, Larry Weaver, having had his colon blown out by a rocket, was lying on a table in sick bay. "I could feel a lot of warmth from the blood," he said. "They said, 'Stand by for torpedo run, starboard side.' And I said, 'Fred, get me a life jacket, get one on me.' . . . Well we got hit by the torpedo and it's like a giant grabbed the ship and threw it. . . . And right afterwards they called [prepare to] abandon ship."

Despite his injuries, Weaver tried to make it to one of the life rafts.

"And I was going as fast as I could and I remember my feet were going through blood that was running down the deck like a small river, I will never forget that." But by the time he reached his life raft, it had been destroyed. "My life raft was all blown to smithereens, there just wasn't anything left of it. . . . And there was a guy beside me, a couple feet beside me, and you could just hear the incoming shells. All of a sudden he was there and the next thing I knew he wasn't and I was slipping, trying to hold on to the rail, and there was a lot of blood and I looked down and I was standing on what was left of his thigh. I remember the skin and the hair from his legs underneath my foot. And I was sliding."

The firing continued, now from the torpedo boats. Weaver and a number of other wounded were placed on gurneys between metal barriers. "We were laying there," he recalled, "and if I was to summarize what it sounded like, we were all praying. And it just almost sounded like a guru type of chant, like a mum-mum-mum-mum, that's the way it sounded because all these guys were wounded and we were all praying and almost in the same tone. And I remember the sound of that. And we could hear them [shells] hitting the bulkhead, just unbelievable. I was so scared to close my eyes because I thought I would never open them again."

Still down near the NSA spaces was Bryce Lockwood, who had been knocked unconscious. When he awoke all he could feel was cold, frigid, oily water. Around him were more than two dozen dead intercept operators, analysts, and communications personnel. The water was pouring in from the massive torpedo hole below the waterline, and smoke, oil, and darkness filled the space. Lockwood heard a groan behind him and found one sailor alive, Petty Officer Joseph C. Lentini. The sailor's leg had been smashed by an armor-piercing bullet and then crushed by a bulkhead when the torpedo struck. In spite of the difficulties, Lockwood managed to free the sailor's leg, put him over his shoulder, and climb up the ladder to the next level, where he again passed out.

Once again he awoke as the water, climbing still higher, washed over him. Desperate to escape, he again put the sailor on his shoulder and climbed a second ladder—but now the top hatch had been sealed shut to help prevent the ship from sinking. Two, three, four times Lockwood dropped Lentini into the rising water as he pounded on the hatch with one hand, held a flashlight with the other, and screamed at the top of his lungs. Each time he would retrieve Lentini, reclimb the ladder, and continue pounding. Finally, a sailor doing a damage control survey opened the hatch and found Lockwood with the wounded Lentini, who, his leg shredded, was still clinging to life. Lockwood was later awarded the Silver Star for his heroism. Lentini survived. He was one of two sailors Lockwood saved.

Immediately after the attack, one of the boats signaled by flashing light, in English, "Do you require assistance?" McGonagle, with no other means to communicate, hoisted the flags indicating that the ship was maneuvering with difficulty and that they should keep clear. Instead, the torpedo boats continued to terrorize the crew, firing at the ship, at firefighters, at rescue personnel, and even at the life rafts in their racks. Larry Weaver, whose raft was destroyed, said: "They must have known where they [the rafts] were. They tried to blow them out in their racks."

To prevent anyone from escaping the badly wounded ship, the Israelis even destroyed the few surviving life rafts that were put into the water following the call to abandon ship. "I watched with horror as the floating life rafts were riddled with holes," said Lieutenant Lloyd Painter, in charge of the evacuation. "No survivors were planned for this day!" Stan White, the top enlisted man on the ship, also witnessed the lifeboat attack. "When 'prepare to abandon ship' was announced, what was left of our lifeboats were released overboard; these were immediately machine-gunned by the torpedo boats. It was obvious that no one was meant to survive this assault."

Jumping overboard to escape the sinking ship was also not an option. "If you don't go down with the ship," said Seaman Don Pageler, "you're going to jump overboard. If you jump overboard, the way these people were attacking us, we knew they would shoot us in the water. We did firmly believe that there was no way they intended to capture anybody."

Earlier that day, the Israelis had massacred civilians and prisoners in the desert; now they were prepared to ensure that no American survived the sinking of the *Liberty*. Another witness to the lifeboat attacks was shipfitter Phillip F. Tourney. "As soon as the lifeboats hit the water they were sunk. They would shoot at us for target practice, it seemed like. They wanted to kill and maim and murder anyone they could. . . . One of the torpedo boats picked a life raft up and took it with them."

"They made circles like they were getting ready to attack again," added former petty officer Larry B. Thorn, who also witnessed the sinking of the life rafts. "Our biggest fear was that the Israeli commandos . . . would come back and get us that night and finish the job," said Phillip Tourney.

The Israelis, not knowing what intelligence NSA had picked up, would have had reason to suspect the worst—that the agency had recorded evidence of the numerous atrocities committed that morning only a few miles away. This would be devastating evidence of hundreds of serious war crimes, approved by senior Israeli commanders.

Indeed, many Israeli communications had been intercepted. "We heard Israeli traffic," said section supervisor Charles L. Rowley. Much of what was recorded was to be listened to and analyzed later, either at the secret processing station in Athens or back at NSA.

As the *Liberty* continued to burn and take on water from the forty-four-foot hole in its starboard side, damage control crews dodged Israeli shells to try to save it. Commander McGonagle, however, was quietly considering killing it himself. He had glimpsed an Israeli flag on one of the torpedo boats, and he feared that next the Israelis would attempt to board the ship, kill everyone not yet dead, and capture the supersecret NSA documents. (Because of the constant strafing by the fighters and the torpedo boats, the crew had been unable to throw overboard any of the ditching bags.) Rather than let that happen, he told his chief engineer, Lieutenant George H. Golden, about the Israeli flag and, said Golden, "told me that he wanted to scuttle the ship. I told him that we were in shallow water [the depth was 35 to 40 fathoms], that it would be impossible to do that. If it came to that point we would need to get our wounded and everybody off the ship and move it out into deeper water where we can scuttle it. And he asked me how long it would take me to sink the ship. And I gave him a rough idea of how long it would take for the ship to sink after I pulled the plug on it. But we had to be out in deep water—we were too shallow, and people could get aboard the ship and get whatever that was left that some of them might want."

High above, the intercept operators in the EC-121 ferret continued to eavesdrop on voices from the war below, but they heard no more mentions of the American flag. "Finally," said Chief Nowicki, "it was time to return to Athens. We recorded voice activity en route home until the intercepts finally faded. On the way home, the evaluator and I got together to try to figure out what we copied. Despite replaying portions of the tapes, we still did not have a complete understanding of what transpired except for the likelihood that a ship flying the American flag was being attacked by Israeli air and surface forces."

After landing on the Greek air force side of the Athens airport, Nowicki and the intercept crew were brought directly to the processing center. "By the time we arrived at the USA-512J compound," he said, "collateral reports were coming in to the station about the attack on the USS *Liberty*. The first question we were asked was, did we get any of the activity? Yes, we dared to say we did. The NSA civilians took our tapes and began transcribing. It was pretty clear that Israeli aircraft and motor torpedo boats attacked a ship in the east Med. Although the attackers never gave a name or a hull number, the ship was identified as flying an American flag. We logically concluded that the ship was the USS *Liberty*, although we had no idea she was even in the area and could become the object of such an attack." At the time, based on the fractured conversations he heard on the intercepts, Nowicki just assumed that the attack was a mistake.

The question then was whether to send a CRITIC to NSA, CRITIC being the highest priority for intercept intelligence. "After much deliberation," Nowicki said, "we decided against the CRITIC because our information was already hours old. To meet CRITIC criteria, information should be within fifteen minutes of the event. . . . It had been quite a day and other days remained before us. We returned to the Hotel Seville for rest and relaxation, feeling a sense of exhilaration but not comprehending the chaos and calamity taking place on the *Liberty* at that very moment as she struggled to leave the attack area."

The message sent by the *Liberty* shortly after the attack requesting immediate help was eventually received by the Sixth Fleet, which was then south of Crete, 450 miles to the west. Suddenly high-level communications channels came alive. At 2:50 P.M. (*Liberty* time), fifty minutes after the first shells tore into the ship and as the attack was still going on, the launch decision was made. The aircraft carrier USS *America*, cruising near Crete, was ordered to launch four armed A-4 Skyhawks. At the same time, the carrier USS *Saratoga* was also told to send four armed A-1 attack planes to defend the ship. "Sending aircraft to cover you," the Sixth Fleet told the *Liberty* at 3:05 P.M. (9:05 A.M. in Washington). "Surface units on the way."

At 9:00 A.M. (3:00 P.M. *Liberty*) bells sounded and the first CRITIC message, sent by either the *America* or the *Saratoga*, stuttered across a role of white Teletype paper in NSA's Sigint Command Center. The senior operations officer then passed it on to Director Marshall Carter. With Carter in his ninth-floor office was Deputy Director Tordella. At 9:28 A.M. (3:28 P.M. *Liberty*) Carter sent out a CRITIC alert to all listening posts. "USS *Liberty* has been reportedly torpedoed by unknown source in Med near 32N 33E," said the message. "Request examine all communications for possible reaction/reflections and report accordingly."

Eleven minutes after the CRITIC arrived at NSA, the phone rang in the Pentagon's War Room and European Command Headquarters told the duty officer that the *Liberty* had been attacked by unknown jet fighters.

At that moment in Washington, President Johnson was at his desk, on the phone, alternately shouting at congressional leaders and coaxing them to support his position on several pieces of pending legislation. But four minutes later he was suddenly interrupted by Walt Rostow on the other line. "The *Liberty* has been torpedoed in the Mediterranean," Rostow told Johnson excitedly. A minute later, the adviser rushed into the Oval Office with a brief memorandum. "The ship is located 60 to 100 miles north of Egypt. Reconnaissance aircraft are out from the 6th fleet," it said. "No knowledge of the submarine or surface vessel which committed this act. Shall keep you informed."

In the Pentagon, Secretary of Defense Robert S. McNamara called Carter at NSA for precise information on the ship, its personnel, and other details. Carter told him what he knew but said that the Naval Security Group, which manned and operated the ship, would have the most up-to-date facts. Carter told McNamara that he would have Captain Ralph E. Cook, the Security Group's director, call him immediately. Carter then called Cook's office, only to discover that he was at the dentist's. Cook's deputy, a Captain Thomas, got on the phone, and Carter told him to call McNamara at once. About ten minutes later McNamara again called Carter and said he still hadn't heard from anyone. After a few more minutes of crossed wires, McNamara and Thomas finally talked.

NSA's worst fears had come true. "After considerations of personnel safety," said Tordella, "one of General Carter's and my immediate concerns, considering the depth of the water and the distance of the ship off shore, had to do with the classified materials which she had on board." Tordella got on the phone to the Joint Reconnaissance Center and spoke to the deputy director, a Navy captain named Vineyard. "I expressed my concern that the written material be burned if at all possible and that the electronic equipment be salvaged if that were possible," he said.

But Tordella was not prepared for what he heard. According to NSA documents classified top secret/umbra and obtained for *Body of Secrets,* Tordella was told that some senior officials in Washington wanted above all to protect Israel from embarrassment. "Captain Vineyard had mentioned during this conversation," wrote Tordella, "that consideration was then being given by some unnamed Washington authorities to sink[ing] the *Liberty* in order that newspaper men would be unable to photograph her and thus inflame public opinion against the Israelis. I made an impolite comment about the idea." Almost immediately Tordella wrote a memorandum for the record, describing the conversation, and then locked it away.

Concern over the secrets on the ship grew and Carter said he was prepared to order the ship scuttled to prevent their loss. He only reconsidered when informed that the shallowness of the water made compromise of materials and equipment "a distinct possibility." Then he began worrying about the security of the material if the ship ended up sinking. "If it appeared the ship was going to sink," Carter told Vineyard, "it was essential that the security of the sinking site be maintained. . . . It would be necessary to get down and remove the sensitive material from the ship."

Also, there was discussion of sending in a replacement ship, the USS *Belmont.* A cover story for the *Liberty* was then quickly devised. "She was a communications research ship that was diverted from her research assignment," it said, "to provide improved communication-relay links with the several U.S. embassies around the entire Mediterranean during the current troubles."

On the *America* and *Saratoga*, the pilots were instructed to "destroy or drive off any attackers who are clearly making attacks on the *Liberty*." They then catapulted into the air toward the *Liberty* at 3:45 P.M. *Liberty* time (9:45 A.M. Washington).

At 4:00 P.M. on the *Liberty* (10:00 A.M. Washington), the crew was still screaming for help. "Flash, flash, flash," Radioman Joe Ward shouted into his microphone. "I pass in the blind. [That is, he didn't know who was picking up the transmission.] We are under attack by aircraft and high-speed surface craft. I say again, flash, flash, flash." By then, unencrypted voice messages had been filling the open airwaves for two hours. If the Israelis were monitoring the communications, as they did continuously during the war, they would now have begun to worry how soon the American fighters would arrive.

From the White House Situation Room, Rostow phoned Johnson at 10:14 A.M. (4:14 P.M. *Liberty*) to tell him that the ship was "listing badly to starboard. The *Saratoga* has launched 4-A4's and 4-A1's." Johnson feared that the attack had been conducted by Soviet planes and submarines and that the United States was on the verge of war with Russia. Later he called all his advisers for an emergency meeting in the Situation Room.

About the same moment that Joe Ward was again pleading for help, Commander Ernest C. Castle, the U.S. naval attaché in Tel Aviv, was summoned urgently to Israeli Defense Force Headquarters. There, he was told that Israeli air and sea forces had attacked the *Liberty* "in error." Castle raced back to the embassy and at 4:14 P.M. *Liberty* time (10:14 P.M. Washington), he dashed off a Flash message to Washington concerning this development. Strangely, NSA claims that it first learned of Israel's involvement fifteen minutes before Castle was called by the Israeli Defense Forces and half an hour before Castle's Flash message. It has never been explained how NSA discovered this.

At the White House, Johnson was relieved to learn that the attackers were not Soviet or Egyptian. There would be no war today. But he became very worried that the Russians, through Sigint, radar, or observation, would become aware that a squadron of American fighters was streaking toward the war zone, and that if the USSR suspected that

America had suddenly decided to become involved, it would launch an attack. So at 11:17 AM. (5:17 P.M. *Liberty)* he sent a hot-line message to Kosygin in Moscow.

The small office next to the War Room had lately become a busy place. Supervisor Harry O. Rakfeldt, a Russian-speaking Navy cryptologic chief, was already pounding out a hot-line message to Moscow, one of a number he had sent during the crisis, when the White House phone rang. Army Major Pawlowski, the presidential translator, picked it up, listened for a moment, then told Rakfeldt to notify Moscow to stand by for an emergency message. Immediately Rakfeldt stopped typing, dropped down several lines, and sent "Stand by for an emergency message." Then, as Major Pawlowski dictated, Rakfeldt typed the following alert:

> We have just learned that USS Liberty, an auxiliary ship, has apparently been torpedoed by Israel Forces in error off Port Said. We have instructed our carrier Saratoga, now in the Mediterranean, to dispatch aircraft to the scene to investigate. We wish you to know that investigation is the sole purpose of this flight of aircraft and hope that you will take appropriate steps to see that proper parties are informed. We have passed the message to Chernyakov but feel that you should know of this development urgently.

The message arrived in the Kremlin at 11:24 A.M. Washington time; Kosygin replied about forty-five minutes later that he had passed the message on to Nasser.

Black smoke was still escaping through the more than 800 holes in the *Liberty*'s hull, and the effort to hush up the incident had already begun. Within hours of the attack, Israel asked President Johnson to quietly bury the incident. "Embassy Tel Aviv," said a highly secret, very-limited-distribution message to the State Department, "urged de-emphasis on publicity since proximity of vessel to scene of conflict was fuel for Arab suspicions that U.S. was aiding Israel." Shortly thereafter, a total news ban was ordered by the Pentagon. No one in the field was allowed to say anything about the attack. All information was to come only from a few senior Washington officials.

At 11:29 A.M. (5:29 P.M. *Liberty*), Johnson took the unusual step of ordering the JCS to recall the fighters while the *Liberty* still lay smoldering, sinking, fearful of another attack, without aid, and with its decks covered with the dead, the dying, and the wounded. Onboard the flagship of the Sixth Fleet, Rear Admiral Lawrence R. Geis, who commanded the carrier force in the Mediterranean, was angry and puzzled at the recall and protested it to Secretary of Defense Robert S. McNamara.

Admiral Geis was shocked by what he heard next. According to information obtained for *Body of Secrets*, "President Lyndon Johnson came on with a comment that he didn't care if the ship sunk, he would not embarrass his allies." Admiral Geis told Lieutenant Commander David Lewis, the head of the NSA group on the *Liberty*, about the comment but asked him to keep it secret until after Geis died. It was a promise that Lewis kept.

The hole in the *Liberty*'s twenty-three-year-old skin was nearly wide enough to drive a bus through; the ship had a heavy list to starboard, most of its equipment was destroyed, thirty-two of its crew were dead (two others would later die) and two-thirds of the rest wounded; its executive officer was dead, and its commanding officer was badly hurt. Despite all this, the *Liberty* was heroically brought back to life and slowly made her way toward safer waters. To keep the ship from sinking, the hatches to the flooded NSA spaces had been dogged down, sealing the bodies of the twenty-five Sigint specialists inside.

Throughout the long night, propped up in a chair on the port wing of the bridge, Commander McGonagle continued to conn his ship, using the North Star ahead and the long wake behind for direction. Shortly after dawn, 16½ hours after the attack, help finally arrived. Rendezvousing with the *Liberty*, 420 miles east-southeast of Soudha Bay, Crete, were the American destroyers *Davis* and *Massey*.

Helicopters soon arrived and began lifting litters containing the most seriously wounded to the deck of the *America*, still 138 miles away. There they were transported by plane to Athens and then to the naval hospital in Naples. At the completion of the transfer, after eighteen continuous hours on the bridge, the weary skipper finally headed to what was left of his cabin. Despite his injuries, he remained with the ship until she docked in Malta.

As the wounded landed at Athens Airport, NSA civilians at USA 512J a short distance away finished transcribing most of the tapes from the previous day's EC-121 ferret mission. They then sent the raw information back to NSA over the agency's special channel, SPINTCOMM ("Special Intelligence Communications"). Later, the civilians were instructed to pack up the original tapes and send them by armed courier to NSA as soon as possible.

At NSA, concern had shifted from the rescue of the crew to the possible loss of sensitive documents from *Liberty*'s ruptured signals intelligence spaces. Boats from the destroyers were ordered to search around the *Liberty* for two hours looking for classified papers that might be washing out from the gaping, pear-shaped hole. Later, as the *Liberty* sailed slowly toward Malta, a major concern was the possibility that Russian ships would attempt to retrieve the flotsam. "Do whatever is feasible to keep any Soviet ships out of *Liberty*'s wake," the Sixth Fleet commander was told. "Maintain observation of *Liberty*'s wake and if possible find out what sort of documents are being lost in the wake . . . take whatever steps may be reasonable and appropriate to reduce possibility of compromise, noting that a compromise could have both political and technical aspects."

Like a shark sensing blood, a Soviet guided-missile destroyer did tag along with the *Liberty* for a while, but the two American destroyers and a fleet ocean tug trailed *Liberty* to recover any papers before the Russians had a chance to grab them. Along the way, the tug used boathooks and grab nets to pick up the top secret material. When the tug could not recover a document, it ran over it with the propeller and then backed down over it to shred the paper into small pieces. Despite this vigilance, the bodies of five technicians washed out of the hole and were never recovered.

Another concern at Fort Meade was the three NSA civilian Arabic linguists on the ship. They had earlier been flown to Rota, where they joined the crew. One, Allen M. Blue, had been killed; another, Donald L. Bullock, had been injured; and a third, Robert L. Wilson, had survived unscathed. Marshall Carter ordered an NSA official to meet the ship in Malta and provide maximum assistance in getting Bullock and Wilson back to the United States as quickly and as quietly as possible.

Once the *Liberty* pulled into Malta on June 14, the effort to bury the incident continued at full speed ahead. A total news blackout was imposed. Crewmembers were threatened with courts-martial and jail time if they ever breathed a word of the episode to anyone—including family members and even fellow crewmembers. "If you ever repeat this to anyone else ever again you will be put in prison and forgotten about," Larry Weaver said he was warned.

Now that the ship was safely in dry dock, the grisly task of searching the NSA spaces, sealed since the attack six days earlier, also began. "I took a crew . . . down in the spaces to inventory the classified equipment and info," said former senior chief Stan White. "The smell was so awful it can't be described. We got the bodies out and then the pieces of bodies were picked up and put in bags and finally the inventory. The sights and smells I am still sometimes aware of today." Seaman Don Pageler also spent two and a half days helping to search and clean out the cavernous compartment. At one point he lifted a piece of equipment only to make a grim discovery. "Below it was this guy's arm. . . . I looked at the muscle structure and I knew whose arm it was. I didn't know him well but I knew who he was."

In July 1967, the *Liberty* returned to Norfolk from Malta. There it languished while NSA tried unsuccessfully to obtain $10.2 million from the Pentagon to restore her to signals intelligence operational status. When that effort failed, the *Liberty* was decommissioned, on June 28, 1968. In 1970 the ship was turned over to the U.S. Maritime Administration and sold for $101,666.66. In 1973 the ship came to an ignominious end in Baltimore's Curtis Bay shipyard as welders' torches at last did what the Israeli attack hadn't. She was cut up and sold for scrap.

On April 28, 1969, almost two years after the attack, the Israeli government finally paid about $20,000 to each of the wounded crewmen. This compensation was obtained, however, only after the men retained private counsel to negotiate with Israel's lawyers in Washington. A substantial portion of the claim, therefore, went to lawyers' fees. Ten months earlier, the Israelis had paid about $100,000 to each of the families of those killed.

Finally, the U.S. government asked a token $7,644,146 for Israel's destruction of the ship, even though $20 million had been spent several years earlier to convert her to a signals intelligence ship and another $10.2 million had gone for the highly sophisticated hardware. Yet despite the modest amount requested, and the agony its armed forces had caused, the Israeli government spent thirteen years in an unseemly battle to avoid paying. By the winter of 1980, the interest alone had reached $10 million. Israeli ambassador Ephraim Evron then suggested that if the United States asked for $6 million—and eliminated the interest entirely—his country *might* be willing to pay. President Jimmy Carter, on his way out of office, agreed, and in December 1980 accepted the paltry $6 million.

In the days following the attack, the Israeli government gave the U.S. government a classified report that attempted to justify the claim that the attack was a mistake. On the basis of that same report, an Israeli court of inquiry completely exonerated the government and all those involved. No one was ever court-martialed, reduced in rank, or even reprimanded. On the contrary, Israel chose instead to honor Motor Torpedo Boat 203, which fired the deadly torpedo at the *Liberty*. The ship's wheel and bell were placed on prominent display at the naval museum, among the maritime artifacts of which the Israeli navy was most proud.

Despite the overwhelming evidence that Israel had attacked the ship and killed the American servicemen deliberately, the Johnson administration and Congress covered up the entire incident. Johnson was planning to run for president the following year and needed the support of pro-Israel voters. His administration's actions were disgraceful. Although Captain McGonagle was awarded the Congressional Medal of Honor for his heroism in saving the ship and bringing it back to safety, senior White House officials decided to keep the occasion as quiet as possible. Because the medal, the nation's highest honor, is only rarely awarded, it is almost always presented by the president in a high-profile White House ceremony. But McGonagle's award was given by the secretary of the Navy in a low-profile, hastily arranged gathering at the Washington Navy Yard, a scrappy base on the banks of the smelly Anacostia River.

"I must have gone to the White House fifteen times or more to watch the president personally award the Congressional Medal of Honor to Americans of special valor," said Admiral Thomas H. Moorer, who became Chief of Naval Operations within weeks of the attack. "So it irked the hell out of me when McGonagle's ceremony was relegated to the obscurity of the Washington Navy Yard and the medal was presented by the Secretary of the Navy. This was a back-handed slap. Everyone else received their medal at the White House. President Johnson must have been concerned about the reaction of the Israeli lobby."

Later, a naval officer connected with the awards told Jim Ennes, a lieutenant on the ship, the reason. "The government is pretty jumpy about Israel," he said. "The State Department even asked the Israeli ambassador if his government had any objections to McGonagle getting the medal. 'Certainly not!' Israel said. But to avoid any possible offense, McGonagle's citation does not mention Israel at all, and the award ceremony kept the lowest possible profile."

In the period immediately after the incident, several quick reviews were conducted by the Navy and CIA, among other agencies. However, they dealt principally with such topics as the failure of the Naval Communications System and how the crew of the ship performed during the crisis. No American investigators ever looked into the "why" question or brought the probe to Israel, the scene of the crime. Investigators simply accepted Israel's bizarre "mistake" report at face value. This was a document which included such statements as a claim by the torpedo-boat crew that the *Liberty*—an ancient World War II cargo ship then loitering at five knots—was attempting to escape at an incredible thirty knots (the *Liberty*'s top speed was seventeen knots)—outracing even their torpedo boats. This was the reason, the report said, for calling in the air force.

The Israeli report then said that their observers checked in *Jane's Fighting Ships* and misidentified the *Liberty* as *El Quseir*, an Egyptian troop and horse transport. But *Jane's* gave the top speed of *El Quseir* as only fourteen knots; how could a ship supposedly doing thirty knots have been mistaken for it? *Jane's* also contained details on the *Liberty*, the same details that Commander Pinchas Pinchasy, at air force headquarters, had used to positively identify the ship. (And Pinchasy had reported the identification to Israeli naval headquarters.)

The Israeli report also said that the whole reason for the attack was to stop the *Liberty*, with its few short-range machine guns, from bombarding the town of El Arish, more than a dozen miles away. This was nonsense.

Nevertheless, most of the U.S. investigations took the path of least resistance, the one onto which they were pushed by the White House, and accepted the "mistake" theory. Incredibly, considering that 34 American servicemen had been killed and 171 more wounded, and that a ship of the U.S. Navy had been nearly sunk (no U.S. naval vessel since World War II had suffered a higher percentage [69 percent] of battle casualties), Congress held no public hearings. With an election coming up, no one in the weak-kneed House and Senate wanted to offend powerful pro-Israel groups and lose their fat campaign contributions.

But according to interviews and documents obtained for *Body of Secrets*, the senior leadership of NSA, officials who had unique access to the secret tapes and other highly classified evidence, was virtually unanimous in their belief that the attack was deliberate. They strongly believed that Israel feared what the *Liberty* might have intercepted, and therefore ordered it killed leaving no survivors.

Israel has never wavered on one critical point: that no one ever saw a flag flying from the *Liberty* during either the air or sea attack, despite the virtually unanimous agreement among survivors that flags were flying during both periods. "Throughout the contact," said the "mistake" report, "no Israeli plane or torpedo boat saw an American or any other flag on the ship."

But former Chief Marvin Nowicki, the senior Hebrew linguist on the EC-121 flying above the scene, knows what he heard. "As I recall, we recorded most, if not all, of the attack," he said. "I heard a couple of references to the flag during an apparent attack." Nowicki, who later received a Ph.D. in political science and taught public administration at the college level, is an enthusiastic supporter of Israel, who originally assumed his information would help clear Israel. Instead, it convicts the government. If the Israelis did see the flag, then the attack was cold-blooded murder—like the hundreds of earlier murders committed by Israelis that day at El Arish.

As soon as the incident began, Marshall Carter appointed a small task force led by Walter Deeley, a senior official in the Production Organization, the agency's Sigint operations division. The task force was to keep track of all information regarding the *Liberty* and prepare a report for the director. Unlike the other probes, this one included all the signals intelligence details—the intercept tapes from the EC-121, and interviews with the signals intelligence survivors from the *Liberty*. Because of the enormous secrecy in which NSA held its Sigint operations, and especially because the information involved its most secret activity—eavesdropping on a close ally—the details were never shared with anyone else. In the end, Walter Deeley came to the only possible conclusion, given his knowledge of Israel's intelligence capabilities. "There is no way that they didn't know that the *Liberty* was American," he said, suggesting premeditated murder.

NSA Director Carter agreed. "There was no other answer than that it was deliberate," he told the author in a 1980 interview, although he asked that the information be kept off the record at the time. Carter has since died.

NSA's deputy director, Dr. Louis Tordella, also believed that the Israeli attack was deliberate and that the Israeli government was attempting to cover it up. According to highly classified and long-hidden NSA documents obtained for *Body of Secrets,* Tordella not only put his belief in an internal memorandum for the record but also expressed his view to Congressman George Mahon (D-Texas) of the House Appropriations Committee. "Mr. Mahon probed several times to discover the reason for the Israeli attack," wrote Tordella on June 20, 1967, nearly two weeks after the incident. "I told him we simply did not know from either open or intelligence sources but that, by now, there probably was a fair amount of denial and cover-up by the Israelis for the sake of protecting their national position. He asked my private opinion of the attack and I said that, for what it was worth, I believed the attack might have been ordered by some senior commander on the Sinai Peninsula who wrongly suspected that the *Liberty* was monitoring his activities.

"He asked if a mistake of this sort was common or should be expected," Tordella continued. "I told him that I thought a ship the size of the *Liberty* was unlike and much larger than Egyptian ships and that an obviously cargo-type vessel should not reasonably be mistaken by competent naval forces or air pilots for an Egyptian man-of-war. At best I estimated that the attacking ships and planes were guilty of gross negligence and carelessness." So angry was Tordella over the attack and cover-up that he scrawled across the top of the Israeli "mistake" report: "A nice whitewash."

Finally, U.S. Air Force Major General John Morrison, at the time the deputy chief—and later chief—of NSA's operations, did not buy the Israeli "mistake" explanation, either. "Nobody believes that explanation," he said in a recent interview with the author. "The only conjecture that we ever made that made any near sense is that the Israelis did not want us to intercept their communications at that time." When informed by the author of the gruesome war crimes then taking place at El Arish, Morrison saw the connection. "That would be enough," he said. "Twelve miles is nothing. . . . They wouldn't want us to get in on that." He added: "You've got the motive. . . . What a hell of a thing to do."

Even without knowledge of the murders taking place nearby in the desert, many in NSA's G Group, who analyzed the intercepts sent back by both the *Liberty* and the EC-121, were convinced that the attack was no mistake. And among the survivors of the *Liberty*, the conviction is virtually unanimous. "The Israelis got by with cold-blooded, premeditated murder of Americans on June 8, 1967," said Phillip F. Tourney, president of the USS *Liberty* Veterans Association, in July 2000. "There is widespread cynicism that our elected officials will not go up against the powerful Israeli lobby out of fear. . . . This cover-up must be investigated, now."

For more than thirty years, Captain William L. McGonagle refused to say a single word on the issue of whether the killing of his crew was done with foreknowledge or by mistake. Finally, dying of cancer in November 1998, he at last broke his long silence. "After many years I finally believe that the attack was deliberate," he said. "I don't think there has been an adequate investigation of the incident. . . . The flag was flying prior to the attack on the ship." McGonagle died less than four months later, on March 3, 1999, at the age of seventy-three.

Even without the NSA evidence, many people in the administration disbelieved the Israeli "mistake" report. "Frankly, there was considerable skepticism in the White House that the attack was accidental," said George Christian, Johnson's press secretary at the time. "I became convinced that an accident of this magnitude was too much to swallow. If it were a deliberate attack the question remains, of course, of whether it was a tactical decision on the part of elements of the Israeli military or whether it was ordered by high officials."

Another NSA review, conducted fifteen years later and classified Top Secret/Umbra, ridiculed the decision by the Israeli court of inquiry that accepted the "mistake" theory and exonerated all Israeli officials. "Exculpation of Israeli nationals," it said, "apparently not being hindmost in the court's calculations." Next the review accused the Israeli fighter pilots of outright perjury:

> Though the pilots testified to the contrary, every official interview of numerous *Liberty* crewmen gives consistent evidence that indeed the *Liberty was* flying an American flag—and, further, the weather conditions were ideal to assure its easy observance and identification. These circumstances—prior identification of the *Liberty* and easy visibility of the American flag—prompted the Department of State to inform the Israeli Government that "the later military attack by Israeli aircraft on the USS *Liberty* is quite literally incomprehensible. As a minimum, the attack must be condemned as an act of military recklessness reflecting wanton disregard for human life." (Emphasis in original.)

The pilots, said the report, were not the only ones lying: the story told by the torpedo-boat crewmen who blew up the ship—after missing with their first four torpedoes—was also unbelievable. The torpedo-boat crew claimed that they had mistaken the *Liberty* for an Egyptian troop transport, *El Quseir.* At the time of the attack, the Egyptian ship was rusting alongside a pier in the port of Alexandria, 250 miles from where the *Liberty* was attacked, and along that pier *El Quseir* remained throughout the war. The location of every Egyptian ship would have been a key piece of intelligence before Israel launched its war. According to the long-secret 1981 NSA report:

> The fact that two separate torpedo boat commanders made the same false identification only raises the question of the veracity of both commanders. The *El-Kasir* [*El Quseir*]

was approximately one-quarter of the *Liberty*'s tonnage, about one-half its length, and offered a radically different silhouette. To claim that the *Liberty* closely resembled the *El-Kasir* was most illogical. The Department of State expressed its view of the torpedo attack in these words:

"The subsequent attack by Israeli torpedo boats, substantially after the vessel was or should have been identified by Israeli military forces, manifests the same reckless disregard for human life. The silhouette and conduct of USS *Liberty* readily distinguished it from any vessel that could have been considered hostile. . . . It could and should have been scrutinized visually at close range before torpedoes were fired."

Finally the NSA report, fifteen years after the fact, added:

A persistent question relating to the *Liberty* incident is whether or not the Israeli forces which attacked the ship knew that it was American . . . not a few of the *Liberty*'s crewmen and [deleted but probably "NSA's G Group"] staff are convinced that they did. Their belief derived from consideration of the long time the Israelis had the ship under surveillance prior to the attack, the visibility of the flag, and the intensity of the attack itself.

Speculation as to the Israeli motivation varied. Some believed that Israel expected that the complete destruction of the ship and killing of the personnel would lead the U.S. to blame the UAR [Egypt] for the incident and bring the U.S. into the war on the side of Israel . . . others felt that Israeli forces wanted the ship and men out of the way.

"I believed the attack might have been ordered by some senior commander on the Sinai Peninsula who wrongly suspected that the *Liberty* was monitoring his activities," said Tordella. His statement was amazingly astute, since he likely had no idea of the war crimes being committed on the Sinai at the time, within easy earshot of the antenna groves that covered the *Liberty*'s deck.

On the morning of June 8, the Israeli military command received a report that a large American eavesdropping ship was secretly listening only a few miles off El Arish. At that same moment, a scant dozen or so miles away, Israeli soldiers were butchering civilians and bound prisoners by the hundreds, a fact that the entire Israeli army leadership knew about and condoned, according to the army's own historian. Another military historian, Uri Milstein, confirmed the report. There were many incidents in the Six Day War, he said, in which Egyptian soldiers were killed by Israeli troops after they had raised their hands in surrender. "It was not an official policy," he added, "but there was an atmosphere that it was okay to do it. Some commanders decided to do it; others refused. But everyone knew about it."

Israel had no way of knowing that NSA's Hebrew linguists were not on the ship, but on a plane flying high above. Nevertheless, evidence of the slaughter might indeed have been captured by the unmanned recorders in the NSA spaces. Had the torpedo not made a direct hit there, the evidence might have been discovered when the tapes were transmitted or shipped back to NSA. At the time, Israel was loudly proclaiming—to the United States, to the United Nations, and to the world—that it was the victim of Egyptian aggression and that it alone held the moral high ground. Israel's commanders would not have wanted tape recordings of evidence of the slaughters to wind up on desks at the White House, the UN, or the *Washington Post.* Had the jamming and unmarked fighters knocked out all communications in the first minute, as they attempted to do; had the torpedo boat quickly sunk the ship, as intended; and had the machine gunners destroyed all the life rafts and killed any survivors, there would have been no one left alive to tell any stories.

That was the conclusion of a study on the *Liberty* done for the U.S. Navy's *Naval Law Review,* written by a Navy lawyer, Lieutenant Commander Walter L. Jacobsen. "To speculate on the motives of an attack group that uses unmarked planes and deprives helpless survivors of life rafts raises disturbing possibilities," he wrote, "including the one that the *Liberty* crew was not meant to survive the attack, and would not have, but for the incorrect 6th Fleet radio broadcast that help was on its way—which had the effect of chasing off the MTBs [motor torpedo boats]."

Since the very beginning, Admiral Thomas H. Moorer, appointed Chief of Naval Operations shortly after the attack, has also been convinced that the assault was deliberate. "I have to conclude that it was Israel's intent to sink the *Liberty* and leave as few survivors as possible," he said in 1997, on the thirtieth anniversary of the assault. "Israel knew perfectly well that the ship was American."

And in a CIA report received by that agency on July 27, 1967, a CIA official quotes one of his sources, who seems to be an Israeli government official:

> [Regarding the] attack on USS *LIBERTY* by Israeli airplanes and torpedo boats . . . He said that, "You've got to remember that in this campaign there is neither time nor room for mistakes," which was intended as an obtuse reference that Israel's forces knew what flag the *LIBERTY* was flying and exactly what the vessel was doing off the coast. [Deletion] implied that the ship's identity was known six hours before the attack but that Israeli headquarters was not sure as to how many people might have access to the information the *LIBERTY* was intercepting. He also implied that [deletion] was no certainty on controls as to where the intercepted information was going and again reiterated that Israeli forces did not make mistakes in their campaign. He was emphatic in stating to me that they knew what kind of ship the USS *LIBERTY* was and what it was doing offshore.

The CIA called the document "raw intelligence data," and said it was one of "several which indicated a possibility that the Israeli Government knew about the USS *Liberty* before the attack."

In fact, another CIA report, prepared in 1979, indicates that Israel not only knew a great deal about the subject of signals intelligence during the 1967 war, but that Sigint was a major source of their information on the Arabs. "The Israelis have been very successful in their Comint and Elint operations against the Arabs," said the report. "During the Six-Day War in 1967, the Israelis succeeded in intercepting, breaking, and disseminating a tremendous volume of Arab traffic quickly and accurately, including a high-level conversation between the late President Gamal Abdel Nasser of the UAR and King Hussein of Jordan. Over the years the Israelis have mounted cross-border operations and tapped Arab landline communications for extended periods. The Israelis have also on occasion boobytrapped the landlines."

The same CIA report also made clear that after collecting intelligence on the Arab world, spying on the United States was Israel's top priority: "The principal targets of the Israeli intelligence and security services are: . . . (2) collection of information on secret U.S. policy or decisions, if any, concerning Israel."

A mistake or mass murder? It was a question Congress never bothered to address in public hearings at the time. Among those who have long called for an in-depth congressional investigation was Admiral Thomas Moorer, who went on to become chairman of the Joint Chiefs of Staff. "Congress to this day," he said, "has failed to hold formal hearings for the record on the *Liberty* affair. This is unprecedented and a national disgrace." Perhaps it is not too late, especially for a Congress that rushes into lengthy hearings on such momentous events as the firing of a few employees from a travel office in the White House.

Throughout its history, Israel has hidden its abominable human rights record behind pious religious claims. Critics are regularly silenced with outrageous charges of anti-Semitism—even many *Liberty* crewmembers who managed to survive the bloody attack and dared call for an investigation. Evidence of Israel's deliberate killing of civilians is as recent as May 2000. The British Broadcasting Corporation has charged that the death of one of its drivers that month was caused by a deliberate and unprovoked strike on civilian targets during an Israeli tank attack.

The driver was Abed Takkoush, a news assistant for the BBC in Lebanon for twenty-five years. Takkoush was killed on May 23, when an Israeli Merkava tank, in Israel, fired an artillery shell across the southern Lebanon border at his blue Mercedes. "I saw Abed lurch out of the driver's side of the car and then fall to the ground," said Jeremy Bowen, the BBC reporter whom Takkoush had driven to the scene. As Bowen rushed to help the driver, Israelis opened up on him with machine-gun fire. They also fired at a Lebanese Red Cross truck as it attempted to come to the rescue.

According to the BBC's account, which is supported by extensive video footage from its own camera crew and those of four other television news organizations, the killing was totally unprovoked. "Everything was quiet," said Bowen. There had been no gunfire, rocket attacks, or artillery exchanges during the day as Israeli forces withdrew from southern Lebanon, which they had occupied for more than two decades. Bowen was close enough to the border to wave at residents of a local kibbutz across the fence. Predictably, as it did in the case of the attack on the *Liberty*, the Israeli government claimed the shooting was a "mistake." But the BBC was not buying that, and instead began investigating whether Israel could be accused of a war crimes violation under the Geneva Convention.

Even more damningly, the BBC contends that its news film shows that the Israeli Army "appeared to be sporadically targeting vehicles" driven by Lebanese civilians along the same stretch of road earlier on May 23 and on May 22, despite the absence of any "retaliatory fire from the Lebanese side of the border."

Since the Israeli attack on the *Liberty*, U.S. taxpayers have subsidized that country's government to the tune of $100 *billion* or more—enough to fund NSA for the next quarter of a century. There should be no question that U.S. investigators be allowed to pursue their probe wherever it takes them and question whoever they need to question, regardless of borders. At the same time, NSA should be required to make all transcripts available from the EC-121 and any other platform that eavesdropped on the eastern Mediterranean on June 8, 1967. For more than a decade, the transcripts of those conversations lay neglected in the bottom of a desk drawer in NSA's G643 office, the Israeli Military Section of G Group.

The time for secrecy has long passed on the USS *Liberty* incident, in both Israel and the United States. Based on the above evidence, there is certainly more than enough probable cause to conduct a serious investigation into what really happened—and why.

CHAPTER EIGHT

SPINE

VGWEQVSM SVWEDQSNV AUSMYD NFEDV YE BVWAVW SAWVVBVMY
UJSK HLK LKHUE OX LXNN IXXD JD PXOXL SJOE SHIJDX
EVFCMV TSEX MI JBVTRFB FCXRIO, RILWCX-TSEOWBJ VBEVMI
UMSBHWSEC HRCHWRFV KMSJ TCMURVB DMC WSFCEDEVF HMUTWFBCV
YVBXFWY YOLZ GLAYVSFBY, IOWYEGETAY ESITREFAR ZERO OSLY

Despite the trauma of losing a ship and many of its men, neither the NSA nor the Navy learned much; in less than a year more blood would run across gray decks, and another seagoing listening post would be lost.

Long before the *Liberty* was attacked, the Navy had become disenchanted with the entire NSA oceangoing program. Navy personnel had become little more than seagoing chauffeurs and hired hands for NSA, permitted to eavesdrop on targets of great interest to the Navy only when doing so could not in any way interfere with the program's primary mission of monitoring NSA's targets. To listen to foreign naval signals, the Navy had to stick its analysts in awkward, antenna-covered mobile vans placed aboard destroyers and destroyer escorts. But doing so meant pulling the ships out of normal service to patrol slowly along distant coasts, rather than taking part in fleet exercises and other activities. It was a highly inefficient operation, combining the minimum collection capability of a crowded steel box with the maximum costs of using a destroyer to cart it around.

"The Navy was very interested in having a trawler program of their own," said Gene Sheck, formerly a deputy chief within NSA's collection organization, K Group. Sheck managed the mobile platforms, such as the Sigint aircraft, ships, and submarines. "The Navy position pretty clearly was that they wanted a Navy platform controlled by Navy, responsive to Navy kinds of things." The Navy said they needed their own fleet not just for collecting signals intelligence, but also for a wide variety of intelligence activities. A fleet would be useful, they said, for such things as hydrographic intelligence—analyzing the salinity of the ocean at various locations, which could enable better tracking of Soviet submarines.

But NSA was not buying that. "It was totally Sigint," Sheck said. "When they tried to tell us about all this other collection, it consisted of a rope and a bucket, and it pulled water out of the ocean. . . . I said, 'You're not going to get away with [this] garbage. The director of NSA is going to have a lot to say about what you do with Sigint platforms.' "

Nevertheless, despite the NSA's serious misgivings over its loss of control, the Navy began laying out ambitious plans for its own Sigint fleet. "We talked once . . . about having small intelligence gathering ships . . . two hundred of them," said one Navy admiral who was involved. Chosen as the maiden vessel for the Navy's own spy fleet was the U.S.S. *Banner* (AGER—Auxiliary General Environmental Research—1), a humble little craft that had spent most of its life bouncing from atoll to atoll in the Mariana Islands and was then on its way back to the United States to retire in mothballs. At 906 tons and 176 feet, the twenty-one-year-old ship was a dwarf compared with the 10,680 tons and 455 feet of the *Liberty*.

Like a short football player overcompensating for his size, the *Banner* wasted no time in sailing into harm's way. It was assigned to the Far East, and its first patrol, in 1965, took it within four miles of Siberia's Cape Povorotny Bay to test the Soviets' reaction to the penetration of their twelve-mile limit. At the time, the United States disputed the U.S.S.R.'s assertion of that limit. As the *Banner* chugged north toward Siberia, a frigid storm began caking ice forward and on the superstructure. Still closer, and Soviet destroyers and patrol boats began harassment exercises, darting in and out toward the bobbing trawler, sometimes closing to within twenty-five yards before veering away. But as a fresh storm began brewing, the fear of capsizing under the weight of the ice predominated, and the *Banner*'s skipper, Lieutenant Robert P. Bishop, radioed his headquarters in Yokosuka and then swung 180 degrees back toward its base in Japan. Several hours later a reply came through, ordering him back and warning him not to be intimidated. Bishop obeyed and turned back into the storm, but finally gave up after progressing a total of minus two miles over the next twenty-four hours.

During sixteen missions over the next two years, the *Banner* became the tough gal on the block, always looking for a fight. And on its patrols off Russia, more often than not it found one. It had been bumped, nearly rammed, buzzed by Soviet MiGs and helicopters, and come under threat of cannon fire. In each case, the *Banner* managed to wiggle out of the potentially explosive situation.

Sam Tooma was a civilian oceanographer on the ship who helped maintain the cover story. Employed by the U.S. Naval Oceanographic Office, he would take various readings from the ocean during the missions. "We were operating twelve miles (at least) off [the Soviet port of] Vladivostok in February," he recalled. "The wind was blowing off the mainland at a ferocious speed. It was sort of raining, sleeting, and God knows what else. . . . I wear glasses, and they were coated with ice, as was the rest of my face. It took forever to take a station. I don't know how many times I thought that if Hell were the worst place on earth, then I was in Hell. I have never been more miserable in my whole life as when I was on the deck of the *Banner* trying to collect oceanographic data.

"We were constantly being harassed by the Russians," said Tooma, who would frequently discuss with the captain what would happen if the ship were attacked or towed into Vladivostok. "Right now there are aircraft on standby ready to take off if they pull some fool stunt like that," he was told. "Our aircraft would destroy the naval base, including this ship." One March, Tooma was on the bridge when a Soviet ship began heading straight for the *Banner*. "Some of the watch-standers started to act quite excited and began yelling about the 'crazy Russians,' " he said. "The captain ordered the helmsman to maintain course. According to international rules of the road, we had the right of way. Meanwhile, the distance between them and us was closing quite rapidly. We continued to maintain course, until I thought that we were all doomed. At the last second, the captain ordered the helmsman to go hard right rudder. I'm glad that he didn't wait any longer, because all we got was a glancing blow. We had a fairly nice dent in our port bow." Later Tooma was ordered never to mention the incident.

Codenamed Operation Clickbeetle, the *Banner*'s signals intelligence missions became almost legendary within the spy world. The reams of intercepts sent back to Washington exceeded expectations and NSA, now the junior partner, asked that the scrappy spy ship try its luck against China and North Korea. The change in assignment was agreed to and the harassment continued. The most serious incident took place in the East China Sea off Shanghai in November 1966, when eleven metal-hulled Chinese trawlers began closing in on the *Banner.* However, after more than two and a half hours of harassment, Lieutenant Bishop skillfully managed to maneuver away from the danger without accident. "There were some touchy situations," said retired Vice Admiral Edwin B. Hooper. "At times she was harassed by the Chinese and retired. Occasionally the Seventh Fleet had destroyers waiting over the horizon. . . . *Banner* was highly successful, so successful that Washington then wanted to convert two more. The first of these was the *Pueblo.*" The second would be the USS *Palm Beach.*

A sister ship of the *Banner,* the *Pueblo* was built in 1944 as a general-purpose supply vessel for the U.S. Army. She saw service in the Philippines and later in Korea, retiring from service in 1954, where she remained until summoned back to duty on April 12, 1966. Over the next year and a half she underwent conversion from a forgotten rust bucket into an undercover electronic spy at the Puget Sound Naval Shipyard at Bremerton, Washington. She was commissioned in May 1967.

"The *Liberty*[-size] ships were owned by NSA pretty much and were designed and operated in support of their operations, strictly collection for NSA," said Lieutenant Stephen R. Harris, a Harvard graduate who was selected to run the Sigint operation on the ship. "*Pueblo* and company were supposed to be more tactical support to the fleet, although I don't think that ever came to be, so we were operating in support of the Navy. However, all the data that we would have gathered went to NSA for their more detailed analysis." Before his assignment to the *Pueblo,* Harris was assigned to a naval unit at NSA headquarters and also went on hazardous Sigint missions aboard submarines cruising close to hostile shores.

Chosen to skipper the *Pueblo* was Lloyd Mark (Pete) Bucher, a Navy commander with a youth as rough as a provocative cruise on the *Banner.* Bounced from relative to relative, then put out on the street at age seven, he eventually ended up in an orphanage and, finally, at Father Flanagan's Boys Town. Then he dropped out of high school, joined the Navy, and eventually was commissioned after receiving his high school diploma and a degree from the University of Nebraska. A submariner, he had always dreamed of skippering his own sub. Instead, he was put in charge of a spy boat that spent most of its time sailing in circles.

Adding to the insult, he discovered that a large section of his own ship was only partly under his command. He had to share responsibility for the signals intelligence spaces with NSA and its Naval Security Group. In these spaces, he had to first show Harris, a junior officer, that he had a need to know before he could learn some of the secrets held by his own ship.

In October 1967, Harris flew to Washington for briefings on the ship by NSA and the Naval Security Group. "The location of the first mission hadn't been decided upon," he said, "but I was sure we were going to do some productive things. So I selected a list of countries which I thought were significant, and went around to various offices at NSA and talked to people about them. North Korea was on my list. I remember feeling, 'Well, we might go there.' "

Through an agreement between the Navy and NSA, it was decided that the *Banner* and *Pueblo* "would do one patrol in response to Navy tasking and then one patrol in response to NSA tasking," said Gene Sheck of K Group. "It was decided that because the *Banner* . . . had completed a patrol off the Soviet coast, that why don't you guys, Navy, you take the first patrol of the *Pueblo* and designate where you want it to go. . . . They, the Navy, determined that the ship ought to operate off North Korea in 1967. And we, NSA, at that particular point in time, had no problem with that." The *Pueblo*'s missions would be codenamed Ichthyic, a word that means having the character of a fish.

A few weeks later, the *Pueblo* departed the West Coast on the first leg of its journey to Japan, where it was to join the *Banner* on signals intelligence patrols in the Far East.

While Harris was walking the long halls at NSA, getting briefings, reading secret documents, and scanning maps, a man with darting eyes was walking quickly up a sidewalk on Sixteenth Street in northwest Washington. A dozen blocks behind him stood the North Portico of the White House. Just before reaching the University Club, he made a quick turn through a black wrought-iron fence that protected a gray turn-of-the-century gothic stone mansion. On the side of the door was a gold plaque bearing the letters "CCCP"—the Russian abbreviation of "Union of Soviet Socialist Republics."

A few minutes later, Yakof Lukashevich, a slender Soviet embassy security officer with stiff, unruly hair, greeted the man. "I want to sell you top secrets," the man impatiently told the Russian. "Valuable military information. I've brought along a sample." With that, he reached into the front pocket of his jacket and handed Lukashevich a top secret NSA keylist for the U.S. military's worldwide KL-47 cipher machine. With it, and the right equipment, the Russians would be able to break one of America's most secret cipher systems. "My name is James," the man said. "James Harper." It was the beginning of a long and profitable relationship. Within weeks Harper would also be selling the Soviets keylists for the KW-7, a cipher system more modern and secret than the KL-47. Over KW-7 passed some of the nation's most valuable information.

The afternoon was as gray as the *Pueblo*'s wet bow when the ship steamed gently into the Yokosuka Channel. Sailors in midnight-blue pea coats and white Dixie Cup hats raced about in the frigid December wind arranging thick brown lines and shouting instructions as the ship nudged alongside Pier 8 South at Yokosuka Naval Base, just south of Tokyo. After nearly a year of preparation, the *Pueblo* was now positioned for the start of its first mission.

Across the Sea of Japan sat its target, North Korea, a mysterious volcano sending out increasingly violent tremors after a decade of lying dormant. Starting in May, teams of heavily armed agents began landing in rear areas of South Korea with orders to test the guerrilla environment. Since September, trains had twice been sabotaged. In October and November there were seven attempts to kill or capture U.S. and South Korean personnel in or near the DMZ. Finally, several ambushes resulted in the death of six American and seven South Korean soldiers. Between January 1 and September 1, 1967, there had been some 360 incidents of all types, compared with 42 for the entire previous year.

Despite the growing storm clouds, the approval process for the *Pueblo*'s first mission was moving ahead like a chain letter. The outline for the operation was contained in a fat three-ring binder, the Monthly Reconnaissance Schedule for January 1968. Full of classification markings and codewords, it was put together by the Joint Chiefs of Staff's

Joint Reconnaissance Center. Inside the black notebook was a menu of all of the next month's technical espionage operations, from U-2 missions over China to patrols by the USNS *Muller* off Cuba to deep penetrations into Russia's White Sea by the attack submarine USS *Scorpion*. The Navy had evaluated the *Pueblo*'s mission, a dozen miles off the North Korean coast, as presenting a minimal risk.

On December 27, at 11:00 in the morning, middle-ranking officials from an alphabet of agencies gathered in the Pentagon's "tank," Room 2E924, to work out any differences concerning the various platforms and their targets. The action officers from the CIA, NSA, DIA, JCS, and other agencies routinely gave their approvals, and the binder—"the size of a Sears, Roebuck catalogue," said one former official—was sent on its way. Two days later, a courier hand-carried it around to the various agencies for final approval. At the Pentagon, Paul H. Nitze, the deputy secretary of defense, signed off on it, and at the White House, the National Security Council's secret 303 Committee, which reviews covert operations, gave the *Pueblo* mission an okay. There were no comments and no disapprovals.

But at NSA, one analyst did have some concerns. A retired Navy chief petty officer assigned to B Group, the section that analyzed Sigint from Communist Asia, knew that North Korea had little tolerance for electronic eavesdropping missions. Three years earlier, they had attempted to blast an RB-47 Strato-Spy out of the air while it was flying in international airspace about eighty miles east of the North Korean port of Wonsan. This was the same area where the *Pueblo* was to loiter—only much closer, about thirteen miles off the coast.

Codenamed Box Top, the RB-47 flight was a routine Peacetime Airborne Reconnaissance Program (PARPRO) mission. It departed from Yokota Air Base in Japan on April 28, 1965, and headed over the Sea of Japan toward its target area. "We were about six hours into one of those ho-hum missions on a leg heading toward Wonsan harbor, approximately eighty nautical miles out," recalled one of the Ravens, First Lieutenant George V. Back, "when the hours of boredom suddenly turned into the seconds of terror." Raven One, Air Force Captain Robert C. Winters, intercepted a very weak, unidentifiable airborne intercept (AI) signal that he thought might have come from somewhere off his tail. "At approximately the same time," said Back, "we received a message that there were 'bogies' in the area. Neither the pilot nor the copilot observed any aircraft and we continued the mission."

A short while later, Back, down in the cramped, windowless Sigint spaces, intercepted a signal from a ground control radar and began recording it. By then the plane was about thirty-five to forty miles off Wonsan Harbor. "Suddenly the aircraft pitched nose down and began losing altitude," he said. "The altimeter was reading about twenty-seven thousand feet and unwinding." "They are shooting at us," yelled Henry E. Dubuy, the co-pilot, over the intercom. "We are hit and going down." Back began initiating the ejection process and depressurized the Raven compartment. Next the co-pilot requested permission to fire. "Shoot the bastard down," shouted Lieutenant Colonel Hobart D. Mattison, the pilot, as he made repeated Mayday calls into his radio. He then asked for a heading "to get the hell out of here."

"By this time," recalled Back, "all hell had broken loose. The pilot had his hands full with the rapidly deteriorating airplane; the co-pilot was trying to shoot the bastards visually; the navigator was trying to give the pilot a heading; the Raven One was dumping chaff, and the second MiG-17 was moving in for his gunnery practice." The two North Korean MiG-17s came in shooting. "There was no warning, ID pass, or intimidation," said Back, "just cannon fire." The planes were too close for the RB-47's fire control radar to lock on to them.

By now the Strato-Spy was severely wounded. The hydraulic system failed and fire was coming from the aft main tank. Two engines had also been hit, and shrapnel from number three engine exploded into the fuselage. Nevertheless, said Back, "both engines continued to operate but number three vibrated like an old car with no universal joints."

Dubuy, the co-pilot, fired away at the MiGs but without tracers it was hard to tell where he was shooting. The MiGs would dive down, then quickly bring their nose up and attempt to rake the underside of the plane with cannon fire. Down in the Raven compartment, Robert Winters released a five-second burst of chaff during one of the firing passes, hoping to throw off the MiG's radar. Dubuy watched as the MiG nearly disappeared in the chaff cloud before breaking off. Finally the MiGs began taking some fire. One suddenly turned completely vertical and headed toward the sea, nose down. The other MiG headed back toward Wonsan.

As Colonel Mattison leveled out at 14,000 feet, the plane was still trailing smoke. The aft wheel well bulkhead was blackened and nearly buckled from the heat of the fire, and the aircraft was flying in a nose-down attitude because of the loss of the aft main fuel tank. Mattison assured the crew that he had the plane under control but told them to be ready to bail out. Despite the heavy damage, the Strato-Spy made it back to Yokota and hit hard on the runway. "We porpoised about eighty feet back into the air where we nearly hit the fire suppression helicopter flying above us," said Back. Once the plane had come to a stop, he added, "we exited, dodging emergency equipment as we headed for the edge of the runway."

With that incident and others clearly in mind, the Navy chief in B Group went down to the operation managers in K Group. "This young fellow had a message drafted," said Gene Sheck of K-12, "that said, 'Boy, you people have got to be complete blithering idiots to put that ship off North Korea, because all kinds of bad things are going to happen. Therefore cancel it.' It had very strong [language], not the kind of political message you'd ever get out of the building." An official from K Group therefore rewrote the message, the first warning message Sheck had ever sent out:

> The following information is provided to aid in your assessment of CINCPAC's [Commander-in-Chief, Pacific] estimate of risk:
>
> 1. The North Korean Air Force has been extremely sensitive to peripheral reconnaissance flights in the area since early 1965. (This sensitivity was emphasized on April 28, 1965, when a U.S. Air Force RB-47 was fired on and severely damaged 35 to 40 nautical miles from the coast.)
> 2. The North Korean Air Force has assumed an additional role of naval support since late 1966.

3. The North Korean Navy reacts to any ROK [Republic of Korea] naval vessel or ROK fishing vessel near the North Korean coast line.

4. Internationally recognized boundaries as they relate to airborne activities are generally not honored by North Korea on the East Coast of North Korea. But there is no [Sigint] evidence of provocative harassing activities by North Korean vessels beyond 12 nautical miles from the coast.

The above is provided to aid in evaluating the requirements for ship protective measures and is not intended to reflect adversely on CINCPACFLT [Commander-in-Chief, Pacific Fleet] deployment proposal.

Marshall Carter approved the message and at 10:28 that Friday night it rattled onto a cipher machine at the Defense Intelligence Agency's Signal Office in the Pentagon. There a clerk routed it up to the War Room, where a watch officer sent a copy to the chief of the JCS's Joint Reconnaissance Center, Brigadier General Ralph Steakley.

"This was the first voyage in which we were having a vessel linger for a long period of time near North Korean waters," Carter recalled. "It therefore was a special mission as we saw it. We knew that she was going to stay in international waters. We had no evidence that the North Koreans at sea had ever interfered with or had any intentions to interfere with a U.S. vessel outside of their acknowledged territorial waters. Nevertheless, our people felt that even though all of this information was already available in intelligence community reports it would be helpful if we summed them up and gave them to the Joint Chiefs of Staff for whatever use they might make of them or assistance in evaluating this particular mission."

Had NSA wished, it could have called off the entire mission. But because this first *Pueblo* operation was being run solely by the Navy, officials were reluctant to use their big foot. "NSA has a pretty strong voice," said Sheck. "If NSA had gone out with a message or a position on that book [the monthly reconnaissance schedule] in that time frame, I'm sure the mission probably would not have gone. . . . There have been a few cases where NSA has done that. An airborne mission that might provoke the director of NSA to say, 'We don't want to do that.' . . . But nobody did that. Even this message is a little wishy-washy, because of the position NSA's in. It was a Navy patrol proposed by Navy people in response to Navy tasking, and we were an outsider saying, 'You really ought to look at that again, guys. If that's what you want, think about it.' "

On January 2, 1968, after the New Year's holiday, General Steakley found his copy of the warning message when he returned to his office. But rather than immediately bringing it to the attention of the Joint Chiefs of Staff, DIA, and the 303 Committee, which had only a few days earlier approved the mission, he buried it. First he changed its NSA designation from "action"—which would have required someone to actually do something about it—to "information," which basically meant "You might find this interesting." Then, instead of sending it back to the people who had just signed off on the mission, he pushed it routinely on its way to the office of the Commander-in-Chief, Pacific, in Hawaii. At CINCPAC headquarters, the message was first confused with the *Pueblo* approval message, which arrived at about the same time, and then ignored because of the "information" tag.

An earlier "action" copy had also been sent to the Chief of Naval Operations, Admiral Thomas H. Moorer, but because the DIA Signal Office mistakenly attached the wrong designator, it wound up in limbo and was lost for the next month.

There was still one last chance for NSA's warning message to have an impact. One copy had been passed through back channels to the head of the Naval Security Group in Washington. When Captain Ralph E. Cook saw the "action" priority tag, he assumed that the matter would be debated among senior officials in Hawaii, among them his own representative, Navy Captain Everett B. (Pete) Gladding. Nevertheless, he passed a copy on to Gladding to give him a heads-up.

With rosy cheeks and a web belt that stretched wide around his middle, Gladding looked more like Santa Claus than an electronic spy. As director of the Naval Security Group, Pacific, he managed a broad range of signals intelligence missions, including those involving the *Banner* and the *Pueblo.* Located behind a cipher-locked door on the top floor of the old U.S. Pacific Fleet Headquarters at Pearl Harbor, his offices were close to the World War II codebreaking center. And as in the disastrous series of events that led to the devastating attack on Pearl Harbor, once again a warning message was lost or ignored and men would be put in peril. Although Gladding later denied ever having received the message, other officers said he did get it. In any case, rather than NSA's warning, the approval with its "minimal risk" advisory was sent from Hawaii to Japan, and the *Pueblo* made preparations to get under way.

The highly secret operations order instructed the *Pueblo* to:

- Determine the nature and extent of naval activity [in the] vicinity of North Korean ports of Chongjin, Songjin, Mayang Do and Wonsan.
- Sample electronic environment of East Coast North Korea, with emphasis on intercept/fixing of coastal radars.
- Intercept and conduct surveillance of Soviet naval units.
- Determine Korcom [Korean Communist] and Soviet reaction respectively to an overt intelligence collector operating near Korcom periphery and actively conducting surveillance of USSR naval units.
- Evaluate USS *Pueblo*'s (AGER-2) capabilities as a naval intelligence collection and tactical surveillance ship.
- Report any deployment of Korcom/Soviet units which may be indicative of pending hostilities or offensive actions against U.S. forces.

Finally, the order added: "Estimate of risk: Minimal."

Lieutenant Stephen Harris, in charge of the signals intelligence operation on the ship, was disappointed when he read the *Pueblo*'s operational order a few weeks before departure. "I was very upset when we found out we were going to North Korea," he said, "because we were configured to cruise off the [Soviet Union's] Kamchatka Peninsula . . . primarily Vladivostok and secondarily Petropavlovsk. That's where we were supposed to be going, and that's where all the training for our guys came from. And then to find out we were going to North Korea, I thought what a waste. . . . It was our first mission and somebody thought, Well, this will give these guys a chance to learn how to do it. Well, we had all done this before.

"Supposedly our inventory of intelligence information on North Korea was not very current so they thought, Well, here's a chance to update that. But it just caused no end of trouble for us, I mean even before we got under way, because I had a bunch of Russian linguists on board. We had to get these two Marines from [the naval listening post at] Kamiseya who, they knew about ten words of Korean [Hongul] between the two of them. . . . They were good guys but they had not been really seasoned in the language and this type of collection."

"Answer all bells," shouted the officer of the deck. "Single up." In the pilothouse, Boatswain's Mate Second Class Ronald L. Berens held the ship's wheel in his two hands and gently turned it to port. Heavy, low-hanging clouds seemed to merge with the gray seas on the morning of January 5, 1968, as the *Pueblo* slipped away from her berth. Over the loudspeaker came the sounds of a guitar—Herb Alpert and the Tijuana Brass playing "The Lonely Bull," adopted by Commander Bucher as the ship's theme song. It would be the most prescient act of the entire voyage. As the *Pueblo* disappeared over the horizon, the North Korean volcano began to erupt.

One of the Sigint technicians, Earl M. Kisler, later began a long poem:

> *Out of Japan on the fifth of Jan.*
> *The* Pueblo *came a-steamin'.*
> *Round Kyushu's toe, past Sasebo,*
> *You could hear the captain a-screamin',*
>
> *"XO!" he said,*
> *"Full speed ahead! We've got us some spyin' to do!*
> *Timmy, be sharp!" Then with Charley Law's*
> *charts,*
> *Away like a turtle we flew.*

For several months now, Pyongyang KCNA International had been broadcasting frequent warnings in English about U.S. "espionage boats" penetrating North Korean territorial waters. These messages had been picked up by the CIA's Foreign Broadcast Information Service. "It [the United States] infiltrated scores of armed boats into the waters of our side, east of Chongjin port on the eastern coast to conduct vicious reconnaissance," said one broadcast on November 27. Chongjin was to be one of the *Pueblo*'s key targets. Another report, on November 10, quoted a "confession" by a "spy" caught from one of the boats. "Drawn into the spy ring of the Central Intelligence Agency," he said, "I had long undergone training mainly to infiltrate into the north in the guise of a fisherman."

As the weeks and months progressed, the warnings grew more belligerent. Often they quoted the accusations of North Korean major general Pak Chung Kuk. "As our side has declared time and again," he said in a report on December 1, "it had no alternative but to detain the ships involved in hostile acts, as a due self-defense step." In January, a warning aimed directly at the *Pueblo* was even quoted in a Japanese newspaper, the *Sankei Shimbun:* North Korean forces would take action against the *Pueblo* if it continued to loiter near territorial waters. All of this "open source intelligence" was readily available to NSA and Naval Security Group officials in Hawaii and Japan.

One day after the *Pueblo* parked herself little more than a gull's breath outside North Korea's twelve-mile limit, still another warning was issued. "The U.S. imperialist aggressor troops again dispatched from early this morning . . . spy boats disguised as fishing boats into the coastal waters of our side off the eastern coast to perpetrate hostile acts. As long as the U.S. imperialist aggressor troops conduct reconnaissance by sending spy boats, our naval ships will continue to take determined countermeasures." The *Pueblo* had sailed into a spider's web.

Late on the evening of January 19, a group of thirty-one North Korean army lieutenants quickly navigated their way through a labyrinth of mines, brush, barbed wire, fences, and other obstacles. They were penetrating the formidable demilitarized zone, a machetelike scar that sliced North from South Korea. For weeks they had been training with sixty-pound packs on their backs, mapping the route, and clearing a path. Now, armed with submachine guns, nine-inch daggers, and grenades that hung from their South Korean army fatigues, they were heading in the direction of Seoul at about six miles an hour.

At that moment the *Pueblo*, unaware of the tremors taking place little more than a dozen miles to the west, was sailing slowly south toward Wonsan. After leaving Japan, the ship had been hammered by a fierce winter storm and had taken several dangerous rolls while tacking. By the time she reached her northernmost point, an area where North Korea meets Russia, the weather was so cold that ice covered the ship's deck and superstructure. Wearing the warmest clothing he could find, Seaman Stu Russell ventured on deck to take a look around. "Although the seas were calm, the humidity was rising, and as a result, ice was forming on every surface of the ship," he recalled. "Had anyone seen the ship in this condition it would have appeared to be a ghost ship floating on a gray sea."

Then Russell turned his attention toward the bleak shoreline. "The world looked black and white with shades of gray," he said. "There was no color to it. The sky was overcast, the sea had a leadlike sheen to it, and the mountains in the distance were black, with a coating of white on their northern flanks. . . . Few if any of us had ever experienced cold such as this, and we were ill prepared for it." The heavy ice worried Bucher, and he ordered the crew to begin chipping it away with sledgehammers, picks, whatever they could find.

From morning til dark,
A gray Noah's ark,
We bounced and quivered along.
But instead of a pair of all animals rare,
We carried agents, about 83 strong.

The mercury dropped the further north that we got,
So cold, frost covered my glasses,
So cold, ice covered the fo'c'sle and bridge,
So cold we froze off our asses.

The *Pueblo* was hardly bigger than an expensive yacht; space was tight, and within the Sigint area it was at a premium. In addition to the

KW-7, one of the most modern cipher machines in the U.S. government, the space held a WLR-1 intercept receiver, an assortment of typewriters, and nearly five hundred pounds of highly secret documents. Another hundred pounds were generated during the voyage. About twenty-two weighted and perforated ditching bags were stored on board—not enough to hold all the documents in the event of an emergency. For routine destruction of documents at sea, a small incinerator was installed against the smokestack. Since it could only handle about three or four pounds of paper at a time, it was not considered useful for emergency destruction. The ship also had two shredders that could slice an eight-inch stack of paper in about fifteen minutes. To destroy equipment, there were sledgehammers and axes in both the Sigint and cipher spaces.

Because the twenty-eight enlisted Sigint specialists labored mysteriously behind a locked door and seldom socialized with the other members of the crew, friction occasionally developed. "We had a crew meeting and we were told that the mission of this ship was none of our business," said one member of the ship's crew, "and we were not to discuss anything about it or speculate about it. And if we went by the operations spaces and the door was open we were to look the other way. And these guys were all prima donnas and they reported to NSA and there was always friction between the guys that had to do the hard work and the [Sigint crew]."

On January 20, the warnings of General Pak once again vibrated through the ether. "In the New Year, the U.S. imperialist aggressors continued the criminal act of infiltrating armed vessels and spy bandits, mingled with South Korean fishing boats, into the coastal waters of our side. . . . Major General Pak Chung Kuk strongly demanded that the enemy side take immediate measures for stopping the hostile acts of infiltrating fishing boats including armed vessels and spy boats into the coastal waters of our side." The messages, broadcast in English, were repeated ten times in Hongul, the Korean language, creating great public anxiety in North Korea about unidentified ships. But Bucher was never informed of the warnings.

As Bucher maintained radio silence off the North Korean coast, the clandestine force of North Korean lieutenants dressed as South Korean soldiers reached the outskirts of Seoul. Three hours later they arrived at a checkpoint a mile from the entrance to the Blue House, the residence of South Korean president Park Chung Hee. When questioned by a guard, the lead lieutenant said that his men belonged to a counterintelligence unit and were returning from operations in the mountains. They were allowed to pass, but the guard telephoned his superior to check out the story. Minutes later the night lit up with muzzle flashes and the still air exploded with the sounds of automatic weapons. Through much of the early morning the fighting went on. The guerrillas were massively outnumbered; most were killed and a few surrendered. Had they succeeded, the assassination might have triggered an all-out invasion from the North. The calls for retaliation were quick and strong.

By noon the next day, January 22, the *Pueblo* lay dead in calm waters. A short twenty miles to the south and west was Wonsan.

On the way to this spot, the ship had begun trolling for signals through its three operational areas, codenamed on the map Pluto, Venus, and Mars. In the Sigint spaces, the technicians, under the command of Stephen Harris, worked twenty-four hours a day in three shifts. But the electronic pickings were slim near two of their key targets, the ports of Chongjin and Songjin. Adding to the problems, the two Hongul linguists weren't fully qualified and some of the equipment had been malfunctioning. As the men fought off boredom, Bucher began thinking the entire mission was going to be a bust.

Then, as they approached their third key target, Wonsan, the activity suddenly began picking up. Signals were logged, recorded, and (if any words were recognizable) gisted.

From "Venus" to "Mars,"
Charley shootin' the stars,
Songjin, Chongjin, and Wonsan,
The Pueblo *a-bobbin',*
Our receivers a-throbbin',
Us sly secret agents sailed along.

If a ship passing by were to see us they'd die.
"Ha! A harmless and leaky ill craft."
Our ship may be leaky,
But by God we're sneaky,
In the end we'll have the last laugh.

Soon the *Pueblo* had company. A pair of North Korean fishing boats approached, and one made a close circle around the ship. There was no question; they were had. "We were close enough to see the crew looking back at us," recalled Stu Russell, "and they looked upset. On the bridge we could make out what looked like several military personnel who were looking back at us with binoculars. Maybe they were political commissars who kept an eye on the crewmembers to make certain they didn't defect. But this group didn't look like they wanted to defect, they looked like they wanted to eat our livers."

Bucher ordered photographs taken of the boats and then decided it was time to break radio silence. He drafted a situation report and gave it to his radioman to send out immediately. But because of the *Pueblo*'s weak transmitting power and low antenna, as well as difficult propagation conditions in the Sea of Japan, the message was not going through.

That night the crew watched Jimmy Stewart in *The Flight of the Phoenix,* about a group of people stranded in the Sahara Desert after a plane crash. Others played endless games of poker or read in the berthing compartment.

In South Korea, television viewers watched as the one live captive from the failed Blue House raid was paraded on national television—a great humiliation for North Korea. Although most of the people of North Korea did not have televisions, their officials at Panmunjom, where northern, southern, and American negotiators met, had access to TVs and witnessed the spectacle. They may have been left with the feeling that one humiliation deserves another.

The next morning, January 23, a hazy mist obscured the North Korean island of Ung-do, sixteen miles west. Bucher considered it the best place from which to sit and eavesdrop on Wonsan. From there, the sensitive Sigint equipment could pick up some of the more difficult signals as far inland as fifteen miles. About 10:30 A.M., an Elint specialist in the Sigint spaces sat up, adjusted his earphones, and began listening intensely as he studied the green scope in front of him. He had just intercepted two radar signals from subchasers although he could not determine their range or bearing.

Half an hour later, the ship managed to connect with the Naval Security Group listening post at Kamiseya. Once the right circuit was found, the signal was clear and strong and the situation report was finally sent. Then the ship reverted to radio silence.

About noon, as the *Pueblo* was broadcasting to Kamiseya, an intercept operator there began picking up signals from a North Korean subchaser, SC-35. It was the same one that the Elint operator on the *Pueblo* was following. The captain of the subchaser reported to his base his position, about eighteen miles off the coast and twenty-five miles from Wonsan. That was very close to where the *Pueblo* sat dead in the water.

By now Bucher was on the flying bridge, peering through his "big eyes"—twenty-two-inch binoculars. He could see that the fast-approaching boat was an SO-1 class subchaser, hull number 35. He could also see that the boat was at general quarters and that its deck guns—a 3-inch cannon and two 57mm gun mounts—were manned and trained on his ship. A quick check through the files indicated that the SO-1 also carried two rocket launchers. Bucher ordered flags raised indicating that the *Pueblo* was engaged in hydrographic research, its cover. But the subchaser just drew closer and began circling the ship at a distance of about 500 yards. On the *Pueblo,* all hands were ordered to remain below decks to disguise the number of persons on board.

In North Korea, a shore station reported the contact to higher command. "Subchaser No. 35 has approached a 300-ton vessel which is used for radar operation. . . . it is believed the vessel was not armed and that it was an American vessel."

At 12:12, SC-35 signaled the *Pueblo,* "What nationality?"

Bucher ordered the ensign raised and then the hydrographic signal. Next he called the photographer to the bridge to get some shots of the incident and ordered the engines lit off in preparation for some fancy maneuvering if necessary. Despite the worrisome guns pointed his way, he thought that this was simple harassment and decided to report it to Kamiseya. After all, the captain of the *Banner* had told him about a number of similar incidents.

"A guy comes steaming back from that kind of thing," said NSA's Gene Sheck, referring to the captain of the *Banner*, "and he says to the skipper of the *Pueblo,* 'Lloyd, baby, you got nothing to worry about. They do that every day. They'll come out. They'll harass you. You wave back. You blink a few things at them and they'll go away. Everybody knows that. We knew it. They do it to our reconnaissance, airborne reconnaissance missions. Nobody gets excited about that."

But, added Sheck, "Here come these guys—only they weren't playing."

At 12:20, Chief Warrant Officer Gene Lacy noticed a number of small dots on the horizon, approaching from Wonsan. Through the big eyes, Bucher identified them as three North Korean P-4 motor torpedo boats headed his way.

Seven minutes later, on its third swing around the *Pueblo,* SC-35 hoisted a new signal: "Heave to or I will open fire on you." Lieutenant Ed Murphy, the executive officer, again checked the radar and confirmed that the *Pueblo* was 15.8 miles from the nearest land, North Korea's Ung-do island. Bucher told the signalman to hoist "I am in international waters." Down in the Sigint spaces, First Class Petty Officer Don Bailey, who had just transferred to the *Pueblo* from NSA's USNS *Valdez,* kept in continuous contact with Kamiseya. "Company outside," he transmitted to the listening post in Japan, then asked them to stand by for a Flash message.

Although Bucher had no way of knowing it, as far as the North Koreans were concerned the game was already over. At 12:35, the shore station reported that "subchaser has already captured U.S. vessel." About that time, the three torpedo boats had arrived and were taking up positions around the ship while two snub-nosed MiG-21s began menacing from above.

Bucher passed the word over the internal communications system to prepare for emergency destruction. He then turned to his engineering officer, Gene Lacy, and asked him how long it would take to scuttle the ship. Lacy explained that the *Pueblo* had four watertight bulkheads. Two of those would have to be opened to the sea. They could be flooded with the ship's fire hoses, but that would take a long time, about three or more hours. A quicker method, Lacy told Bucher, would be to open the cooling water intakes and outlets in the main engine room and cut a hole into the auxiliary engine room from the main engine room. Once this was done, Lacy said, the ship could go down in forty-seven minutes. But the problem was that many of the life rafts might be shot up during an attack; without enough life rafts, and with the bitter January water cold enough to kill a person exposed to it in minutes, Bucher gave up on the idea.

New flags were going up on one of the torpedo boats: "Follow in my wake. I have pilot aboard." Then a boarding party transferred from the SC-35 to one of the torpedo boats, and PT-604 began backing down toward the *Pueblo*'s starboard bow with fenders rigged. Men in helmets with rifles and fixed bayonets stood on the deck. Next came the signal "Heave to or I will open fire."

Bucher, hoping to somehow extricate the ship, ordered hoisted the signal "Thank you for your consideration. I am departing the area." Bucher knew there was no way his tub could outrun the forty-knot torpedo boats. He considered manning the 50mm machine guns but decided against it, believing it was senseless to send people to certain death. He was still hoping to somehow make a "dignified" departure. Yet, with the North Koreans about to board his ship, he still had not ordered emergency destruction down in the Sigint spaces. Bucher gave the quartermaster instructions to get under way at one-third speed.

As the *Pueblo* began to move, the torpedo boats began crisscrossing the ship's bow and SC-35 again signaled, "Heave to or I will fire." Bucher ordered the speed increased to two-thirds and then to full speed. SC-35 gave chase, gaining rapidly on *Pueblo*'s stern. To the side, sailors aboard PT-601 uncovered a torpedo tube and trained it on the ship. Down in the Sigint spaces, Don Bailey's fingers flew over the keyboard. "They plan to open fire on us now," he sent to Kamiseya.

SC-35 then instructed all North Korean vessels to clear the area. He said he was going to open fire on the U.S. vessel because it would not comply with North Korean navy instructions.

Seconds later the boat let loose with ten to twenty bursts from its 57mm guns. At almost the same moment, the torpedo boats began firing their 30mm machine guns. The men in the Sigint spaces threw themselves on the deck. Personnel on the flying bridge dove into the pilothouse for cover. About four minutes later, general quarters was finally sounded. But Bucher immediately modified the command, forbidding personnel from going topside. He wished to keep anyone from attempting to man the 50mm guns.

SC-35 let loose with another burst of heavy machine fire. Most of the rounds were aimed over the ship, but something struck the signal mast. Bucher collapsed with small shrapnel wounds in his ankle and rectum. Everyone then hit the deck. "Commence emergency destruction," Bucher ordered. Bailey notified Kamiseya, "We are being boarded. Ship's position 39-25N/127-54.3E. SOS." Over and over he repeated the message. In the Sigint spaces, sailors were destroying documents. Bailey was pleading. "We are holding emergency destruction. We need help. We need support. SOS. Please send assistance." It was now 1:31 P.M.

In the Sigint spaces, the emergency destruction began slowly and with great confusion. Fires were started in wastepaper baskets in the passageways outside the secure unit. About ten weighted ditching bags were packed with documents and then stacked in the passageways. Using axes and sledgehammers, the cipher equipment was smashed.

Back at Kamiseya, intercept operators heard the subchaser notify its shore command that he had halted the U.S. ship's escape by firing warning shots. One of the torpedo boats then informed its base that two naval vessels from Wonsan were taking the U.S. ship to some unidentified location.

By now, U.S. forces in the Pacific were becoming aware of the desperateness of the situation. Flash messages were crisscrossing in the ether. Although some 50,000 U.S. military personnel were stationed in South Korea, most near the demilitarized zone, the ongoing war in Vietnam had sapped American airpower in South Korea. The U.S. Air Force had only six Republic F-105 Thunderchief fighter-bombers in the country. These "Thuds," the largest single-engine, single-seat fighters ever built, were capable of carrying 18,500-pound bombs. But at the time, they were armed only with nuclear weapons, to take out targets in China in the event the balloon went up. Removing the nuke-alert packages and replacing them with air-to-ground weapons would take hours.

Also on runways in South Korea were 210 combat-ready South Korean fighters and interceptors that could reach the *Pueblo* before dark. "The Koreans requested from the United States permission to save the *Pueblo,*" said one U.S. Air Force fighter pilot. But the U.S. officer in charge of American and UN forces in South Korea, Army General Charles H. Bonesteel III, refused to allow them to launch. He feared the

South Korean air force might respond "in excess of that necessary or desired" and thus launch an all-out war, impossible to contain.

The next closest aircraft were in Japan, where the U.S. had seventy-eight fighters parked on runways. But because of agreements with the Japanese government prohibiting offensive missions from bases in that country, these were also unavailable on short notice.

Four hundred and seventy miles south, steaming at twenty-seven knots toward Subic Bay in the Philippines, was the USS *Enterprise*, the largest aircraft carrier in the world. On the rolling decks of the nuclear-powered flat-top were sixty attack aircraft, including twenty-four F-4B Phantoms capable of Mach 2 speed. But by the time the confused messages regarding the *Pueblo* reached the carrier, it was too distant for its aircraft to reach the *Pueblo* before it would arrive in Wonsan.

That left Okinawa, which was nearly as distant as the *Enterprise*. Although it was part of Japan, at the time it was also an American protectorate and could be used to launch hostile attacks. The island was home to the 18th Tactical Fighter Wing, made up of combat-experienced fighter jocks who had flown numerous missions against targets in Hanoi and Haiphong in North Vietnam. Some wore the famous "100 Missions/North Vietnam" patch on their flight jackets. Others, who had flown across the Red River on missions into the heart of North Vietnam, wore the "River Rats" patch.

An orange-red flash exploded from the end of a huge J-75 turbojet engine and a deep-throated roar vibrated across Okinawa's Kadena Air Base. The first of a dozen F-105s screeched down the runway. The pilots wanted to fly straight to the *Pueblo*, attack the North Korean torpedo boats, and then fly to Osan Air Base in South Korea for refueling. But instead they were ordered to refuel first at Osan.

By now Bucher realized that there was no escape. He considered that any further resistance would result in the needless slaughter of the crew. Depending on how well the destruction was going in the Sigint spaces, he decided, he would offer no more resistance and would surrender the ship. At 1:34 P.M. he ordered "All stop" and instructed the signalman to hoist the international signal for "Protest." The 57mm fire halted but the 30mm fire continued sporadically. Bucher estimated that he was now about twenty-five miles from the North Korean shore. "We are laying to at present position," Bailey transmitted. "Please send assistance. We are being boarded."

Bucher left the bridge and ran to his stateroom to check for classified information. Finding nothing revealing the *Pueblo*'s true mission, he handed a few documents and his personal sidearm to someone in the passageway and ordered him to throw them overboard. On his way back, he looked in on the destruction taking place in the Sigint spaces and then headed back to the bridge. On SC-35 was the signal, "Follow me. I have pilot on board." Bucher complied and ordered his quartermaster to make a slow, five-degree turn. Bailey notified Kamiseya, "We are being escorted into probably Wonsan." A few minutes later he again pleaded for help: "Are you sending assistance?" Kamiseya replied, "Word has gone to all authorities. COMNAVFORJAPAN [Commander, U.S. Naval Forces Japan] is requesting assistance."

At NSA headquarters near Washington it was the middle of the night when the CRITIC and Flash messages began stuttering from cipher machines. "For ten days," said NSA's Henry Millington, who conducted a highly secret study of the incident, "nobody knew where they were."

"That happened around two o'clock in the afternoon, Korean time," recalled Gene Sheck of NSA's K Group, "which was like two o'clock in the morning here. I got a call to come to work and I came in and General Morrison was at work." At the time, Major General John Morrison was NSA's operations chief. "And General Morrison decided that he was going to be the guy in charge of the *Pueblo*, whatever problem we had with them. He called all kinds of other people, but Morrison was kind of running the show at that particular time." A short time later, Marshall Carter arrived—but he didn't stay long. "You know," he told Morrison, "there's no sense both of us standing here while this thing is trying to work itself out. You stay here, gather all the data, and I'm going to be back in at six-thirty or seven o'clock in the morning."

In addition to the safety of the crew, one of the chief concerns at NSA through the early-morning hours was whether the North Koreans had been able to capture the *Pueblo*'s cipher material, especially old NSA keylists, which would enable easy deciphering of U.S. material already intercepted. These lists—one per month—explained the daily settings for the cipher machines. Across the top of the eight-by-ten sheets of paper were the words in bold red ink: "TOP SECRET—SPECAT": "Special Category." The keylists consisted of instructions on which numbers to set the dozen rotors in the machine on, and other technical details. With these lists and the right equipment, the North Koreans would be able to break the code of every naval unit using the same ciphers.

From Kamiseya the question went out to the *Pueblo.* "What keylists do you have left? . . . Please advise what keylists you have left and if it appears that your communications space will be entered."

At about two o'clock, Bucher suddenly ordered another "All stop" in order to check on the progress of the destruction and to give more time for its completion. But almost immediately SC-35 closed to a range of about 2,000 yards and fired. Upward of 2,000 rounds pounded the ship's thin quarter-inch steel skin. Rapid-fire bursts sent shells into the laundry room, the small-arms locker, the wardroom, and a number of passageways. Near the captain's cabin, Fireman Duane Hodges was picking up some papers to destroy when he was thrown to the deck, his leg nearly severed and his intestines torn from his lower abdomen. As he lay dying, blood from his severed arteries washed from one side of the passageway to the other as the ship rolled with the waves. Nearby, Fireman Steven Woelk suddenly felt a burning in his chest and groin from razor-sharp shrapnel. Blood also poured profusely from the thigh of Marine Sergeant Robert Chicca, a linguist. Sprawled across another passageway was Radioman Charles Crandal, jagged shards of hot metal spiking from his leg.

In order to stop the firing, Bucher ordered full ahead at one-third speed. He then turned the conn over to Lacy and raced down to check on the destruction. Along the way he saw the broken, twisted form of Duane Hodges in the crimson passageway. He pushed open the door to the Sigint spaces and saw some of the men hugging the deck. "Get up and get going!" Bucher shouted. "There's a man with his leg blown off out there." He then saw three large mattress covers overflowing with secret documents. Turning to Stephen Harris, he shouted, "Get this stuff out of here."

Rushing into the cipher spaces, at 2:05 P.M. Bucher dictated a message:

> HAVE 0 KEYLISTS AND THIS ONLY ONE HAVE. HAVE BEEN REQUESTED TO FOLLOW INTO WONSAN. HAVE THREE WOUNDED AND ONE MAN WITH LEG BLOWN OFF. HAVE NOT USED ANY WEAPONS NOR UNCOVERED FIFTY CALIBER MACHINE GUNS. DESTROYING ALL KEYLISTS AND AS MUCH ELEC EQUIPMENT AS POSSIBLE. HOW ABOUT SOME HELP. THESE GUYS MEAN BUSINESS. HAVE SUSTAINED SMALL WOUND IN RECTUM. DO NOT INTEND TO OFFER ANY RESISTANCE. DO NOT KNOW HOW LONG WILL BE ABLE TO HOLD UP CIRCUIT AND DO NOT KNOW IF COMMUNICATIONS SPACES WILL BE ENTERED.

Two minutes later, Kamiseya replied:

> ROGER WE ARE DOING ALL WE CAN CAPTAIN HERE AND HAVE COMNAVFORJAPAN ON HOT LINE. LAST I GOT WAS AIR FORCE GONNA HELP YOU WITH SOME AIRCRAFT BUT CAN'T REALLY SAY AS COMNAVFORJAPAN COORDINATING WITH I PRESUME KOREA FOR SOME F-105. THIS UNOFFICIAL BUT I THINK THAT WILL HAPPEN, BACK TO YOU.

Back in the pilothouse, Bucher again asked about the possibility of scuttling the ship but once again he was told it could not be done quickly. Down in the Sigint spaces, Don Bailey was at last hearing some encouraging words. Kamiseya was reporting that everyone was turning to, doing everything they could, and "figure by now Air Force got some birds winging your way." "Sure hope so," replied Bailey. "We are pretty busy with this destruction right now. Can't see for the smoke. . . . Sure hope someone does something. We are helpless."

On shore, concern over the NSA material was growing. At 2:18, Bailey was again asked about the status of the classified material and cipher machines. In the choking darkness, Bailey said that the KW-7 and some of the printed circuit boards for the KW-37 and the KG-14 remained. Time was quickly running out and there was no way everything would be destroyed. The major problem was Lieutenant Harris's decision to attempt to burn the documents rather than jettison them overboard. This was because the regulations said that jettisoning was not permitted in water less than 600 feet deep, and the *Pueblo* was then in water little more than 200 feet deep. Bucher authorized a message sent saying that destruction would not be complete.

In the passageways, technicians built small bonfires of dense cryptographic manuals. Into the inferno went stacks of raw intercept forms covered with row after row of intercepted five-number code groups; keylists classified "Top Secret/Trine"; and NSA "Techins"—technical instructions on how to conduct signals intelligence. Supersecret manual after supersecret manual, file drawer after file drawer. But the space was too small, the fires too weak, and the smoke too thick. Ninety percent of the documents would survive.

Destruction was also on the minds of the North Koreans. About 2:20 one patrol craft instructed another to watch for attempts by U.S. personnel to throw things into the water. SC-35 reported that the U.S. crew was ditching some items and burning others. The Koreans then ordered Bucher to come to all stop. Without consulting any of the other officers, Bucher agreed to surrender and allow the boarding party to come aboard. The twin screws spun to a halt, sending large bubbles to the surface. A few minutes later Bailey, hunched over his cipher machine, notified Kamiseya. "Destruction of publications has been ineffective," he wrote. "Suspect several will be compromised." Kamiseya then requested a list of what had not been destroyed.

Back on deck, Bucher passed the word to lay aft and assist the boarding party. The carbine normally kept on the bridge was thrown overboard. At someone's suggestion, he then notified everyone that the only information they were required to give was name, rank, and serial number.

Realizing that he did not have on his officer's cap, Bucher then left the bridge, went to his cabin, where he wrapped his wounded ankle with a sock, put on his cap, and returned to the bridge. It would be a dignified surrender. No small arms would be broken out, no machine guns manned, no attempt made to scuttle the ship or destroy the engines. The tarps would never even be removed from the 50mm machine guns, a process that would have taken about three minutes.

At 2:32, officers from the North Korean People's Army (KPA), in charge of the attack boats, boarded the *Pueblo.* "We have been directed to come to all stop," Bailey notified Kamiseya, "and are being boarded at this time." A minute later, he transmitted his last message. "Got four men injured and one critically and going off the air now and destroy this gear. Over." Kamiseya answered, "Go ahead," and then asked the ship to transmit in the clear. But there would be no more messages from the *Pueblo.*

Met by Bucher, the boarding party came aboard without resistance. It consisted of two officers and eight to ten enlisted men. All were armed and none spoke English. Accompanied by Bucher, they went to the pilothouse and the bridge, where crewmembers were ordered to the fantail. All hands below decks, said Bucher, were to immediately lay up to the forward well area. The helmsman was then brought back to the wheelhouse to take the helm. "Each time the mike was keyed there was a very audible click which preceded whatever was being said," recalled Stu Russell. "Each time that thing was clicked, I was sure that they were giving the order to fire into us. It was possible that no one in the free world, no one in the U.S. military knew we had been captured and that the Koreans might as well kill us then and there and cover the whole thing up."

For the first time since 1807, when Commodore James Barron gave up the USS *Chesapeake* after it was bombarded and boarded by the crew of the HMS *Leopard* off Cape Henry, Virginia, an American naval commander had surrendered his ship in peacetime.

Back at Kamiseya, intercept operators kept close track of the *Pueblo* by eavesdropping on the SC-35 and the other escorts as they radioed their positions, about every five minutes, to their shore command in North Korea.

About 4:00 P.M., a second boarding party arrived with a senior North Korean colonel and a civilian pilot. The pilot relieved the *Pueblo*'s helmsman, who was taken to the forward berthing compartment. Together with Bucher, the colonel inspected the ship. White canvas ditching bags, bursting at the seams with highly classified documents and equipment, still lined the passageway; only one had ever been thrown overboard.

When Bucher and the North Korean colonel entered the cipher-locked Sigint spaces, a bulging white laundry bag stuffed with documents sat in the middle of the floor. The WLR-1 intercept receivers were still in their racks; only the faces had been damaged. Also undamaged was perhaps the most secret Sigint document on the ship: NSA's Electronic Order of Battle for the Far East. The EOB was a detailed overlay map showing all known Russian, Chinese, and Korean radar sites and transmitters as well as their frequencies and other key details. The information was critical in case of war. Knowing where the radar systems were located and on what frequencies they operated would allow U.S. bombers and fighters to evade, jam, or deceive them through electronic countermeasures. Knowing that the United States possessed that information, the various countries might now change the frequencies and other technical parameters, thereby sending the NSA back to square one. Within days the document would be on a North Korean desk. "That's guys' lives. That's pilots' lives," said Ralph McClintock, one of the *Pueblo*'s cryptologic technicians, years later.

Following the inspection, about 4:30 P.M., Bucher was ordered to sit on the deck outside his cabin. At that moment, U.S. Air Force officials were notified by Kamiseya that the *Pueblo* was now within North Korean waters. All help was called off. The F-4s in South Korea had not finished converting to conventional weapons, and the F-105s from Okinawa were still an hour away from their refueling base in South Korea. They were ordered to refuel as scheduled but not to attack. The United States had given up on Bucher and his crew.

"They were on their own," said NSA's Gene Sheck. "They were literally one hundred percent on their own."

At about 8:30 P.M., the *Pueblo* arrived in the Democratic People's Republic of Korea (DPRK) and was tied up at a pier about ten miles northwest of Wonsan. Several high-ranking officers from the KPA then came on board to interview Bucher in his cabin. Afterward the crewmembers were blindfolded, had their hands bound, and were led off the ship. A crowd of people who had gathered near the pier shouted and spat at them and then tried to grab them, only to be restrained by guards using rifle butts. They were then put on a bus for the start of the long journey to Pyongyang. "We were, it seemed, being guided to the crowd," said Stu Russell. "I was amazed that only a few minutes before, I thought I was scared as much as I could possibly be. I was beyond scared. No, now I was beyond that feeling and entering into emotional arenas that I didn't know existed. My feet and legs were no longer part of my body, they were part of a mechanical system over which I had no control."

We sailed quiet free until Jan. 23,
When out of nowhere there came
Six boats from the west,
The KPA's best.
Six hunters, and Pueblo *fair game.*

What a sensation we caused in this nation,
When caught red-handed that day.
A slight irritation, quite advanced inflammation,
In the rectum of the DPRK.

As the North Koreans were tying the spy ship to the pier in Wonsan, Lieutenant General Marshall Carter was walking to his corner office on the ninth floor of NSA's Headquarters Building. Eight-thirty P.M. in Korea on January 23 was 6:30 A.M. in Washington on that same day, fourteen hours earlier. There to greet Carter was Air Force Major General John Morrison, his operations chief. He had been at work for hours attempting to make sense of events. Others soon arrived at the director's office for a briefing. Among those standing in front of his mahogany desk, near an oversize globe, were Gene Sheck of K Group; Milt Zaslow, chief of B Group; and Louis Tordella.

Because the *Pueblo* was a joint NSA-Navy operation, Carter knew he was going to have a great deal of explaining to do, particularly about why such a risky mission was launched in the first place. Then Milt Zaslow, who was responsible for analysis of Sigint from Communist Asia, handed Carter a copy of the earlier warning message that NSA had sent out for action. By now most, including Carter, had forgotten about it. "General Carter read it, and then he got up and [took] what I thought was the greatest political position anybody could take," recalled Sheck. "He said, 'I don't want anybody in this room to call or to bring to anybody's attention the existence of this message. They will find out themselves, and when they do they will be sufficiently embarrassed about the whole situation that I don't have to worry about that and you don't have to worry about that, but I consider that message as kind of saving our ass."

Following the briefing, NSA officials began planning what to do next. Zaslow argued that they should immediately bring the *Banner* up from Japan to take the *Pueblo*'s place, only with a destroyer or two for protection. The operation could be accomplished within fifty-seven hours, he said. Sigint flights would also be increased south of the demilitarized zone and unmanned drones would be used over North Korea. In addition, President Johnson personally approved the use of the superfast, ultra-high-flying SR-71 reconnaissance plane to overfly North Korea in an attempt to precisely locate the ship and its crew. Another top priority was recovering any highly secret material jettisoned from the *Pueblo*.

However, Gene Sheck was totally opposed to now putting the *Banner* in harm's way after what had happened to the *Pueblo*. "Our reaction was," he said, "you ought to be careful, Mr. Zaslow, because you know, if they've done that to the *Pueblo* . . . We would say, 'That's kind of a dumb thing to do.' . . . and there was a lot of argument in the building whether that made sense or not." Eventually it was decided to position the *Banner* within the safety of a naval task force south of the 38th Parallel.

Twenty-five miles south of NSA, at the White House, President Lyndon Johnson was secretly planning for war. Within hours of the incident, Secretary of Defense Robert S. McNamara and his generals were leaning over curled maps, revising America's war plan for North Korea. At 10:00 A.M. on the day following the attack, McNamara called a war council to discuss preparations for combat with North Korea. It was to be an enormously secret deliberation. "No word of the discussion in the meeting should go beyond this room," everyone was warned. "Our primary objective is to get the men of the *Pueblo* back," said McNamara. "Return of the ship is a secondary objective."

There would be a limited call-up of the reserves. Upwards of 15,000 tons of bombs were to be diverted to the area from the war in Vietnam. "There are about 4,100 tons of aircraft ordnance in Korea now," said General Earle G. Wheeler, the chairman of the Joint Chiefs of Staff, "with about 10,000 more on the way. We need Strike, Bullpup, Walleye, Falcon, Sparrow, and Sidewinder missiles."

Admiral Moorer said that he could maintain two aircraft carriers off Korea for about six weeks without affecting the war in Vietnam. A plan to mine Wonsan harbor would also be drawn up and nine surveillance/attack submarines would be sent into the area. "This could be done completely covertly, and within a week," said Moorer. More naval gunfire support—cruisers and destroyers—could be brought in. A blockade of selected harbors was also a possibility, as were "reprisal" actions against North Korean ships on the high seas.

The Joint Chiefs recommended moving fifteen B-52 bombers to Okinawa and eleven more to Guam. "We had F-4s lined up wingtip to wingtip," said General Charles Bonesteel, in charge of U.S. and UN forces in Korea, "and if the North Koreans had wished to run the risks and indulge in a five-day war of their own, they could have really provided Time-Life Incorporated with some ghastly sights."

Known as Operation Combat Fox, what followed became the largest strategic airlift in U.S. Air Force history. More than 8,000 airmen, hundreds of combat-ready aircraft, and millions of pounds of bombs, rockets, ammo, and supplies were flown in. Among the options were selective air strikes against North Korea. "Our first action, should we become involved," said the Air Force Chief of Staff, "should be to take out the North Korean air capability."

At the same time, according to NSA documents obtained for *Body of Secrets*, the Pentagon began planning still another trumped-up "pretext" war, this time using the *Banner* to spark a full-scale conflict with Korea. "They wanted to provoke the North Koreans into doing something so they could get back at them," said NSA's Sheck. Manned by only a crew of two—a captain and an engineman—the *Banner* would be sent to the same location the *Pueblo* was at when it was fired on. Then it would just wait for the torpedo boats to attack. "They were going to do that with carriers over the horizon, out of radar range," said Sheck, "and having air cover . . . out of range. And the minute the ship indicated the North Koreans were coming after them, they would then [send an alert]. That was the signal to launch all the fighters."

But, said Sheck, the logistics and the risk to the American prisoners made the idea unfeasible. "It took some time to get the carriers over there," he said. "It took time to get the *Banner* ready for sea, and by then, the reaction of the United States was, Let's cool it, because we don't want to lose the eighty guys and all that sort of thing. So they didn't do that."

Another proposal, said Sheck, came from the four-star admiral in charge of U.S. forces in the Pacific. "CINCPAC [Commander-in-Chief, Pacific] wanted to go in and tie a lasso on it and pull it out of Wonsan harbor. Literally! He said he'd propose a message that said, 'I will send a fleet of destroyers in with appropriate air cover. I will tie a rope on the goddamn tub and I'll pull it back out.' But some cooler heads at the Pentagon said, 'No, forget that.' "

On January 26, three days after the *Pueblo*'s capture, an aircraft as black as a moonless night slowly emerged from its steel hangar at Kadena Air Base on Okinawa. With stiletto-sharp edges, windscreens like menacing eyes, a skin of rare titanium, and engines pointed like shotgun barrels, the CIA's secret A-12 was at once threatening and otherworldly. Beneath the cockpit canopy, dressed in moon boots and space helmet, Frank Murray pushed forward the throttles to the mid-afterburner position. Fuel shot into the engines at the rate of 80,000 pounds per hour and fireballs exploded from the rear of the shotgun barrels. In the distance, a flock of birds flapped for safety. Looking at his control panel, Murray saw that he had reached decision speed and all was go. Ten seconds later he pulled gently back on the stick and the A-12's long nose rose ten degrees above the horizon. Murray was on his way to find the *Pueblo*.

By January 1968, CIA pilot Frank Murray was a veteran of numerous overflights of North Vietnam. But following the capture of the *Pueblo*, he was ordered to make the first A-12 overflight of North Korea. An attempt had been made the day before but a malfunction on the aircraft had forced him to abort shortly after takeoff. Following takeoff on January 25, Murray air-refueled over the Sea of Japan and then pointed the plane's sharp titanium nose at the North Korean coast.

"My first pass started off near Vladivostok," he recalled. "Then with the camera on I flew down the east coast of North Korea where we thought the boat was. As I approached Wonsan I could see the *Pueblo* through my view sight. The harbor was all iced up except at the very entrance and there she was, sitting off to the right of the main entrance. I continued to the border with South Korea, completed a 180-degree turn, and flew back over North Korea. I made four passes, photographing the whole of North Korea from the DMZ to the Yalu border. As far as I knew, I was undetected throughout the flight." (Actually, NSA Sigint reports indicated that Chinese radar did detect the A-12 and passed the intelligence to North Korea. No action was taken, no doubt because of the plane's speed, over Mach 3, and its altitude, 80,000 feet.)*

Murray's film was quickly flown to Yokota Air Base in Japan, where analysts determined that North Korea was not building up its forces for any further attacks.

Shortly after the January 26 A-12 mission, another set of spies made preparations for the waters off North Korea. They would travel via the opposite route: under the sea. Navy Chief Warrant Officer Harry O. Rakfeldt, a career cryptologic officer, and three other Sigint technicians based at Kamiseya were ordered to report to the USS *Volador*, a diesel-powered attack submarine then docked at Yokosuka. "Our mission was to support the captain with special intelligence received from Kamiseya," said Rakfeldt, "and intelligence we might obtain on our own." The sub was part of the Navy's buildup in the days following the attack, to put subs in place to locate Soviet submarines should war begin with North Korea.

On January 31, the *Volador*'s loud Klaxon sounded twice, the hatch was slammed shut, and the sub slipped beneath the waves to periscope depth. Sailing north, the *Volador* quietly crept into the crowded Tsugaru Strait separating the main island of Honshu from the northern Japanese island of Hokkaido, and entered the Sea of Japan during daylight. "We entered the Sea of Japan covertly," said Rakfeldt, "the first chal-

* On May 8, while the *Pueblo* crew was imprisoned near Pyongyang, CIA pilot Jack Layton flew another A-12 mission over North Korea. (Although he did not know it, this was to be the last operational flight of the CIA's prize A-12. The fleet of the spy planes was to be scrapped for a newer, two-seat version being built for the Air Force, the SR-71.)

lenge. A current runs from the Sea of Japan to the Pacific Ocean and there is a lot of surface traffic in the strait."

The *Volador*'s operational area consisted of a 10,800-square-mile stretch of water in the middle of the Sea of Japan; for a while, it seemed the mission would be fairly routine. Its first priority was to locate the Russian subs before being discovered itself. Every night the *Volador* had to come up to periscope depth and raise its hydraulic breathing tubes, like chimney tops, above the surface of the sea. That evening, the sub discovered company nearby.

Sitting in front of a round green screen, the sonarman watched the deep sea as a plane's navigator scanned the sky. Gradually he began noticing a pinging in his earphones, coming from the *Volador*'s passive sonar. It was a Soviet sub that had surfaced. Despite the darkness, the *Volador*'s captain decided to maneuver close enough to be able to read the hull number and identify the sub. Closer and closer he edged the *Volador*, quietly heading directly toward the Russian boat, broadside. "Damn it, it's turning on us," the captain shouted as the Soviets suddenly embarked on a collision course. "Dive!" The hatch to the conn was quickly closed, sealing Rakfeldt and other officers off from the rest of the boat. They avoided a crash by diving under the Russian sub. "It was a close one," said Rakfeldt. "We did it without being detected."

Later, as the *Volador* was snorkeling, the tables were turned. "We were found by a Soviet sub," said Rakfeldt. Once again the sonarman heard the distinctive metallic pinging of a Russian boat. The captain began maneuvers to determine if the *Volador* had been detected. "It was confirmed that the sub was tracking us," said Rakfeldt. "What evolved was a hide-and-seek operation." To keep as quiet and invisible as possible, all operations were kept to a minimum and the snorkel was retracted. "It took many hours but it worked, as the Soviet sub was finally detected snorkeling," Rakfeldt recalled. "We then became the hunter and maintained covert contact on the sub for a period before it moved out of our area of operations."

But now another problem developed. After the long period of deliberate inactivity, one of the diesel engines refused to start because the oil had become too cold. Finally, after hours of work, the chief in the engine room jury-rigged a temporary pipe system connecting the oil supplies for the two engines. "It wasn't pretty," said Rakfeldt. "The temporary piping was suspended overhead." By circulating the cold oil from the dead engine into the working engine, the chief was able to warm it up enough to restart the dead engine, and the crew sailed back to Yokohama without further incident.

Following a bus and train ride to Pyongyang, Bucher and his crew were locked in a worn brick building known as the "barn." Dark and foreboding, it had hundred-foot-long corridors; bare bulbs hung from the ceilings. From the moment they arrived, they were regularly beaten, tortured, and threatened with death if they did not confess their espionage.

To Pyongyang we were taken,
All comforts forsaken,
When into the "barn" we were led.
All set for the winter,
Cords of bread you could splinter,
A rat ate my turnips, now he's dead.
. . . .
"What's your status?! Your function?!
Could it be in conjunction
With spying on our sovereign territory?!"
Said the captain, "Goddamn! I'm a peace-loving
man,
Same as you and your crummy authorities!"

In the meantime, the KPA removed the papers and equipment from the *Pueblo,* and the highly secret information was shared with the Russians. Major General Oleg Kalugin was deputy chief of the KGB station at the Soviet embassy in Washington. "The KGB did not plan to capture the *Pueblo,*" he said. "The KGB was not aware of the *Pueblo*'s capture until the Koreans informed the Soviets. So the Soviets were taken unaware. But they were very interested because they knew that it was a spy ship. And in fact, the Koreans managed to capture a lot of classified material aboard the ship. They also picked up the code machines. They picked up the keylists. . . . And this, of course, for the Soviets, had very great operational importance."

The North Koreans, said Kalugin, permitted the Soviets to go over what they found. "The Soviets had been allowed to inspect the captured material because they were the only ones who knew how to handle this stuff. They knew how to make use of it. I know the code machines, KW-7, [were] supposedly smashed by the crew of the *Pueblo*. But," said Kalugin, laughing, "I think that was probably not quite that."

According to Kalugin, nothing is more valuable than cryptographic material. "The ciphers and codes are considered the most important piece of intelligence because they provide you authentic material on the problems and events which are of interest. . . . When you pick up a cable and you decipher it, you break the code, you read the genuine stuff, it's no rumor."

But while the Russians received a KW-7 cipher machine from the *Pueblo,* it and the keylists were useless: the minute NSA learned the ship had been captured, they changed the keylists throughout the Navy and also slightly modified the KW-7. What NSA didn't know, however, was that among the recipients of the new keylists and the technical changes for the cipher machine was the Kremlin.

Since that chilly October day in 1967, when James Harper had walked into the Soviet Embassy in Washington, the Russians had had a key piece of the puzzle: "James Harper" was actually John Walker, a U.S. Navy communications specialist. From him they would regularly receive top secret NSA keylists and technical modifications for the cipher equipment.

The Soviet agent who ran Walker was Major General Boris A. Solomatin, the hard-drinking, chain-smoking KGB chief of station in Washington from 1965 to 1968. As Oleg Kalugin's boss, he was considered "perhaps the best operative the KGB ever produced," according to one high-ranking FBI counterintelligence official. "Walker showed us monthly keylists for one of your military cipher machines," said Solomatin, now retired. "This was extraordinary. . . . Walker was offering us ciphers, which are the most important aspect of intelligence. . . . For more than seventeen years, Walker enabled your enemies to read your most sensitive military secrets. We knew everything. There has never been a security breach of this magnitude and length in the history of espionage. Seventeen years we were able to read your cables!"

Supplied with the keylists since October 1967, all the KGB needed was an actual working machine. The capture of the *Pueblo* answered their wishes. "So John Walker's information, on top of *Pueblo*," Kalugin said, "definitely provided the Soviets with the final solutions to whatever technical problems they may have had at the time. And I think this combination of two really brought about, you know, tremendous results for the Soviet side. . . . We certainly made use of the equipment from the *Pueblo*."

In addition to the KW-7, the North Koreans also salvaged two other valuable cipher machines from the *Pueblo*—the KW-37 and the KG-14—and turned them over to the Russians. One member of John Walker's spy ring, Jerry Whitworth, was later stationed at the U.S. Navy base on the remote Indian Ocean island of Diego Garcia. There he had access to the KW-37, the KG-14, and other cipher machines and sold key materials for them to the Russians.

It is hard to overestimate the value of the Soviet code break. "Using the keylists provided by John Walker," Kalugin said, "[We] read all cryptographic traffic between the United States Naval Headquarters and the Navy across the world. . . . So by keeping control of the movement of U.S. nuclear submarines, by controlling the coded traffic between the Navy and the units in the open seas, we could really protect our country's security. . . . I think this was the greatest achievement of Soviet intelligence at the time of the Cold War."

In March, the crew of the *Pueblo* was moved to a newer detention facility outside Pyongyang, and the physical mistreatment became less frequent and less severe. Three months later, a number of the Sigint technicians were interrogated about cipher equipment by officials with obvious knowledge of the subject. In some instances, classified information was passed on and block diagrams and explanations of the KW-37 and KG-14 cipher machines were provided.

In the end, despite the thirst for retaliation back in Washington, diplomacy won out over military action in the efforts to gain the release of the *Pueblo* crew. But for nearly a year the cumbersome talks dragged on.

"Americans were shocked at President Lyndon Johnson's inability to 'free our boys,' " said William Taylor, Jr., of the Center for Strategic and International Studies. "Coming on top of repeated disasters in the Vietnam War, congressional opposition to Johnson grew rapidly. This was the beginning of the end of a failed presidency." Two months after the capture, on March 30, 1968, Johnson stunned the nation when he announced that he would not run for a second term.

By the fall of 1968, the *Pueblo* had become a hot political issue. Richard Nixon, running for the presidency against Vice President Hubert Humphrey, pounded on a podium and called for revenge. "When a fourth-rate military power like North Korea will seize an American naval vessel on the high seas," he said, "it's time for new leadership."

On December 23, 1968, Major General Gilbert Woodward, the American representative to the Military Armistice Commission in Panmunjom, signed a North Korean–prepared apology admitting to the espionage and the intrusion. However, before it was signed, Woodward denounced the papers as false. "I will sign the document," he said, "to free the crew and only free the crew." Nevertheless, the North Koreans accepted the fig leaf, and later that day all the *Pueblo* crewmen—along with the body of Duane Hodges—crossed the bridge linking North and South Korea. It had been exactly eleven months since the ordeal began.

Imprisoned [eleven] months,
A grand collection of lumps
We've gathered since the dawn of detention.
But do you think we're resentful?
Hell no! We're repentful!
How *repentful it's safer not to mention.*

Following the crew's release, a Navy court of inquiry was harshly critical of Bucher's performance during the crisis. He was accused of not recognizing in time the serious threat to his ship. "A determination to resist seizure was never developed in *Pueblo* prior to or during the incident," it said. "Commander Bucher had the responsibility for developing the best defensive capability possible in his ship utilizing all weapons and personnel available. This he did not do."

He was also severely criticized for giving up his ship and its secrets.

"He should have persisted—increased speed, zigzagged, and maneuvered radically. No boarding party could have come aboard had the ship so maneuvered. In view of the absence of fire or flooding and few minor casualties at the time the Commanding Officer made the fatal decision to stop and follow the SO-1 into Wonsan, his ship was fully operational. . . . He should have realized that the greatest service to his country could have been performed by denying to a foreign government classified material and personnel with knowledge of sensitive information on board." Finally, the court said, "He decided to surrender his ship when it was completely operational without offering any resistance. He just didn't try—this was his greatest fault. . . . He made no apparent effort to resist seizure of his ship. He permitted his ship to be boarded and searched while he still had the power to resist."

On the other hand, the court gave Bucher high marks for the way he held the crew together and kept up their morale while in custody "in a superior manner."

The court also had harsh words for Lieutenant Stephen Harris, the head of the Sigint operation on the ship, with regard to his ineffective destruction of the classified material in the spaces. It was estimated that only about 10 percent of the material within the Sigint area was actually destroyed. In light of that record, the court concluded, Harris "failed completely in the execution of emergency destruction of classified material."

Finally, the court found the conduct of most of the crew, and the Sigint personnel in particular, was greatly lacking. "With few exceptions the performance of the men was unimpressive. Notably the performance of the [Sigint personnel] in executing emergency destruction was uncoordinated, disappointing and ineffective. A general description of the crew of the *Pueblo* might be summarized by noting that in most instances CPOs [chief petty officers] and petty officers simply did not rise to the occasion and take charge as the emergency demanded."

The court recommended that Bucher and Harris be court-martialed.

But the crusty admirals on the court had been reading too many biographies of John Paul Jones when they should have been watching *Mission: Impossible*. No one, especially in peacetime, is required to commit either suicide or murder. The prosecutable offense should have been ordering anyone out on the open deck as a fleet of torpedo boats fired 3-inch shells at anything that moved. It would have taken a sailor between five and ten minutes just to undo the gun's cover, unlock the ammunition locker, and load the weapon. He would have been dead before he even reached the gun. And as a spy ship the *Pueblo* was supposed to maintain its cover as long as possible, not go to general quarters every time a foreign ship came by for a look.

"You're surrounded," said NSA's Gene Sheck. "You're literally surrounded. You've got to make a judgment. Do I lose all eighty-one guys? Those days of John Paul Jones, as far as I'm concerned, are long gone. While the Navy shudders and shakes at the thought that somebody surrendered a Navy ship, I don't think he had any choice. . . . You can imagine that thing being surrounded by all these gunboats out there and patrol boats and these guys just pulled right up to them and just literally climbed on board. They had nothing to fight back with. One .50-caliber machine gun, a couple of small guns, maybe a rifle or two, I don't know. But nothing that made sense."

Those who should have been court-martialed instead were the desk-bound Naval Security Group officers at Pacific Fleet Headquarters in Hawaii who planned the operation so carelessly. First they paid no attention to either the NSA warning message or the mounting North Korean threats—in English—against "U.S. spy ships" sailing off its eastern coast. Then they sent a bathtub-sized boat on its way lined bulkhead to bulkhead with unnecessary documents and a destruction system consisting of matches, wastebaskets, and hammers. Finally, they made no emergency plan should the ship come under attack. Said Sheck: "Folks out there said, 'Ain't no NSA bunch of guys going to tell us what not to do. And besides that, who's going to capture one of our Navy combat ships?' "

General Charles Bonesteel, who was in charge of both U.S. and UN forces in Korea at the time of the incident, said Bucher had no choice but to give up his ship. "They had total incapacity to do anything except die like heroes, and they couldn't have even done that. [The North Koreans would] have taken the damned ship," he said. "I think they probably did about all they could do under the circumstances."

Those who were at fault, said Bonesteel, were the Naval Security Group planners in Washington and Hawaii. "The degree of risk was totally unnecessary," he said. "Now, I wanted intelligence. I didn't have any damned intelligence, real intelligence, that could provide early warnings against a surprise action from the North. But we didn't need it in superfluous Comint. This was the intelligence wagging the dog. . . . North Korea wasn't a very serious threat to the continental U.S. . . . [North Korea] had made it very plain that this was an area they didn't want bothered. Sitting around there for several days relying on international law of territorial waters was just asking for it. I don't think this was very much of a planned action on the part of the North Koreans. I think our actions were just so blatant and obvious that they just couldn't resist the temptation. . . . The people who were responsible were totally out of touch with what the situation was in North Korea."

In the end, the Commander-in-Chief of the Pacific Fleet, Admiral John J. Hyland, approved letters of reprimand instead of court-martials for Bucher and Harris. Secretary of the Navy John H. Chafee then declared, "They have suffered enough," and dropped all charges against Bucher and Harris.

"The *Pueblo* incident, I think, was one of the remarkable episodes of the Cold War," said the KGB's Kalugin. "It was remarkable not only because it allowed the North Koreans and the Soviets to get hold of the . . . highly classified equipment and cryptographic material. It was also important because it allowed the Soviets and North Koreans and the Chinese to play this propaganda game. . . . great propaganda value.

"The *Pueblo* is still in the hands of the North Koreans. They keep it as a symbol of American interference, American arrogance, and a symbol of American defeat of sorts. For them it's a symbol of North Korean ability to deal with the greatest power in the world. . . . [Then North Korean President] Kim Il Sung raised his own stature to a level unthinkable before. He challenged the United States. He kept Americans in prison. He kept the *Pueblo* in the hands of the North Koreans and never let it go."

By 2001 the *Pueblo* had been moved to a pier on the Taedong River, which flows through Pyongyang, and opened to tourists. Visitors hear from two North Korean sailors who took part in the capture and watch a video recording of the incident.

Nevertheless, for some former senior NSA officials, the *Pueblo*'s last battle is not yet over. Led by a former NSA contractor who installed much of the ship's Sigint equipment, they were angry that the United States did not grab the *Pueblo* back as it was moved, past South Korea, from one side of the country to the other. They also quietly pressured the Clinton administration to seek the return of the freshly painted and battle-scarred ship. "The sooner, the better!" agreed retired Navy Commander Lloyd Bucher.

CHAPTER NINE

ADRENALINE

I.G. EOPVJEVRG GJRMESKRG JWJSRGE MOSRJ KDVP MKQLPSWOE YSWOE
HWAMQGW MEAG CWILCH, KXI HENA LX HLSQKEKIW SEN FW LBWC
NDII TCEASVDQ WKZQDW TCPVGPSD VC WIGND ZLVDQ AQCLGV HZQPGPB
BXQFDMAB' QXO KWSS OMGSR KSMET VMAX SMFQB DM VXPWEM
ZASQD XB BLSYRXCM PCQQALLSYZ UOKYTAM BLSYRA CYQX PXKLYCYT

In the penultimate days before the North Korean attack on the *Pueblo*, NSA's focus was on another troubled land severed along a degree of latitude: Vietnam. For the 2 million people packed as tightly as bullet casings into the twenty square miles of Saigon, the morning of January 22, 1968, began with a frenzy of activity. Emergency vehicles, rushing to a trio of separate terrorist incidents, performed pirouettes around fruit-laden shoppers. Overhead, a swarm of helicopter gunships, like heavily armed locusts, searched back and forth across an open field for Communist guerrillas. In front of a cloud of hazy blue exhaust fumes, an American-made tank tore at a downtown pavement as the driver took a shortcut to a convoy of vehicles heading north.

Amid the war, life went on as normal. At a restaurant near the Central Market, passersby inspected the barbecued chickens with their shiny lacquerlike coatings, hanging from hooks in an open window. U.S. Air Force commandos in big hats and low-slung revolvers sipped bitter espresso at a stand-up counter, like gunslingers at a Wild West saloon. In the malodorous Ben Nghe Canal, gray wooden sampans pushed slowly past shacks perched on narrow, spindly legs. Policemen in tropical whites directed swirls of traffic at the broad circular intersections.

In the far north on that Monday in January, at Firebase 861 near Khe Sanh, enemy soldiers lobbed mortar rounds and rifle grenades. American troops fought back through mailboxlike slits in the thick cement walls that protected them. Between explosions, a Marine battalion arrived to reinforce the garrison. Landing nearby were pallets containing 96,000 tons of ordnance. The day before, North Vietnamese Army forces had begun a siege of the hilltop outpost, and the United States was engaged in an all-out effort to save it.

In charge of the American war was Army General William Westmoreland. On the afternoon of January 22, at his Saigon headquarters, his major worry was the powerful attack in the north on Khe Sanh. He compared it to the bloody assault on the French at Dien Bien Phu more than a dozen years earlier. But Westmoreland was intent on proving that massive firepower would allow the United States to succeed where the French had dismally failed. He believed that sometime prior to Tet—the Vietnamese New Year, nine days away—the guerrillas would launch a major attack in the far north, at Khe Sanh and some of the surrounding bases. Thus, he began focusing his men, munitions, and might in that high province. "I believe that the enemy will attempt a country-wide show of strength just prior to Tet," he cabled the Joint Chiefs of Staff in Washington, "with Khe Sanh being the main event." At the White House, President Johnson, following the action like a front-row fan at a championship boxing match, had a sand model of Khe Sanh built in the Situation Room.

But behind the cipher-locked door leading to NSA's headquarters in Vietnam, a different picture was beginning to emerge from analysis of enemy intercepts.

Twenty-three years earlier, a large and excited crowd had gathered in Hanoi's Ba Dinh Square, a grassy, festively decorated field a short distance away from the graceful homes in the French district. They had walked there on callused feet as tough as rawhide from the flooded rice fields of the Tonkin Delta, the muddy banks of the Red River, the docksides of Haiphong, and the sampans of Halong Bay. Bac Ho, the man they came to see and hear, stood before them, awkward and slightly stooped. A frayed khaki tunic covered his skeletal frame, his feet were clad in worn rubber sandals, and wispy black hairs hung from his bony chin like dandelion fluff.

As the din of the crowd began to fade, Bac Ho stepped forward on a wooden platform, his glasses flashing in the sunlight. "We hold the truth [*sic*] that all men are created equal," he said solemnly, borrowing a phrase from the American Declaration of Independence, "that they are endowed by their Creator with certain unalienable rights, among them life, liberty, and the pursuit of happiness." The men and women in their drab pajamas and conical straw hats exploded as Bac Ho, a onetime resident of Brooklyn, gave birth to the Democratic Republic of Vietnam. By then, most knew him simply as Uncle Ho. Those in the United States would later know him more formally as Ho Chi Minh—Bringer of Light.

In a land that had known little but torment, for a brief afternoon in September 1945, the sun had never shined brighter. Like a tired horse that has bucked off its last abusive owner, Vietnam had finally rid itself of its French and Japanese masters. Gangly and serious, Ho Chi Minh looked more like a shy chemistry professor than the leader of a guerrilla army. Born in central Vietnam in 1890, he traveled widely as a merchant seaman, spent time in the United States, learned seven languages, and saw communism as the most effective way to unite his country to expel the colonialists. After an absence of thirty years, Ho slipped back into Vietnam in 1941 disguised as a Chinese journalist. There he formed the Vietnam Independence League—the Viet Minh—to beat back the French colonizers, who had enslaved his country for decades, and the Japanese warlords, who were attempting to take over much of Asia.

As the Allied and Axis powers battled in Europe and Japan, Ho fought his own war in the jungles of Vietnam—then French Indochina—using ambushes in place of howitzers, and sabotage instead of bombers. After four years of trial and error, he could have taught a doctorate-level course on the strategy of guerrilla warfare. Finally, with the end of World War II and the defeat of Japan, which was then occupying the country, Ho saw Vietnam's opportunity for independence, which he proclaimed on September 2, 1945. Unbeknownst to Ho, by the time of his proclamation America was already secretly eavesdropping on his new country.

Although defeated by Allied forces in August 1945, the Japanese occupiers remained in Vietnam for another six months. During that time, American intercept operators and codebreakers monitored communications to Tokyo from Japanese outposts in Hanoi and Saigon. "Japanese reports back to Tokyo in the days before and immediately after the surrender," said a later NSA report, "provide some indication of how deep was the desire to throw off the yoke of colonialism, how strong the will to resist the return of the French." The intercepts carried reports of Ho's forces secretly taking into custody important Frenchmen, and "at nighttime there was gunfire." Another said, "when one considers the situation after the Japanese Army is gone, he cannot fail to be struck with terror."

Not yet willing to give up their profitable rubber plantations and their global prestige, the French colonizers moved back in the spring of 1946 as the Japanese were pulling out. In so doing they arrogantly rejected the postwar trend to begin loosing the chains of foreign domination, and once again began to brutally exploit their distant colony. The moment of sunlight had passed; Ho's war would continue in the darkness. In November shooting erupted in Haiphong and the French bombarded the city, killing some 6,000 Vietnamese. On December 19, the Vietnamese attacked the French. As an NSA report says, "Thus began the Indochina War."

In the United States, State Department Asian experts cautioned President Truman that Vietnam was a powder keg and that pressure should be put on France to grant the country "true autonomous self-government." The alternative, it warned pointedly, would be "bloodshed and unrest for many years, threatening the economic and social progress and peace and stability" of the region. CIA analysts counseled that providing military aid to France to crush its indigenous opposition "would mean extremely adverse reactions within all Asiatic anti-'colonial' countries and would leave the U.S. completely vulnerable to Communist propaganda."

Nevertheless, while mouthing hollow platitudes about freedom and independence throughout the world, Truman agreed to help France remount its colonial saddle, sending millions of dollars in aid, weapons, and U.S. forces to help them fight Ho and his rebels. At one point in 1952, a witless CIA officer at the U.S. embassy in Hanoi hired a team of Chinese saboteurs, gave them some plastic explosives from his stockpile, and sent them off to blow up a bridge. That they failed in their mission should have been taken as a sign, like a fortune in a Chinese cookie. But the blunders would only grow larger and more violent over the next two decades.

Eisenhower also weighed in on behalf of colonialism, sending the CIA to help the French beat back Ho and his forces. In November 1953,

French paratroopers occupied Dien Bien Phu in northwestern Vietnam, ten miles from the Laotian border. Their plan was to lure Ho's rebel army into a trap in which they would be slaughtered by superior French firepower. But the French miscalculated and suddenly found themselves isolated, unable to keep resupplied by air. As a result, Eisenhower agreed to an airlift using CIA men and planes to fly supplies back and forth from Hanoi's Cat Bi airfield to Dien Bien Phu.

The operation began on March 13, 1954, but the beleaguered French stood little chance and Dien Bien Phu fell on May 7. Over the two months it operated, the CIA flew 682 airdrop missions. One plane was shot down and its two pilots were killed; many other C-119s suffered heavy flak damage, and one pilot was severely wounded.

Meanwhile, NSA secretly eavesdropped on the conflict. "I recall very dramatically the fall of Dien Bien Phu," said Dave Gaddy, an NSA official at the time. "There were people with tears in their eyes. . . . We had become very closely attached to the people we were looking over the shoulders of—the French and the Viet Minh. And we could very well have sealed the folders, put everything away, locked the files, shifted on to other things, and didn't. As a result, we had a superb backing for what came along later."

Taking up where the French left off, CIA operations continued in Indochina after the fall of Dien Bien Phu. Between mid-May and mid-August, C-119s dropped supplies to isolated French outposts and delivered loads throughout the country. The French, driven by greed, would be replaced by the Americans, driven by anti-Communist hysteria. This despite a secret State Department intelligence report at the time saying that the department "couldn't find any hard evidence that Ho Chi Minh actually took his orders from Moscow."

By the time John F. Kennedy entered the White House in January 1961, Vietnam was a wave in the distant ocean, barely visible; a thin white line slowly growing and building. The French, at Dien Bien Phu, had been forced out after eight years of fighting and scores of thousands of deaths. Left as a reminder was a ragged demilitarized zone (DMZ) that cut across the narrow middle of the country like a haunting dead zone; a no-man's-land separating the pro-Communist forces in the North from the pro-Western forces in the South. Six hundred and eighty-five American advisers were now in Vietnam and the financial commitment since 1954 topped $2 billion.

Pressured by the Pentagon, which was concerned over growing reports of Communist infiltration into South Vietnam, Kennedy ordered a few helicopter and Special Forces units to the area. Then the Army began lobbying to also send signals intelligence assistance. For years South Vietnamese officials had asked for NSA's help in locating and eliminating Ho's infiltrators from the North, the Vietcong. But Eisenhower had long rejected the requests, considering the information and techniques far too secret.

Kennedy reluctantly gave in to the Army's pressure. During a meeting of the National Security Council on April 29, 1961, he authorized NSA to begin providing Sigint support to the South Vietnamese Army. Sharing such sensitive information with a foreign government was highly unusual, as reflected in the Top Secret/Codeword "Communications Intelligence Regulation" that authorized the transfer. Because "the current situation in South Vietnam is considered to be an extreme emergency involving an imminent threat to the vital interests of the United States," said the order, dissemination of Sigint to the South Vietnamese military was authorized "to the extent needed to launch rapid attacks on Vietnamese Communists' communications."

Vice Admiral Laurence H. Frost, the director of NSA, ordered his military arm, the Army Security Agency (ASA), to begin immediate preparations. Within weeks the 400th ASA Special Operations Unit (Provisional), using the cover name 3rd Radio Research Unit and the classified NSA designation "USM 626," was airborne. On May 13, 1961, the spit-shined boots of ninety-three Army cryptologists stepped from a silver C-130 transport onto the tarmac of Saigon's Tan Son Nhut Air Base. It was the Year of the Buffalo, symbolizing patience, fruitful toil, and peaceful contentment, concepts that would be difficult to find in a country on the precipice of all-out war. Green to combat, the Sigint experts would have a difficult time hearing the enemy.

Ho's twenty years in the underground taught him not only the art of guerrilla warfare, but also how to keep a secret. Within days of his declaration of independence, officials of the rebel government began addressing the issue of codes and ciphers. "In the first days of the revolutionary regime," said a North Vietnamese document obtained and translated by NSA, "an urgent requirement was to research methods of using cryptography so as to ensure communications security." Ho himself warned a class of budding codemakers: "Cryptography must be secret, swift, and accurate. Cryptographers must be security conscious and of one mind."

By the time of the war with America, Ho was calling his codemakers "cryptographic warriors" and ordering them to prevent loss of their crypto materials at all cost. He would give examples of heroic deeds to emulate. In 1962, they were told, Petty Officer Third Class Bui Dang Dzuong, a cryptographer on a small ship, ran into fierce weather. Nevertheless, as the boat was sinking he "destroyed the entire set of [cryptographic] materials. . . . Big waves, heavy wind, and sapped of strength—Comrade Dzuong gave his life." In another example, two cryptographers were injured during an attack; one stepped on a mine "that snapped his leg" while the other's "ears deafened and ran blood." Nevertheless, they "calmly preserved the cryptographic system," and only after they were relieved by a replacement did they go to the hospital. Following the lectures, the youthful codemakers were sent "down the Ho Chi Minh trail into the South to strike America."

The Vietcong cryptographers learned their lessons well. While throwing an electronic fishing net into the ether, they regularly reeled it back in bulging with American communications; but they seldom used radios themselves. While they listened to broadcasts from Hanoi on inexpensive transistor radios, they sent messages back to their commands with couriers, except in dire emergencies. For local communications, they often used radios with very low power, frustrating American eavesdroppers.

From dusk to dawn, the Vietcong ruled, in varying degrees, more than half of the South. They marched over, under, and around the DMZ like worker ants. In the South, supporters were recruited and resisters often shot.

Locating the guerrillas so they could be killed or captured was the job of the radio direction-finding specialists. Another operation, codenamed White Birch, involved eavesdropping on the nests of Vietcong infiltrators. A third, dubbed Sabertooth, trained the South Vietnamese soldiers to intercept, locate, and process plaintext voice communications.

The art of codebreaking, however, was considered too sensitive to pass on to South Vietnamese students.

Home for the 3rd Radio Research Unit was an old hangar within the South Vietnamese Army's Joint General Staff Compound at Tan Son Nhut Air Base. Temperature inside the un-air-conditioned building regularly exceeded 100 degrees, and when a monsoon downpour came, the water would rush in through the front door and flood the space several inches deep.

Separating the various sections were walls made of stacked C-ration boxes. The analysts worked on long tables constructed of plywood and scrap lumber, but because there were so few chairs, the table was made about four feet tall so they could stand up while working. The NSA official assigned to the unit did little better. "As a civilian from NSA," he said, "I was fortunate. They made me a desk—two stacks of C-ration boxes with a piece of plywood laid across them—and gave me a folding chair." Living conditions for the NSA chief were much more comfortable. First assigned to the Majestic Hotel in downtown Saigon, he was later moved to a two-bedroom villa he shared with an ASA officer.

Within seven months the Sigint force more than doubled. By December 1961, the secret organization had grown to 236 men, along with eighteen intercept positions. Listening posts stretched as far north as Phu Bai, near the DMZ, a choice spot to pick up valuable cross-border communications. The school for training South Vietnamese soldiers was set up at the South Vietnamese Army Signal Compound.

In the field, the work was nerve-racking and dangerous. It was, said President Kennedy, a "war by ambush rather than combat," one made up of "guerrillas, subversives, insurgents, assassins." Among the first Army cryptologists to arrive in Vietnam was twenty-five-year-old James T. Davis, a pharmacist's son from Tennessee whose words rolled off his tongue with a honey-coated twang. Based at Tan Son Nhut, the specialist-4 was assigned to search for Vietcong guerrillas in the tangled, overgrown jungle of giant ferns and dirt paths near Saigon. Traveling with heavily armed South Vietnamese soldiers, he needed to get close enough to the rebels so that his PRC-10 mobile radio direction-finding equipment could pick up their short-range signals. But if he got too close, he would become the hunted rather than the hunter. It was a deadly game of hide-and-seek, in which the loser was attacked and likely killed and the winner survived for another day.

Three days before Christmas in 1961, Davis climbed into his jeep and, accompanied by his team of South Vietnamese soldiers, set off for a new location to the west of Saigon. But about eight miles from the air base, muzzle flashes from automatic weapons cut across his path and he zigzagged to avoid the fire. A split second later he heard a loud boom and was thrown to the ground as a powerful land mine blew his jeep apart.

Davis grabbed for his M-1 carbine and he and the others opened fire. But by now they were surrounded, and within minutes nine of his South Vietnamese troops had been killed by machine-gun fire. A bullet crashed into the back of Davis's head and he collapsed on the ground. The Vietnam War had claimed its first American victim—a Sigint specialist. Two weeks later, the 3rd Radio Research Unit's secret headquarters at Tan Son Nhut Air Base would be named Davis Station. Eventually, a barracks at NSA headquarters would also bear his name.

In Washington, that remote wave was beginning to swell and head toward shore. Kennedy further Americanized the civil war, ordering the CIA to beef up its covert operations far above the DMZ. Late at night, out of carbon-black skies, billowing parachutes glided gracefully to earth. But the missions, to infiltrate heavily armed South Vietnamese commandos into the North, were doomed before they began as a result of poor security. Automatic fire instead of friendly faces greeted most of the teams as they touched down at their landing spots in the northern regions of North Vietnam.

Soon after President Johnson moved into the White House, following Kennedy's assassination in November 1963, the once far-off swell became a tidal wave about to crash. By mid-1964 there were 16,000 U.S. troops in the country and the war was costing American taxpayers about $1.5 million a day. Giving up on the disastrous CIA infiltration scheme, Johnson instead ordered the Joint Chiefs to develop a much more aggressive—but still "plausibly deniable"—operation that would convince Ho to give up his war for the South. The answer was Operational Plan 34A—OPLAN 34A, in Pentagonese—an ill-conceived CIA/Pentagon scheme for sabotage and hit-and-run attacks against the interior and coast of North Vietnam.

For a quarter of a century Ho had fought for an independent, unified Vietnam, successfully driving the heavily armed French back to Paris. Even Secretary of Defense Robert S. McNamara thought OPLAN 34A made no sense. "Many of us who knew about the 34A operations had concluded they were essentially worthless," he recalled years later. "Most of the South Vietnamese agents sent into North Vietnam were either captured or killed, and the seaborne attacks amounted to little more than pinpricks."

Just as U.S. and South Vietnamese forces fought back against the guerrillas from the North, the North Vietnamese fought back against the commandos from the South, on both land and sea.

Into the middle of the fighting sailed NSA. According to an NSA report, "By midsummer of 1964 the curtain was going up on the main event, and no single element in the United States government played a more critical role in national decisions, both during and after the fact, than the National Security Agency."

For several years NSA's seagoing eavesdroppers, the Naval Security Group, had been searching for ways to conduct signals intelligence along the coastal areas of their high-priority targets. Long-range high-frequency North Vietnamese naval communications could be collected at large, distant listening posts, such as at Kamiseya in Japan and San Miguel in the Philippines. Other medium-range signals could be snatched by the large NSA listening posts at Davis Station in Saigon and at Phu Bai, near the DMZ. But to snare short-range signals, such as walkie-talkie and coastal communications, the antennas and receivers would have to get close to the action. Off limits were the large eavesdropping factories owned exclusively by NSA, such as the USS *Oxford.* And far in the future were the smaller, Navy-owned Sigint ships, such as the *Pueblo.*

The only alternative was to build Sigint shacks inside large steel antenna-sprouting boxes. These shipping-container-like huts would then be lowered onto a destroyer and sealed to the deck. The ship would then cruise close to a shoreline, like a spy at a party with a bugged olive in his martini glass.

They were far from ideal. Unlike the dedicated Sigint ships, which were virtually unarmed and unthreatening in appearance, the heavily armed destroyers were designed to be threatening and their presence was provocative. At the same time, the amount of signals intelligence that could be collected in the steel box on the deck was minuscule compared with what the dedicated ships could gather.

The Naval Security Group began conducting these Sigint patrols, codenamed DeSoto, in April 1962 with missions off China and North Korea. In January 1964, as they were planning the OPLAN 34A hit-and-run operations, the Joint Chiefs ordered additional DeSoto patrols off the North Vietnamese coast, in the Gulf of Tonkin. The signals generated by the surprise coastal attacks, they assumed, would be a good source of naval intelligence for the Sigint collectors. In addition to voice communications, the locations and technical details of coastal radar systems could be captured.

The first mission was conducted by the USS *Craig* in late February 1964. Resting on the ship's deck were both a Comint van for communications intelligence and an Elint van for radar signals. But upon spotting an American warship idling suspiciously a half-dozen miles off their coast, the security-conscious North Vietnamese navy quickly switched off virtually all nonessential radar and communications systems. Thus the Sigint take was poor.

At the request of U.S. officials in Saigon who were planning the raids into North Vietnam, another DeSoto mission was scheduled for the end of July 1964. It was felt that if a DeSoto mission coincided with coastal commando raids, there would be less chance of another washout. Chosen to host the electronic spies was the USS *Maddox,* a standard Navy "tin can," as destroyers were known. But whereas other ships had been ordered to stay at least thirteen miles off the coasts of such countries as China, North Korea, and the Soviet Union, the *Maddox* was authorized to approach as close as eight miles from the North Vietnamese coast, and four miles from offshore islands.

Like itinerant seamen, the Sigint vans would bounce from ship to ship, sailing off the coast of China on one tin can and then off the coast of North Korea on another. The crews also would change. One month a van might be filled with Russian linguists and the next with Chinese. "Home" for the vans was the port of Keelung in Taiwan. Because there were only a few available to cover a large area, they were very much in demand. The one lowered onto the deck of the *Maddox* had earlier been lifted from the deck of the USS *MacKenzie,* where, loaded with Russian linguists, it had eavesdropped off the Soviet coast.

As the *Maddox* was about to enter the Gulf of Tonkin, tensions were very high. At My Khe, a gritty stretch of coarse, hard-packed sand at the base of Monkey Mountain, U.S. Navy SEALs were teaching South Vietnamese marines the science of inflicting the maximum amount of death and destruction in the minimum amount of time. The main base from which the raids to the north took place, the My Khe compound was made up of a series of "compartmented" camps divided along ethnic lines, and long wooden docks. Secretly run by U.S. forces, it was a land of white phosphorus rockets and black rubber boats.

Late on the night of July 30, 1964, as moonlight rippled across the choppy Gulf of Tonkin, a raiding party of South Vietnamese commandos climbed aboard four large, fast patrol boats. Several of the type known as PTFs—or, appropriately, *Nasty*-class boats—were powered by diesel engines. The others were standard American-made, gasoline-driven PT boats. The vessels were armed with 57mm light infantry cannon. Bluish-gray exhaust gas shot from the rear of the guns, rather than the muzzle, to reduce the amount of recoil so that they would be steadier when used out of their mounts.

In the early morning hours of July 31, about halfway up the North Vietnamese coast, the boats blasted away at two offshore islands, Hon Me and Hon Ngu, in the most violent of the South Vietnamese–U.S. raids thus far.

As the boats were returning to My Khe later that same morning, their wake passed within four miles of the *Maddox,* then just north of the DMZ. Viewed by North Vietnamese coastal defense radars, the ships would have appeared to be rendezvousing. The *Maddox* may also have been perceived as standing guard, ready to fire at any boats seeking to cross the DMZ in hot pursuit of the heavily armed patrol boats. It was well known that the United States was behind virtually every South Vietnamese raid on the North.

Throughout the day, the *Maddox* bobbed lazily about eight miles off the North Vietnamese coast, just above the DMZ, an area of good signal hunting. Sitting in front of racks of receivers in the cramped Sigint van, which had received a new coat of gray paint a few days earlier to make it look like a normal part of the ship, the intercept operators worked twelve hours on and twelve hours off. One of the intercept positions was dedicated to short-range VHF communications, picking up hand-held radios and the chatter between vessels off the coast. The proficiency of the voice linguists was limited at best, but they had a tape recorder attached to the monitoring equipment and could save the conversations for later analysis.

Two other positions were for intercepting high-frequency Morse code signals. Because of the vagaries of radio wave propagation, some of the North Vietnamese high-frequency signals could be better heard in the Philippines than right off the coast. But because the ship was mobile, it could also pick up high-frequency signals that might escape the fixed, land-based listening posts. Unlike some DeSoto missions, the *Maddox* did not have a separate Elint van; the two Elint operators worked instead on the ship's standard radar receivers, alongside the crew. Also in the van was an on-line encrypted teleprinter, which could print out highly classified messages from NSA exclusively for the Sigint-cleared cryptologic team. This link bypassed the ship's normal communications channels.

Unlike the job of the *Oxford* and the other seagoing eavesdropping factories then being launched by NSA, the DeSoto patrols were "direct support" missions. Part of the job of the Sigint detachment was to collect intelligence on naval activities along the coast for later reports. But another was to provide area commanders with current, immediate intelligence support, including warning intelligence. On the *Maddox,* those cleared to receive such reports included the ship's captain, Commander Herbert Ogier, and also Captain John Herrick, the commander of the Seventh Fleet's Destroyer Division 192.

The twin missions of the *Maddox* were, in a sense, symbiotic. The vessel's primary purpose was to act as a seagoing provocateur—to poke its sharp gray bow and American flag as close to the belly of North Vietnam as possible, in effect shoving its 5-inch cannons up the nose of the Communist navy. In turn, this provocation would give the shore batteries an excuse to turn on as many coastal defense radars, fire control systems, and communications channels as possible, which could then be captured by the men in the steel box and at the radar screens. The more provocation, the more signals. The ship even occasionally turned off all its electronic equipment in an effort to force the shore stations to turn on additional radar—and begin chattering more—in order to find it.

The mission was made more provocative by being timed to coincide with the commando raids, thus creating the impression that the *Maddox* was directing those missions and possibly even lobbing firepower in their support. The exercise was dangerous at best, foolish at worst. In the absence of information to the contrary, the Navy had assumed that North Vietnam, unlike most U.S. targets, did not claim a twelve-mile limit. Thus the decision was made to sail far closer to shore than on normal patrols in Communist Asia despite the fact that the United States happened to be engaged in combat with North Vietnam. In fact, North Vietnam also claimed at least a twelve-mile limit and viewed the *Maddox* as trespassing deep within its territorial waters.

On August 1, when the *Maddox* was about halfway up the North Vietnamese coast, intercept operators in the van were busy eavesdropping on the shore stations tracking the ship's progress. Upon hearing them report the *Maddox*'s distance and bearing they could "back-plot" the signal to the station's location.

About 8:30 P.M. (local time) the ship approached the island of Hon Me; the island was now within easy range of the *Maddox*'s powerful cannons. Although no one on board likely knew it, survivors on shore were still cleaning up from the grave damage produced by the American-planned South Vietnamese commando boat raid just two nights earlier. It may be that when those on Hon Me saw the U.S. warship loom large on the horizon in the gray twilight, the alarm went out that the shelling was going to begin again, this time with more powerful guns.

Hours later in the Sigint van, the tenor of the messages suddenly changed. A high-level North Vietnamese message was intercepted indicating that a decision had been made to launch an attack later that night. Although no targets were named, Captain Herrick was awakened immediately and informed of the situation. The next message, however, mentioned an "enemy" vessel and gave the *Maddox*'s location. The conclusion was that an order had gone out to attack the *Maddox*. By then it was about 2:45 A.M. Captain Herrick ordered all personnel to go to general quarters, increased the ship's speed, and turned away from shore.

At about 11:30 A.M. the next day, August 2, crewmembers on the *Maddox* sighted five North Vietnamese navy attack boats about ten miles north of Hon Me. They had been sent from the port of Van Hoa, 145 miles to the north, to help defend the island from further attacks and hunt for the enemy raiders. Nevertheless, despite the danger, the *Maddox* continued its patrol, reaching the northernmost point of its planned track at 12:15 P.M. At that point it turned south, remaining about fifteen miles from shore. In the Sigint van, the messages intercepted had again become routine—supply orders, pier changes, personnel movements.

Suddenly the mood in the box changed. An odd message had been intercepted, and as it was being translated its seriousness became clear. It was an order to attack the ship with torpedoes.

By then three North Vietnamese torpedo boats had already pulled away from the island, waves lathering their bows like shaving foam as they reached thirty knots. Their goal was to trap the *Maddox* in a pincers move. They would pass the *Maddox* and then turn back, trapping the ship between them and the coast, preventing its escape to the safety of the high seas. Told of the message, Captain Herrick immediately turned southeast toward the open ocean. The intercept had turned the tide. By the time the PT boats arrived the *Maddox* was racing out to sea, leaving them in its wake as they fired at the destroyer's stern.

On board each swift sixty-six-foot aluminum-hulled PT boat were torpedoes packing a deadly wallop, each fitted with warheads containing 550 pounds of TNT. The three boats each launched one torpedo, but the fast-moving *Maddox* was beyond reach.

After this near miss, Captain Herrick suggested that the remainder of his Sigint mission be called off. But the general perception in the Pentagon was that such action would set a bad precedent, since in effect the United States would have been chased away. Herrick was ordered to continue the patrol and another destroyer, the USS *Turner Joy*, was provided as protection.

Shortly after the attack on the *Maddox*, it was clear to officials in Washington that the principal reason for the incident was the North Vietnamese belief that the ship was directing the commando raids. "It seems likely that the North Vietnamese and perhaps the Chi-Coms [Chinese Communists] have assumed that the destroyer was part of this operation," Michael Forrestal, the State Department's Vietnam expert, told Secretary of State Dean Rusk on August 3. "It is also possible that

Hanoi deliberately ordered the attack in retaliation for the harassment of the islands."

Yet with the *Maddox* still on its DeSoto Sigint patrol, it was decided to launch more commando raids on the day following the attack, August 3, this despite Secretary of Defense McNamara's firm belief that the operations were useless. Departing from My Khe, the same location as the previous mission, the four-boat raiding party sped seventy-five miles up the North Vietnamese coast to Cape Vinh Son and Cua Ron. There they shelled a radar station and a security post, the first South Vietnamese–U.S. attacks against a mainland target. In response, a North Vietnamese patrol boat took off in hot pursuit for about forty minutes before giving up. And once again, the government of North Vietnam connected the raid with the still-present *Maddox*.

Captain Herrick was worried about how stirred up the North Vietnamese were over the latest OPLAN 34A shelling. Early the next morning, August 4, he cabled his superiors:

> Evaluation of info from various sources indicates that the DRV [North Vietnam] considers patrol directly involved with 34-A operations and have already indicated readiness to treat us in that category. DRV are very sensitive about Hon Me. Believe this PT operating base and the cove there presently contains numerous patrol and PT craft which have been repositioned from northerly bases.

Later, an analyst at NSA received intercepts indicating that another attack on U.S. destroyers in the Gulf of Tonkin was imminent. One of the messages, sent from North Vietnamese naval headquarters in Haiphong to a patrol boat, specified the location of the destroyers. Another message included an order to prepare for military operations, using the patrol boats and perhaps a torpedo boat if it could be made ready in time. NSA immediately notified the Pentagon and a few minutes later, at 7:15 P.M. (Vietnam time), informed Captain Herrick on the *Maddox*.

An hour after NSA's warning, the *Maddox* sent out emergency messages indicating that it had picked up radar signals from three unidentified vessels closing fast. Fighters were launched from the *Ticon-*

deroga but thick, low-hanging clouds on the moonless night obscured the sea and they reported that they could see no activity. Nevertheless, over the next several hours, the two ships issued more than twenty reports of automatic weapons fire, torpedo attacks, and other hostile action. But in the end, no damage was sustained, and serious questions arose as to whether any attack actually took place. "Freak radar echoes," McNamara was told, were misinterpreted by "young fellows" manning the sonar, who "are apt to say any noise is a torpedo."

Nevertheless, regardless of the doubts raised by talk of "radar ghosts" and "nervousness," in testimony before Congress McNamara spoke of "unequivocal proof" of the new attack. That "unequivocal proof" consisted of the highly secret NSA intercept reports sent to the *Maddox* on August 4 as a warning. Based largely on McNamara's claims of certainty, both houses of Congress passed the Tonkin Gulf Resolution, thus plunging the United States officially into the open-ended quagmire known as the Vietnam War.

But it later turned out that that "unequivocal proof" was the result of a major blunder by NSA, and the "hard evidence" on which many people based their votes for the war never really existed. Years later Louis Tordella quietly admitted that the intercepts NSA used as the basis for its August 4 warning messages to the *Maddox* actually referred to the first attack, on August 2. There never were any intercepts indicating an impending second attack on August 4. The phony NSA warning led to McNamara's convincing testimony, which then led to the congressional vote authorizing the Vietnam War.

"What in effect happened," said Ray S. Cline, who was CIA's deputy director for intelligence at the time, "is that somebody from the Pentagon, I suppose it was McNamara, had taken over raw Sigint and [had] shown the President what they thought was evidence of a second attack on a [U.S.] naval vessel. And it was just what Johnson was looking for." Cline added, "Everybody was demanding the Sigint; they wanted it quick, they didn't want anybody to take any time to analyze it." Finally, he said, "I became very sure that that attack [on August 4] did not take place."

A quarter of a century earlier, confusion in Washington over Sigint warning messages resulted in calm at Pearl Harbor when there should have been action. Now, confusion over Sigint warning messages in Washington led to action in the Gulf of Tonkin when there should have been calm. In both cases a long, difficult pass was successfully intercepted, only for the players in Washington to fumble a few feet from the goal line.

For nearly four decades the question has been debated as to whether the Pentagon deliberately provoked the Gulf of Tonkin incident in order to generate popular and congressional support to launch its bloody war in Vietnam. In 1968, under oath before the Senate Foreign Relations Committee, Robert McNamara vigorously denied any such plot:

> I must address the suggestion that, in some way, the Government of the United States induced the incident on August 4 with the intent of providing an excuse to take the retaliatory action which we in fact took. . . .
>
> I find it inconceivable that anyone even remotely familiar with our society and system of Government could suspect the existence of a conspiracy which would have included almost, if not all, the entire chain of military command in the Pacific, the Chairman of the Joint Chiefs of Staff, the Joint Chiefs, the Secretary of Defense and his chief assistants, the Secretary of State, and the President of the United States.

McNamara knew full well how disingenuous this was. The Joint Chiefs of Staff had become a sewer of deceit. Only two years before the Gulf of Tonkin incident, his Joint Chiefs had presented him with a plan to launch a conspiracy far more grave than "inducing" the attack on the destroyers. Operation Northwoods had called for nothing less than the launch of a secret campaign of terrorism within the United States in order to blame Castro and provoke a war with Cuba.

More than three years after the incident in the Gulf, about the same time McNamara was feigning indignation before the Senate committee, the Joint Chiefs were still thinking in terms of launching "pretext" wars. Then the idea was to send the Sigint ship *Banner*, virtually unmanned, off dangerous North Korean shores, not to collect intelligence but to act as a sitting duck and provoke a violent response. Once the attack occurred, it would serve as an excuse to launch a war.

These proposed wars would be hidden for decades from Congress and the public under classification stamps and phony claims of national security.

George Ball, under secretary of state when the Tonkin Gulf incident took place, later came down on the side of the skeptics. "At the time there's no question that many of the people who were associated with the war," he said, "were looking for any excuse to initiate bombing. . . . The 'DeSoto' patrols, the sending of a destroyer up the Tonkin Gulf was primarily for provocation. . . . I think there was a feeling that if the destroyer got into some trouble, that it would provide the provocation we needed." Ball had no knowledge of Operation Northwoods.

Restless from a decade of peace, out of touch with reality, the Joint Chiefs of Staff were desperate for a war, any war. Thanks in large part to the provocative Sigint patrols and NSA's intercept mix-up, now they had one.

With the passing of the Tonkin Gulf Resolution, the tidal wave that had begun as distant whitecaps came crashing down, eventually sweeping tens of thousands of Americans to their death.

At the same time the war was being fought in the steamy jungles, it was also being waged high in the ether. This was the Sigint war, an invisible battle to capture hidden electrons and solve complex puzzles. As in World War II, it can often be the decisive battle. But the glory days of solving the German Enigma code and the Japanese Purple code had long since passed. With the North Vietnamese military and the Vietcong, NSA was discovering, the old rules had been changed. The eavesdroppers would have to start from scratch.

Hidden from view, NSA rapidly increased its buildup in Vietnam. By 1964 the number of cryptologic personnel in the country had reached 1,747. Three hundred men now packed Davis Station at Tan Son Nhut in Saigon. The Navy sent a Marine Sigint detachment to Pleiku, where they targeted Laotian and North Vietnamese communications. And U.S. Air Force intercept operators began setting up shop in Da Nang. To coordinate the growing numbers of units, a secure communications network was built linking sites at Nha Trang, Can Tho, Bien Hoa, Pleiku, Da Nang, and Ban Me Thuot. Then, in order to communicate quickly and securely with NSA headquarters, an undersea cable was laid from Vietnam to the Philippines. Codenamed Wetwash, the cable carried a variety of traffic ranging from high-speed CRITIC circuits to intercepted North Vietnamese messages too difficult to decrypt in Vietnam. In the Philippines, the Wetwash cable connected to another secure undersea cable that eventually terminated at NSA, in Fort Meade.

In the far north, near the demilitarized zone separating North from South, 1,000 Sigint personnel were sent to Phu Bai, which became the cornerstone of NSA's expansion. Like electronic border police, intercept operators manned 100 positions in a windowless operations building, listening for indications of infiltration and guerrilla activity. Others eavesdropped on tactical communications by both North Vietnamese and Laotian Communist forces. The expansive base was supported by another 500 people and surrounded by high fences, barbed wire and concertina wire, and eleven guard posts manned twenty-four hours a day.

But just as the numbers of people continued to grow, so did the problems. Although the school to train South Vietnamese soldiers was built and fully equipped, for years it had virtually no students because of the inability of the indigenous soldiers to pass NSA's rigorous security clearance requirements. More equipment and personnel in the field meant more intercepts, but most of them were not being analyzed because of the lack of trained linguists. "U.S. personnel with the ability to read Vietnamese texts were in short supply," said one NSA document, "and people competent to deal with spoken Vietnamese, with very few exceptions, were not to be found." Despite a crash training program at NSA, said the report, "the linguist problem became worse, not better." Communications problems were also frequent.

Most incredibly, NSA deliberately refrained from mounting a massive World War II–style Enigma or Purple effort against North Vietnamese cipher systems. According to one of the key NSA officials overseeing the cryptologic effort in Vietnam, "We found that we had adequate information without having to do that. In other words, through a combination of traffic analysis, low-level cryptanalysis, and plaintext/clear voice. The situation didn't justify the major effort." According-ing to another former official, mounting an enormous effort against North Vietnam would have diverted limited resources away from "the Soviet problem" and other areas, which nobody wanted to do. "And of course there was always the question of whether there was any utility in working on one-time pads," said the former official. "But my argument always was, How do you know it's a one-time pad if you don't work it?" This was an allusion to the surprising "Venona" breakthrough in Soviet onetime pads.

For most of the intercept operators, used to the monotonous routine of peacetime listening posts, there was an air of unreality about Vietnam. The constant *wharp-wharp-wharp* of steel helicopter blades echoing off rusty corrugated roofs. Gunships on a hunt, flying in formation as they skimmed the ground. Open crates of green rocket-propelled grenades and saucer-shaped claymore mines resting haphazardly beside delicate flame trees and baskets of lotus blossoms.

The Sigint war was fought by both sides. Although no one knew it at the time, the North Vietnamese Central Research Directorate, which managed the North's Sigint operations, was successfully collecting almost all South Vietnamese and U.S. communications passing over a number of key traffic lanes. North Vietnam did not need to break high-level American codes, because the Americans continuously chose expediency over security. Rather than take the time to send the information over secure, encrypted lines, they would frequently bypass encryption and simply use voice communications. The problem became, according to NSA, America's Achilles' heel during the war. "There was no blotter large enough to dry up sensitive, exploitable plain-language communications in Vietnam," said one NSA report.

Over the years, U.S. forces would occasionally capture enemy Sigint operators who would shed light on the problem. "Through interrogation of these men and study of the documents and signals intelligence materials seized," said a secret NSA analysis, "a clear, even frightening picture of Vietnamese Communist successes against Allied communications gradually emerged." Even as late as 1969, major clandestine listening posts were being discovered, such as one in Binh Duong Province. "Evaluation of the equipment showed that the enemy unit could hear virtually all voice and manual Morse communications used by U.S. and Allied tactical units. The documents proved the enemy's success—2,000 hand-copied voice transmissions in English and signals intelligence instruction books of a highly professional caliber."

U.S. intelligence sources estimated that North Vietnam had probably as many as 5,000 intercept operators targeting American communications. "The inescapable conclusion from the captured documents in U.S. hands," said the NSA report, "is that the enemy is conducting a highly sophisticated signal intelligence operation directed against U.S. and Allied forces in South Vietnam. He has developed the art of intercept to the point where his operators receive training materials tailored to the particular U.S. or Allied units against whom they are working. The training materials captured list selected [U.S.] units, the frequencies on which they communicated, their communications procedures, the formats and numerous examples of their messages, and other characteristics to guide the communist operator."

The consequences of the poor U.S. communications security coupled with the advanced state of North Vietnamese Sigint were serious. NSA labeled the careless procedures "deadly transmissions." Lieutenant General Charles R. Myer, a career signals officer who served twice in Vietnam, outlined the problem. "The enemy might disappear from a location just before a planned U.S. attack," he said. "B-52 bomber strikes did not produce expected results because the enemy apparently anticipated them."

Strikes from sea were equally vulnerable. On February 11, 1965, the aircraft carrier USS *Hancock* was preparing to launch a bombing raid against certain shore targets in the North. But details of the mission were discussed over plain-language channels days before the attack. As a result, North Vietnamese naval units were ordered to use camouflage and systematically disperse before the morning of February 11. On other occasions, when the American planes arrived over their targets, anti-aircraft weapons were waiting, pointing in their direction, with deadly results.

Again in an attempt to avoid the time-consuming task of encrypting information using approved NSA ciphers and equipment, Americans would often make up their own "homemade" codes. "Their continued appearance on the scene has constituted one of the major Comsec [communications security] headaches of the war," a Top Secret/Umbra NSA report noted. "Even as late as the spring of 1969, the U.S. Air Force attaché in Laos, who was coordinating semi-covert U.S. air and other operations in that country, was sending most of his messages in a code he had made up himself." NSA's Air Force communications security specialists secretly eavesdropped on the attaché's communications. "They could completely reconstruct his code within eight to ten hours after each change," said the NSA report. "Since the attaché changed codes only every five weeks, most of his messages were susceptible to immediate enemy Sigint exploitation. The appearance and reappearance of codes of this type demand constant Comsec alertness."

Even if U.S. forces did use secure encryption to pass sensitive information, such as dates and times for attacks, problems arose when that information was passed to the South Vietnamese military and *they* discussed it over less secure channels. The South's communications were particularly vulnerable to the Vietcong. For example, using captured American equipment the guerrilla force was able to pick up U.S. Special Forces communications transmitted through the South Vietnamese Air Force network. "It was . . . likely that they could gain all the intelligence they needed on the growing U.S. presence in Vietnam from [South Vietnamese Air Force] communications," said an NSA study of the problem. One former Vietcong soldier later told U.S. officials that as a result of Sigint his unit had never been taken by surprise over a ten-year period and that they never had enough English-language linguists for all the communications they intercepted.

Another major problem was the lack of secure telephones. The Vietnam-era secure phone, the KY-8, was far from the compact handset of today; it looked more like a small safe. In 1965 there were 800 of the crypto machines in a warehouse in the U.S., but they had neither mounting brackets nor connecting cables. After what was described as "some tortuous evolutions," the first KY-8s eventually arrived in South Vietnam late in 1965 and over the next three years they were all distributed. An aircraft version, the KY-28, and a mobile unit, the KY-38, were also distributed. But there were not nearly enough secure phones. They were also very temperamental and prone to failure. Because they broke down in direct sunlight and high heat, they were also useless in places like bunkers. As a result, they did not solve the problem of classified talk on unsecure phones. "Signal security, particularly in voice radio transmissions," said General Myer, "was a major problem area throughout the period of combat operations in Vietnam."

To help guard against sloppy procedures and compromises, NSA and its naval, air, and military arms conducted what was known as communications security monitoring. "In conventional Comsec operations," said one NSA study of the Vietnam War, "the monitor places himself in the role of the enemy. Selectively, he intercepts the communications of his own service and then reports on the intelligence he has—and the enemies could have—gleaned from them." The Comsec personnel would frequently work from the back of hot, antenna-covered, three-quarter-ton trucks. Surrounding them would be a variety of monitoring equipment, such as the TPHZ-3, which could listen to thirty telephone lines simultaneously. During 1967, Comsec operators eavesdropped on 6,606,539 radio-telephone conversations and more than 500,000 conventional telephone calls.

At one point, such operations possibly saved the life of Lieutenant General Creighton W. Abrams, the deputy chief of the U.S. military command in Vietnam. As Abrams was about to board a helicopter on a flight north from Saigon to Phu Bai near Hue, the details of the mission, including the time, altitude, and route, and the names of the passengers, were transmitted in the clear. Comsec monitors overheard the transmission and reported it immediately. As a result, the flight plan was changed. North Vietnamese intercept operators also overheard the transmission. Although Abrams flew by a different route, one of the other helicopters scheduled to make the trip was not told of the change. As a result, "it was shot at the whole way from Saigon to Phu Bai—an unusual effort by the VC who did not usually shoot at helicopters on such flights," said an NSA report on the incident. "This I believe was a certain example of enemy Sigint use."

North Vietnamese Sigint experts were also able to pass false and deceptive information over U.S. communications links and at other times were able to trick American personnel into passing sensitive information to them over the phone. NSA called such "imitative communications deception (ICD)" the "capstone of the enemy's Sigint operations." During one period, at least eight American helicopters were downed as a result of ICD.

At the U.S. air base in Da Nang, a Vietcong guerrilla killed an American base guard and then picked up his phone. Speaking English, he announced that the far end of the base was being attacked. When the guards rushed off to the far end of the field, the Vietcong attacked with little resistance. The damage to the base and its planes was estimated to be around $15 million. The incident could have been prevented if the guards had simply used a proper authentication system.

At another point, guerrillas were able to lure American helicopters into a trap by breaking into their frequencies, using correct call signs, and then directing the choppers to a landing spot where they were ambushed. There were also numerous times in which American air and artillery strikes were deliberately misdirected to bomb or fire on friendly positions. At other times, the guerrillas were able to halt attacks by giving false cease-fire orders.

Even the best NSA encryption systems then available were potentially vulnerable. These included the KY-8 for secure voice communications and the KW-7 for highly sensitive written messages. "All of our primary operational communications were passed on KW-7 secured circuits," one U.S. commander in Vietnam told NSA. "Thus, for the more important traffic, we had good security."

But both the KW-7 and the KY-8 were captured by North Korea and turned over to Russia in 1968, and for years, until long after the Vietnam War ended, the Soviets were also getting up-to-date keylists for the machines from the Walker spy ring. This has led to speculation that the Soviets passed some of this information to the North Vietnamese.

Former KGB Major General Boris A. Solomatin, chief of station at the Soviet Embassy in Washington from 1965 to 1968, denies that Walker contributed to America's defeat: "Walker is not responsible for your failures in bombing in North Vietnam." Solomatin, who retired from the KGB and still lives in Moscow, added, "If you decide that the information from Walker was not handed over to the North Vietnamese or our other allies, you will be making the correct one."

But Solomatin's deputy at the time, KGB Major General Oleg Kalugin, who defected to the United States and now lives in Washington, disagrees. Although the machines and their keylists were considered far too sensitive to turn over to the North Vietnamese, the Russians certainly helped the North Vietnamese whenever they could. "We certainly provided the Vietnamese with some of the product we had obtained through John Walker, and ultimately with the *Pueblo*'s stuff we had from the North Koreans," said Kalugin. "The Soviet military were . . . quite involved in Vietnam. Not only in terms of providing military equipment, hardware and weapons, but also in helping the Vietnamese to conduct military operations, and to brief them on certain issues which the Soviets thought would have winning implications for the Vietnamese side." Kalugin added, "By providing the intelligence we had obtained . . . I'm sure we would help the Vietnamese. I'm sure we did."

The Soviets also provided help in other ways. On June 18, 1965, on a runway on Guam, twenty-seven Strategic Air Command B-52 bombers lined up like a rehearsal for doomsday. They were a fearsome sight: planes as long as sixteen-story buildings, their swept-back, fuel-laden wings spanning more than half the length of a football field and drooping so close to the ground that they needed to be supported by bicycle-like outriggers. Weighing them down were eight Pratt & Whitney J-57 turbojets capable of generating more than 100,000 pounds of earth-shaking thrust. Their cavernous bomb bays were roomy enough to house limousine-size nuclear bombs.

In the cockpit of the lead aircraft, the gloved right hand of the pilot grasped the eight throttles, one for each engine. Slowly, in a single motion, he shoved them forward, hurling the mighty machine ever faster down the runway. Seconds later the plane lifted into the sky from Anderson Air Force Base, bearing fifty-one conventional bombs totaling sixteen tons. More than two dozen Stratofortresses followed, flying to a point over the measureless Pacific Ocean where they rendezvoused with a fleet of KC-135 tankers. There, through long steel straws, they took in fuel at 6,000 pounds a minute while performing a delicate ballet five miles above the sea at 300 miles an hour.

Codenamed Operation Arc Light, their mission was to lay waste South Vietnam—the country the U.S. was trying to save. The targets were Vietcong guerrilla bases, which were to be bombed back into the days of flint and stone axes. Launched on their nonstop, 5,000-mile round-trip missions, the B-52s cratered the South Vietnamese countryside like the face of the moon. Twelve hours after taking off, they would land back on Guam. Month after month, 8,000 tons of iron rain fell on South Vietnam, spreading death, dismemberment, and destruction on whomever and whatever it touched. An average of 400 pounds of TNT exploded somewhere in the small country every second of every hour for months on end.

As preparations got under way days in advance for each mission, a growing cloud of electrons would form over Guam. Messages would have to go out requisitioning new bomb fuses and brake pads, target recommendations would flow back and forth, authorizations and go orders would be transmitted. The volume of signals would increase every day, like a bell curve.

Shortly after the Tonkin Gulf Resolution was passed, a Soviet trawler, the *Izmeritel*, took up residence three miles off Apra, Guam's major harbor. Like a seagull hovering around a fish factory, the antenna-covered Sigint boat was scavenging for signals. With the start of the Arc Light missions, the feeding became a frenzy. Guam served as a key communications center for many of the Navy's operations in Southeast Asia, and during the early part of the war was the only staging area for B-52 bombing missions over Vietnam. Soon after the beginning of Arc Light, mission planners began noticing that on many occasions the element of surprise had been lost. It would be more than a year before they began to understand why.

Bobbing innocently in the waves off Apra, the *Izmeritel* was able to gain a clear picture of launch times for the B-52s. Through traffic analysis of pre-strike encrypted transmissions, they were able to identify alerts from the indicators that marked Flash messages. About an hour before launch, the short-range VHF radio network would swell with clear-text transmission by aircraft and munitions maintenance personnel. This increased volume tipped off the Soviets to an impending launch like a signalman waving a flag. Also, thanks to radio talk such as "652 must be ready by 0900," they were able to identify the launch aircraft by tail numbers and even to learn the names of the crew. Unencrypted weather forecasts by SAC over certain areas of the Pacific gave away the aerial refueling locations.

Similar Sigint operations by the Vietcong in South Vietnam would reveal the target areas. And because the B-52s carried no encryption equipment, except for the Triton codes for nuclear authorization, all their communications were in clear voice. Captured enemy documents included a transcript of two and a half hours of detailed discussion of a particular planned B-52 raid, including the exact time of the attack and the coordinates of the target.

Only after a highly secret NSA, Air Force, and Navy investigation at Guam and other locations was it determined how the North Vietnamese and Vietcong were able to eliminate Arc Light's element of surprise. The probe uncovered "a number of insecure communications practices that made vital intelligence available to the enemy."

The NSA was also concerned about the Soviet trawler's ability to break its codes by discovering a "bust." Known technically as a *cipher-signal anomaly*, this is when an electrical irregularity occurs during encryption that "might permit an alert enemy to recover plain language or other data," according to an NSA document. Then, as now, it is a key way to break an otherwise unbreakable cipher.

Even without a bust, the Soviet trawler might still be able to defeat the cipher systems by intercepting the radiation emitted from the cryptographic equipment. For years NSA had worried about the amount of intelligence that might be gained by monitoring the radiation emitted by sensitive communications and encryption equipment—even by power cords. Through careful analysis, these radiated signals might reveal the contents of a secret message as it was being typed on a cipher machine—that is, before it was encrypted. Likewise, an incoming message might be detected as it was being printed out, and thus at a time when its protective ciphers have been stripped away. To help eliminate or at least decrease this radiation, the agency has long had a program known as "Tempest testing."

An NSA team was flown to Guam and put aboard the USS *Charles Berry*, a destroyer, which was then positioned near the *Izmeritel*. Working inside a cramped Sigint van, the intercept operators began testing the electronic environment to determine just what the Soviet trawler was capable of hearing. Then the destroyer moved to other locations, eventually working its way around the island, staying three miles offshore. During the course of the test, the NSA team obtained over 77,000 feet of magnetic tape recordings. Happily, while in the vicinity of the Sigint trawler, the team could detect no "compromising cipher-signal anomalies," nor any Tempest problems. Nevertheless, at every point around the island they were able to clearly hear Air Force ground maintenance crews. "The communications were in plain language," said the

NSA report, "and the NSA analysts could thus predict B-52 mission launchings at least two hours prior to take-off."

After their seagoing survey, the NSA team tested the land-based circuits and found that signals from teletypewriters that were rapping out decrypted, highly secret messages were leaking onto unencrypted voice channels. Thus by intercepting and then closely analyzing the voice communications, the Soviets might be able to read the classified messages.

As a result of the investigation, NSA conducted several other large-scale analyses of communications leaks. One, codenamed Purple Dragon, determined that the North Vietnamese were learning the locations of planned strikes by several means, among them the monitoring of unencrypted radio traffic from the fleet of KC-135 tankers.

To many at NSA, the results were shocking. "U.S. air strikes were of dubious success against an enemy who mysteriously faded from target areas," said a former NSA deputy director for communications security, Walter G. Deeley. "Ground sweeps seldom encountered more than the aged and the very young; and Marine amphibious forces stormed virtually deserted shores. It was apparent that the success of the enemy in evading our forces was probably predicated on advance knowledge of our intentions."

More shocking, said Deeley, was the fact that even after being informed by NSA of the devastating security lapses, the military refused to take any corrective action. U.S. military commanders in Vietnam frequently looked down on Comsec and paid no attention to the warnings. And communications personnel referred to them as "buddy fuckers" because they eavesdropped on American forces. In such cases there was little NSA could do. "Comsec monitors and analysts had an advisory role only and no power themselves to effect changes," said an NSA report. "For a variety of reasons commanders frequently ignored, or read sympathetically without action, the findings of the Comsec units." The consequences were often deadly.

One U.S. Army commander at 1st Infantry Division headquarters was talking over his desk phone when someone came into his office and mentioned that a specific operation was to take place in a location "35 kilometers north of here tomorrow." A Comsec monitor, eavesdropping on the call, heard the mention of the location of the operation and notified the officer. But the officer never bothered to change the plans. "On landing, the assault force met unexpectedly heavy resistance," said an NSA report. "U.S. losses were approximately 58 men killed and 82 wounded." The ASA commander on the scene "regarded the outcome as the results of an enemy reaction to a security breach." The number of deaths caused by poor U.S. communications security and successful North Vietnamese Sigint became alarming. NSA spoke of "a veritable flood of intelligence for enemy Sigint exploitation and tactical application, a flood that spelled defeat or losses during many U.S. combat operations."

Incredibly, the United States was losing the code war the same way Germany and Japan lost it in World War II. With the aid of the Russians, the North Vietnamese may have been getting access to intelligence from NSA's most secure encryption systems, gaining information like that obtained by breaking the German Enigma and Japanese Purple codes during World War II. Even without that, they were obtaining enormous amounts of Sigint, which frequently allowed them to escape destruction and, instead, target American forces.

From the very beginning, American commanders had an arrogant belief in U.S. military superiority. They believed that the North Vietnamese military and jungle-based Vietcong—the "gooks"—were far too unsophisticated to be able to make sense of U.S. communications networks. After all, many commanders reasoned, how could an army of soldiers who marched on sandals made of used tire treads be taken seriously? "Most U.S. commanders in Vietnam," said an NSA study, "doubted that the enemy could conduct successful Sigint operations. These commanders reasoned that U.S. superiority in training, firepower, and mobility made Comsec of little importance." The commanders, like their defeated German and Japanese counterparts during World War II, would be wrong.

Compounding the problem, the American military commanders would also ignore a second lesson of World War II: they paid little heed to warnings derived through their own signals intelligence.

On March 8, 1965, two Marine battalions stormed ashore at Da Nang, the first official combat troops to be sent into the war. By the end of the year, the number of American forces in Vietnam would swell to nearly 200,000. After a period of relative calm, the Vietcong erupted throughout the country on May 11. More than 1,000 poured over the Cambodian border, a growing weak spot, and brought down Songbe, a provincial capital about fifty miles north of Saigon.

To help plug the Cambodian hole, the decision was made to send NSA's flagship, the USS *Oxford*, into the war zone. The *Oxford* would be the first seagoing Sigint factory assigned to Vietnam. The orders were transmitted to the ship on May 26 to set sail immediately for Southeast Asia. At the time, the *Oxford* was just completing a nearly four-month cruise off West Africa, where it had stopped at Lagos and Durban, among other ports. Now not only were the crew going to war rather than home, they were also told that from now on the ship's homeport would be San Diego instead of Norfolk, a blow to those with families on the East Coast.

"In Africa we were looking at some of the local links," recalled George A. Cassidy, an Elint intercept operator on the ship. "Anything that could be Communist related. If we ever got anything Communist or Russian it was like a feather in our cap. That was our main goal, to get something that had to do with Russia."

Then came the message from NSA. "We left Durban and were going around the other side of South Africa for some reason," said Cassidy. "It was about three o'clock in the afternoon. The captain came on and made an announcement. Guys were really worried. I mean, you had guys who had marriages almost on the rocks, and here they are, they're across on the other side of the world. Guys had houses, families, cars, kids, wives, lovers, whatever, everything on the East Coast, and we all said, Now we're going to Vietnam. . . . I can tell you it was probably almost the same lowering of morale, in a different way, which we felt when Kennedy was shot."

On the long voyage to Southeast Asia, Cassidy found a way to boost morale: he created a photomontage of pictures taken by crewmembers in the various houses of prostitution they had visited while on their many NSA Sigint voyages. "Crewmembers would take photos in the whorehouses and bring them back where another crewmember would develop the film," he said. "I would swear them to secrecy that they wouldn't show it to anyone on the ship, especially the officers, and I would keep an extra print of the good stuff. I kept it locked away, a place nobody could find. It was in a big metal can up in an air vent in the photo lab.

"So after this happened [the orders to Vietnam], I was talking to some of the guys, and they said why don't you make up a big poster board of all these pictures and try to raise the morale a little. I said, 'I can't do this, I'll get killed.' So I went to the captain and I told him what my idea was and he said, 'Well, if they're not really bad, explicit photographs it probably won't be a bad idea.' So I went to each guy and asked if they would mind and nobody really minded. And we put it up in the mess deck one afternoon. And I'll tell you, it kind of brought the morale up a little bit. It was from photographs of guys with women in Durban, the Canary Islands; I had some from the Caribbean, even. And there were some from the Zurich Hotel in Valparaiso, Chile."

In Asia, as elsewhere, all information concerning the *Oxford* was considered very secret. Unfortunately, that made life difficult for those who were sent from the United States to join it. One of those was John De Chene, who was trying to get to the *Oxford* from California. "They tried to keep the *Oxford* movements very highly classified," he said. "First we went to Subic Bay, Philippines, because that's where they had the *Oxford* listed. We arrived at Clark Air Force Base and took a bus for four hours over back roads to Subic. Once there, they told us it was actually at Yokosuka, Japan. So we took the bus back to Clark and flew to Yokosuka, only to be told they'd never heard of the ship. Later, however, someone said the ship was now off Saigon. So we flew to Saigon and they said no, not here, she's now at Subic. We went back to Subic and it wasn't there. Finally they sent out a fleet search. Well, it had been sitting for two months in dry dock in Sasebo, Japan. So they flew us in to a Marine base in Japan and then we had to take a Japanese train all the way down to the lower islands and got to Sasebo the next morning and there she was. We were probably in transit about a week."

Once out of dry dock, the *Oxford* sailed to its assigned station in the Gulf of Thailand, a remote area near An Thoi on the southern tip of Phu Quoc Island. "We generally spent two months on station at our position on the border of Cambodia/Vietnam, copying and recording all communications, both foreign and friendly," said De Chene. "A lot of the time we were only about two miles off the coast." It was a very good position to eavesdrop on and DF [direction-find] the hundreds of units in the area."

The ship would occasionally pull in to An Thoi so that Ray Bronco, the ship's postal clerk, could pick up and drop off mail. One day he accidentally discovered that An Thoi was also home to a prison camp for captured Vietcong. "I was on the back of a flat pickup truck with all these bags of mail going to the U.S.," he said. "A C-130 troop transport flew in and landed on an airstrip. I was probably about fifty yards or less away. It turned and the tail end almost lined up to the back of the truck. The back door opened up and out ran about thirty to fifty screaming Vietcong. They came charging toward me. The Marines fired over their head. They didn't realize that there was an innocent bystander there. I still have flashbacks and post-traumatic stress over it."

Later, the *Oxford*'s sister ship, the USS *Jamestown*, was also ordered to the area. The *Jimmy-T*, as it was known, was assigned to the South China Sea around Saigon and the Delta region. "There was always a rivalry between our sister ship . . . and us," said Richard E. Kerr, Jr. "In the aft ops area, we had a huge wooden hand carved into the classic 'the bird' position. I do not know the story behind it, but I think it had some funny inscription like, 'From one sister to another.' "

Down below, in the *Oxford*'s forward NSA spaces, intercept operators listened with highly sensitive KG-14 multichannel receivers. To translate the information, the Sigint unit had linguists qualified in Lao/Thai, several Chinese dialects, Russian, and Vietnamese. Among the intercept operators on board was at least one qualified in Tagalog, the language of the Philippines. "We did as much processing as we could," recalled De Chene. "Fort Meade wanted both recordings and transcripts and our breakdowns of it. Pretty much full scope of as much as we could cover . . . For about two weeks we had one NSA guy on board. He kept to himself. I don't think anybody knew why he was there." In the aft area, Elint operators collected the signals of hundreds of radar systems on huge reels of Mylar tape attached to 32-track Ampex recorders.

Among the most important assignments during the *Oxford*'s years in Southeast Asia was the Seven Nations Manila Summit Conference, which took place in the Philippine capital on October 23–27, 1966. Anchored in Manila harbor, right across from the Stanley Point Naval Air

Station, the ship was able to eavesdrop on the negotiations. Thus, American negotiators got a leg up by discovering the strategies and arguing points of the other players. At one point, intercept operators on the ship "uncovered a plot," said De Chene, "to assassinate [U.S. President Lyndon B.] Johnson, [Philippine President Ferdinand E.] Marcos, and I think Nguyen Cao Ky." The plotters were members of the Communist-inspired Huk movement. As a result of the intercept operators' warning, every member of the ship received a letter of commendation.

The Sigint personnel and the rest of the ship's crew, referred to as general service personnel, were in effect segregated. "The general service personnel had no idea what we did, or how we did it," said De Chene. "All they knew was at the commencement of the workday, we would file behind those security doors, both fore and aft of the ship, and we would reappear at noon for chow. For the most part, they stayed away from us and in greater or lesser degrees, we, them. It was as if there were two different *Oxfords*, and I guess there really were." Ray Bronco agreed: "They [the Sigint personnel] were in a world of their own."

In July 1966, NSA decided to have the *Jamestown* temporarily relieve the *Oxford* and send *Oxford* to conduct signals intelligence operations along the coast of mainland China. At the time the secretive and violent Cultural Revolution was going on. "After about two weeks of cruising up and down China's coastline," said De Chene, "our results were fairly meager at best. From all appearances, the Chinese knew when and where we were going to be and for the most part, their communications transmissions were held to a bare minimum, or none at all."

But while the eavesdropping proved quite boring, the South China Sea gave them more excitement than they desired. Typhoon Ora was moving rapidly toward the *Oxford*. "We were taking severe rolls," De Chene recalled, "and the storm was growing stronger. The following day all hell broke loose. We lost a boiler and we were now dead in the water, almost at the center of the typhoon. We were drifting, and the wind was pushing us right into the coastal waters of Red China."

An emergency message went out for help and a fleet tug was dispatched for rescue. But more than a day went by without any sign of help. "All hands were now briefed on our full situation," said De Chene, "and advised that an abandon ship order might be given, and the CTs [communications technicians] were put on standby to destroy all equipment and documents. The captain also considered putting our utility boat and his gig in the water to possibly either start towing the ship or at least slow her drift. At this point we were approximately twenty miles from the beach, or eight miles from Chinese coastal waters. Finally, after drifting inland for two more miles, the tug made its appearance and shot us her lines. She then towed us back to Taiwan and out of harm's way of both capture and the storm."

The war in Vietnam was layered, like a wedding cake, and it was fought from the ground up. After the ambush death of James Davis as he prowled through the jungle near Saigon attempting to pinpoint enemy signals, NSA began experimenting with direction finding from the air. "Since radio wave propagation in Southeast Asia required that DF equipment be very close to the transmitter," said an NSA report, "the obvious answer was to go airborne."

While some airborne Sigint and DF missions required enormous planning, others were seat-of-the-pants, such as the chopper missions. Flying near treetop level just south of the DMZ were intercept operators in UH-1H "Huey" helicopters. With antennas duct-taped to the chopper's skids, the operators searched for North Vietnamese Army communications signals. Inside, a Vietnamese linguist listened for infiltrators through earphones attached to a captured North Vietnamese Army backpack radio. "They used to make them out of their beat-up green .50-caliber ammo cans," said one intercept operator. "It had a few dials on it with Chinese characters."

The pilots on board had KY-38 secure voice systems to quickly and secretly pass the time-sensitive information back to base. "Most of the time we were flying we picked up their communications," said the intercept operator, "so you would get a lot of information. But it would be very time-critical. The units were always on the move, so if you didn't get the information back really quick it would be of little use. Tactical intelligence is very of-the-moment, versus strategic, which is long-range, overall planning." Once NVA units were located, airborne or ground troops would be sent in after them.

Unlike the other services, the Army had paid little attention to airborne Sigint since the end of World War II. Throughout the 1950s,

Army intercept operators flew missions in Navy aircraft. The codename of one of their operations in the early 1960s, also aboard a Navy Sky Warrior, seemed to sum up the problem: Farm Team. It was at that point that the Army decided to invest both manpower and funds in developing its own professional team of aerial eavesdroppers. By March 1962 the Army Security Agency had its first airborne DF platform, the RU-6A De Haviland Beaver, a single-engine aircraft that flew low and slow and had room for very few operators. Within days, intercept operators in the unit were calling it TWA: Teeny Weeny Airlines.

Far from the sleek, high-flying U-2 or the lightning-fast SR-71, the early Sigint planes in Vietnam were almost comical. "The operators hung a long wire out the back of the aircraft for a crude direction-finding antenna," said one veteran. "Crews flew in hot, humid conditions in very loud aircraft. Missions were often four hours long, but could be longer depending on the operational tempo of the forces in contact." The planes may have looked funny, but they provided vital information. "It has been said," the veteran reported, "that air missions produced as much as one-third of the intelligence known to ground forces."

Later, a more advanced aircraft joined the fleet of Beavers. This was the RU-8D Seminole, a stubby black twin-engine with room for five passengers. Tall thin blade antennas protruded vertically from the tips of the wings, giving the diminutive spy plane a somewhat menacing look.

Richard McCarthy was one of those who volunteered for the 3rd Radio Research Unit's 224th Aviation Battalion. Flying out of Tan Son Nhut Air Base, McCarthy would often be assigned to the Saigon River Delta area, an inhospitable, mosquito-ridden wedge of swamp that stretched from Saigon to the sea. Because it was also the main shipping channel to Saigon, it became a haven for pirates and small groups of Vietcong guerrilla fighters. "Whoever controlled the shipping channel controlled Saigon," said McCarthy.

Because the Delta area was so compact, the single-engine Beaver was preferred. Wedged behind the copilot, the plane's skin to his back and two Collins 51S1 receivers in front of him, McCarthy would be listening for enemy communications through one of his helmet's earphones, and to the Beaver's pilot and copilot through the other. Navigation consisted of looking out the window for landmarks, and wads of masking tape were applied to the doors to prevent the plotting sheets from being sucked out.

Two hours into one mission over the Delta, McCarthy's earphones began buzzing—the familiar sound of a guerrilla tuning his transmitter for a call. "He was good and he was loud," said McCarthy. "It was show time." In an attempt to locate the guerrilla's transmitter, the pilot would twist and turn the plane back and forth to obtain different bearings on the target. Once the enemy forces were plotted, the crew would call in an air strike.

As NSA began sending more and more airborne eavesdroppers to Vietnam, the sky became an aviary of strange-looking metal birds hunting for signals to bring back to their nests. Two miles above the choppers and puddle jumpers was the EC-121M "Big Look," a Lockheed Super Constellation with monstrous radomes on its top and bottom. To some, the plane resembled a humpbacked and pregnant dinosaur. Because it was heavy and the cabin wasn't pressurized, it was limited to about 10,000 or 12,000 feet. Lined up along the windowless bulkheads, the intercept operators attempted to squeeze every electron of intelligence out of the ether during each twelve-hour mission, providing warnings to U.S. attack aircraft.

Warnings were critical. In the late spring of 1972, General John Vogt dispatched an eyes-only message to the Air Force Chief of Staff, General John Ryan, frankly stating that the 7th Air Force was losing the air war. The problem, Vogt said, was the increased proficiency of North Vietnamese pilots and their ability to make single, high-speed passes while firing Atoll missiles. Facing them were inexperienced U.S. pilots rotating into the combat zone every year.

NSA came up with Teaball, a system in which detailed warnings based on Sigint were quickly sent to the pilots. Many at the agency opposed the idea of broadcasting in the clear such secret information, but the concept was eventually approved.

Teaball was set up in a van at NSA's large listening post at Nakhon Phanom in northern Thailand. There, intercept operators would broadcast to the fighters, via a relay aircraft, the latest Sigint on surface-to-air missile sites and MiG fighters in their area. When Sigint revealed that a specific U.S. aircraft was being targeted for destruction, the pilot, nicknamed "Queen for the Day," would be instantly notified. "Naturally, that particular flight element began to sweat profusely," said Doyle Larson, a retired Air Force major general involved in Teaball, "but all other strike force elements relaxed a bit and let Teaball take care of them." A veteran pilot and Sigint officer with over seventy combat missions in Vietnam, Larson said that "Teaball was an instant success." The kill ratio for American fighters attacking North Vietnamese MiGs "increased by a factor of three."

Above the choppers, the Beavers, the Seminoles, and Big Look were the RC-135 flying listening posts—Boeing 707s filled with intercept operators and super-sophisticated eavesdropping equipment. From Kadena, Okinawa, the planes would fly daily twelve-hour missions, codenamed Burning Candy and Combat Apple, to the Gulf of Tonkin.

Eventually, as the war heated up, more and more missions were flown, until an RC-135 was constantly on station in the northern Tonkin Gulf twenty-four hours a day. It was an incredibly demanding schedule. Each mission lasted just over nineteen hours, including twelve over the Gulf. Two missions were flown every day, with a third aircraft on standby, ready for immediate launch if the primary aircraft had a problem. All the while, the five RC-135s in the Far East were also needed to cover the numerous Sino-Soviet targets. The missions took their toll not only on the crews but on the aircraft, the corrosive salt spray and high humidity ulcerating the planes' aluminum skin.

The North Vietnamese air force knew full well the purpose of the aircraft and would occasionally try to shoot it down. "MiG-21s would streak out over the Gulf at supersonic speeds and make a pass at the RC-135," said veteran Sigint officer Bruce Bailey. "Both fuel and fear limited them to only one pass. They would fire everything they had and run for the safety of their AAA [anti-aircraft artillery] and SAM [surface-to-air missile] umbrella back home." Although the RC-135 was a prize target, none was ever lost to a MiG.

Wherever they flew, the RC-135s were electronic suction pumps, especially the RC-135C, nicknamed the "Chipmunk" because of its large cheeklike antennas. The reconnaissance systems on board were programmed to automatically filter the ether like kitchen strainers, "covering the electronic spectrum from DC [direct current] to light," said Bailey. "It had such a broad coverage and processed so many signals at such an incredible rate it became known as the 'vacuum cleaner.' It intercepted all electronic data wherever it flew, recording the information in both digital and analog format."

At the same time, the Chipmunk's numerous onboard direction finders were able to automatically establish the location of each emitter for hundreds of miles. Sophisticated computers located signals that in any way varied from the norm, and highlighted them. Other key voice and data frequencies were preprogrammed into the computer and instantly recorded when detected. "The volume of data collected by that system was sufficient to require an entire unit and elaborate equipment to process it," said Bailey. "That large and impressive operation became known as 'Finder.' The amount of intelligence coming out of Finder was staggering.

"With its vacuum cleaner capability and very little specific tasking in the war zone," said Bailey, "the Chipmunk spent only a couple of hours in the combat area on those missions. It went in, sucked up all the signals, let the two high-tech operators look around a little, then resumed its global tasks."

Still another RC-135 variation, sent to Vietnam late in the war, was the RC-135U "Combat Sent," which had distinctive rabbit-ear aerials. It has been described as "the most elaborate and capable special mission aircraft ever . . . with technical capabilities that seemed like science fiction."

Still higher in the thinning layers of atmosphere above Vietnam were the unmanned drones that could reach altitudes in excess of 12½ miles. "They were designed to intercept communications of all sorts: radars, data links, and so forth," said Bruce Bailey. "The intercepted data was then transmitted to other aircraft, ground sites, or satellites." Based at Bien Hoa Air Base near Saigon, the diminutive drones contained so many systems as to give rise to a joke: the Ravens claimed that they also contained "a tiny replica of a field-grade officer to take the blame for anything that went awry."

The program proved very successful. On February 13, 1966, one of the Ryan drones "made the supreme sacrifice," said Bailey, but in the seconds before it became a fireball it intercepted and transmitted to an RB-47 critical information on the SA-2 missile, including the fusing and radar guidance data. The assistant secretary of the Air Force called it "the most significant contribution to electronic reconnaissance in the past twenty years."

Above even the drones flew the U-2, the Dragon Lady of espionage. Following the shootdown of Francis Gary Powers over the Soviet Union in 1960 and Eisenhower's declaration that the U.S. would never again overfly Russia, the U-2 had been reduced to air sampling missions for nuclear-test detection and to peripheral missions; its glory days were seemingly behind it. Eventually, intelligence officials began to nickname the plane the "Useless Deuce." The Cuban missile crisis was only a brief shot in the arm, but after the Gulf of Tonkin incident in 1964, the U-2 was drafted into service for the Vietnam War. Although the aircraft started out performing the job it was most famous for—high-altitude photography—that soon changed. Because of the growing numbers of SA-2 missile sites—the U-2's weak spot—in North Vietnam, the planes were soon assigned exclusively to Sigint.

Based initially in Bien Hoa Air Base near Saigon, and later moved to Thailand, the U-2s in Indochina were now the responsibility of the Strategic Air Command, not the CIA. Although happy with the new responsibility, the Air Force pilots found eavesdropping far more tedious than snapping pictures over hostile territory. "All I had to do was throw a switch and recorders on board would collect the bad guy's radar frequencies and signals, and monitor everything," said former U-2 pilot Buddy Brown. The Armed Forces Courier Service would then ship the tapes to NSA.

The missions called for the planes to circle for a dozen or more hours in areas over the Gulf or Laos, listening primarily to Chinese communications targets. As more and more antenna blades were stuck to its skin, the once-graceful U-2 was beginning to resemble a porcupine. On board, the receivers were becoming increasingly automated. All the pilot had to do was to stay awake. The antennas would pick up the preprogrammed signals, and the onboard receivers would automatically transmit them down to Sigint analysts in South Vietnam, who could then retransmit them via satellite in near real time right to NSA. There, computers and cryptanalysts could immediately begin attacking them.

"The pilot did not operate the receivers, as they were either automatic or remotely controlled," recalled Bruce Bailey. "He sat there boring holes in the sky for hours with very little to do or see. The only relief came from tuning in on the war, listening to radio calls from strike aircraft and rescue attempts. That helped keep him awake."

As the systems became ever more automated, Sigint analysts on the ground were able to remotely switch from target to target via the U-2's electronics. "Those systems enabled the specialists to select signals of the most interest," said Bailey, "search for suspected emitters, operate the equipment as if they were aboard the U-2 and to relay their intelligence to users around the world via satellite and other communications." Eventually, the main thing keeping the pilots awake, according to Bailey, was simple discomfort. "Twelve hours is agonizingly long to wear a pressure suit, sit in one position, endure extremes in heat and cold, control your bowels, and feel your body dehydrating from the extremely dry air and the oxygen they had to breathe constantly." Nevertheless, he said, the aircraft's ability to linger in one area for extended periods, capturing thousands of conversations, made it "the king of Comint."

"Throttles to Max A/B," said Air Force Major Jerry O'Malley just before his SR-71 nosed into the sky over Kadena Air Base. From Okinawa, just after noon on Thursday, March 21, 1968, the Blackbird set out on its very first operational mission: to penetrate North Vietnamese airspace, record enemy radar signals, photograph missile sites, and be back in time for dinner.

As the Blackbird sped at more than three times the speed of sound toward the hot war in Vietnam, it left behind a bureaucratic war in Washington. For nearly a decade the CIA and the Air Force had been secretly at war with each other over whose aircraft would become America's premier spy plane—the CIA's A-12 or the Air Force SR-71. They were virtually the same aircraft except that the A-12 was a single-seater, covert (that is, its very existence was secret), and a bit smaller and older; and the SR-71 was overt and had room for a pilot and a reconnaissance systems officer. President Johnson decided to go with the Air Force version and, eventually, the CIA was forced out of the spy-plane business entirely.

One step above the U-2 and one step below the Sigint satellites, the bullet-fast SR-71 Blackbird could penetrate hostile territory with impunity. It flew sixteen miles above the earth, several miles higher than the U-2, at more than 2,000 miles per hour; no missile had a chance against it.

As Major O'Malley approached the Gulf of Tonkin at a speed of Mach 3.17 and an altitude of 78,000 feet, the top of his Blackbird was brushing against outer space. Outside, the air temperature was about minus 65 degrees Fahrenheit, yet the leading edges of the plane were beginning to glow cherry red at 600 degrees and the exhaust-gas temperatures exceeded 3,400 degrees. Above 80,000 feet, the curvature of the earth had a deep purple hue. In the strange daylight darkness above, stars were permanently visible.

The Comint and Elint sensor-recorders were already running when O'Malley prepared to coast in for a "front-door" entry into North Vietnam at two miles a second. As the Blackbird followed a heading of 284 degrees, the onboard defensive systems indicated that the North Vietnamese clearly had them in their Fan Song radar, one of the types used by SA-2 missile batteries. Behind O'Malley, Captain Ed Payne, the reconnaissance systems officer, flipped a few switches and the Blackbird's electronic countermeasures prevented the radars from locking on as they passed over Haiphong harbor near Hanoi.

"The SR-71 was excellent for 'stimulating' the enemy's electronic environment," said retired U.S. Air Force Colonel Richard H. Graham, a former SR-71 pilot. "Every time [they] flew in a sensitive area, all kinds of radars and other electronic wizardry were turned on to see if they could find out what was flying so quickly through their airspace. In fact, our missions were generally not Elint productive unless 'they' were looking for us with electronic signals." To capture the signals, the SR-71 used a piece of equipment known as the electro-magnetic reconnaissance (EMR) system. At first, said Graham, "the EMR would literally sit there and record signals from hundreds of miles around the aircraft. It had no discretion on what signals it received, and made it very difficult to find specific frequencies out of the thousands recorded on one mission."

But after an upgrade, known as the EMR Improvement Program (EIP), the SR-71's Sigint capability improved considerably. "The EIP continuously recorded signals from horizon to horizon along our flight path," said Graham, "a distance of around 1,200 nautical miles. If the system recorded a specific frequency for a short period of time, computers could plot the precise position of the transmitter on the ground within approximately one half mile, at a distance of three hundred miles from the SR-71. . . . The EIP was very efficient at its job, at times often recording over five hundred emitters on a single operational sortie. . . . It was a Star Wars version of eavesdropping."

As the Blackbird entered North Vietnam's "front door," each of its two Pratt & Whitney J-58 engines was generating as much power as all four of the enormous engines on the *Queen Mary*. Just twelve minutes after entering, the Blackbird had crossed the country and was about to exit through the "back door." Passing over the Red River, O'Malley flicked the Inlet Guide Vane switches to the "Lockout" position and eased the throttles out of afterburner. After a second in-flight refueling from a "boomer"—a tanker—over Thailand, the Blackbird headed back to Vietnam. This time it passed over the DMZ in search of the heavy guns that had been assaulting Khe Sanh. In its few minutes over North Vietnam, analysts later discovered, it located virtually every missile site.

For all the sophisticated ships, planes, and foreign listening posts, there were many who fought the Sigint war in the muddy swamps and steamy jungles, right alongside the combat troops.

"As a member of the Army Security Agency you will never end up in a war zone," the reddish-haired Army recruiter in the neatly creased uniform confidently assured Dave Parks. "The ASA, because of the high level of security clearance, is not allowed to serve in a combat zone." That made sense, thought Parks as he walked out of the Atlanta recruiting station in 1965, having just signed up for four years.

Two years later Parks, now an Army intercept operator, arrived in Saigon for a one-year tour in Vietnam. The recruiter had kept his promise, but Parks had volunteered. "I wanted to see a war," he said, "and Vietnam was the only one we had." Assigned to the 303rd Radio Research Unit at Long Binh, near Saigon, Parks quickly became aware of the dangers involved in the assignment. "In the event that you are severely wounded would you like your next of kin notified?" a clerk casually asked him without ever looking up from the form. "Okay, in the event you are severely wounded do you want the Last Rites administered? We will need to make arrangements in case of your dying over here." Finally Parks asked what kind of a unit he was in. "Infantry," he was told. "A unit called the 199th Infantry." Parks gulped.

"I had spent my six months of Advanced Individual Training at Fort Devens being threatened by the ASA instructors that if we students washed out of the course we would get a one-way ticket to the 196th Light Infantry," Parks recalled. "Now here I was eighteen months later being assigned to its sister unit. This might be more adventure than I'd bargained for. Volunteer for Vietnam, I should have known better."

Parks's Sigint unit, the 856th Radio Research Detachment of the 199th Light Infantry Brigade, was made up of about fifty troops, headquartered at Long Binh. "Light infantry" meant light and mobile. The troops were equipped with only the most basic armament, such as rifles, machine guns, and grenade launchers. The largest caliber of weapon carried in the field was a 90mm hand-held recoilless rifle.

The men were housed in a two-story wood-frame barracks surrounded by several layers of protective sandbags and topped with a corrugated-tin roof. The Sigint operations compound was encircled by a tall barbed-wire fence with coils of razor wire on top and to either side. Cover music blared from speakers to hide escaping signals; loud, rasping generators ran twenty-four hours a day; and there was a sandbagged guard shack at the only entrance. Intercept operations were conducted from two windowless vans that were parked backed up to the building.

Parks, however, would spend little time in the operations compound. The mission of the 199th in November 1967 was to patrol, with South Vietnamese rangers, the vast rice bowl known as the Mekong River Delta. Spreading south of Saigon like a soggy sponge, the area was a maze of swamps, rice paddies, and waterways. Soldiers called walking in it "wading in oatmeal." In places it was covered by triple-canopy jungle, sometimes so dense that light had difficulty getting through. The map gave areas such descriptive names as Parrot's Beak, the Iron Triangle, and the Rung Sat Special Zone. The 199th's orders were to seek out and destroy Communist guerrilla infiltrators, mostly from Cambodia, and to act as a sort of quick reaction force in the event of a firefight.

Operations were based at Cat Lai, a small village on the banks of the Song Nha Be River, a winding snake fed by a lacework of muddy canals and narrow streams. Like a liquid highway, the river carried countless cargo ships to the docks of Saigon, where they unloaded heavy tractors and foodstuffs and filled up with dusty bags of rice. As they lined up, bow to stern, waiting for their turn at the docks, the lightly protected ships were prime targets for the Vietcong, who would attempt to sink them. It was up to Parks and his fellow troopers to prevent that.

Unlike most Sigint soldiers, who worked regular shifts at heavily protected listening posts, most far from the action, Parks fought side by side with the combat troops. A bandolier of ammo was strapped over one shoulder, and an M16 hung from the other. Canteens, poncho, bayonet, camouflage blanket, sleeping bag, and first-aid kit clung to his back or hung from his web belt. His job, as a DF operator, was to find the Vietcong before they found his fellow troopers.

Cat Lai was little more than a few rows of grass huts and some red bougainvillea on the bank of a muddy river. The troops lived in tents erected over wooden platforms that served as floors. Two olive-drab vans were used as listening posts, with two intercept operators in each one. Wooden walkways led to a club, constructed out of plywood, that served Vietnamese "33" beer and mixed drinks. A short way down the road, alongside the river at the edge of the village, was an open-sided restaurant/bar/whorehouse patronized by the crews from ships lining the waterway. Like the small, rusty tubs anchored nearby, the crews came from every part of the world and the background conversations had a musical quality. Years later, when Parks saw the bar scene in the film *Star Wars*, he was reminded of the club.

The prostitutes who served the crew also came from many parts of the world. One, a stunning woman with sparkling eyes and coal-black skin, came from Cameroon in West Africa. Her ex-lover had recently tossed her off one of the transports. With halting French and a little German, Parks agreed to a price.

The work of the direction-finding teams had changed little in the seven years since DF specialist James Davis became the first American soldier killed in the war. It had only grown more dangerous. "Being on a DF team was about as far forward as you could get in the ASA in Vietnam," said Dave Parks. The Vietcong had shifted their priority targets from the South Vietnamese to the Americans. In a nearby province, the casualty rate for one American unit was running 40 percent. Out of about forty men, eighteen had been killed or wounded in the field and another had a grenade dropped on him in the shower.

After a brief break-in period, Parks was sent out to the front lines, to an area where Highway 5A slithered out of the Vietcong-infested Delta like a black lizard. "The whole reason for the infantry being there," said Parks, "was to act as a checkpoint for the motor traffic coming out of the Delta headed for Saigon." Parks's weapon would be his DF device, a PRD-1, simply called the Purd. He kept it hidden from prying eyes, inside an octagonal tent. "Learning the Purd was not too difficult," Parks said. "Learning the ins and outs of staying alive was. . . . One learned to watch where to place each step as you walked, for there were snakes in the Delta that could kill you in seconds. The snakes of Vietnam were named according to how far a victim walked before dying from a bite, beginning with the 'three-pace snake,' the green krait, which had to chew its poison into you." Before turning in at night, Parks would take his bayonet and see what might have crawled into his bunk while he was at work. "Lizards mostly," said Parks, "but sometimes snakes, including the king cobra. We were in the Delta."

There were many more rules to live by, according to Parks. "Don't pick up something without checking it for booby traps. Inside the bunker line, stay on the paths; outside of it, stay off of them. Don't venture outside the perimeter unless you were willing to die. Don't walk around at night inside the perimeter for danger of being shot by your own troops. There was plenty to learn and not much time to learn it."

On a typical mission, the PRD-1 would be transported by jeep to what was thought to be a good spot from which to locate Vietcong in the Delta. Once at the site, a tactical DF post would be established. A bunker made of double or triple sandbags would be set up, then encircled with rolls of barbed wire and concertina wire, perhaps fifteen feet across. A variety of antennas would be set up and warning signs would be posted. "Signs telling," said Parks, "that this was a classified site and not to enter on pain of death and according to some regulation or another." In the center, sitting on a tripod, would be the PRD-1, which was about eighteen inches square and crowned with a diamond-shaped antenna that could be rotated. At its base was an azimuth ring marked off in degrees.

Once he was set up, the DF operator would put on his earphones and begin listening for enemy signals. "Time to get on the knobs and kill a Commie for Mommy," said Parks. In order to cover the operational area, a "net" of three DF sites would have to be set up. This would allow the operators to triangulate the enemy signals and get a fix on their exact locations. " 'Find them, fix them, and fuck 'em over!' was our unofficial motto," said Parks. " 'Better Living Through Electronics' was another one."

Once a DF station picked up an enemy transmission, the operator would take a bearing on it. The information would then be encrypted and sent up the chain of command and an attack order would frequently be given. Heavy artillery fire would then plaster the site, and the infantry would sweep in.

Unfortunately, the Vietcong were wise to the game; they knew the United States was probably listening and they avoided transmitting as much as possible. Or they would place their transmitting antenna up to a mile from the actual transmitter, in order to avoid fire. "It was a great and intricate game of fox and hounds played silently between us," said Parks. "Each side aware of the other though we never met. It was a life-or-death game for them, too. To place it bluntly, the DF teams were there to aid the 199th in its task of killing those Vietnamese radio ops and all of their buddies, if at all possible. We hounded them unmercifully. . . . Their radio ops became worse as time went by due to the better-trained ones having been killed."

But DF missions were a double-edged sword, as Specialist Davis had discovered. Since the range of the PRD-1 was only about five miles—on a very good day—the Sigint soldiers had to be almost in the enemy's camp to locate them. "They were practically in our lap most of the time," said Parks. "Once, we DF'd a transmission that was coming from a grass hut not three hundred yards from me—easy rifle shot if I could have caught him coming out of the hut."

For Parks, the constant tension took its toll. "It was a rough way to live and work, and it took a lot out of men even as fit and young as we were," he recalled. "I'm not talking about the mission—I'm talking about being in that environment and doing everything it took to try and stay alive. I myself ended up in the hospital suffering from sheer exhaustion about three-quarters the way through my one-year tour. Truth is, I awoke in the 'hospital' after passing out cold one fine day. The 'hospital' was actually more like a ward on the upper floor of a barracks a block from the 856th. They needed to keep an eye on their own, you know—can't have me giving away any secrets in my delirium."

By January 1968 NSA had placed Vietnam under a massive electronic microscope. Sigint specialists even scanned every North Vietnamese newspaper for pictures of communications equipment. Hardly a signal could escape capture by one of the agency's antennas, whether in a mud-covered jeep slogging through the Mekong Delta or in the belly of a Blackbird flying sixteen miles over Hanoi at three times the speed of sound. Yet the signals were useless without adequate analysis, and analysis was useless if military commanders ignored it.

A few years earlier the Joint Chiefs of Staff had calmly approved committing acts of terrorism against Americans in order to trick them into supporting a war they wanted against Cuba. Now that they finally had a war, the senior military leadership once again resorted to deceit—this time to keep that war going. Somehow they had to convince the public that they were winning when they were really losing.

"If SD and SSD [both were Vietcong Self Defense forces—militia] are included in the overall enemy strength, the figure will total 420,000 to 431,000," General Creighton Abrams, the deputy U.S. commander in Vietnam, secretly cabled the chairman of the JCS in August 1967. "This is in sharp contrast to the current overall strength figure of about 299,000 given to the press here. . . . We have been projecting an image of success over the recent months. . . . Now, when we release the figure of 420,000–431,000, the newsmen will . . . [draw] an erroneous and gloomy conclusion as to the meaning of the increase. . . . In our view the strength figures for the SD and SSD should be omitted entirely from the enemy strength figures in the forthcoming NIE [CIA National Intelligence Estimate]."

As intercept operators trolled for enemy communications, the results flowed back to NSA, where analysts deciphered, translated, and traffic-analyzed the massive amounts of data. Reports then went to the CIA and other consumers, including General Westmoreland's headquarters, the Military Assistance Command, Vietnam (MACV). Westmoreland's staff included NSA's Sigint reports in the command's highly classified publications, including the Weekly Intelligence Estimate Updates and the Daily Intelligence Summaries, both read by Westmoreland. Nevertheless, MACV refused to include any NSA data in its order-of-battle summaries, claiming that the information was too highly classified.

There may have been another reason. NSA's Sigint was making it increasingly clear that enemy strength was far greater than the military commanders in Vietnam and the Pentagon were letting on, either publicly or in secret. CIA Director Richard Helms saw the difference between the estimates and told his top Vietnam adviser, George Carver, that "the Vietnam numbers game" would be played "with ever increasing heat and political overtones" during the year. To help resolve the problem, he asked analysts from the CIA, NSA, and the Defense Intelligence Agency to travel to Saigon and meet with General Westmoreland's staff to resolve the differences in numbers.

The meeting took place in Saigon in September at the U.S. embassy. Over a conference table strewn with intercepts and secret reports, the Washington analysts attempted to make their case, but it was useless. Rather than rely on NSA's Sigint for enemy strength figures, the military instead relied on questionable prisoner interrogations. "MACV used mainly Confidential-level documents and prisoner interrogation reports," said a recent CIA study, "and, in contrast with CIA's practice, did not generally use data derived from intercepted enemy radio signals, or Sigint."

George Carver, the lead CIA analyst at the meeting, expressed his anger in an "eyes-only" cable to Helms, characterizing the mission as "frustratingly unproductive since MACV stonewalling, obviously under orders." Despite the evidence, he said, Westmoreland's officers refused to accept any estimates of enemy forces larger than 298,000, and "the inescapable conclusion" must be drawn that Westmoreland "has given instructions tantamount to direct order that VC strength total will not exceed 300,000 ceiling." He added that he was planning to see Westmoreland the next day and would "endeavor to loosen this strait-jacket. Unless I can, we are wasting our time."

In the end, the military refused to budge. Westmoreland's top military intelligence officer, Major General Phillip Davidson, told Carver to buzz off. "I was frequently and sometimes tendentiously interrupted by Davidson," Carver cabled Helms, "[who] angrily accused me of impugning his integrity," and who stated that the figures MACV had tabled were its "final offer, not subject to discussion. We should take or leave it." Eventually, caving in to the pressure, Carver and the CIA took it, greatly angering many of the other analysts.

In November 1967, NSA began reporting that two North Vietnamese Army divisions and three regiments were heading toward South Vietnam. Follow-up reports continued over the next several months until the units arrived in South Vietnam, or in staging areas in the DMZ and Laos, in late 1967 and early 1968.

Other reports began coming in January 1968 that a major attack was in the works. William E. Rowe, with the ASA's 856th Radio Research Detachment near Saigon, picked up intelligence that two Vietcong regiments were planning to overrun the U.S. compound at Long Binh, Bien Hoa Air Base, and several other locations around the Saigon area. In addition to passing the information to NSA, the Sigint detachment "also told MACV headquarters personnel about reports of the planned attack on the Bien Hoa Air Base and several sites in Saigon such as the MACV headquarters building, the U.S. Embassy, the relay station, the radio station and the Phu Tho racetrack," said Rowe. "MACV headquarters personnel sloughed off the information. They ignored intelligence reports indicating the Vietcong were assembling in tunnels, caves, and foxholes."

On January 17, NSA issued the first in a series of intelligence bulletins reviewing recent Sigint from Vietnam. It was likely, said the report, that NVA units were preparing to attack cities in Kontum, Pleiku, and Darlac provinces. Other attacks were being planned against the coastal provinces of Quang Nam, Quang Tin, Quang Ngai, and Bin Dihn. Still other intercepts indicated that Hue would be attacked. NSA reported that Sigint had also picked up indications of increased enemy presence near Saigon.

Despite all these reports, the mood within Westmoreland's headquarters was upbeat, like the bridge on the *Titanic*. Although he was being warned that there were icebergs ahead, Westmoreland knew his massive ship was unsinkable. According to a recent CIA analysis, "A 'we are winning' consensus pretty much permeated the Saigon-Washington command circuit; intelligence reports and analyses that deviated from it tended to be discounted."

Off the coast of North Korea, the USS *Pueblo* was attacked on January 23, suddenly turning attention from the growing threat of a North Vietnamese invasion to the possibility of North Korean invasion. Many in the Johnson administration saw a connection. "It would seem to us that there is a relationship," said Westmoreland. Johnson and McNamara agreed. Nevertheless, there has never been any indication that the two events were in any way linked.

Incredibly, despite the fact that NSA's Sigint warnings on Vietnam were becoming more and more alarming, the USS *Oxford*, NSA's premiere spy ship, was given permission to leave its station. On January 23, as North Korea captured the *Pueblo* and North Vietnam was on the verge of a major offensive, the *Oxford* sailed to Bangkok for a week of R&R. It was an enormous gaffe.

The following day, NSA reaffirmed an earlier report that attacks against cities were imminent in northern and central South Vietnam. On January 25, NSA issued another alert, "Coordinated Vietnamese Communist Offensive Evidenced." The Sigint report gave clear evidence that a major attack was about to take place, citing an "almost unprecedented volume of urgent messages . . . passing among major [enemy] commands." The analysis went on to predict imminent coordinated attacks throughout all of South Vietnam, especially in the northern half of the country. Tet, the Vietnamese lunar New Year, was only five days off.

Richard McCarthy also noticed unusual activity in the days before Tet. He was on a direction-finding patrol near the Cambodian border in his small RU-6A Beaver. Nearby was a large rubber plantation, Loc Ninh. "Evening missions were usually very quiet," he said. "The Americans were all lagging [*sic*] into their night defensive positions, and the VC were preparing for their night activities. This night was no exception. There was a large component of the 1st Infantry Division lagging in on the golf course at Loc Ninh, and I could see the smoke from white phosphorus, as smaller units around the area were setting in their final protective fires.

"Suddenly I started picking up a familiar sound. I quickly identified the target as the reconnaissance element of the VC division that controlled the area. This was very unusual, because this guy usually didn't come on the scene until the last phases of planning an attack! When we finished the fix, we knew that we had something big. The target was located 300 yards outside of the American perimeter at Loc Ninh. We tried to contact the [ASA unit] at Loc Ninh, but they had shut down for the night. I elected to return to base and report that fix, instead of flying the full four hours that we were scheduled to fly." McCarthy later learned that his alert had thwarted one of the rehearsal attacks for the coming offensive.

On January 30, Westmoreland finally saw the iceberg dead ahead. He had just been handed several warnings, based on Sigint, from the commander of the U.S. forces in the region around Saigon. The commander, Major General Frederick C. Weyand, had become convinced, by intercepts, traffic analysis, and DF indications he had just received, that a major offensive was about to take place. Westmoreland immediately canceled a previous Tet cease-fire he had issued and ordered that "effective immediately all forces will resume intensive operations, and troops will be placed on maximum alert." "These precautionary moves," said a recent CIA analysis, "doubtless saved Saigon and the U.S. presence there from disaster."

That night Dave Parks noticed something very unusual. "At twelve midnight, the enemy went on total radio silence," he said. "It was just as if someone had switched off a light—'Nil More Heard' on any frequency. Now, that spooked the hell out of me. I had never experienced anything like it. Military units go on radio silence for only one reason: they're up to something. In this case they were on the move to their assigned targets." One of his colleagues, serving a second tour in Vietnam, told Parks, "If anything is going to happen it will happen at three A.M.—we may as well go and get some sleep." "He was dead on," said Parks, "we got the hell rocketed out of us at precisely three A.M. . . . What we didn't expect was the scale and intensity of the attacks."

About the same hour, the 856th Radio Research Detachment at Long Binh, which weeks earlier had attempted to warn Westmoreland of the coming attack, came under bombardment. "They had been hiding in tunnels and foxholes in the area for about two weeks, awaiting orders from Hanoi," said William E. Rowe. "For the next two and a half hours the Vietcong initiated probing attacks against our bunker line and other positions along our perimeter. . . . Most of my buddies were in the operations building setting satchel charges and incendiary grenades to all the filing cabinets, equipment (radios and receivers), maps and reports—everything that should not fall into the hands of the enemy."

It was a ferocious attack. "Each time they attacked," said Rowe, "some would get hung up in the wire. Each time they attacked, we went crazy, yelling expletives as we went out to meet them, firing and firing each time they approached. A mound of enemy dead was forming in front of the concertina, body upon body. The frontal attacks lasted for another two hours. After each advance, we would pace up and down the bunker line, nervously anticipating the next attack. After each attack, the mound of enemy dead got bigger and bigger."

As the fighting continued, Rowe's unit began running out of ammunition. "Those not swearing loudly were praying, preparing for close-in fighting. We knew if we did not get more ammunition, it would be a one-on-one struggle for each of us." The Sigint soldiers were ordered to hold their fire until the last instant, to preserve ammo. "When we could wait no longer," said Rowe, "we started to run toward the wire to meet them head on." A short while later, six helicopter gunships came to the rescue. Nevertheless, the ferocious battle went on for days. By the time it was over, enemy soldiers were stacked five deep around the listening post. "The plows pushed about four hundred dead Vietcong into a low drainage area to the right and in front of our bunker line."

Gary Bright, a stocky, sandy-haired Army warrant officer, woke to the ring of the phone beside his bed in Saigon's Prince Hotel. It was 2:30 A.M. "They've hit the embassy and palace. The airfield is under attack," said the excited voice. "I'm going to blow the switch." The call was from a sergeant at NSA's newly installed Automatic Secure Voice Switch at the MACV compound on Tan Son Nhut Air Base. The switch was the key link for highly secret phone calls between Saigon and Washington, and the sergeant was afraid that the facility and all its crypto equipment would soon be captured. Bright, in charge of the switch, told the soldier to get ready for a destruct order but not to pull the plug before he arrived.

Bright quickly threw on his tan uniform, grabbed his glasses, and ran down three flights of stairs to his jeep. "As we got in I armed my grease gun—a .45-caliber submachine gun—and watched the street," he said. Bright and his partner sped down Plantation Road, the main traffic artery, toward the MACV compound. As they rounded the traffic circle near the French racetrack they passed another jeep with its lights on. Seconds later Bright heard a loud explosion and turned around to see the second jeep demolished and in flames. Then he started taking fire from the top of the racetrack wall, bullets crashing into his vehicle. Bright swiveled around and opened fire with his submachine gun, knocking some of the Vietcong shooters off the wall.

Upon reaching the secure switch, Bright began to prepare for emergency destruction. Later a call came in from the U.S. embassy. "The VC were on the first floor," Bright said. The caller was shouting, worried that enemy forces would soon capture the sensitive communications and crypto equipment. To make matters worse, the embassy had no destruct devices and Bright was asked to bring some over. "I got on the phone and told them that it was impossible to get out, much less get downtown to them," Bright recalled. "I told them the best thing to do was to shoot the equipment and smash the boards as much as possible if emergency destruction became necessary."

At the time of the attack, the *Oxford*'s crew was living it up in Bangkok. The ship would not sail back until February 1, a day after the start of the biggest offensive of the war.

Battles were taking place simultaneously throughout South Vietnam, from Hue in the north to Saigon in the south. By the time the acrid cloud of gunsmoke began to dissipate, on February 13, 4,000 American troops had been killed along with 5,000 South Vietnamese and 58,000 North Vietnamese soldiers. Although the United States eventually turned back the Tet offensive, the American public now realized what price was being paid for a war without end.

The sole winner to come out of Tet was NSA. Of all the intelligence agencies, it was the only one to come up with the right warning at the right time. That the intelligence was not acted on much sooner was the fault of Westmoreland and the generals and politicians in Saigon and Washington who refused to pay attention to anything that might detract from their upbeat version of the war and their fantasy numbers. "The National Security Agency stood alone in providing the kind of warnings the U.S. Intelligence Community was designed to provide," concluded a 1998 CIA review of the war, which gave only mediocre reviews to the agency's own intelligence. "Communications intelligence often afforded a better reading of the enemy's strength and intentions (and was better heeded by command elements) than did agent reports, prisoner interrogations, captured documents, or the analytic conclusions derived from them. But in Washington the Sigint alerts apparently made little impression on senior intelligence officers and policymakers."

Finally, the CIA study concluded, "Senior intelligence and policymaking officers and military leaders erred on two principal scores: for having let concern for possible political embarrassment derail objective assessments of the enemy order of battle, and for ignoring NSA's alerts and Saigon Station's warnings that did not accord with their previous evaluations of probable enemy strategy."

Pleased with his agency's performance, Director Marshall S. Carter, on May 8, 1968, sent a telegram to former president Harry S. Truman on his eighty-fourth birthday. "The National Security Agency extends its heartiest congratulations and warm wishes," he wrote. "You will recall establishing the National Security Agency in 1952 and we will continue to strive to accomplish the objectives you laid down for us at that time."

Back in Washington, Lyndon Johnson was being compared in the press to General George Custer at the Battle of the Little Big Horn. About a month after the heavy fighting ended, he announced he would no longer be a candidate in the upcoming presidential election. In Vietnam, American troops suddenly began to realize they might be fighting a losing war.

Some soldiers who physically survived Tet nevertheless died inside. Following one fight, an injured American soldier and two wounded Vietcong were brought to an aid station at a firebase named Stephanie. After attempting, unsuccessfully, to save the U.S. soldier, an Army medic went off to have a beer while leaving the two Vietcong, a father and his young son, to bleed to death.

Nearby was Dave Parks, working his PRD-1 direction finder. "Nothing had been done to attend to their wounds," he said. "The younger one, despite having several chest wounds and his left leg shot nearly in two below the knee, was alert; we looked into one another's eyes as I paused briefly to look them over. There was fear in the eyes, and pain. The older fellow was pretty far gone. His eyes were glazed over and half closed. . . . Without help they were not going to live. Even my untrained eye could see that."

Parks returned to his direction finder, expecting that the medic would treat the men. But a short while later he looked back and saw they had never been attended to. "I got up and went over to them, expecting to find them dead," he said. "The older fellow was dead now, his eyes filmed over but still open in death. The young one was alive but not nearly as alert as before; his dark eyes briefly locked into mine when I approached. I felt the need to do something for him; it looked as if the medic had forgotten these two."

Returning to his DF site, Parks grabbed a canteen to give the young Vietcong some water, but first thought he would check with the medic to see if water was the right thing to give him. "I wondered why nothing was being done . . . ," said Parks. "I found the medic inside the bunker drinking a warm beer and asked him what would be done with the VC, adding that one looked as if he was already dead. 'Fuck those gooks,' he swore at me, voice rising. 'Leave them the fuck alone, they can just hurry up and die 'cause I'm not touchin' those filthy bastards!' " Confused by the medic's reaction, Parks returned to the injured boy. "The sergeant had done a good job of intimidating me into doing nothing," he said, "but I was still left with the feeling that I should try something.

"Looking down on the VC," Parks continued, "it dawned on me that the medic knew full well their situation. He was allowing them to die; it was his payment to the dead American. I spent a moment or two looking at the young VC. His eyes seemed duller now, and the flies were all over his wounds. I knelt beside him and brushed at the flies to no real effect. 'Screw him,' I thought, thinking of the medic. I pulled the stretcher into the shade. I ripped a square off of the old fellow's shirt and wet it from my canteen. I wiped the teenager's forehead, upper chest, and arms."

Parks attempted to get the help of a nearby Army captain. " 'Sir, one of the VC that came in with that kid is still alive. He looks like he's going to die if something isn't done. The sergeant says he won't touch him.' The captain looked at me, looked over toward the aid station, and back at me. He said, 'If I were *you*, Specialist, I'd keep *my* goddamned nose out of it. The sergeant is in charge over there, and you just might need his services someday. Let him run the aid station any damned way he sees fit!'

"Not the answer I had expected. The subtext of the man's statement was clear enough, though. The good captain just might need the sergeant's services someday, too, and he wasn't about to screw with that. Defeated, I returned to my war, and my area of responsibility in it. By sundown the young VC was dead.

"I have lived with that day's events for thirty-plus years now, I am positive I will live with them for the rest of my life. . . . The Vietcong teenager is my personal guilt. I should have moved heaven and earth to do more for him, but I failed him."

Following the Tet offensive, the war, like the young Vietcong, slowly began to die. The next year, NSA pulled its Sigint ships from Vietnam and then scrapped the whole fleet. "My opinion of 1969 on *Oxford* thirty years later," said Richard E. Kerr, Jr., "[is that] we proved to the NSG [Naval Security Group] Command and the CNO [Chief of Naval Operations] that operations like this at sea . . . were obsolete. You cannot combine large numbers of NSG personnel with uncleared officers and crew. All the ships . . . were too slow, too old, and had no business being in tense situations. . . . Events of the *Liberty* and *Pueblo* (1967 and 1968) had already placed this type of platform in jeopardy. Vietnam was over in 1968 and the [Sigint] fleet was dead in 1969."

By then, largely as a result of the war in Vietnam, NSA's cryptologic community had grown to a whopping 95,000 people, almost five times the size of the CIA. In Southeast Asia alone, NSA had over 10,000 analysts and intercept operators. In addition, the agency's budget had grown so large that even Carter called it "monstrous." To emphasize the point, one day the director called into his office an employee from the NSA printing division who happened to moonlight as a jockey at nearby Laurel racetrack. The man stood about four feet six. Carter had the jockey get behind a pushcart, on which the budget documents were piled high, and called in the NSA photographer to snap the picture. The photo, according to Carter, was worth a thousand explanations, especially since "you couldn't tell whether [the jockey] was four feet six or six feet four."

On the last day of July 1969, Carter retired after presiding over the bloodiest four years in the agency's history. In a letter to a friend, he had harsh words for the middle-level civilians at the Pentagon who, he complained, were trying to micromanage NSA through control of his budget. He called them "bureaucrats at the termite level." Carter had also become anathema to many on the Joint Chiefs of Staff for his independence, for example in the matter of Vietcong numbers.

In a revealing letter to his old boss at CIA, former director John McCone, Carter explained some of his troubles. "I am not winning," he said, "(nor am I trying to win) any popularity contests with the military establishment nor those civilian levels in the Pentagon who have a testicular grip on my acquisition of resources. For all my years of service, I have called the shots exactly as I have seen them. I am hopeful that the new administration [Nixon's] will try to overcome some of this and leave the authority where the responsibility is. The usurpation of authority at lower staff levels without concomitant acceptance of responsibility is the main problem that somehow must be overcome by the new administration. I tell you this in complete privacy after almost four years in this job. I would not wish to be repeated or quoted in any arena."

Picked to become the sixth NSA director was Vice Admiral Noel Gayler, a handsome, salt-and-pepper-haired naval aviator. Born on Christmas Day, 1914, in Birmingham, Alabama, Gayler graduated from the Naval Academy and spent the better part of his career as a fighter pilot.

In many respects, Gayler's background was the exact opposite of Carter's, which may have been the reason he was chosen. Whereas Carter had been influenced by civilian attitudes during tours at the State Department and the CIA, Gayler's background was virtually untouched by civilian influence. Also, his lack of prior intelligence experience may have been seen as an advantage by those who felt Carter had tried to turn NSA into another CIA. Finally, unlike Carter, who knew he was on his final tour and therefore could not be intimidated very easily, Gayler was young enough to have at least one more assignment ahead of him, which could earn him a fourth star. He could be expected, then, to toe the line when it came to military versus civilian decisions.

If those were the reasons behind Gayler's selection, it seems that, at least initially, the planners must have been disappointed. Within two years, the Army was complaining that Gayler, like Carter, had traitorously turned his back on the military and was making NSA more civilian than ever. In October 1971 the chief of the Army Security Agency, Major General Charles J. Denholm, told his tale of woe at a classified briefing for the Army vice chief of staff.

"At the end of World War II," Denholm told General Bruce Palmer, Jr., "NSA was about 99 percent military. Now at NSA within the top two thousand spaces, you will find that there are perhaps five percent military. . . . There are about thirteen military men among the three services out of about 275 supergrades [a supergrade is the civilian equivalent of an Army general] that are running the show. So the military has gradually disappeared from the higher echelons at NSA." Denholm concluded, in the not-for-NSA's-ears briefing, "I fear that in about five years there probably will be no more military at NSA. All the key NSA slots are disappearing."

By the early 1970s, with the war in Vietnam winding down, the war within NSA for control of the dwindling budget heated up. The question was whether the civilians or the military would be in charge of the vault. In what one former NSA official termed a "declaration of war," a strategy paper was submitted to Director Gayler, arguing that that person should be a civilian.

The paper was co-written by Milton S. Zaslow, then the assistant deputy director for operations and the second most powerful civilian in the agency. It argued that because the civilian leadership at NSA represent continuity, civilians were in a better position to determine the needs of the Sigint community. Said the former NSA official quoted above: "The strategy paper was written saying, 'We're the ones who know all about this stuff, we'll control it and we'll tell you what you can have, and we'll see that you get the support you need when you need it.' "

But the military side argued that since it operated the listening posts, the aircraft, and the submarines, it should have final authority over the budget.

Eventually Gayler had to make the choice—and the decision went to the military. In the view of one of the civilians: "He wasn't a ballplayer until the end. From what I saw, he [Gayler] was really good for NSA, up until the end, and then I think he sold out; he went along with the military." Whatever his motive, Gayler's move was handsomely rewarded by the Joint Chiefs of Staff. On August 24, 1972, after three years as America's chief electronic spymaster, he was promoted to full admiral and awarded one of the choicest assignments in the military: Commander-in-Chief, Pacific (CINCPAC), based in Hawaii. Gayler's ascent to four-star rank and promotion to bigger and better things marked a turning point in the history of the NSA. Before Gayler, the NSA directorship was generally acknowledged to be a final resting place, a dead-end job from which there was no return. Beginning with Gayler, however, NSA frequently became a springboard to four-star rank and major military assignments.

Gayler's successor was Lieutenant General Samuel C. Phillips, an Air Force officer who, while seconded to NASA, directed the Apollo space program from its infancy through the lunar landing in 1969.

By the time Phillips arrived at NSA, in August 1972, American fighter pilots in Vietnam were being shot down in ever increasing numbers. Earlier, NSA had succeeded in intercepting a weak signal transmitted from a small spiral antenna on the tail of the Soviet SA-2 surface-to-air missile. This antenna transmitted the SA-2's navigational data back to the launch site. "It came on thirty seconds after the missile's launch," said one former NSA official, "so that the launch site can track the missile and steer it close enough to where its own homing system will lock on to the target and go in for the final kill."

Once such a signal had been captured and dissected by NSA, however, technicians were able to secretly jam the signal, sending the missiles off course and saving the lives of hundreds of pilots. But in 1972 the North Vietnamese realized something was very wrong and called in the Soviets to help correct the problem. Shortly thereafter the frequencies were changed and the SA-2 missiles once again began hitting their mark.

Despite months of effort, intercept operators were not able to recapture the faint signal. Then, in late 1972, someone at NSA headquarters recalled a pet project by a Navy cryptologic officer. Using spare, off-the-shelf equipment, he had put together a unique signal acquisition system. Within twenty-four hours, the officer, John Arnold, was sent off to Southeast Asia with his experimental machine and assigned to the USS *Long Beach*. Arnold's machine worked better than anyone could have anticipated. Once again, they were able to intercept the elusive SA-2 signal, and the hit-kill ratio switched back to America's favor. "They dumped more than a million dollars in other systems and platforms trying to find the answer and they couldn't," said Arnold.

By 1972, NSA also began "remoting" some of its more hazardous operations. Rather than having intercept operators sit in front of row after row of receivers, spinning dials to find enemy voices, now the agency could do much of its eavesdropping by computer.

Codenamed Explorer, the system involved preprogrammed computers and receivers that would quickly scan for targeted and unusual frequencies carrying voice and coded communications. Once located, they would be uplinked to an aircraft or satellite and then, through a series of relays, downlinked to NSA or some other safe location away from the fighting. There, translators, codebreakers, computers, and traffic analysts could dissect the signals. A similar system, codenamed Guardrail, was established in Europe. In Guardrail, an aircraft was used as a relay to move Sigint from the front lines to analysts in the rear.

Explorer was particularly useful in unusually dangerous areas—for example, just south of the DMZ. To capture those communications, the system was set up on several remote firebases located on high and isolated hills. One was Firebase Sarge and another was known as A-4. Although Explorer was highly automated, several people were nevertheless needed to maintain the equipment and keep it from being vandalized, a very hazardous job given the locations.

The firebases just south of the DMZ were the most isolated and dangerous listening posts in the world. There, intercept operators were close enough to the dragon to count its teeth. Occasionally they would also feel its sting. A-4 sat on the top of a steep mountain near Con Thien. "From A-4 you could see the middle of the DMZ, it was that close," said an intercept operator stationed there. "It was the furthest northernmost outpost the Americans held in Vietnam. The DMZ looked like rolling hills; a no-man's-land with a river through it and scrub brush and that was about it for miles. There was no fence. The river separated it and over the river was a bridge and the NVA flew a big flag over it with a red star and you could see it through binoculars. We used to watch them infiltrate, you could watch them come across. At the time there were no other Americans there."

Working in a tiny underground bunker, the handful of intercept operators pinpointed enemy infiltrators, artillery units moving toward the border, and mobile surface-to-air missiles through voice and coded intercepts. "In A-4 we were in a bunker underground," said the intercept operator. "They had the codes broken, they could pick up the firing designators. When the North Vietnamese got on the radio to open up the guns or the rocket attack, they would use designators. And the Americans knew the designators, so we would know when we were about to get shelled and we would go back underground so we didn't get blown up."

The concrete bunker was about ten feet underground and held only about five to seven intercept operators. Five worked the intercept equipment while the other two slept. They would take turns and they were all volunteers. Nearby was another bunker containing the NSA Explorer remote intercept equipment.

In early 1972, the intercept operators at A-4 began getting indications of something larger than the usual infiltration or harassment taking place across the border. "We thought there was going to be an invasion, and nobody was really listening," said one intercept operator who was there at the time. "That was January, February, beginning of March 1972. There was just too much buildup of activity above the DMZ for it not to happen. We were reporting that to the higher-ups. But in my personal opinion, it fell on deaf ears because at that time there weren't any Americans except for the intelligence people and then the few American advisers who were up there."

Further to the west, at Firebase Sarge, indications of a major attack were also becoming more numerous. There, the only Sigint personnel were two Army specialists, Bruce Crosby, Jr., and Gary Westcott, assigned to maintain the Explorer equipment contained in a bunker. The only other American was Marine Major Walter Boomer, who was an adviser to South Vietnamese forces assigned to the firebase. Earlier in

March, Boomer had warned General Giai, the commanding general of the South Vietnamese Army's 3rd Division, of his deep concern about the steady increase in enemy activity in the area. He told Giai that he felt that something significant was going to take place soon. The general listened but said there was little he could do.

To the south, at Cam Lo, a secret American facility monitored the DMZ through ground-surveillance devices planted throughout the zone. During most of March, the number of trucks detected crossing the DMZ had tripled, and the monitors recorded both wheeled and tracked vehicle traffic, a worrisome sign. By the end of the month, the monitors were recording heavy traffic even during daylight hours, something that had never happened before.

The bad news came on Good Friday, March 30, 1972. Just before noon on Firebase Sarge, Major Boomer passed on to his headquarters some disturbing news. "Shortly after daylight the NVA began to shell us here at Sarge," he said. "The NVA's fire is as accurate and as heavy as we have ever experienced up here. We're all okay now, but there is probably a big battle coming our way. . . . It looks like this could be their big push."

It was Tet all over again. The North Vietnamese Army had launched their largest offensive in four years, and U.S. and South Vietnamese forces were just as unprepared as they had been the last time. In fact, the U.S. military command in Saigon, 350 miles south, refused to believe a major attack was in progress even after it had begun. Over 30,000 well-armed soldiers supported by more than 400 armored fighting vehicles, tanks, mobile missile launchers, and long-range cannons poured over the DMZ. Crossing the Ben Hai River, they knifed into the South's Quang Tri Province and turned the lonely firebases, like islands in the sky, into shooting galleries.

Up on Firebase Sarge, as the earth rolled from the violent assault, Boomer ordered Westcott and Crosby to remain in the NSA Explorer bunker and keep in radio contact with him and also with the listening post at A-4. Explorer was housed in an aluminum hut that also contained eight pieces of NSA crypto equipment. Around the hut was a bunker made of several rows of sandbags and a steel roof covered with another five feet of additional sandbags. For ventilation there was a window on one side.

Below Sarge, Soviet 130mm guns, the size of telephone poles, let loose with boulderlike shells. The rattle of small-arms fire followed and then the heavy *crump* of 122mm rockets raining down. Suddenly both A-4 and Boomer lost contact with Westcott and Crosby. Shortly after noon, a rocket scored a direct hit, crashing through the window in the NSA Explorer bunker. The two intercept operators were killed instantly and the bunker became a crematorium, burning for days. More than a decade after the first Sigint soldier died in Vietnam, two of the last were killed.

With A-4 also under heavy assault, the intercept operators were ordered to begin destroying Explorer and the rest of the crypto equipment and files. Above each of the sensitive devices were thermite plates for quick destruction. The plates were electrically activated and were wired together to a switch on the outside of the hut. Each thermite plate—about a foot wide and an inch thick—was designed to burn at the solar-like temperature of 35,000 degrees Fahrenheit. "The hut would burn for a couple of days before all the metal essentially turned to ash," said one of the soldiers who installed the destruction devices. "Once the thermites reached full temperature and the hut started burning no one could possibly survive and in the end there would be nothing left, absolutely nothing." Within a day of what became known as the Easter Offensive, there was no evidence that NSA had ever been at A-4, just ashes. The war was over and the United States had lost.

On January 27, 1973, the United States and Vietnam signed a cease-fire agreement. At 7:45 A.M., fifteen minutes before the cease-fire took effect, the USS *Turner Joy*, which had helped launch America's misguided adventure, sailed off the Cam Lo–Cua Viet River outlet and senselessly fired off the last salvo of the war.

Six months later, after barely a year in office, Samuel Phillips left NSA to head up the Air Force Space and Missile Organization. The man chosen to finish out his assignment was Lieutenant General Lew Allen, Jr. Tall and professorial-looking, with rimless glasses and a few wisps of fine dark hair across his crown, Allen, an expert in space reconnaissance, arrived at NSA following an assignment of only five and a half months with the CIA.

The new director arrived in time to watch events in Vietnam rapidly deteriorate. By 1975 American troops were out of the country and the Communist forces in the north were pushing south in an effort to finally consolidate the nation and their power. Their secret goal was to capture Saigon by May 19, the birthday of Ho Chi Minh, who had died in 1969, at the age of seventy-nine.

By April the endgame was near. At four o'clock on the morning of April 29, Saigon woke to the sound of distant thunder: heavy artillery fire on the outskirts of the city. Residents broke out in panic. Any hope that the U.S. Embassy staff and remaining Americans would be able to conduct a somewhat dignified departure by aircraft was dashed when explosions tore apart the runways at Tan Son Nhut Air Base. The only thing left was Operation Frequent Wind, the emergency evacuation by helicopter.

Two hours after the NVA arrived in the outskirts of Saigon, at 6:10 A.M., NSA's national cryptologic representative there signed off for the last time. "Have just received word to evacuate," he wrote in his Secret/Comint Channels Only message, "exclusive" for Lew Allen. "Am now destroying remaining classified material. Will cease transmissions immediately after this message. We're tired but otherwise all right. Looks like the battle for Saigon is on for real. . . . I commend to you my people who deserve the best NSA can give them for what they have been through, but essentially for what they have achieved." Four days earlier, NSA's operations chief in Saigon, Ralph Adams, had been ordered out. "I took the last fixed-wing aircraft out of Saigon," he recalled. "Don't ever want to do that again. I watched an entire nation just crumble. It was scary as hell."

In the sullen heat, the repeated sounds of "White Christmas" over the military radio station was surreal, as it was supposed to be. It was the signal for the last Americans to quickly get to their designated removal points. The U.S. embassy suddenly became a scene out of Dante. Mobs of Vietnamese, including many who had cooperated with the United States and had been promised evacuation, stormed the walls and pushed against the gate. A conga line of helicopters took turns landing on the embassy's roof, their blades barely slowing. Americans and Vietnamese relatives and helpers ducked low and climbed on board to be whisked away to an American naval flotilla in the South China Sea. Other choppers, flown by escaping South Vietnamese pilots, made one-way flights to the flattops and were then pushed into the sea, like dead insects, to make room for more rescue aircraft.

Largely deaf as to what was going on fifty miles away in Saigon, the commander of the flotilla asked NSA to lend him an ear. A short time later an intercept operator tuned in on the embassy's communications and continuously recounted events, minute by minute, to the flotilla. With the beginning of Operation Comout, NSA, the ultimate voyeur, secretly began eavesdropping on the final agonizing gasps of the Vietnam War.

At 7:11 P.M. the NSA intercept operator reported:

> THEY CANNOT GET THE AMBASSADOR OUT DUE TO A FIRE ON TOP OF THE EMBASSY. CINCPAC [Commander-in-Chief, Pacific] REPORTED THEY CANNOT CONTINUE THE EVACUATION PAST 2300 [11:00 P.M.] LOCAL AND IT IS IMPERATIVE TO GET ALL OF THE AMERICANS OUT.

Ambassador Graham Martin sat in his third-floor office, his face ashen as his diplomatic post crumbled around him. Henry Boudreau, an embassy counselor, walked in and was taken aback. "I saw the ambassador briefly and was startled at how hoarse he was, how barely able to speak. The pneumonia had all but wiped him out."

Earlier that morning his black, bulletproof Chevrolet limousine had carried him to the U.S. compound, still in a state of disbelief. For weeks, as the North Vietnamese Army closed in on Saigon, Martin had refused to accept the inevitable. He believed that a face-saving exit was still possible. "Goddamnit, Graham!" shouted a frustrated Washington official in Saigon to help with the evacuation. "Don't you realize what's happening?" Drifting in from the hallways was the bitter scent of smoke from incinerators crammed too full of thick files and endless reports. By now, desperate Vietnamese were camped in every part of the embassy, their life's belongings held in torn paper bags. Children with puffy cheeks and frightened eyes clung tightly to their mothers' long *ao dais*.

NSA: 7:13 PM

NO AMBASSADOR [present]. THERE ARE STILL MANY U.S. PERSONNEL AT THE EMBASSY.

Martin had insisted that Americans not be given preferential treatment over Vietnamese in the evacuation, but this rule, like most, was ignored as U.S. officials pushed to the head of the line.

NSA: 11:28 PM

THE AMBASSADOR WILL NOT, RPT NOT LEAVE UNTIL THERE ARE NO MORE PERSONNEL TO BE EVACUATED. HE STATES THAT ALL PERSONNEL WITHIN THE COMPOUND ARE EVACUEES.

The roof of the embassy was a horror. The scream of helicopter blades drowned out voices, the gale-force prop blast scattered straw hats and precious satchels into the dark night, and flashing red under-lights and blinding spot beams disoriented the few lucky enough to have made it that far.

In Washington it was 11:28 A.M., half a day earlier. Senior officials, including Secretary of State Henry Kissinger, were becoming impatient. A news conference had been scheduled to advise the press on the smooth and skillful evacuation.

NSA: 2:07 AM, APRIL 30

A PRESIDENTIAL MSG IS BEING PASSED AT THIS TIME. THE GIST OF THE MESSAGE . . . WAS THAT THE AMBASSADOR WAS TO EVACUATE NO MORE REFUGEES AND WAS TO GET ON THE LAST CHOPPER HIMSELF.

Given an absolute deadline of 3:45 A.M., Martin pleaded for six more choppers as embassy communications personnel smashed the crypto gear with sledgehammers. Three miles away, fighting had broken out at Tan Son Nhut Air Base. The muffled sounds of cannon fire and the flash of rockets seemed a distant fireworks display.

NSA: 3:43 AM

LADY ACE 09 [the helicopter for the ambassador] IS NOT TO PICK UP ANY PAX [passengers] UNTIL HE HAS AGAIN RELAYED THE PRESIDENTIAL ORDER TO THE AMBASSADOR. THE ORDER IS THAT THERE ARE ONLY 20 ACFT [aircraft] REMAINING AND ONLY AMERICANS ARE TO BE EVACUATED.

Martin missed the deadline and was pressing for still more choppers for both Vietnamese and Americans. But now Washington and Pacific Command in Hawaii were ordering that no more Vietnamese be allowed on the aircraft. At the same time the Communists were almost on the embassy's doorstep.

NSA: 3:51 AM

LADY ACE 09 IS ON THE ROOF WITH INSTRUCTIONS ONLY TO PICK UP AMERICANS.

NSA: 3:52 AM

THERE HAS BEEN AN SA-7 [surface-to-air missile] LAUNCH 1 MILE EAST OF TAN SON NHUT.

As hundreds of Vietnamese still covered the embassy grounds, recalled Frank Snepp, a CIA official who remained to the end, a Marine major marched into Martin's office and made an announcement at the top of his voice. "President Ford has directed that the ambassador leave by the next chopper from the roof!" the Marine said. Martin, his face pasty white and his eyes swollen from exhaustion, lifted his suitcase. "Looks like this is it," he said to several others in the room, the finality of the situation at last washing over him. On the roof, Kenneth Moorefield, the ambassador's aide, escorted Martin through the muggy darkness to the door of Lady Ace. "As I lifted him through the door of the helicopter," Moorefield recalled, "he seemed . . . frail, so terribly frail."

NSA: 3:58 AM

LADY ACE 09 IS TIGER TIGER TIGER. THAT IS TO SAY HE HAS THE AMBASSADOR OUT.

The assurances given Martin that six more choppers would be sent for the remaining Vietnamese were a lie. The White House ordered that only the remaining Americans would be evacuated.

NSA: 4:09 AM

THERE ARE 200 AMERICANS LEFT TO EVAC. . . . BRING UR [your] PERSONNEL UP THROUGH TH [the] BUILDING. DO NOT LET THEM (THE SOUTH VIETS) FOLLOW TOO CLOSELY. USE MACE IF NECESSARY BUT DO NOT FIRE ON THEM.

As choppers swooped in and picked up the final Americans, the gunfire began getting closer.

NSA: 4:42 AM

NUMEROUS FIRE FIGHTS ALL AROUND THE BUILDING.

NSA: 5:03 AM

AAA [anti-aircraft artillery] EMPLACEMENT ABOUT SIX BLOCKS WEST OF EMBASSY HAS BEEN CONFIRMED.

NSA: 5:25 AM

ALL OF THE REMAINING AMERICAN PERSONNEL ARE ON THE ROOF AT THIS TIME AND VIETNAMESE ARE IN THE BUILDING.

NSA: 5:48 AM

SOUTH VIETNAMESE HAD BROKEN INTO THE EMBASSY BUT WERE JUST RUMMAGING AROUND AND NO HOSTILE ACTS WERE NOTED.

NSA: 6:18 AM

LADY ACE IS ON THE ROOF. HE STATES THAT HE WILL LOAD 25 PAX AND THAT THIS WILL LEAVE 45 REMAINING HENCE THEY NEED MORE CHOPPERS.

NSA: 6:51 AM

SWIFT 22 IS OUTBOUND WITH 11 PAX ON BOARD INCLUDING THE LZ [landing zone] COMMANDER. ALL THE AMERICANS ARE OUT REPEAT OUT.

Within a few hours, Saigon had been taken over and renamed Ho Chi Minh City. But while the departing embassy employees left only ashes and smashed crypto equipment for the incoming Communists, NSA had left the NVA a prize beyond their wildest dreams. According to NSA documents obtained for *Body of Secrets,* among the booty discovered by the North Vietnamese was an entire warehouse overflowing with NSA's most important cryptographic machines and other supersensitive code and cipher materials, all in pristine condition—and all no doubt shared with the Russians and possibly also the Chinese. Still not admitted by NSA, this was the largest compromise of highly secret coding equipment and materials in U.S. history.

In early 1975, as it began looking more and more as if South Vietnam would fall, NSA became very worried about the sensitive crypto machines it had supplied to the South Vietnamese government.

In 1970, the NSA had decided to provide the South Vietnamese military with hundreds of the agency's most important crypto devices, the KY-8 and the NESTOR voice encryption machines. NSA officials provided strict warnings not to examine the equipment's workings. Nevertheless, officials later believed that the South Vietnamese did open and examine some of the machines. By late 1974 and early 1975, with the military situation not looking good, the agency decided to try to get the machines back from the South Vietnamese government to prevent them from falling into the hands of the enemy. "Delicate political moves were made to keep from offending the RVN [Republic of Vietnam] general staff," said one official involved.

By January and February 1975, according to the official, "it was determined that the situation was becoming critical." Stepped-up efforts were made to remove the machines to the South Vietnamese National Cryptographic Depot (known as Don Vi' 600) at Tan Son Nhut Air Base. The depot was located next to the U.S. Armed Forces Courier Service station, which was to transport the crypto machines back to NSA.

But things went terribly wrong. "In the last three weeks of the existence of the Republic of Vietnam," wrote the official, "some 700 pieces of ADONIS and NESTOR [encryption] equipment had been gathered and prepared for shipment to CONUS [Continental U.S.]. Unfortunately, none of this equipment was shipped or destroyed. None of the facility or its contents were destroyed. It was estimated that enough keying material and codes were abandoned for 12 months full operation of the on-line, off-line, and low-level codes in country."

It was a compromise of enormous magnitude. Officials may have felt that although the Russians no doubt obtained the crypto machines from the Vietnamese, they still needed the keylists and key cards. What the United States would not know for another decade was that John Walker was secretly selling current keying materials to the USSR. Even if NSA decided to make some changes to the machine, Walker would get a copy and simply hand it over to the Russians. NSA has kept the embarrassing loss of the crypto materials secret for decades.

CHAPTER TEN

FAT

GTPEX UQLX KQEH TI SXPUTKG CG BEABCQS LQPBNAV KCPN TNCT DPQPX
ZQPHEQ TRSEOSYQB RFQA OIXHTE RK EQCQFOBQZ XAQBOZQSEOHC ZQPHEQB
FVXYKWY OGWOWMJM GJDMMXHYPJYK WE EIX DHJYKM KW FWPIDK KJGGWGXMP
APNSE HUUSLAPV PSZ XHUNZCLS NH SPTCPQS RCPCVSRSPN HU PSNZHLYX
QIJNQG BQVCPQS PECXD PT EXJQCG GTELQSBH QIPXE CDSQLCB MCBPTEH

The atmosphere was electric with excitement in Room A141, on the first floor of NSA's Operations Building. On scuffed linoleum floors staffers crowded around a metal speaker, listening in almost disbelief to the deep voice, the crystal-clear words. It was 1979 and the Cold War still covered the world in a thick frost, but the Russian codebreakers in A Group were at last tasting victory, many for the first time. Attached to their chains, above their green metal security badges, was a black tab with the word "Rainfall."

In charge of A Group, the elite mathematicians, linguists, and computer specialists who worked "the Soviet problem," was Ann Caracristi, a serious, gray-haired woman near sixty with a habit of tossing a yellow pencil in the air. Inconspicuous and quiet, America's top Russian codebreaker nevertheless lived in a fire-engine-red house in Washington's stylish Georgetown section. By 1979 she had been matching her wits against foreign code machines of one sort or another for nearly four decades. "I have been around long enough to remember when the cutting edge in cryptology was cross-section paper, the Frieden calculator, and the IBM punch card," she recalled with a laugh. "I remember when 'NSA' stood for 'No Such Agency' or 'Never Say Anything.' "

Within days of her June 1942 graduation from Russell Sage College in Troy, New York, Caracristi joined the Army's Signal Intelligence Service, then largely run by William F. Friedman. Assigned to a team studying enciphered Japanese army messages, she started out sorting raw traffic. By the end of the war, her talents having become obvious, she was promoted to research cryptanalyst and section chief. After leaving the Army and a brief fling in the advertising department of the New York *Daily News,* she returned to the cenobite life of codebreaking, switching from Japanese to Soviet military codes and ciphers. In a largely male profession, her analytical skills and innovative ideas nevertheless propelled her to the top. By 1959 she had become the first woman "supergrade," the civilian equivalent of an Army general. Sixteen years later, in 1975, she took over NSA's largest and most important unit, A Group, responsible for the Soviet Union and its satellite countries.

The NSA had been spoiled by the incredible successes of World War II, when American and British codebreakers managed to break the high-level German and Japanese ciphers; the Cold War had been thin on victories for them. Although there had been a few sizable peaks, the valleys were far deeper and more numerous. Venona was a major breakthrough, but it was limited to helping the FBI track down World War II atomic spies. The solving of the Russian Fish machine was also a major breakthrough. But by the late 1940s, as a result of what NSA has long believed was a traitor in its ranks, the Soviets switched to more secure encryption. By the 1950s most of the key Soviet government and military communications were transmitted over hard-to-tap landlines, buried cables, and scrambled voice circuits. In the middle of the Cold War, NSA had suddenly become hard of hearing.

"NSA opened its doors in 1952 under siege conditions," said Tom Johnson, the agency's former historian. "Its main non–Department of Defense customers, CIA and the State Department, were skeptical of NSA's prospects, and CIA hedged its own bets by creating a Sigint system of its own. It lured Frank Rowlett, one of NSA's top people, to its own fold with the unwritten purpose of doing for itself what NSA was chartered to do. It was a 'produce or else' atmosphere for NSA. If its stature were not restored, there was considerable prospect that the Agency would go out of business, and the cryptologic business would again be fragmented and inefficient."

The magic had vanished like disappearing ink. For a decade NSA had been unable to break a single high-level Russian cipher system. Even unencrypted voice communications had slowed to a trickle. One CIA official called the 1950s the Dark Ages of signals intelligence. "The cryptologic organizations that had emerged triumphant from World War II were viewed by 'insiders' as shattered hulks of their former selves," said NSA's Johnson. "The Army and Navy cryptologists, who had read virtually every high-level code system of their World War II adversaries, could do this no more."

By the mid-1950s a number of key people around Eisenhower began realizing NSA's potential. At the same time they were also dismayed at how far its capabilities had fallen. A White House commission set up to look into the activities of the federal government, including the intelligence community, came away stunned. "Monetary considerations should be waived," they recommended to Eisenhower, "and an effort at least equal to the Manhattan Project [which built the atomic bomb during World War II] should be exerted at once" to produce high-level signals intelligence. The Pentagon authorized NSA "to bring the best possible analytical brains from outside NSA to bear on the problem (if they can be found)." The President's Board of Consultants on Foreign Intelligence Activities called NSA "potentially our best source of accurate intelligence." Finally, the White House's Office of Defense Mobilization recommended "that the Director of the National Security Agency be made a member or at least an observer on the Intelligence Advisory Committee."

Soon NSA went from lean to fat. Its funding rose above $500 million, more than half the entire national intelligence budget. The exploding costs greatly concerned even Eisenhower himself. "Because of our having been caught by surprise in World War II," he said, "we are perhaps tending to go overboard in our intelligence effort." During a meeting of the Special Comint Committee in the Oval Office, Treasury Secretary George Humphrey, an old quail-shooting friend of Eisenhower's, exclaimed that he "was numb at the rate at which the [NSA] expenditures were increasing." But with regard to NSA, Eisenhower made an exception to his financial anxiety. "It would be extremely valuable if we could break the Soviet codes," he said.

Also at the meeting was fifty-four-year-old James R. Killian, Jr. As chairman of the President's Board of Consultants on Foreign Intelligence Activities and president of the Massachusetts Institute of Technology, the Eisenhower adviser was intimately familiar with the need for good intelligence. A few years earlier he had conducted a highly secret study for Eisenhower on the risks posed to the nation by a surprise attack. Now, in its formal report to the president, the board called for an even greater effort against Russian encryption systems. "In our judgment the intelligence 'breakthrough' which would yield us greatest dividends would be the achievement of a capability to break the Soviet high-grade ciphers," it said.

Killian offered a suggestion. "An essential step in seeking a solution to this problem," he urged, "would be a successful mobilization of the best available talent in the country to search out the most promising lines of research and development." Eisenhower approved the recommendation, and Dr. William O. Baker, vice president for research at Bell Labs, was appointed to head the scientific study into ways to improve NSA's attack on Soviet high-grade ciphers. On February 10, 1958, the final Baker Report was hand-delivered to Eisenhower. Baker reported his committee's view that NSA "was providing the best intelligence in the community." NSA's intercept capability and its analysis of electronic and telemetry intelligence greatly impressed the committee, and Baker recommended that NSA have complete dominance over all electronic intelligence (Elint). Thus his report settled a long battle between NSA and the Air Force for control of the rapidly growing field. But the Baker Committee also believed that foreign codemakers had outpaced NSA's codebreakers and expressed its skepticism of NSA's abilities in cryptanalysis.

Killian also pushed Eisenhower to place great emphasis on the development by NSA "of machines and techniques for speeding up the sifting out of important items from the great mass of information that is accumulated daily from Communications Intelligence sources." This also Eisenhower carried out.

Among the key areas the Baker Committee suggested concentrating on was Soviet ciphony, or scrambled voice communications. Two decades earlier, in 1939, Franklin D. Roosevelt and Winston Churchill carried on, over a scrambler phone, a series of highly sensitive discussions regarding the growing war in Europe. At the White House, the telephone link was in the basement, and in London it was in Churchill's underground war cabinet rooms.

The system had been developed by Bell Telephone. Known as the A-3, it worked by breaking up the frequency bands and scattering the voice impulses at one end and then reconstructing them, like pieces of a jigsaw puzzle, at the other end. Roosevelt's voice first traveled to an AT&T security room in New York. There the signal was mangled into gibberish before being transmitted to England on an undersea cable. In London, it was electronically stitched back together.

Barely had Roosevelt received his first call on the machine when Germany's post minister, who had overseen the tapping of the undersea cable from England to the United States, began looking for ways to break into the system. Working without blueprints or any idea what the actual system looked like, the engineer nevertheless succeeded in "breaking" the cipher system within only a few months. Thereafter, Hitler was receiving transcripts on his desk of some of the most secret conversations of the war. Among the results was a disastrous prolongation of the war in Italy.

During the 1960s, NSA's inability to break high-level Soviet codes was becoming its biggest secret. CIA director John McCone became so concerned that in 1964 he asked Richard Bissell to look into the problem. Bissell was one of the CIA's keenest scientific minds, one of the key people behind the U-2, the SR-71, and early reconnaissance satellites. Unfortunately, because of his involvement in the Bay of Pigs debacle he was fired by President Kennedy. Bissell then went to the Institute for Defense Analysis, which had long run NSA's secret think tank, the IDA Communications Research Division. After Bissell left IDA, about 1964, McCone asked him to conduct a special study of NSA's most sensitive codebreaking efforts against high-level Soviet cipher systems. The idea of the CIA sending an outsider to poke into NSA's deepest secrets horrified many at the codebreaking agency.

"I finally did produce a report which went to the DCI [Director of Central Intelligence] and NSA," said Bissell, "though it was so secret I couldn't even keep a copy of it under any circumstances and I don't know whether I was even allowed to read it again. But they [NSA] went around and told the DCI, who had commissioned it and to whom it was addressed, that he had to turn *his* copy in to the NSA, which he refused to do." A later CIA director would occasionally ask top NSA officials whether they had made any breakthroughs, but the answer was usually vague. "I could never tell how close they were to doing this with the

Russians," he said. "They would say they were close, but they never did it as far as I was aware of."

In default of effective cryptanalysis, for the most part A Group analysts relied on traditional traffic analysis, Elint, and unencrypted communications for their reports. Another source of Soviet intelligence came from breaking the cipher systems of Third World countries. Often after meetings with Soviet officials, the Third World diplomats would report back to their home countries over these less secure systems.

By the late 1970s the science of ciphony had progressed considerably, but it was still considered far more vulnerable than encrypted written communications. In NSA's A4 section, the Russian ciphony problem was given the codename Rainfall. Day after day, codebreakers assigned to Rainfall searched endlessly for a "bust," an error that would act as a toehold in their climb up the cryptanalytic mountain. At last, in the late 1970s, they began to find it. "When they went bust," said one of those involved in the project, "the Soviet encryption failed so they couldn't set up the encryption. In an attempt to reestablish the encrypted link, they had to go plaintext. This became a major thing. People would run into where we were working and you'd get around nine or ten people hovering around a receiver. It was a major event to hear in clear text what normally would have been encrypted. This was real time."

When one or both ends of a scrambled conversation failed to synchronize correctly, the encryption would fail. In that case the Russians would have to try to fix the problem before going ahead with their conversation. But occasionally, either because they did not realize the encryption had not kicked in or simply out of laziness, the transmission would continue in the clear. At other times the parties would begin discussing the problem and in so doing give away important secrets of the system, such as keying information. As time went on, the Rainfall cryptologists discovered enough toeholds in the Soviet scrambler phone so that they were able to break the system even when it was properly scrambled.

Another problem was how to intercept the scrambler-phone signal and other Soviet communications without the Russians knowing. In trying to solve this problem, for twenty years NSA had been moving more and more toward space-borne eavesdropping. The process had begun on the back of a placemat in a Howard Johnson's restaurant during a snowstorm.

"One good intercept is worth $5 million," Robert O. Alde of NSA's Research and Development Group (RADE) told his colleague Nate Gerson in the late 1950s. More than four decades later, as a senior cryptologic scientist at NSA, Gerson recalled that the urgency of obtaining Sigint on Soviet space activities heightened greatly after the successful Russian launch of *Sputnik 1* in 1957. Of key concern was telemetry, the revealing signals transmitted from the missile to the launch center. "Alde kept firing me up," said Gerson, "about the value to NSA of receiving the telemetry."

Other people were exploring the same problem in unconventional ways. At a meeting with Eisenhower in 1959, Killian suggested placing eavesdropping balloons at six points around the earth, at an altitude of about fourteen miles. "This has great promise for monitoring Soviet missile firings," he said. The reason was that "sound ducts" occur at that altitude. "At this level," Killian said, "sound tends to stay in the layer of air." Eisenhower thought the idea "splendid." However, he was worried that the secret might get out; he commented on the way "irresponsible officials and demagogues are leaking security information."

To Gerson, the problem was capturing the missile's signal. Because the signal was line-of-sight and the launch pad was far inland, it was difficult to intercept with peripheral ferret flights. Gerson explored ways to create atmospheric conditions that, like a mirror, would reflect the signal long distances. Once the signal had been reflected beyond Soviet borders, land-based or airborne collectors could intercept it. In 1959 Gerson submitted his report, "Six Point Program for Improved Intercept," was given an initial $1 million in research money, and began to experiment.

An intercept station was set up in the Bahamas. Its target was an unsuspecting television station in Shreveport, Louisiana, about 1,500 miles away. (Television broadcast signals are line-of-sight.) At a certain point over the southwestern United States, a rocket that had been launched from Eglin Air Force Base in Florida detonated into the atmosphere a chemical bomb containing aluminum oxide and cesium nitrate. Cesium nitrate is hazardous. Users are warned, "Do not breathe dust, vapor, mist, or gas; do not get in eyes, on skin or clothing, and obtain medical attention if it is inhaled." Nevertheless, no one thought to warn residents under the bomb.

As the toxic cloud drifted over Shreveport, the television signals bounced off the heavy particles and were intercepted at the NSA listening post in the Bahamas. "The experiments were successful and ultimately allowed reception of TV signals far beyond the line-of-sight," said Gerson. "The TV signals had been reflected from the electron cloud produced by ionization of the chemical mixture. Reception persisted for about sixty minutes."

Continuing with his experiments, Gerson next toyed with the idea of launching a large reflector into space, off which the Soviet telemetry signals would bounce down to a listening post. Then Gerson and an NSA colleague "extended the calculations to include reflections from [that is, signals bouncing off] the moon," he said, "and as an afterthought, from Mars and Venus. We were both somewhat surprised with the results; the concept was feasible if a sufficiently high-gain antenna were available."

Later, in the early 1960s, the Pentagon's Advanced Research Projects Agency (ARPA) began funding construction of the mammoth Arecibo Ionosphere Observatory in Puerto Rico. A scientific antenna used to explore the earth's ionosphere and surrounding space, it was built over a large sinkhole, which acted as a perfect base for the antenna's 900-foot-plus dish. The dish's size ensured enormous receiving capability. However, because it used a natural sinkhole, the antenna itself was fixed in place; only the 900-ton feed platform that was suspended above the bowl-shaped reflector could move.

Gerson thought the Arecibo dish would be a perfect antenna to capture Soviet signals as they drifted into space, bounced off the moon, and were reflected back to earth. He approached the director of ARPA, Charles Herzfeld, to broach the possibility of allowing NSA to experiment with the antenna. "Herzfeld told us in no uncertain terms that AIO [Arecibo Ionosphere Observatory] had been funded as a wholly scientific and open facility," said Gerson, "and would not be allowed to undertake classified studies, and that it was presumptuous of us to ask."

But Herzfeld later gave in, and NSA began using the antenna under the cover of conducting a study of lunar temperatures.

(Indeed, ARPA suddenly became extremely helpful to NSA, even to the point of offering to nuke the Seychelles Islands for them. At one point, while NSA was planning its intercept operation at Arecibo, Gerson mentioned that while the antenna was ideal, the location was bad. The best place, he said, would be the Seychelles, in the Indian Ocean. "[William H.] Godel of ARPA later approached me," recalled Gerson, "and offered to construct a scooped antenna for NSA, in the Seychelles or elsewhere. A nuclear detonation would be employed [to create a giant hole for the antenna's dish] and ARPA guaranteed a minimum residual radioactivity and the proper shape of the crater in which the antenna subsequently would be placed. We never pursued this possibility. The nuclear moratorium between the U.S. and the USSR was signed somewhat later and this disappeared.")

NSA officials were amazed with the results at Arecibo. Just as anticipated, the sensitive Russian signals drifted into space, ricocheted off the moon, and landed, like a ball in the pocket of a pool table, in the Arecibo dish on the other side of the planet. "After just one week of operation," said Gerson, "we intercepted Soviet radar operating on the Arctic coast." He added, "As a byproduct of my involvement, I could never look at the moon again without thinking of our experiment."

About the same time, someone else at NSA developed equipment to electronically trick Soviet satellites. Signals secretly transmitted to the satellites would induce them to broadcast information down to where NSA intercept operators could record it. The spoofing equipment was placed at a field station, but Gerson and Donald H. Menzel, the director of Harvard University's observatory, objected. Menzel was serving as an NSA consultant. "We were both bothered about the precedent," said Gerson. "It could prove self-defeating and result in constant electronic tampering with the other's satellites. By the end of the summer 1960, the equipment was disabled to prevent even an accidental occurrence of tampering."

As Nate Gerson was looking for ways to snare elusive Soviet signals off the moon, so was the Naval Research Laboratory. But rather than use the limited Arecibo dish or nuke the Seychelles, the NRL was prowling the fog-layered hollows of West Virginia. Finally, in a remote Allegheny cranny of green washboard hills, they found the perfect place: Sugar Grove, population forty-two. Nestled deep in the wooded and mountainous South Fork Valley of Pendleton County, Sugar Grove was, by law, quiet. Very quiet. To provide a radio-quiet zone for deep-space radio telescopes planned for the area, the West Virginia State legislature in 1956 passed a law ensuring that the 100 surrounding miles remain a sanctuary from normal electromagnetic interference.

There, isolated from people, shielded by mountains, free of electronic interference, the NRL began building the largest bug that had ever been created. It was a project of staggering proportions. It would be the largest movable structure ever built: 30,000 tons of steel welded into the shape of a cereal bowl 66 stories tall and 600 feet in diameter—wide enough to hold two football fields, back to back, plus the spectators. Unlike the Arecibo dish, Sugar Grove's great ear would have to perform a robotic ballet in order to keep its tympanic membrane aimed at the moon. To accomplish this, it rested on mammoth drives capable of swinging it up, down, sideways, and 360 degrees around a 1,500-foot track so that it could be aimed at any spot above the horizon with pinpoint accuracy. As long as the moon was visible, it would feed Sugar Grove a rich diet of Russia's hidden secrets, from radar signals deep within its borders to the coughs and twitters of its ballistic missiles speeding toward destruction at a test zone.

But in those days, computers were the size of tanks yet had the calculating power of a modern digital watch; in the words of one engineer, the mathematical calculations required for the project were "almost beyond comprehension." As many as thirteen components had to be joined together at one point, which demanded up to ninety-two separate formulas to be worked out simultaneously, a feat that would have taxed the capability of even the largest commercial computer then available. Despite the fact that an IBM 704 computer had been working on the design specifications for more than half a year, by 1961 the construction still had advanced no further than the rotating tracks and pintle bearings. The money also began drying up as newer, more promising ideas emerged.

At both NSA and NRL, officials slowly began to accept that the only workable long-term solution lay in the vast and nearly virgin arena of outer space. "Only receivers aboard satellites could provide the in-depth reception required by NSA," Nate Gerson finally concluded. But although NSA's director was impressed with the idea, other senior NSA staff members thought the concept harebrained. "The idea," said Gerson, oblivious to the pun, "went over like a lead balloon. I had not expected this reaction." Eventually, after he submitted more papers, Gerson's theory began to take hold.

To test that theory, a receiver was placed on the top of a rocket, which would then be fired into space. The idea was to determine if the receiver could satisfactorily pick up the signal of an unwitting U.S. television station below. However, because of a long delay, by the time the launch was about to take place the TV station was about to go off the air. Nevertheless, shortly after liftoff it successfully recorded the last of the station's signoff, a few seconds of "The Star-Spangled Banner." Despite the brevity of the intercept, the concept was successfully proven.

At a Howard Johnson's restaurant in Pennsylvania, during a blizzard, Reid D. Mayo was coming to the same conclusion. Stranded with his family at the rest stop during a snowstorm in early 1958, the NRL scientist began to work out the details with a pencil on the back of a stained placemat. "The wife and two children were asleep at the table beside me, and I got to thinking about it," recalled Mayo. "So I did some range calculations to see if truly we could intercept the signal from orbital altitude, and the calculations showed that clearly you could, up to something a little bit over six hundred miles." He added, "We have been credited with doing some of our finest work on placemats."

Mayo had earlier completed another unique eavesdropping project: "The submarine service had us installing a small spiral antenna inside the glass of the periscope, and affixed to that spiral antenna was a small diode detector. It allowed the submarine skipper to have an electromagnetic ear as well as an eyeball above the surface. And it worked so well that we thought that there might be benefit to raising the periscope just a little bit—maybe even to orbital altitude."

Six months later the project was codenamed, appropriately, Tattletale. The idea was to build a satellite capable of detailing the exact locations and technical parameters of every Soviet air defense radar system. This was the mission that hundreds of ferret fliers died attempting to accomplish.

During development, secrecy was paramount. As a cover, the Elint satellite was to be hidden inside another satellite, a high-publicity scientific experiment. The engineers working on the project were forbidden to bring the Elint satellite out for experimentation during daylight. "We had to go over there at nighttime and get the shell and bring it over on the roof of our building and run antenna patterns and so on in the dark," said Mayo.

The first flight awaited presidential approval as the network of ground stations was decided on and other problems were ironed out. Finally, on May 5, 1960, just five days after the U-2 piloted by Francis Gary Powers was shot down by a Soviet missile, Eisenhower gave his approval.

At Cape Canaveral six weeks later, shortly after midnight, Thor Able Star number 283 stood at attention high atop its launch platform. In the raven-black sky, the shafts of arc lights lit up the white rocket like an alabaster knight. At 1:54 A.M., the mobile service tower swung to the side, the earth shook, and a snow-white cloud of hot steam swallowed the lower stages. Slowly the rocket lifted from the platform, straining against gravity to achieve the 17,000 miles per hour needed to reach orbit. Packed tightly in its fiberglass shroud was the world's first operational spy satellite.

The world was told that the package aboard the Thor contained two scientific satellites, one to measure solar radiation, known as SolarRad, and the other to aid in navigation. "Piggy-back Satellites Hailed as Big Space Gain for U.S. Satellite," said the headline in the *Washington Post* on the morning of June 23. But hidden within the SolarRad satellite was NRL's Elint bird, codenamed GRAB, for "Galactic Radiation and Background." At a dwarfish six watts and forty-two pounds, GRAB looked a bit like a silver soccer ball.

As GRAB orbited about 500 miles over Russia, it would collect the beeping pulses from the hundreds of radar systems throughout the forbidden land. The signals would then be retransmitted instantly on narrow VHF frequencies to small collection huts at ground stations in Turkey, Iran, and elsewhere, where they would be recorded on reels of magnetic tape. Flown to Washington aboard courier flights, the tapes would go to NRL scientists, who would convert the data into digital format and pass them on to NSA for analysis.

"At its altitude, being able to see clear to the horizon," said Mayo, "the circle that we were able to intercept from instantaneously was about three thousand or thirty-two hundred miles in diameter, depending on the altitude." On the other hand, he said, the ferret flights could hear only about 200 miles over the border. "NSA examined our data in great detail," Mayo added, "and found the first intercept of an ABM—an anti-ballistic missile—radar."

Despite the pint-sized spy's orbital altitude, Eisenhower was extremely concerned that the Soviets would discover its true mission. As a result, on each pass over Soviet territory his personal approval was required to turn on the receiver. "With Eisenhower's concern," said Mayo, "we turned it on [during] one pass. And then we'd leave it off, or take a holiday for the next pass. We were very conservative in using it over the Soviet Union."

An episode when Soviet ground control temporarily lost contact with a returning cosmonaut proved to be a bonanza for NSA—and GRAB—as Russian radar systems lit up like a Christmas tree. "They lost communications with him," said Mayo, "and turned on everything in their inventory to see if they could reestablish [contact]."

While the first mission concentrated on radars associated with air defense missiles, later launches relayed signals from Soviet long-range air surveillance radars and other systems. A second GRAB was launched on June 29, 1961, and remained operational through August 1962, when it was replaced with a more advanced system, codenamed Poppy. At the same time, NSA and the National Reconnaissance Office (NRO), which took over the building and management of all spy satellites, began working on a new generation of Sigint satellites. While the celestial soccer balls successfully charted the Soviet radar architecture, they were inefficient in eavesdropping on microwaves—thin, narrow beams of energy that carried sensitive voice and data communications. In their low orbits, the small satellites whizzed right through those beams with barely enough time to pick up a syllable.

More and more the Soviets began using microwaves and satellite communications rather than high-frequency signals and buried cables. High-frequency signals were unreliable, bouncing around the world like Ping-Pong balls and susceptible to sudden changes in the atmosphere. And because vast distances separated one side of the country from the other, and the ground in Siberia was frozen much or all of the year, buried cables were too expensive and difficult to install. Microwaves, on the other hand, needed only cheap repeater towers every twenty or so miles; satellite signals were not affected by the weather.

As a result, the Russians began sticking conical microwave antennas on buildings around major cities and setting up long rows of repeater towers, like steel sentries, linking officials in Moscow with commands in the Far East and elsewhere. The numerous repeater towers were necessary because microwave signals travel in a straight line, like a beam of light, rather than following the curve of the earth, like a train crossing the United States. For the eavesdroppers at NSA, the straight line was the key. With nothing to stop them, the microwave signals continue right into deep space, like an open telephone line. And because the numerous repeaters were fixed, the signals always ended up in the same place in space, creating a giant arc of communications. Thus, if NSA could set up its own receiver in space, at the point where those microwaves passed, they would essentially be tapping into tens of thousands of telephone calls, data transmissions, and telemetry signals.

The problem was gravity. If a low-orbiting satellite stopped in its tracks to pick up the microwave signals, it would tumble back to earth. The only way to avoid that was to put the satellite into a "geosynchronous" orbit, one that exactly matched the speed of the earth, like two cars traveling side by side on a freeway. But that geosynchronous orbit was a long way out—22,380 miles above the equator in deep space. Thus, more powerful rockets would be needed to get the heavy satellite out there, enormous antennas would have to be attached to pick up the weak signals, and new ground stations would have to be built to capture the flood of information.

For much of the 1960s engineers and scientists at NSA, NRO, and the aerospace firm TRW tested new lightweight screens, shrank components, and finely tuned receivers. The result was Rhyolite. NSA's first true listening post in space, it was designed to capture the line-of-sight signals that traveled like a flashlight beam into the deep black. TRW constructed the spacecraft in its M-4 facility at Redondo Beach, California, a windowless building with a large white dome on the roof, like the top of a grain silo. Known as the High Bay Area, it was where the satellite was fully assembled and tested. As in a hospital operating room, technicians in starchy white uniforms and lint-free nylon caps bent over their patient with delicate instruments, adjusting its miles of veinlike electrical lines and sensitive eardrums.

Far from the silver soccer balls, Rhyolite was a complex microwave receiver the size of a minibus with a large dish-shaped antenna pointed at earth. For electricity, the space bug had two long wings made of silicon cells to convert solar light to energy.

The first launch took place in 1970 from Cape Canaveral. Boosted into space atop a powerful Atlas-Agena D launch vehicle, it was eventually placed in geosynchronous orbit above the equator near Indonesia. There it was in a good position to collect signals from both the Soviet Union and China.

Chosen for Rhyolite's ground station was a godforsaken patch of earth at the center of Australia. Surrounded by a fearsome Mars-scape of red, sunburned desert, corrugated scrubland, waterless rivers, and parched saltbrush, Alice Springs had everything NSA wanted: isolation. To minimize the satellite's weight, its size, and its power requirements, encryption systems were never installed. Thus it was essential to keep the Soviets as far away from Rhyolite's downlink as possible. If a Sigint trawler, such as those off Guam and Cape Canaveral, or a listening post, like the one in Cuba or one within an embassy, were able to tap into the beam, the USSR would discover how NSA was eavesdropping and would take countermeasures.

"The satellites would pick up the signals and then they would be transmitted without encryption directly down to the ground station," said one former NSA official who worked on the project. "The satellite had about twenty-four receivers on it. The reason they put it in Alice Springs was because they didn't want the Russians to know what the satellite was sending down. By placing it in Alice Springs, the 'footprint' [of the signal] was small enough so that you couldn't eavesdrop on it outside Australia. They didn't want the Russians hearing it from their trawlers. They [NSA technicians at Alice Springs] would encrypt it and send it up to another satellite and then have it studied at NSA. Alice Springs would just receive the unencrypted signal, encrypt it, and retransmit it back to Fort Meade. They would do no codebreaking there. They didn't do anything except acquire the signal, lock the signal on, and when we had receiver problems they would work on them." Once completed, the NSA base at Alice Springs was named Pine Gap.

One of the problems with the earlier Rhyolite satellites, said the official, was their inability to discriminate among a plethora of signals. "They would pick up signals that they didn't necessarily know where they were coming from," he said. "They would have a language identification officer who would pick out what language it was and then bring in the person who handled that language to see if it was important enough to listen to. They would occasionally pick up [Soviet leader Leonid] Brezhnev."

Throughout the 1970s, NSA's Sigint satellites grew in size and sophistication. Larger, more capable spacecraft were launched into geosynchronous orbits, enough to eavesdrop on the entire earth except for the extreme northern regions. To cover these blind spots, "Jumpseat" satellites were developed. Rather than being placed in geosynchronous orbit, Jumpseat spacecraft flew an elliptical pattern that allowed them to, in essence, "hover" over the northern regions of Russia for long periods.

"They were huge umbrellas," said a former NSA official, "about forty meters [120 feet] across. There aren't any weak signals in space. What makes a signal weak is going through the atmosphere—hitting mountains and trees and so forth. But once they go into space there's nothing for it to hit so it's a real clear signal. Going from ground-based listening posts to satellites was like listening to an AM station from five hundred miles away to moving right into the same room the person is broadcasting from. We couldn't move in orbit but we could angle in orbit. We could point at Moscow or go over [to] the Far East. We always dealt in footprints—where's our footprint right now, what can we pick up."

Additional ground stations were also built or upgraded, both to receive downlinks from the Rhyolite-type satellites and from Russia's own military and civilian communications satellites. In addition to Pine Gap, NSA established major overseas satellite listening posts at Bad Aibling in Germany; Menwith Hill in Yorkshire, England; and Misawa, Japan. As one generation of satellites replaced another and more variations were added, codenames multiplied: Canon, Chalet, Vortex, Magnum, Orion, Mercury.

Just as NSA was soaring ahead in collection, it was also suddenly making great strides in codebreaking. "Around 1979 we were able to break into the Russian encrypted voice communication," said a former NSA official. "We would receive a signal and in order to understand the signal we would have to build a machine to exactly duplicate the signal before we could understand what it was. 'Rainfall' was secure, encrypted voice communications. I think what was so important is we were probably hearing secure encrypted voice communications better than they were hearing each other."

It was an enormous breakthrough, one of the most important since World War II. Thus it surprised few when A Group Chief Ann Caracristi was appointed deputy director of the agency in April 1980. Deputy director is the highest position to which an NSA civilian can rise.

While NSA was extending its electronic ear far into outer space, it was also reaching deep to the bottom of the oceans. In the summer of 1974, John Arnold, at NSA, was called to a private briefing on one of the agency's most secret operations: Ivy Bells. Over the course of two decades, Arnold had worked his way up from seaman to lieutenant commander, a highly unusual accomplishment. Along the way he had become an expert in undersea eavesdropping, leading teams on numerous submarine espionage missions close to the Soviet coast, including the 1962 mission to photograph and record the last of the Soviet aboveground nuclear tests, on Novaya Zemlya. It was he who later developed the device that saved the lives of hundreds of pilots in Vietnam by intercepting the signals generated by SA-2 missiles.

At the briefing, Arnold was told that for several years a small team of Navy Sigint specialists had been attempting to tap a key Soviet undersea communications cable on the bottom of the Sea of Okhotsk in Russia's Far East. Nearly surrounded by the Russian landmass, Okhotsk was more like a giant Soviet lake than a sea. The cable ran from the Kamchatka Peninsula, home of some of Russia's most sensitive submarine and missile testing facilities, to land cables connecting to Vladivostok, headquarters of the Soviet Pacific Fleet. An earlier submarine mission had located the cable by using its periscope to find a sign, posted on a small beach area, warning anyone present to be careful to avoid harming a buried cable. But while the sub, the USS *Halibut,* had succeeded in briefly tapping the cable, the results had been disappointing.

"They came back with very, very poor quality material and the NSA and the Navy were very upset," said Arnold. "NSA said, 'Hey, don't tease us like this. There's great stuff there if you could get some decent recordings.' " According to Arnold, "They had people who were Sigint qualified but not for cable tapping and they weren't versed in broadband recording and they weren't properly equipped either." As a result, Arnold was told to put together the best team of cable tappers he could find. "They basically said you can go anywhere in the world you want and pick your team because they didn't want another black eye." Arnold flew down to the Navy's Sabana Seca listening post in Puerto Rico and picked the first of four highly experienced chiefs for the job. Those four would join half a dozen other Navy Sigint experts, four divers, and the rest of the *Halibut*'s crew for nearly a year of secret training at NSA and elsewhere.

The mission got under way from Mare Island, near San Francisco, in June 1975. About a month later, the *Halibut* quietly arrived in the mouth of the bear—the Sea of Okhotsk—and, after several days of searching, located the cable. Like a moon lander, she slowly settled down on the mucky bottom, black clouds of silt rising in the total darkness. Specially designed to sit on the floor of the sea for weeks at a time, the *Halibut* was equipped with unique sledlike skis to keep the round bottom from rolling.

On board, excitement built as preparations were made to begin the tap. By now, despite the secrecy of the operation, everyone on board had been briefed, from the cooks to the senior officers. "If you know the truth you respect it and handle it accordingly," said Arnold. "But if you treat them like dumdums and they aren't supposed to know anything, that irritates them and a lot of times, the speculation is worse than the truth."

Arnold and his team worked out of a tiny converted storeroom, amidships just forward of the reactor compartment. On the other side was the radio shack, which was crammed with additional Sigint specialists, mainly Russian linguists. The four divers were sealed in a diving-bell–like contraption. The device looked like a deep-sea rescue vehicle, but it wasn't going anywhere—it was welded to the top deck. Inside the cramped, uncomfortable decompression chamber the divers had lived for about a week. Special gases in the pressurized, tube-shaped room were mixed to equalize their bodies to the 400-foot depths where the sub was parked. The room consisted of four cots and a "poop bucket."

With the pressure equalized to that of the sea outside, two of the divers opened the hatch of the lockout chamber and made their way out into the frigid blackness. Inside their wetsuits, warm water was pumped by an umbilical cord to keep them from freezing. Other tethers supplied a witches' brew of gases to breathe and a communications cable. A third diver stood at the hatch and fed out the cord while the fourth, also suited up, remained behind as a backup.

Once free of the hatch, the two divers went to a sealed compartment on the side of the sub and pulled out a long, thick electrical cord, like a giant set of jumper cables. In fact, this was the tap, plugged into the side of the boat. After some searching, the divers found what they were looking for: a large round metal cylinder known as a repeater. In fact, the sub had landed right on top of the cable—standing above it on its snowmobilelike skis. Located every twenty or thirty miles along the fist-thick cable, the repeaters boosted the signals like amplifiers. "That's where you get the best signal," said Arnold, "because on the one side of the repeater you've got strong signals coming out going [in] one direction and on the other side of the repeater you've got strong signals coming out going in the opposite direction. So you have the best of situations—strong signals in both directions."

As they began securing the tapping device around a cable in the repeater, one of the divers was suddenly attacked: "They had a big fish glom on to the arm of one of the divers," said Arnold. "Tried to bite him. He couldn't shake him off so he took his knife out and had to kill it to get it off. It was a good-size fish." On the way back to the sub, the divers picked up a few crabs for dinner.

Meanwhile, in the special operations spaces panic was beginning to break out. Arnold and his team were turning dials and flipping switches but could hear absolutely nothing. Some feared the Soviets might have discovered the operation and shut off the cable. The divers returned to the repeater, where they discovered they had attached the tap to a "pigtail"—a short spiral wire double-wrapped in both directions so that there would be no signal leakage. This time they attached the tap to one of the active, unshielded cables and again returned to the sub. "It's done by induction," said Arnold. "There's no physical penetration or damage to the cable. It worked on the inductive leakage of the cable." In a sense, such a tap is a complex version of the suction cup on the receiver used by many people on their home and business phones to record their conversations.

This time there was a collective sigh of relief in the special operations room: the sounds were loud and clear. "This is what we came for, guys," Arnold said. The Soviet cable contained scores of channels using "frequency division multiplex." "We could separate them for analysis purposes, but we recorded the entire thing on a broadband recorder. Plenty of channels." The recording was done on tape decks using ten-inch-wide reels and thick, two-inch tape. "We could tune in to any of the channels and listen to them. It had all kinds of stuff—you name it, it was there," said Arnold.

Flowing through the cables and onto NSA's tape recorders were the voices of Soviet military commanders discussing military and naval operations and data transfers between commands. Some transmissions were in the clear, some encrypted.

After the sub had spent about fourteen days on the bottom, filling reel after reel with sensitive Soviet communications, an alarm went off. A gushing leak had occurred in a pipe connecting a diesel engine—used to provide an emergency start—to the hull. To make matters worse, divers were out of the sub, at the repeater, and they might not have enough time to return. "It was a difficult decision for the skipper to make," said Arnold. "He's got the decision, do I blow off the bottom and save the ship and lose the divers, or do I stay on the bottom and potentially lose the ship and can't control the flooding? The water's twenty-eight degrees, so the guys that are working on stopping the flooding are getting numb real quick." Luckily, the flooding was stopped before that decision had to be made.

Following the near disaster, the captain cut the mission a bit short and sailed to Guam for repairs. But it was to be a brief stay; the plan was for the *Halibut* to return for a second mission after the repairs were completed, in about three weeks. Arnold had all the tapes strapped to several pallets and loaded on an Air Force C-141 for a flight back to Washington. "We turned in probably seven hundred recordings, broadband recordings," said Arnold. "NSA was elated. They had never seen such good recordings—and such significant material. It was a gold mine for them. . . . The stuff was so good that NSA wanted more as soon as they could get it."

About a month later, Arnold and the ship returned for another three weeks on the bottom of the Sea of Okhotsk, eventually providing NSA with hundreds of additional tapes. Over the following years, mammoth twenty-foot-long pods were built and installed on the Okhotsk cable, as well as on one up in the Bering Sea. This allowed the subs to leave the tap on the cable for up to a year before returning to recover it. But much of the project was compromised when a former NSA employee, hurting for money, sold details of the operation to Soviet intelligence around 1980. Nevertheless, for as long as the tap lasted, NSA was able to go where no one could have ever dreamed.

At the height of the cable tapping operation, a new director moved into Room 9A197 in the Headquarters Building—a director who was thoroughly familiar with the project long before he arrived at Fort Meade. On the day after Independence Day, 1977, Vice Admiral Bobby Ray Inman became the youngest director in NSA's history.

It had been a long ride from the tumbleweed hamlet of Rhonesboro, the East Texas town where Inman grew up. Far from any thoroughfares and absent from most maps, Rhonesboro was a forgotten backwater halfway between Dallas and the Louisiana border. Gangly, gap-toothed, Inman seemed out of place in the hardscrabble town of 200, where his father operated the local Sinclair gasoline station. He soon found that the best way to keep from becoming a punching bag in the restroom of Mineola High was to turn his enemies into his protectors. He did this by ingratiating himself with his bullies, helping them with their homework so they could squeak by in class. At the same time he curried favor with the school's social and political elite by helping them in their campaigns for class office. These were lessons he would long remember.

By the mid-1970s the fast-rising admiral had been named director of Naval Intelligence. There, he worked closely with NSA on the cable tapping operation. He also worked on a highly secret operation to spy on Russian naval activities south of South Africa. This led him to a long relationship with a shady American businessman who ran a small company started in a chicken coop behind his Pennsylvania home.

Named International Signal and Control, the company was run by James Guerin, who was anxious to find a way to sell electronic equipment to South Africa. The major problem with this scheme was the U.S. ban on all economic commerce with South Africa as a result of that government's apartheid policies. Guerin's solution was to agree to become a covert agent for Project X, the unoriginal codename for a questionable joint NSA/Naval Intelligence operation whose purpose was to help the racist Pretoria government upgrade its secret listening post at its Simontown naval station, off the Cape of Good Hope. NSA would give the South African intelligence service superadvanced eavesdropping and optical equipment to spy on Russian ships and submarines as they transited past the southern tip of Africa; in return, the U.S. agency would get access to the raw information.

To hide the shipments of secret equipment to an embargoed nation, a civilian cutout was needed. That was where Guerin and his ISC came in. But—apparently unbeknownst to Inman—Guerin had his own agenda. Not only would he act as the conduit to transship the bugging equipment, he would also use the covert channel to supply South Africa with desperately needed electronic equipment, providing him with a tidy profit. Guerin was to work secretly for Inman until 1978.

When Inman moved into his office on NSA's "Mahogany Row," in July 1977, it was not his first assignment to the agency. In 1961 he had become an operations intelligence analyst at the Navy Field Operational Intelligence Office at the agency. "I was an analyst for thirty-three months looking at the Soviet Navy as my prime occupation in a complete all-source environment," said Inman. "That means no category of intelligence were restricted in their flow for my consideration so long as they dealt with the general topic of the Soviet Navy. I was watching them at a time when they rarely sent any ships two hundred miles beyond their waters, and when they did the units frequently broke down and had to be towed back. By the time I left three years later I had seen them develop a permanent presence in the Mediterranean and off West Africa, and they were building a framework for their presence in the Indian Ocean."

Now the junior analyst had returned as the director, like the prodigal son. "The idea of going back to be director had always been one of those wishful dreams that appeared to be unobtainable," Inman recalled. "When I became the director of Naval Intelligence, which is after I had gotten my first star, suddenly the prospect that I might be around long enough to get a three-star job was there. So NSA was clearly top of the list. . . . I very much wanted the NSA job. . . . There had never been any doubt that in my view it was the best of all the [intelligence] agencies."

To help bring Inman up to date on the issues affecting NSA, the outgoing director, Lew Allen, gave him some highly classified reading. An Air Force general, Allen had been promoted to four-star rank and would shortly take over the Air Force as Chief of Staff. It was a major reward for guiding the agency through the various intelligence probes of the mid-1970s.

Among the documents given Inman to study was one on the problems involved in breaking Soviet encryption systems. At the time, A Group had not yet achieved its breakthrough. The document, said Inman, "had all kinds of VRK [Very Restricted Knowledge—a supersecret NSA classification] restrictions on it. But it was an extraordinarily thoughtful examination of the A5 problem [A5 was part of A Group] and the absolute critical role in going forward, finding success in those areas if the mission was going to be successful."

Looking out the ninth-floor window on his new empire, Inman quickly began to build a cadre of loyal spear-carriers. He was looking for what he called "the water walkers." Those, he said, "who were the people at that stage of the game who looked to be potential major leaders of the agency." Inman also began looking for a new deputy director. At the time, Benson K. (Buff) Buffham, a former deputy chief of operations, held the job, but his term was almost up. It was widely assumed that Robert E. Drake, the deputy director for operations, was next in line. Without much enthusiasm, Inman named him to the post. "I had it in my mind from the beginning," he recalled, "that about two years for Bob and then time to get on to the next generation. [But] I was not persuaded that any of them were quite ready . . . so I sort of shocked the place by picking Ann Caracristi. I had watched the job she had done running A [Group]."

Inman added, "I decided to go with one more of the World War II generation. Ann knew that I wanted to be *the* director in a somewhat different role than in the long years when Lou Tordella had been the deputy [and éminence grise]. She had no problem." Inman also didn't want to see deputy directors overstaying their time. "I set out to try to get a pattern where deputy directors did somewhere between two and four years," he said. "I think [Tordella] stayed too long in the process."

Inman wanted not just to represent NSA throughout the intelligence community, but also to run the day-to-day operations, something previous directors had left to the cryptologic professional, the deputy director. "I had a sense in my first couple of months that the internal agency's view of the director was sort of like, Treat him like the pharaoh. Bear him around. Put him down for honors and ceremonies. Send him off to deal with the outside world and not get very involved in what went on inside. I am a very hands-on person who likes to get all over an organization." Inman began walking around and sticking his head in the various offices—another highly unusual behavior for a director. At one point he stopped in G Group, which was responsible for the noncommunist parts of the world. "I walked into G7 spaces on about the fourth of these visits," he said, "and there was a banner on the wall in case I came. It said, 'Welcome, Admiral Inman. You will be the first director to visit G7 since General Canine.' "

When Inman arrived, the agency was still recovering from the trauma of dual Senate and House investigations into the intelligence community. Determined to rebuild congressional confidence in NSA, Inman worked, as he had in high school, to turn his adversaries into allies. Instead of tutoring his bullies, he would tutor the powerful chairmen and members of the Senate and House Intelligence Committees. The committee members had long been accustomed to absolute secrecy and a "Don't worry, we'll tell you what you need to know" attitude; Inman would win their praises with heavy doses of uncharacteristic candor and gushing flattery. "Few could understand this but you," he would privately tell members, beaming boyishly. Such remarks, said former intelligence committee staffer Angelo Codevilla, "were enough to convince most of Inman's contacts, liberal and conservative, that they were fellow geniuses."

Inman's plan worked as well as it had back at Mineola High. To Congress he was the wonder boy, the spook who could do no wrong; hearings became love-ins. "You have my vote even before I hear your testimony," said the Senate Intelligence Committee chairman, Barry M. Goldwater, adding, "I don't know of a man in the business that is more highly regarded than you." Delaware's senator Joseph Biden dubbed him the "single most competent man in the government."

At the same time Inman neutralized much of the elite Washington press corps by currying their favor, becoming their leaker-in-chief. No one in the press, he correctly calculated, would risk eliminating one of their best—or only—"senior intelligence sources" by criticizing him or his agency. He also developed as allies the senior editors and executives of the most powerful newspapers and networks, installing them as honorary members of his club so that they would keep in check any rogue reporter who might contemplate breaching his fortress.

In a city where someone can be transformed from a hero to a Hitler between commercial breaks, Inman became a near divinity. *Omni* magazine, in an article entitled "The Smartest Spy," called him "simply one of the smartest people ever to come out of Washington or anywhere," while *Newsweek* referred to him as "a superstar in the intelligence community." The *Washington Post,* in an editorial, once said, "Inman's reviews are extraordinary, almost hyperbolic." Inman's philosophy boiled down to a few understated words: "I have over the years practiced a general theory of conservation of enemies."

"He certainly knew how to play the game," said John Walcott, a former reporter for *Newsweek*, the *Wall Street Journal,* and *Time,* who often dealt with Inman. Another reporter later described him as "the single biggest leaker of intelligence information in the last 10 to 15 years." The *New York Times,* years later, also acknowledged that Inman, indeed, "was a valued source of news for the paper's Washington bureau."

Some saw Inman's approach to both Congress and the press as more sinister than cynical. As the head of the NSA, said Suzanne Garment of the American Enterprise Institute, "Inman was in control of unequaled information—and, say his critics, disinformation—that put him in a dominant position in these exchanges." Given the NSA's "ability to listen in on all overseas phone calls," she said, "he could protect people and give the impression of including them in the inner circles of power. Some were happy to pay for these privileges with sympathetic writing and legislative action. Some did not know they were paying."

Another writer put it more bluntly: "There were certain rules, of course: You never named him; you never attributed the tidbits he gave you; you never, in fact, did anything he didn't want you to do, or the invitations to breakfast stopped. . . . During his time at NSA, exposés of the agency all but disappeared."

When Inman wasn't whispering his own leaks to the media, he was trying to get others plugged. A few months after he arrived at NSA, a *New York Times* article that crossed his desk enraged him. Republican Illinois Congressman Edward J. Derwinski, the paper alleged, was under investigation for tipping off top South Korean officials that their country's New York intelligence chief was about to defect. What burned Inman was a reference to the fact that the way the FBI got on to the alleged leak was through NSA intercepts of calls between Derwinski, who was never charged with any wrongdoing, and the South Korean officials.

Inman flew to New York to complain in person to publisher A. O. (Punch) Sulzberger. During the lunch at the *Times* Manhattan offices, Inman made his pitch that he be called prior to any future stories involving NSA. On his flight back he believed he had a secret agreement in his pocket, but Sulzberger apparently had a different opinion. He never passed any formal instructions on to his editors. Nevertheless, in the course of normal journalistic reporting, editors frequently ran NSA-related stories past Inman. "The truth is there was nothing nearly as formal as [Inman] suggested," said Nicholas Horrock, who headed the *Times* investigative unit at the time, "but lots of reporters, at the *Times* and elsewhere, called Inman to check out stories."

Also among those with Inman's phone number close at hand was the *Washington Post*'s Bob Woodward. But Woodward occasionally proposed a story Inman didn't like, and in that case the admiral would go over his head, to Ben Bradlee or Howard Simons, then the *Post*'s managing editor, seeking to get the offending material removed.

Despite his boy-wonder reputation, Inman suffered from a deep sense of insecurity. His self-image never reached much higher than the tops of his spit-polished Navy shoes. Rhonesboro had followed him to Fort Meade and would never leave him. Embarrassed by his gapping teeth, he was almost never photographed with his lips open. He would also drop the "Bobby Ray" from his official correspondence, preferring simply "B. R. Inman." "My name is really Bobby Ray, much as I hate it," he once said, "but that is my real name."

At work, he saw himself as the consummate outsider, always seeking but never quite reaching the inner circle. After a day of lavish praise, he would wake up in the middle of the night, unable to sleep because of a single word of criticism. Once, following a whispering campaign about whether he was a closet homosexual, because he hadn't fired a gay NSA employee, he felt it necessary to deny publicly that he was gay. For "proof," he pointed to a lie detector exam in which he had denied any homosexuality. The polygraph examiner, said Inman, had found his answer "not deceptive." Nearly obsessed with the issue, he went out of his way to tell others that the reason he had gay friends was that he "deliberately [sought them out] to try to understand them."

While most saw only the confident, super-smart admiral, beneath his membrane-thin shell was a boiling caldron of anger and arrogance, a man "wound tighter than a hummingbird in Saran Wrap," according to one observer. Another was reminded of Captain Queeg of *The Caine Mutiny*. Still others saw a man who had lived so long in the hidden world of spies that he now saw plots everywhere.

Among the first to get a peek of the other Inman was *New York Times* columnist William L. Safire. Unaware of the secret "deal" Inman had supposedly made with the publisher of his newspaper, Safire telephoned Inman a few weeks later seeking information for a column. Inman refused to provide any help or information to Safire, a former Nixon speechwriter who felt he deserved a leak as much as anyone. As a result, according to Inman, the columnist "was very direct that if I didn't become a source, I would regret it in subsequent coverage." Safire denied having made any such threat.

A few years later, in 1980, Safire wrote another column, this one devoted to "Billygate," the scandal involving allegations that President Jimmy Carter's brother, Billy, was working as a business agent on behalf of the Libyan government. The tip-off came as a result of NSA's secret monitoring of all communications into and out of Libya. In his column Safire congratulated Inman for his "considerable courage" in reporting to the attorney general about the president's brother.

Inman was livid at Safire for bypassing his secret standing order that any mention of NSA's operations first be sent to him for "guidance." He believed that Safire's article had caused the loss of "critical access that gave us a lot of information on terrorists." Sitting at his oversize wooden desk, Inman picked up the "red" telephone used for unclassified outside calls and dialed Safire's number. According to the columnist, the admiral "denounced [me] for doing . . . irreparable harm . . . by revealing our sources and methods." But Safire would have none of it, instead asking Inman how a "grown man could go through life calling himself Bobby." At that point, said Safire, Inman "slammed down the phone."

Safire, however, would have the last word. In a column published shortly after the phone-slamming incident, he raked Inman over the coals for appearing as a guest on ABC's *Nightline,* a strange decision for the director of the nation's most secret spy agency. "The nation's chief eavesdropper," Safire wrote, was "blabbing about sources and methods on late-night TV."

Much of Inman's tenure was divided between trying to ensure an NSA monopoly in the field of cryptography and working out protective legislation for NSA's Sigint operations with the Senate and House Intelligence Committees. To eliminate outside competition in the cryptographic field, Inman took the unprecedented step of going public in a number of lectures and interviews. Most of these, however, were low-key affairs, intended to attract little attention and to produce even less substance.

With regard to his unusual decision to make public appearances, Inman told one group, "I try to do it out of any glare of publicity, because of my conviction that the heads of the intelligence agencies should not be public figures. . . . If they are, if the work force sees their profiles day after day on the front page of the paper, on television, on the weekly magazine cover, and sees them getting all the credit for what they're doing, it's a little hard for them to enforce the discipline of protecting secrecy."

In 1981, with the election of Ronald Reagan as president, Inman left NSA to become the deputy director of the CIA under William J. Casey. But the two never hit it off. Casey saw Inman as "a brittle golden boy, worried about his image." The following year he resigned and entered private industry, where he accepted a paid position on his old friend James Guerin's "proxy board," required to guard against the transfer of sensitive defense information to foreign governments. But within a few years, while Inman was on the board, Guerin had reopened his illegal pipeline to South Africa, this time sending highly sensitive military equipment, such as photo-imaging systems and advanced radar-controlled antiaircraft parts, to the apartheid government. Casey's CIA, which knew of the operation, had turned a blind eye.

About the same time, Guerin also became a major arms dealer, specializing in deadly cluster bombs. In 1984 it was discovered that sensitive bomb-making design information had been illegally transferred to a company in Chile that was manufacturing cluster bombs for the armed forces of Iraq. Although a long federal investigation followed, the Justice Department was never able to make any arrests. Also, there is no evidence that Inman was aware of the deals.

But by the end of the decade, Guerin's greed had finally gotten the best of him. He was convicted of masterminding a $1.4 billion fraud, which one federal judge described as "the largest . . . ever perpetrated in North America." He was also convicted of money laundering and of smuggling $50 million in weapons to South Africa. Other allegations had Guerin improperly selling missile technology to Iraq. Sentenced to fifteen years in prison, Guerin still had Bobby Inman's support. At Guerin's sentencing, Inman wrote a letter praising his "patriotism."

Once NSA was the unwanted stepchild of powerful spymasters such as Allen Dulles, who refused its director a seat on the Intelligence Advisory Committee. But by the late 1970s the agency had grown so secret and powerful that the head of the CIA was complaining that it was almost beyond control. By then NSA had become a well-oiled spying machine, with its own army, navy, and air force; hundreds of secret listening posts throughout the world; and massive bugs deep in space. Its printing plant worked twenty-four hours a day turning out its own reports, analyses, high-level transcripts, and projections. Powerful congressmen were treating Bobby Inman as the dark prince of intelligence, an infallible all-knowing wizard. Suddenly NSA had gone from a 98-pound weakling, rubbing the CIA's sand from its eyes, to a superstar.

With billions of dollars at stake, there followed a war of the admirals—Inman at NSA and Stansfield Turner at CIA—over gargantuan satellite programs. Inman pushed to fill the skies with more and bigger ears, and Turner argued instead to seed the heavens with electronic eyes. Little wonder that palace intrigue abounded. For Inman, it was Mineola High, only for bigger stakes. Now instead of currying favor with a class officer, he was quietly passing highly secret reports to a powerful congressman to win support for his projects.

When Senator Daniel Inouye (D-Hawaii) of the Intelligence Committee said he needed some secret NSA files, Inman didn't wait to get White House or CIA approval. "I said, 'Sure,' " Inman recalled, "and sent a guy running off down to deliver them to Inouye." A short while later, Inman heard from a boiling Zbigniew Brzezinski, the president's national security adviser. "Admiral, I understand that you are sending sensitive material to Inouye. Who authorized that?" he demanded. "I authorized it!" Inman shot back. "You didn't consult Stan Turner or the secretary of defense?" asked Brzezinski. "I said, 'It is within my authority and I authorized it,' " said Inman. "And he hung up." As always, Inman got away with it and his legend grew within Congress as a man who could be trusted, a man who got things done.

Administration officials seldom said no to Inman. When he proposed a budget-busting project, every effort was made to accommodate him. "What we wanted to do was so massive that there was no way you could do it within the existing budget," he said of one super-expensive Soviet collection project. At the Pentagon, Secretary of Defense Harold Brown suggested that rather than adding money to NSA's budget, they cut something. "I told him he couldn't," said Inman. "That this had to be an augment. That its potential, if it could ever be successful, had enormous value, primarily for defense." Inman got his money. "Turner later gave me hell for not having developed it through him," said Inman, arrogantly adding, "At the time I was polite and let it just roll off."

Congress was a cakewalk. Inman briefed the chairmen of the House and Senate Intelligence Committees and Congressman George Mahon (D–Texas) of the House Appropriations Committee. "He did not understand a word I said," said Inman, mockingly. "Then it was just simply, 'Son, if that's [what] you-all think is what ought to be done, that is just fine. We'll take care of it.' "

At the CIA, Turner was rapidly becoming worried about NSA's obsession with secrecy and power. According to Turner, matters had reached the point where the NSA no longer even trusted the CIA and other members of the intelligence community with some of its most important information. "My concern was over the stuff that didn't get out of NSA at all," he said after leaving the CIA. "They were sitting on it, waiting for a scoop, or saying, 'This is too sensitive to let out.' "

According to Turner, Inman was not satisfied with simply overtaking the CIA in espionage, he also wanted to surpass it in analysis. "The NSA is mandated to collect intelligence, not analyze it," Turner said. "It must do enough analysis about what it has collected to decide what to collect next. In intelligence jargon, this level of analysis is called processing. Processing is regularly stretched by NSA into full-scale analysis."

Some of the intelligence NSA released to other American spy agencies, according to Turner, was so sanitized—stripped of sensitive information—that it was almost useless. This amounted, he said, "to deliberate withholding of raw information from the true analytic agencies. NSA wants to get credit for the scoop." While NSA defended the practice by arguing that it was simply protecting its supersecret "sources and methods," Turner had a different view. He said there was no doubt in his mind that NSA regularly and deliberately drew the curtain in order "to make itself look good rather than to protect secrets."

In the NSA-CIA spy war, Inman began having similar complaints about Turner's obsession with secrecy. During the planning for the elaborate 1980 attempt to rescue the American embassy employees held hostage by radical Iranian forces in Tehran, NSA was cut out of the loop. "We weren't getting into the quest for support or anything else," said Inman. "It turned out that Turner was providing all the intelligence support for the hostage rescue planning." In fact, Inman only learned about the planning accidentally, through NSA's own Sigint. One day someone brought some suspicious intercepted messages up to him. "I agreed instantly that it had all the connotations of being a U.S. operation going on, some kind of planning," he recalled. "It was pretty early."

When the rescue attempt took place, NSA played a major role, and then it was Turner complaining that the CIA was being cut out. "When the time came," said Inman, "we were able to provide, in a minute-by-minute way, what was happening to [the Joint Chiefs at the Pentagon and] directly to [Secretary of Defense] Harold Brown, who was sitting over in the White House. And to Turner's later allegation that he was deliberately cut out of it to diminish his role or whatever is simply—he had no interest!"

According to Inman, NSA unwittingly played a role in the mission's eventual failure. Angered that his agency had been cut out of the planning, Inman warned Air Force General David C. Jones, the chairman of the Joint Chiefs of Staff, that NSA had discovered it because of poor communications security procedures. Shocked, Jones ordered drastic radio silence procedures; he even ordered that the choppers not be flown until the last minute, so that no stray signal might be intercepted.

"Jones was so stunned by the potential of blowing the security at the beginning," said Inman, "that he then imposed awesome communications security constraints and it probably directly impacted on the readiness of the forces. The fact that the helicopters were put on carriers, sent for five weeks, never flown until they left the carrier—all of this out of concern that [they] would be detected in the process . . . He was directly driven to it by the impression made on him [by NSA] that the cat was almost out of the bag because he had not brought NSA into the process." The radio silence, the lack of pre-mission helicopter training, and the choppers' condition after they sat unused on the carrier deck for so long all contributed to the disaster.

Years later, President Clinton nominated Inman to replace Les Aspin as secretary of defense. During his speech in the White House Rose Garden accepting the nomination, Inman stunned many people by making an arrogant reference to a need to find a "comfort level" with the man who had just nominated him.

But during the routine background investigation the old rumors about Inman being gay came up. Inman had denied the rumors to Joel Klein, the White House lawyer assigned to supervise the background check—the same type of check performed when he went to NSA. But Clinton aide George Stephanopoulos was worried. "If the rumors of Inman's being gay could be proved true, there was no way he'd be confirmed as secretary of defense," he said. "He'd get hit from both sides: by conservatives who believed that homosexuality was a disqualifying condition and by gay-rights advocates who would argue, justifiably, that it was hypocritical to have a homosexual defense secretary when gays and lesbians were prohibited from serving openly in the military."

Suddenly Inman had a confession. "When the president was first considering my appointment," he told Klein over the telephone from his vacation cabin in Vail, "I told you only ninety percent of the truth. Here's the other ten." Although still denying that he was gay, he disclosed parts of his private life that he had kept from the initial background check. "Had we known the full story a month earlier, the president would not have chosen Inman," said Stephanopoulos. "Once the Senate investigators finished digging through Inman's life, everything would be public, and Inman would not be confirmed."

Strobe Talbott, one of Inman's most ardent supporters, called the White House to argue the admiral's case. He said that Inman had explained away the concealed behavior as "a way to get attention." "The rest of us rolled our eyes," said Stephanopoulos. "Then Joel told Talbott about his most recent conversation with Inman. Even if you made the dubious assumption that Inman's private life would remain private during the confirmation process, we had a problem: the fact that Inman had misled the White House."

The decision was to dump him, fast. But because Inman had deliberately placed Clinton in an embarrassing position, the responsibility was on him to make a graceful exit. "The only option was for him to withdraw quietly, but the flinty and flighty admiral wasn't ready for that," said Stephanopoulos. Instead, Inman decided to go out blaming everyone but himself for his problems. He did it in a live television news conference the likes of which no one had ever seen before. Over an hour peppered with rambling accusations, Inman charged that he was the victim of a "new McCarthyism," that Senator Bob Dole and the columnist William Safire had conspired against him, and that he had been the target of "hostile" press coverage. To Stephanopoulos, Inman looked "like a man who was broadcasting instructions transmitted through the fillings in his teeth."

Rather than admit he had been dumped, Inman later tried to make it sound like he never really wanted the job in the first place. "I'm arrogant," he said. "And I've got a temper. And people are probably right when they say I should have a thicker skin. But I was pissed off. . . . Hell, I didn't want the job in the first place. The dumb decision was accepting."

Named on March 10, 1981, to fill Inman's chair at NSA was his old friend Lincoln D. Faurer, a fifty-three-year-old Air Force lieutenant general with gray hair and a buzz cut. A native of Medford, Massachusetts, Faurer graduated from West Point and spent most of his career carrying out intelligence and strategic reconnaissance assignments, commanding RB-47s in the 1950s, and taking over a surveillance squadron on the frigid Aleutian island of Shemya during the late 1960s. During the 1970s, Faurer served variously as the director of intelligence for the U.S. Southern Command; Air Force deputy assistant Chief of Staff for Intelligence; vice director for production at the Defense Intelligence Agency; director of intelligence at the U.S. European Command; and deputy chairman of the NATO Military Committee.

When Faurer arrived, Crypto City was undergoing the largest construction boom in its history. The enormous building program was adding a million square feet to his headquarters/operations complex, at a cost of $130 million, plus another million square feet with new buildings for the Technology and Systems Organization and other facilities. Under President Reagan, money for the spy world would flow as if from a faucet with the handle broken off. Fat times were coming to NSA.

Unlike Inman, Faurer was determined to keep out of the spotlight; he began rebuilding the agency's wall of anonymity. Speaking to a group of NSA retirees, he gave them a not-so-subtle warning to forever keep their mouths shut. "Leaks are not the answer," he scolded. "They are dangerous, destructive, and inexcusable. Both the source and user of leaked classified information should be met with public disapprobation, and media judgment in disclosing intelligence accomplishments should be criticized. If free speech and free press are to remain the cornerstone of our society, given the growing strength of our adversary, 'free' must not be synonymous with 'irresponsible.' " He then quoted George Washington: " 'The necessity for procuring good intelligence is apparent and need not be further urged—all that remains for me to add is that you keep the whole matter as secret as possible.' "

Blunt, lacking Inman's tact and charisma as well as his many friends in Congress, Faurer was allegedly pushed out the door. After four years in office, the general was due to retire in August 1985. But over the previous winter he had become embroiled in a major budget fight. In order to divert money to NSA, the Pentagon, and the rest of the intelligence community, Reagan dammed up the flow to many social programs. Angered at the rising federal budget deficits and worried about their impact on the 1986 congressional elections, Democrats and many Republicans lit a fire under the administration to cut back on defense spending. In response, Secretary of Defense Caspar W. Weinberger began targeting a number of programs for cuts. High on his agenda was placing NSA's overweight frame on a diet.

But Faurer would have none of it. He believed that NSA's Crypto City should continue its rapid growth, not slow down. At the same time, Faurer wanted still another new building constructed in NSA's city to house the National Cryptologic School, which was located at its annex a few miles away. Speaking to former NSA employees in 1982, he boasted how well NSA was doing. "The health of the Agency is great," he said. "There's no question about that . . . and can get nothing but greater." He then went on to complain of the need for even more space and people. He pointed out that in 1960, only about 35 percent of NSA office space was occupied by computers and other equipment but that now the figure had almost doubled, to 65 percent. "You can imagine what that does for crowding people in," he protested. "It has left us with a significant workspace problem." Despite all the new construction going on and planned for the future, Faurer said only that Congress had been "somewhat" responsive.

He also blasted those in the Congress and the Pentagon who were attempting to slow down the growth of his secret city. In particular, he pointed to what he called the "negative impact" of "budget constraints," especially the cutback in analysts. "The analysts' numbers have been excessively drawn down," he said, "the scope of their target unwisely narrowed, their confidence eroded by uninformed criticism, and the language of their judgments too often hedged against the inevitable cry of 'intelligence failure.' "

Faced with the ordered cuts, Faurer fought back, arguing that the reductions could lead to erosion of future intelligence capabilities. His continued resistance "created a big fuss in the intelligence community," said one official. As a result, "to put an end to the agonizing over this issue," Cap Weinberger reportedly suggested that Faurer speed up his retirement. Faurer then decided to "go out in a blaze of glory," said one report, by submitting his retirement papers immediately, on March 19. A week later he was gone. The Pentagon denied that Faurer was pressured to leave.

Faurer's premature departure put the Pentagon on the spot to quickly come up with a replacement. The Joint Chiefs of Staff recommended to Weinberger the name of a Navy admiral, but the CIA's Casey reportedly found him unacceptable because he had only one year's experience in the intelligence field. Next in line was Lieutenant General William Odom, the Army's intelligence chief. Despite objections from some within the Reagan administration, who were unhappy that Odom had served in the Carter White House, and others, who wanted to see Odom instead take over the Defense Intelligence Agency, he was formally installed on May 8, 1985, six weeks after Faurer's stormy departure.

A balding, owl-faced officer with large round glasses, who once taught Russian history at West Point, Odom had risen rapidly in rank and position as a result of the backing of Zbigniew Brzezinski. The two met at Columbia, where Brzezinski was a professor and Odom was attending graduate school while in the Army. Eventually Odom, an archconservative military hard-liner, became Brzezinski's military assistant, picking up the nickname "Zbig's Super-Hawk." While in the Carter administration, Odom worked on such issues as the Soviet invasion of Afghanistan and the Iranian capture of the U.S. embassy in Tehran. He quickly rose to the rank of brigadier general. Shortly after President

Reagan moved into the White House, Odom took over the top job in Army intelligence.

Odom, stern, abrasive, and humorless, was widely disliked at NSA and was considered by many the most ineffective director in the agency's history. He also developed a reputation as a Captain Queeg of secrecy, claiming that intelligence leaks to the news media had resulted in "paralysis" and "major misjudgments" in U.S. foreign and military policies and could lead to war. As examples he cited the diminution in the U.S. ability to follow and deal with terrorist activities and the failure to properly gauge Soviet strategic force growth in the 1960s and 1970s. "Quite simply," Odom told a group of old spies, "there is no comprehensive 'right to know' included, either explicitly or implicitly, within the First Amendment." He added, "Perhaps if the public were informed of the damage done, the media would be compelled to provide a better accounting for their actions." But Odom was an extremist on secrecy, equating journalists with spies and calling one an "unconvicted felon" for daring to write about NSA.

Odom was also critical both of Congress and of other officials within the Reagan administration whom he blamed for leaks. "There's leaking from Congress," he informed the group; "there's more leaking in the administration because it's bigger." Then he seemed to name President Reagan as the worst leaker of all. The previous year Reagan had publicly blamed Libya for the terrorist bombing of the La Belle discothèque in West Berlin—a club known to attract off-duty U.S. servicemen—which killed two American soldiers and a Turkish woman, and injured 230 other people. Reagan ordered a retaliatory strike against Tripoli and then appeared on national television. In order to justify the attack by American aircraft, Reagan summarized three Libyan messages intercepted by NSA as "irrefutable" proof of Libya's involvement in the bombing. In doing so he no doubt made it clear to the country's leader, Muammar Qaddafi, that he'd better change his codes or get new crypto equipment. In his blast over leaks Odom said, "Leaks have damaged the system more in the past three to four years than in a long, long time." Then, asked about the disclosure of the Libyan intercepts, which had been revealed by President Reagan, Odom said, "Libya, sure. Just deadly losses." He refused, however, to elaborate.

Odom also created a storm over his handling of the aftermath of the Iran-contra scandal. In December 1985, as a cabal of Washington officials, including William Casey, plotted to send missiles to Iran in exchange for the release of hostages being held in Lebanon, Lieutenant Colonel Oliver L. North of the National Security Council staff turned to NSA for help. He wanted a number of specially designed "KY-40" laptop computers containing secure encryption chips so he and his fellow conspirators could communicate secretly via e-mail while traveling.

At the suggestion of a fellow staffer on the NSC, North was referred to John C. Wobensmith, a senior official in NSA's Information Systems Security Directorate, which is responsible for developing, distributing, and keeping track of all codemaking equipment. North told Wobensmith the machines were needed for his work with American hostages in Lebanon. Because it was a covert operation, North said, he decided to deal with NSA himself.

Wobensmith claims that shortly after he was approached by North he walked up to Odom, who was passing between offices, and had a brief stand-up conversation with him. "I know you are supporting Colonel North," Wobensmith says Odom told him. "I authorize you to continue doing that support, give him what he needs, give him a couple of KY-40s if he needs them." Odom later said he did not recall the conversation. Wobensmith passed on the computers to North but failed to have him sign a receipt for them, a fact that would later come back to haunt him.

Two years later, following the devastating scandal that erupted as a result of the Iran-contra affair, a senior official at NSA recommended that Wobensmith be suspended without pay for fifteen days for the slip-up over the receipt and for giving inadequate instructions to North about the KY-40s' use. But a four-member appeals board, after five days of hearings, recommended that no disciplinary action be taken and awarded Wobensmith about $50,000 to reimburse him for his legal fees.

Odom was incensed. He believed that Wobensmith was responsible for casting the agency into the public spotlight, a rare and unforgivable sin in NSA's secret city. He was also worried that Lawrence E. Walsh, the Iran-contra independent prosecutor, might now have reason to turn his attention to NSA. "You didn't hear the name of this agency come up in the hearings," Odom once boasted. "The reason was I understood Oliver North's ilk long before most others did. I made damn sure this place was straight." According to one person with knowledge of the events, Odom was also upset that Wobensmith seemed to enjoy his contacts with the "political scene" in Washington. He told another person that the violation of proper procedure was inexcusable and that if Wobensmith were a soldier, he would have had him court-martialed.

As a result, Odom reversed the panel's decision, ruled that Wobensmith should be reprimanded, that he receive only $1,229 for legal fees, and that he be ordered hidden behind the "green door"—away from any public contact—as quickly as possible.

Many NSAers were outraged, some believing that Wobensmith had been scapegoated by the director. Wobensmith's boss, Edwin R. Lindauer, Jr., the deputy director for information security and one of the agency's most senior officials, protested Odom's action to the appeals board. "I personally am very upset," he said, "when I find a person dedicated to performing his duty has to defend himself against his own director, and pay considerable funds to accomplish that." Lindauer went on to say that the incident was one of the "significant factors" that drove him into retirement. "I am totally disgusted with the management and policy of this agency," he said, "that castigates a person such as John."

Wobensmith didn't know what had hit him. Before the charges arising out of his failure to get receipts from North, his supervisors had been preparing to recommend him for a bonus. Several years earlier he had been one of four people nominated by the agency for a Federal Career Service Award as a result of his extensive voluntary public service—he spent between thirty and forty hours a week doing volunteer work in his community.

After his demotion, people turned away from him. "I was pretty much isolated," Wobensmith said. "I saw a lot of fences going up, a lot of doors closing." The shunning was especially difficult to bear given the unique hardships of working in NSA's secret city. "We deal with our families in a very special way when we work in this place," he said. "That is, we can't tell them what we do. I think they understand that growing up, but when there comes a time that they know you've worked so hard, and they see this kind of thing, they say: 'What's happening? This is a place you're dedicated so much to. Why is [it] that, suddenly, you're in essence being abandoned?' "

Eventually, Odom himself was basically shown the door. He was reportedly passed over for promotion to four-star rank as a result of differences with Reagan's secretary of defense, Frank Carlucci. At the same time, the Joint Chiefs of Staff unanimously recommended against extending his tenure at NSA beyond the typical three years. "It was made clear to him he was no longer welcome," one source told Bill Gertz of the *Washington Times*. Odom had a different take. "I've had a hell of an impact on this agency," he said. "I've really kicked this agency into line."

Odom's departure opened the way for the Navy to sail back to NSA. The first naval officer to become DIRNSA since Bobby Inman, Vice Admiral William O. Studeman seemed almost his clone—apart from the new director's likeness to Wallace (*My Dinner with Andre*) Shawn. Like Inman, Studeman was born in Texas and, also like Inman, he had most recently been director of Naval Intelligence. "I think it was just fortuitous that all the stars happened to be in the right place in the heavens," he said of getting the job. "This is clearly the main gun of the intelligence community."

He was sworn in as the twelfth NSA director on August 1, 1988; upon moving into his office on the top floor of Operations Building 2B, he found a number of problems left over from Odom's disastrous reign. "There were some morale problems when I came here," Studeman recalled. "I got the impression that NSA had become quite insular." Odom also tried to push on Studeman a number of his pet projects. "He clearly wanted his thrusts to continue and had a vested interest in his thrusts," said Studeman.

On top of Odom's agenda was his plan to spend enormous amounts of money to make his eavesdropping satellites "survivable" in the event of a Soviet attack. Most senior officials at NSA thought the idea loony. "It was clear this agency did not want to spend the money on survivability," said Studeman. "They wanted to spend it on Sigint . . . and there was a sort of a major effort down there to wait out General Odom or to slow-roll him on the issues." Studeman also rejected Odom's arguments. "Early on," he said, "I chopped all those survivability initiatives off. . . . I think General Odom had some frustrations about his ability to make decisions," Studeman concluded, "or talk about issues and actually have the system respond around here."

Studeman also found the agency widely split along cultural lines.

"This place is cut seven ways from Sunday with cultures," he said. "You have the way NSA itself is organized, whether it's linguists or engineers or mathematicians or cryptologists or support people. . . . Or if it's Army, Navy, Air Force, or NSA, or whether it's research people and operators, or whatever."

When Studeman arrived, the Cold War was still hot and the Reagan largess continued to flow. Besides expanding its own network of listening posts around the world, NSA began helping to beef up its partner Sigint agencies in Britain, Canada, Australia, and New Zealand. Since the signing of the UKUSA Communications Intelligence Agreement on March 5, 1946, the partnership had grown continuously. By the late 1980s, there was barely a corner of the earth not covered by a listening post belonging to one of the members, or by an American satellite.

A key member of the UKUSA club is Canada's diminutive but resourceful Communications Security Establishment (CSE), which grew out of the World War II Examination Unit. In 1946, the Canadian Department of External Affairs recommended the creation of a new national signals intelligence organization. Thus was created the Communications Branch of the National Research Council, with a total of 179 employees. Britain supplied many of the intercepts for the fledgling agency, which, by 1962, had grown to about 600 staff members.

In 1975, when the CBNRC still had about the same number of employees, a series of orders transferred it to the Department of National Defence, where it took its present name. Situated near the Rideau River in a suburb of Ottawa known as Confederation Heights, CSE is headquartered in the nondescript Sir Leonard Tilley Building, at 719 Heron Road. Five stories high and L-shaped, the brown brick building is surrounded by a high fence and barbed wire. An underground tunnel connects it to an annex, a windowless $35 million block of cement designed to prevent any signals from escaping. On the roof is a silver forest of antennas. By 1996 CSE had more than 900 employees and its budget was about $116.8 million (Canadian) a year. Manning listening posts in various parts of Canada are about 1,100 military intercept operators. Inside, desks are grouped according to the regions of the world and many employees sit in front of computer screens, their ears cupped in plastic muffs.

For a time during the late 1970s, as NSA was celebrating its enormous success with satellite eavesdropping, the CSE was becoming a dinosaur. The more satellites circled the earth, transmitting rivers of intercepted data, the less NSA depended on the CSE ground stations sweeping in over-the-pole signals from the Soviet Union. At the same time, the CSE's codebreaking organization, O1 Division, was on life support. Much of the information was still being processed by hand. Only one person, Ed Cheramy, truly qualified as a cryptanalyst, and even he worked only on ancient, manual systems. When he died in early 1981, CSE effectively went out of the codebreaking business for a time. The agency's computer setup was primitive. According to Canadian documents, CSE's targets "had become very sophisticated and difficult to analyze" and its cryptanalytic department "had a poor reputation as a dead end, being unproductive." In the words of one insider, O1 "had become obsolete and unreliable."

Thus, in early 1980 a decision was made to bring the organization back to life. New blood was pumped in. In 1979, Peter Hunt, formerly the CSE liaison officer to NSA, had taken over as director general of production, replacing Jack Dornan, who had held the job since way back in the late 1950s. Within a year, Hunt was named chief of the entire CSE. As a first step he reached out to NSA for help, sending down one of his organization's most gifted scientists, Thomas Johnston, who held a Ph.D. in physics and was a dynamo with advanced math. Johnston returned with an expensive prescription. It called for aggressive hiring of mathematicians expert in such esoteric fields as stochastic and Markov processes, shift register, and polynomial theory. The entire cryptanalytic staff needed to be rebuilt, and a powerful supercomputer was required. At the time, CSE's Sigint database was loaded on IBM 370 mainframes, and obsolete PDP-8 and PDP-11 computers were used for linguistic analysis.

The multimillion-dollar price tag for the supercomputer was resisted by the budget office. Nevertheless, Johnston continued to argue his case. (In the meantime, he managed to convert one of the IBM computers into a codebreaking machine able to supply him with the critical daily key on a foreign cipher system he had been attacking.) At first Johnston pushed for the purchase of a $3 million–$5 million Control Data Corporation Cyber 740, largely because NSA was also considering buying one. Eventually, however, NSA went with the newer, more expensive Cray X-MP and Johnston was forced to plead for even more money to keep up.

Faced with what NSA calculated was "a 40-year catch-up" in computer cryptanalysis, the Canadian government finally bit the bullet and approved the purchase of a slimmed-down Cray, the X-MP/11 (modified). It cost $12,082,000 (Canadian) with the required Cray maintenance contract and instantly became the most powerful computer in the country.

The mighty machine was set up in an expansive, air-filtered computer center. At beige terminals, sixteen cryptanalysts tapped out complex questions while their mechanical wizard quietly crunched numbers, spitting out results in illionths of a second. Instructing the whirring brain was an NSA Sigint software package, the Folklore operating system. NSA also trained a number of Canadian cryptanalysts and computer operators in the Cray's use.

Catching up in cryptology was an expensive undertaking. By 1994, the CSE had spent a whopping $34 million (Canadian) on the X-MP alone. Over the 1980s, it has been estimated, the modernization of CSE cost upwards of $100 million. By 2001, the staff had grown to about 900, upping the annual budget to $98 million. Adding to the cost was a new twenty-four-hours-a-day, seven-days-a-week Canadian Sigint Operations Center (CANSOC).

Much of the collection is done by intercept operators attached to the Supplementary Radio System, whose headquarters are at Tunney's Pasture, in Ottawa. Among the CSE's listening posts are those located at Canadian Forces Station (CFS) Leitrim, just south of Ottawa in Ontario. Its antenna farm includes four large satellite dishes, and it listens to diplomatic communications in and out of Ottawa. At its Gander, Newfoundland, post the CSE has a giant elephant-cage antenna and concentrates mostly on naval intercepts. The Gander listening post is connected with NSA's worldwide Bullseye high-frequency direction-finding network. Several others are largely operated remotely. These include Alert on Ellesmere Island in the Northwest Territories, which for decades has monitored Russian over-the-pole communications, and CFS Masset in British Columbia, which also has a giant elephant-cage antenna.

Among CSE's targets are such allies as Japan, South Korea, and Mexico. As at NSA, trade intelligence has become a big priority. During negotiations leading up to the 1992 North American Free Trade Agreement, CSE intercept operators were very busy. "They spied on the Mexican trade representative during the NAFTA negotiations," said Jane Shorten, a former CSE linguist. "I just remember seeing those summaries. I know my colleagues who were Spanish linguists were working really hard at that, doing extra hours." Under Project Aquarian, Shorten monitored South Korean diplomatic reaction to meetings with Canadian trade officials about the CANDU nuclear reactor. She also eavesdropped on communications in and out of the South Korean Embassy in Ottawa.

"Knowledge is power," said Liberal Member of Parliament Derek Lee. "When we as Canadians sit down with another country to negotiate an agreement, our negotiators must be possessed of as much knowledge as they can get their hands on. There isn't a country in the world that wouldn't do that."

While the Canadians may be the new kids on the block when it comes to signals intelligence, the British virtually invented Sigint—hundreds of years before signals even came along. As early as the Elizabethan period, at least a few people in England knew that the Crown secretly read everyone's mail. In Stratford, a place of gentle green hills and straw-thatched cottages along the Avon, William Shakespeare mentioned the practice in *Henry V:*

> *The King has note of all that they intend,*
> *By interception which they dream not of.*

During World War II, the cryptanalytic activities of both Britain and the United States reached their zenith with the breaking of the Enigma, Fish, and Purple cipher machines. Following the war, to obscure the purpose of the burgeoning codebreaking organization, all references to cryptology were dropped from its name. Thus the Government Code and Cypher School became the Government Communications Headquarters (GCHQ). About the same time, Bletchley Park was turned into a training center and GCHQ moved to the Cotswolds. There in Cheltenham, among medieval villages of stone cottages and endless fields, GCHQ built its sprawling headquarters in 1953.

Among the differences between NSA and GCHQ for many years was unionization. Codebreakers, intercept operators, and others at GCHQ were allowed to join unions and even engage in brief work stoppages. That came to an end in 1984 when Prime Minister Margaret Thatcher used her iron fist to ban the unions. Much of the pressure to deunionize GCHQ came from the United States.

On February 23, 1979, in a little-noticed action, a few hundred members of two civil service unions walked out for the day in support of a pay hike, briefly halting long-term analysis of intercepted messages. Then, in December 1979, after the Russians invaded Afghanistan, intercept operators began a "work-to-rule" action that limited the degree to which GCHQ could eavesdrop on Soviet tank and troop movements. Work-to-rule meant that intercept operators would do such things as tune their receiver to exactly the frequency of the desired target and not move from that frequency even though the signal might drift slightly to either side.

Because NSA always has a sizable number of its own personnel working at GCHQ, the agency immediately became aware of the action. For the director of GCHQ, Sir Brian Tovey, it was extremely embarrassing. He ended up apologizing to NSA's then director, Bobby Ray Inman, for his agency's poor performance. "It made us look ridiculous," he recalled. "That was the turning point for me. From that time onwards, there was always an undercurrent of worry in some part of the office. It might be the radio [intercept] operators this week, the communications officers the next, and the computer operators the week after, but there was always something one was trying to contain."

"Some sixty percent of the GCHQ radio [intercept] operators obeyed the call to work to rule," said one GCHQ supervisor, "creating such great damage to communications intelligence information that a major row erupted between GCHQ and NSA, with the latter threatening to terminate the UKUSA Agreement and withdraw all financial assistance and exchange of intelligence." He added, "NSA's faith in GCHQ's ability to deliver the goods was on the wane."

Tovey saw trouble ahead. In the spring of 1981, he said, the unions made it "brutally clear" that they now regarded GCHQ as an attractive target—"a damn good place to hit." He added, "Hitting GCHQ doesn't hit the public, but it does bother and embarrass HMG [Her Majesty's Government]."

In 1980, GCHQ intercept operators at one listening post had conducted a work-to-rule slowdown just at the time the Soviet Union was heavily involved in Afghanistan, causing a great deal of teeth-gnashing at NSA. As a result, Tovey wrote a classified letter to the staffers who had caused the disruption. "I was able to spell out the consequences of their action and the considerable anxiety it had caused to some of our customers and our major allies," he said.

The most serious job action took place on March 8, 1981, during a critical period when there were numerous major international events taking place. These included the assassination attempt on President Reagan in Washington and a call for a national strike by the Solidarity union in Poland. At GCHQ, the unions called for a one-day strike and then mounted "selective disruptive action" at a number of the agency's listening posts around the world. "The massive response to the strike call by intercepting personnel rendered a number of the intelligence gathering stations completely inoperable for more than a week," said one GCHQ supervisor. "This lost not only the current intelligence available through interception, but deprived the organization of information necessary for the reception of valuable information for months ahead."

According to Tovey, it became essential that actions at one of those monitoring stations be halted immediately "for the most vital security reasons." But when a senior GCHQ official pleaded with a union official to call off the work stoppage at that station, explaining in vague terms the nature of the threat, the union official replied bluntly, "You are telling me where I'm hurting Mrs. Thatcher."

Thus when Tovey told the NSA director shortly after the incident that he was going to get the unions banned, Inman smiled and exclaimed, "That's marvelous." "We do not interfere with each other," said Tovey. "But having said that, the Americans could not be unconcerned if a major partner fell down on the job. We noticed a reluctance to enter into work-sharing and we read this as a message. It was the beginning of a reluctant feeling that 'Oh Lord, we don't know whether we can rely on the Brits.' . . . They had always been puzzled by the presence of unions. They have a cast-iron organization at the NSA. If anyone goes on strike there they get the sack. We used to have to tell them: 'We've had to drop this because of industrial unrest; could you pick it up for us?' The Americans found this bizarre."

Arguing to Britain's Joint Intelligence Committee that unions should be banned at GCHQ, Tovey asserted that their past actions had put "unfair stress on the Americans" and that the tempo of union disruptions was increasing. Once Thatcher approved the recommendation, buff-brown envelopes appeared on employees' desks explaining the order. "Some people went white," said one GCHQ worker, "some people started to giggle. You could say they were in a mild state of clinical shock." To protest the action, the Trades Union Congress paid for an advertisement in a London tabloid. "At GCHQ," it said, "the Government listens to everyone except the people who work there."

The worry that NSA might someday distance itself from GCHQ has had a major impact on the British organization, never more than during the 1982 war with Argentina over the Falkland Islands. At that point, the British government realized how much they relied on NSA for help with Sigint. "Dependence is total," said one official. One report indicated that NSA broke the Argentine code and that as much as 98 percent of the intelligence on Argentina's naval and military movements came from NSA. "We can ask the Americans to do things," said one former official, "but we cannot compel them. There may be targets they don't want to cover."

As a result of this worry, the British government in 1983 gave secret approval for a massive undertaking, the development of their own Sigint satellite, codenamed Zircon. GCHQ originally recommended the project to the Ministry of Defence as far back as the early 1970s, following the success of NSA's Rhyolite program. But they were constantly turned down until 1983, after the Falklands War.

Originally scheduled for a 1988 launch, Zircon was to be disguised as a military communications satellite and was to focus primarily on Europe, Russia, and the Middle East. Not everyone, however, was happy with the decision. A few dismissed it as "macho politics," simply an attempt to keep up with the United States in an endless Sigint space race. Worse, the Ministry of Defence kept the entire $700 million project hidden from Parliament.

But the costs soon doomed Zircon. The satellite itself bore an enormous price tag, and it was estimated that yearly maintenance requirements would have added about another $150 million to the project. "The UK simply isn't able to afford that coverage," said Lieutenant General Derek Boorman, the chief of Defence Intelligence. Instead, Britain agreed to contribute money to the United States in return for a sort of time-share arrangement with a new generation of NSA's Sigint satellites, codenamed Magnum. Under the new agreement, London would be allowed to "task" the satellites on targets of interest to the United Kingdom for up to one-third of the time.

The first Magnum was launched in 1994 with an eavesdropping dish 160 feet in diameter. Now that they were part owners of the Sigint satellite, senior British officials began taking a closer interest in Cheltenham. That same year Prime Minister John Major paid his first visit to GCHQ, and early the next year the Queen herself and the Duke of Edinburgh were given a tour. At the time, the agency employed 6,228 people at its headquarters, with about 3,000 more at overseas listening posts, and had a budget of about $900 million.

By 2001, GCHQ was busy constructing a new $500 million space-age complex to replace its headquarters buildings. Nicknamed "the doughnut," the circular structure was being built on a 176-acre site in Benhall, a section of Cheltenham about four miles from the old headquarters in Oakley. Plans called for the bombproof, four-story signals intelligence center to be seventy feet high and more than 600 feet in diameter—easily big enough to hold London's Royal Albert Hall. In addition to rooms full of receivers and computers, the doughnut would also resemble a small town with banks, shops, a health center, a gym—and a small pond in the center "hole" bordered by dish-shaped antennas. Surrounding the revolutionary building would be spaces for 1,750 cars and 200 bikes, arranged in concentric rings.

Auditors have recently warned that the doughnut's costs appear to be on the verge of spiraling out of control. Nevertheless, other GCHQ facilities are also planned for the site, including a science park of high-tech buildings. It was hoped that the project would be completed by

2003. At that time, the old headquarters would be turned into a 500-house development with a supermarket, video shop, and takeout restaurant.

Despite the end of the Cold War, the dawn of the new century, and the many internal and external changes at GCHQ and NSA, the secret relationship between the two partners promises to remain as close as it was sixty years ago, during the darkest days of World War II. Addressing a group in NSA's Friedman Auditorium in the fall of 1999, director Hayden said he had just returned from a visit with his counterparts in England. Then he added enthusiastically: "We must go back to our roots with GCHQ."

Like GCHQ, the Australian Defence Signals Directorate (DSD) rose from the ashes of World War II, during which its Central Bureau played a large role in eavesdropping on the Japanese and attacking their codes. Following the war, a number of listening posts were built, and Australian intercept operators worked jointly with employees of GCHQ at listening posts in Hong Kong and Singapore.

Today DSD is headquartered at Victoria Barracks, a modern glass government facility on St. Kilda Road in Melbourne. Compared with NSA and GCHQ, DSD is tiny, with about 500 civilians, most of whom work at headquarters, and about 500 military intercept operators. Despite the agency's small size, because of Australia's strategic location it is able to contribute considerable signals intelligence on its neighbors to NSA and the other UKUSA partners. According to Australian intelligence documents, this material has included such things as Japanese, South Korean, and Pakistani diplomatic traffic, rebel communications in southern Africa, and border conflicts between Iran and Iraq. For years DSD was also able to provide early tipoffs on French nuclear tests in the South Pacific. This allowed the United States to position aircraft and naval vessels to monitor the detonations and determine the bombs' yield and other technical details.

Next to Victoria Barracks is a boxy, windowless building that looks like a warehouse for dry goods. In fact, for many years it was a major listening post for eavesdropping on China and western Russia. In the early 1980s, many British and Australian intercept operators were pulled out of Hong Kong and the antennas became largely remoted. Giant dishes automatically collected the signals, which were in turn retransmitted by satellite to Melbourne, nearly 5,000 miles away. The listening post's cover name was the Joint Telecommunications Unit Melbourne.

Finally, the newest and smallest member of the UKUSA club is New Zealand's Government Communications Security Bureau (GCSB), formally established in 1977. During World War II, as the Japanese war machine pushed rapidly across the Pacific, gobbling up islands, New Zealand quickly built a number of signals intelligence stations, which contributed to the British and American Sigint effort. They were controlled from Defence House, a seven-story building on Stout Street in Wellington.

After the war, the intercept service was abandoned and New Zealand contributed some members to Australia's postwar codebreaking and eavesdropping organization, the Defence Signals Bureau. Nevertheless, a small listening post was built on a bleak volcanic plateau at Waiouru in the central part of North Island. Eventually named the New Zealand Combined Signals Organisation, it contributed to the Sigint effort during the war in Vietnam.

Today, the headquarters for the GCSB occupies the top floors of the Freyberg Building, opposite Parliament, in Wellington. Concentrating mostly on the Pacific Rim and small island nations, it has a high-frequency listening post at Tangimoana Beach, about 225 miles north of Wellington. A satellite interception facility was opened at Waihopai; it targets, among other things, diplomatic communications to and from Japanese embassies around the Pacific. In 2001 GCSB employed about 200 people and had a budget of about $20 million (Australian). Its director was Warren Tucker, who joined the agency in 1982 and before that served as liaison to NSA.

With the admission of New Zealand's GCSB in 1977, the major English-speaking nations of the world were joined in a highly secret agreement to eavesdrop on the rest of the world, friend as well as foe. Over the years, the UKUSA partnership would develop into a unique supranational body, complete with its own laws, oaths, and language, all hidden from public view. As a sovereign nation has a body of laws, so UKUSA has a body of secrets. The International Regulations on Sigint govern the actions of the multinational cyberspies, from the wording of their indoctrination oaths to the format of their intercept forms to their unique cryptospeak of codewords and covernames.

Once those rules were firmly in place in the 1970s, NSA set out to weld the individual members together into a virtual nation, with Crypto City as its capital. It did this by building a massive computer network, codenamed Platform, which tied together fifty-two separate computer systems belonging to all the members around the world. The focal point, or "host environment," for the massive network was NSA headquarters at Fort Meade. Finally, to do away with formal borders, a software package was developed to turn the partners' worldwide Sigint operation into a unified whole. Agencies would be able to submit targets to one another's listening posts and, likewise, everyone would be allowed to share in the take—to dip their electronic ladles into the vast caldron of intercepts and select what they liked. The software package that established this was codenamed Echelon.

During the 1980s, fax machines and computers began to proliferate. More and more information once sealed tightly in envelopes began zipping through the ether. Everything from private letters to tax returns to contracts to business negotiations to foreign unclassified military and diplomatic messages suddenly went from opaque to transparent. All spies needed was steel nets to catch the signals as they plunged from the international communications satellites (INTELSATs). Perched like chattering magpies in geostationary orbits above the earth, the seventeen INTELSAT satellites provide telephone, fax, e-mail, and other international communications to over 200 countries and territories around the world. The system is managed by the International Telecommunications Satellite Organization, a Washington, D.C.–based cooperative. "We link the world's telecommunications networks together," says the company.

As commercial earth stations were built around the world to transmit and receive millions of private messages and telephone calls to and from the INTELSATs, NSA and its partners quietly began constructing mirror sites hidden nearby. Massive ninety-foot dishes resting on thick cement pedestals, they looked like great silver chalices containing offerings to the gods. The first ones were built in an isolated valley in Sugar

Grove, West Virginia (using parts from the failed Moonbounce project); on a vast, restricted Army firing range in Yakima, Washington; and at the edge of a Cornish cliff near Bude, England. As more INTELSATs began dotting the distant skies, the UKUSA partnership began building more ground stations to eavesdrop on them.

By the end of the 1980s, the revolution was in full swing. Wholesale satellite eavesdropping would change the nature of signals intelligence forever. "We grew so fast in the '80's we got buried," recalled Robert L. Prestel, who took over as deputy director in 1990.

CHAPTER ELEVEN

MUSCLE

CNAMIIN TQSWGIMY'C CMOK GWNOK ASKMO QY BKVMB TQVEC
ZMNZJK NTO EKMAJO SRB JUEJABJX BR XJBRQK YTATBMRS EDTSO
MWCUPQI QXC OQWC HQUU KXZ QWHIKXZQ OKDSR ZSUKMMCKWU
KDXGWX QDV QWOWXLDF FSGWE FWV WFADT OD AYWOFSG
PUILSC RUXXWD UXZR UIKIED GL SILRUOE OPUGSOL UIWZKEGS

The southern French city of Toulouse has developed a pinkish tint as a result of the centuries-old blending of brick and red tile. Houseboats line the Canal du Midi, the waterway linking the Atlantic Ocean with the Mediterranean Sea, and a labyrinth of alleyways leads to the embankments of the Garonne River. On the northern outskirts of the city sits a small factory on the winding Chemin du Pont de Rupé. There, in December 1997, a salesman by the name of T. Dècle* became a fly caught in UKUSA's worldwide electronic web. In the shadow of the nearby Pyrenees, where the Visigoths and also Charlemagne once ruled, the complex system of eavesdropping satellites, hidden antennas, and powerful supercomputers began telescoping down to the beige phone on the unsuspecting salesman's desk.

In the equatorial forests of French Guiana, the air was leaden with humidity during the brief interludes between fierce downpours. Forty miles west of the capital of Cayenne, the Kourou River feeds into endless mangrove swamps and tropical marshlands. There, on March 14, 1996, a sleek white Ariane 44P rocket rose above the green canopy of coconut palms and screeching macaws at the European Space Agency. After three months of testing and calibration, INTELSAT 707 was nudged into its geostationary orbit high above the tiny West African island nation of São Tomé and Principe. There, like an orbital switch-

*To protect the privacy of the salesman, a pseudonym has been used.

board, it was capable of relaying up to 90,000 telephone calls and data transmissions simultaneously throughout Europe, Africa, and Asia.

Twenty-two thousand miles below and to the north, on a mist-hazed cliff in England's Cornwall, intercept operators at GCHQ's Morwenstow listening post, near Bude, were working around the clock. Like an outfielder under a high fly ball, the Morwenstow station was ideally positioned to secretly catch the new satellite's beam containing thousands of simultaneous messages and conversations. In the days following the satellite's activation, technicians in the station worked overtime attempting to log and program into their computers and Echelon software the channels with the highest intelligence value.

Sitting high above the Celtic Sea on the edge of Sharpnose Point, the base has nearly a dozen dishes pointed to the heavens. It was originally built in the late 1960s, largely with money from NSA, to eavesdrop on communications flowing down to Europe from the early INTELSAT satellites. A brief sixty miles away, also in Cornwall, was Britain's commercial ground station for the satellites, at Goonhilly Downs.

Once the Morwenstow station was completed, the director of GCHQ at the time, Sir Leonard Hooper, sent his personal thanks to Marshall Carter. "I know that I have leaned shamefully on you, and sometimes taken your name in vain, when I needed approval for something at this end," Sir Leonard wrote. "The aerials at Bude ought to be christened 'Pat' [Carter's nickname] and 'Louis' [Tordella]!" Hooper added, "Between us, we have ensured that the blankets and sheets are more tightly tucked around the bed in which our two sets of people lie and, like you, I like it that way."

Later Carter commented on the letters, explaining Hooper's budget problems and how he would approach his superiors for the money. "He says, 'Well, look, you can turn me down from the British viewpoint, but I'm in bed with Pat Carter on this thing—this is a joint requirement; he needs it as badly as I do. The product that he is going to develop for us will come right to us, so would you take another look at this, because he wants it, it will help him in his business. We'll get the results of it.' "

Today, among UKUSA's key targets are Iran, China, and North Korea. Just as Morwenstow eavesdrops on INTELSAT communications to Europe, INTELSAT signals to the Far East are monitored from a large

American listening post in Japan. There, at Misawa Air Base on the northern tip of Honshu Island, the antenna area looks like a soccer field for giants. Fourteen large radomes, like mammoth soccer balls, sit on a stretch of green. Nearby is an elephant-cage antenna, over 100 feet tall and nearly a quarter-mile wide.

The signals collected by the antennas are piped into a modern windowless building known as the Misawa Cryptologic Operations Center. Inside, NSA civilians and 1,800 tri-service (Army, Navy, Air Force) military Sigint specialists work in shifts. Among them are the Naval Security Group and the Air Force 301st Intelligence Squadron, which performs "satellite communications processing and reporting." One of the satellites on which Misawa performs "processing and reporting" is an INTELSAT 8 launched over the Pacific on June 27, 1997, with a capacity for up to 112,500 simultaneous phone calls.

The Army's 750th Military Intelligence Company is also there. Of the Army intercept operators and analysts, many are so-called 98Ks: signals collection/identification analysts. They are involved in the "collection, identification, exploitation, and analysis of digital and analog communications, to include voice, teleconferencing, videoconferencing, facsimile, computer-to-computer traffic, and telemetry." In other words, everything that might go through an INTELSAT.

The days of intercepting Morse code are long gone. Today the focus is on intercepting and analyzing far more complex digital satellite communications. According to an Army intelligence publication, "98Ks will 'break' digital signals into a recognizable form so that the 98C (signals intelligence analyst), 98G (voice interceptor), 98H (communications locator/interceptor), and 98J (electronic intelligence interceptor/analyst) soldiers can further exploit the intelligence within the 'digital window.' "

Some of the advanced training is done at the Navy's Technical Training Center at Corry Station in Pensacola, Florida. Other courses are given remotely, from NSA's National Cryptologic School. Among the courses are FORNSAT (Foreign Satellite Collection), COMSAT (Communications Satellite Collection), Cellular Communications Collection, Overhead Collection Management, Computer/Signals Analysis, Bit Stream Analysis, Modems, Multiplexing, Geolocation, Antenna Selection, and Target Development. Among the FORNSATs the Misawa analysts likely focus on are the several domestic China Sats in orbit, also known as DHF-3s.

Another course is VSAT (Very Small Aperture Satellite [Terminal]) Collection. This type of collection is aimed at intercepting communications using small dishes, such as those used with DirecTV. India's nuclear weapons establishment, for example, uses this method to send and receive encrypted digital messages by satellite.

Also busy eavesdropping on INTELSATs over the Pacific are New Zealand's listening post at Waihopai and Australia's station at Geraldton, 230 miles north of Perth. A port on the Indian Ocean in the extreme westernmost part of the country, Geraldton was designed primarily to eavesdrop on the two INTELSATs over the Indian Ocean. It is also able to monitor the Pacific Ocean satellites. The station was opened by DSD in 1994, about the same time as GCHQ's Hong Kong station was closing.

In the post–Cold War years, the proliferation of both nuclear and conventional weapons has joined the chief concerns of the U.S. government. A particular worry is the possible sale by China of nuclear components and missile parts to Pakistan and Iran. Thus, NSA receives numerous requests from the CIA, the State Department, and other "customers" for intelligence on such transfers. Analysts at these agencies submit to NSA long, detailed watch lists containing keywords and names.

After NSA receives the watch lists containing the keywords, names, phrases, telephone and fax numbers, analysts assign four-digit numbers to them—search codes—and then pass them on, through the Echelon computer system, to the various UKUSA listening posts. There a computer, codenamed Dictionary, searches for those words and numbers among the millions of messages passing through the intercept antennas. It does this much as computers use search engines such as Alta Vista to locate keywords and phone numbers almost instantly in the vast Internet.

No doubt high on the list of keywords submitted to NSA is the name of Jin Xuekuan, the president of China National Precision Machinery Import & Export Corporation. This Chinese government–owned company, a sort of Missiles 'R' Us on Fu Cheng Road in Beijing, is responsible for foreign sales of missiles and other weapons. Once a listening post gets a hit on Jin, the intercept will automatically be forwarded to NSA. There, an analyst need only enter the search number for Jin and any intercepts from, to, or mentioning him will appear on the analyst's screen.

Despite the very secret nature of weapons deals, communications about them are seldom encrypted, because each country has separate and incompatible systems. So the parties are forced to resort to commercial faxes, phone calls, and electronic mail. Also, as in any complicated sale, a great deal of electronic "paperwork" is always generated—contracts, warranties, price negotiations, service agreements: the same type of paperwork as is involved if Burger King sells a franchise to a company in Holland. For the UKUSA partners, this enormous "paper" trail is collectable over the open airwaves through their worldwide electronic dredging operation.

Terrorists also frequently use unencrypted communications, because for encryption the caller and the receiver must have compatible systems. Since at least one party is often traveling, carrying encryption equipment can be cumbersome.

According to information obtained for *Body of Secrets,* NSA regularly listens to unencrypted calls from suspected terrorist Osama bin Laden, in hiding in Afghanistan. Bin Laden uses a portable INMARSAT phone that transmits and receives calls over spacecraft owned by the International Maritime Satellite Organization. This is the same system used by most ships and some people who travel to remote locations, such as oil explorers. According to intelligence officials, Bin Laden is aware that the United States can eavesdrop on his international communications, but he does not seem to care. To impress cleared visitors, NSA analysts occasionally play audiotapes of Bin Laden talking to his mother over an INMARSAT connection.

When targets do use encryption, or when the information is sent by diplomatic pouch, cyberspies have to be creative. "With regard to encryption," said one former official, "you look for places outside the zone. At some time he has to go to the Danish freight forwarder or Danish shipping guy to ask him a question—'I need a ship with extra-heavy reinforced decking with a hatch this size.' So we just need to look other places. Yeah, it's going to be harder. Look for letters of credit being cut—they almost always have to go to a regular bank."

Vast numbers of messages and phone calls are intercepted from the INTELSATs, and likewise the power and speed of the NSA computers that sift through the sea of information are enormous. According to William Studeman, "U.S. intelligence operates what is probably the largest information processing environment in the world. Consider this: Just one intelligence collection system alone can generate a million inputs per half-hour. Filters throw away all but 6,500 inputs; only 1,000 inputs meet forwarding criteria. Ten inputs are normally selected by analysts and only one report is produced. These are routine statistics for a number of intelligence collection and analysis systems which collect technical intelligence."

Despite sophisticated software, watch lists, and powerful computers, signals intelligence analysis is an attempt to solve a puzzle whose pieces are difficult to see, include only small bits of the much larger picture, and are constantly changing. Sometimes the pieces of the puzzle lead to dead ends, and sometimes they lead to great discoveries. Occasionally they may lead to serious consequences for innocent, unsuspecting citizens of friendly countries. Sometimes the answers are just gray and ambiguous. The piece of the puzzle fits but the words don't match.

Highly secret documents reviewed for *Body of Secrets* describe in detail how NSA and its UKUSA partners spent years following one difficult trail—that of China's C-802 missile and Iran's attempts to build one of its own. They offer unique insight into the controversial and misunderstood Echelon program, showing the system at its best and also at its most questionable. The documents were reviewed at the National Security News Service in Washington, a nonprofit group that has researched the C-802.

Four thousand miles west of Toulouse, in Washington, concern had been growing over the help China was giving the Iranian missile program. A particular worry was the deadly C-802, a sleek, sharklike antiship cruise missile that could also deliver a chemical or biological payload. The sales brochure of its manufacturer, China National Precision Machinery Import & Export, boasted that the C-802 had "mighty attack capability" and "great firepower"; it had a range of 120 kilometers and resembled the Exocet cruise missile that had killed thirty-seven U.S. sailors on the USS *Stark* in 1987. C-802s, said James Lilly, the former U.S. ambassador to China, pose a "clear and present danger to the United States fleet." At the time, more than 15,000 U.S. servicemen were stationed in the Persian Gulf.

For years, Iran had purchased C-802s from China, but officials in Tehran were becoming increasingly troubled about the prospects for future sales. They felt that as China nudged closer to the United States, it might eventually slow down or halt weapon sales to Iran, as it had been doing with Pakistan.

By the summer of 1997, NSA intercepts of phone calls and faxes among Tehran, Beijing, and Hong Kong were beginning to indicate that Iran might be attempting to build the missiles themselves. The prospect made many in Washington very nervous, because if Iran produced its own missiles the United States would have even less ability to monitor and control its inventory. The near-supersonic weapons could wreak havoc against American ships sailing in the Persian Gulf. But the key to the missile was the complex, high-precision turbojet engine that powered it. It was built by Microturbo, SA, a firm based in Toulouse. Few believed that Iran would be able to successfully build such a machine on its own.

Then, in July 1997, NSA delivered some bad news to the White House. Its electronic vacuum cleaner had intercepted a phone call from Tehran to Hong Kong revealing that Iran was attempting to reverse-engineer the French Microturbo engine—to acquire one and then peel it back, layer by layer, until it understood the engine well enough to build one. Then Iran would attempt to obtain engine parts for as many as 100 missiles from Microturbo by disguising the parts' ultimate destination. According to the intercepted conversation, instead of having Microturbo ship the parts to Tehran, Iran would have them sent to a Hong Kong company called Jetpower. Jetpower would then forward them on to Iran, although it is unclear from the intercepts whether or not the company knew of the deception. To further screen the true nature of the shipment, the equipment would be labeled "Generator 4203 mini–jet engine."

Iran seemed to be pulling out all the stops. GCHQ, through its Morwenstow antennas, intercepted a call from an Iranian official in Paris to Tehran indicating that Iran was considering hiring a notorious arms dealer to help obtain the Microturbo engine. On July 29, 1997, an overcast but warm Saturday in Paris, the Iranian official, a Mr. Mehrdad, met with Syrian arms trafficker Monzer al-Kassar.

Flabby and gray-haired, the forty-nine-year-old al-Kassar had traveled to Paris from his home in Marbella, Spain, where he operated a company called Conastra Trading. In 1992, al-Kassar was arrested in Spain on charges of providing weapons and financing for the 1985 hijacking of the Italian luxury liner *Achille Lauro* but was later acquitted. A man of many passports as well as identities, al-Kassar had been part of the covert network run by Lieutenant Colonel Oliver North during the days of the Iran-contra scandal. It was revealed that al-Kassar had received $1.5 million to purchase weapons. When he was questioned about al-Kassar, former U.S. national security adviser John Poindexter said, "When you're buying arms, you often have to deal with people you might not want to go to dinner with."

Mehrdad told his contact in Tehran that "the meeting had gone very well" and that they should invite both al-Kassar and another international arms dealer, the French-born Bernard Stroiazzo-Mougin, to Tehran for further discussion on ways to acquire the Microturbo engine. According to the GCHQ report, "Stroiazzo-Mougin is Director of North Atlantic Airways. In August 1996, he was noted [in earlier GCHQ intercepts] supplying electron tubes and Boeing 707 and 747 aircraft spare parts to an Iranian company."

Mehrdad concluded the July 29, 1997, conversation by telling al-Kassar that he was certain they would be able "to do very big things." A few weeks later al-Kassar faxed to Tehran details concerning the half dozen people he was going to bring with him on his visit to Iran—mostly engineers from South Africa, as well as Stroiazzo-Mougin—to discuss the missile project. GCHQ dutifully intercepted the list, which included such key data as dates of birth and passport numbers.

By September, Iran's fears about the Chinese connection seemed to be coming true. Chinese officials told their Iranian counterparts that the latest shipment of C-802 missiles had been temporarily halted because of "technical problems." There were no "technical problems." According to U.S. intelligence reports, the Chinese government had quietly decided to cease delivery of the missiles until at least after the late October summit meeting in Washington between China's president Jiang Zemin and Bill Clinton. Also according to the intelligence reports, General Mohammad Vahid-Destjerdi, the Iranian deputy minister of defense, didn't buy the "technical problems" excuse and accused the Chinese of being unprepared to stand up to Western pressure and lacking in resolve.

In Washington on October 29, behind blue and white sawhorses across from the White House, protesters chanted and shouted. But as the long black armor-plated limousine arrived with President Jiang Zemin, a military band drowned out the demonstrators with the national anthems of both the United States and China.

Following the summit talks, a news conference was held in the Rose Garden. In the crisp fall air, under a bright sun, Clinton addressed the issue of nuclear proliferation. "President Jiang and I agree," he said, "that the United States and China share a strong interest in stopping the spread of weapons of mass destruction, and other sophisticated weaponry in unstable regions, and rogue states, notably Iran." In part on the basis of President Jiang's assurances that China had halted missile sales to Iran, Clinton granted permission for U.S. companies to sell nuclear power plant equipment to China. But Clinton was relying on more than Jiang's word: behind the scenes, away from the press and the public, he was relying far more heavily on NSA to tell him whether China was keeping its agreement.

In November, NSA intercepted messages confirming earlier reports: Iran had decided to go it alone and build its own missile. Plucked from an INTELSAT were faxes indicating that six months earlier, in May, a deal had been struck between Iran and Microturbo. The intercepts included a letter of credit, valued at over $1.1 million, issued by Iran's Defense Ministry to Microturbo. The terms of the contract indicated that there was little time left: the "goods" were to be shipped to Iran by December 3, less than a month away. They were to be loaded on an Iranian ship in Antwerp, Belgium, which would take them to Bandar Abbas, Iran.

At the White House there was outrage over the NSA report on the backdoor deal between Microturbo and Tehran's generals. In June the United States had sent a démarche—a diplomatic protest—to France complaining about earlier sales of Microturbo engines to China. In response, the French Foreign Ministry agreed to prohibit future sales by the company to China as well as "to other pariah states such as Iran out of principle."

Now, as a result of the NSA intercepts, a second démarche was issued, this time requesting an investigation into the Microturbo contract with Iran. More U.S. protests followed. Officials from the American embassy in Paris approached the French Foreign Ministry again about the same time, and Pentagon officials called on the French defense attaché in Washington. But the French would only say, unofficially, that the Microturbo contract simply involved "generators," not missile engines.

Finally, when no formal reply was forthcoming, an unusually high-level and blunt protest was made to the French Foreign Ministry. "It is our understanding," it said, "that Microturbo's generators and jet engines are almost entirely identical, and only slight modifications are necessary to turn the 'generator' into a jet engine."

Although it was December, the atmosphere in Microturbo's offices was decidedly hot following the U.S. diplomatic protests over who their clients were and what they were shipping. The issue was especially sticky because Microturbo had a subsidiary located in Grand Prairie, Texas, and that subsidiary depended greatly on U.S. government contracts for sales of its turbojet engines.

What employees of Microturbo did not know was that they had become entangled in UKUSA's electronic web. Thus when T. Dècle, a company official, faxed a message to Mr. R. Heidari, an Iranian defense official, it was intercepted by GCHQ's Morwenstow antenna, several hundred miles away. Transferred to the agency's headquarters at Cheltenham, it arrived on the desk of an analyst who specialized in weapons systems and had been following the C-802 closely. The analyst concluded that Microturbo was attempting to "mask involvement in Iranian anti-ship [C-802] cruise missile component deal."

In his report, the GCHQ analyst wrote that Dècle had informed the Iranian military officials "that he would advise them in the next few days of Microturbo's position. To avoid any faxes being mis-sent to Microturbo's U.S. subsidiary, Dècle requested that in the future the headers of faxes should not show the name of the U.S. subsidiary, and he also asked them to use a specific French fax number."

The secret intercepts offered clear, hard evidence that the Jiang-Clinton summit was having a positive effect. Inside a low, pale-colored government building near a busy intersection in Tehran, Hossein Jafari, the official responsible for buying the C-802 missiles from Beijing, was becoming more and more angry at the Chinese, who were reneging on their contract. His anger was specifically directed at China National Precision Machinery Import & Export Corporation.

In early December, Jafari marched over to China Precision's office in Tehran and demanded some answers from Wen Bo, the local representative. Like a man who had been conned, Jafari laid into Wen. He demanded to know why China Precision had not returned his calls, why the contracts had not been fulfilled, and why he had been given no explanations. Jafari said he had instructed his financial department to cease all payments and then demanded that Wen Bo immediately call China Precision's president, Jin Xuekuan, or its vice president, Ji Yanshu, for an explanation.

Wen Bo did as Jafari asked and made the call to Beijing. While Jafari listened to Wen Bo's side of the conversation, NSA was eavesdropping on *both* sides. Over the telephone, Wen Bo told an official at China Precision that he was in an embarrassing position because he had received no instructions on the missile deal. He then listed Jafari's complaints and asked to speak to the top executives. In response, an official suggested to him that although both Jin Xuekuan and Ji Yanshu were both in the building, he should tell Jafari that the executives were temporarily out and could not be reached. Wen Bo did as he was told, and Jafari left as angry as he arrived. However, he said, he did not blame Wen Bo but rather the "policymakers" in Beijing.

The Jiang-Clinton summit, according to the NSA intercepts, also affected a long-planned trip to Tehran by a delegation of China Precision engineers. They were scheduled to travel to Tehran in October, just before the summit, to help repair and service the missiles already delivered. The trip was then delayed for several months. Finally, in December, just before the team's rescheduled arrival, Beijing sent Wen Bo some disappointing news. "The future looked bleak," the NSA report quoted the Chinese officials. The delegation had been shrunk to just three persons and they were going to Tehran only to carry out some nonspecific discussion about contract matters, "not to actually do anything about them." When the delegation finally arrived at Tehran's Mehrabad Airport on December 4, a still-boiling Jafari asked them why the two top executives of the company had never got back to him. He was simply told that "the current situation had already gone beyond the realm of CPMIEC's [China Precision's] control; consequently, Jin and Ji were not able to reply."

For Jafari, things did not get better. In February 1998 he learned from press accounts what he was never told directly: China had pledged not to sell any more cruise missiles to Iran. In a further meeting with officials of China Precision, the Iranian officials demanded renewed commitment within two weeks; otherwise, cooperation between Iran and China might be suspended.

These intercepts brought smiles to normally glum officials at the White House and State Department. "The complaints lodged by Tehran suggest Beijing is holding firm on the original pledge," said a State Department intelligence report. "Since the commitment was made, the U.S. has detected only one possible shipment to Iran of small components related to the air-launched version of the C-802." Giving up on China, Iran began working hard at reverse engineering and attempting to build its own missiles with the parts already received. "Iran may already have received some or all of the equipment necessary to assemble C-801 or C-802 missiles before the commitment was made," said the State Department report.

In March, the U.S. defense attaché based in Tel Aviv reported that an Israeli military intelligence official had passed on some hot information. "According to IDF DMI [Israeli Defense Force, Directorate of Military Intelligence], Iran signed a contract in 1993 with the Chinese corporation CPMIEC for the procurement of C-801 and C-802 missiles for its naval units and shore-to-sea missile batteries." The U.S. defense attaché could barely keep from laughing at this report, which, he warned, might include "circular reporting from U.S. intelligence exchange program." That is, he felt it was simply something Israel had happened to pick up from U.S. intelligence and was feeding right back to U.S. intelligence for "credit." "Caution should be exercised in using this information for direct reporting. . . . It is interesting that the Israelis are dredging up old information to serve as a vehicle for renewed request for information on the Iranians, or, in the alternative, are just now obtaining information on six-year-old contracts."

(According to a former intelligence official involved in nonproliferation issues, "Ninety percent of what we did we relied on Sigint—ninety percent of nonproliferation comes through NSA. We get some Humint [human intelligence], some from the attachés, some from the Israelis—they had a reporting requirement with us, they had to send us something through the attaché every week to justify their $5 billion a year.")

Six months after the summit, intercepts indicated that China was keeping its pledge to refrain from selling the cruise missiles to Iran. "Recent intelligence reports suggest Iran is dissatisfied with China's failure to implement existing ASCM [antiship cruise missile] contracts," said an April 1998 intelligence report. Nevertheless, Tehran planned one last-ditch effort. Iranian officials made plans to fly to Beijing on April 15 to air their frustration and discuss future cooperation. If the trip was ever made, it was of little avail.

With China having backed out of its contract, Iran turned inward. In December 1998, Iran's then president, Ali Akbar Hashemi Rafsanjani, claimed that Iran had become "technologically self-sufficient" in missile development.

After analysts at NSA review intercepts, such as those between Tehran and Microturbo, they write up reports and send them out to customers. Many of the reports are stamped with exotic codenames, such as "Gamma," which is reserved for Sigint of the highest sensitivity. "Within Gamma they had double G, which was higher than Gamma," said one former official. "Double G material was sent to people by hand—[Director of Central Intelligence George] Tenet, [Secretary of State Madeleine] Albright, and so forth. This included material from friendly-nation wiretaps. 'EG' was Executive Gamma, blue cover sheet."

The analysts also mark reports with a three-letter code indicating where the intercept was obtained. "FRD," for example, indicates that the information in the report came from intercepted French diplomatic communications. "ILC" indicates that it was intercepted from an "international licensed carrier," such as a commercial telecommunications channel. There is also a subject tag, such as "ABIG," for "Arms Investigation of Tracked Vehicles," which indicates that the intercept concerns tracked weapons vehicles. Thus the analyst need only enter "ABIG" into his computer and all intercepted messages over the past few days dealing with that topic would pop up.

The analysts are searching through the world's private whispers every day, yet after a while even that becomes routine. "I looked for black-market arms sales," said one former customer, an analyst for a federal agency. "I would arrive in the morning, go to my NSA web site—they had a search engine—pull it down. Keywords were 'letter of credit,' 'contract,' 'bill of lading,' 'middleman,' 'dealer,' 'broker.' I had eight to ten categories. In about an hour I would go through all my message traffic [intercepts]. It would say, 'We searched and we found twenty-seven things that meet your criteria.' And then you have the subject lines. You click on the subject line and the message will come up. These will be the reports, you never see the raw intercepts. It would say something like, 'On the fourteenth of March some person in the Iranian Ministry of Defense contacted so and so at the embassy in blah blah. They discussed the following topics.' It would give a description of the conversation, it would reference other cables on the same issue. And then if they faxed something—the letters of credit or contracts—they would be in there."

The analysts in NSA work, for the most part, in standard cubicles. On their desks are several computer monitors. As a security measure, the one on which they read the intercepts is not connected to the outside world. A second computer is connected to the public Internet, and analysts are forbidden to input classified material into it, for fear of hackers. Many analysts have reel-to-reel tape recorders for listening to the intercepted voice conversations. "They had pictures above their desk of the guys they were listening to," said one person who spent time in the area. He said that often such photographs were obtained by intercepting the fax when someone transmitted a copy of his or her passport in applying for a visa. After listening to the voices of the same unsuspecting individuals, hour after hour, day after day, many analysts begin to feel they know them. "They used to tell me, 'Even if I have never seen these guys, if I ever got on an elevator and heard their voice I'd jump through the roof. You get to know these voices as well as your wife's.' "

The question of whether or not to bring a démarche to a foreign government is always a difficult issue, especially when the discovery of a violation comes from NSA's Sigint. The State Department is usually in favor of issuing a démarche, but NSA is occasionally opposed because it might reveal to the foreign country that its communications are being intercepted. "In order to bring a démarche to a foreign country," said one official, "we would first have to get permission from NSA to declassify or reduce the classification of the information. They were usually pretty good about it."

The CIA, however, was a different story. "The Agency [CIA] guys never bothered telling you what they were doing, if they bothered showing up at the meeting," said the official. "The NSA would at least make it usable. The Agency [CIA] would say, 'You're not to démarche this country because we've got an op going.' We say, 'What's the op?' And they say, 'We can't tell you.' They never tell you when it's over, unless you follow it up with them. It's like they almost didn't care, they had other fish to fry. You know nonproliferation just wasn't important."

Normally, to hide the source of the underlying information, a certain period of time was allowed to pass before a démarche was issued. "We'd never go in doing this stuff right away, because they'd know," said one former official. "We'd have to sit on the stuff for weeks sometimes. And then they'd think that some guy talked to his girlfriend or blabbed to a hairdresser. You've got to put time and distance between it."

Through UKUSA's worldwide eavesdropping web, NSA and its partners were able to peek behind scenes and determine how well the agreement between the United States and China was holding up. In the days of the Cold War, "verification" simply involved photo satellites snapping images, and analysts counting missile silos and launchers. But today, it is not what is planted in the ground but what is planted in someone's mind that is critical to know. For that, imaging satellites are useless and only signals intelligence can provide the answers. Without Sigint, Washington would have been left in the dark. No other intelligence source—

human, military, diplomatic, photo, Israeli—provided the answers produced by the Echelon system. (Echelon is a software program whose name has become a generic term for eavesdropping on commercial communications.)

But the history of the C-802 problem also shows the dangers associated with Echelon. Once GCHQ intercepted the fax Microturbo's T. Dècle sent Iran's Heidari, it was passed on to NSA, the Canadian CSE, and Australia's DSD, as well as to the British Secret Intelligence Service (MI-6) and customs offices. Like most of the other intercepts dealing with the cruise missile deal, it was not sent to New Zealand's GCSB, possibly because of continued bitterness over that country's declaration that it was a nuclear-free zone.

At NSA the information on Dècle went to W9P3, the Missile Proliferation section of W Group, the Global Issues and Weapons Group. NSA in turn sent the report on Dècle to a number of CIA stations around the world, including those in Paris and Bonn, as well as to the U.S. Commerce Department and to Customs. Thus, within a few days of Dècle's fax, there were probably hundreds of people in at least four countries around the world reading it and possibly putting Dècle's name on some blacklist, as if he were an enemy of the state. The question, however, was whether the analysts were correct. Was Microturbo sending a missile engine to Tehran, as they suspected, or was it simply an innocent generator, as France was claiming? As with many cases in the gray, shadowy world of Echelon, little is strictly black and white.

To resolve the issue, French export inspectors flew to Antwerp as the ship containing the "special items" was preparing to sail to Iran. Upon opening the crates, they later told U.S. authorities, they confirmed that the "special items" were generators. This caused U.S. authorities to conduct a "reevaluation" of the NSA and GCHQ transcripts. In light of the French information, NSA concluded that some of the intercepted conversations were more ambiguous than originally believed. They admitted that the equipment sent by Microturbo in fact could have been a generator, but one with potential military uses. "It doesn't mean we were necessarily wrong" in the earlier reports, said one U.S. official. "But if we'd known of the doubts before, we wouldn't have done things [written the reports] that way."

The chairman of Microturbo, Jean-Bernard Cocheteux, also flatly denied that the generator had any usefulness as a missile engine. They were "very different from engines used to propel missiles," he said, and not useful in building missile engines. "Microturbo, SA, never assisted Iran in any way" on any missile, he added.

The issues involving Dècle are central to the debate over the potential harm caused by UKUSA's worldwide eavesdropping system. Had he been a citizen of one of the UKUSA nations, his name would have been deleted before the report was ever sent out. But because he was not, his name made its way into the computers and possibly onto the watch lists of intelligence agencies, customs bureaus, and other secret and law enforcement organizations around the world. It is unknown with whom those organizations might then have shared the information.

If this did happen, maybe nothing would come of it, or maybe the next time Dècle tried to enter the United States or Britain he would be refused without explanation. Maybe he could even be arrested. Also, after the NSA "reevaluation," were the new conclusions casting doubt on the earlier reports sent to everyone who had received the originals? Or were those recipients left only with the reports indicating that Dècle and Microturbo were secretly selling a cruise missile engine to Iran? Complex issues involving innocent non-UKUSA persons, similar to those raised by the Microturbo intercepts, are likely to occur hundreds of times a week throughout the UKUSA countries. As government surveillance technology becomes even more pervasive, the risks to individual rights grow proportionally.

By 2001, the UKUSA partners had become an eavesdropping superpower with its own laws, language, and customs. It operated secret antennas in nearly every corner of the planet and deep into outer space. Just as mighty navies once ruled the high seas, UKUSA's goal is to rule cyberspace. On a wall at NSA is a plaque presented to Kenneth A. Minihan by GCHQ shortly after his arrival as director in 1996. "Celebrating fifty years of successful partnership," it says, and then notes the "special relationship" of "the English-speaking peoples."

In the late 1990s, for the first time since the in-depth congressional hearings a quarter of a century earlier, NSA was facing probing questions about its eavesdropping activities. This time they were coming mostly from European parliaments, skeptical reporters, and an unusual alliance of left and far-right groups in the United States. In Europe, the principal concern was the suspicion that NSA was eavesdropping on business communications and passing on trade secrets to European firms' American competitors—stealing from Airbus and giving to Boeing, for example.

Interviews with dozens of current and former NSA officials indicate that the agency is not currently engaged in industrial espionage, stealing data from one company and giving it to a competitor. But there is no law preventing the agency from doing so, and because its customers, including the White House and the CIA, dictate NSA's targets, it could conceivably engage in such espionage in the future. The only prerequisite would be a secret verbal order from the president or the director of Central Intelligence that industrial espionage was now a national security requirement. According to information obtained for *Body of Secrets,* something like that came close to happening in 1990, during the administration of President George Bush.

At the time, Vice Admiral William O. Studeman was the director of NSA. "There are a substantial number of legal problems associated—legal and ethical problems—associated with the concept of trying to provide intelligence information directly to business in the United States," said Studeman in 1990. "And so I believe that this decision has not yet been made. I believe that we are going to move in the direction of considering this with great caution. . . . I believe that it's going to be years, and a very slow process and one that's going to be very deliberate as to what kinds of decisions are going to be made."

Direction, said Studeman, would come from above. "We would not be the ones to make that decision," he said. "I would have to defer to the director of Central Intelligence and receive his guidance on this particular subject." The 1990s were a time, said Studeman, when "clearly the area of economics is now becoming the area of principal concern to the American citizen. This is being reflected in the polls. More people are concerned about economic competitiveness than they are concerned about military problems or many other issues in the world today."

In short, the time was ripe to begin quietly turning America's big ear on Airbus and other tough foreign competitors, and had the decision been made, NSA would have begun complying. The issue for the agency was not ethics but mechanics, according to Studeman.

"If economic intelligence and economic competition are defined as a national security interest, the intelligence community is essentially going to have to spread its resources across a lot more of the problem, and the problem is still very big," he said. "When you take all the geographic distribution possibilities and add on top of it the military, political/diplomatic, economic, sociological, ecological, and every other kind of area we're being asked to look at now . . . it's a new world and it's possible we could be caught short and have some cold starts." He added, "The real issue for us is whether or not we can find a way to, number one, successfully collect that intelligence, which is a nontrivial achievement in and of itself, if it were ever directed. And secondly, how do we use it? . . . There isn't any use to collecting it if it cannot be used."

For years NSA had collected economic intelligence, but the agency had not specifically eavesdropped on particular companies for the purpose of industrial espionage. "Right now what broad information NSA collects on trade and that sort of thing in the world," said Studeman, "we provide to federal agencies whether it's Commerce or Treasury or the State Department. We provide that information directly and they are a federal consumer."

Rather than supply direct competitive intelligence to American business, NSA was directed to increase support for the business community—and the American economy—in more indirect ways. One means was to beef up efforts to discover illegal and deceptive tactics, such as bribery, used by foreign competitors to win contracts away from American companies. The other was to devote more resources to providing intelligence to U.S. government negotiators during important trade talks.

NSA had long played a "defensive" role in helping to prevent foreign countries from spying on American companies. "What we use the intelligence instrument for is collecting against other people who are collecting against us for industrial espionage purposes," said Studeman, "or to collect against other people who are not playing by internationally accepted rules of the road or business ethics." But in 1990 the question being debated in the Bush White House and at CIA was whether the NSA would begin going on the "offensive." "We will be definitely helping out on the defensive side," said Studeman. "But the school's out on the offensive."

In one "defensive" case, the CIA obtained details of an offer by

French business executives to allegedly bribe Brazilian officials to steer a $1.4 billion contract toward Thomson-CSF and away from the Raytheon Corporation. Raytheon later won the contract. In 1995, a report presented to Congress cited "almost one hundred cases of foreign firms using bribery to undercut U.S. firms' efforts to win international contracts with about $45 billion." It added, "The foreign firms that offer bribes typically win about eighty percent of the deals."

"If we had any certain evidence," said Studeman, "that someone was essentially targeting an American company, the [intelligence] community would essentially go to that company and actively inform them they are being targeted and also might provide them some kind of advice on how to enhance their security or at least make recommendations about how technically . . . [to] reduce their vulnerability."

Former CIA director R. James Woolsey was far more blunt about NSA's eavesdropping on European companies to detect crooked tactics. "Yes, my continental European friends, we have spied on you," he said.

> And it's true that we use computers to sort through data by using keywords. . . . That's right, my continental friends, we have spied on you because you bribe. Your companies' products are often more costly, less technically advanced, or both, than your American competitors'. As a result you bribe a lot. So complicit are your governments that in several European countries bribes still are tax-deductible.
>
> When we have caught you at it, you might be interested [to know], we haven't said a word to the U.S. companies in the competition. Instead we go to the government you're bribing and tell its officials that we don't take kindly to such corruption. They often respond by giving the most meritorious bid (sometimes American, sometimes not) all or part of the contract. This upsets you, and sometimes creates recriminations between your bribers and the other country's bribees, and this occasionally becomes a public scandal. We love it.

As mentioned earlier, during the 1990s NSA also became more aggressive in providing intelligence during key international trade conferences. Fifty years ago to the day after NSA's predecessor the Signal Security Agency eavesdropped on the San Francisco conference that led to the United Nations, American signals intelligence specialists were preparing to bug another conference. This time, in June 1995, the participants were the United States and Japan, and the subject Japanese luxury car imports to the United States. As before, American negotiators tried to have the conference entirely on U.S. soil, where eavesdropping would be much easier: the Japanese wanted to meet on their own home turf. But a compromise was reached: the talks were to be held partly in Geneva, Switzerland, and partly in Washington.

The dispute was over a $5.9 million punitive tariff on fourteen Japanese luxury cars, scheduled to take effect on June 28. On Sunday night, June 25, U.S. Trade Representative Mickey Kantor arrived in Geneva for the start of the latest round of talks aimed at averting the rapidly approaching deadline. The next morning, at the Intercontinental Hotel near Lake Geneva, in the shadow of the Swiss Alps, Kantor held a press conference. President Clinton, he said, "has directed me to come here and make our best efforts to see if there is any way to open Japanese markets and expand trade as we have been trying to do."

To help Kantor's negotiating team make those "best efforts," an NSA team had been flown in weeks earlier and was housed nearby. They were there to supply the team with intercepted conversations among auto executives from Toyota and Nissan, who were pressuring their government for a settlement. Fortunately for the eavesdroppers, the Japanese negotiators frequently bypassed secure, encrypted phones because insecure hotel telephones were more readily available and easier to use.

But while NSA looks for bribery and eavesdrops on trade missions, there is no evidence that it is a handmaiden to corporate America. Nor, apparently, does GCHQ engage in industrial espionage. In 1984 Jock Kane, a former supervisory intercept operator with thirty years' experience at GCHQ, wrote a blistering manuscript accusing the agency of mismanagement and sloppy security. Before it was published, however, the manuscript was seized by the British government under the Official Secrets Act and never saw the light of day. Publication, said the order, "would be a breach of duty of confidentiality owed to the Crown, and contrary to the provisions of the Official Secrets Act."

In a copy of the manuscript obtained by the author before the seizure, Kane discusses what is clearly the Echelon system, although he does not use the codename. Of industrial espionage, he points out:

> Much of the targeting is ILC—International Licensed Carriers. . . . Thousands of messages are processed every week from these links, on every possible subject, from diplomacy to business, oil supplies, crop failures in any part of the world, down to ordinary domestic telegrams.
>
> From these intercepts pours a wealth of industrial intelligence information into the memory cells of GCHQ's vast computer complex, information that would have been a tremendous asset to British industrialists, but British industry has never had access to this information because GCHQ chiefs, not the Cabinet, took the decision that British industry, which to a large extent finances this vast bureaucracy, should not be one of their "customers."

The issue for Europe is not whether UKUSA's Echelon system is stealing trade secrets from foreign businesses and passing them on to competitors; it is not. The real issue is far more important: it is whether Echelon is doing away with individual privacy—a basic human right. Disembodied snippets of conversations are snatched from the ether, perhaps out of context, and may be misinterpreted by an analyst who then secretly transmits them to spy agencies and law enforcement offices around the world.

The misleading information is then placed in NSA's near-bottomless computer storage system, a system capable of storing 5 *trillion* pages of text, a stack of paper 150 miles high. Unlike information on U.S. persons, which cannot be kept longer than a year, information on foreign citizens can be held eternally. As permanent as India ink, the mark may remain with the person forever. He will never be told how he was placed on a customs blacklist, who put him there, why he lost a contract—or worse.

One snippet of NSA or CIA information concerned an Egyptian immigrant, Nasser Ahmed, who was seeking asylum in the United States. The secret information led to his arrest; he was denied bail and held for more than three years in solitary confinement pending his deportation. Despite years of efforts by his attorney, Abdeen Jabara, once a subject of illegal NSA surveillance himself, he was never told what the "secret evidence" consisted of, where it came from, or how the United States obtained it. In this Kafkaesque world, he could not fight the charges because he was not told what they were: they were secret. It was only after considerable pressure from the Arab-American community that the Justice Department finally ordered some of the information released. Ahmed was then able to successfully challenge it and win his freedom. "With a better understanding of the government's case," wrote the judge in August 1999, the secret evidence "can no longer be viewed as sufficiently reliable to support a finding that [Mr. Ahmed] is a danger." At the time, more than two dozen other people around the country were being held on such "secret evidence." A few months later, another federal judge ruled that to hold someone, whether or not a U.S. citizen, on the basis of "secret evidence" was unconstitutional.

Unchecked, UKUSA's worldwide eavesdropping network could become a sort of cyber secret police, without courts, juries, or the right to a defense.

Whether NSA spies on American citizens has long been a troubling question. Its past record is shameful, not only for what the agency did but for how it went about it. In the late 1960s NSA was an agency unrestrained by laws or legislative charter and led by a man obsessed with secrecy and power. By then Louis Tordella had been deputy director for a decade, during which he had taken the agency from a sleepy backwater to the largest and most secret intelligence organization in American history. Never before or since has any one person held so much power for so long in America's spy world. But where most top officials are drawn to public recognition like moths to streetlights, Tordella was drawn to the darkness. So dark was Tordella's world that he became lost in it, unable anymore to recognize the boundary lines between U.S. citizens and foreign enemies and between a government of open laws and one of secret tyranny. All ears and no eyes, Tordella was leading his agency and his country toward a deep abyss.

Thus in the fall of 1967, when the U.S. Army began requesting intercepts on American citizens and groups, the agency blindly complied.

At the time, the military was worried about a massive "March on the Pentagon," organized to protest the war in Vietnam. Army officials compiled a list of protesters and asked NSA to put their names on its watch lists. Over the following months, other agencies, including the CIA, FBI, and DIA, followed suit. The folksinger Joan Baez was considered a threat and placed on the list, as were the well-known pediatrician Benjamin Spock, the actress Jane Fonda, and Dr. Martin Luther King, Jr. Like weeds in an untended lot, the lists multiplied as more and more people were added and as people who had dealings with the targets became targets themselves.

The domestic watch list program took on added importance on July 1, 1969, when it was granted its own charter and codeword: Minaret. "MINARET information specifically includes communications concerning individuals or organizations," it said, "involved in civil disturbances, antiwar movements/demonstrations and Military deserters involved in the antiwar movements." An equally important aspect of Minaret was keeping NSA's fingerprints off the illegal operation. "Although MINARET will be handled as Sigint and distributed to Sigint recipients, it will not," said the charter, "be identified with the National Security Agency."

Frank Raven, in charge of G Group, which focused on the non-Communist world, was upset by the sudden switch to domestic eavesdropping but could do little about it. At one point, after being given the name of a U.S. citizen to target, he protested. "I tried to object to that on constitutional grounds as to whether or not it was legal—as to whether or not we should do it," he said, "and I was told at that time that you couldn't argue with it—it came from the highest level." Some of the targets, he said, were downright "asinine." "When J. Edgar Hoover gives you a requirement for complete surveillance of all Quakers in the United States," recalled Raven, "when Richard M. Nixon is a Quaker and he's the president of the United States, it gets pretty funny." Hoover apparently believed that the religious group was shipping food and supplies to Southeast Asia.

Since taking office in January 1969, Richard Milhous Nixon had waged a two-front war, one in Southeast Asia against North Vietnam and the other at home against a growing army of antiwar activists. Convinced that foreign interests were financing the antiwar movement, on

June 5, 1970, he met in the Oval Office with Vice Admiral Noel Gayler, who was then the director of NSA, and the chiefs of the CIA, DIA, and FBI. Also present was Tom Charles Huston, a thirty-year-old Hoosier who had been on Pat Buchanan's research and speechwriting staff. A lawyer and recently discharged Army intelligence officer, the young White House counsel had been appointed the point man on the issue.

"Based on my review of the information which we have been receiving at the White House," Nixon told his spy chiefs that Friday afternoon, "I am convinced that we are not currently allocating sufficient resources within the intelligence community to the collection of intelligence data on the activities of these revolutionary groups." According to the DIA's Lieutenant General Donald V. Bennett, "The president chewed our butts."

At Fort Meade, Tordella regarded the change of policy as "nothing less than a heaven-sent opportunity for NSA." At last, he would be able to turn his massive parabolic antennas inward on the unwitting American public. Following submission of an "Eyes Only" memorandum entitled "NSA Contribution to Domestic Intelligence" and signed by Gayler, Huston drew up a proposal for Nixon's signature. It authorized NSA "to program for coverage the communications of U.S. citizens using international facilities." No warrant or probable cause would be required; anyone's international telephone calls or telegrams could be intercepted and distributed. "The FBI does not have the capability to monitor international communications," said the document, which became known as the Huston Plan. "NSA is currently doing so on a restricted basis and the information it has provided has been most helpful. Much of this information is particularly useful to the White House." Restrictions were also lifted on other spy agencies.

But if there was jubilation in Tordella's office, there was outrage at the FBI. J. Edgar Hoover "went through the ceiling" after reading the report. Tordella had earlier warned Gayler: on matters relating to domestic intelligence, no one challenged Hoover. The old lawman saw the move by NSA and the other intelligence agencies into his territory as a direct threat to his exclusive domain.

Out of character as a champion for civil liberties, Hoover stormed into the office of Attorney General John Mitchell and demanded the order be withdrawn. Mitchell agreed. The illegalities spelled out in the memorandum, he said, could not be presidential policy. Mitchell eventually convinced Nixon to drop the program; five days after authorizing it, the president withdrew his approval.

At NSA, Tordella and Gayler were angry over Hoover's protest and the cancellation of the Huston Plan. Nevertheless, they had been conducting domestic intelligence targeting without authorization for many years, and they saw no reason to stop just because the president had formally withdrawn his approval. In fact, the watch lists of American names flowed into NSA faster than ever.

Huston was informed that a new White House aide would be taking over responsibility for internal security matters and that from now on he would be on the new aide's staff. He was then introduced to his new boss, a young lawyer who had worked under Mitchell at the Justice Department and had been transferred to the White House only a few days earlier: John Wesley Dean III. Dean tossed the Huston Plan in his office safe and spun the dial.

Three years later, like a body discovered in the woods, the Huston Plan came back to haunt Nixon. By then the Watergate scandal had brought his presidency to disaster and the Oval Office resembled a shell-torn bunker. Every day, new revelations sent cracks down the cream-colored walls. Among the most serious problems was the recent defection of John Dean. He had given the Huston Plan to the prosecution as a bargaining chip in his plea for immunity. Because few in the White House recalled the plan's contents, there was a scramble to grasp the document's importance.

On May 16, 1973, a worried Richard Nixon met in the Oval Office with his lawyer, J. Fred Buzhardt, Jr., to discuss the new development. "Well, what the hell is this?" said Nixon.

"What he has, Mr. President," Buzhardt explained, "there was a plan for intelligence gathering, primarily in the domestic area."

Nixon smelled blackmail. "Oh—it's in the domestic area, so he thinks that's gonna scare us," he said. "What in the name of God is this? Why do you think he's played this game?"

"I have no idea, Mr. President," replied Buzhardt. "But we have managed to identify from his remarks—I have found a copy of this thing, at NSA—I just talked to Lou Tordella."

That late Wednesday afternoon, Buzhardt was particularly worried because the document clearly showed that Nixon had ordered NSA to begin illegally targeting American citizens. But even after more than four years in the White House, Nixon had no idea even what NSA was—despite the fact that he had signed the order.

"Now, I'm fairly sure NSA . . . ," Buzhardt began, but then Nixon cut in. "What is the NSA?" he asked. "What kind of action do they do?"

"I don't know the specifics," replied Buzhardt. "They pick up communications stuff, they don't actually tap."

"Anything the NSA did is totally defensible," Nixon instinctively shot back.

"I think it's defensible," said Buzhardt, "but I think that they move into a broader category with respect to domestic affairs."

Nixon was again confused. "Right, meaning, picking up by—what do you mean, electronic surveillance?"

"Targeting—yes sir—targeting U.S. citizens' conversations that were on international circuits," explained Buzhardt.

"Doing so because of their concern about their being involved in violence?" Nixon asked.

"Yes, sir," agreed Buzhardt.

Not only had Nixon forgotten signing the document, he had also forgotten canceling it five days later. But the Defense Intelligence Agency had earlier reminded Buzhardt of the fact.

"DIA says that—thinks it was terminated?" asked Nixon.

"They think it was terminated," said Buzhardt. "And they told me independently from Huston that they think the approval was recalled, and that's what Huston said. Now we're going to check this thoroughly with NSA, and the reason it's important is because if you remember, they [NSA] were the most aggressive group to go forward."

"NSA," said Nixon.

Buzhardt agreed, "NSA."

"NSA probably did something," added Nixon, finally catching on. "The electronic work."

They also began discussing NSA's long battle with the FBI over embassy break-ins in Washington. Tordella had long pressured Hoover to send his black-bag specialists into various embassies in Washington in order to steal codes and bug cipher machines. This was far less time-consuming than attempting to break the codes at NSA using computers, a method known as brute force. For many years Hoover had approved such operations, but in 1967, worried about the scandal that might result if one of his teams was discovered, he stopped the practice.

In an effort to force Hoover to begin cooperating again, Gayler met with him and Attorney General John Mitchell on March 29, 1971. NSA, he said, was "most desirous" of having the black-bag coverage resumed. Hoover erupted, saying he "was not at all enthusiastic" about such an extension of operations, in view of the hazards to the FBI. Despite the meeting, the feud continued and it was only after L. Patrick Gray took over as acting FBI director, following Hoover's death on May 2, 1972, that the Bureau once again began embassy break-ins on behalf of NSA.

During the May 1973 Oval Office meeting with Buzhardt, Nixon brought up the embassy black-bag jobs, adding them to his growing list of problems that might surface as a result of Dean's defection.

"They never quite got a handle on it until Pat Gray was appointed," said Buzhardt.

"Shit," exclaimed Nixon.

"Pat went out to visit NSA, and took four of his assistants with him, and he told Lou Tordella, 'I understand we used to do things with you that were very helpful.' Pat was putting back together the assets."

"[Who] told you this?" asked Nixon.

"Tordella told me this," said Buzhardt.

Nixon later made a cryptic remark to his top aide, H. R. Haldeman, that seems to indicate that black-bag jobs at the embassies of India and Pakistan may have led to the breaking of their ciphers.

"In fact, the India-Pakistan one," said Nixon, "that's the way it was broken. . . . Although that's one we've got to bury forever."

Nixon's meeting with Buzhardt went late into the night and then continued the next morning. The two were worried not just about the documents but also about whether NSA might have secretly recorded any of its officials' conversations with White House officials concerning the targeting of Americans and the black-bag jobs.

"I don't know," said Buzhardt. "I wouldn't be surprised if they [NSA] tape the conversations going in and out of there. I don't think they would admit it."

"No, they shouldn't," said Nixon, apparently supporting NSA's secret taping of all calls to and from the agency.

"Even to me," replied Buzhardt. "But I had the definite impression."

"They're a (starry-eyed?) bunch," said Nixon. (The parenthesis is in the original.)

Buzhardt added, "There are (75,000?) people there." (Parenthesis in original.)

"I think Hoover taped all his conversations," said Nixon.

During his May 16 and 17, 1973, discussion with Nixon, Buzhardt also brought up another of NSA's enormously secret and illegal operations, one codenamed Shamrock. It involved an agreement whereby the major U.S. telegraph companies, such as Western Union, secretly turned over to NSA, every day, copies of all messages sent to or from the United States. (Indeed, by the 1970s, NSA had developed a watch list consisting of the names of more than 600 American citizens. These names had been placed in NSA's computers and any communications containing one of those names—such as the telegrams obtained through Shamrock—would be kicked out, analyzed, and sent to whoever in the federal government wanted the information thus obtained.) "Well, Mr. President," Buzhardt said, "the way the collection operation works—on some in and out line, this foreign collection—what some of the communication companies here use to pick those communications up, that go to the foreign country and back."

Nixon had little interest in this, because it did not directly relate to his Watergate problems. "But at least that's one Watergate story that's—"

Buzhardt completed the sentence. "That's going to be a dud," he said. "NSA participation in anything domestic—they define it as foreign politics."

Luckily for NSA, Buzhardt and Nixon said no more about Shamrock. But in 1975, two years after Nixon resigned, another investigation began picking up clues to the operation. This time it was a probe by Idaho's Senator Frank Church into possible illegal actions by the U.S. intelligence community.

One of the investigators assigned to the committee was L. Britt Snider, a thirty-year-old lawyer. "I was given the task," he said, "of trying to crack what was perceived to be the most secretive of U.S. intelligence agencies, the National Security Agency." His boss warned him, "They call it 'No Such Agency.' "

Snider began by asking the Congressional Research Service for everything on the public record that referred to NSA. "The CRS soon supplied us with a one-paragraph description from the *Government Organization Manual*," he said, "and a patently erroneous piece from *Rolling Stone* magazine. . . . In 1975, NSA was an agency that had never before had an oversight relationship with Congress."

Early clues to NSA's darkest secrets came from comments in the final report of an earlier investigation into the intelligence community, this one led by then Vice President Nelson Rockefeller. "The first was a reference to an office in New York that CIA had provided NSA for the purpose of copying telegrams," said Snider. "The other disclosed that CIA had asked NSA to monitor the communications of certain U.S. citizens active in the antiwar movement. At last we had something to sink our teeth into."

For weeks, NSA stonewalled all questions and requests for documents on the two areas. Finally, the Church Committee sent formal interrogatories to NSA, but the agency claimed that the subject was so sensitive that only Church and John Tower, the ranking minority member, would be permitted to be briefed. But then a story appeared in the *New York Times* alleging that NSA had eavesdropped on the international communications of U.S. citizens. "With the allegations now a matter of public record," said Snider, "NSA wanted to explain its side of the story." At NSA, Snider was briefed on Operation Shamrock, which was so secret that only a few even within the agency knew of its existence.

"Every day," the briefer told Snider, "a courier went up to New York on the train and returned to Fort Meade with large reels of magnetic tape, which were copies of the international telegrams sent from New York the preceding day using the facilities of three telegraph companies. The tapes would then be electronically processed for items of foreign intelligence interest, typically telegrams sent by foreign establishments in the United States or telegrams that appeared to be encrypted." Although telegrams sent by U.S. citizens to foreign destinations were also present on the tapes, the briefer added that "we're too busy just keeping up with the real stuff" to look at them. The briefer then said the program had been terminated by the secretary of defense the previous May, as the Church Committee began looking into NSA. "I asked if the secretary had ended it because he knew the Committee was on to it," said Snider. "Not really," the briefer said, "the program just wasn't producing very much of value."

But whenever Snider attempted to probe into the background of the operation—how it started, who approved it, and how long it had been going on—he was constantly told, "I don't know." The keeper of the secrets, the briefer said, was Dr. Louis Tordella, who had retired in April 1974 as deputy director.

On a Sunday afternoon in September, Snider knocked on the front door of Tordella's Kensington, Maryland, home. "Tordella was clearly uncomfortable with the whole idea of confiding in someone like me," said Snider. "He said he was not so worried about me as about the Committee and what it might make of the 'facts.' He asked me what I knew about Shamrock. I told him. He sighed a long sigh and then began a discourse on Shamrock that lasted into the early evening."

Tordella told Snider about Shamrock's origins in the days following World War II. "All the big international carriers were involved," Tordella said, "but none of 'em ever got a nickel for what they did." The companies had been assured at the time that President Harry S. Truman and Attorney General Tom Clark were aware of the program and approved its continuation. But Tordella knew of no further high-level approval until he finally told Secretary of Defense James R. Schlesinger in 1973. "To his knowledge," said Snider, "Schlesinger had been the only secretary to have such a briefing," even though NSA reports to the secretary of defense.

Like an inmate making a jailhouse confession, Tordella outlined the illegal scheme. Snider later summarized it:

> During the 1950s, paper tape had been the medium of choice. Holes were punched in the paper tape and then scanned to created an electronic transmission. Every day, an NSA courier would pick up the reels of punched paper tape that were left over and take them back to Fort Meade. In the early 1960s, the companies switched to magnetic tape. While

the companies were agreeable to continuing the program, they wanted to retain the reels of magnetic tape. This necessitated NSA's finding a place to make copies of the magnetic tapes the companies were using. In 1966, Tordella had personally sought assistance from the CIA to rent office space in New York City so that NSA could duplicate the magnetic tapes there. This lasted until 1973, Tordella said, when CIA pulled out of the arrangement because of concerns raised by its lawyers. NSA then arranged for its own office space in Manhattan.

Tordella recalled that while many NSA employees were aware of Shamrock, only one lower-level manager—who reported to him directly—had had ongoing responsibility for the program over the years. . . . Tordella recalled that years would sometimes go by without his hearing anything about Shamrock. It just ran on, he said, without a great deal of attention from anyone.

I asked if NSA used the take from Shamrock to spy on the international communications of American citizens. Tordella responded, "Not per se." NSA was not interested in these kinds of communications as a rule, he said, but he said there were a few cases where the names of American citizens had been used by NSA to select out their international communications, and to the extent this was done, the take from Shamrock would have been sorted in accordance with these criteria. He noted that . . . the Nixon administration had thought about turning over Shamrock to the FBI, but the FBI did not want it.

When I asked if it was legal for NSA to read the telegrams of American citizens, he replied, "You'll have to ask the lawyers."

I noted that I would have expected the companies themselves to be concerned, and Tordella remarked that "the companies are what worry me about this." He said that whatever they did, they did out of patriotic reasons. They had presumed NSA wanted the tapes to look for foreign intelligence. That was NSA's mission. If the telegrams of

> American citizens were looked at, the companies had no knowledge of it.
>
> I countered with the observation that, by making the tapes available to the government, the companies had to know they were providing the wherewithal for the government to use them however it wanted. They had to bear some responsibility.
>
> The comment caused Tordella's temper to flare for the first time during our interview. The companies were not responsible, he reiterated, they were just doing what the government asked them to do because they were assured it was important to national security. If their role were exposed by the Committee, it would subject them to embarrassment, if not lawsuits, and it would discourage other companies from cooperating with U.S. intelligence for years to come. I told him that the Committee had yet to determine how the whole matter would be treated, including the involvement of the companies. We parted amicably, but he clearly had misgivings about how this would turn out. His distrust of politicians was manifest.

Following Tordella's mea culpa, Snider began probing what the companies knew and when they knew it. Only one former employee, from RCA Global, had been on the job at the beginning of the program. "He said the Army had come to him and asked for the company's cooperation," said Snider, "and, by damn, that was enough for him." An executive from ITT, on the other hand, "came to the deposition surrounded by a phalanx of corporate lawyers who proceeded to object to every question once I had gotten past the man's name and position." Snider said, "I pointed out to them that this was the United States Senate—not a court of law—and, if they wanted to object to the questions I was asking I would have a senator come in and overrule every one of their objections. They piped down after that."

When the committee's report was being drafted, Snider argued against the public release of the names of the companies. But the committee's chief counsel, Frederick A. O. Schwartz, disagreed. "The companies had a duty to protect the privacy of their customers," he said;

"they deserved to be exposed. If the Committee did not do it, it would become the subject of criticism itself." Pushed by Church, the committee voted to make its report public—over NSA's vehement objections, and to the great displeasure of its Republican members.

President Gerald Ford telephoned Church and other senators, imploring them to reconsider. But Church was determined to go forward and the next day, Lieutenant General Lew Allen, the NSA director, was scheduled to testify before the committee in public session—a situation unprecedented for NSA. (The testimony on which the report was based had, of course, been given in closed session.) There, in the packed hearing room with television cameras rolling, Allen faced the full committee. Church himself raised the issue of Shamrock, although he did not name the companies. "In his view," said Snider, "the program was illegal, and its disclosure would not harm national security." But after a flurry of objections by Republican members of the committee, including Senators Barry Goldwater and Howard Baker, Church agreed to reserve any further discussion of Shamrock for closed session.

Over the next few days, the White House continued to plead with the committee to drop all mention of Shamrock from its final report. "For the first time since the Committee began operations," said Snider, "Attorney General Edward Levi, speaking expressly on behalf of the president, personally appealed to the Committee not to publish the Shamrock report on the grounds that publication would damage national security." But the weight of opinion among committee members was for disclosure. "Senators were bothered that the telegrams of Americans had for years been handed over to an intelligence agency," said Snider. "Whatever its legality, it should not have happened. . . . Why was the identification of the companies a national security concern? Yes, the report might be embarrassing to them and they might even get sued because of it, but why should that make it classified?"

So the committee voted to disregard the White House objections and leave in the damning material. "It remains to this day the only occasion I know of where a congressional committee voted to override a presidential objection and publish information the president contended was classified," said Snider.

Months later, in March 1976, the committee was notified that "a lower-level employee" at NSA had discovered a file relating to Shamrock—the first such file found. (The committee's report had been based on testimony it heard.) "The file proved to be a mother lode of information," said Snider. "The documents also cast doubts on the veracity of the companies' claims that they could find no documentation pertaining to Shamrock. After all, this had concerned the highest levels of their corporate management for at least four years."

By 2000 Snider had risen through the intelligence community to become the CIA's inspector general. Looking back, he said, "I came to see that relations between intelligence agencies and the private sector endured. Lawyers became more involved than they used to be, but questions of legality were no longer ignored or unresolved. Agreements were put in writing and signed by the responsible officials.

"I also came to think that the investigation, in the long term, had a beneficial effect on NSA. With no desire to undergo another such experience, NSA adopted very stringent rules in the wake of the Church Committee to ensure that its operations were carried out in accordance with applicable law. Where the communications of U.S. citizens were concerned, I can attest from my personal experience that NSA has been especially scrupulous. As upsetting and demoralizing as the Church Committee's investigation undoubtedly was, it caused NSA to institute a system which keeps it within the bounds of U.S. law and focused on its essential mission. Twenty-three years later, I still take some satisfaction from that."

Among the reforms to come out of the Church Committee investigation was the creation of the Foreign Intelligence Surveillance Act (FISA), which for the first time outlined what NSA was and was not permitted to do. The new statute outlawed wholesale, warrantless acquisition of raw telegrams such as had been provided under Shamrock. It also outlawed the arbitrary compilation of watch lists containing the names of Americans. Under FISA, a secret federal court was set up, the Foreign Intelligence Surveillance Court. In order for NSA to target an American citizen or a permanent resident alien—a "green card" holder—within the United States, a secret warrant must be obtained from the court. To get the warrant, NSA officials must show that the person they wish to target is either an agent of a foreign power or involved in espionage or terrorism.

But because these issues fall under the jurisdiction of the FBI within the United States, NSA seldom becomes involved. Thus, according to a senior U.S. intelligence official involved in Sigint, NSA does not target Americans at home. "I want to make it clear," said the official, "[that] we do not intentionally target known U.S. persons in the United States—period. And therefore, we don't go to court to get a warrant to target any such people because we don't do any of those . . . FBI worries about spies in the United States." The same goes for foreigners suspected of terrorism, he said. "Osama bin Laden . . . comes into the United States, he crosses the border," said the intelligence official. "We wouldn't do the guy. It would be FBI who'd do him, because he's a terrorist in the United States." Thus, the vast majority of the 886 eavesdropping warrants approved by the Foreign Intelligence Surveillance Court in 1999—the highest number ever—were from the FBI.

Judicial protections, however, stop at the border. "FISA doesn't cover the U.S. person who's outside the United States," added the official. To target Americans outside the country, all that is needed is the approval of the U.S. attorney general. Nevertheless, the number of Americans targeted by NSA overseas is very small. "At any one time," said the senior intelligence official, "there may be five. . . . These persons are—there's virtually no doubt that they are agents of foreign powers. Either they're terrorists or they're some kind of officer or employee of a foreign government. We're not talking about Jane Fonda."

He added: "We'll find out that person *X* in a foreign country is a terrorist. And maybe he has a green card and he used to live in the United States. He's got a green card, we treat him as a U.S. person. So most of the people that we're after are not citizens but resident aliens who have gone back to another country."

On the other hand, NSA does not need a FISA Court order to spy on foreign embassies and diplomats within the United States, just an okay from the attorney general, which is good for a full year.

The deliberate targeting of Americans is only one issue. The other is what is done when an American—or a citizen of one of the other UKUSA nations—incidentally turns up in the reams of intercepted traffic. This is becoming more and more likely as technology advances. "The networks have collapsed into one another," said one senior NSA official, "and many of our targets are on the same network that we use. It is now just 'the network'—the global telecommunications infrastructure."

Heavy restrictions are placed on the dissemination of names of UKUSA residents. This is in stark contrast to the freewheeling use and distribution of European names, such as Dècle's. NSA's bible governing "whom we may target, how we collect, select, and store such information, and how we disseminate information on U.S. persons" is United States Signals Intelligence Directive 18 (USSID 18), "Limitations and Procedures in Signals Intelligence Operations of the United States Sigint System." It was first drawn up in May 1976, shortly after the Church Committee investigation, and it is occasionally updated.

By 1999 a number of people were questioning whether USSID 18 should be completely rewritten to better reflect the workings of modern-day signals intelligence. "These concerns are legitimate," said an NSA operations panel. "USSID 18 is not easy to read and understand. It deals with a complicated subject and, therefore, is a document that must be read carefully. This is not justification, however, for it to be rewritten."

Key to the directive is the definition of "U.S. persons," because it determines whether a given intercept will be swept in, analyzed, and disseminated. "A person known to be currently in the United States," it says, "will be treated as a United States person unless positively identified as an alien who has not been admitted for permanent residence; or unless the nature or circumstances of the person's communications give rise to a reasonable belief that such person is not a United States person."

On the other hand, "A person known to be currently outside the United States, or whose location is unknown, will not be treated as a United States person unless such person can be positively identified as such, or the nature or circumstances of the person's communications give rise to a reasonable belief that such person is a United States person."

In 1994 a forty-seven-page document entitled "U.S. Identities in Sigint" was issued to further clarify under what circumstances the names of U.S. persons must be deleted or may be retained in Sigint reports. While in most cases U.S. names must be removed, the document said, this rule does not apply under certain circumstances—for example, in the event of an emergency "such as a hijacking or a terrorist attack."

"When specific, actionable threat information involving U.S. persons is obtained," said one instruction, "reporting elements issue a report with as much information as possible, including U.S. names, in the interest of protecting U.S. persons." NSA uses "Implied Consent Procedures" in cases such as kidnappings or hijackings, "where a U.S. person is held captive by a foreign power or a group engaged in international terrorism and consent for NSA collection could be implied."

Another exception allows for reporting the communications of U.S. persons when there is "evidence of a crime." These are cases, said the present NSA director, Michael Hayden, where "we bump into violations, or potential violations of law—threats to physical security, possible espionage, possible disclosure of classified information. . . . In the last sixteen months, that has happened a total of eighteen times. In those eighteen instances, there were ten instances in which the information was about U.S. persons. Six instances in which it appeared the information was about U.S. persons but we were far, far from definite. And two others—the remaining two other instances, the information was about individuals of unknown nationality. We simply didn't know."

In 1980, while intercepting everything in and out of Libya, NSA analysts discovered that President Jimmy Carter's brother Billy was doing business with and acting as an unregistered agent of the Libyan government. Bobby Ray Inman, who was then the NSA director, showed the intercepts to the U.S. attorney general and an investigation was launched, leading to what became known as the Billygate scandal.

Analysts are forbidden to mention in their reports not only the actual names of U.S. citizens and green card holders but also the names of U.S. companies. "As a general rule," says one internal document, "analysts must select generic terms to replace the U.S. identity and must present the report details in such a way that the customer cannot determine the identity."

Any time a U.S. identity is mentioned in a Sigint report, the Operations Directorate must keep a record of it for a quarterly report sent to the agency's inspector general. "Please remember," said one internal memorandum, "that if a U.S. identity is disseminated in any fashion, e.g., product, analytical exchange, etc., NSA is then required to account for the times the identity is disclosed outside of the Sigint System, whether the disclosure is intentional or not."

In an attempt to prevent inappropriate intercepts and dissemination, frequent training sessions are conducted for intercept operators and analysts (seventeen such sessions were held in November 1998, for example). Analysts are offered difficult hypothetical scenarios similar to situations they might encounter, and correct responses are taught. "You have reason to believe that the [cell phone] user is involved in international narcotics trafficking," says one hypothetical, "but you have no information telling you whether or not he is a U.S. person: Can you collect?"

Despite all the hypotheticals, real-world operations frequently give rise to complex questions concerning just what names and titles to leave in or take out of finished Sigint reports. The following issues have come up in the past few years.

- In January 1993, a few weeks before President-elect Clinton was going to be sworn in as president, a question arose concerning how to refer to him and his cabinet choices when their names turned up in intercepts. While it violates USSID 18 to refer to U.S. persons by name, senior U.S. executive branch officials can be referred to by *title* without special permission. The problem was that they were not yet sworn in.

"The NSA Office of the General Counsel," said an NSA document, "has advised that titles of these candidates may be used in reports . . . as follows: title of position to which candidate has been nominated followed by the word 'designee' (e.g., Secretary of Defense Designee). These titles should be used until such time as the candidates have been confirmed and the Clinton Administration assumes responsibility. Names of the candidates should not be used without prior approval. . . . As always, titles should only be used if they are necessary to understand or assess foreign intelligence."

It is interesting to note that NSA analysts must also delete the names of United Nations officials from reports and, in the case of senior officials, must include only their titles. Generic terms—such as, perhaps, "UN official"—must be substituted for the names of lower-ranking officials.

- Six months after the inauguration, NSA analysts found the name of Hillary Rodham Clinton turning up in intercept reports. What was her status?

A federal court had determined that her work on health care policy put her in the category of a full-time government official. As a result, "Mrs. Clinton may be identified in reports," said an internal NSA memorandum, "only by title (currently, Chairperson of the President's Task Force on National Health Care Reform) without prior approval when that title is necessary to understand or assess foreign intelligence and when the information being discussed relates to her official duties. Should Mrs. Clinton be assigned to other task forces or official duties in the Executive Branch, those titles may also be used, as necessary. Reports containing information about Mrs. Clinton that is not clearly foreign intelligence must be checked, at a minimum, through Office and Group level 05 [policy] elements. As with other senior officials of the Executive Branch, no reports may be published concerning Mrs. Clinton's private life or activities absent evidence of criminal wrongdoing and even then only after review by senior NSA management and the OGC [Office of the General Counsel]."

- In 1994, former president Jimmy Carter was invited to travel to Bosnia and Herzegovina by Bosnian Serb president Radovan Karadzic to participate in efforts to help end the war that had been raging there. In December 1994, Carter tentatively accepted the offer and stated that he would travel to Bosnia as a representative of the Carter Center for Peace.

The Balkans were a key target area for NSA, so the Operations Directorate anticipated that a number of intercepts would mention Carter or would even be to or from him. For this reason, it issued a directive regarding whether Carter's name would appear in NSA reports sent out to "customers":

> The current U.S. Administration [that of President Clinton] has cautiously welcomed this development, but has

> made it clear that Former President Carter would be traveling to Bosnia as a private U.S. citizen and not as a representative of the U.S. Government.
>
> Since Former President Carter will not be officially representing the U.S. Government, any reports that reflect either his travels to Bosnia or his participation in efforts to end the war may identify him only as a "U.S. person." Only if Former President Carter eventually becomes an official envoy of the U.S. Government in this activity, could he then be identified as a "former U.S. president."

- In 1995, there was great concern in Washington over the fate of Michael DeVine, an American who ran a hotel in the Guatemalan rain forest, and Efraín Bamaca Velásquez, a guerrilla leader married to an American lawyer. The evidence indicated that they had both been killed by a Guatemalan military officer on the CIA's payroll and that the agency may have known of the murders. Outraged, Senator Robert Torricelli of New Jersey wrote to President Clinton: "The direct involvement of the Central Intelligence Agency in the murder of these individuals leads me to the extraordinary conclusion that the agency is simply out of control and that it contains what can only be called a criminal element."

As a result of a number of calls for investigations by both the CIA and Congress, NSA was asked to check its massive database—years' worth of stored raw traffic—for "any information concerning events in Guatemala from January 1987 to the present" relating to DeVine and Velásquez. Seeing that NSA could be dragged into a quagmire by the request, NSA's general counsel reminded the Operations Directorate that federal law "prohibits the collection of communications to, from, or about U.S. persons without approval of either the Director, NSA, the Attorney General, or the FISA Court depending on the circumstances." He added, "NSA is not authorized to collect Sigint for law enforcement or investigative purposes." The lawyers were no doubt worried about intercepts turning up in civil lawsuits or criminal proceedings.

- In June 1996, as former senator Bob Dole and President Clinton began squaring off for the fall elections, analysts were specially reminded to be careful to avoid mentioning any candidate or political party that might be picked up in an intercept. "The political parties of the U.S. are," said the memorandum, "considered U.S. persons, as are the candidates themselves. Since a U.S. identity is considered to be revealed whenever the reader of a report can recognize a particular U.S. person, avoid identifying the political parties or the candidates by name, unique title, personal identifier, or textual context."

The memo went on, "We anticipate that as the 1996 election campaigns go on, there may be instances when references to political parties and candidates will be necessary to understand foreign intelligence or assess its importance. In such cases . . . refer to the U.S. identity in generic terms only: a U.S. political party, a U.S. presidential candidate, a U.S. Senate candidate, etc. Remember that even when such terms are used, the context of the report could constitute an identification."

- During the October 1997 summit in Washington between President Clinton and China's Jiang Zemin, greatly expanded eavesdropping operations were planned. The planning required extensive searching through satellite and microwave channels—"search and development"—for key circuits of potential intelligence value.

Four months earlier, in preparation for the event, the lawyer assigned to NSA's Operations Directorate sent out a Top Secret/Comint Channels Only briefing memorandum to those preparing for the complex operation. "USSID 18 procedures for Search and Development are broader than those identified in the main body of the USSID," it said; this may have meant that domestic communications channels were to be searched. "During the course of search and development any signals with communications to, from, or about U.S. persons should be handled in accordance with the processing section of the USSID."

The memorandum then laid out a series of questions the intercept operators and analysts should ask themselves, among which were the following: "Will you get the information through a database?" "Who is the target? What is his/her status as a U.S. person?" "What is the foreign intelligence purpose?" "What do you reasonably expect to get from the proposed electronic surveillance and what is the basis of that belief?"

The memorandum also established a number of guidelines. "If your focus is a foreign target and you incidentally have a U.S. person on one side of the communications," it said, "the foreign intelligence may be reported as long as you focus on the foreign aspect and minimize out the U.S. side. The U.S. information must be replaced with a generic term unless it meets [certain other] criteria. . . . If someone requests U.S. person information you must have them contact P022 [NSA's Special Product Control Branch]."

Officials anticipated that analysts would make heavy use of what one document referred to as NSA's "raw traffic storage systems which contain identities of U.S. persons." As a result, analysts were cautioned, "Do your research before you get on the system and try to anticipate what type of information you will get back when you type in your query."

As tight as the laws, regulations, and internal guidelines governing the NSA are, a few potential loopholes exist. Although NSA takes great pains to eliminate the names of U.S. persons in the reports it sends out, any customer (for instance, CIA or DIA) can obtain the names simply by faxing a request to NSA. The request must offer a reason and state that the name "is necessary to understand the foreign intelligence or assess its importance." In case such a request is received, NSA keeps the names in its database for up to a year. And the agency will not disclose how often names are released through this backdoor procedure.

"Americans were never listed" in reports, said one of NSA's customers. "It would say 'U.S. Person.' Also for the Brits. If you [the customer] needed the name you could make a request—there's an office called U.S. Identities, and you [the customer] could call them [the U.S. Identities Office] up and send them a letter and say, I need to know who that guy is. They [U.S. Identities] could tell you, if you . . . sent them a letter explaining why. You would tell them the transmittal number, serial number. It didn't make any difference if the U.S. person was in the

U.S. or overseas. As long as you give them a reasonable explanation as to why you needed it. And then they [NSA] call you back and they say, 'Hi, we're calling about your letter, serial number so and so,' and they [NSA] would say, 'Here's the name and here's the control number,' so they'd [NSA] have a tracking number."

"If the [Sigint] report goes out to twenty people, not all twenty people get the identity," said a senior intelligence official involved in Sigint. "Maybe only five people will come in and ask for it. The five people who come in and ask for it have to ask for it in writing, and they have to demonstrate they need it for their official duties and that it's necessary to understand the foreign intelligence or assess its importance. If they don't, we don't give it to them. If they do, then they get the identity of the U.S. person, but there's a record that that has happened."

Although USSID 18 directs that "communications identified as domestic communications shall be promptly destroyed," there is an exception: "Domestic communications that are reasonably believed to contain foreign intelligence information shall be disseminated to the Federal Bureau of Investigation (including United States person identities) for possible further dissemination by the Federal Bureau of Investigation in accordance with its minimization procedures."

Also, international and foreign communications between two Americans can be retained and distributed at the discretion of the director of NSA, providing that he determines that the intercept contains "significant foreign intelligence or possible evidence of a crime." U.S. Attorney General Janet Reno approved these revised guidelines on July 1, 1997.

While the federal government allows a number of exceptions to its privacy constraints when it comes to average Americans, no exceptions are permitted concerning the government's own communications. If an intercept operator inadvertently picks up a conversation one party to which is a U.S. official, the tape must be destroyed immediately—even if the official is talking to one of NSA's key targets.

For Americans, the greatest danger of NSA is its involvement with law enforcement. During the Nixon years, NSA was used to secretly target antiwar protesters and others in disfavor with the White House. Today, among NSA's key targets areas are the "transnational" threats: narcotics trafficking, terrorism, international organized crime, weapons proliferation, and illicit trade practices. "The primary purpose of the collection activity," says one NSA document, "will be the production of foreign intelligence information on the foreign aspects of international narcotics trafficking. No collection for law enforcement purposes or in support of law enforcement operations is authorized. All collection must be designed to satisfy national Sigint requirements. Information pertaining to the international narcotics trafficking activities targeted for collection will be forwarded to NSA for analysis and reporting."

"If the Sigint business can tell the president, 'When you're dealing with this guy, you're effectively dealing with the XYZ cartel,' " said one senior intelligence official involved in Sigint, "that's pretty good information for the president to know."

One of those most opposed to NSA involvement in law enforcement is the agency's former top lawyer, Stewart A. Baker. "When I was at the National Security Agency," he said, "we used to joke about the predictable stages traversed by prosecutors who sought intelligence reports in connection with big investigations. The first reaction was open-mouthed wonder at what the intelligence agencies were able to collect. That was followed by an enthusiastic assumption that vast quantities of useful data must lie in our files. Next came the grinding review of individual documents and the growing realization that the reports were prepared for other purposes and so were unlikely to contain much of relevance to the investigator's specific concerns. Last came ennui, and a gritted-teeth plod through the reports, mostly to avoid a later charge that the examination was incomplete."

NSA's major push into law enforcement came with the fall of the Berlin Wall and the collapse of communism. "Because the Soviet Union was no longer a threat," said Baker, "some of the resources devoted to extracting its secrets could be turned to other tasks, to other foreign targets. But some of those foreign targets had a domestic tinge. As topics like international narcotics trafficking, terrorism, alien smuggling, and Russian organized crime rose in priority for the intelligence community, it became harder to distinguish between targets of law enforcement and those of national security."

Soon, common centers were formed for counterdrug, counterterrorism, counterproliferation, and counter-international-organized-crime activities. They were populated by both law enforcement and intelligence personnel, again dangerously mixing the two areas. "Few foresaw any danger in nibbling a bit at the principle that intelligence and law enforcement must remain separate undertakings," said Baker. "Today the risk to civil liberties is largely theoretical. However theoretical [those] risks . . . may be, they cannot be ignored. . . . One of my office's jobs at the agency was to review requests for intelligence from drug enforcement agencies. In some cases, we suspected they were trying to shortcut constitutional or statutory limits, and their requests were denied. But I have no illusions that our objections would have prevailed if a different message had been coming from the leaders of the agency and the government."

In the end, the question of whether NSA is secretly abusing its enormous powers comes down to trust. " 'Trust us' is the NSA's implicit message," said David Ignatius of the *Washington Post.* "Trust us to distinguish between the good guys and the bad guys, and to use our powerful surveillance tools for the good of humankind. As an American and a trusting soul, I want to extend that confidence to General Hayden and his beleaguered colleagues. The United States needs an NSA that can shed its threadbare old clothes—and, when necessary, can crack the codes and monitor the conversations of people who could get us all killed. But it is unrealistic to expect the rest of the world to be enthusiastic. People will be glad when the NSA bags that biological terrorist as he's about to deliver the anthrax bomb—even those dyspeptic European parliamentarians. But don't expect them to give the global policeman much help along the way—or to stop demanding the same privacy rights that Americans have."

On a Monday evening in January, everything suddenly went quiet. NSA's brain, overworked, had a sudden seizure, a blackout. Its ears continued to hear, pulling in the millions of messages an hour, but its mind could no longer think.

Three miles away in his stately brick home on Butler Avenue, NSA Director Michael Hayden, an Air Force lieutenant general, had just finished his dinner and was watching television when his secure STU-III phone rang. The entire system had crashed, he was told. It was January 24, 2000.

While it was 7:00 P.M. at NSA, it was midnight deep within the computers, which operate on Greenwich Mean Time. For some reason, at that moment a piece of software malfunctioned, setting off a systemwide shutdown. "It was the whole net by which we move, use, abuse, process—everything we do with information here at Fort Meade went down," said Hayden. "Everything on the Fort Meade campus went down. Everything."

The director ordered an emergency response. Computer scientists, electrical engineers, mathematicians, anyone who could shed light on the problem was told to report in. " 'What do I tell the workforce?' " Hayden said he thought. "I called [Director of Corporate Communications] Bill [Marshall] in here and I said, 'Bill, I need a concept; we need to communicate this to the workforce. What should we do?' " Marshall suggested a town meeting. "And that's exactly what we did." Taking to the stage in the Friedman Auditorium, Hayden warned everyone not to say a word about the crash. "I said the fact that we're down is an operational secret," Hayden recalled. "Our adversaries cannot know that our intelligence capabilities have been crippled."

On the second floor of the Tordella Supercomputer Facility, scientists pulled apart spaghettilike mazes of multicolored wires, covered desks and floors with unwieldy schematics and wiring diagrams, and probed, inch by inch, the computer's nervous system.

To Hayden, the crash came as a shock—especially because only three weeks earlier, on New Year's Day 2000, he had successfully dodged the Y2K bullet. But for nearly a decade, pressured by ever-increasing demand and overuse, NSA's brain had been heading for a stroke. The first signs appeared in the early 1990s, when it became obvious that the agency's massive system for processing, storing, and distributing Sigint—codenamed Universe—had become technologically outdated. Universe required 130 people to administer, took up 20,000 square feet of floor space, and ate up enormous amounts in operations and maintenance costs.

In an effort to replace Universe before it crashed, a new system was developed in 1993 that used standard workstations, servers, and supercomputers. Codenamed Normalizer, the new system took up 15,000 fewer square feet of floor space, saved $300,000 a year in costs, and cut the number of people needed to operate it to just ten. But as the system became smaller, the demands placed on it grew exponentially. Delivery time for processed Sigint, for example, was shrunk from more than an hour to only ten minutes. Given such pressures, an electronic aneurysm was inevitable—and the most vulnerable time was millennium eve. In addition to performing its normal hefty workload, the agency's computer system would also have to figure out that switching from 99 to 00 meant moving ahead to 2000, not behind to 1900.

In the weeks leading up to the new century, Hayden ordered that contingency plans be developed "to maintain continuity of operations of our critical intelligence mission" in case of a massive crash. His predecessor, Lieutenant General Kenneth A. Minihan, had called the Y2K problem "the El Niño of the digital age." In August 1998 he said, "As each day passes we are coming closer to the date of one of the largest technological and managerial challenges ever faced by our workforce."

As early as October 1996, the agency had set up the Millennium Program Management Office, later named the Year 2000 Oversight Office. NSA also began demanding that, as a prerequisite of doing business with the agency, vendors state in writing that their products contained no Y2K problems. Charged with coming up with a solution was Ronald Kemper, NSA's chief information officer. Desperate for staff who could help repair the millennium bug, the agency implemented an "Emergency 911" operation to quickly find and recruit people with critical knowledge of some of the older and more obscure computer languages. Incentives were offered. General Minihan promised money bonuses and time off.

By 1998, however, agency officials were discovering that many companies that early on claimed to be Y2K compliant were suddenly retracting their words. "In some cases," said one NSA report, "the Agency may not know there is a problem until something breaks." Said Minihan: "Solving the Y2K problem is a tedious job and we are fighting a battle against a deadline that will not move under any circumstances."

As the date approached, the systems governing the agency's thousands of computers were assessed and stickers were placed on the terminals. A green "Y2K OK" sticker indicated that the system would pass over the threshold without problem; a yellow sticker marked systems concerning which there was still some question, and a red sticker warned, "Y2K NOT OK."

Less than a year before the critical date, NSA was still behind schedule. Only 19 percent of the agency's computers were ready, and repairs on nearly 60 percent were late. But as a result of a crash program, computer programmers managed to bring 94 percent of the computers into compliance by July 1999. The remaining 6 percent were expected to be ready by the end of September. Ultimately, as in most of the world, the millennium's arrival caused little or no disruption to NSA's powerful computers and software; the agency continued to eavesdrop as though nothing had happened. Until January 24.

Finally, after the agency spent thousands of staff hours and more than $3 million on repairs, the system was patched together. After three days, NSA awoke from its electronic coma, its memory still intact. "We had the ability to store that which we collected over this three-and-a-half-day period," said Hayden. "When we were able to go back and process the information when that capability came back, it took eight to twelve hours to process and analyze the information that we had collected." During the outage, much of intercept traffic that would have normally gone to NSA shifted instead to GCHQ. "We covered the whole thing for them," said one GCHQ official, "to their acute embarrassment."

A year after the crash, with computer management now more centralized, NSA's brain was again functioning normally, at about 12 to 15 percent of capacity. Nevertheless, Hayden concluded, "The network outage was a wake-up call to our stakeholders and us that we can no longer afford to defer the funding of a new infrastructure. And the challenge doesn't stop there."

With his pudgy face, rimless glasses, and hairless dome, Hayden more closely resembled a John Le Carré spymaster than an Ian Fleming secret agent. He also lacked the background of the stereotypical super-high-tech spy chief. Shortly after his arrival on the eighth floor of OPS 2B, he told his staff that arithmetic had never been his best subject. "I'll state right up front," he admitted, "I am not a mathematician or a computer scientist and I won't pretend to be one. I will be relying heavily on all of you who are." To make the point, he added, "When I think about the intellectual and mathematical brainpower that comes to work here every day, I can recall the same intimidating feeling I experienced as a child when Mrs. Murphy introduced me to the times tables in the second grade."

Born on March 17, 1945, Hayden grew up in Pittsburgh. In college and graduate school at Duquesne University he avoided hard math and science courses and instead studied history. During the height of the antiwar era, the late 1960s, Hayden excelled in ROTC, becoming a Distinguished Graduate of the program. He entered the Air Force in 1969, shortly after finishing his master's degree in history, and was assigned as a briefer at Strategic Air Command headquarters at Offutt Air Base in Omaha, Nebraska. Two years later he was assigned to Guam as chief of current intelligence for the headquarters of the 8th Air Force. He spent the last half of the 1970s at various schools, mostly teaching ROTC at St. Michael's College in rural Vermont.

In June 1980 Hayden, newly promoted to major, was sent to Osan Air Base in South Korea as chief of intelligence for a tactical fighter wing. Two years later it was back to the good life again, as a student and then, in Sofia, Bulgaria, as air attaché. From there Hayden moved into a policy job in the Pentagon and then over to the Bush White House, on the National Security Council, until 1991. After an intelligence assignment at U.S. European Command Headquarters in Germany, he took over the Air Intelligence Agency and became director of the Joint Command and Control Warfare Center at Kelly Air Force Base, Texas. There he became heavily involved in the concept of information warfare. Finally he was made deputy chief of staff for the United Nations Command in South Korea, where he dealt with the issue of missing servicemen from the Korean War.

Hayden was in Korea when he secretly received word of his new assignment to NSA. Shortly afterward, on a Friday night, he went to the base movie theater with his wife. Playing was a film he had not heard of, *Enemy of the State*, in which Will Smith plays an average citizen eavesdropped on by NSA, and Gene Hackman plays a retired NSA official worried about the agency's enormous power.

"Other than the affront to truthfulness," said Hayden, "it was an entertaining movie. And I will tell you, I walked out of there saying, you know, that's not a good thing, to portray an agency so inaccurately. But I'm not too uncomfortable with a society that makes its bogeymen secrecy and power. That's really what the movie's about—it was about the evils of secrecy and power. Then they tacked NSA on, that was the offensive part. But making secrecy and power the bogeymen of political culture, that's not a bad society."

When Hayden arrived at Crypto City, it was under siege. Congress was lobbing mortar rounds. Morale was lower than a buried fiber optic cable. Senior managers had become "warlords," locked in endless internecine battles. "The term 'warlordism' has been going around for years," said one NSA official. "It means that each deputy director acts like a feudal warlord in a fiefdom. He will not give up anything for the greater glory of the NSA mission. If we have something that requires taking some of my stuff and putting in another deputy directorate, I won't do it. It's like rearranging the deck chairs on the *Titanic.* The directors are, by and large, afraid to tell the deputy directors to leave. They feel perhaps unsure of themselves." The deputies, he added, "tend to stake areas out like dogs marking their territory."

Another problem was that the Senior Policy Council, which advised the director on major issues affecting NSA, comprised so many feuding "warlords" that to reach agreement on anything was impossible. "I don't know how anything gets done," said one member of the council. "There are thirty-five of us in that room and we don't get anything done. Anybody who was anybody was on the damn leadership team. It was impossible for the director to get a consensus on anything."

Hayden also arrived to find the agency's financial system in shambles. "The budget is one of his biggest problems," said an official in January 2000. "He doesn't know where it is, he can't account for it, that's what's driving him nuts." Adding to the management problems were the enormous technical challenges facing the agency at the dawn of the new century.

Hayden candidly admitted that at stake was nothing less than the survival of NSA. "As an agency, we now face our greatest technological and analytic challenges—diverse and dynamic targets; nontraditional enemies and allies; a global information technology explosion; digital encryption; and others. Make no mistake, we are in a worldwide competition for our future."

Hayden had been at NSA less than a year when the computer crash came. It likely confirmed the worst predictions he had been hearing about his agency's failing health. "The NSA used to have the best computers in the world, bar none," said an official who had been briefed on the crash. "Now they can't even keep them running. What does that tell you? Do you know a modern company that goes off-line for four days? They're struggling."

The agency that once blazed the trail in computer science, going where the private sector feared to go or could not afford to go, was now holding on to technology's tail for dear life. "Most of what they were expert in is no longer relevant," said a former director. "Getting them to embrace the new world has been traumatic. . . . All they're trying to do is hang on and survive." Florida congressman Porter J. Goss, one of those who did see the computer crash coming, was more blunt. "Believe me," he said, "it's patch, patch, patch out there. We no longer are capable of doing what we used to do." Goss also said, "This should have come as a surprise to no one. Indeed, the [House Intelligence] Committee has, for at least three years, warned NSA and the intelligence community of concerns in these areas."

"Signals intelligence is in a crisis," said House Intelligence Committee staff director John Millis more than a year before NSA's crash. Like a worried first mate seizing the ship's wheel from a captain who is headed for the shoals, the committee began forcing change on NSA. Both Millis and Goss had served for about a dozen years in the CIA's Operations Directorate. Millis had also spent some time in the executive offices of NSA. Now the two teamed up to reinvigorate NSA's sensitive Sigint operations.

"We have been living in the glory days of Sigint over the last fifty years, since World War II," said Millis. "Sigint has been and continues to be the 'int' of choice of the policymaker and the military commander. They spend about four or five times as much on it as they do on clandestine collection, and the fact of the matter is, it's there quickly when needed. It's always there. Or it has always been there. In the past, technology has been the friend of NSA, but in the last four or five years technology has moved from being the friend to being the enemy of Sigint."

In the past, a major communications revolution—telephone, radio, television, satellite, cable—might happen at most once every generation. The predictable pace gave NSA time to find new ways to tap into each medium, especially since many of the scientists behind the revolutions also served on NSA's secret Scientific Advisory Board. Today, however, technological revolutions—PCs, cell phones, the Internet, e-mail—take place almost yearly and NSA's secret advisers no longer have a monopoly on the technologies. "Increasingly," said Mike McConnell, the NSA's director from 1992 to early 1996, "we will have to deal with a much more diverse electronic environment, cluttered not only with human communications and sensor signals, but also with machines *speaking* to other machines."

One major problem confronting NSA is a change in the use of technologies throughout the world. Some of NSA's targets still use traditional methods of communications—unencrypted faxes and phone calls, transmitted over microwaves and satellites. As can be seen from the intercepts surrounding Iran's attempt to acquire the C-802 missile, NSA is still very capable of performing its mission on these technologies. But other targets are switching to far more complex communications systems—circuit encryption, fiber optics, digital cellular phones, and the Internet. The problem is to spend the vast amounts of money, time, and expertise needed to develop ways to penetrate the new systems, and yet not to overlook the old ones.

"We've got to do both," said Hayden, sitting in his office. He had walked into the middle of the problem when he joined the agency. "Do more without giving up what you used to do. . . . Part of the world looks like this now and is moving hell bent for leather in that direction, but in this different part of the world it still looks like it did fifteen years ago. And things of interest are happening to the United States in both universes. . . . How do you do the new while the old is still important to you—in a budget that doesn't allow you to create two Sigint systems, one for the old, one for the new? You've captured the precise dilemma of this agency."

Deputy Director Barbara McNamara outlined in stark numbers another of NSA's key problems today: too much communication. "Forty years ago there were five thousand stand-alone computers, no fax machines, and not one cellular phone. . . . In 1999 there were over 420 million computers, most of them networked. There were roughly 14 million fax machines and 468 million cell phones and those numbers continue to grow. The telecommunications industry is investing a trillion dollars to encircle the world in millions of miles of high bandwidth fiber-optic cable." McNamara might have added that there were also 304 million people with Internet access in 2000—up 80 percent from just the year before. And for the first time, less than half of those people live in North America.

Not only is NSA spreading itself thin attempting to listen in on ever-expanding modes of communications, the tasks assigned to it by the White House, CIA, Pentagon, and other customers are also exploding. In 1995, the agency received about 1,500 "immediate" requests for intelligence—known as *ad hoc requirements.* By the fall of 2000, the number of such requests had already grown to 3,500—a 170 percent increase. Analysts, said one senior NSA official, "brute force" their way through massive amounts of information.

The problem is not just interception of ever-increasing quantities of communications, it is moving the information back to NSA. "Well, what are all these communications you're going to bring back to the building and process?" asked a senior intelligence official involved in Sigint. "You've got to have a pipeline to bring them back. You've got to have bandwidth, which is expensive, and which is limited. It's finite. You can't just get all the bandwidth in the world and ship everything back here. So you've got a physics problem. . . . You've got to get a real big pipe and there is no such big pipe that exists."

Even if the avalanche of signals could successfully be diverted back to Fort Meade, there would never be enough people to process it all. "Supposing you pipe every communication that goes on in China back to the United States," said the senior Sigint official. "Then you've got to have somebody process it. You've got to have a linguist listen to it. And the chances of your ever digging out from under the pile of information and finding what's important [are] miniscule. . . . You don't have the linguistic resources to deal with that kind of problem."

The answer is using powerful computers to filter as much intercepted information as possible at the front end—the point of interception—such as at Menwith Hill Station, NSA's massive satellite listening post in central England. "You've got the antenna," said the senior Sigint official, "and now, next to it, in a building, you've got the filter. . . . You filter it by finding out some identifier of a person or an entity that will allow you to pick off that person's communications and throw away everybody else's. . . . You're going to run some identifier in the message against a category of identifiers that you have in a dictionary [computer] somewhere."

One such identifier, he said, is the target's telephone number. "And what you're looking for is a communication going to that telephone number. So in comes a dialed number that's a different dialed number—[the filter] ignores it, goes away until it hits on one. . . . All we're doing is we're comparing the communications that are out there against a target list, and if they don't hit, nothing ever happens to the ones that get rejected. You don't see them, they don't get stored. . . . The stuff that does hit goes to an analyst—maybe they're back here [NSA headquarters] someplace—to look at it. . . . Reality of life is that you're talking about a small percentage of everything out there that even gets vacuumed. . . . So what I'm saying is that there's a first cut. You've got to decide where you're going to vacuum."

Given this burgeoning increase in worldwide telecommunications now confronting NSA, concern has been growing in Congress. Some believe that NSA, through years of mismanagement, is depending far too heavily on the old, reliable systems while failing to prepare for the tidal wave of new technologies now beginning to crash down on the agency. Barbara McNamara candidly agrees. "So far," she said, "the National Security Agency is lagging behind."

High on NSA's worry list is the shift from microwave and satellite communications—whose signals NSA was adept at capturing with its eavesdropping satellites and ground-based stations—to buried fiber optic cables. "Technology has now become a two-edged sword," said Hayden. "On the dark days it has become the enemy."

According to a senior NSA official, by the fall of 2000 only 2 percent of AT&T's voice and data communications were transmitted over microwave towers in the United States. And AT&T had virtually given up on domestic satellite communications, except for Alaska. Instead, it is selling its satellite voice and data circuits to the rapidly growing direct-TV industry. "AT&T invested very heavily in the '70s in satellites in order to move great volumes of information," said the official. "Right now AT&T is selling off all of their domestic satellite coverage. . . . There's a lot of change going on here, and a Sigint enterprise has to look like that which it targets."

By turning instead to buried fiber optic cables, said the senior NSA official, AT&T was able to double its capacity in just ninety days. Made up of bundles of tiny, hair-thin glass strands, fiber optic cable offers greater volume, more security, and higher reliability. Thus, where satellite communications are as easy to collect as rain, fiber optic signals require the skills of a mole.

So worried was NSA about the difficulty of eavesdropping on fiber optics that in the early 1990s it fought against export of the technology to Russia. For example, the United States denied an export license to US West, Inc., for a proposed trans-Siberian cable project. Now NSA must deal with a second, far more sophisticated generation of fiber optic technology.

Greater and greater volumes of material—from 400-page books to megabyte-hogging animated graphics to full-length movies—are being shoved through the narrow straws that make up the communications networks. Says MIT's David Clark, "The ability to get bits down a fiber is growing faster than Moore's law," which predicts that computer power will double every eighteen months. The carrying capacity of fiber, said Clark, is doubling every twelve months.

Scientists are now developing methods to greatly multiply the numbers of fiber optic channels in existing cables while at the same time rolling out miles and miles of new cable. The new technology, known as wavelength division multiplexing (WDM), consists of sending multiple signals down the same straw at different wavelengths. The technique has been called the fiber optic equivalent of parallel processing. By 2001 WDM had become a $4 billion business, and fiber optic cable was flying out of factories as if tied to a speeding harpoon. According to John MacChesney, an optical fiber pioneer at Bell Labs, the factories were "producing hundreds of kilometers of fiber drawn to precise dimensions at a rate approaching sixty miles an hour." At the same time, the production costs had dropped from $1 a meter in 1980 to about $.05 a meter in 2001.

One such system is known as Project Oxygen, so called because it is an attempt to breathe new life into an old technology. If signals are sent at sixteen different wavelengths through each of four pairs of optical fibers, information can be transmitted through a single transatlantic cable at 640 gigabits per second—the equivalent of 10 million simultaneous telephone calls.

In 1998 Lucent Technologies unveiled its new WaveStar OLS 4006 system, which it claimed could carry over a single strand of fiber the equivalent of the entire Internet. Its speed was such that it could also transmit the equivalent of over 90,000 encyclopedia volumes in one second. The company achieved this capability by using what it called ultradense WDM. "Leapfrogging current competitive offerings," said the company, "Lucent's new optical networking system can be configured to handle up to eight fibers, each transmitting 400 gigabits per second, to give communications providers a maximum capacity of 3.2 terabits (or 3.2 trillion bits) per second of voice, video and data traffic."

AT&T was to be the first customer for Lucent's new system, and by 2001 the company had signed contracts with firms in Europe and Asia. Among them were the Netherlands' KPN Telecom B.V., Spain's Telefónica de España, Korea Telecom, and even China's Posts and Telecommunications Administration.

The system was designed by Lucent's subsidiary Bell Labs, which for many years has had a very close and very secret relationship with NSA. For two decades William O. Baker served on NSA's Scientific Advisory Board. At the same time he also served, at various points, as research chief, president, and chairman of the board of Bell Labs. The first operational fiber optic system was developed under Baker at Bell Labs. Among the members of what is now the NSA Advisory Board are former State Department official Arnold Kanter; former DIA director Lieutenant General James Clapper; and James Adams, chairman of iDefense, Inc. The executive secretary is NSA's David P. Kokalis.

NSA has also joined with Lucent and a number of domestic telecommunications companies, including Verizon, to form a consortium called Multiwavelength Optical Networking (MONET). MONET will research advanced fiber optic techniques, including routing/switching and optical monitoring.

In 1998, the first large submarine cable designed for multiwavelength operation was turned on. It forms a loop connecting the United States with Britain, the Netherlands, and Germany. When the newer

WDM technology is in place, its capacity will be more than 1,000 times greater than that of the first fiber optic cable, which began service only about a decade earlier. Engineers are planning to lay 168,000 kilometers of the cable, enough to circle the earth four times. More cable will be laid by other companies. Said David Clark of MIT, "We're going to drown in fiber."

Another problem facing NSA is the growing difficulty of tapping into the Internet—a series of complex, interconnected communications lines that encase the earth like a tangled ball of sewing yarn. Every one hundred days the Internet doubles in size. Also up is voice traffic, which increases in volume at 20 percent a year. This is largely as a result of new digital cellular communications, which are far more difficult for NSA to analyze than the old analog signals. Rather than consisting of voices, the digital signals are made up of data packets that may be broken up and sent a myriad of different ways. "Today you have no idea where that information is being routed," said one intelligence official. "You may have somebody talking on a telephone over a land line and the other person talking to them on a cell phone over a satellite. You don't know how it's being routed, it's going through all kinds of switches, the information is not where you think it is, and that's what has created the complexity and that's what we have to figure out how to deal with."

"The mere fact of digitizing the signals gives it some level of protection," said one former NSA official. "But if you really hit it with a hard encryption system, digital encryption, it's a forget-it situation."

Encryption was once an area where NSA held a monopoly. But after a disastrous period during the 1990s when the agency attempted to outlaw the export of powerful encryption software, it has now virtually given up. "Crypto policy is the wave of the past," said former NSA general counsel Stewart Baker. To worry about encryption sales was like locking a door on a house without walls. Restricting American sales would do nothing to prevent foreign nations from selling equally powerful encryption tools. "No matter what we do, encryption is here and it's going to grow very rapidly," said John Millis. "That is bad news for Sigint, so it is going to take a huge amount of money invested in new technologies to get access and to be able to break out the information that we still need to get from Sigint." According to one senior NSA official, in the fall of 2000 only 10 percent of communications were encrypted. But for NSA, the projections were frightening. Within seven years, he estimated, fully 85 percent of all communications will be hidden in complex ciphers.

As a result of the House Intelligence Committee's push to focus attention on NSA's problems, news reports began painting the agency as losing its hearing. "Difficulties posed by new technologies also threaten to make the NSA's 'big ears' increasingly deaf," said one report, on CNN. A headline in *Newsweek* read: "Hard of Hearing," adding, "The National Security Agency has fallen behind in the high-tech battle against terrorists, hackers and other threats."

Although life may be somewhat more complicated for NSA, and eavesdropping may become even more difficult years down the road, much of this criticism is overblown. The agency is certainly not going "deaf" today—a point made by Michael Hayden. "One criticism is that we're omniscient and reading everybody's e-mail," he said, "and the other is that we're going blind and deaf. It can't be both."

According to information obtained for *Body of Secrets,* NSA has managed to find ways to tap into all of these new technologies—including fiber optic cables—and is pulling in more communications than ever. This was revealed in a highly classified closed-door discussion at NSA on September 30, 1999, between NSA Deputy Director for Services Terry Thompson and members of the agency's technical workforce.

"The projections that we made five, six, eight years ago," said Thompson, "about the increasing volumes of collection and what that's going to mean for our analysts have all come true, thanks in large part to the work that you-all and others have done. We're much further ahead now in terms of being able to access and collect network data, fiber optics, cellular data, all the different modalities of communications that we are targeting, and that results in a lot of output for our analysts. Our tools are coming along okay to help process and reduce the backlog, but there's still a huge requirement for human beings at the end of the day to figure out what's important, and that boils down to language work and IA [intelligence analysis] work."

Thompson explained how NSA breaks into the Internet by hiring people who have special knowledge of key U.S. companies that make critical components for the network. With their help, the agency reverse-engineers the components in order to eavesdrop on the systems. Among the most critical components of the Internet are routers made by Cisco Systems, a California company. These are specialized microcomputers that link two or more incompatible computer networks. They act as a sort of postal service, deciding where to route the various messages carried over the network. "Virtually all Internet traffic travels across the system of one company: Cisco Systems," says a Cisco television ad. By discovering the weak spots and vulnerabilities in this "postal service," NSA can target and intercept much electronic mail.

During the discussion with the technical workforce about short-term hiring by NSA, Thompson said, "If you can see down the road two or three or five years, and say, Well, I only need this person to do reverse engineering on Cisco routers, that's a good example for about three or five years, because I see Cisco going away as a key manufacturer for routers and so I don't need that expertise. But I really need somebody today and for the next couple of years who knows Cisco routers inside and out and can help me understand how they're being used in target networks." In fact, NSA recently recruited a Cisco engineer to be the top technical adviser to its new transformation office, which is charged with moving the agency forward in the new century.

As communications shift from satellites to fiber optics, NSA may have to return to tapping undersea cables—if it hasn't already done so. But now, instead of copper cables connecting parts of Russia, the targets may be major commercial WDM fiber optic cables connecting continents. And instead of the USS *Halibut*, the new cable-tapping submarine may be the USS *Jimmy Carter*, called the most advanced spy sub ever built, which is due to be completed in 2004. In December 1999, Electric Boat was awarded a $887 million contract by the Navy to extensively modify the *Jimmy Carter* for "surveillance, mine warfare, special warfare, payload recovery and advanced communications." When completed, said a source quoted in the *Los Angeles Times*, the Seawolf-class sub "will be able to place and recover top-secret 'pods' that will tap undersea fiber-optic cables for the first time."

To cope with what Michael Hayden referred to as "the massive volume of stuff" flowing into NSA every day, the agency plans to "move processing more forward in our process so that you're not moving raw unprocessed stuff—so much so far."

That may mean giving more responsibility to NSA's three large Regional Sigint Operations Centers (RSOCs). The Medina RSOC, located at Medina Annex in Lackland, Texas, focuses on the Caribbean and on Central and South America. The second, in an underground bunker at Kunia, Hawaii, focuses on Asia. And the third, at Fort Gordon, Georgia, processes and analyzes intercepts from Europe and the Middle East. Manned jointly by NSA and its three military Sigint organizations, the RSOCs were set up to consolidate on U.S. territory much of the intercept activity that was previously done at the scores of worldwide listening posts. Much of the Sigint flowing into these centers comes from satellites and remotely operated stations.

Another problem created by the rapid changes in worldwide communications technology is how to design the newest Sigint satellites to target these systems. The enormously expensive eavesdropping birds may be programmed in 2001 for a system or technology that becomes obsolete by 2003. "We spend more money on one satellite in one year than we do on all the analytic capabilities combined," said John Millis. "It doesn't make a lot of sense doing Sigint from there anymore. Excepting Elint, you shouldn't be spending one dollar more than we do to try and intercept communications—regular voice and data-type communications—from space. But we do make that investment. This is something that we think that we have to move away from." The change in philosophy is revolutionary in an agency that, since the late 1950s, has moved nonstop toward space.

Because of the change, there have been repeated delays in completing the next generation of NSA satellites, called Integrated Overhead Signals Intelligence Architecture–2 (IOSA-2), while experts attempt to decide which collection systems would be best. Originally the National Reconnaissance Office, which builds NSA's satellites, said the new Sigint constellation—a constellation is several satellites operating in concert—would be defined by the end of 1999 and acquisition would begin about 2002. But now it appears that because of "the magnitude of the job," the first systems will not be operational before 2010.

These are all areas where the House Intelligence Committee is attempting to throw NSA a financial life buoy. "NSA now faces new, more robust challenges, thanks to the explosion of the technology and telecommunications industries," said its chairman, Porter Goss, in 2000.

"Each type of communications—radio, satellite, microwave, cellular, cable—is becoming connected to all the others. Each new type of traffic shows up on every type of communication. Unfortunately, as the global network has become more integrated, NSA's culture has evolved so that it is seemingly incapable of responding in an integrated fashion."

Tim Sample, who became staff director on Millis's death in June 2000, minced no words in a talk to a group at NSA. He made it clear that for years NSA's leadership had simply ignored the agency's many problems. Some on the House Intelligence Committee have been especially critical of Barbara McNamara, a member of the agency's old school, who was deputy director up until June 2000 and is now NSA's liaison officer to England. "There was an attitude of, We'll do it ourselves, thank you very much," said Sample. "We understand that there are some changes, but we've been doing pretty well with what we've been doing, thank you. We'll keep going." Sample assessed NSA's management problems harshly:

> When it came to Sigint, we turned to NSA and we got a lot of resistance. There was an issue of financial accountability, and that was at best elusive. There was a sense of protecting fiefdoms—and again we understand, we were hunkering down here, for God sake, Congress is coming, don't let them cut us again. We saw multiple efforts at projects throughout the organization that in some cases were duplicative, and were done more in the sense of the bureaucracy is not quite working for me, I'll do it internal to my organization and that way something might get done. Or there was a sense of ownership within each organization.
>
> We saw, we believe, that the agency was too insular. It was that sense of we can do everything internally. It was a sense of protection of people—which isn't bad, as long as it's mixed with what kind of people do you need for the future. What skill mix do you need to have. And then you help your workforce get there.
>
> From a management standpoint, we saw a major protection of bureaucracy. Many managers, especially at the more senior levels, didn't accept the writing on the wall. Not just the Congressional writing on the wall, but the

intelligence, the target writing on the wall. That somehow in our view, some of the management lost touch with the workforce. And one of the most rewarding things I think I've seen in the last four or five years is, if you dive down into the workforce, the young people that have gotten into this game. They have the same infection that almost all of us have had when we started our careers in intelligence. It's a sense of patriotism, it's a sense of accomplishment, it's a sense of protecting national security. And many of them, we thought—and not just NSA but other agencies—were scratching their heads trying to figure out where are we going? And that was important to us. So we're on a defensive posture instead of an offensive one.

There was—and I know I'll probably get a lot of people upset at this one—but there really was a philosophy of feel better. Let's do some things to feel better about where we are. And one of those areas was—without taking swipes at it, because it was important—but one of the areas that was emphasized was management awards. And I'm fully supportive of rewarding people and of having agencies rewarded for their efforts, of how they manage people and how they manage organizations and how they do things. It is an important part of life. It is an important part of human value. It is not *the* most important part of intelligence. But that's not the feeling that we had. We got the feeling that that was a big priority.

And if you think I'm making this up, let me tell you one of the phone calls that I got, that I will never, ever, forget. And I will not tell you who called me. I will just tell you that this individual was at the senior levels of NSA. And we were about to produce a bill, and we were about to send it out the door, and I got a phone call one morning—and this individual said, "Tim, whatever you write, would you do me a favor and not put it in the public bill." And I said, "Why? It's unclassified." And the response was, "Because we're in line for some management awards and if the media sees that, it may ruin that opportunity." To us, that spoke

> volumes. To us that said that many of the managers, including the senior managers, were not quite with the picture, in our view.
>
> . . . .
>
> And what we said basically was we see a lot of management and very little leadership. And there is a major difference. And we said that we saw a lot of people trying to do a lot of good work, but that Sigint in the future was in peril. And they were fairly harsh words, and they got a lot of people upset, though my sense is for those in the workforce, there was a lot of head shaking up and down, going, Yeah, how do we fix this. And I will say this now, and I will say it again and again, the issue here was facing change.

Asked in 2000 whether he believed Congress was attempting to micromanage NSA—take over command of his ship—Hayden was diplomatic. "Not Congress," he said. "We have occasionally skirmishes with particular staffers, and those are honest differences of opinions. I've got a natural inclination to think they're too detailed. We have a fair amount of attention from Congress. . . . That's a good thing. What I communicate to the workforce is: that says that what we do is important, they're paying attention.

"Now the dark side of that is they may have views on some things that we're doing that we don't totally agree with. We'll get over it. The important thing is that they care, and actually I have used that with the workforce. I say we occasionally get the harsh words from our overseers. Even when it's the harsh word—I'll tell you the exact metaphor I used. You're watching somebody's kids playing down the street a little bit out of sight, and they're soaping somebody's car windows. You kind of get a little smile on your face—till you suddenly realize it's your kid. And what happens then, you run out, you grab him by the ear, and you bring him back in. That's a little bit like us and Congress. If they didn't care about us, they wouldn't be making these statements that occasionally make us less comfortable or embarrassed or feel that it's unfair criticism and so on. But the underlying point is . . . how important [Congress] thinks the agency is."

"I think in the history of the agency, we were never a big player downtown," said one NSA official. "Until Bobby Ray Inman. Bobby Ray knew how to manipulate and he knew how to punch the buttons and he knew how to ingratiate himself, and he had a reputation, and it was well earned, as a straight shooter. But the problem was nobody else in the agency knew how to do that. And they saw what he was doing but they didn't understand how he was doing it or why he was doing it. So they thought, If we ingratiate ourselves downtown, if we train our people to respond to congressional inquiries, that this is okay. We'll figure out how to do it. But they don't understand how to deal with Congress. I think part of it is that the directors they brought up are political clowns, klutzes, they don't understand how to deal with politicians. They think that the aura of the agency will fake everybody out. And the problem is that song isn't being bought anymore downtown. You can't go down and say, 'Trust us' because it's no longer a question of secrets, it's a question of money."

Realizing that NSA's very existence depended on reform, Hayden issued an edict: "Our agency must undergo change if we are to remain viable in the future." Nevertheless, he acknowledged that the attempt to move an iceberg like NSA would inevitably produce fractures and fissures. "There has been much discussion about this change," he told the residents of Crypto City, "much agreement that it is necessary, but some reluctance to take the actions to implement it."

Like someone who had just inherited an old car, Hayden decided to call in the repairmen to explain what was wrong and offer suggestions on how to fix it. He put together two groups to take a close look at what makes NSA tick and directed them to write up report cards. One group was made up of nineteen middle-ranking insiders, the other of five outside experts on management.

The insiders, known as the New Enterprise Team and led by the former deputy director for technology and systems, Jack Devine, were brutal in their criticism. Hayden jokingly referred to them as "responsible anarchists." "Absent profound change at NSA," they told Hayden, "the nation will lose a powerful weapon in its arsenal. . . . NSA is an organization ripe for divestiture: its individual capabilities are of greater value than is the organization as a whole. The legacy of exceptional service to the nation that is NSA is in great peril. We have run out of time."

The team also made no bones about the source of the troubles: current and past leadership. Without naming names, they were clearly referring to then deputy director Barbara McNamara and past director Kenneth Minihan as well as their predecessors. "NSA has been in a leadership crisis for the better part of a decade," Hayden was told. "It is the lack of leadership that is responsible for both NSA's failure to create and implement a single corporate strategy, and for the complete breakdown of the NSA governance process. . . . These short comings have put us in dire straits. . . . Leadership has failed on multiple fronts. It has not provided a corporate vision or strategy. It has been unable or unwilling to make the hard decisions. It has been ineffective at cultivating future leaders. And despite a decade of criticism from stakeholders [Congress], it has failed to bring about real change. . . . Indeed, the workforce has carried the NSA institution on its backs for the better part of a decade."

The team also described the climate within the thick walls and high fences in harsh terms, referring to "our insular, sometimes arrogant culture."

Other criticisms included focusing on building bigger and better bugs while paying little attention to the needs of NSA's customers—the White House, Pentagon, CIA, and other users of Sigint. "[You] care more about technology than about the customer," one critic told the team. Another problem was duplication.

The outside team was no less sparing in its candor. Among the criticisms was NSA's "slowness" in moving from old, comfortable targets, such as microwave interception, to newer, more difficult targets, such as the Internet. "Whatever the attractiveness of known targets and technologies," Hayden was told, "leadership must decide smartly when to move to more difficult but potentially more lucrative targets."

Like its in-house counterpart, the outside team also criticized the agency's secrecy-driven culture. "Much of this can be attributed to the historic insularity of the Agency," they said, "which grew up in a culture of 'NSA doesn't exist and doesn't talk to people who don't work at NSA.' " At another point, the team noted "the 'Super Secret NSA' image . . . is no longer useful to Agency needs."

Again, much of the blame was directed at the current and former senior management, which cultivated not only a culture of excessive secrecy but also one of fear. "We are concerned the present mindset fostered a society where people were afraid to express their own thoughts," the outside team told Hayden. "Even though people spoke to us with true candor, they always wanted to avoid attribution because of the perception that the information was going to be used against them." Nevertheless, the employees made it clear that NSA was heading for the rocks. "The staff knows NSA is falling behind and is not properly addressing the inherent problems of the emerging global network," said the team, "and the present management infrastructure does not appear to be supporting the required changes."

"In a broad sense," Hayden said, both panels painted a picture of "an agency that did not communicate with itself, or with others, well. Which—my view now, not theirs—is the by-product of a great deal of compartmentalization and insularity built up over almost half a century. A management culture that found it difficult to make the tough decisions, largely because the decisions were so tough." Also, he said, "They found that accountability was too diffuse throughout the agency. I've used the phrase, 'You damn near have to rent Camden Yards to get everybody that thinks he has a piece of the action in on a meeting.' Smaller team, which gives us a little more agility."

Hayden immediately set about implementing many of the panels' recommendations. On November 15, 1999, he instituted "100 Days of Change," an ambitious plan to put many of the reforms into place in a little more than three months. At the same time, he sought to consolidate his power in order to blunt any opposition from the conservatives. "Even the best game plan," he warned, quoting legendary University of Alabama football coach Paul (Bear) Bryant, "ain't got no chance if the players don't execute it." So Hayden threw out the unwieldy senior management groups that held much of the power. The Senior Agency Leadership Team (SALT), the Critical Issues Group, and the Corporate Management Review Group vanished overnight. The one management group he kept, the Executive Leadership Team, he stripped to the bone, leaving only the director, deputy director, deputy director for operations, and deputy director for information security.

To help correct the budget problems that caused so much grief for his predecessor, Hayden hired a chief financial manager, a first for NSA. Going outside the agency, he chose Beverly Wright, a Harvard MBA with a background in investment banking. At the time of her selection she was chief financial officer at Legg Mason Wood Walker, in Baltimore. Her job, according to Hayden, was to develop a management strategy for the agency and to "ensure that our mission drives our budget decisions" and not the other way around.

He also ordered the personnel promotion process streamlined and even began taking the first baby steps to opening the door to the outside world a crack. Hayden would announce these fiats in agency-wide memorandums called DIRgrams.

Finally, in June 2000 Barbara McNamara received her long-expected transfer to London, which paved the way for Hayden to name his own choice for deputy. Ironically, rather than pick a young lion to help set the course for the new century, he picked a retired agency employee who had started work at NSA even before McNamara. Tapped was William B. Black, Jr., an old hand with thirty-eight years of experience with the agency. But the last ten were no doubt the reason for his selection; they were spent in areas promising to be most important for NSA in the years to come. These included chief of NSA Europe from 1990 to 1993; chief of A Group, the Russian codebreakers, from 1994 to 1996; and then special assistant to the director for information warfare from 1996 until his retirement in 1997. He also served a tour as chief of the Special Collection Service, the covert joint NSA/CIA organization that specializes in worldwide bugging, black-bag jobs, and bribery in order to penetrate foreign communications facilities. Finally, because Black had worked as a senior executive with Science Applications International Corporation (SAIC), a major defense contractor, following his NSA retirement, he also brought some insight from the corporate world.

By 2001 Congress was so pleased with the way Hayden was steering his ship away from the shoals that it was looking for ways to keep him in place for up to five years—two years over the normal three-year term.

The rise of NSA's star since the end of the Cold War has been at the direct cost of the CIA and its dwindling ranks of clandestine officers. Human spies have proved no match when measured against the trusted rapid-response eavesdroppers at NSA. No love is lost between the two agencies; former NSA director William Odom, a retired Army lieutenant general, offered a caustic view of his agency's rival across the Potomac. "The CIA is good at stealing a memo off a prime minister's desk," he said, "but they're not much good at anything else."

A former CIA director, Robert Gates, said that the Gulf War might have proved a Waterloo of sorts for the clandestine service: "Perhaps the most compelling recent example of the gap between our technical and human capabilities was the Persian Gulf War. U.S. military commanders had superb imagery and signals intelligence, but we had only sketchy human intelligence on Iraq's intentions prior to invading Kuwait, Iraq's ability to withstand sanctions, and the status of Iraq's weapons program."

By 1998, the CIA had no more than ten or fifteen clandestine espionage operations active at any one time around the world, and the Directorate of Operations (DO), home of the spies, had shrunk to well below 1,000 officers.

Reuel Marc Gerecht, an officer in CIA's clandestine service from 1985 to 1994, called into serious question not only the quality but even the veracity of much of the reporting by DO officers in sensitive parts of the world. Writing in the February 1998 *Atlantic Monthly*, under the pseudonym Edward G. Shirley, Gerecht called the DO "a sorry blend of Monty Python and Big Brother." "The sad truth about the CIA," he said, "is that the DO has for years been running an espionage charade in most countries, deceiving itself and others about the value of its recruited agents and intelligence production." By the mid-1980s, he noted, "the vast majority of the CIA's foreign agents were mediocre assets at best, put on the payroll because case officers needed high recruitment numbers to get promoted. Long before the Soviet Union collapsed, recruitment and intelligence fraud—the natural product of an insular spy world—had stripped the DO of its integrity and its competence."

Gerecht complained that even in critical field positions, the agency paid little attention to matching skills to countries. "Not a single Iran-desk chief during the eight years that I worked on Iran could speak or read Persian," he said. "Not a single Near East Division chief knew Arabic, Persian, or Turkish, and only one could get along even in French." Another former agency officer pointed out that the CIA teams dispatched to northern Iraq to assist the political opposition in the mid-1990s "had few competent Arabic-speaking officers."

"The CIA's spy service has become an anachronism," argues Melvin A. Goodman, a twenty-four-year veteran Soviet analyst of both the CIA and the State Department. Now a professor at the National War College, he gave a number of examples to show why the cloak-and-dagger spies have become an endangered species. "CIA sources failed to decipher Leonid Brezhnev's intentions toward Czechoslovakia in 1968, Anwar Sadat's toward Israel in 1973, and Saddam Hussein's toward Kuwait in 1990. . . . It's time," he concluded, "to jettison the myth that only clandestine collection of information can ascertain the intentions of foreign leaders."

So far had the CIA's human capabilities dwindled by 1998 that it led House Intelligence Committee chairman Porter Goss—himself a former CIA case officer—to declare, "It is fair to say that the cupboard is nearly bare in the area of human intelligence."

Over the 1990s, the CIA's staff was slashed by 23 percent and the agency's slice of the intelligence budget pie became a narrow wedge. When handing out about $27 billion to the intelligence community as part of the 1999 federal budget, Congress gave NSA a "huge increase," said one staffer, while leaving CIA's funding about level. A few weeks later Congress awarded an additional $1.5 billion in emergency supplemental funds. The technical spies received what one observer called "a windfall"—nearly $1 billion—while less than 20 percent went to the CIA's human agents.

Robert Gates thought his agency should completely scrap its covert, paramilitary capability and make its analytic staff "much smaller." Noting the irony, the longtime head of the agency's Directorate of Intelligence pointed out in 1996, "I say that after having spent a good part of the eighties building it up!"

Not only had CIA's status as an intelligence collection and covert action agency hit rock bottom by the end of the century, so had the director's role as chief of the entire intelligence community. Although in theory the CIA director is responsible for all U.S. spy agencies, Gates said that in practical terms this is no longer so. "We don't really have a Director of Central Intelligence [DCI]," he said in a CIA publication. "There is no such thing. The DCI at CIA controls only a very small portion of the assets of the Intelligence Community, and there are so many entities you don't have any director."

Nor does the DCI have any real power over the community's purse strings. A commission on intelligence reform headed by former defense secretary Harold Brown and former senator Warren B. Rudman of New Hampshire noted in 1996 that the director of central intelligence controls only 15 percent of the U.S. intelligence budget. Two years later even that estimate had dropped. Speaking about the authority of the DCI, John Millis in late 1998 said, "It is very difficult to exercise authority over the National Foreign Intelligence Program and all its agencies because ninety percent of them are funded and owned and operated by the Department of Defense." That, in Millis's view, has led to another problem: "an absolute and total fixation on near-term, tactical intelligence" at the cost of strategic—political and diplomatic—intelligence. "Since Desert Shield/Desert Storm," he said, "we have abandoned the strategic mission in large part to meet the pressing requirements the military has made for tactical intelligence."

In an effort to rebuild the Clandestine Service, the CIA, in the late 1990s, began the largest recruitment drive for new case officers in its history. From 1998 to 1999 the number of job offers jumped 52 percent. Director George Tenet also directed the rebuilding of the CIA's overseas presence and the overhauling of the agency's clandestine training facility—"the Farm"—at Camp Perry near Williamsburg, Virginia. The number of clandestine and covert action specialists trained annually had dropped to less than a few dozen. But by 1999 the number of students, most of whom were between the ages of twenty-seven and thirty-two, had jumped to 120 and was expected to rise to 180 over the next few years. At an average cost of $450,000 to train a case officer, rebuilding the Clandestine Service is a significant investment. To further beef up the human spy capability, Tenet has allowed the Defense Humint Service, the Pentagon's human intelligence agency, to send its students to Camp Perry for training.

Tenet made rebuilding the CIA into a significant intelligence agency his top priority. In a speech at Georgetown University in the fall of 1999, he clearly signaled that he preferred human spies over machines. "At the end of the day," he said, "the men and women of U.S. intelligence—not satellites or sensors or high-speed computers—are our most precious asset."

In fact, the combination of human and machine spies may, in the end, save both. According to senior intelligence officials, in 1978 a covert joint intelligence organization was formed, which marries the clandestine skills of the CIA with the technical capabilities of the NSA. The purpose of this Special Collection Service (SCS) is to put sophisticated eavesdropping equipment—from bugs to parabolic antennas—in difficult-to-reach places and to target key foreign communications personnel for recruitment.

The SCS, whose headship alternates between NSA and CIA officials, is an outgrowth of the CIA's former Division D, established in the early 1950s by William F. Friedman's first employee, Frank Rowlett. Worried about competition from the upstart NSA, Allen Dulles hired Rowlett away to set up a mini-NSA within the CIA. At the time, Rowlett was upset because AFSA/NSA Director Ralph Canine wanted him to switch jobs, going from chief of Sigint to that of Comsec, the codemaking side of the business. "As it happened," recalled fellow pioneer Abraham Sinkov, "Rowlett was made quite unhappy by this suggestion; he wasn't very keen about moving over to Comsec, and he transferred to the CIA." (After about five years, Rowlett transferred back to the NSA.)

Over the years the mission of Division D was to assist the NSA in stealing foreign cipher materials and recruiting foreign crypto clerks and communications employees. After Rowlett left in the late 1950s, the division was taken over by William Harvey, a balding, overweight, bug-eyed veteran spook. Harvey had long been the CIA's link to NSA. In the 1950s he ran the CIA's Berlin tunnel operation, which succeeded in secretly tapping a key East German telephone network.

In his work as chief of Division D, Harvey came up with a project known as ZR/RIFLE, which was designed to locate agents who could help him steal foreign code secrets and bribe cipher clerks. In longhand on sheets of yellow legal paper, he outlined the joint NSA/CIA operation:

1. *IDENTIFICATION:* THE PURPOSE OF PROJECT ZR/RIFLE IS TO SPOT, DEVELOP, AND USE AGENT ASSETS FOR DIVISION D OPERATIONS. AGENTS WILL BE SPOTTED IN SEVERAL AREAS, INCLUDING THE UNITED STATES, BUT FOR OPERATIONAL SECURITY REASONS WILL PROBABLY NOT BE USED IN THEIR COUNTRIES OF RESIDENCE. PRESENT DEVELOPMENT ACTIVITY IS BEING CONDUCTED IN THE WE [WESTERN EUROPEAN] AND EE [EASTERN EUROPEAN] AREAS, BUT IT IS ANTICIPATED THAT THIS WILL BE EXTENDED TO OTHER DIVISIONS ALSO. THE PROJECT WILL BE OPERATED AGAINST THIRD-COUNTRY INSTALLATIONS AND PERSONNEL.

2. *OBJECTIVE:* THE OBJECTIVE OF THIS PROJECT IS THE PROCUREMENT OF CODE AND CIPHER MATERIALS AND INFORMATION CONCERNING SUCH MATERIALS, IN ACCORDANCE WITH REQUIREMENTS LEVIED ON THE CLANDESTINE SERVICES, PRIMARILY BY THE NATIONAL SECURITY AGENCY. SINCE THESE REQUIREMENTS ARE SUBJECT TO FREQUENT REVISION, NO LISTING OF TARGETS WOULD BE VALID FOR THE DURATION OF THE PROJECT. SPECIFIC OPERATIONS WILL BE REQUESTED ON THE BASIS OF NEED AND OPPORTUNITY. THE PROJECT WILL BE CONDUCTED BY DIVISION D WITH ASSISTANCE FROM AREA DIVISIONS AND STATIONS AS NEEDED.

3. *BACKGROUND:* IN RESPONSE TO THE INCREASING REQUIREMENTS FOR THE OPERATIONAL PROCUREMENT OF FOREIGN CODES AND CIPHER MATERIALS, DIVISION D IN 1960 BEGAN THE SPOTTING OF AGENT ASSETS AS A DEVELOPMENTAL ACTIVITY. DURING THE SAME PERIOD REQUIREMENTS FROM NSA BECAME MORE REFINED AND IN MANY RESPECTS MORE SENSITIVE. BECAUSE MOST STATIONS ARE NOT EQUIPPED TO CONDUCT THIS TYPE OF OPERATION AND BECAUSE OF THE DESIRABILITY OF COMPLETELY CENTRALIZING CONTROL OVER THIS ENTIRE EFFORT, IT WAS DETERMINED THAT DIVISION D, WHICH IS IN CLOSEST TOUCH WITH NSA ON PROCUREMENT REQUIREMENTS, COULD BEST CONDUCT THE ACTIVITY.

Although ZR/RIFLE was designed to recruit "black bag" experts to break into diplomatic facilities in order to plant bugs and photograph cryptographic documents, in late 1960 a new mission was added. Besides engaging in burglary, Harvey was now told, ZR/RIFLE was to act as cover for "executive action" operations. The unit would become the home of the CIA's assassination unit. Harvey, who carried a .45-caliber pistol wherever he went and enjoyed tough-guy assignments, seemed the right man for the job. And the joint NSA/CIA ZR/RIFLE project, buried deep within Division D, was the perfect place to hide the new capability. Eventually, however, the CIA's attempted assassinations were revealed during congressional hearings and such activities were later banned.

Today, the SCS is the successor to Division D. As encryption, fiber optics, the Internet, and other new technologies make life increasingly difficult for NSA's intercept operators and codebreakers, the SCS has greatly expanded and become increasingly important. Its goal, like that of television's old Impossible Missions Force, is to find unique ways around problems. "Yesterday's code clerk is today's systems administrator," said one very senior CIA official. The easiest way to acquire many secrets is to get into foreign databases, and the best way to do that is to recruit—by bribery or otherwise—the people who manage the systems. Also, by bribing someone to plant bugs in the keyboards or other vulnerable parts of a computer network, NSA can intercept messages before cryptographic software has a chance to scramble them.

The SCS is headquartered in a heavily protected compound of modern buildings on Springfield Road in Beltsville, Maryland, a few miles south of NSA. There, in what is known as the live room, the electronic environment of target cities is re-created in order to test which antennas and receivers would be best for covert interception. Elsewhere, bugs, receivers, and antennas are fabricated into everyday objects so they can be smuggled into foreign countries. "Sometimes that's a very small antenna and you try to sneak it in," said former CIA director Stansfield Turner. "Sometimes the signal you're intercepting is very small, narrow, [of] limited range, and getting your antenna there is going to be very difficult. I mean, under Mr. Gorbachev's bed is hard to get to, for instance."

While on occasion NSA or SCS has compromised a nation's entire communications system by bribing an engineer or telecommunications official, often much of the necessary eavesdropping can be done from special rooms in U.S. embassies. But in difficult countries, clandestine SCS agents must sometimes fly in disguised as businesspeople. An agent might bring into the target country a parabolic antenna disguised as an umbrella. A receiver and satellite transmitter may seem to be a simple radio and laptop computer. The SCS official will camouflage and plant the equipment in a remote site somewhere along the microwave's narrow beam—maybe in a tree in a wooded area, or in the attic of a rented farmhouse. The signals captured by the equipment will be remotely retransmitted to a geostationary Sigint satellite, which will relay them to NSA. At other times, no other solution is possible except climbing a telephone pole and hard-wiring an eavesdropping device.

The SCS will also play a key role in what is probably the most profound change in the history of signals intelligence—the eventual switch from focusing on information "in motion" to information "at rest." Since the first transatlantic intercept station was erected on Gillin Farm in Houlton, Maine, just before the close of World War I, Sigint has concentrated on intercepting signals as they travel through the air or space. But as technology makes that increasingly difficult and prohibitively expensive, the tendency, say senior intelligence officials, will be to turn instead to the vast quantity of information at rest—stored on computer databases, disks, and hard drives. This may be done either remotely, through cyberspace, or physically, by the SCS.

In a large sense, the changing philosophy represents the American spy world turned full circle, back to where the best way to get secrets is to steal them from where they are stored. Only now the storage site may be a single hard drive containing all the world's information.

CHAPTER TWELVE

HEART

WZEEFCIE OCRT ASKFAI KA RAKT LAW "IAIT AL KOT CDART"
UHVQ HKBJMMT GVKMLFQ BCFBKHFT CWKH GUJ JEEHCWJM EHCBKTT
XIXAL, DXJMDDH ZXGDA GUU JG DXJ UXDMZ UGTI
CFWF LNJHB WFVW NH'W THWRICWJMDH BIT UJWWJIC BFJDPTHW
RXIBB DWNEDCI FCHZ CR VYHHCAD WAHCEW FNXXYACHZ NABCAW

Beneath the surface—past the razor wire, the bomb-sniffing dogs, the hundreds of armed police, the SWAT teams, the barriers, and the signs with their dire warnings—Crypto City functions, on one level, like any other town.

Although it is not found on any map, Crypto City, if incorporated, would be one of the largest municipalities in the state of Maryland. Each working day more than 32,000 specially cleared people—civilians, military, and contractors—travel over its thirty-two miles of roads, which are named in honor of past NSA notables. They park in one of the 17,000 spaces that cover 325 acres and enter one of fifty buildings whose combined floor space totals more than seven million square feet. In terms of growth, Crypto City is one of the most vibrant metropolises in the country. Between 1982 and 1996 it undertook more than half a billion dollars' worth of new construction. Another nearly $500 million was spent leasing 1.5 million square feet of office space. And $152.8 million more was spent for new construction in the final years leading up to the millennium.

Crypto City's budget, long a closely held secret, has been revealed in a closed-door meeting in the City's Engineering and Technology Building. Addressing a group of technology employees in September 1999, Deputy Director for Services Terry Thompson said, "Were we a corporate company based on our four-billion-dollar budget and the number of employees that we have, we kind of bench ourselves against Hewlett-Packard."

In fact, NSA's overall budget for 1995–1999 totaled $17,570,600,000.

Another $7,304,000,000 was sought for 2000–2001. As for its personnel, NSA employs approximately 38,000 people, more than the CIA and FBI combined. Another 25,000 are employed in the agency's Central Security Services, which operates the scores of listening posts; these staffers do not count as NSA employees.

More than 37,000 cars are registered in Crypto City; its post office distributes 70,000 pieces of mail a day. Guarding and patrolling it all are the secret city's own cops, with law enforcement authority in two states. Ranking in size among the top 4.8 percent of the nation's 17,358 police departments, it even has its own SWAT team. Patrolling the city, NSA police cars average 3,850 miles each month and respond to 700 emergency calls a year.

By the 1990s Crypto City's police force had grown to over 700 uniformed officers. Their equipment is specially designed so that they can not only react to an emergency but also do so in total secrecy. The officers have available an Emergency Response Communications Command Post equipped with STU-III secure cellular telephones and encrypted closed-circuit television systems. This technology enables the command post to communicate secretly with the city's Emergency Management Center and its Support Services Operations Center, a twenty-four-hour command, control, and communications center.

Should a threat be detected, Crypto City also has its Special Operations Unit/Emergency Reaction Team. Dressed in black paramilitary uniforms and wearing special headgear, they brandish an assortment of weapons, including Colt 9mm submachine guns. Attached to the team are two military medics assigned to NSA's Medical Center. During periods of heightened alert, and at other times as a deterrent, the team, known as the Men in Black, are posted at the perimeter gates. Another special unit, the Executive Protection Unit, provides the drivers and bodyguards for NSA's director and deputy director and conducts advance security at locations where the top two officials are scheduled to appear.

As part of NSA's increased perimeter security antiterrorism program, new fences and barriers are being constructed around the entire metropolis. When completed, every nonregistered vehicle will have to first be inspected for bombs and other threats at a new $4 million screening center before being allowed to enter Crypto City. There, a team of handlers and eleven specially trained Dutch shepherd and Belgian Malinois bomb-sniffing dogs will closely examine every car and truck. The canines, imported from Holland, are also used for operational support and in emergency-response situations. They are transported throughout the city in specially designed Jeep Cherokees equipped with a kennel, a remote door-release system, and temperature-monitoring equipment to protect the animals in hot weather. Currently in limited operation, the Explosive Detection Canine Unit inspects an average of more than 750 vehicles per week.

Crypto City's yearly consumption of electricity—409,005,840 kilowatt-hours, carried over 662 miles of wires—equals that of Maryland's capital, Annapolis. And with over six acres of computers, twenty-five tons of air-conditioning equipment pumping out over 6 billion cubic feet of cool air a year, and more than half a million lightbulbs to power, the city burns up 54 million watts of electricity a day. That leaves the secret city with a shocking monthly electric bill of nearly $2 million, which makes it the second largest user of electricity in the entire state. In 1992 Crypto City consumed 3.5 trillion BTUs of oil, electricity, and gas—the equivalent of 33 million gallons of fuel oil.

Despite the enormous energy available, Crypto City still suffers blackouts, resulting occasionally in the loss of "critical mission information," according to an NSA document. To handle such outages, the city has its own generating plant capable of quickly producing up to twenty-six megawatts of electricity, enough to power a community of over 3,500 homes.

In winter, 243,000 pounds of blistering steam race through thirty-seven miles of insulated piping every hour to keep the city warm. To satisfy its thirst, ninety-five miles of water pipes crisscross the community, joining forty-two miles of sewage and drain lines to keep the top secret–cleared plumbers busy. The city is equipped with its own fire department as well as twenty-three separate alarm systems and 402 miles of sprinklers feeding 210,000 sprinkler heads. And in case they don't work, there are approximately 5,000 fire extinguishers in the city. In 1998, the busy fire department responded to 168 alarms, 41 medical assists, 44 automobile accidents, 8 natural gas investigations, and 5 brush fires.

It is far easier to get blood out of NSA employees than secrets. NSA is the largest contributor to Maryland's blood donor program, donating approximately 6,500 pints of blood per year. As a result, NSA employees and their families are eligible to receive blood whenever they need it. In fact, so many gallons of donated blood flow out of Crypto City every day that it is used to aid victims in terrorist incidents. Places as divergent as Oklahoma City, following the bombing of the Alfred P. Murrah Federal Building in 1995, and Africa, after the 1998 embassy bombings in Kenya and Tanzania, have received blood from NSA's codebreakers.

For entertainment, Crypto City offers its own movies, although none that would ever be found in a cineplex in the world beyond the barriers. Recent films have included *Pathfinder*, in Lapp; *My Village at Sunset*, in Khmer; *Touki Bouki*, in Wolof, one of the languages used in the West African nation of Mauritania; and *Wend Kuuni*, in Mõõre, a language used in Burkina Faso.

The city even has an annual film festival, sponsored by the Crypto-Linguistic Association. Entries have ranged from *This Land Is Ours,* a Nigerian picture in the Hausa language about a corrupt businessman who tries to buy up an entire village without revealing that precious stones are buried beneath the land, to an Iranian black comedy, *The Suitors,* in Farsi, which deals with a group of Iranians who sacrifice a sheep in their Manhattan apartment and end up facing a SWAT team. Others have included *Harvest: 3000 Years,* in Ethiopia's native Amharic; *Letters from Alou*, in Senegalese; *Children of Nature,* in Icelandic; and *Hedd Wyn,* in Welsh. The 2000 festival featured *A Mongolian Tale,* in Mongolian. Like a very unusual video store, the Crypto-Linguistic Association has more than 105 films in 48 foreign languages available for loan to city residents.

For those interested in more conventional forms of entertainment, the city has its own ticket agency, which, during one recent year, sold over 217,000 tickets, worth nearly $1.8 million, to local sports, theater, and other events. Short on cash for a ticket to the opera? The city has its own private bank, the Tower Federal Credit Union, the second largest in the state and the twentieth largest in the country, with over 75,000 members and $412 million in assets.

In need of day care? Crypto City offers its own Children's World, for children aged six weeks to five years, complete with its own kindergarten approved by the State of Maryland. With room for 305 youngsters, it is the largest facility of its kind in the state. Cotton swabs can be purchased in the NSA's own drugstore, where the most popular items are candy bars. "NSA has a lot of junk food addicts," said Maryellen Smith, standing behind the cash register. "They eat a lot!" Not surprisingly, the second most popular item is headache medicine.

Although the invisible city has no docking facilities or even any waterfront, it has its own, very exclusive yacht club, complete with commodore. Membership is restricted to the city's security badge–carrying citizens. The clubhouse for the Arundel Yacht Club, founded in 1967, is in Room 2S160 of the OPS 1 Building. There, in secure spaces protected from hostile eavesdroppers, the 120 members attend seminars on such topics as "Boarding Ladders—Mounting and Storage Methods." In May 2000 members went on a moonlight cruise and had a rendezvous in Lovely Cove, off Maryland's Chester River.

Elsewhere in Crypto City, NSA's Bayside Big Band may be playing, while the Parkway Chorale performs *Cats* or *Phantom of the Opera* or even Mozart's *Requiem.* On the softball diamond, Hot Flash may be pitching out Huge Batting Egos to a cheering crowd. More than 3,200 employees participate in such intramural sports programs. A bulletin board across from the barbershop lists the next meeting of the Family Historians Genealogy Club: "Mexican War Records: Adventures of the Baltimore and Washington, D.C., Battalions." For those who enjoy a bit more stimulation, members of WIN (Women in NSA—men are allowed to join) recently aired the daring video *Sex Hormones vs. GS Ratings.*

For pianists, there is the Klavier Club; warriors have their Battlegaming Club; and for hedonists there is the Sun, Snow & Surf Ski Club, with trips to Austria and Switzerland. For hams there is the Freestate Amateur Radio Club (call letters K3IVO) which sponsors regular radio "foxhunts" where members, using radio direction-finding equipment, attempt to track down other members out in the wilderness who transmit brief messages on handheld radios. And for those wishing to send a signal beyond the ionosphere, the city offers the Good News Bible Club.

Finally, in what would have been unthinkable only a few years ago, NSA's hidden city even has its own Gay, Lesbian, or Bisexual Employees (GLOBE) club, complete with its own internal web address (GLOBE@nsa). The chapter is named in honor of Alan Turing, the brilliant British mathematician who played a key part in breaking the enormously complex German Enigma cipher machine during World War II. After the war, he was declared a security risk because of his homosexuality. After being convicted in Manchester of being a practicing homosexual, he died of cyanide poisoning in a suspected suicide.

Every June the city holds a weeklong "All American Festival." Open to "all badged personnel," the gala is intended to highlight the cultural diversity within NSA's community. "What better way to acknowledge the vast array of similarities and differences of all Americans," said the Festival Steering Committee. In 2000, residents of Crypto City could play "Who Wants to Be a Millionaire?" in the Friedman Auditorium, watch some Polynesian dancers, take salsa dance lessons, try out fencing, or listen to Scottish bagpipe music, a gospel choir, a barbershop quartet, or the disc jockey Wite Noyze.

Bucking political correctness, the keynote speaker addressed the issue of "White Men in America . . . A Historical Perspective." "For many years, much attention has been focused on the changing roles for women and minorities in America," said the *NSA Newsletter* about the talk by Dr. Anthony J. Ipsaro, a clinical psychologist specializing in the psychology of men. "Ipsaro will present one of the first accounts of the status and power of American white men in a diverse and democratic society—their contributions, their failures, and their futures in the 21st Century."

With eleven cafeterias and a VIP dining room, it would be difficult to go hungry in the invisible city. The OPS 1 Building alone has a mammoth cafeteria—over 45,000 square feet, with 75 employees. It prepares 200 gallons of soup a day and is capable of serving lunch to over 6,000 people. Designed like a food court in a suburban mall, the Firehouse Grill serves up dogs, fries, onion rings, and a variety of daily specials, while at the New York Deli customers can have a sandwich made to order or prepare their own and pay by the ounce. The city also has a Taco Bell and a Pizza Hut.

Although it's unlikely that any study exists to substantiate the proposition, there appears to be a direct correlation between codebreaking and appetite. When the new OPS 1 cafeteria opened on December 13, 1993, a total of 9,743 people showed up. Before they left they consumed 2,127 tacos and enchiladas from the Taco Bell stand, 176 pounds of salad, and about 20,000 other items. In 1993, food sales totaled more than $7 million—and employees dropped another $2 million in quarters into the city's 380 vending machines.

To help residents convert their nachos and deep-dish pizzas from a solid into a liquid by means of sweat, half a dozen SHAPE Fitness Centers—16,000 square feet of floor space—are located in the invisible city. There, residents can exercise to their cardiovascular delight on StairMasters, treadmills, LifeCycles, Nordic Tracks, stationary and recumbent bikes, rowers, cross-country-ski simulators, upper-body ergometers, gravitrons and Cybex resistance equipment. In the OPS 2B Building every Tuesday and Thursday morning, technospooks are taught to carry the tiger to the mountain, grasp the bird's tail, wave their hands like clouds, step back and repulse the monkey, and perform more than fifty other intricate moves of Tai Chi. Other courses include Shorinji Kempo Martial Arts, Plyometrics Training, and Flexible Strength, a yoga-type class. SHAPE also sponsors an annual 5K run for city residents. After a hard day of stressful codebreaking, SHAPE offers "seated massage therapy" by licensed massage therapists at a cost of $1 a minute, or guided meditation for free.

Crypto City also has a unique collection of professional associations, known as Learned Organizations. One of the first established was the Crypto-Linguistic Association, which itself has a number of subgroups. The members of the Special Interest Group on Lexicography (SIGLEX), for example, strive to push ahead the state of the art of dictionary and glossary making, including even dictionaries for unwritten languages. Two other special interest groups are SIGVOICE, concentrating on topics ranging from accents to spoonerisms, and SIGTRAN, dedicated to the art of translation.

Other Learned Organizations include the Crypto-Mathematics Institute, the Computer Information Sciences Institute, and the International Affairs Institute. The traffic and signal analysts have their Communications Analysis Association, the cryptanalysts have their Kryptos Society, and the intercept operators have their Collection Association, which presents an award to the best eavesdropper of the year.

While in many respects Crypto City is unique, and, to many, even incomprehensible, it can also be very ordinary. Like other large communities, it has its share of dirt, fear of crime, and other problems. The same NSA police who guard the inner sanctum of codebreaking also, during 1993, gave out thousands of parking tickets and responded to 236 traffic accidents and 742 other emergencies. NSAers complain about poor working conditions. "Accumulated along every hallway leading to those few stairways," said one employee whose branch moved into the basement of the old OPS 1 Building, "are mounds of trash, pallets of cast-off equipment, old racks, and dilapidated shelves." Another complained of a burned-out car that had been in a city parking lot for days, and of trash accumulating in front of OPS 2A.

Some residents are afraid to walk through remote tunnels and hallways late at night. "If I use the south tunnel, I am really asking for it," said one late-night worker. "Although the tunnel has a row of overhead lights, only one works—and that one is very dim . . . someone could wait there . . . follow me into the tunnel, and grab me once no one was in sight."

At the heart of the invisible city is NSA's massive Headquarters/Operations Building. With more than sixty-eight acres of floor space, the entire U.S. Capitol Building could easily fit inside it four times over. A modern, boxy structure with floor after floor of dark one-way glass, from the outside much of the complex looks like any stylish office building. But looks, like most else at NSA, are meant to deceive.

Hidden underneath this reflective glass is the real building. This one is protected by a skin of orange-colored copper and unique windows—a thick, bulletproof-like outer pane, five inches of sound-deadening space, a thin copper screen, and an inner pane. The elaborate shielding is designed to keep all sounds and signals—indeed all types of electromagnetic radiation—from ever getting out. Known by the codename Tempest, this protective copper shielding technique is used throughout much of the city and is designed to prevent electronic spies from capturing any telltale emissions. Like a black hole, NSA pulls in every signal that comes near, but no electron is ever allowed to escape. At least that is the way NSA would like it.

The massive Headquarters/Operations Building is an interconnected labyrinth of 3 million square feet that stretches in all directions. Entrance is first made through the two-story Visitor Control Center, one of more than 100 fixed watch posts within the secret city manned by the armed NSA police. It is here that clearances are checked and visitor badges are issued.

Far more than a simple piece of plastic, the NSA badge, about the size of a playing card, with the employee's picture on the front, represents life itself to Crypto City's tens of thousands of daytime residents. Take it away, and their livelihood suddenly disappears; change the color, and their status goes up or down. If they forget it, their day is a mess; if they lose it, they come under suspicion. Add a tab, and their universe grows slightly larger.

Blue badges are worn by those who have passed a lengthy background investigation, suffered through a nerve-racking polygraph exam, received a top secret codeword clearance, and, finally, been "indoctrinated" into the supersecret world of Sigint and codemaking. The "indoctrination" is NSA's version of at last being let in on the club's secret handshake, finally being allowed to look behind the thick black curtain. It is something like a Mafia induction ceremony without the drop of blood. The fresh initiates may now be told how their country eavesdrops on other countries, breaks their codes, and reads their most secret communications.

Next, in solemn tones, the new blue-badgers are told the meaning of certain secret codewords, such as Umbra, which, when stamped on a document, means that it reveals the highest-level signals intelligence sources and methods. Some are indoctrinated for additional codewords, such as Gamma, which means that the information comes from a particularly sensitive source, such as internal foreign communications systems or cipher systems that NSA was able to defeat. Others, such as Zarf, indicate that the information was obtained from electronic intelligence picked up by eavesdropping satellites. Like an endless spiral, there are secret classification systems within secret classification systems. In 1974, a new category was approved exclusively for NSA's most secret secrets: VRK, Very Restricted Knowledge.

Although they predominate in NSA's secret city, the blue badge is only one of twenty-six different styles and colors that make up the security rainbow. Fully cleared contractors wear green; those with only a secret clearance have LIC (Limited Interim Clearance) printed on top; students at the National Cryptologic School have a turquoise border around their badges; and former directors and deputy directors have red and blue stripes around them. Important visitors have PV ("privileged visitor") badges, while uncleared visitors must wear a badge with a large red *V* and be accompanied by a person with an additional *E* (for "escort") badge.

Additionally, for admittance into certain supersecure areas, a small plastic plate must sometimes be attached to the neck chain above the picture badge. Workers in the National Security Operations Center, for example, wear a plate bearing the letters "NSOC." And at the agency's giant listening post at Menwith Hill Station in central England, only NSAers with a badge plate bearing a blue diagonal strip are allowed into the building that houses Operation Silkworth. This is a satellite eavesdropping mission targeting Russian microwave communications.

And then there is the red badge—the NSA equivalent of the Scarlet Letter, awarded to those who have had their clearance taken away. Although officially it stands for "clearance status not indicated," and is normally worn by people working in the "Red Corridor"—the drugstore and other concession areas—for ex–blue-badgers it is the ultimate humiliation. Those with a red badge around their necks are forbidden to go anywhere near classified information and are restricted to a few corridors and administrative areas—the bank, the barbershop, the cafeteria, the credit union, and the airline and entertainment ticket counters. A clearance may be yanked for reasons ranging from bad debts to an unauthorized meeting with a foreign official to an unfounded third-hand rumor twice removed.

Regardless of their badge's color, all employees are warned, "After you leave an NSA installation, remove your badge from public view, thus avoiding publicizing your NSA affiliation."

Once inside the white, pentagonal Visitor Control Center, employees are greeted by a six-foot painting of the NSA seal, an eagle clutching a silver key in what the agency describes as "sinister talons." In front of the seal are ten Access Control Terminals, watched over by a central security command post. Employees insert their security badges into the terminals, punch in their personal identification numbers on the keyboard, and wait for the green light to signal that the turnstile is unlocked. At unannounced times, a special cadre of NSA police officers assigned to the Aperiodic Inspection Team conduct surprise inspections, looking for anyone attempting to smuggle out secret documents, or to sneak in cameras, tape recorders, computer disks—or Furbys.

In December 1998, worried security officials sent out a "Furby Alert" on the agency's Intranet, banning the small furry toys. Because the homely, bug-eyed creature contains a small device allowing it to mimic words, officials worried that a Furby might retain snippets of secret conversations in its microbrain. NSA employees "are prohibited from introducing these items into NSA spaces," the warning said. As for those improbable few who might already have one sitting on their desk, the notice sternly instructed them to "contact their Staff Security Officer for guidance." In a recent year more than 30,000 inspections were conducted at the Visitor Control Center and the other gatehouses. There are no statistics on how many people were arrested with illegal Furbys.

From the Visitor Control Center one enters the eleven-story, $41 million OPS 2A, the tallest building in the City. Shaped like a dark glass Rubik's Cube, the building houses much of NSA's Operations Directorate, which is responsible for processing the ocean of intercepts and prying open the complex cipher systems.

Beyond the Visitor Control Center, secrecy and security permeate the air. Above escalators, moving electronic words on "Magic Message" boards warn employees against talking about work outside the secret city. Along hallways and in the cafeteria, signs hanging from the ceiling warn "Don't Spill the Beans, Partner. No Classified Talk!" Other warnings are posted on bulletin boards throughout the city. No meetings of any kind may be held in the Visitor Control Center, where an uncleared person may be present. Classified talk in "corridors, restrooms, cafeterias . . . barber shop, and drugstore" is forbidden, according to the NSA Security Handbook.

Every month, NSA's Office of Security pumps out 14,000 security posters designed by "security awareness officers" to line Crypto City's rest rooms, snack bars, hallways, and stairwells. Others are sent to overseas listening posts and contractor facilities. One design pictured a noose hanging from the branch of a tree, with the caption, "For Repeated Security Violations." Some posters appear to have been concocted in a time warp. On the very day that East and West Germany were unified in the Federal Republic, security officials unveiled a new poster showing East German troops standing on the Berlin Wall. The caption was a menacing 1931 prediction by a Soviet official: the USSR would win a military victory over the capitalists by duping them with bogus peace overtures. Another poster shows Uncle Sam asleep under a tree while a skulking Soviet ogre prepares to take advantage.

The posters prompted one NSA employee to question whether the campaign represents "a not-too-subtle form of political indoctrination in a format reminiscent of traditional Cold War propaganda." Another complained that visitors to NSA "must find them surreal."

More recently, the posters have begun to reflect pop culture. One is designed like a scene from the popular television quiz show *Who Wants to Be a Millionaire?* "What should you do if approached by a foreign intelligence officer?" reads the question. "*A:* Answer Questions; *B:* Accept Gifts; *C:* Negotiate Payment." Circled is answer *D:* "Report Contact." Finally, the poster adds, "And This Is OUR Final Answer." Another poster bears a picture of a wastebasket containing copies of *Newsweek,* the *New York Times,* and other news publications below the caption "Snooper Bowl."

In 1996 agency artists put a grim-faced Cal Ripken, Jr., on a poster. Knees flexed and glove at the ready, the Baltimore Orioles player stood below a lime-green banner that read, "Security. Our Best Defense." Unfortunately, no one had asked Ripken's permission, which provoked a protest by his business management firm. "If Cal's identified, they need our permission," complained Ira Rainess, general counsel of the Tufton Group. "His publicity right is violated if they use any elements of Cal's persona without consent. Even if they are just using it promotionally, they are deriving some value from using Cal's image."

In a basement beneath OPS 2A, behind the door to Room 2A0114, is the security command post for Crypto City. The Support Services Operations Center (SSOC) is dominated by a tall, curved console consisting of banks of computer screens and secure television and telephone equipment. In operation twenty-four hours a day, the Center oversees security throughout the city. It also serves as the city's crisis hub through its Emergency Management Center. Officers handle more than 1,500 calls a day—lockouts, requests for assistance, trespass alarms, and radio dispatch instructions. The hundreds of closed-circuit television cameras that peer down from the city's rooftops and line its hallways are also monitored here—as are the cameras that keep the director's house under constant surveillance.

Whenever someone in Crypto City dials 911, the call is answered in the SSOC. Security officers can immediately determine the exact location of the telephone. The Center handles an average of forty emergency calls each month. It is also responsible for tracking NSA couriers and locating missing employees. When a danger to the city—a bomb threat or a terrorist attack, for instance—arises, the SSOC has authority to undertake "hostile emergency action plans."

Hidden far from the spotlight, the agency has seen few external assaults; when one is detected, no matter how minor, NSA immediately goes to battle stations. On July 3, 1996, for example, both the SSOC and the National Security Operations Center, the focal point of NSA's worldwide eavesdropping network, were tipped off about a planned demonstration at the agency. The group sponsoring the demonstration was identified as the Baltimore Emergency Response Network (BERN), a small, nonviolent organization that promotes peaceful solutions to conflicts rather than armed intervention. Its leader was Philip Berrigan, a longtime veteran of peaceful demonstrations.

The protest was scheduled for the following day, the July Fourth holiday. At NSA, the director and his senior staff were immediately notified. The FBI and other government agencies were quickly asked to provide background information on BERN. "Members of the SSOC, Facilities Security, Public and Media Affairs, and Protective Services convened to enact an NSA Emergency Management Plan to address the threat," said an internal document. "Protective Services activated their Special Operations Unit." They then notified the military police at Fort Meade, "who mobilized a contingent to augment the Protective Service Officers' force."

Prepared for anything except all-out nuclear war, the agency must have been disappointed. About 10:30 A.M. a motley group of about thirty late-sleeping activists arrived at the outer fence, carrying a few placards protesting illegal NSA operations. They then began to read Scripture. Next someone recited a "Declaration of Independence from the National Security Agency," which was mounted on a large placard for presentation to the director, Lieutenant General Kenneth A. Minihan. After a few hours in the warm sun, the group headed back to Baltimore.

Pleased that the agency had once again been saved from imminent peril, the author of a classified internal document declared the operation "an unequivocal success. The orchestration of a multitude of NSA and non-NSA emergency response resources proved extremely effective." Even Philip Berrigan was impressed. "Very efficient," he said, "very sterile."

After leaving the SSOC, the visitor walks down a passageway and enters the $56.3 million OPS 2B Building, a rectangle of black glass, and is immediately impressed by the large polished wall of black granite. Carved in the structure, twelve feet wide and eight feet high, is a triangle containing the NSA seal. Above, inlaid in gold, are the words "They Served in Silence." And below, in eight columns, are the names of 152 military and civilian cryptologists, intercept operators, and analysts who have given their lives in the line of duty. Among those listed on the National Cryptologic Memorial Wall, which was dedicated in February 1996, is Army Specialist James T. Davis, the first American soldier killed in Vietnam. Also listed on the wall are the seventeen airmen who died when their C-130 ferret was shot down over Soviet Armenia in 1958 and the thirty-four crewmembers of the USS *Liberty* who died when it was attacked by Israel.

The highly polished black granite was designed to allow workers viewing the memorial to see their own reflections and thus remind them that they, too, serve in silence and support the cause for which those honored gave their lives.

Nearby is the Canine Suite, named after the first director. It is often used to host visiting VIPs.

Up on the eighth floor of OPS 2B, the mayor of Crypto City, Air Force Lieutenant General Michael V. Hayden, has his suite of offices. On a typical day, Hayden's alarm wakes him up about 5:45 A.M. but he stays in bed, eyes closed, listening to National Public Radio's six o'clock news summary. After a quick shower, he climbs into his Volvo and drives the three miles to the NSA. "I drive myself, or my son or wife will drop me off if they need the car," he says, "and more often than not they will drop me off."

Arriving about 6:50, Hayden enters the lobby, inserts his badge into the CONFIRM reader, and pushes through the turnstile. If he is in a hurry, he can slip a key into his small private elevator, off to the right. But on most days he simply crowds with the other early-morning arrivals into one of the large employee elevators.

On the eighth floor, he walks to the end of the hallway and enters the executive suite, which includes the offices of the director, deputy director, and chief of staff. The suite was once referred to as Mahogany Row, but today there is no mahogany. Instead, past the receptionist, the walls are covered with large framed pictures of NSA's largest listening posts, including Menwith Hill Station with its dozens of eavesdropping antennas hidden under radomes. Hayden takes a left through an unmarked wooden door and enters his corner office.

Standing at the eavesdropping-proof windows he can look out on his burgeoning empire, stretching far into the distance. Against a beige wall is a large bookcase containing mementos from his hometown football and baseball teams, the Pittsburgh Steelers and Pirates. On another wall is a framed, yellowing newspaper article from October 1941 announcing that his father, Harry V. Hayden, Jr., has been inducted into the service as a private and has arrived in Northern Ireland. In the center of the large office is a dark conference table surrounded by eight green chairs; a couch with a gold print design stands off to the side. There is also a lectern, so the director can work standing up.

Hayden sits in a green high-back chair. Nearby is a small space heater to keep out the winter chill. On his walnut desk rests a pen holder from his days as the number two commander in Korea, a notepad printed with the word "DIRECTOR," and a Brookstone world clock. On a table behind him, next to his NSA flag, are three computers—one for classified work, another for unclassified work, and a secure laptop linking him with members of his NSA Advisory Board, a small group of outside consultants. There are also several telephones on the table. One is for secure internal calls; another is a secure STU-III for secret external calls; and a "red line" with buttons that can put him through instantly to the secretary of defense, the Chairman of the Joint Chiefs of Staff, and other senior officials.

No phones, however, connect the director to the White House; indeed, during Hayden's first year in office, he never once spoke directly to

President Clinton. "When I've talked to the people who've been in the chair before," he said, "it seems to me that it's been pretty distant in the past that the director of NSA has had routine contact with the president. My routine contact has been—I've met with Jim Steinberg, who's the deputy national security adviser, I wouldn't say 'routinely,' but the fact is if I picked the phone up I could talk to Jim if I wanted to. John Hamry, the deputy secretary of defense, although routinely I talk to Art Money, his assistant secretary. At the CIA it's both [Director George] Tenet and [Deputy Director Lieutenant General John A.] Gordon routinely on anything that comes to mind."

To the side of his desk are two Sony television sets, one connected to the outside world with the Weather Channel muted, and the other connected to Crypto City's own secret television network. Over that set, every Monday, Wednesday, and Friday at 7:15 A.M., Hayden gets a private intelligence briefing from an NSOC official.

Next, on those same days, is an early morning briefing by his staff. "I'll have a stand-up meeting in here with just my personal staff," said Hayden, "public affairs, inspector general, lawyers, each of the key components represented. It's real quick. Literally a stand-up, everyone's standing, including me. The room is about a third full. We'll go quickly around—hot news of the day."

On Tuesdays and Thursdays, Hayden walks down to the NSOC for an 8:00 A.M. meeting with all his senior officials. "It's something I started here because I wanted the seniors to get a sense of the ops tempo. And so we'll get a briefing in the NSOC from the ops officer, right there—about five to seven minutes, and I keep beating them to keep it shorter. And then we'll retire to a little room privately next door and have a quick staff meeting. . . . By eight or eight-thirty we've kind of gotten the burst communications and now you're into your work schedule."

Next comes a round of meetings and phone calls. Monday, January 31, 2000, for example, was spent cleaning up from the massive computer crash a week before. Hayden's morning meetings centered on NSA's Information Technology Backbone program; he spoke on the phone with Arthur L. Money, the assistant secretary of defense for Command, Control, Communications and Intelligence, and with Charles E. Allen, the CIA's assistant director for collection. He also talked with Judith A.

Emmel, the chief of public affairs, about a candidate for the job of legislative affairs officer.

Lunch also varies depending on the day. "Today [February 2, 2000] I had lunch with the [NSA] Advisory Board," said Hayden. "Yesterday I had lunch with four randomly selected employees up here. The day before I had lunch in the cafeteria. Every now and again we'll have a visitor. Tomorrow Chris Mellon [the principal deputy assistant secretary of defense for intelligence] . . . will be here and we'll have a formal lunch. I have a little dining room off to the side here, seats eight comfortably."

After lunch there are more meetings, often out of the building. Much of Hayden's time is spent being driven to and from Washington in his official black Ford Grand Marquis, "going to [CIA headquarters at] Langley [Virginia], over to the Pentagon. And so frankly that's the reflective time, that's when I can work the telephones, that's when I can get a little reading done. It's sort of a chockablock day of going from meeting to meeting to meeting."

Hayden tries to leave by around 5:30 P.M., but he frequently brings home a briefcase packed with secrets for late-night homework. "I've got secure comms [communications] at home. I bring work home. I have a vault at home where I can keep materials," he said. "And the big thing I do the night before is this: my to-do list for the day, people I want to call, hot things, long-term things." When Hayden isn't working, he enjoys going to movies and reading about the Civil War. "I'm really a fan of the Civil War," said Hayden. "I hate to be called a buff, but in my darker moments my kids would call me that. I like battlefields. My wife and I love movies, we see a lot of movies. All kinds of movies—you'd be surprised."

An inner door in Hayden's office, past his private bathroom labeled WATERCLOSET and a framed picture of the Pittsburgh Steelers, connects him to his deputy director next door. That office, about half the size of the director's, had a French provincial motif while Barbara McNamara occupied it and southwestern after her successor, William Black, moved in. A few steps away, behind the door to Room 2B8020, is the Director's Large Conference Room—a circular, futuristic center where high-level briefings are conducted. At the center is a wooden, doughnut-shaped conference table with twenty-four rose-colored padded chairs. Behind, like a mini-theater, are another sixty-six seats, and on the opposite wall are three large, silvery multimedia screens. During Operation Desert Storm the room was turned into a crisis center, and it was also here where many of the crisis meetings were held during the U.S. air attacks on Kosovo.

Also nearby is Barbara G. Fast, an Army brigadier general, who is deputy chief of the little-known Central Security Service (CSS). In addition to being the director of NSA, Hayden also commands the CSS, NSA's own army, navy, and air force. In that second universe, he is responsible for operational control of all signals intelligence collection, "in consonance" with the commanders of the individual security services—Naval Security Group Command, Army Intelligence and Security Command, and Air Force Intelligence Agency. As deputy chief of CSS, Fast helps manage NSA's vast network of worldwide listening posts.

In addition to his own armed forces, Hayden also has his own "ambassadors," Special U.S. Liaison Officers (SUSLOs), who represent NSA in various parts of the world. The job of SUSLO London is so choice that it frequently serves as a preretirement posting for NSA's deputy directors. Thus it was no surprise when Hayden's first deputy, Barbara McNamara, decided to spend her final NSA days sipping tea and shopping at Harrods. Other SUSLOs are located in Ottawa, Canada; Canberra, Australia; and Wellington, New Zealand. Hayden also has senior representatives to the major military commands. Based in Hawaii, the chief, NSA/CSS Pacific, serves as the top cryptologic liaison with the commander of American forces in the Pacific and the chief, NSA/CSS Europe, has similar responsibilities with respect to the top U.S. commander in that region. Finally, other officials, known as NSA/CSS representatives, are posted in a variety of countries and with other agencies, such as the Pentagon and the State Department.

Other residents of the eighth floor include the agency's chief scientist, mathematician George R. Cotter. He is responsible for keeping NSA abreast of fast-changing technologies in the outside world. Another is Robert L. Deitz, NSA's general counsel, who manages the agency's forty-five lawyers. For two decades, NSA has picked its top attorney, who usually serves for about three years, from private practice. Deitz was formerly a product liability lawyer.

Down the hall from Robert Deitz is Rear Admiral Joseph D. Burns, the chief of staff. Among other things, his office helps formulate the top secret United States Signals Intelligence Directives (USSIDs), which govern NSA's worldwide eavesdropping operations. The USSIDs tell eavesdroppers *what* to do; Technical Instructions (Techins) are then issued to explain *how* to do it. The office also deals with the agency's legislative, contracting, and budget issues.

Past the Russian Technical Library, through a breezeway decorated with an American flag made up of photographs of NSA personnel, and one is in OPS 1, the original A-shaped building built in the 1950s. Today, as then, it is the principal home of the Directorate of Operations (DO). First among equals, the DO constitutes the agency's largest single division. With its legions of eavesdroppers, codebreakers, linguists, and traffic and signals analysts, it encompasses the entire spectrum of signals intelligence, from intercept to cryptanalysis, high-level diplomatic systems to low-level radiotelephone chatter, analysis of cleartext to analysis of metadata—information about information. Its brief covers the analysis of cipher systems belonging to friend as well as foe, democracies as well as dictatorships, microcountries as well as giants. It is the Black Chamber's Black Chamber.

Behind the door to Room 2W106—once the director's office before OPS 2B was built—is James R. (Rich) Taylor, the deputy director for operations. Formerly the agency's executive director, Taylor began his civilian career at NSA in 1974, having graduated from the Air Force Academy and spent five years as an officer with the NSA's air arm, the Air Force Security Service. During the 1990s he became one of the agency's top weapons experts. He also served as director of the RAMPART National Program Office, a big-budget and highly secret joint intelligence community activity "pursuing an area of major investment for future U.S. intelligence operations."

"Operations," Taylor says, "encompasses all the activities that enable analysts to provide intelligence to meet customer requirements. Many agency personnel, in different jobs, have a stake in ensuring that Sigint continues to be America's most valued source of intelligence." Essential, he says, is a close relationship between those who collect the information and those who build the ultra-advanced systems that make the collection possible. "The key to our success is a strong dynamic partnership between DT [the Directorate of Technology and Systems] and DO."

Taylor's deputy is Air Force Major General Tiiu Kera, a stocky woman with reddish hair. A native of Germany, she was born in Balingen/Württemberg at the end of World War II. In 1969, during the height of the antiwar period, Kera received a master's degree in political science from Indiana University. Four years later she was commissioned a second lieutenant in the Air Force. During much of her career she held a number of routine assignments as a personnel officer, mostly within the United States. But in 1987 her career got a boost when she was sent to the National War College for nine months. Kera spent the Gulf War not making policy in the Pentagon or directing air missions over Baghdad but hanging out in Harvard Square as a student, this time at Harvard's Center for International Affairs. After her tour in Cambridge, she became the first U.S. defense attaché to Lithuania and later was named director of intelligence for the U.S. Strategic Command in Omaha, Nebraska.

Because of the growing closeness between NSA and CIA—especially through the joint Special Collection Service, which uses clandestine personnel and techniques to assist NSA—one of Taylor's top deputies always comes from the CIA.

For nearly forty years the DO was organized along geographic lines. The codebreakers of A Group focused on the Soviet Union, while those of B Group analyzed the communications of Communist Asia and G Group tackled the cipher systems of all other areas. But when the Cold War ended, so did the preoccupation with borders. The new nontraditional threats—terrorism, nuclear weapons proliferation, and drugs—have no borders.

Thus, in 1997 the old geographically based groups were replaced with two new organizations. W Group, the Office of Global Issues and Weapons Systems, was formed to focus the agency's powerful eavesdropping platforms on these new transnational adversaries, irrespective of geography. The other, M Group, the Office of Geopolitical and Military Production, would concentrate on the cyber infrastructure of potential adversaries, looking, for example, for vulnerabilities in their telecommunications systems.

Chief of M Group in 2000 was Jeanne Y. Zimmer, who was awarded the Pentagon's Distinguished Civilian Service Award for her "leadership and management of a newly formed organization with worldwide responsibilities [that] had a lasting impact for the United States." The NSA's organizational changes, said former NSA director Minihan, "lets you think in a more agile and dynamic way. Now you are not looking at airplanes, tanks, ships, and soldiers. You are looking at the infrastructure within which the operating capability of the adversary exists."

Room 3E099 of OPS 1 is the home of the National Security Operations Center, the very heart of NSA's worldwide eavesdropping activities. Located on the building's third floor, the NSOC (pronounced "N-sock") is reached through a set of automatic glass doors. Above are the seals of the three organizations that make up the NSA's own military, the Central Security Service, and below, inlaid in the flooring, are the Center's initials.

Inside is a quiet, windowless, war room–like command center, staffed around the clock by five rotating teams of civilian and military personnel. Waist-high cubicles separate target areas, such as terrorism and transnational threats; large video screens cover the walls; and computer monitors glow like electronic candles in the dim light. On the top of the wall, clocks tick off time in various places—Bosnia, Moscow, Iraq. If an uncleared visitor enters, red warning lights begin to whirl. The NSOC directs critical and time-sensitive signals intelligence and information security operations. When it was established in 1972, the NSOC was known as the National Sigint Operations Center. The name was changed in 1996 when the NSOC also became the center for the information security side of the agency, responsible for developing cipher machines and assisting in protecting the nation against cyber attacks. Its director in 2000 was Colonel Joe Brand. Reporting to him is the senior operation officer (SOO), the NSA duty officer. If a listening post suddenly picks up an indication of a far-off assassination, or a sudden attack by Russia on a neighboring republic, a CRITIC message containing that information will be flashed immediately to the NSOC. Shortly after the USS *Cole* was attacked by terrorists in the port of Aden in October 2000, a CRITIC was zapped to the NSOC. Within minutes of the early morning message, a call was placed to the director, Michael Hayden.

Elsewhere in the NSOC, information security specialists monitor critical networks for indications of threats and intrusions. During a crisis, senior officials meet in the nearby conference room, where they sit around a highly polished, wedge-shaped conference table with a secure conference speakerphone in the center.

Just down the hallway, in Room 3E132, is Special Support Activity, which provides sensitive assistance to military commanders and federal executives around the world. Units known as Cryptologic Service Groups (CSGs) bring the NSA, in microcosm, to the national security community and forces in the field. Among the more than thirty CSGs is one assigned to the U.S. Operations Command at MacDill Air Force Base in Tampa. Another is at the State Department in Washington. There, the CSGs are most useful when they can provide diplomats with intercepts containing details of their opponents' positions during important negotiations.

Further down the hallway in OPS 1 is NSA's Worldwide Video Teleconferencing Center, which allows headquarters employees to conduct highly secret meetings with their counterparts at various listening posts around the world or with officials from NSA's foreign partners, such as Britain's GCHQ. The Center conducts about 200 conferences a month. It consists of a large conference room, with space for twenty-five participants, and a wall of television monitors. This allows the faraway participants to be seen and heard simultaneously. Data can also be exchanged, by computer and fax. All communication to and from the teleconferencing center is heavily encrypted and highly secure.

Among the most secret organizations in OPS 1 is the Defense Special Missile and Astronautics Center (DEFSMAC). At the entrance to Room 1E069 is the organization's seal: an orbiting satellite and a patch of stars above the earth. Even within the intelligence community, DEFSMAC (pronounced "deaf-smack"), a joint project of the NSA and the DIA, remains little known.

Robert McNamara established the organization on April 27, 1964, largely as a result of the Cuban missile crisis, in order to evaluate foreign missile activity and threats. "You didn't want NORAD [the North American Air Defense Command] fooling around in technologies that they didn't understand, or trying to evaluate a bunch of raw data, so DEFSMAC was put in," said Lieutenant General Daniel O. Graham, a former director of the Defense Intelligence Agency. Since its beginning, the organization has always been headed by an NSA civilian, with a DIA colonel as deputy director.

Today the organization operates as the nation's chief warning bell for the launch of foreign rockets—whether in ballistic missile tests by China or North Korea, or in an attack from a rogue launch site in Russia. The focal point for "all source" intelligence—listening posts, early warning satellites, human agents, seismic detectors—on missile launches, DEFSMAC provides the "initial analysis and reporting on all foreign space and missile events."

As other organizations have shrunk with the end of the Cold War, DEFSMAC has more than doubled its size, to more than 230 people, eighty-five of whom staff a new operations center. Where once DEFSMAC had only Russia and China to monitor, its widely dispersed targets now also include India, North Korea, Iran, Israel, and Pakistan.

DEFSMAC watches the earth as a physician listens to a heart, hoping to detect the first irregular beat indicating that a missile is about to be launched. "It has all the inputs from all the assets, and is a warning activity," explained one former NSA official. "They probably have a better feel for any worldwide threat to this country from missiles, aircraft, or overt military activities, better and more timely, at instant fingertip availability, than any group in the United States." According to another former NSA official, "DEFSMAC not only detects them but . . . [also has] the capability to relatively immediately determine what kind of a vehicle was launched, what trajectory it's on, and based on all these parameters they can say either it's a threat or it's not a threat." A recent director of DEFSMAC, Chary Izquierdo, referred to her organization as "the [nation's] premier missile and space intelligence producer."

Once DEFSMAC receives a tip-off, an indication that a launch is soon to take place somewhere in the world, a complex chain of events is set in motion. For example, in October 1998 NSA satellites and listening posts, such as those in Germany, picked up indications that Russia was about to test a new missile from its launch site in Plesetsk, in the country's far northwest. Electronic signatures intercepted from Russian instruments being prepared to measure the rocket's telemetry gave one of the first clues that the missile was a Topol-M single-warhead intercontinental ballistic missile. Signals intelligence satellites also likely picked up phone conversations between the launch site and Moscow.

Upon receiving such indicators, DEFSMAC officials would immediately have sent out near-real-time and in-depth, all-source intelligence alerts to almost 200 "customers," including the White House Situation Room, the National Military Command Center at the Pentagon, the DIA Alert Center, and all listening posts in the area of the launch site. At the same time, elsewhere within DEFSMAC, analysts would have closely monitored all intercepts flooding in from the area; examined the latest overhead photography; and analyzed data from an early-warning satellite 22,300 miles above the equator. This satellite would have been first to spot the missile's rocket plume and signal back to earth that a launch had occurred.

DEFSMAC would then have flashed the intelligence to one of the specially designed Boeing 707s that on such missions are codenamed Cobra Ball. Fitted with a wide array of receiving equipment, the RC-135 aircraft would immediately have begun eavesdropping on the missile's telemetry as it reentered the atmosphere near its target zone on the Kamchatka peninsula. Through its super-wide windows, Cobra Ball would also have photographed the missile in flight, using high-speed and multispectral photography. Also receiving DEFSMAC intelligence, whenever enough warning time was received, would be the USNS *Observation Island*, which is packed with antennas and satellite dishes that would monitor and photograph the final stage and splashdown of the missile. Such preparations would have been of little use during the October 1998 test, however. The rocket, of a type that is the centerpiece of Russia's shrinking nuclear shield, exploded shortly after launch.

Working closely with DEFSMAC is NSA's National Telemetry Processing Center, the final destination of intercept tapes from missile tests. Here analysts study the various measurements on the magnetic tapes, identify the transducers, and develop performance estimates for the missiles and spacecraft. In 1969, the center took delivery of its first large-scale telemetry processor—twenty-two racks of whirring equipment codenamed Tellman. In the early 1980s, Tellman was replaced by Rissman, which had just fifteen racks of equipment and at the same time could process a greater variety of signals. Rissman was a busy machine—often processing tapes around the clock—from the day of its delivery until the end of the Cold War. By the 1990s, it had been retired and in its place was a relatively compact telemetry processing system codenamed Outcurve, consisting of four racks of equipment and a sixteen-megabyte memory.

Down Corridor C in OPS 1, past the drugstore and Bank of America, is Crypto City's medical center, staffed by an emergency medical response team. Nearby is an urgent care unit, where ambulances occasionally come and go. NSA even has its own mobile medical center to take medical services to people in distant parts of the city so they don't have to come to the clinic. The large, streamlined, bus-sized vehicle can accommodate wheelchairs and even has its own examination room with table. It is equipped to perform a variety of tests, including EKGs. As might be expected, the mobile medical unit is equipped with secure telephones and cell phones for communicating with the various buildings.

Nearby, in Room 1E145, is the Geographic Library, containing a unique collection of worldwide maps, many on CD-ROM. Analysts can also access these digital maps directly at their workstations through the library's Automated Mapping System. Among the products developed by NSA is a high-resolution interactive geographic-based software system codenamed Oilstock. It is used to store, track, and display near-real-time and historical signals-intelligence-related data over a map background.

A short distance away on the South Corridor, near the drugstore and barbershop, is NSA's Main Library. It contains probably the world's largest collection of cryptologic materials. It also holds a major collection of foreign telephone directories, very useful in finding key telephone numbers to target. Nearby are the Main Research Center and Digital Library.

Walking along the long, broad hallways, one passes the Crisis Action Center, the Advanced Reconnaissance Programs Office, and the Office of Unconventional Programs, where chief Coy R. Morris attempts to penetrate targets not accessible by conventional means. In 1999 Morris was awarded the Department of Defense Distinguished Civilian Service Award for amassing "an astounding record of successful operations."

Also in OPS 1 is the National Signals Analysis Center (NSAC). Before an encrypted message can be broken, it first has to be found, and that is the job of the NSAC's engineers, mathematicians, and computer scientists. They locate important streams of communications, whether hidden in thin air or in a blanket of noisy static. "With today's rapidly evolving global communications, NSA's signals analysts are seeking to recover, understand, and derive intelligence from all manner of foreign signals," says one NSA document. Another adds: "Consider that hundreds or thousands of channels of mixed information types may be multiplexed together and transmitted digitally over a satellite or terrestrial link to form a single signal."

Flowing between earth stations and distant communications satellites are millions of telephone calls, fax transmissions, television signals, and computer and multimedia data transfers. They are all squeezed together in thousands of channels. Once they have been intercepted by NSA, it is up to the signals analysts to untwist them and make them understandable. "Demodulating and unraveling the internal structure of such complex signals, to recover their information content and related data, is one job of the signals analyst," according to NSA. Other signals, such as covert communications, may be deliberately hidden deep within such signals as television transmissions, or broken into thousands of jigsawlike pieces and sent on hundreds of different channels. They may even be spread so thin as to be almost invisible. Within the center, many of the signals analysts have had multiple tours at overseas listening posts. Once a year, at NSA headquarters, there is a week-long conference to discuss new ways to discover, and eavesdrop on, the elusive signals.

Within these hallways, offices are protected by heavy steel doors containing a variety of padlocks, combination dials, and cipher locks. Some doors also bear round, color-coded seals. A red seal indicates an "Exclusion Area"—an office containing what one NSA document calls "*extremely sensitive* (i.e., compartmented) classified materials or activities" [emphasis in original]. All classified documents, when not in use, must be kept locked in safes. Blue seals indicate areas where the volume of sensitive materials is so great that some may be left out on desks provided they are covered "completely by a black cloth."

During the Christmas season employees compete to see who can come up with the most original door decorations. In 1999, the door to Room 1W070 in OPS 1 bore a replica of a signals intelligence spacecraft entitled "The Malfunctioning Santallite."

To enter other offices, such as the NSA's Special Processing Laboratory, a person must first pass through a complex, unmanned station known as a High Security Portal. After entering a glass-enclosed booth, the person wishing to go farther must swipe a security badge through a credit card–like reader. The computer then checks the person's name against an access list known as CONFIRM.

Next an eye scan is performed, providing for positive identification by recording the pattern of blood vessels in the retina, at the back of the eye, and comparing it with the person's pattern as stored in the CONFIRM database. An individual's retina is unique and does not change during his or her life. Finally, load cells take body weight measurements and once again check them against the CONFIRM system to ensure that only one person is inside the portal. Only after everything matches can the door be opened.

NSA is continually developing more and more complex biometric identification systems. "Using biometrics for identifying and authenticating human beings offers some unique advantages," said Jeff Dunn, NSA's chief of biometrics and protective systems. "Only biometric authentication bases an identification on an intrinsic part of a human being. Tokens—such as smart cards, magnetic strip cards, physical keys, and so forth—can be lost, stolen, duplicated, or left at home. Passwords can be forgotten, shared, or observed."

In 1999, NSA installed a number of multi-biometric security stations on a pilot basis. The stations incorporate fingerprint recognition, voice verification, and facial image recognition technologies into a single system. In face recognition, a computer is programmed with a "statistical knowledge of human faces" so that it can break down and reconstruct images of faces.

Once past the High Security Portal, some employees must enter still another supersecure area in order to work. As its name implies, the Vault Type Room (VTR) resembles a large, walk-in bank safe, with a heavy, thick steel door and fat combination dial.

But even inside Crypto City, inside one of its buildings, inside a red-seal room, and finally inside a Vault Type Room, one occasionally needs to open, like a Chinese puzzle, another locked door. To accomplish this, one must first go to a tall, steel, closetlike device, an Automated Key Access Machine (AKAM). After one enters one's badge and PIN numbers, the computer searches key access lists, determines eligibility, retrieves the key, and dispenses it with a robotic arm. Each machine stores 406 keys on a carousel, has a response time of less than thirty seconds, and provides complete tracking of key movements.

Although one might assume that a security-obsessed scientist thought up the AKAM in a dark corner of NSA, it was actually designed for use in auto dealerships. While out shopping for a new car, an NSA security employee spotted the device and recognized its potential. The agency then worked with the manufacturer, Key Systems, to modify the equipment for use in Crypto City.

Finally, another passageway leads to the Headquarters Building. Like OPS 1, it is primarily occupied by personnel from the Directorate of Operations.

Inside the offices, some people scribble away on green chalkboards while others talk in "teaming areas," informal meeting spaces designed to increase the sharing of ideas. Most work in bland, shoulder-height cubicles, tapping away at a UNIX system built by Sun Microsystems or at a Dell workstation. Many employees have two separate computer terminals on their desk and some, especially voice analysts, also have reel-to-reel tape recorders to listen to voice intercepts. Two recorders are occasionally required in order to listen to both sides of a conversation.

Every desk is equipped, as well, with two types of telephones: "black" phones for unclassified conversations and "gray," secure phones known as STU-IIIs (for Secure Telephone Unit 3; pronounced Stew-3). The STU-III was developed under an NSA contract in the mid-1980s. Before that, NSA used the far more cumbersome STU-I and STU-II systems, which were developed in the 1970s. The principal drawback of these earlier secure phones was the need to call a "Key Distribution Center" in order to set up each call, which resulted in a delay of two to three minutes.

The STU-III can be used both as a secure phone for conversations classified as high as Top Secret/Codeword, or as a POTS ("plain old telephone system") for normal, unclassified calls. To "go secure," both the caller and the person on the other end insert a thin black plastic "Crypto Ignition Key" into their STU-III. Many employees attach the key to the neck chain that holds their security badge. Once the key is inserted, a small display screen on the phone tells the person on the other end what security clearance—Secret, Top Secret, or Top Secret/Codeword—the key's holder has. The STU-III has reduced to about fifteen seconds the time needed to go secure; it also has secure fax, data, and video capability. Once the key is removed, the phone is again usable for unclassified calls.

Gradually, the STU-III is being replaced by a new, more sophisticated system known as the STE (for Secure Terminal Equipment). Made by L3 Corporation, the STE is digital as opposed to analog and can therefore also be used to send and receive secure data. The "key" used is not thin and plastic but similar to the small metal cards used in computers. In addition to increasing the quality of the sound and making it nearly identical to a normal phone, the new STE has the advantage of virtually eliminating the wait time to "go secure." By the time the receiver is placed to the ear, the system is encrypted. According to Michael J. Jacobs, head of NSA's codemaking organization as deputy director for Information Systems Security, the encryption within the STE is so powerful that, given projected foreign codebreaking capabilities, it will remain fully secure for at least fifty years.

Among the places within NSA an employee can call once his or her Crypto Ignition Key is inserted is an automated, classified information network. Need "SIGINT Operations and Intelligence Information"? Simply dial 9-555-1212 on the secure phone and you are connected to NSA's ACCESS menu, where you just press "1."

Crypto City's operators average 250,000 assisted calls per year—60 percent of which are on the "unclassified" phones, 40 percent on the secure phones. A computer program known as Searchlight provides directory assistance for secure calls.

Highly classified documents once could be whisked from one part of the city to another over ninety-five miles of pneumatic tubes in less than ninety seconds. To ensure security, the system contained over

10,000 sensors to monitor the progress of the documents. But repair costs eventually became too great and the system was abandoned. Today the city is interconnected by a network of fiber optic cables not shared by the outside world. The cable contract was offered to the small start-up fiber network company Qwest, said one person, "because it was the only bidder that offered the agency its own fiber path that would not have to be shared with commercial users."

When not attacking crypto systems, residents of the secret city can switch their TV sets to Channel 50, the NSA Broadcast Network. Programs are beamed from Crypto City's own state-of-the-art Television Center, in the FANX II building. ("FANX" means "Friendship Annex"; Friendship was the old name for the nearby Baltimore-Washington International Airport.) The facility is completely soundproof and has two video-edit suites, a sound booth, an audio-sweetening room, a studio, and three-D computer-graphics capability.

Among the programs produced at the Television Center and transmitted throughout the city is *Newsmagazine,* which features a variety of live presentations. NSAers may also tune their television sets to the live call-in show *Talk NSA.* "If you enjoy *Larry King Live, Imus in the Morning,* or any of the many other interactive talk shows, you might want to give *Talk NSA* a try," gushed one enthusiastic NSAer. On March 25, 1998, Kenneth Minihan was the guest on the show's forty-fifth broadcast. Seated "on location" in an NSA warehouse, he spent an hour taking questions from viewers who dialed 968-TALK.

Lieutenant General Minihan also was the first director to conduct a Worldwide Electronic Town Meeting for NSA employees around the world, using an NSA computer chat room. "Ask short, straightforward questions," the workforce was cautioned. More than 6,000 people across the globe, many in secret listening posts, took part in the virtual event, generating 36,711 lines of text.

In search of something a bit more exciting, an NSAer can switch channels to the intelligence community's own encrypted and highly secret version of CNN. As the Defense Intelligence Network (DIN) logo fades from the screen, an anchor introduces "Global Update," a Top Secret roundup of world events. Although the lead story might be the same as the one on Ted Turner's twenty-four-hour news network, DIN has unique advantages: up-to-the-second photos from spy satellites, secret conversations from NSA intercepts, and the latest diplomatic gossip from the DIA's worldwide corps of defense attachés.

Another difference from CNN is that the classification (Secret, Top Secret/Umbra, and so on) of the intelligence or the commentary appears in the corner of the screen, sometimes changing as often as every twenty seconds. While on occasion a bit slower than CNN to pick up a story, DIN often soars ahead, as it did when viewers were able to watch reports of the attempted coup in Venezuela "long before CNN made the world aware of it," said one DIN official.

Tired of TV, an NSAer can boot up his or her computer and log on to Crypto City's own, very secret intranet. Based on the ideas and technologies that are currently wrapping the world in an ever-tightening mesh of interactive electrons, NSA's "Intelink" has one key difference: it is totally hidden from the outside world.

At the same time that NSA's money and personnel were being cut back as a result of the post–Cold War intelligence drawdown, more and more data were streaming into the agency's earth station atop a small wooded hill on the northern edge of the city. The problem was similar throughout the intelligence community. The solution was to go online, using cyberspace to move, distribute, and access the mountains of intelligence reports.

Connected through a system of highly secure and encrypted cable networks, Intelink allows NSA's technospies and analysts to surf through secret home pages and databases. Within seconds, they can download everything from the latest intercepts on Chinese submarine activity off the Paracel and Spratly Islands to satellite imagery and video footage of Pakistani tank movements near Kashmir. "If Warren Christopher wants to know about Korea," said Ross Stapleton-Gray, a former CIA official, "he just goes over to the Korea page and he can see the DIA analysis, the CIA analysis, the NSA intercept, and an FBI report on Korea."

Linking NSA with the CIA, the National Reconnaissance Office, and other members of the intelligence and defense community, the new system is "a major breakthrough," according to a senior Pentagon intelligence official. "Intelink," he said, "for the first time, in a user-friendly environment, allows every element of the intelligence community and every element of the Department of Defense to reach into every other element." A CIA official added, "Essentially, to a great extent we've cloned the technology from the Internet into our communications system."

Over Intelink, NSA now publishes documents containing hypertext links that allow customers to instantly obtain details concerning the original raw signals intelligence data on which the conclusions were based, so that they can understand the basis of an analyst's views.

High praise for the system reaches all the way to the White House, which in the past had to wait for the CIA's most secret reports to be delivered by the agency's "pizza truck," as the courier van was called. Intelink can now provide these documents almost instantly. Former Vice President Al Gore has called the system "a brilliant use of cyberspace" that is "bringing the intelligence community closer together than ever before."

The idea had its origins in a dusty, little-known "back room" of the U.S. intelligence community: the Intelligence Systems Secretariat (ISS), set up in 1994. Key to the system was to make it completely separate and secure from the publicly used Internet in order to prevent anyone from hacking into it. Thus, rather than an Internet, it would be an extranet, a private system connecting all of the supersecret internal networks and databases of the spy community, with a thick firewall separating it from the crowded and open Internet. Among those databases would be NSA's own internal intranet, Webworld.

In the past, getting intelligence from the collector to the ultimate user in the field in time to be helpful was the Achilles' heel of the system. One NSA linguist, Fredrick T. Martin, assigned to a remote outpost in the Middle East during the Cuban missile crisis, recalled the frustration. "Collaboration with our counterparts elsewhere," he said, "and with NSA Headquarters meant asking a question, forwarding it on a special teletype circuit, and waiting until your shift the next day (if you were lucky) for the reply. Although many improvements were made to this basic approach over the next thirty years, the fundamental set of dissemination and collaboration problems remained."

More recent complaints came from General H. Norman Schwarzkopf, who warned that delays in receiving intelligence reports had a serious impact on his direction of the Gulf War. Another example is the shootdown of Air Force Captain Scott O'Grady over Bosnia in June 1995. It was later discovered that anti-aircraft missile batteries had been spotted earlier but the intelligence did not reach O'Grady in time. Over Intelink, troops on the front line can now obtain information at the same time that it is received within the White House.

With the click of a mouse, the Netscape browser opens up to Intelink Central and the warning, "Anyone using this system expressly consents to monitoring." Scrolling down, the user can choose from a long list of hyperlinks to the classified home pages of about ninety intelligence organizations. These range from the Arms Control Intelligence Staff to the CIA's Office of Advanced Projects to DIA's Central MASINT [measurement and signature intelligence] Office to the Intelligence Community Librarians' Committee. For signals intelligence information, there are links to such sites as NSA, the Regional Sigint Operations Center at Fort Gordon, Georgia, and the National Sigint Committee.

Intelink has its own Yahoo!-style search tool called Wer'zit!? Users can also use five commercially available search engines, such as Alta Vista.

In a major innovation for the intelligence community, Intelink even offers secret, around-the-clock chat rooms with the program WebChat. "If you have the need to consult in real time via keyboard chat with a peer anywhere in the world," said James P. Peak, the Intelink director, "WebChat is for you." Among the chat rooms are Analyst Rooms, where issues affecting intelligence analysts are discussed. More general discussions can be conducted in Office Rooms. And for chat about specific areas of the world, such as the Middle East, a person can enter Geographical Regional Rooms. Topical Rooms are for those who wish to exchange or solicit information on specific topics. An example is the International Organized Crime chat room.

Despite their sensitive jobs and high clearances, the elite participants in WebChat have caused concern within the intelligence community with "obscene and boorish behavior." This has led to close monitoring by Intelink managers. The posted rules on Intelink include a prohibition on the "use of fantasy role-playing 'personas' and postings describing imaginary activities."

NSA serves as the home for Intelink, though the intranet is used by other intelligence agencies. Its Intelink Service Management Center operates a twenty-four-hour command post known as Intelink Central, a spacious room with a wraparound console crowded with computer monitors and telephones. Because Intelink serves a wide customer base, it comprises four separate networks with different security classifications. The first created was "Top Secret–SCI" ("sensitive compartmented information"). More than 50,000 people with codeword clearances at over 100 different locations have access to this network. For those cleared only to the Secret level, there is "Intelink-S," which has about 265,000 users at some 160 locations.

The most secret and restricted network is "Intelink-P," also known as "Intelink-PolicyNet." Those authorized access are limited to the president and vice president, the national security adviser, the directors of Central Intelligence and NSA, and a small number of other officials. It operates on a private, secure, high-bandwidth network and is used primarily to distribute supersensitive reports not available on the other levels.

At the other end of the spectrum there is "Intelink-U," the newest network, which is designed to provide exclusively unclassified and open-source materials. It is said to be the single largest data repository in the world.

Intelink is now expanding worldwide, connecting the intelligence agencies of the United Kingdom, Canada, Australia, and the United States in a unique, private, Top Secret–SCI network known as "Intelink-C" for Intelink-Commonwealth. Officials are considering expanding even further, creating a unique, and somewhat unsettling, invisible international espionage web.

Another—more limited but far speedier—communications network at NSA is the Advanced Technology Demonstration Network, which links the agency with the Pentagon's Defense Advanced Research Projects Agency, the DIA, NASA, the Defense Information Systems Agency, and the Naval Research Laboratory. Using a variation of a hyperspeed technology known as ATM (for "asynchronous transfer mode"), information can be transferred at the astonishing rate of 2.5 billion bits a second—fast enough to send the text from nearly 500 copies of *Moby-Dick* in one second. The applications of such a hyperfast system are especially significant given the growing requirements to transfer near-real-time pictures and video from spy satellites and reconnaissance aircraft. A program known as Fastlane was recently created by NSA to develop encryption techniques for ATM.

If Intelink is the intelligence community's Internet, the *National SIGINT File* is its *New York Times.* It contains, said Fredrick T. Martin, one of NSA's Intelink founders, "a *feast* of the world's most significant events of the day that were derived from the codebreaking side of NSA's mission." For years, NSA's premier publication was the *SIGINT Summary,* or *SIGSUM.* But despite the fact that it contained the end product of the world's most advanced intelligence agency, it "was published and distributed by techniques that would be used if the *SIGSUM* were not much more than a club newsletter," said Martin in his book *Top Secret Intranet.* Well into the 1990s, the *SIGSUM* was published the old-fashioned way, on paper, and was manually distributed by courier.

Eventually, though such pioneering internal projects as Beamrider, NSA began disseminating its highly classified Sigint reports over secure NSA communications lines to senior officials in Washington. This led to the replacement of the *SIGSUM* with an electronic version known as the *NSA SIGINT Digest.* Finally, in October 1997, NSA inaugurated its "virtual" newspaper, the *National SIGINT File,* which completely replaced both the regular and exclusive versions of the *SIGINT Digest.*

Unlike anything before in the spy world, the *National SIGINT File* provides a "virtual window" into NSA's vast ocean of intercepted communications. Its exclusive recipients can click on such options as the National SIGINT Update, which can be specially tailored to the person's interest—nuclear weapon transfers in Iran or terrorist movements around Africa. Updates appear periodically throughout the day. Another option allows one to view the latest signals intelligence on a menulike list of general topics. Still another offers a *TV Guide*–like listing of available Sigint "finished intelligence."

The "customer" can also define key world hot spots in which he or she has a particular interest. Someone interested in the conflict in the Middle East, for example, can receive all relevant finished Sigint every half-hour. A Sigint search can be done to locate previously issued reports on the subject. Also, a new feature will allow the viewer to see finished intelligence in video format on the computer screen.

Of special significance is the capability to instantly display CRITIC messages on screen. Critical Intelligence reports are of the highest importance, and the CRITIC system is designed to get them to the president in ten minutes or less from the time of an event. When Saddam Hussein pushed into Kuwait in 1990, for example, the first alert came in the form of a CRITIC. The issuance of a CRITIC is instantly noted in the *National SIGINT File* by a flashing message in the top left corner of the screen.

Among the dozens of buildings in the invisible city is a strange yellow structure, across the street from the headquarters complex, with a large round smoke pipe on its roof. Deep inside, in a cavernous vat, a chunky man with a frowning mustache jabs a shovel into a soggy pile of gray sludge. A few seconds later he plops it over a drain several feet from his frayed green knee boots. America's most closely held secrets—transcripts of North Korean diplomats' conversations, plans for the next generation of eavesdropping satellites, algorithms for a high-level crypto system—have been transformed into a pastelike pulp. For the nation's secrets, it is the penultimate stop in their metamorphosis into pizza boxes.

"Is the National Security Agency literally burying itself in classified material?" a curious senator once asked. He probably did not anticipate the response of the NSA assistant director seated across from him: "It would seem that way." According to a report by congressional auditors, the NSA classifies somewhere between 50 million and 100 million documents a year. "That means," the General Accounting Office report concluded, "that its classification activity is probably greater than the combined total activity of all components and agencies of the Government." With more secrets than are held by the CIA, the State Department, the Pentagon, and all other agencies of government combined, NSA likely holds the largest body of secrets on earth.

Every week, couriers from the Defense Courier Service lug nearly a million pounds of materials stamped "Top Secret" and above to and from the city. Formerly known as the Armed Forces Courier Service, the DCS is responsible for transporting highly classified materials for all the services and the Pentagon. Nevertheless, it is chiefly the NSA that packs its well-guarded trucks and fills its thick canvas pouches. The NSA produces approximately 80 percent of the 60 million pounds of material that the courier service handles annually. Because of this, the NSA once attempted, unsuccessfully, to take over the courier service.

While for most at NSA, the problem is how to acquire secret information, for a few others the problem is how to get rid of it. At one point the agency tried to have secret documents exported to a pulp plant. The material, sealed in plastic bags, was trucked to the Halltown Paperboard Company (apparently the only company that would have anything to do with the scheme), several hundred miles away in Halltown, West Virginia, where NSA would then take over the plant for twenty-four hours. Dumped into a macerator, the NSA's secrets emerged as low-quality cardboard. The problem with this system was that some paper was just not acceptable, and the agency was left with 20,000 square feet of warehouse space full of paper that had to be burned.

Finally, in desperation, the agency turned to the American Thermogen Corporation of Whitman, Massachusetts, for construction of what came to be known as White Elephant No. 1. NSA officials journeyed up to the Bay State to view a pilot model of a "classified waste destructor" and came away impressed. According to the company, the three-story machine was supposed to swallow the agency's mountains of secrets at the rate of six tons an hour and cremate them at temperatures of up to 3,400 degrees Fahrenheit.

When this marvel of modern pyrotechnics was finally completed, it had only one problem: it didn't work. Instead of being converted into gases and liquids, which could be piped off, the top secret trash would occasionally congeal into a rocklike mass and accumulate in the belly of the Elephant, where jackhammers were needed to break it up. On at least one occasion, horrified security personnel had to scurry around gathering up bits and shreds of undigested intercepts, computer printouts, and magnetic tapes that had managed to escape destruction. Twenty-ton Army trucks had to be drafted into service, along with armed guards, to cart the undigested secrets to secure storage at Army Intelligence headquarters at Fort Holabird, just outside Baltimore.

In all, the destructor managed to operate for a total of fifty-one days out of its first seventeen months. By the time the agency canceled its contract with American Thermogen, it had already paid off all but

$70,000 of the $1.2 million construction price. Said one red-faced NSA official, "Our research will continue."

That research prompted NSA to turn from fire to water in order to shrink its Mount Everest of forbidden papers. "Try to imagine," said one NSA report, "a stack of paper six feet wide, six to eight feet tall and twenty yards long traveling along a conveyor belt towards you every ten minutes all day long." By the mid-1990s, Crypto City was annually converting more than 22 million pounds of secret documents into cheap, soluble slurry. And in case the paper flow increased, the new system was capable of destroying three times that amount.

To transport the huge heaps of "burn bags" crammed with discarded secrets, NSA turned, appropriately enough, to Florida's Disney World. In Fantasyland and the rest of the Magic Kingdom, accumulated trash is transported automatically by underground conveyor belt to a central waste disposal facility. Similarly, burn bags from NSA, the intelligence community's Fantasyland, are sent down a Rube Goldberg–like chute-and-conveyer-belt contraption known as the Automatic Material Collection System. The 6½-foot-wide conveyer belt then dumps the bags into a giant blenderlike vat that combines water, steam, and chemicals to break the paper down into pulp. The pulped paper is processed, dried, funneled through a fluffer, and finally, fifteen minutes later, baled. Within a few weeks, the documents that once held the nation's most precious secrets hold steaming pepperoni pizzas. In 1998, the agency took in $58,953 in profit from the sale of its declassified pizza boxes.

Problems arise, however, when thick magnetic tapes, computer diskettes, and a variety of other non-water-soluble items are thrown into the burn bags. Once a week, destruction officers assigned to Crypto City's Classified Materials Conversion Plant have to use rakes, shovels, and hacksaws to break up the "tail," the clumps of hard, tangled debris that clog up the room-sized Disposall. Among the stray items that have found their way into the plant are a washing machine motor, a woman's slip, and an assortment of .22-caliber bullets. Because this residue, totaling more than fifty-two tons a year, still may contain some identifiable scrap bearing an NSA secret, it is left to drain for about five days and then put in boxes to be burned in a special incinerator.

NSA was able to turn an additional thirty tons of old newspapers, magazines, and computer manuals into pizza boxes as a result of a spring cleaning program, dubbed "The Paper Chase," in 1999. But paper is not the only thing NSA recycles. It also converts metal from the tiny chips and circuit boards in the agency's obsolete computers into reusable scrap. So many computers hit the junk pile every year that the agency is able to recycle more than 438 tons of metal annually from the small components.

Despite the unfathomable amount of information destroyed by NSA every year, it is almost negligible compared to the amount of data it actually saves, mostly in the form of magnetic tapes. In Support Activities Building 3, a flat, nearly windowless structure in Crypto City, NSA's Magnetic Media Division maintains the agency's 95,000-square-foot tape library containing approximately 1.6 million data tapes. NSA is nearing the point—if it hasn't reached it already—where it will be able to store the equivalent of more than half a million typed, double-spaced pages (up to ten gigabytes) on a square inch of tape. Thus its mammoth tape library may soon reach the point where all the information on the planet can be placed inside, with room left over.

To cut down on the expense of purchasing new tapes, NSA uses large "degaussers" to erase used reels. Because of the enormous volume of tapes, however, worries have developed over the degausser operators' exposure to electromagnetic fields. More than a thousand current and former degausser operators were surveyed in 1998 by the agency's Office of Occupational Health, Environmental and Safety Services. Although the question of adverse health effects is still unanswered, shielding was installed and the operators were told to keep a distance from the powerful magnetic coils.

While copies of secrets are regularly destroyed, the original information is seldom given up. Down the street from the tape library, in Support Activities Building 2, is the NSA Archives and Records Center. Here, more than 129 million documents, all more than a quarter of a century old, are still hidden from historians and collecting dust at enormous cost to taxpayers. Even NSA has a hard time comprehending the volume of material. "The sheer number of records is astounding," said one internal report. A stack of them would be over nine miles tall, higher than the cruising altitude of a Boeing 747.

Also held are tens of millions of recent documents, including

11 million "permanent records" that trace the history of the secret city. In April 1996, NSA finally declassified a January 1919 memorandum from U.S. Army Colonel A. W. Bloor, a commander of the American Expeditionary Force in France. "The German was a past master at the art of 'Listening In,' " the memorandum said. "It was therefore necessary to code every message of importance." However, many other documents from that same period, and even earlier, are still classified.

As a result of a tough executive order issued by President Clinton in 1995, NSA must now declassify over 10 million pages of yellowing secrets. According to the internal report quoted above, "The agency must review these records or they will be considered automatically declassified on 17 April 2000." (The deadline was later extended to 2001.)

To accomplish this Herculean task, NSA established a project appropriately named Plethora. As part of the project, a unique facility was built: the Automated Declassification System. With advanced imaging technology, boxloads of ancient documents—including delicate onionskin and smudgy carbon copies—are scanned into the system from various workstations. Then, after consulting databases containing declassification guidance, specialists magically erase still-sensitive information from the now electronic documents. The sanitized pages are then optically stored in a memory capable of holding up to 17 million pages. But in the end, given NSA's numerous exclusions from the Freedom of Information Act, the odds that the public will ever see even a small fraction of those documents remain less than slim.

That NSA has the technical capability to intercept and store enough information to wallpaper much of the planet is unquestionable. What is in doubt, however, is the agency's ability to make sense of most of it. "Sometimes I think we just collect intelligence for the thrill of collecting it, to show how good we are at it," said former CIA director Robert Gates. "We have the capacity to collect mountains of data that we can never analyze. We just stack it up. Our electronic collection systems appear to produce far more raw intelligence data than our analysts can synthesize and our policymakers can use."

The city's brown, boxy OPS 3 building is the home of NSA's Information Systems Security Organization and the agency's naval service, the

Naval Security Group. It is also where the agency's mammoth 66,000-square-foot printing plant pumps out code and cipher materials for the U.S. government's sensitive communications. Among the cryptographic items produced in the NSA Print Plant are the "go codes," used to authorize nuclear war; small, square one-time pads—row after row of scrambled numbers and letters—designed to be used only once and then destroyed; and perforated cipher "key tape." Packaged in sealed Scotch tape–like holders, the cipher strips are pulled out, torn off, and inserted in cryptographic machines. The key tape is changed every day to ensure security.

Across the street is the ultramodern Special Processing Laboratory, NSA's state-of-the-art microelectronics fabrication and printed-circuit-board factory. There, cloaked head to toe in white clean-room apparel, agency scientists develop and produce the chips and other components used in the country's most sensitive encryption equipment. Among those special chips is the CYPRIS microprocessor, designed to operate at 40 megahertz and able to obtain nearly 35 MIPS (million instructions per second). At one time NSA accounted for 50 percent of the world's integrated circuit market. Other scientists regularly attempt to redefine the limits of an array of key technologies—from electron-beam maskmaking to "direct write" wafer lithography.

Another windowless building a few blocks away, the Systems Processing Center, houses a series of bizarre anechoic chambers. Like something out of a nightmare, every inch of these vast baby-blue rooms is covered with giant dagger-shaped cones of various sizes—up to eight feet high. The chambers are used to test intercept antennas designed and built in the City. Chamber A, the largest, measures 42 feet wide, 42 feet high, and 90 feet long. It was designed to test antenna frequencies up to 26.5 gigahertz. A transmitting antenna is placed on a raised platform at one end of the chamber and a receiving antenna is installed at the opposite end. Each of the cones, which are composed of special foam impregnated with chemicals, is sized to absorb different frequencies.

A little further on is the Research and Engineering Building, a massive, handsome, dark-gray mausoleum dedicated to advanced eavesdropping. It houses the agency's Technology and Systems Organization, which is responsible for the design, development, and deployment of signals intelligence systems at NSA headquarters and worldwide.

Among the projects worked on was one to greatly extend the life of batteries needed to run eavesdropping equipment hidden in foreign countries. "The problem of providing power for years or decades for electronics in harsh environments remains an unsolved dilemma," said one NSA technical report. One possibility was the microencapsulated betacell, or "beta battery," which is a nuclear battery. Beta batteries operate by converting the electrons from beta radiation into light and then converting the light into usable electric energy with photovoltaic cells. Such batteries are now in use.

Most of the Technology and Systems Organization's several thousand employees are computer scientists and engineers. The deputy director for technology and systems in 2000 was Robert E. Stevens. High on his list of priorities was pushing signals intelligence technology well into the twenty-first century. Known as the Unified Cryptologic Architecture, it is a blueprint for taking NSA's technology up to the year 2010.

Within the Research and Engineering Building is NSA's Microelectronics Research Laboratory, which works on such projects as thinning technology to reduce the thickness of circuitry on computer wafers to half a micron, so that the circuits virtually vanish.

Across the Baltimore-Washington Parkway is another tall glass office building belonging to the Technology and Systems Organization. Known as NBP-1, for National Business Park, it is the centerpiece of NSA's highly secret crypto-industrial complex. Stretching out below NBP-1, hidden from the highway and surrounded by tall trees, National Business Park is a large compound of buildings owned by NSA's numerous high-tech contractors, such as Applied Signal Technology, which builds much of NSA's sophisticated satellite eavesdropping equipment. The crypto-industrial complex, like the military-industrial complex of the Cold War, is a cozy fraternity of business executives with close, expensive contractual ties to NSA. According to one study, signals intelligence is a $2 billion market. In just one year (1998) and in Maryland alone, NSA awarded more than 13,000 contracts, worth more than $700 million.

A quick-turning revolving door allows frequent movement of personnel between the agency and industry. To help swing even more NSA contracts their way, Applied Signal Technology in 1995 named John P. Devine, just retired as NSA's deputy director for technology and systems, to its board of directors. Likewise, TRW hired former NSA director William Studeman, a retired Navy admiral, as its vice president and deputy general manager for intelligence programs. The massive consulting firm Booz-Allen & Hamilton, which frequently bids for NSA contracts, hired Studeman's successor as director, retired vice admiral J. Michael McConnell. And McConnell's former deputy director, William P. Crowell, left NSA to become vice president of Cylink, a major company involved in encryption products. Crowell had been through the revolving door before, going from a senior executive post at NSA to a vice presidency at Atlantic Aerospace Electronics Corporation, an agency contractor, and then back to NSA as chief of staff. Another deputy director of the agency, Charles R. Lord, left NSA in 1987 and immediately became a vice president at E-Systems, one of NSA's biggest contractors.

Headquarters of the crypto-industrial complex is in a white two-story office building at 141 National Business Park, just down the street from NSA's Technology and Systems Organization in NBP-1. Behind the double doors to Suite 112 is a little-known organization called the Security Affairs Support Association (SASA), which serves as the bridge between the intelligence and industrial communities. SASA's president is Lieutenant General Kenneth A. Minihan, who retired as director of NSA in 1999. Its executive vice president for many years was retired Air Force Major General John E. Morrison, Jr., a former head of operations at NSA and long one of the most respected people in the intelligence community.

SASA holds symposiums and lectures throughout the year, and every May its awards gala attracts a *Who's Who* of the intelligence community and the blacker parts of private industry. In April 1997 SASA held a two-day symposium at NSA to discuss the agency's cryptologic strategy for the next century. SASA's 1999 Awards Dinner, which honored former NSA deputy director Ann Caracristi, attracted senior executives from over eighty companies involved in technical intelligence, and scores of officials from NSA, the National Sigint Committee, and other intelligence agencies.

The new century promises to be good to NSA's contractors. In its 2001 budget authorization, the House Intelligence Committee recommended that NSA begin reaching beyond its high fences. Listing the agency's many new problems—fiber optic communications, the Internet, and so on—the committee practically ordered NSA to begin bringing in more expertise from the outside. "During the 1980s budget increases," said the committee, "NSA decided to build up its in-house government scientists and engineers and the agency now seems to believe that in-house talent can address the rapidly evolving signals environment better than outsiders can. . . . The culture demanded compartmentation, valued hands-on technical work, and encouraged in-house prototyping. It placed little value on program management, contracting development work to industry, and the associated systems engineering skills."

The House committee believed it was time for a change. "Today, an entirely new orientation is required," said the 2001 budget report. "The agency must rapidly enhance its program management and systems engineering skills and heed the dictates of these disciplines, including looking at options to contract out for these skills." According to Michael Hayden, "The explosive growth of the global network and new technologies make our partnership with industry more vital to NSA's success than ever before."

Like many large communities, NSA's secret city has its own university, the National Cryptologic School. It is located a short distance to the north in the NSA compound called FANX.

"The magnitude of their education, of their mental capacity was just overwhelming to me," former director Marshall Carter recalled of the people he found himself surrounded with when he left the CIA to direct NSA. "I made a survey . . . when I got there and it was just unbelievable, the number of Ph.D.s that we had at the operating levels—and they weren't sitting around glorying like people do."

To channel all that mental power in the right direction, NSA established what must be the most selective institution of higher learning in the country: the National Cryptologic School. The NSC was the final metamorphosis of the Training School, which started out on the second floor of a rambling wood-frame building known as Temp "R" on Jefferson Drive between Third and Fourth Streets in southwest Washington. There, in the early 1950s, the students would clamber up the creaking stairway between Wings 3 and 4, past the guard post, and disperse into the five wings of the school.

Opened on November 1, 1965, the NCS is located in a two-story building containing more than 100 classrooms. Over 900 courses are offered, from Basic Sigint Technology to three years of intensive technical training in the Military Elint Signal Analysis Program. Also offered is the advanced National Senior Cryptologic Course (Course No. CY-600), a seven-week, full-time course for senior signals intelligence managers.

At Crypto City's new NSA Graduate Studies Center, students can even obtain a "master of eavesdropping" degree—actually a master of science in strategic intelligence, with a concentration in Sigint. The program, which consists of two years of part-time study, includes ten prescribed intelligence core courses and four Sigint-related electives, along with a thesis. The NSC also boasts what is believed to be the largest computerized training facility in the country. Tests in 154 languages are available on new state-of-the-art machines.

For the most advanced students of cryptology there is the Senior Technical Development Program, which exposes a select group of employees to advanced cryptanalysis and other specialized fields. The program may take up to three years to complete. The seventeen graduates of the class of 1998 held their commencement ceremony in OPS 1's Friedman Auditorium, with Director Minihan calling them the "best of the best."

Following a brain-cracking exam on the latest Sigint applications for high-temperature superconductivity, or a quiz on local dialects of Lingula, students can go down the hall to the Roadhouse Café for a quick gourmet coffee and a focaccia sandwich.

In 1993 the NCS awarded certificates to over 38,000 NSA students. It also paid colleges and universities around NSA $5 million for additional courses taken by NSA employees. Additional contracts were awarded in other parts of the country. During the 1980s, for example, the University of Wisconsin at Madison was awarded more than $92,000 to develop proficiency tests in modern Hindi. University officials were warned to keep their eyes out for anything or anyone that might "have the potential for adversely affecting the national security"—i.e., spies.

The first "dean" of the National Cryptologic School was Frank B. Rowlett, Friedman's first employee in the newly formed Signal Intelligence Service in 1930. In 1958, after five years with the CIA, he replaced the retiring Friedman as special assistant to the director, a position Rowlett held for seven years under four directors. While there, he led the study group that prepared the way for the National Cryptologic School's founding and stayed on as commandant to give it some direction. He retired two months later, on December 30, 1965.

On March 2, 1966, Rowlett became the third NSA employee to win the intelligence community's top award when President Johnson presented to him the National Security Medal during a ceremony at the White House. If the surroundings looked familiar to him, it was because he had been there a brief nine months earlier to receive the President's Award for Distinguished Federal Civilian Service, the highest award given to a civilian in the federal government. "His brilliant achievements," read the presidential citation, "ranging from analyses of enemy codes to technological advances in cryptology, have become milestones in the history of our Nation's security."

Rowlett, the last of the original band of codebreakers who started the SIS with Friedman in 1930, died on June 29, 1998. On January 27, 1999, Kenneth Minihan stood in the late-morning sun near a large canopy in Crypto City. Behind him was the boxy, chocolate-brown headquarters of NSA's Information Systems Security Organization, the agency's codemakers. As a small group watched, shivering in the chill, Minihan unveiled a large granite boulder that resembled a grounded meteorite. On the flat face of the stone was a large brass plate with an inscription. "This building," it said, "is dedicated to Frank B. Rowlett—American Cryptologic Pioneer—Head of the team that broke the Japanese 'PURPLE' cipher device in 1940—Principal inventor of SIGABA, the most secure cipher device used by any country in World War II."

It was only the second building in the city to be named for an individual, the first being the Supercomputer Facility named after Dr. Louis Tordella. The effort to name buildings is part of a new trend to bring a sense of history to the residents of Crypto City. A by-product of NSA's preoccupation with secrecy is a lack of knowledge of the agency's past. What few histories exist are so highly classified with multiple codewords that almost no one has access to them. The author of an article in the Top Secret/Umbra *Cryptologic Quarterly* emphasized the point. "Despite NSA's size and success," he wrote, "its sense of its own history (an important part of any organizational and professional culture) is astonishingly weak. . . . Where clues to the Agency's past are not absent altogether, they are in some cases seriously misleading." The author had a recommendation: "We need to name our buildings for our heroes; we need their photographs and plaques commemorating their efforts in the corridors or our buildings. . . . We simply must do a better job indoctrinating our people with the history and traditions of the cryptologic service."

But in 2001, the light of the outside world was pushed even further away as construction continued on one more high fence stretching for miles around the entire city. By then Crypto City had become an avatar of Jorge Luis Borges' "Library of Babel," a place where the collection of information is both infinite and monstrous, where all the world's knowledge is stored, but every word is maddeningly scrambled in an unbreakable code. In this "labyrinth of letters," Borges wrote, "there are leagues of senseless cacophonies, verbal jumbles and incoherences."

CHAPTER THIRTEEN

SOUL

TRZAV DUZR QYKZYVTQXY DQUVT SZYBQYGVT BZ SFZGK VSZYZRQVT
ODPUW RDAAZGGWW ROZWI UPUBZRZDPU DI YOZGW ODPUW GSBWU
NMMNDWKWNS MOIKWRD PROVWSC WS OICRSKWSR FNSCRDD RPRFKWNSD
SEYEAKO RHAZ ACR OZHNEDL, YEUU LCZFBNBLC FCABSHZEBA
JBYYF TAFHOUR: HOAKR HOPJU HFA MCYOHFAEOC TJFEB MFEUACMU

As mysterious as the agency itself are the tens of thousands of nameless and faceless people who populate NSA's secret city. According to various agency statistics, the average employee is forty-three years old, with between fourteen and eighteen years of experience. About 59 percent of the workers are male and 10 percent are members of racial and ethnic minorities. Sixty-three percent of the workforce has less than ten years' experience; 13 percent are in the military (including four generals and admirals), 27 percent are veterans, 3.3 percent are retired military, and 5 percent are disabled. In addition to civilian and military employees, 2,300 contractors are employed full-time at the agency.

If NSA were considered as a corporation, then, in terms of dollars spent, floor space occupied, and personnel employed, it would rank in the top 10 percent of *Fortune* 500 companies. In 1993 NSA spent over $9.4 million on air travel; more than 90 percent of the flights originated at nearby Baltimore-Washington International Airport. On behalf of NSA employees residing in Maryland, NSA paid approximately $65 million in 1993 state income taxes on gross salaries totaling approximately $930 million.

But beyond the numbing statistics, the men and women who disappear through the double steel fences every day are both extraordinary and ordinary. They constitute the largest collection of mathematicians and linguists in the country and possibly the world, and they are civil servants angry over how far they must park from their building. Some spend their day translating messages in Sinhalese (spoken in Sri Lanka), or delving into the upper reaches of combinatorics and Galois theory.

One woman knows everything on earth about tires. "She's known as the 'tire lady,' " said one of NSA's customers in the intelligence community. "She's the tire specialist. Embargoed airplanes need tires and when you're trying to embargo somebody it's the little things that take on major importance. If somebody is shipping jet fighter tires to Iran you want to know what kind of fighter they go on."

Most NSA staffers could be anyone's neighbor. Some wear suits to work every day, but most dress less formally. "There is no dress code at all," complained one fashion-conscious former Russian linguist, who called NSA a "haven for geeks and nerds." "I saw a guy wearing yellow pants, yellow shirt, and yellow sweater vest," she said. "A lot of guys don't dress *that* well."

When he has time, Brent Morris performs magic at his children's school in Columbia, Maryland. At NSA, he is a senior cryptologic mathematician. Morris got hooked on magic at the age of five when he saw Buffalo Bob perform a trick on the *Howdy Doody* television show. In high school he learned the perfect card shuffle while studying the connection between math and magic. At NSA, Morris used the perfect shuffle to help develop a method of random and sequential accessing of computer memories. Later the shuffle helped him work out a method of sorting computer information. Morris also served as the executive secretary of the NSA Scientific Advisory Board.

By day Eileen Buckholtz works in NSA's Telecommunications and Computer Services Organization. But by night she is "Rebecca York," the author of a series of romantic suspense novels published by Harlequin. Her co-author is married to another NSAer. And Frederick Bulinski of the agency's Programs and Resources Organization was inducted into the Polka Music Hall of Fame, has released eight albums, and organizes "Polkamotion by the Ocean," a popular yearly festival in Ocean City, Maryland.

One unique study, done by longtime NSA employee Gary L. Grantham, examined the character, styles, traits, and personalities of NSA's management. "The results show that the personality of NSA leadership is substantially different as a group from the general population of the United States," he concluded. "NSA management is more introverted in dealing with situations, more impersonal in making judgments, and more likely to come to conclusions about their environment than is the general population." Grantham explained that the reason that NSA managers were more shy and impersonal had largely to do with "the highly technical mission of the organization and the large numbers of college-trained employees and those with military background where similar personality traits are found."

The study, "Who Is NSA," was conducted as part of a program at the National War College. NSA granted Grantham access to the results of a test, the Myers-Briggs Type Indicator, which was given to NSA senior executives and supervisors. The tests indicated that almost two-thirds of the officials were introverted in the way they dealt with "the outer world." "This contrasts markedly with the general population in the U.S.," said the study, "where extraverting [*sic*] types make up about 75 percent." NSA officials were also far more "thinking" oriented than the outside world, which was more "feeling" in its professional relationships. "The average NSA manager is more introverted than the general public, much more intuitive, more thinking, and more judging." "You can always tell an NSA extrovert," goes one old agency joke. "He looks at your shoe tips instead of his."

"The great predominance of introverts (64%) means that most NSA managers have greater powers of concentration," the study concluded, "and go deeply into their work by focusing on the underlying concepts and ideas in the pursuit of real understanding. They may be reluctant to consider their work finished and get rid of it. They are not likely to be affected by a lack of praise or encouragement since their focus is on their inner world. If they assume that everyone around them has the same attitude about the world as they do, they may fail to recognize the needs of the extraverts around them for praise. By the same token, the introverts' inner-directed view of the world is often confusing to those around them, including other introverts."

Finally, the study suggested a secret city run by a cold, aloof, detached management. "The predominance of thinking types among managers at NSA is significant in that their preferred way of judging is impersonal, logical, and analytic. While that approach is decidedly more useful in solving task-oriented problems, the people side of managing will suffer. Thinking types expect to be recognized for their competence. Their rewards are responsibility, titles, and raises. They may forget, or not be aware, that one-fourth of their subordinates are feeling types who occasionally need praise and need to be appreciated for who they are, doing a job. According to one observer, 'a "T" [thinking type] thinks that if you haven't been fired, you should know you are doing a good job.'

"The overwhelming preference among NSA managers for judging reflects a choice for system and order. They are organizers who thrive on making decisions, schedules, and programs, and are disconcerted by disruptions or unplanned occurrences. They are less tolerant, less open-minded and less flexible than their perceptive co-workers who often put off making a decision because they are not sure they have enough information. The potential for conflict is great."

For many, if not most, the initial excitement of working in the nation's largest and most secret spy agency gradually gives way to routine. "From my perspective," said Tami McCaslin, associate editor of the *NSA Newsletter*, "isolated in the depths of the *Newsletter* office, I sometimes fail to see how the rest of the world can be so intrigued by this (in my mind) typical government bureaucracy."

As diverse as the workforce is, there is one thing they all have in common: you won't find them talking about their jobs, even when they're sharing a meal in the cafeteria with someone from the next office. The operative rule is "Don't tell, don't ask" about work. The very first subject addressed in the *NSA Handbook*, given to all new residents of the secret city, is the "practice of anonymity." "Perhaps one of the first security practices with which new NSA personnel should become acquainted is the practice of anonymity. . . ." says the report. "Anonymity means that NSA personnel are encouraged not to draw attention to themselves nor to their association with this Agency. NSA personnel are also cautioned neither to confirm nor deny any specific questions about NSA activities directed to them by individuals not affiliated with the Agency." Finally, the handbook warns: "The ramifications of the practice of anonymity are rather far reaching."

Those seeking employment with NSA are told little about the actual work of the organization. "It has become commonplace in recent years to describe NSA as super-secret—'the hush-hush Agency,' " said an editorial in NSA's highly secret *NSA Technical Journal*. "NSA, with missions so interwoven in the fabric of national security, necessarily has had to forgo all custom of public statement, to eschew the press releases which over the years might build an inviting public image and make its worth known to the American people. Though mindful of the dictates of security, NSA knows too that security can have an adverse effect on recruitment—the lifeline of any institution. Indeed, so little can be said that the acceptance of employment with NSA is virtually an act of faith."

Concerned over the failure to reach recruits with critical high-tech abilities because of the agency's obsession with secrecy, the editorial's author suggested getting the following message out to the scientific academic community: "We in NSA comprise a scientific and technological community that is unique in the United States, unique in the western world and perhaps unique in the entire world. We work on problems which no other agency works on. We develop and utilize devices which are in advance of those that have been developed or are utilized by any other agency or any organization in the entire United States. We are confronted with an ever-changing challenge of greater complexity, of greater scope, and of correspondingly greater depth and difficulty than any other changing challenge on the rapidly evolving frontier of science and technology. If you can qualify, you will find NSA a stimulating and rewarding place to work. If you are interested, we can tell you a little more but not much more. One of the qualifications is faith." Still nervous even over that bland description, the editorial added, "Before you send it—better check it out with Security."

More recently, the agency has made a few reluctant public references to cryptology and signals intelligence. "Your challenge," says one brochure directed at mathematicians, "is to use algebra, number theory, combinatorics, statistics, even cryptology and other skills to create—or break—nearly impenetrable codes and ciphers." Another said, "The challenge is to use probability, statistics, Fourier analysis, Galois theory, stochastic processes and other techniques to outwit the world experts in creating or breaking codes and ciphers." But beyond that, no more is said.

"We're looking for those special few," goes one NSA recruitment pitch, "who are up to this ultimate test." Some are hired while still in college, through a minority scholarship program known as the Undergraduate Training Program. The students work at NSA during summers, then receive full-time offers upon graduation. The program is highly competitive. Of the 600 to 800 high school students who apply each year, only a small percentage are selected. In 1999 there were seventy-nine participants attending a variety of schools, including Harvard, MIT, Princeton, and Cornell. Not everyone, however, is happy about the program. "It is appalling," complained one employee, "to see such a blatant case of reverse discrimination being sponsored by the Agency."

Other opportunities for those in college are offered by the agency's Co-operative Education Program, which allows about four dozen students to spend their college years alternating semesters between full-time work and full-time study. In 1997, about 80 percent of the graduates chose to remain with the agency. "Our recruiting strategy has historically been built on excitement of the mission," said Deputy Director for Services Terry Thompson in 1999. "And that's why our Co-op programs are so vital to us because when we get people in here before they make the big career decision when they graduate, and find out about the excitement of the mission."

Traditionally, prospective employees were marched in groups through the agency, like draftees, for numerous interviews, tests, and polygraph exams. Only at the completion of the process—it normally took about seven months—would some of those prospects be matched to a particular job and offered employment. But by then many had already accepted better-paying jobs from private industry, and the agency was forced to dig deeper in the pool. Those not called would remain in limbo.

Stung by tough competition paying top dollar for information technology personnel, the agency in 1999 initiated a streamlined hiring process based more on private industry than on the local draft board. Only a few schools were targeted, so that strong relationships with them could be established. Students were given more detailed job descriptions than the agency had offered in the past, as well as a better explanation of the benefits of working at the cutting edge of technology. A private firm was hired to scan résumés into an NSA-only Internet site. The company then helped match the résumés to specific jobs. An e-mail address was created (njobs@fggm.osis.gov) for the submission of résumés. Finally, in order to accelerate the process, initial screening was done over the telephone.

Those selected are then brought to headquarters for interviews; they undertake a battery of standardized tests and are assigned NSA "buddies" to help sell them on the agency and the surrounding community. The exams are designed to measure a person's general knowledge as well as his or her "cipher brain"—the special abilities needed for the tedious, sometimes mind-numbing, work of a cryptanalyst or other cryptologic staffer. Although codebreaking and codemaking are what most people think of in terms of occupations at NSA, "they undoubtedly represent a declining percentage of the Agency's work force," said a recent internal document. This results from growth in other areas, such as personnel and employee services.

One math major who recently went through the process, hoping to become one of the agency's 600 mathematicians, found it "very humanely organized." He was fingerprinted and asked to fill out a thick "Statement of Personal History" containing detailed questions concerning addresses, travel, and activities over the past ten years. "Getting through that required me to think plenty about whether I wanted to go through it all," he said.

Next, he was invited down to Fort Meade, assigned an escort, and paraded through a gauntlet of interviews. The escort, a fellow mathematician, took on the buddy role, answering questions in a candid, off-the-record manner, and putting in occasional plugs for the agency. The candidate was surprised to find that every official who interviewed him was very familiar with his résumé, down to the marks on his transcripts. "I've never had that happen before," he said.

His first interview was with the head of the mathematicians' training unit, who described the three-year program the applicant would have to complete, beginning with a long course at the National Cryptologic School. He and about forty other newly hired students, some just out of college and some with Ph.D.s, would get a quick review of higher algebra followed by deep involvement in the cryptologic aspects of mathematics. Normally the course work would involve two hours of lectures every day, followed by six hours of study. Lining one wall of the official's office were photos of the three classes of mathematician trainees then in the pipeline.

After a candidate undergoes interviews and submits a variety of paperwork, such as letters of reference, his or her name is sent to the twenty-four-member Mathematicians Hiring Committee. During one of the committee's monthly meetings, the person is discussed and voted on. The views of the escorts are never solicited nor are they questioned on their conversations with the candidate. Results of the vote, yea or nay, are immediately sent out by e-mail.

Those who make the final cut—in recent years, about 100 of the 2,000 or so people who applied annually—are then given a conditional offer of employment. Next they begin their processing at the agency's four-story Airport Square Building a few miles away in the FANX compound. There, the new recruits spend their first day filling out forms and getting a medical checkup.

The next hurdle is the intensive background investigation conducted on all prospective employees by the Defense Security Service. Known as an SSBI (for Single-Scope Background Investigation; it is also known within NSA as a Special Background Investigation), it includes a "National Agency Check"—a check of all federal investigative agencies for derogatory information. Birth records and citizenship are verified. Finally, education, employment, credit files, and local court records are checked for the previous ten years. A neighborhood search for dirt is also conducted at addresses listed for the past decade.

Rob Fuggetta, who lives in Odenton, Maryland, near NSA, recalled when a government investigator knocked on his door in the mid-1980s and began quizzing him about his neighbor, a high school student looking for a summer job at NSA. The questions started off routine, he said, but soon turned very personal. "Do you know if he's a homosexual? Does he use drugs or alcohol? Does he go to church frequently? What can you tell me about his home life? Does he get along with his parents?"

"Appropriate character" is what NSA was looking for, according to Bill Shores, in charge of NSA's college recruitment program at the time. That someone is homosexual or a drug user, per se, "does not mean [he or she] can't come to work for NSA," he said, but "a person that has something to hide would not be a good security risk."

NSA officials are fighting a new proposal by the Defense Security Service to abandon neighborhood in-person visits in favor of simple telephone calls. The DSS argues that it can no longer afford such costly and time-consuming procedures. Pointing out that NSA is only one of its customers, DSS officials say that they must conduct more than 250,000 background investigations of government and contractor personnel each year, leading to tremendous backlogs. At the same time, the agency is behind on tens of thousands of five-year updates required for the 3 million federal employees and contractors who hold active security clearances. Thus, by 2000, DSS's total backlog was a whopping 900,000 investigations. On top of those problems, DSS personnel have been cut back about 40 percent in recent years, from 4,300 employees in the mid-1980s to 2,500 in 1998.

A survey done in 1999 discovered that 94 percent of the background investigations DSS conducted for NSA were incomplete and not up to federal standards. That same year, a routine reinvestigation polygraph examination resulted in the arrest of Daniel King, a Navy petty officer working for NSA. King, an eighteen-year veteran, was arrested on October 28 and charged with espionage for allegedly confessing to mailing a computer disk to the Russian embassy five years earlier. The disk allegedly contained supersensitive details on NSA's undersea cable-tapping operations against the Russians.

After the SSBI is completed, the results are sent back to NSA for evaluation.

The next phase takes them down a narrow passageway to an area of small offices that sends shivers down the backs of most candidates: Polygraph Services. Within the tiny beige offices, new, computerized polygraph machines sit on wood-grain desktops and are attached to monitors that display the recruit's physiological responses in a variety of formats. Among the data recorded, according to an NSA document, are the individual's "respiration, electro-dermal responses, pulse rate, pulse amplitude, vascular volume, capillary volume, vascular pressure, capillary pressure, and bodily movement as recorded by pneumograph, galvanograph, cardiosphygmograph, plethysmograph and cardio activity monitors, which are sections of polygraph instruments." Watching the graphics form sharp peaks and deep valleys is one of the agency's several dozen certified examiners. Many of the questions they ask come from the results of the SSBI.

On the other side of the desk, the applicant sits in a large, heavily padded, executive-type swivel chair. Electrodes are attached to the fingers; rubber tubes are strapped around the chest; and a bulky blood pressure cuff fits around the upper arm. What the examiners are looking for are significant changes from the subject's baseline chart. These may be as dramatic as a total cessation of breathing or a major increase in blood pressure—or as subtle as a slight decrease in skin resistance.

The Armed Forces Security Agency began the polygraph program in May 1951 with the hiring of six examiners at annual salaries of $6,400. The program was introduced because the agency was growing so quickly that background investigations could not be completed fast enough for the hiring program. More than 1,000 people had been hired but could not be cleared until their background investigation was finished, which because of the Korean War was taking from nine to eighteen months. By 1953 NSA was giving polygraphs to all job applicants. The questioning was originally conducted in a well-guarded, ominous-looking building at 1436 U Street, NW, in Washington, before the office moved to the Operations Building and then to FANX.

The polygraph remains the most dreaded part of NSA's admission ritual. "Polygraph! The word alone is enough to set your nerves on edge," began one article on the machine in NSA's in-house newsletter. It is also, by far, the most important part of that ritual. According to a study at NSA, 78 percent of all information used in evaluating an applicant as a security risk comes from the polygraph reports. Only 22 percent of the information is based on the background investigations.

From July 1983 to June 1984 the agency administered a total of 11,442 examinations. Of those, 4,476 were given to job applicants. From that group, 1,875 dropped out voluntarily for a variety of reasons. Of the remaining 2,601, 793 were rejected by the agency's Applicant Review Panel, composed of personnel, security, and medical managers. As an example of the power of the box, a whopping 90 percent of those (714 of 793) were booted because of bad polygraph results. During the first half of 1984 a total of 1,202 contractors were strapped to the machine, and 167 were shown the door after leaving the polygraph room.

The polygraph sessions earned a black eye during the 1950s and early 1960s because of the agency's heavy dependence on the EPQ, or embarrassing personal question. EPQs are almost inevitably directed toward intimate aspects of a person's sex life and bear little relationship to his or her honesty or patriotism. Following a congressional investigation and an internal crackdown, the personal questions became somewhat tamer but abuses have occasionally continued.

"The worst experience of my life," said one former NSA Russian linguist, "was the lie-detector test." After starting out with questions about shoplifting, the polygraph operator quickly turned to sex, asking if she was into bestiality. "If you have sex, they want to know how much. If you have too much sex, they get scared. If you don't have sex, they think you're gay. At the time I wasn't dating anybody and they kept wanting to know, 'Why don't you have a boyfriend?' " That test was given in 1993. More recently, NSA claims, the questions have been less intrusive.

Contractor employees were first required to take polygraphs in 1957. And in 1982, following a damaging spy scandal at Britain's GCHQ, military personnel assigned to NSA were first required to be strapped to the box. The military entrance polygraph is conducted by the military services on military assignees before their acceptance for a position at NSA and is directed toward counterintelligence questions.

At the same time, a five-year reinvestigation polygraph examination, which also focuses on counterintelligence-related questions, was introduced for all employees. Still another polygraph program, the special access examination, was instituted to test employees about to be assigned to especially sensitive programs within NSA. Those tested under this program are asked both counterintelligence and, under certain circumstances, "suitability"—personal—questions.

Finally, again in 1982, NSA instituted a dreaded policy of unscheduled "aperiodic" counterintelligence polygraph examinations. One purpose of these tests is to look for spies; another is to look for leakers. According to a memo from the director, civilian employees who refused to consent faced "termination of employment." The agency, said one senior NSA official, asked the Justice Department to investigate about four leaks a year during the first half of the 1980s.

Among the topics covered during NSA's counterintelligence polygraph examination are the following.

- knowledge of, participation in, or commission of acts of espionage or sabotage against the United States

- knowledge of, approaches to, or giving or selling any classified information or material to unauthorized persons
- unauthorized or unreported foreign contacts

The idea of suddenly being called from an office, strapped to a machine, and asked whether you have been selling secrets to the Russians or leaking information to the press might leave "the work force at NSA . . . shocked," said Philip T. Pease, the chief of the Office of Security at NSA. As a result, employees were called to the Friedman Auditorium for a series of town meetings during which the new procedures were discussed.

Under the aperiodic exam program, the agency, without notice, pulled 1,770 people into the polygraph rooms in 1983. Of those, 1,699 were thanked and sent on their way. Seventy-one, however, were asked to come back for a further interview, which cleared all but four. They returned for a third round of drilling but were eventually also allowed to return to work, presumably a few pounds lighter. According to the chief of the Polygraph Division, Norman Ansley, the problems ranged across the board. One individual had kept a classified manual at his residence for several years. Another person knew of the improper destruction of crypto keying material. Still another described a suspicious approach by foreign personnel but had failed to report the incident at the time it took place.

After the test, the examiner reviews the individual's charts and makes a final decision on the results. "NSR" (no significant response) means that there were no unresolved issues. "SPR" (specific physiological response) signifies that the individual reacted consistently to a specific question. "INC" (inconclusive) means that the test results could not be interpreted. And "incomplete" signifies that the test was not finished. When issues are unresolved, the individual is requested to return to the box for retesting.

Once completed, the examiner's report is forwarded to quality control for an independent review of accuracy and analysis and to ensure that all issues have been covered. From there it travels to the Clearance Division for adjudication. The polygraph examiner does not make any clearance decisions. His or her sole purpose is to verify the validity of the information being provided during the interview and to resolve any matters that are causing the person difficulty in passing the test.

A unique insight into the NSA polygraph program comes from an analysis of 20,511 applicants between 1974 and 1979. Of those, 695 (3.4 percent) admitted to the commission of a felony. In nearly all cases the perpetrator had gone undetected. The admissions included murder, armed robbery, forcible rape, burglary, arson, embezzlement, hit-and-run driving with personal injury, thefts of expensive items or large amounts of money, smuggling, and wholesale selling of illegal drugs.

One person who applied to NSA proved to be a fugitive who, during questioning under the polygraph, admitted firing a rifle into his estranged wife's home in an attempt to murder her. Another confessed to firing his shotgun at six people, and hitting all of them. He had been charged with attempted murder but not tried because of lack of evidence. Still another told of setting fire to the trailer in which his ex-wife and their child lived. A veteran admitted to a polygraph operator that while in Vietnam he had murdered a young girl. On a later occasion he stabbed a stranger in the face with a knife in an argument over some beer. And an applicant for an engineering position—who was employed as an engineer by another government agency—blurted out that he had shot and wounded his second wife and that his present wife was missing under unusual circumstances, which he would not explain. He also suddenly declared that his engineering degree was phony.

Even espionage has turned up during polygraph examinations. One applicant with access to Top Secret/Codeword intelligence who was about to retire from the military described making several visits to the Soviet embassy to make arrangements to defect to the Soviet Union. The Russians took copies of his classified documents and when they found out he had applied to NSA for employment, they encouraged him to continue.

Another applicant, who had access to classified information while in the military, confessed that he would sell classified information to a foreign intelligence service if he could get enough money. And one person looking for a job at NSA eventually admitted that much of his background was falsified and that he had worked as a scientific adviser to the chief of a foreign military intelligence agency.

Most significantly, the NSA study indicated serious questions about highly cleared military personnel assigned to NSA's Central Security Service. At the time, service members were not subject to the polygraph. During the five-year period of the survey, 2,426 of these SCI-cleared military personnel applied for employment with NSA as civilians. Of that number, thirteen admitted that either they themselves or someone they knew had been involved in espionage. Another twenty-five told of passing classified information to Communists or terrorists.

In the early 1990s NSA became the first intelligence or defense agency to completely computerize its polygraph program—the first major change in the art of polygraphy since 1940. According to NSA officials, the computerized polygraph equipment was found to be more accurate than conventional methods because it could record signals at maximum sensitivity. The computer also allows the examiner to change how the data are displayed on the screen without changing the base data, thus protecting the validity of the test.

The agency is currently working on ways to almost completely eliminate all human involvement in the polygraph process. In the near future an Orwellian computer, programmed with an individual's history, will ask the questions, analyze the answers, and decide whether a person is lying or telling the truth.

In 1991 the Office of Security Services, working with the Mathematics Branch of the Research and Sigint Technology Division, issued a contract aimed at elevating the computer from simply a passive display to an active analyst. The lead contractor on the project, Johns Hopkins University's Applied Physics Laboratory, was able to develop a system called Polygraph Assisted Scoring System (PASS) using a briefcase-sized AXCITON computerized polygraph. Unlike evaluation by humans, which sometimes took days or even weeks to produce a final decision, the computerized procedure finishes within two or three minutes of the exam. Using both a history of the individual's past tests and his or her own physiological makeup, the computer comes up with a statistical probability concerning the meaning of test results.

Although with the PASS system examiners would still make the final determination, their future does not look bright. Early testing indicates that computerized analysis is more accurate and produces fewer inconclusive results than human-administered tests. According to one

NSA document, "In the near future, it may even be possible for the computer to ask the test questions—eliminating any possibility of the examiner's affecting the test results."

But despite the growing dependence on the polygraph, the box is far from infallible, as Norman Ansley, chief of NSA's Polygraph Division during the 1980s, once admitted. Asked whether someone addicted to drugs and alcohol could beat the box, his answer was "Possibly," if that person "had practiced dissociation by thinking of something else." Which is precisely why many both inside and outside government distrust the machines. "Polygraphing has been described as a 'useful, if unreliable' investigative tool," said the Senate Select Committee on Intelligence in 1999. Given such questionable data, the panel asked CIA director George J. Tenet and FBI director Louis J. Freeh to assess "alternative technologies to the polygraph." The newest agency to use the polygraph is the Department of Energy, in its nuclear weapons labs. One scientist noted in the DoE employee newsletter that the expected error rate is about 2 percent. "In our situation," he said, "that's 100 innocent people out of 5,000 whose reputations and careers would be blemished."

After the polygraph, NSA applicants undergo a battery of psychological tests to determine their suitability for both employment and access to the agency's highly classified materials. A clinical psychologist interviews 90 percent of all applicants.

All the information obtained about an applicant from the polygraph, psychological testing, and the full field investigation is then put together and brought before NSA's Applicant Review Panel, comprising representatives from the personnel, medical, and security offices. The board examines each applicant on what the agency calls the "total person" principle and either gives the candidate a thumbs-up or refers the case to the director of personnel for a "We regret to inform you" letter.

The second day of the two-day program for job applicants consists mainly of more briefings, including a security briefing and an unclassified operational briefing. A few of the most desirable prospects may get a tour of an operational area. This, however, requires the sanitizing of the entire area—everything classified must be removed—so it is seldom offered.

Following their forty-eight hours at FANX, the recruits head back to school to finish their last semester and, in the meantime, to sweat out the background investigation.

For many years, NSA security officials rated homosexuality near the top of its list of security problems to watch out for.

In 1960, during the Eisenhower administration, irrational fear of homosexuality extended right into the Oval Office. "The Soviets seem to have a list of homosexuals," Attorney General William P. Rogers nervously told Eisenhower during a Top Secret National Security Council meeting. What really concerned him, he said, was "the possibility that there is an organized group of such people." Rogers, who would later become President Richard Nixon's secretary of state, apparently feared a worldwide conspiracy of homosexuals. "The Russians had entrapped one individual," he told the president, "who, in his confession, had stated that there was an international group of homosexuals."

A month before, two NSA cryptologists had appeared before cameras on a stage in Moscow, asked for political asylum, and confessed the agency's deepest secrets like sinners at a revival meeting. It was the worst scandal in NSA's history. All evidence pointed clearly to ideology as the reason for William Martin and Bernon Mitchell's drastic action. But once it was discovered that one of the men had engaged in some barnyard experimentation as a youth, sexuality was quickly seized on as the real cause of the defections. According to documents obtained for *Body of Secrets*, the fear of homosexuals caused by the men's defection became pathological within the White House. The FBI secretly drew up a nationwide list of everyone it thought might be gay and, in a throwback to McCarthyism, Eisenhower ordered them blacklisted.

At the National Security Council meeting described above, Treasury Secretary Robert Anderson was also concerned. He asked "how good a list we had of homosexuals." J. Edgar Hoover replied that his bureau "did have a list and that local authorities notified federal authorities when they obtained such information." Eisenhower then ordered a secret, systematic blacklisting of the listed individuals throughout the federal government. "Such lists," he said, "should be given to someone who would have responsibility for watching to ensure that such individuals were not employed by other Government agencies. Everyone who applied for a job should be fingerprinted. Then if you had a fingerprint and an indication that the individual had been rejected for such reasons [as homosexuality], you would have a basis for preventing his future employment." Hoover agreed. "This was a useful idea." Eisenhower concluded the meeting with the comment, "It was difficult to get rid of such people once they were employed and that the time to catch them was when they came into the Government."

The harsh attitude of the White House translated into a massive purge at NSA. Anyone who showed even the slightest gay tendencies, whether that person was actively homosexual or not, was out. Dozens were fired or forced to resign. The fear would last for decades. But by 2001, the attitude had changed considerably. The most striking example is the authorized formation within the walls of NSA of GLOBE, the group for gay, lesbian, and bisexual employees, whose regular monthly meetings, in NSA offices, are advertised in the *NSA Newsletter.*

Less than a year after the Berlin Wall crumbled, the first post–Cold War conflict erupted. Following the Iraqi invasion of Kuwait, U.S. and coalition forces launched the Desert Storm operation against Saddam Hussein. As the smoke began to clear, NSA director Studeman rated the performance of U.S. spy agencies during the conflict as mixed—except for what he called the excellent monitoring of sanction-busters. The principal problem, he said, was converting a former friend into an enemy almost overnight. "Clearly during the Iran-Iraq war," Studeman said, "we viewed Iraq as an ally. So, Iraq was an area where we didn't have a lot of basic collection, or a lot of idea of the depth and breadth of the Iraqi capabilities. We had that on a monitoring basis, but few would call it in-depth knowledge of the target, the kind you would want to have if you go to war. We simply didn't have that."

Studeman also said that because Saddam Hussein had been an intelligence partner, NSA was now at a disadvantage. "Having had about four years' or more worth of U.S. delivering intelligence to it with regard to Iran's conduct of the war, Iraq had a substantial knowledge and sensitivity of our capabilities in the area of imaging and other intelligence collection methods such as signals intelligence. If you go back to the fundamental principles of intelligence, we had already failed on the first count. That is, our security had been penetrated because we were dealing with this target to whom we had spent so many years displaying what our intelligence capabilities were. Add the fact that Iraq is a very secretive country itself and places a great premium on security, and you then have a target that is probably the most denial-and-deception-oriented target that the U.S. has ever faced. It is a country that goes out of its way to create a large number of barriers to allowing any Western penetration of its capabilities and intentions."

Especially troublesome during the war were such areas as intelligence "fusion"—bringing all the U.S. intelligence organizations together—and information management. A key problem for NSA was getting intelligence from the intercept operators to the codebreakers to the analysts to the commanders in desert tents in time for it to be useful. "Essentially, from the threat of the invasion of Kuwait in late July until the outbreak of hostilities on 15 January," Studeman said, "the time was spent creating the environment for collection, processing and analysis, and the connection between the national side of it and the theater side."

As troops began boarding planes for the trip back home, Studeman looked ahead to the long decade leading up to the new century. "The world of the future is going to be an entirely different intelligence world," he said. By 1990 the fat years for NSA and its partners had come to an end. The Cold War had been won and it was time for the soldiers to return home. Suddenly a group that had known only growth was faced with cutbacks, budget slashing, and layoffs.

At an intercept station in Marietta, Washington, the gray operations building lies abandoned and ghostlike. "While standing amongst the weeds, trash, and wrecked automobiles," said a former technician who decided to return for a visit, "my ears caught a faint sound coming from the remains of the ops building." Then he realized what he was hearing: "Several hundred rats rummaging through the piles of garbage."

The powerful wave of Cold War fears that decades earlier had swept listening posts onto remote mountaintops and Arctic wastelands and into hidden valleys was now receding like a fast-falling tide.

During deactivation ceremonies at Edzell, Scotland, near the elephant cage that had captured so many Soviet voices, the only sound was the piercing skirl of a lone bagpipe playing the haunting farewell "We're No' Awa' Tae Bide Awa'."

At Key West, Florida, where reports had flashed to the White House during the Cuban missile crisis, a bugler sounded "Taps" and an NSA official watched the flag descend for the final time.

In the Command Conference Room at Kamiseya, Japan, once the Navy's largest listening post, the commanding officer solemnly read from a classified message ordering the station's closure.

At Skaggs Island, California; Karamürsel, Turkey; and dozens of other listening posts around the world, massive antennas were disassembled as quietly as they had been built.

Once a forbidden and frozen land populated exclusively by eavesdroppers, the Alaskan island of Adak was put up for sale on the Internet. Satellite dishes, power plant, the Adak museum, schools, even the church were to go to the highest bidder.

After seventy-nine years of operation, the last watch was stood at the naval listening post at Imperial Beach, California, near San Diego.

Many listening posts not closed were virtually abandoned and turned into remotely controlled operations. At the small monitoring station atop Eckstein, a high German peak overlooking what was once Czechoslovakia, the intercept operators were replaced with automatic antennas controlled in Augsburg, more than five hours away by car. The only people left were a few security guards and several maintenance staff.

The drawdown was not limited to NSA. In the far north, on the doorstep of the North Pole, several hundred people were cut from the Canadian listening post at Alert, the most important in the country. As with Eckstein and many other listening posts around the world, technology now permitted the station to be operated remotely from thousands of miles away.

Across the Atlantic, Britain's GCHQ was going through the same post–Cold War trauma. In 1995, 900 of 6,000 jobs were ordered cut from the headquarters in Cheltenham over four years. Listening posts were also nailed shut, including the monitoring station at Culmhead in Devon, cutting 250 jobs.

As at NSA, a number of GCHQ's overseas stations switched to remote control. Perched high on a cliff in Hong Kong, the joint British-Australian Chung Hom Kok listening post had long been one of the most important in the Far East. But all except a skeleton crew pulled out and moved thousands of miles away, to downtown Melbourne. There, in a windowless two-story gray stone building, intercept operators from Australia and New Zealand eavesdropped on Chinese and Russian communications picked up by British antennas in Hong Kong. "Most of the [intercepted information] went back to the NSA," said one of the staff. Among the key targets were Chinese testing of nuclear and other advanced weapons, and of space flight and military activities on the troublesome Paracel Islands in the South China Sea. Melbourne also monitored Russian communications from Vladivostok to the Russian base at Cam Ranh Bay in Vietnam.

But that all came to an end in the mid-1990s as Britain prepared for the return of Hong Kong to China. GCHQ officials ordered all its Hong Kong buildings razed to eliminate any chance that secrets would be compromised. By July 1997, when the handover took place, the windowless operations buildings had been reduced to rubble and the guard post was occupied by a vagrant sheltering from the rain. GCHQ did leave some equipment behind, however. Planted in the walls of the British army's former Prince of Wales barracks, which was turned over to the Chinese, was an assortment of listening devices.

Some at GCHQ feared that if staff numbers dropped below 4,500, the agency would begin to seem minor in the eyes of NSA. "If we can stay at 4,500 we can be a vibrant and effective organization," said Brian Moore, a GCHQ staff officer. "If we don't stabilize at 4,500, there must be a question mark over GCHQ's core business." But for the first time an outsider—and one known for his budget cutting—was appointed director. David Omand, deputy undersecretary of policy at the Ministry of Defence, had made his name by championing a series of initiatives designed to cut costs and boost the efficiency of the U.K.'s armed forces.

For many cryptologists, watching their secret world vanish into thin air was a difficult and painful experience. In the Texas hill country, just north of Austin, Robert Payne sat on his porch beneath an umbrella of stars. In the cool night, as fireflies danced, he puffed on a long cigar and took sips from a pale green coffee cup. "Who remembers what we did, how we did it, and why?" he once wrote.

> We were young sailors and marines, teenagers, sitting with headphones and typewriters copying and encrypting and decrypting and sending and receiving. Always on the alert, ever vigilant . . . Who understands the contributions we made in those far-flung outposts where we listened and watched through the endless days and nights of a very real Cold War? Who knows, for certain, what our work accomplished? I wonder what difference we made in the overall scheme of things.
>
> I sit here in the soft summer darkness and try to remember the names of all the places, and ships, and stations where we served. And I wonder if somewhere down the long, cold corridors of history, there will be monuments or memorials to these special ships and secret places that have served their country so well. . . . Places with strange-sounding names, surrounded by fences, gates, armed Marines, and signs that warned "Authorized Personnel Only." Secret places with funny-looking antenna arrays called "giraffe" or "dinosaur cages." Places with names people have never heard.

Another former intercept operator lamented, "Technology has progressed, so yesterday's way of doing business is no longer today's way. . . . The circle tightens and grows smaller; our bases in the Philippines are gone. Keflavík, Iceland, is gone. San Vito, Italy, is gone. Galeta Island, Panama, is gone. Pyong Taek, Korea, is gone. Adak, Alaska, is gone."

On the pages of the prestigious *Naval Institute Press,* a retired Navy cryptologist wrote that the Naval Security Group had outlived its usefulness and that the precious money used to run it would be better spent elsewhere in the Navy. The future looked so dim that Rear Admiral Isaiah Cole, the Security Group's director, was forced to reassure worried cryptologic veterans that their organization was not going to fold. "There will continue to be a Naval Security Group," he bravely asserted. But he had to admit that because of budget cuts "these are troubled times."

As the Cold War passed, so did NSA's boom years. In the early 1980s, "people [were] stacked almost three deep," said one congressional aide. In 1983, NSA building projects (totaling $76 million, with another $212 million slated for the following year) accounted for almost 20 percent of the Pentagon's entire construction budget worldwide. The addition of two new operations towers provided the agency's headquarters complex with more space than eleven New York City World Trade Centers.

But by 1997, the intelligence community budget had shrunk to what it had been in 1980, during the last years of the Carter administration and just before the Reagan administration gave the spooks the key to Fort Knox. At the same time, many of NSA's precious eavesdropping satellites were dying of old age and not being replaced. In the few years between 1991 and 1994, the number of spy satellites dropped by nearly half. "NSA's relative piece of the intelligence resource pie will likely diminish," Admiral William O. Studeman had told his workforce in a frank farewell memorandum on April 8, 1992. "Things will be tight, and the demand will be to continue to do more with less."

Studeman's concerns were well founded. Between 1990 and 1997 the agency was forced to cut its staff by 17½ percent and was scheduled to increase the total to 24 percent by 2001. A commission headed by former defense secretary Harold Brown said that at least 10 percent more staff should be cut throughout the intelligence community. On top of that, a Pentagon inspector general's review in 1991—the first one ever done at NSA—found that the agency was too top-heavy and that management was asleep at the wheel in the oversight of a number of key areas. "We found that the growth of the Agency had not been centrally managed or planned," the inspection report concluded, "and that the NSA did not have sufficient internal oversight mechanisms to ensure the

Agency efficiently accomplished its mission." The result was a serious bureaucratic shake-up. On October 1, 1992, Mike McConnell, Studeman's successor, instituted a major restructuring, slashing by 40 percent the number of deputy directors and by 29 percent the number of middle managers. Lower management was reduced by an average of 50 percent. At the same time, the number of people reporting directly to the director was cut from ninety to fifteen.*

"NSA personnel will be deeply affected by these changes," declared the *NSA Newsletter*. McConnell told a group of his senior staff, "As resources diminish we must reduce the Agency's overhead and build a structure that will make us more efficient." But, the cutbacks in personnel seemed to have a contradictory effect on the agency's budget. The cost of the shrunken workforce grew because of inflation, promotions, and the higher cost of benefits. These factors drove NSA's civilian payroll from about 30 percent of its budget in 1990 to nearly 40 percent in 1996. A White House study called the problem "acute" and said these "growing amounts allocated to meet the payroll have crowded out investments in new technologies and limited operational flexibility." It seemed that the more people NSA cut the less money it had for satellites and computers.

When McConnell replaced Studeman in May 1992, the downsizing problem was on his desk waiting for him. "Employees should take this opportunity to return to their areas of expertise," said the *Newsletter*, paraphrasing the new director. "Cross-training, technical tracks, and mission involvement are the buzzwords of the future." The long handle of the budget ax extended even to some of the agency's most remote listening posts. In a further effort to reduce costs, NSA civilians began gradually being replaced by military personnel at some of the listening posts not shut down entirely. As the cuts continued into the new century, employees were encouraged to attend a workshop called "Coping with

*The Pentagon report also criticized the NSA for wasting millions of dollars on warehousing old magnetic tapes, failing to manage properly its highly secret special-access programs, and not adequately measuring whether the intelligence being collected matched the intelligence that was being asked for. Four years later, in 1996, the agency still had not corrected several of the problems.

Change," and a noted speaker was brought in to give a lecture in the Friedman Auditorium on "Thriving in Turbulent Times."

Most believed there were few more secure places to work than NSA, and that downsizing would never happen. "While our neighbors and family members in the private sector faced job uncertainty, we remained secure," moaned one worried worker in 1992. "We are now in the unenviable position of being uncertain about our futures. It is not an easy time to work here." Exit interviews with resigning employees reflected the same concerns. Many of them felt that a bond had been broken.

But others believed that NSA had long been overstaffed. Dr. Howard Campaigne, a driving force in the computerization of codebreaking in the 1950s and 1960s, believed that the machines should have reduced staff costs. "I had visions . . . these would be labor-saving devices," recalled the former research chief, "and we wouldn't need a lot of people around. And it's been a continual disappointment that we had so many people around. Of course, what we've done is use these devices to do more [work] rather than to do what we were doing before more economically. But I still feel we ought to be able to do it with fewer people. More machines and fewer people." For those displaced, the former assistant director had one suggestion: "Join the 'buggy whip' manufacturers. Retire."

To help ease the trauma of drastic personnel reductions, over 4,000 employees were given buyouts in 1999. At the same time, NSA offered a parachute dubbed Soft Landing to many of the employees headed for the door. The idea was to transfer the employees to jobs within the crypto-industrial complex—jobs with defense firms that had significant contracts with NSA. During the first year, the employee would be paid under an NSA contract, and after that he or she might be hired full-time by the contractor.

Many such contracts called for the employee to remain right at NSA, although in a different job and in a different office. For example, Barbara Prettyman retired from her job as chief of staff for NSA's Health, Environmental, and Safety Services. Hired by Allied Signal under the Soft Landing program, she simply moved over to the agency's Information Systems Security offices, where she was assigned to create a national colloquium for information security education.

Other companies taking part in the program included TRW, SAIC, and Lockheed Martin. The money to finance the Soft Landing contracts comes from funds the agency saves by retiring senior employees early. By 1998, after two years in operation, the program had found homes for more than 300 retirees at eight contractors, saving NSA $25 million along the way.

Born in the foothills of the Blue Ridge Mountains in Greenville, South Carolina, during the middle of World War II, Mike McConnell graduated from the local college, Furman University, with a degree in economics in 1966. Shortly afterward he joined the Navy and was shipped off to Vietnam as a damage control officer on the USS *Colleton,* a ship attached to the Mobile Riverine Force in the Mekong Delta. Having survived the conflict, he went on to counterintelligence work with the Naval Investigative Service in Yokosuka, Japan, took a liking to the spy world, attended the Defense Intelligence College, and became an intelligence specialist.

Assigned as the operations officer for the Fleet Ocean Surveillance Information Facility in Rota, Spain, in 1976, McConnell received his initiation into the world of signals intelligence. "Four Navy chiefs and one NSA civilian took me under their wing to teach me Sigint," he recalled. "I learned as a young Navy lieutenant that Sigint is hard; it is complex, esoteric, and difficult to understand over its depth and breadth. . . . It changed my understanding, respect for, and use of Sigint for the rest of my professional life."

Following other assignments, including a tour as force intelligence officer aboard the USS *La Salle* in the Persian Gulf and Indian Ocean, McConnell moved to NSA, where he headed up the Naval Forces Division. Then he went to Pearl Harbor as the top naval intelligence officer for the Pacific Fleet, a job that won him his first star. He earned a second while dealing with such issues as the fall of the Soviet Union and the war in the Persian Gulf as a key intelligence staffer to the Chairman of the Joint Chiefs of Staff.

At NSA, McConnell soon found that it was far easier to eavesdrop than to convert intercepts into finished, usable intelligence. As always, codebreaking—"processing"—was the hardest part. "I have three major problems," McConnell was often heard declaring, "processing, processing, and processing."

Translation was also a major problem. "There now exists a world full of 'Navajo Code Talkers,' in a certain sense," noted McConnell. He was referring to the Native Americans who during World War II were employed to securely communicate sensitive messages because their language was unwritten, almost unknown outside their community, and thus almost impossible for an enemy to translate. "With the rich diversity of potential intelligence targets owing to possible U.S. involvement in low-intensity conflict and regional crisis situations anywhere U.S. interests may be threatened," McConnell continued, "we are confronted by a linguistic challenge of staggering proportion."

Down on the working level, the reductions and changes forced many managers to dig out their old earphones and go back to being operators. Similarly, those with language skills now in excess, such as Russian linguists, had to retrain in another language or develop new skills entirely.

While the end of the Cold War brought a greater sense of tranquility to most parts of the country, it created a seismic shift at NSA. Gone were the old traditional targets, the Soviet Union and Eastern Europe. Taking their place were new trouble spots that seemed to spring up almost anywhere. In 1980, fully 58 percent of the intelligence community's budget was targeted against the Soviet Union. Three years later NSA, desperate for Russian linguists, asked fifteen colleges, including Penn State and Georgetown University, to participate with the agency in a secrecy-shrouded Russian language internship program.

But by 1993 only 13 percent of the intelligence budget was aimed at Russia, and Russian linguists were scrambling to find new vocabularies to master. Suddenly the buzz phrase was "exotic languages."

Exotic languages have long been NSA's Achilles' heel. In 1985, for example, Libyan diplomatic messages were intercepted discussing the planning of the terrorist attack at La Belle discothèque in West Berlin. However, according to intelligence experts, a shortage of Berber translators led to a critical delay of several days in reading the dispatches. By then, the deadly bombing had already taken place.

In 1986, Bobby Inman had warned a congressional committee that "steadily deteriorating language training capabilities" presented "a major hazard to our national security." The message was underscored by the Pentagon's director of intelligence personnel and training, Craig L. Wilson, who spoke of the "dismal ignorance," in the Defense Department and the intelligence community, of Third World languages.

A year after McConnell arrived, as President Clinton was considering military action in the former Yugoslavia, NSA began to get worried about finding enough people who could translate Serbo-Croatian. Thus, on April 23, 1993, a curious advertisement appeared in *Commerce Business Daily*. Placed by NSA's military organization, the Army Intelligence and Security Command, it sought "a group of approximately 125 linguists to provide translation and interpretation support for U.S. forces in Yugoslavia." The work, said the ad, "would be in a hostile, harsh environment." And the government would pick up the cost of "life, dismemberment and medical insurance."

A similar crisis at NSA broke the following year, when President Clinton ordered American troops into Haiti to restore order. "When Haiti blew up a few years ago," said Deputy Director for Services Terry Thompson, "we looked around; there were a total of three Haitian Kreyol linguists in the entire cryptologic system. One in NSA, one in the Navy, and one in the Army, and that was it. So we had to go outsource—hire a lot of Haitian Kreyol speakers, many of whom lived in downtown Washington doing menial labor, and put them in a building over in Columbia [Maryland] and send them the material to transcribe."

One reason for the shortage of linguists is the tedium of the job. "You sit there with a pair of headphones, rocking back and forth with your foot on a pedal trying to figure out what people said," recalled one former NSA Russian linguist. "It is very repetitious, incredibly boring, and very demanding. It could drive you crazy." However, it could also be very educational, said another Russian linguist, who recalled all the Russian curses he learned while eavesdropping on the walkie-talkie conversations of Soviet troops on maneuvers in Siberia.

To help with the language problems, Director McConnell quietly turned to academia. Several colleges were paid to develop textbooks and teaching materials in exotic languages as well as to train university and NSA language teachers. Among the schools chosen was the predominantly black Florida A&M University, which was given a $1.74 million grant to fund courses in the difficult African languages of Zulu and

Xhosa, spoken largely in South Africa; Farsi, which is spoken in Iran; and Punjabi and Bengali, from the Indian subcontinent.

A side benefit of the grant, agency officials hoped, would be to recruit to the agency black students who had successfully completed the courses; this would not only build up the NSA language base but also help increase minority staffing. Unfortunately, however, many of the students enrolled in the courses had far more interest in international business than in eavesdropping on communications networks, and thus never went to work for NSA.

One solution, which NSA for decades has been trying to perfect, is machine translation. In the early and mid-1980s, NSA was focusing on a variety of crises—the Russian invasion of Afghanistan, the fundamentalist Islamic takeover in Iran, and the civil war in El Salvador. "NSA is faced with the growing problem of documents in virtually every language and script," said one agency report. To help find a way to quickly translate the reams of paper flowing into the agency written in unusual languages with strange alphabets, NSA turned to the University of Pennsylvania.

The experimental program, funded on behalf of NSA by the Pentagon, involved designing optical scanning technology to first identify and then read a number of exotic languages. The machine was eventually able to translate Azerbaijani-language newspapers printed in a non-standard version of the Cyrillic alphabet. A Turkic dialect, Azerbaijani is spoken by several million people in the former Soviet republic of Azerbaijan and the contiguous areas of Iran and Afghanistan. Other languages focused on by the project included Somali, Slovenian, and a Mayan Indian language, Chorti, that is spoken in parts of Guatemala, Honduras, and El Salvador.

Today, for more commonplace languages, NSA uses programs such as SYSTRAN that automatically translate text at up to 750 pages per hour using Russian dictionaries containing more than half a million words. The program translates technical texts with better than 90 percent accuracy. On average, human translation takes forty-five minutes per page. NSA has also developed a technique that allows analysts with no prior knowledge of a language to quickly search machine-readable foreign language databases for keywords and topics.

To find key text quickly within a very large collection of foreign language documents—such as Chinese or Devanagari (Sanskrit)—one program NSA uses is Oleada XConcord.

A further breakthrough in NSA's ability to pick out the right tree in a vast forest of words came with the development of the software called Semantic Forests. Semantic Forests allows NSA to sift through printed transcripts of conversations, faxes, computer transfers, or any other written intercepts and intelligently come up with the targeted subjects in which the agency is most interested. The name derives from the software's ability to create a weighted "tree" of meanings for each word in a document. During lab tests, the software quickly sifted through an electronic filter large volumes of printed matter, including transcripts of speech and data from Internet discussion groups. One of the sample questions in the test was "What have the effects of the UN sanctions against Iraq been on the Iraqi people, the Iraqi economy, or world oil prices?" Initial tests proved very successful, increasing the ability to locate target information from 19 percent to 27 percent in just one year.

Far more difficult than machine translation of printed texts is automatic translation and transcription of voice communications, such as intercepted telephone conversations in a variety of languages and accents. The ability to automatically spot targeted words in millions of telephone calls all over the world has long been a goal of NSA. A recent breakthrough was made by biomedical engineers at the University of Southern California, who claim to have created the first machine system that can recognize spoken words better than humans can. The research was largely funded by the Pentagon, long used as a cover for NSA contracts.

According to the university, the system can "instantly produce clean transcripts of conversations, identifying each of the speakers." Known at NSA as "Speaker ID," the USC's Berger-Liaw Neural Network Speaker Independent Speech Recognition System can mimic the way brains process information. This gives the computer the ability to conduct "word spotting" in target communications regardless of who or what pronounces the word.

The new system is also far better than the human ear at picking out words from vast amounts of white noise. It can even extract targeted words or conversations from the background clutter of other voices, such as the hubbub heard during conference calls, meetings, or cocktail parties. "The system can identify different speakers of the same word with superhuman acuity," said university officials.

Despite such progress, by 2001 there was still far more traffic than there were people or machines to handle it. "It's a good-size problem," said Hayden. "It's one that we're paying attention to, but the fixes are not immediate. There's probably no philosophers' stone here that we can touch and say, 'Oh yes, now the linguist problem's fixed.' There's probably a whole bunch of discrete decisions that you make that you begin to reduce the magnitude of the problem. One aspect of the problem is, just given the nature of our business, the demands on linguists are higher."

Some NSA language training takes enormous amounts of time, said Hayden, who himself was trained as a Bulgarian linguist. "Group Three languages, and I believe that's Arabic and Hebrew, take eighteen months," he said. "And Group Four languages take two years. And those are Chinese, Japanese . . . And then there is a whole other addition there to turn someone who has working knowledge of the popular language into a cryptolinguist, which is the specialized vocabulary. . . . It's a long time, these are long-term investments. And you can see why, then, we have trouble mostly with our military linguists who move a lot, whereas a civilian you hire for thirty-five years and you make a front-end investment of five years, you've still got thirty years of return. You've got a GI going through here on an eighteen-month tour."

Realizing NSA's personnel plight, the House Intelligence Committee began a major push in the late 1990s to redirect money away from various fields, ranging from satellites to support staff, and toward analysis and linguists.

"We need to hire a lot more people than we have authorized strength to do," Terry Thompson told a group of employees in late 1999. "The DO has recently told the Human Resources Review Group that they would like to hire twenty-six hundred more people to do language work and IA work, Intelligence Analyst work. And the reason for that is, if they look at their attrition projections, they expect to lose about a thousand people over the next couple of years and so they want to hire those people back. And then they want a plus-up of about sixteen hundred people over and above that, just to be able to do the work that comes in today." According to one senior NSA official, the agency hired about 698 people in 2000. For 2001, Congress gave NSA an additional $3 million to go toward hiring, plus $3.5 million more to use for signing bonuses for particularly desirable candidates.

Just as the fall of the Soviet Union created a need for exotic languages, the proliferation of low-cost, complex encryption systems and fast computers has forced NSA to search for more mathematicians whom they can convert to codebreakers. In a series of lectures at NSA in the late 1950s, William F. Friedman, the father of modern cryptology, argued that cryptology should be considered a separate and distinct branch of mathematics. It is little wonder, therefore, that NSA employs more math majors than any other place in the country, and possibly the world.

Thus the national decline in math test scores, the decreasing focus on math in the classroom, and the paltry number of graduate students seeking doctorates in the subject have become major concerns within NSA. "The philosophy here is that unless the U.S. mathematics community is strong, healthy, vibrant," said James R. Schatz, chief of NSA's mathematics research division, "then we're not going to have the kind of population to recruit from that we need."

Some at NSA trace the growing scarcity of mathematicians back to the early 1980s. It was then, according to one agency official, that "the agency succumbed, as did the rest of the American society, to the increasing gap between its population of technical specialists and a generalist population." As the last editor of the *NSA Technical Journal*, which ceased publication in 1980, the official witnessed the decline in mathematical and scientific education firsthand. It was one of the reasons for the *Journal*'s termination, he said, noting that many of the contributions were becoming increasingly "irrelevant to (and unintelligible to) all but a small audience." He added that if Friedman was correct in including cryptology as a branch of mathematics, "then large numbers of NSA's employees, even at the professional level (and within the professions, even within senior positions), are ill-equipped for their trade."

In an effort to reverse the trend, NSA recently launched a new program to seed the academic soil in order to keep the supply of mathematicians coming. It involved providing $3 million a year, through research grants, to mathematicians and also to summer programs for undergraduates. Yearlong sabbaticals at the agency were even offered to promising number lovers. In a rare foray into the unclassified world, then-director Minihan expressed his worry to a convention of mathematicians in 1998. "The Cold War is characterized by battles not fought, lives not lost," he said. "That era was fought with mathematicians and cryptologists."

"Over a three-year period," said Schatz optimistically in 1998, "we're going to be hiring over a hundred mathematicians with Ph.D.'s. There's nothing like that in the world, really. A university might have one or two openings a year, if that." But just as NSA seems to be getting its need for mathematicians under control, it is facing an even more daunting task in recruiting enough computer scientists. Among the problems, according to Michael J. Jacobs, chief of NSA's codemakers, is 42 percent fewer graduates with computer science degrees now than in 1986.

Among the most sensitive issues facing NSA in the post–Cold War period has been the hiring, as well as promotion, of minorities and women. For years NSA has had serious problems keeping up with the rest of government—and the rest of the intelligence community—in such employment statistics. "I have been here at NSA for over twenty years," wrote one frustrated employee in the mid-1990s, "and as a minority, have experienced racial discrimination like I have never seen before. The minorities here at NSA are so very stigmatized by the 'Do nothing, powerless' EEO [Equal Employment Office] and the IG [Inspector General] organizations . . . there is no adequate or effective process for minority complaints here at NSA. Many racial discrimination and fraud cases have been reported/presented to NSA's EEO and IG, and nothing, absolutely nothing, has been done."

Another complained, "EEO is a joke. . . . Nothing is held confidentially or anonymously. Retaliation is common and well known around the Agency. Most African Americans have stopped complaining and warn younger, less experienced African Americans against complaining in fear of retaliation and retribution." And still another cautioned, "It is a well known fact that if you stand up for your rights it can be a crippling experience, but become a whistle blower, and your career will experience the Kiss of Death!"

In a 1988 study of the intelligence community, done at the request of Congress, the National Academy of Public Administration found women and minorities underrepresented at NSA. Two years later, the Senior Advisory Group, a group of senior black NSA employees, examined the barriers faced by African American applicants and employees in hiring, promotion, and career development. They gave the agency low marks, citing institutional and attitudinal barriers. And in 1993 the Equal Employment Opportunity Commission concluded that little had been done to correct problems identified five years earlier. Finally, in 1994, both Congress and the Pentagon's inspector general hauled the director in for questioning as to progress in hiring and promoting minorities and women.

A key problem, the Department of Defense inspector general pointed out, was the tendency of NSA recruiters to go after the "best and the brightest." "The philosophy," said one senior personnel manager, "is that it is better to hire an applicant with a 3.2 grade point average from Stanford than one with a 4.0 from a school you've never heard of." Although the former strategy keeps the agency well endowed intellectually, it does not help the agency correct its racial and gender imbalance, it was argued.

NSA did make some efforts to recruit minorities, but more often than not they were only halfhearted. In an effort to recruit Hispanic students, the agency set up a Southwestern Recruiting Office in Phoenix in 1989. However, instead of staffing it with a Hispanic recruiter, the agency sent a sixty-year-old black male. The result was a total of eleven people hired in three years—none of whom were Hispanic. The office was closed in 1992.

For Director McConnell, the problem lay in the numbers. Although in 1993 women made up 43.4 percent of the federal workforce, at NSA they represented only 36 percent. And while 27.7 percent of federal government employees were members of minority groups, NSA's minority representation stood at a dismal 11 percent. In his agency's defense, McConnell pointed to the highly technical nature of its work—mathematics, engineering, computer science, and language:

"skill areas," he said, "in which minorities have been traditionally underrepresented."

For example, McConnell noted, "we have probably the highest concentration of mathematicians in the country." But "of the 430 doctoral degrees in mathematics awarded to U.S. citizens in 1992, only 11, or 2.5 percent, went to minorities," he said. "Can you imagine the competition for that 2.5 percent between companies like IBM or GM or whatever and NSA? It's very, very stiff competition."

To help correct the imbalance, McConnell established a policy of encouraging his recruiters to make one-third of their new hires minorities. In fact, the recruiters exceeded the quota, achieving 38.3 percent minority hires. But with NSA hiring fewer than 200 full-time staffers a year between 1992 and 1996, the quota system at this late date amounted to little more than tokenism. In the meantime, McConnell was left to deal with complaints from the agency's white males, who make up 57.5 percent of the workforce. Although no "reverse discrimination" lawsuits had yet been filed, McConnell was holding his breath. "So far I haven't gone to court," he said. "Time will tell."

In an effort to ease tensions, an Office of Diversity Programs was established to help ensure that minorities were fairly represented in programs throughout the agency. Among the units of the office is the Alaska/Native American Employment Program, which in 1999 sponsored a presentation by storyteller Penny Gamble Williams, the tribal chief of the Chappaquiddick Indian Nation of the Wampanoag Indian Nation, relating tales passed down through the generations. A luncheon of buffalo meat in the Canine Suite followed.

After more than four years in the director's chair, McConnell retired on February 22, 1996. His replacement was Kenneth A. Minihan, a tall, broad-shouldered Air Force lieutenant general. Unlike McConnell, who had spent most of his career in staff (as opposed to command) positions, General Minihan arrived at NSA after running two previous intelligence organizations: the Air Intelligence Agency and, briefly, the Defense Intelligence Agency. He was born in 1943, the same year as McConnell, in Pampa, a dusty, oil-soaked town straddling the old Santa

Fe Railroad in the Texas Panhandle. After graduating from Florida State University in 1966, he entered the Air Force as an intelligence officer, serving in Vietnam, Panama, and Italy and in a variety of positions in the Pentagon and at Air Force Headquarters.

In 1981 Minihan went to NSA as chief of the Office of Support to Military Operations and Plans. He also served in the agency's Directorate of Operations, as commander of the Air Force's 6917 Electronic Security Group. Minihan was named director of DIA in July 1995; there, one of his chief assignments was to review tainted information about Russian weapons systems passed by the CIA to the Pentagon. The Pentagon had received this bad intelligence because of the massive compromise of American spies in Russia by CIA turncoat Aldrich Ames.

According to Minihan, NSA's problems had become a great concern to both Secretary of Defense William J. Perry and CIA director John Deutsch. "They would use the phrase 'NSA doesn't get it,' " he said. "And they were somewhat impressed with how I was beginning to take over the reins of DIA, in the sense that we 'got it' at DIA." Thus the decision was made to shift Minihan to NSA. During the transition to his new job, Minihan spoke to a great many people both inside and outside government about the agency and was stunned to find that the reaction was virtually universal. "I would say I spent a good month or so talking with lots of people," he said. "It was almost riveting in the common sense that they all expressed that we [NSA] don't get it."

Once in place at Fort Meade, it didn't take long for Minihan to understand why this was so. "It . . . really surprised me, both how accurate Dr. Perry and Dr. Deutsch were . . . ," he said. "In my mind we had fallen into a—I've never used this phrase before—sort of like a loser's mentality, a loser's mind-set." One cause, said Minihan, was the constant downsizing: "We'd lost about a third of our workforce. What we had done is we were accepting the loss of program and people resources as a norm. You've got another three percent cut. So we're going through our tenth straight year of three percent decline. And we just accepted that."

Another early concern for Minihan was finding a new deputy. When he arrived, the position was occupied by William P. Crowell, appointed by Admiral McConnell two years earlier. A native of Louisiana with an impish grin and a taste for Cajun shrimp, Crowell joined the agency in 1962 and rose quickly, a decade later becoming chief of A

Group, the section responsible for attacking Soviet cipher systems. Crowell foresaw the enormous impact that the personal computer would have on both society and NSA and pushed the agency to begin taking advantage of commercial, off-the-shelf technology. This was the key, he believed, to improving both the way NSA attacked code problems and the way it disseminated the results. Eventually rising to deputy director for operations, Crowell championed the Intelink, the highly secret intelligence community version of the Internet. "He was a 'geek' in the most positive sense," said former NSA official Fredrick Thomas Martin. "He understood technology. He knew the intelligence business."

But Minihan was concerned that the position of deputy director had become too powerful, so that the director was little more than a ceremonial chief. "The DDIR [deputy director] is part of the seducing," he said, "the seduction of the director, so that the director becomes the host for dinners and lunches, the speaker at major engagements and awards and things like that. . . . And so part of the DDIR's efforts are, in my view, to numb the director." Adding, "It is not healthy to numb the director," Minihan also charged that deputy directors became bureaucratic warlords. "They purge those beneath them who are not on their team, and then they elevate those who have been on their team," he said. "Some people go into exile, some people retire."

So Minihan and Crowell began locking horns almost immediately. "I was very disruptive to his definition of what the deputy director [should be]. I took a lot of things that he had on his plate and moved them to my own plate, because I wanted those to be the director's authorities." Minihan also opposed warlordism. "I was asked by Bill, 'Well, who's on your team?' " said Minihan. "I was not willing to participate in a 'Who's on my team.' . . . The answer is, 'They all are.' " Minihan added, "It didn't matter to me a bit who Bill was. It was what I wanted to do."

Nor did Minihan get along with the various senior officials in the agency—the deputy directors for operations, information security, and so on. "My first two or three weeks, maybe a month or so, as I went around, it was pretty clear that I was not going to hit it off that well with the DDs [deputy directors] who were in place. . . . And we were having natural tense sessions." On top of that, according to Minihan, the senior officials didn't even get along with one another. "The DDs not only were resistant to me," said Minihan, "which I could handle, but they were resistant to each other. That's not healthy! And so, part of the grinding was, 'You guys don't even like each other? How is my institution going to be run if it's clear that you all don't even get along?' "

To employees, the result sounded like squabbling parents throwing dishes at each other. "You could hear the groans even down at our level," said Dr. David Hatch, the agency historian. Minihan added, "The workers were telling me the same thing: 'Those guys don't get it. They're always in a fight.' "

Given the tension, there was little surprise when Crowell left in September 1997.

Nearly twenty years earlier, Bobby Inman had arrived at NSA with views similar to Minihan's concerning the need for a strong director and a weak deputy. Inman chose a woman for the position: Ann Caracristi. ("Ann knew that I wanted to be *the* director," he said.) Minihan did the same, choosing Barbara A. McNamara as only the second woman deputy director. "Part of the transition from Bill to Barbara McNamara was to make certain that she understood what, how I thought the two portfolios should be handled," said Minihan. "I had a full expectation that there wasn't going to be any 'numbing' in what we were doing. And that was part of the interview: to be certain that that was . . . a clear message in that sense."

Short, with close-cropped blond hair, Barbara A. McNamara—"BAM," as she was known to many within NSA—was born in Clinton, Massachusetts, and joined the agency as a linguist after receiving a degree in French from Regis College in 1963. At the time of her appointment to the deputyship, McNamara headed up the Operations Directorate and had also served as the NSA's ambassador to the Pentagon: the National Cryptologic Representative, Defense.

"I am honored to have been sworn in before you today," McNamara told the audience in NSA's cafeteria after the ceremony. "I would like to think that years from now, this organization will stand together again on a 'Day of Celebration' and speak about our successes yet unknown."

The new pair inherited not only the outgoing team's adjoining eighth-floor offices but also its quagmire of race and gender issues. McConnell's policies seemed to please few, if any. The number of NSA employees filing complaints with the federal Equal Employment Opportunity Commission more than doubled, going from seventeen in 1990 to forty-five in 1995. Some even began to question whether national security was being imperiled by the promotion of inexperienced employees to sensitive jobs in order to meet hiring quotas. By 1997, following Minihan's arrival, at least a dozen lawsuits had been filed related to race or sex discrimination, and former employees had begun branding senior leadership the "Irish Mafia" while seeing the Office of Discrimination Complaints and Counseling "a party organization for blacks."

Under a new promotion policy, women and minority candidates received at least one round of extra consideration for promotion, thus allowing a minority woman three chances to advance where a white male got one. Such policies provoked anger and frustration from many longtime employees. William J. Sonntag was considered for promotion to deputy division chief in 1993 but failed to get the job; all three slots went to women. He sued, claiming, "I was denied consideration of a management position on the sole basis that white males were not being considered for three such jobs in my office." Sonntag lost his case but the government later settled with him when he appealed.

Sonntag and other employees essentially alleged that NSA used an aggressive brand of affirmative action to deny staffers promotions or, in some cases, even dismiss them. Emile J. Henault, Jr., an attorney who worked at the agency for twenty-seven years, agreed. In the spring of 1997 he received more than twenty requests from NSA employees thinking about bringing suit: "Suddenly it's become overwhelming." Calling the personnel office a "paramilitary group," Henault said that the agency uses information from confidential employee-counseling sessions to revoke security clearances. And losing a clearance at NSA means losing a job. "When you say 'national security,' everybody just wilts," Henault said. "Everybody hides under it."

To resolve internal problems, NSA has an Office of Inspector General, with a number of attorneys and investigators, but some employees feel that the main function of this office is simply to protect the agency and not to redress injustices. Few have greater reason to believe that than Mary Ann Sheehy, who transferred from the FBI to NSA in 1988 and was assigned to an extremely sensitive and covert Pentagon unit in northern Virginia.

In 1994, while stopped at a red light, a car plowed into the rear of her Toyota Tercel, leaving her with a permanent 15 percent disability. As a result, she filed suit against the driver of the other car. In order to establish lost wages as a result of her injuries, she asked the agency to release copies of her employment records to the driver's attorney. As defined by NSA, "employment information" consists simply of verification of an employee's position, grade, salary, and length of service. She also directed that the agency have no communication with the driver's attorney.

Later, to her horror, Sheehy learned that NSA's Office of Personnel not only telephoned the defense attorney but then sent her virtually every paper in her file, including copies of her pre-polygraph psychological records, pre-employment psychological and psychiatric evaluations, personality profiles, and all her agency medical records. It was a clear violation of both the federal Privacy Act as well as NSA's own internal guidelines. Also shocked by the release was NSA psychologist Dr. Michael J. Wigglesworth, who attempted to get the material back from the attorney. "I am quite concerned about this," he wrote to the lawyer. "It is the policy of this office [Psychological Services Division] to release this kind of information only to the employee, their therapist, or their representative. . . . As the material is still protected information under the Privacy Act, I would appreciate your returning all of the psychological information to me." But the attorney never returned the materials.

On November 7, 1994, Sheehy protested the actions of the personnel office to NSA's Office of Inspector General, requesting a formal internal investigation. Three weeks later the opposing attorney used the very private documents, including the polygraph-related documents, in open court. "The files released by NSA were utilized by the defense attorney to embarrass, humiliate, and intimidate me during judicial proceedings," Sheehy said, "as well as jeopardize my future opportunities for employment as a covert intelligence officer."

Undeterred, Sheehy continued to fight within the secret bureaucracy. "I requested an appointment with the IG, Frank Newton, but was denied," she said. "My telephone calls to him were never returned. I followed the chain of command all the way to Ralph Adams, the executive director of NSA. [In October 1995] he told me to sue the agency. I wanted to speak to the director [then Lieutenant General Mike McConnell], but was told that was impossible." Six months later, in April 1996, the Inspector General's Office finally issued its report. Despite the gross violation of her privacy, the IG simply sided with the agency, concluding that "no evidence of improper or illegal activity on the part of Agency officials was found with respect to the release of your records under the Privacy Act."

After years of frustration and lack of promotion, Sheehy sent a scathing letter to Attorney General Janet Reno in 1999. "NSA believes it is above the law, can police itself and is accountable to no one," she wrote. "Instead of helping me, they lied to cover their illegal conduct." Once again she was brushed off with a stock response: "While we sympathize with your circumstances, there is not sufficient evidence of a criminal violation of the Privacy Act for us to take any further action."

Finally, in the spring of 2000, Sheehy asked the U.S. Attorney in Baltimore to look into NSA's treatment of her. The U.S. Attorney's Office responded on April 13, saying it had received her letter. That very day, in what Sheehy considers retaliation, NSA dispatched two officials from the Office of Security to Virginia to strip her of her special agent badge and identification card. Only after two months and the intervention of a high-ranking Pentagon intelligence official did NSA relent and return Sheehy's credentials to her. The U.S. Attorney's Office eventually dismissed her complaint, finding that no federal laws were broken. "You should look for another job," an attorney once warned her, "because they are going to retaliate—they're going to put you in a closet and give you a terrible supervisor and force you out."

By 2000, according to several employees, the IG's office had become more responsive, under the direction of Ethan L. Bauman, an outsider who had previously served as a federal prosecutor.

General Minihan could easily have served as the model for William H. Whyte, Jr.'s, Organization Man. Almost weekly he announced a new program or theme. He came up with "Future Day" and *The Futuregram* to bring "all parts of the Agency together with ideas, concerns, and solutions." ("I think it's magnificent," he later said. "And I thought of it myself!") He created an internal Internet web page outlining his goals and priorities for the next 30, 100, 365, and 1,000 days.

He would throw out slogans, such as "One Team, One Mission," and ask employees to take pledges ("No one will work harder . . . ," "No one will stand watch longer . . . ," etc.).

Minihan also pushed the NSA's normally cenobite senior managers to broaden their experience by seeking an assignment or two with other intelligence agencies. And he would hand out small medallions, "The Director's Coin," when he saw an on-the-spot need to recognize someone's special contribution to the agency. He even started an annual week-long festival to bring together agency staff from diverse cultural backgrounds.

To help break out of the bureaucratic mind-set, Minihan announced, "Out-of-the-box thinking is not only authorized, it is encouraged." He then set up his own personal "secret team," a sort of antibureaucracy commando force designed to carry out his orders in the most expeditious manner possible, regardless of the organizational chart.

Named the Skunk Works, after the famous Lockheed team that built the spectacular U-2 and SR-71 spy planes ahead of schedule, under budget, and in total secrecy, the five-member team worked directly for Minihan. He would turn to them when he needed quick action on a project in order to cut through the agency's red tape. The motto of the Skunk Works was "anytime, anywhere, on time, and right the first time."

It was as though Minihan had taken over a losing football team and was determined to snap it back into shape. "Now is the time for Team NSA to step forward and lead America's entry into the 21st century," he said in his first announcement to the workforce. "We are no longer a world-class organization; NSA is the class of the world."

But some saw Minihan's efforts as a crass attempt to bludgeon workers with tacky slogans and heavy-handed propaganda. "Where are my hip boots?" wrote one employee upset and embarrassed over Minihan's gushing enthusiasm over his "Future Day."

> The propaganda about Future Day just will not end! . . . The truth is that participation in Future Day was mandatory and, worse yet, the *word* came down through management that all responses to Future Day should be positive, *or else*. In

> my many years at the Agency, I have never seen such widespread and blatantly coercive pressure used on employees as was the case with Future Day. All negative or dissenting opinion was quashed, except that of a few people willing to risk their careers by expressing their opinions on ENLIGHTEN [the NSA internal e-mail system].
>
> The fact that NSA's management is resorting to this level of coercion and propaganda is not merely embarrassing or irritating—it is a sure sign that the Agency has lost its corporate integrity and suffers from a deplorable lack of qualified leadership. A first step toward reversing this downward trend would be an official, public acknowledgment by NSA seniors that employees were pressured to provide only positive feedback regarding Future Day and that the proclaimed benefits of Future Day have been grossly overhyped.

To unify his "team," Minihan attempted to break down the thick walls separating the Sigint and Infosec (information security) sides of NSA as well as the cultural barriers that divided the military and civilian workers. Where the National Sigint Operations Center had been the exclusive club of the eavesdroppers and codebreakers, Minihan brought in the Infosec folks and renamed it the National Security Operations Center. He also launched the NSA's first worldwide virtual town meeting. "We now have people talking about both sides of the mission in ways that we haven't seen for a long, long time," said one senior official, "and that's pretty exciting."

While many in NSA welcomed Minihan's aggressive, all-for-one-and-one-for-all management style and his budgetary innovations, the politicians on Capitol Hill who held the key to the agency's strongbox were fuming. In 1998 the House Intelligence Committee even threatened to withhold funds unless the agency made "very large changes" in its "culture and methods of operation." Of particular concern was Minihan's lack of adequate "strategic and business planning" as well as the agency's resistance to ordered budget cuts, and the diversion "from their intended purpose" of funds previously allocated to the agency.

Minihan's accounting system was also a shambles. According to a classified Pentagon inspector general's report released in 1998, auditors found that NSA had not instituted required internal controls and ignored laws and regulations, such as the Chief Financial Officers Act, necessary to produce accurate financial statements. "The NSA FY 1997 financial statements were materially incomplete and inaccurate," said the report. "The financial statements omitted real property located at a field site, a portion of Accounts Payable and a portion of operating expenses." This was not the first time the Inspector General's Office had found NSA's books out of order: in August 1996 it found similar inaccuracies.

The mismanagement left Minihan and NSA open to harsh criticism by House committee members. The agency officials "cannot track allocations for critical functions," the panel said in its report on the fiscal 1999 Intelligence Authorization Act. As a result, "Fences have been placed on portions of the [NSA] budget with the prospect that a considerable amount of money could be programmed for other intelligence community needs if NSA does not develop strategic and business planning."

Even more humiliatingly, about the same time that the House report was released, the Pentagon cut Minihan's direct lines to the Secretary of Defense and the Chairman of the Joint Chiefs of Staff. In a plan approved in late April 1998, Minihan and other senior NSA officials had to first report through an assistant defense secretary several rungs down the ladder, one responsible for command, control, communications, and intelligence, or "C3I" in intelligence jargon.

Adding to Minihan's woes was the discovery that NSA for years had been seriously mismanaging its mega-million-dollar high-tech computer and information technology systems. One organization in NSA would buy a top-of-the-line system only to discover that it was incompatible with other systems in the agency; millions of dollars' worth of new equipment would be bought that duplicated—or was inferior to—equipment already owned by the agency.

To correct the situation, the Secretary of Defense ordered NSA to install a sort of budget czar overseeing all purchasing and use of information technology. In 1997 Minihan named Ronald Kemper to the new post of chief information officer for NSA. Kemper also headed up the agency's new Enterprise Information Technology Office.

From the moment he walked into his spacious office on the top floor of OPS 2B as the fourteenth DIRNSA, Minihan had his eye on the new millennium. He saw a future where wars were fought not on muddy battlefields but in the invisible ether, in cyperspace, and there the NSA was king. "Just as control of industrial technology was key to military and economic power during the past two centuries," he told the citizens of the secret city, "control of information technology will be vital in the decades ahead. . . . In the future, threats will arise and battles will be fought and won in the information domain. This is, and has always been, the natural operating environment of the National Security Agency. . . . Information will give us the power to pick all the locks."

Searching for a catchy phrase, Minihan came up with "Information dominance for America." Said Minihan, "And then a couple of times the Brits and others beat up on me; I figure I got to add 'and its allies.' "

Minihan's metaphor for the future was not a technology superhighway but a technology sword, a sword that could cut both ways. "Though new technologies provide tremendous opportunities to share information and develop new relationships," he warned, "those same technologies are the primary weapons of the electronic road warriors of the future. 'Techno-terrorists,' ranging from mischievous teens to sophisticated nation and state adversaries, have agendas and potential destructive powers far more wide-ranging than we are accustomed to. Their targets will be our information databases, emergency services, power grids, communications systems, and transportation systems. . . . We must continue this fight."

The centerpiece of Minihan's Year 2000 battle plan for NSA was his "National Cryptologic Strategy for the 21st Century," in which NSA would take the lead in the conflicts of the future—both protecting the nation from cyber attacks and taking the offense with information warfare. Minihan put this work on the same level as protecting from nuclear attacks. "Information warfare poses a strategic risk of military failure and catastrophic economic loss and is one of the toughest threats this nation faces at the end of this century," he said. "We must be able to determine if we are being attacked, who is conducting the attack, and what to do if we are attacked. . . . We will also continue targeting intelligence for information warfare at levels of detail and timeliness comparable to those achieved for conventional and nuclear warfare."

But by the end of his tour, Minihan still had not corrected some of

NSA's most grievous problems, and the House Intelligence Committee showed him no mercy. It bluntly declared, "The committee believes that NSA is in serious trouble." Although it continued to pour large sums into the agency's worldwide eavesdropping network, its satellites and code-breaking capabilities, the committee said, "money and priority alone will not revive NSA, nor the overall [signals intelligence] system." The problem, said the panel, is not lack of money but lack of management. "The committee believes that NSA management has not yet stepped up to the line."

In a farewell note to his employees, Minihan talked of both the successes and setbacks of his tour. "Looking back," he wrote, "we have accomplished much together. As is our tradition, those successes remain known only to a few. We have also experienced the continuation of the largest draw-down in our history. At the same time, we have been confronted with a tidal wave of new technologies and transnational threats which some believed threatened our very existence." Privately, in his office, Minihan was more candid. "It's the hardest job I've ever had," he said. "It sucks the life out of you. You know, if you're awake, you're thinking about this job."

In his last days, Minihan feared that his successor would shift from the course he had set for the agency. "I think it will be catastrophic if we allowed the person to drift away from the scheme that we've set up," he said to several employees in his office. Then he said it was up to them to keep the new director on course. "And I think that's actually more a question of you and I and the folks here than it is a question for this guy. So I've done my part with this guy. But his background is actually completely different if you look back at us. I've been in the business a lot. He has not. I was sent here with a 'Do they get it or not?' Now his question is, 'Are you going to stay the course or not.' "

One week later, on March 15, 1999, Minihan walked between a double row of well-wishers, past the shiny turnstiles of OPS 2A, and out into the chilly air of retirement. No more government-paid cook, car, and chauffeur. No more government housing. No more secrets with his morning coffee. Gone was his subscription to the Top Secret/Umbra *National SIGINT File*, gone was his high-speed connection to the supersecret Intelink. Now his daily intelligence summary would be found rolled in a plastic wrapper on the driveway of his new Annapolis, Maryland, home. In place of a briefing on the latest advances against a Chinese cipher system, he now had the daily crossword puzzle to tease his brain.

The moving vans, loaded with Minihan's well-traveled belongings, had barely pulled away from the handsome redbrick house on Butler Avenue when painters and cleaners arrived to spruce it up for his successor. For more than four decades this has been the official residence of the director of NSA. Located in a restricted, tree-shaded corner of Fort Meade, it is equipped with its own Secure Compartmented Information Facility (SCIF). Inside the Vault Type Room is a STU-III crypto phone connected to NSA, about three miles away, and a heavy safe in which to hold highly classified documents brought home for late-night reading.

On a wall near the kitchen is a plaque containing the names of all the NSA heads who have lived there—every director except for the first, Lieutenant General Ralph Canine. After Minihan's departure, a new brass plate was attached to the plaque, one bearing the name of Michael V. Hayden, an Air Force lieutenant general and the fifteenth director of NSA.

In addition to a house, Hayden had inherited an ax. He would have to use it to slice away at NSA's personnel levels more than other directors had done. In order to reduce the personnel rolls, NSA for the first time began turning over to outside contractors highly sensitive work previously reserved to NSA employees. This project, called Groundbreaker, was unveiled in 2000 to the dismay of many in the agency. Projections were that it would "impact more than 3,000 employees." As many as 1,500 employees and 800 contractors would lose their jobs under the project. However, those affected would be guaranteed jobs with whichever contractor won the bidding for the contract. Those who declined to work for the new contractor would be let go.

Hayden called the project "unprecedented" because it involved turning over to private industry the management and development of nearly all of the agency's nonclassified information technology programs. The contracts were worth $5 billion over ten years. The drastic measures were taken largely because of years of poor in-house management. "Our information technology infrastructure is a critical part of our mission and it needs some repair," said Stephen E. Tate, chief of NSA's Strategic Directions Team. "It is a burning platform and we've got to fix it."

But some longtime employees think the agency is sacrificing senior analysts to buy more expensive satellites to collect more information to be analyzed by fewer experienced people. "They're buying all those new toys," said one twenty-six-year veteran, "but they don't have the people to use them. It's always happened that way, but more so in the past seven or eight years. The people who provide the intelligence aren't there anymore. So things are starting to slip through the cracks."

Among those cracks was NSA's failure to warn of India's nuclear test in 1998, a mistake that John Pike of the Federation of American Scientists called "the intelligence failure of the decade." Pike added, "The question of 'toys versus boys' in the NSA budget has been, and will remain, controversial. It's my understanding that Minihan's view of this is, they've got too many people and they need more toys. They're clearly trying to have their cake and eat it, too."

In order to cut as few linguists and analysts as possible, some of the heaviest reductions were made in support functions at NSA—turning the agency into a colder and less personal environment. "There is a significant amount of concern from Congress and from our overseers," Terry Thompson told a group of technical employees, "about how much money and resources we're devoting to human resources activity at NSA." He joked: "We have thousands of people doing resources management at NSA; half of them spend time generating work for the other half. If we had a good business process and a good way of handling our budget . . . we could free up a lot of those to do other things."

Thus, just as NSA's vast unclassified information technology operations were turned over to outside contractors, so were many of the agency's human resources activities. The contract went to Peoplesoft, a California corporation that specializes in automating human resources functions. "The transition from working with a human being down the hall to working with a computer on your desktop to do most of your human resources business is a tough transition for everybody," said Thompson.

For employees stressed out by all the changes, the agency has its own mental health clinic. Hidden away in the Parkway Corporate Center in Hanover, Maryland, to provide "anonymity and confidentiality," the center has a staff of thirteen fully cleared clinical psychologists and social workers. In addition to courses in stress management and coping with organizational change, the NSA's Employee Assistance Service provides a wide range of programs, on topics such as assertiveness training, bereavement, dealing with difficult people, weight control, eating disorders, and even social skills enhancement. A "significant number" of EAS clients, says one report, are treated for depression. The EAS also has branch offices at NSA's major listening posts in England and Germany.

Seventy-two percent of NSA employees who visit EAS are "self-referred"; others are sent by their supervisors. A person's boss may call the psychology office to verify that the employee kept an appointment, but cannot probe into the problems discussed. To ensure confidentiality, all EAS files are kept separate from normal NSA personnel and security files. Nevertheless, the Office of Security is made aware when a person visits the office. And if it is determined that "national security is threatened," the confidentiality of the sessions can be broken.

Ironically, while one group of senior managers at NSA is searching for ways to reduce the employment rolls, another group, in the Information Security Directorate, is attempting to stem the brain drain caused by big-bucks offers from private industry. As computers take over more and more segments of society, so does the demand grow for highly experienced computer and information security specialists to protect that data. At the top of the list of places to which corporate headhunters are now turning is NSA. "It's a real worry," said one senior NSA executive. "If the issue is salary, we're in a noncompetitive position."

"Our hiring program skims off the cream from the available hiring pool year after year," said Terry Thompson. "And so we have a very, very high-quality workforce. All of that says that when you go out, shopping yourself around for a job, if you have NSA on your résumé, it's worth more than the ten thousand dollars or whatever the amount [the increase in salary] is for having a TS/SI [Top Secret/Special Intelligence] clearance. There's a brand-name recognition that goes above that for people who work at NSA."

According to a study by the U.S. Department of Commerce, "While average starting salaries [in the private sector] for graduates with bachelor's degrees in computer engineering grew to more than $34,000 in 1995, the federal government's entry-level salary for computer professionals with bachelor's degrees ranged from about $18,700 to $23,000 that year." To help overcome the disparity, NSA in 1996 raised the pay of its mathematicians, computer scientists, and engineers.

Agency officials, however, say it is not the money that attracts many NSA employees but "the unique nature of our work." In an effort to find new talent, NSA set up its own recruitment web page, which has been responsible for bringing in about 20 percent of its applicants. The agency also began posting job openings on employment web sites like Job Web and Career Mosaic.

By the mid-1990s NSA had scaled back hiring to only about 100 new employees a year. A commission established to look into the intelligence community saw problems down the road in consequence of such drastic cutbacks in hiring. "This is simply insufficient to maintain the health and continuity of the workforce," the report said. It went on to warn that if the pattern continued, NSA would face a future in which large segments of its workforce would leave "at roughly the same time without a sufficient cadre of skilled personnel to carry on the work."

NSA's decade-long diet had left it nearly a third lighter at the start of the new century. "Our budget has declined by almost thirty percent over the last ten years," said Thompson in late 1999. "And our workforce has gone down at a commensurate rate. But our requirements [the work assigned to NSA] have gone up and we have a hard time saying no, so it's hard for us to stop doing things."

Thompson believes that Congress neglected NSA for many years because it had fewer high-cost defense contractors on its payroll than some other agencies, and thus far fewer lobbyists to pressure Congress for more money for NSA. "One of the reasons we don't get more support on the Hill for the budget," he said, "is we don't have a strong lobby in the defense industry. You know the NRO has a seven-billion-dollar budget. And anytime somebody talks about taking a nickel away from them there's people from Lockheed and Boeing—well, especially Boeing . . . and other big, big defense industrial contractors that are down there saying, 'You can't cut this because it's jobs in your district, Senator or Congressman. . . .' "

"The point is," continued Thompson, "they [other agencies] have a very effective defense-industrial lobby because they spend a lot of money in the contract community. We don't have that. We used to have, ten or fifteen years ago. But we don't anymore, because we spend our money on four hundred or four thousand different contracts and it's hard to get a critical mass of people who want to go down and wave the flag for NSA when budget deliberations are going on."

Speaking to a group of military communications officials, Kenneth Minihan once summed up NSA's budgetary problems with an old pilot's saying: "The nose is pointing down and the houses are getting bigger."

CHAPTER FOURTEEN

BRAIN

WDLDXTDKS'B AFSWDX GSADB GSKKYTQ YG CDKSZDC WYQD
RJEPBZYPZA QWXPK QWZLX OXLZ QJB KOXWAAWZR YWNBJKJQA
IBRUITRUL TEF HTHWEF BRTINRXK NTHXKF RU MRLM BRUIF
OHSQSHYJB LGADM-DYJBSL ZDPSW MV DYQS DGK ZPLASLW
UABCHPC QTMQ EJHBC QJDDBH UPJAW MBVAW EGPXGVQQ

It would be one of the most delicate operations ever performed. The doctors and technicians would gather early and work late into the night. Any mistake could be extremely serious. The patient's memory could be lost forever, or the ability to function severely damaged. Crypto City was about to undergo its first brain transplant. According to the director, nothing less than "the continued success of the agency's Sigint mission largely depended on this." The planning had taken years. NSA would create the largest, most powerful, and most secret electronic brain on earth.

But first it would have to build a specialized facility to house the new center. Then it would need to carefully transplant tons of massive and delicate supercomputers—more than 150—from the cavernous basement of OPS 1 to their new home, out of sight in a wooded corner of the secret city nearly a mile away. Whereas most government offices and large corporations measure in square feet the space taken up by their computers, NSA measures it in acres. "I had five and a half acres of computers when I was there," said Marshall Carter, director in the late 1960s. "We didn't count them by numbers; it was five and a half acres." Even though modern computers have more capacity and smaller footprints, one NSA employee more than a decade later commented, "It's double that today."

Once in place, the computers would be brought back to life and linked by a secure fiber optic spinal cord to the Headquarters/Operations Building complex—all without disrupting NSA's critical operations. When it was finally completed, in 1996, NSA's Supercomputer Facility held the most powerful collection of thinking machines on the planet.

Standing in front of the new building on the afternoon of October 29, 1996, Kenneth Minihan held a pair of scissors up to a thin ribbon of red, white, and blue. No press releases had been issued, and even the invitations to the event gave no hint where the ceremony would actually take place. But then, that was precisely how the man in whose name the Tordella Supercomputer Facility was about to be dedicated would have wanted it. This would be the first NSA building to be named for a person. As the scissors sliced through the colorful ribbon, a handheld machine of elegant simplicity opened the way to a building of infinite complexity.

The history of modern codebreaking and the history of computers are, to a large degree, coterminous. Yet because of its "policy of anonymity," NSA's role has been almost totally hidden. When the Association for Computing Machinery sponsored a commemoration of the twenty-fifth anniversary of its founding, NSA simply stayed away. Likewise, when computing pioneers gathered at the quarter-century anniversary meeting of the Institute of Electrical and Electronic Engineers' Computer Society, NSA again exhibited an advanced case of shyness.

But NSA's role in computer development has been, and continues to be, enormous. The man responsible for much of that work—as well as for the thick shroud of secrecy that still surrounds it—was Dr. Louis W. Tordella, NSA's keeper of the secrets.

By the outbreak of the Second World War, the importance of machines to aid in codebreaking was known but their use was limited. At that time the Signal Security Agency had only fifteen machines and twenty-one operators. But by the spring of 1945, the SSA was employing 1,275 operators and supervisors to work on 407 keypunch machines.

Besides its off-the-shelf tabulating machines, the agency had specialized machines custom built for codebreaking. Known as Rapid Analytical Machines (RAMs), they employed vacuum tubes, relays, high-speed electronic circuits, and photoelectrical principles. They were the forerunners of the modern computer, but they were expensive and overspecialized. A number of them were built to attack a specific code or cipher, so if a cipher system was changed or abandoned, the machine was of little value.

The Navy's Op-20-G contracted with Eastman Kodak, National Cash Register, and several other firms to design and build its RAMs. The Army's Signal Security Agency, on the other hand, worked closely with Bell Laboratories. Another major contractor during the war was IBM, which built a specialized attachment for its IBM tabulator, thereby increasing the power of the standard punch-card systems by several orders of magnitude.

Two of the SSA's cryptanalytic machines were immense. Costing a million dollars apiece, an extraordinary sum at the time, they were capable of performing operations which, if done by hand in the old Black Chamber, would have required over 200,000 people. By the end of 1945 another monster machine was nearing completion; it had power equivalent to 5 million cryptanalysts.

Tordella hoped the development by outside contractors of new, sophisticated cryptologic equipment would continue. But with no war to fight he found the contractors less willing to undertake the research. The rigorous security clearances, the oppressive physical security, and the limited usefulness of the equipment in the marketplace made many companies shy away from the field. Because of this, a group of former Navy officers, familiar with cryptography and signals intelligence, banded together to form Engineering Research Associates, which took on some of the Naval Security Group's most complex assignments.

At about the same time, a group of engineers and mathematicians at the University of Pennsylvania's Moore School of Electrical Engineering completed an electronic marvel named ENIAC (for "electronic numerical integrator computer"), and thus gave birth to the computer era. ENIAC was an ungainly giant whose body was a good deal larger than its brain. Its total storage capacity was only twenty numbers, yet its 18,000 electron tubes took up the better part of a room thirty feet by fifty. Nevertheless, the machine offered tremendous possibilities in speed.

The development of ENIAC led to a series of lectures on the theory of computers, presented at the Moore School and sponsored jointly by the Office of Naval Research and the Army's Ordnance Department. Among those attending the lectures, given between July 8 and August 31, 1946, was Lieutenant Commander James T. Pendergrass, a colleague of Tordella's in the Naval Security Group, whose assignment was to assess the potential of computers in cryptography and signals intelligence.

Pendergrass came away from the lectures excited. Computers appeared to offer the flexibility that RAMs lacked. Whereas many of the RAMs were designed to handle one particular problem, such as breaking one foreign cipher system, computers could handle a whole range of problems. "The author believes that the general purpose mathematical computer, now in the design stage, is a *general purpose cryptanalytic machine,"* wrote Pendergrass. "A computer could do everything that any analytic machine in Building 4 can do, and do a good percentage of these problems more rapidly."

Soon after Pendergrass submitted his favorable report, negotiations began between the Security Group and Engineering Research Associates for the design and construction of the signals intelligence community's first computer. But what to name it? A yeoman overheard Tordella and his colleagues discussing ideas and suggested "Atlas," after the mental giant in the comic strip "Barnaby." Atlas lived up to its namesake. When it was delivered to the Security Group in December 1950, Atlas had an impressive capacity of 16,384 words; it was the first parallel electronic computer in the United States with a drum memory. A second, identical computer was delivered to NSA in March 1953.

A key component of the machine was the vacuum tube. "We had the biggest collection of vacuum tube circuitry anyplace in the world there at one time," said former NSA research chief Howard Campaigne. "And we knew more about the life of vacuum tubes and the kinds of vacuum tubes that were used and how they should be maintained than just about anybody else." The vacuum tubes, he said, were as big as lightbulbs. "And then you get a lot of lightbulbs together and you have to have air-conditioning to cool them off. And so we were having fifteen tons of air-conditioning per machine."

Tordella was not the only one impressed by the Pendergrass report. About the same time that he received it, a copy also landed on the desk of Sam Snyder at Arlington Hall, headquarters of the Army Security Agency. "A copy of this report hit my desk in November 1946," Snyder later recalled, "and my reaction was explosive. I immediately ran into the office of Dr. Solomon Kullback, my boss, and said something like, 'We have to get a machine like this. Think what it could do for us!' " Kullback assigned Snyder to investigate the possibilities; Snyder spent the next year meeting with experts such as John von Neumann, at Princeton University's Institute for Advanced Study, and visiting institutions and private companies involved in computer research. "In the agency at that time," Snyder said, "money was no object; we could get whatever we wanted."

Eventually the ASA built its own codebreaking computer, which they named Abner. "We chose the name from Li'l Abner Yokum, the comic strip character who was a big brute, but not very smart," said Snyder, a longtime NSA computer expert, "because we believed that computers, which can be big and do brute-force operations, aren't very bright either; they can only follow simple instructions but can't think for themselves." Abner was originally given only fifteen simple programs, or "instructions" (later doubled to thirty). Nevertheless, when it was secretly completed in April 1952 it was the most sophisticated computer of its time. One could enter or extract information not only with the standard keypunched computer card but also with punched paper tape, magnetic tape, a parallel printer, a typewriter, or a console.

At NSA Tordella became chief of NSA-70, which was responsible for high-level cryptanalysis. He and the others who were pushing for ever-increasing computer power got a boost in 1954. James Killian, a Harvard professor exploring U.S. vulnerability to another surprise attack, concluded that 90 percent of war warnings would inevitably come from signals intelligence. But, he pointed out, since nuclear attack could come in a matter of minutes, it would be necessary to speed up the timeline on eavesdropping and codebreaking to beat the clock. "From then on," said one former NSAer, "the focus of the Sigint process was on speed."

Several years later, in July 1956, one of the most costly as well as far-reaching research programs ever undertaken by NSA was born. Its birthplace, however, was not a chalk-covered blackboard in Research and Engineering but a cocktail party. Over drinks, several high-level NSA equipment planners began discussing with Director Canine a number of the agency's perennial problems. At the top of the list was the battle between the codebreakers, always looking to attack ever-increasing volumes of data, and the engineers, constantly attempting to design and build bigger and faster computers to meet those needs. No matter how powerful the new equipment, the engineers never seemed to catch up. Tordella began pushing for research into second-generation computer technology.

At the time, NSA was using the PACE 10, the first analog desktop computer used at the agency. It was self-contained, to the extent that the logic was in the interior. The output was a printing device. The plug-in units had a wire associated with them and each panel was set up to do a different mathematical function. For a fairly complex mathematical problem, one would plug in all the appropriate panels and hand-wire them together. The computer's operations manual boasted that once it was set up, a problem could be completed in fifteen to sixty seconds.

On the drawing board was a second-generation computer known as Harvest. It was designed to be an estimated hundredfold improvement in speed over the best current computers, but a completion date was still several years away. Exasperated by this situation, Canine exploded: "Dammit, I want you fellows to get the jump on those guys [computer companies]! Build me a thousand-megacycle machine! I'll get the money!"

The head of NSA's REMP (Research, Engineering, Math and Physics) Branch at the time was Howard Campaigne, who had helped uncover the high-level Russian "Fish" cipher system as part of TICOM. "After the ideas of Harvest were started," he said, "we in research tried to think of other things; and one of the suggestions that came up was that we ought to have a big program. We ought to attack it like the Manhattan Project. We ought to really go after it. And so we dreamed up this 'Project Lightning.' "

It was a time, according to Campaigne, when anything was possible. "We were always surprised. We had an idea which looked expensive and we'd go ahead and they'd always be encouraging—'Do it,' " he said. "During most of my career, we always had encouragement from above to do things. If you can see something to do, do it. We made some mistakes, but by and large, most of the things we attacked were at least partially successful." Among the successes was developing the first solid-state computer by replacing vacuum tubes with transistors. Then the transistors were replaced by magnetic cores in a computer named Bogart.

But by the late 1960s, said Campaigne, things began to change. "In the late sixties we weren't getting encouragement. We were being told the budget had to be cut. We had to do without. . . . I used to argue that it [the research-and-development percentage of the overall NSA budget] should be more than five percent. It ought to be up in the seven and eight percent [range]. . . . During the Lightning program, my budget had been as high as nine million dollars a year. And when I left in '69, that was my last full fiscal year, our budget was three million. It had been cut to a third. . . . And we had been pretty much cut down in contract work. All the contracts were much smaller than they had been. So when I became eligible to retire, I figured, Well, gee, no point in staying around here to cut budgets. So I went out." By the late 1990s, the research-and-development portion of the overall NSA budget had dropped even further than during Campaigne's time, to less than 4 percent.

Part of NSA's early success, said Campaigne, was a willingness to take chances. "What the research-and-development people are doing is just trying things out," he said. "They're doing experiments. And so you'd expect them to have a lot of failures and a few successes. Historically, as a matter of fact, they had many more successes than they should have." Later on, as NSA grew, the experiments became less bold. "The reason is they're so damned cautious. See, they're more cautious than we were. At least, more cautious than we should have been. . . . I guess it's because the researchers like to look good. They don't like to have a failure, even though they're there just to experiment. They like to succeed. But, in fact, somebody who was administering a research-and-development activity ought to say, 'You know, you guys are too damn cautious. Get out there and do some experimenting.' "

Campaigne's optimistic push-ahead-at-all-costs philosophy derived from his belief that every cipher machine, no matter how difficult, could eventually be broken. "There is no such thing as an unbreakable cipher," he said, "and it irritates me when people talk about such things without realizing it's nonsense. . . . But people keep thinking there might be such a thing as an unbreakable cipher."

Secrecy was always NSA's best ally when attempting to get money from Congress. "All those committee chairs were very friendly in those days, and secrecy impressed them," said Arthur Levenson, in charge of Russian codebreaking at NSA and also a veteran of TICOM. "We got most of what we wanted, and a free hand in how we used it." Another former official said, of congressional oversight: "We didn't have any in those days." When General Canine was asked a question during a closed budget appropriations committee hearing, his favorite answer was, "Congressman, you don't really want to know the answer to that. You wouldn't be able to sleep at night." Said one former official, "And the members would look at each other and they were content with that."

Awarded $25 million by Congress, and okayed by Eisenhower, NSA's five-year race to develop "thousand-megacycle electronics" was on.

Lightning research began in June 1957. Contractors on the project, the largest government-supported computer research program in history up until then, included Sperry Rand, RCA, IBM, Philco, General Electric, MIT, the University of Kansas, and Ohio State. Though the project's primary goal was to increase circuitry capability by 1,000 percent, the end results went even further, extending the state of the art of computer science well beyond expectations. Research was conducted on cryogenic components, subminiaturization of components, and superfast switching devices, called tunnel diodes.

One of the most rewarding by-products of Lightning was the boost it gave the development of NSA's mammoth Harvest complex, which was designed to be NSA's largest general-purpose computer. For years computers were designed to attack specific codebreaking machines, such as the complex, Swiss-made Hagelin, which was used by many countries around the world. "We had in the past, before that time, we had built a special device for every problem," said Howard Campaigne. "And we'd gotten some very effective devices. But it always took a long time to build it. We had to formulate the problem and design the equipment, and get it constructed, and debugged, and all that had to take place when we ought to be operating."

But a superpowerful computer like Harvest, it was hoped, would be able to attack not only the Hagelin machine but also a variety of cipher machines and systems from multiple countries. "As the computers became more sophisticated," said Solomon Kullback, one of William F. Friedman's original pioneers, it became possible to "program one of these high-speed general purpose computers so that it could simulate the action of the Hagelin and use them for the Hagelin problem." However, the computer would not be limited to the Hagelin machine.

The original name for the computer was to be Plantation, but it was discovered that the White House had already taken the name to use as a codeword for emergency relocation. "The idea . . . was to have a modular computer set up in which you'd have things which resembled barns and stables and that the plantation [would be] a center or central thing," recalled Howard Campaigne. "So they called it Harvest as part of this plantation group of things."

Ironically, Solomon Kullback, who headed NSA's research-and-development office for a decade, never had any real enthusiasm for computers until they started proving their worth. "He didn't interfere with us," said Campaigne. "He didn't try to stop us or anything like that, but he just had no personal enthusiasm for it at all. And later on he was willing to spend plenty of money on them. And there were a lot of people like that."

In 1955 IBM began planning its most ambitious computer, the Stretch. So huge was Stretch that IBM designers believed the market contained only two possible customers: NSA and the Atomic Energy Commission. The AEC signed up for the computer primarily because of its advantages in high-speed multiplication. But NSA, looking for more flexibility as well as the manipulation of great volumes of data, sent the engineers back to the drawing board for a more customized version. In April 1958 a final design was approved, and in February 1962 the agency took delivery of its long-awaited Stretch, now modified and considerably faster. "IBM regarded it as a bad experience because the Stretch as a whole they lost money on," said Howard Campaigne. "And since then, they've been very careful about getting into big computers. They just let Seymour Cray build them."

Once in place as the heart—or, more appropriately, brain—of NSA's enormous Harvest complex, even Stretch began to look somewhat diminutive. Attached was a variety of unusual, complex accessories that more than doubled the computer's original size. One was the Stream Processing Unit, which was able to take over a number of the more tedious and time-consuming cryptanalytic functions. A key to codebreaking is the ability to quickly test encrypted text against every conceivable combination of letters in an alphabet. Because it may take millions of tries before the right combination of letters is found which breaks the cipher, speed is essential. "It was clear to us that one way of getting high capacity was to go fast," said Campaigne. An evaluation conducted by an NSA team concluded that Harvest was more powerful than the best commercially available computer by a factor of 50 to 200, depending on the particular application.

During World War II, the U.S. Navy's codebreaking machine, known as the *bombe*, was able to perform tests on 1,300 characters per second. In other words, it was able to try 1,300 separate keys in the German lock every second, looking for the right one to pop it open. With the new Stream Processing Unit, that speed was increased to some 3 *million* characters each second—a 230,000 percent increase. Thus, to pick the lock, NSA could now try 3 million new keys every second until the right one was found—truly lightning speed.

From one foreign cipher system alone, Harvest was able to process 7,075,315 intercepted messages of about 500 characters each, examining every possible combination, to see if they contained any 7,000 different target words or phrases on a watch list. The watch list might include such words as "submarine" or "battalion," or the names of key leaders. It was all done in just three hours and fifty minutes: an average of over 30,000 intercepted messages per minute.

Like misers hoarding every last penny in a rusted treasure chest, NSA computer scientists hoard microseconds. "You save enough microseconds and lo and behold you've got a tremendously fast machine," recalled Solomon Kullback.

Harvest not only increased NSA's speed, it also enlarged its memory, with a specially designed system that permitted the storage and retrieval of data at nearly 10 million characters per second.

Still another area advanced by Harvest was information retrieval, which used a unit known as Tractor. Tractor was capable of automatically locating desired information from a magnetic tape library of 480 reels, each capable of storing some 90 million characters. The machines would then mount, position, and thread the correct tape, and transfer the information at a then mind-boggling 1,128,000 characters per second—"a rate," said a secret NSA document at the time, "that is still beyond present computer tape technology." Whereas most magnetic tape contained 100 bits to the inch, NSA managed to pack 3,000 bits in the same space, and then whisk them past the reading heads at 235 inches per second.

Feeding streams of intercepts from the worldwide listening posts to the analysts at NSA is a special highly secure Sigint Communications System. First opened on the eve of Pearl Harbor, the system carried over 25 million words a day by the mid-1960s. Analysts using Harvest would then further process the encrypted traffic.

Another system bears critically important intelligence from an intercept operator at a listening post in a distant part of the world straight to the president of the United States at breakneck speed. The surprise launch by the Soviet Union of *Sputnik* in 1957 caused an earthquake within the intelligence community. At the time, it took an average of 8 hours and 35 minutes for a message containing critical intelligence to reach the White House. President Eisenhower demanded that the time be reduced to minutes. At a National Security Council meeting on August 27, 1958, attended by Eisenhower, CIA director Allen Dulles agreed that "there was little purpose in developing critical intelligence overseas unless we had the communications means to insure its rapid transmission to Washington."

A month later, in a meeting in the Oval Office with Eisenhower, Tordella proposed a system known as CRITICOMM. After Tordella outlined the costs and benefits, Eisenhower turned to the deputy secretary of defense and said, "Do it." Within six months NSA was able to reduce transmission time from more than 8 hours to 52 minutes. In another six months the agency was able to have a CRITIC, or critical intelligence message, on Eisenhower's desk within a brief thirteen minutes, regardless of where it had originated. Eventually the time shrunk to between three and five minutes.

Finally, a system codenamed Rye provided remote access to Harvest, thus permitting analysts throughout NSA to access the main computer via several dozen distant terminals. "RYE has made it possible for the Agency to locate many more potentially exploitable cryptographic systems and 'bust' situations," said one secret report at the time. "Many messages that would have taken hours or days to read by hand methods, if indeed the process were feasible at all, can now be 'set' and machine decrypted in a matter of minutes. . . . Decrypting a large batch of messages in a solved system [is] also being routinely handled by this system."

Few could have foreseen Harvest's bright future when the machine was first built. Because the complexity of the system baffled even many of the best analysts, it was originally considered a white elephant. During employee tours, the huge, boxy machine was pointed to and mocked. "It's beautiful, but it doesn't work," officials would scoff. But once the machine was fully understood, Harvest became so successful that it was used continuously for fourteen years. The agency finally switched to a more advanced system only in 1976.

As computers more and more became essential in both codemaking and codebreaking, worries developed over the progress the Soviet Union was making in the field, especially given its early lead in space exploration. In 1959 a top secret panel was created to investigate where the United States stood in its computer race with Russia. The results were encouraging. By then the U.S. government had about 3,000 computers, of which about 300 were high-performance machines valued at more than $1 million each. Russia, however, had fewer than 400 computers, of which only about 50 were large machines.

Although for a time both countries attained comparable speed—the Soviet M-20 was about as fast as the IBM 709—the United States had left Russian computer scientists in the dust with the development of the transistor. Nevertheless, the secret panel's report advised against overconfidence. "The Soviet Union could achieve a computer production capability equivalent to that of the U.S. in 2–3 years, if they place the highest possible priority on the effort." But, the report added, "There is no evidence that they intend to establish such a priority." Nor, the report said, was the Soviet Union engaged in anything equivalent to Project Lightning.

Following Harvest, NSA's brain, like that of a human, was divided into right and left hemispheres, codenamed Carillon and Lodestone. Carillon was at one time made up of IBM 360s, and later of four enormous IBM 3033s linked together and attached to three IBM 22,000-line-per-minute page printers.

Even more powerful, however, was Lodestone. Dominating the center of a yellow-walled, gold-carpeted hall of computers, front-end interfaces, and mass storage units, was a decorative, 4½-foot-wide, 6½-foot-high semicircle of narrow gold and deep green panels surrounded by a black vinyl-upholstered bench-type seat. It appeared to be an ideal resting place for lunch or a mid-morning coffee break. It was, however, the fastest, most powerful, and most expensive computer of its time.

Built by Cray Research at its plant in Chippewa Falls, Wisconsin, a town also known for its Leinenkugel's beer and Chippewa Springs water, the $15 million CRAY-1 may be the ultimate testimony to the old proposition that looks are deceiving. Housed within what one wag once called "the world's most expensive love seat" were more than 200,000 integrated circuits, each the size of a thumbnail, 3,400 printed circuit boards, and 60 miles of wire. So compact was the five-ton, seventy-square-foot unit that enough heat was generated per cubic inch to reduce the machine to a molten mass in seconds had it not been for a unique Freon cooling system using vertical aluminum-and-stainless-steel cooling bars that lined the wall of the computer chassis.

The supercomputer was the brainchild of Seymour Cray, a shy, enigmatic engineer who rarely allowed interviews or pictures but was one of the most influential figures in computer science. The founder of Cray Research, Inc., Cray "is to supercomputers what Edison was to light bulbs," said *Time* in 1988, "or Bell to the telephone." When not in his laboratories, Cray could likely be found deep in the earth beneath his Wisconsin home, slowly tunneling toward the nearby woods. Eight feet high and four feet wide, the tunnel was lined with four-by-four cedar boards. When a tree once crashed through the roof of the tunnel, Cray turned the hole into a lookout with the installation of a periscope.

To Cray, the tunnel was both inspiration and recreation. "I work when I'm at home," he once told a visiting scientist. "I work for three hours and then I get stumped, and I'm not making progress. So I quit, and I go to work in the tunnel. It takes me an hour or so to dig four inches and put in the four-by-fours." Half kidding, Cray continued: "Now, as you can see, I'm up in the Wisconsin woods, and there are elves in the woods. So when they see me leave, they come into my office and solve all the problems I'm having. Then I go back up and work some more." According to John Rollwagen, then chairman of Cray Research, "The real work happens when Seymour is in the tunnel."

Cray began his career by building codebreaking machines in the 1950s with Engineering Research Associates, then headed by future NSA research chief and deputy director Howard Engstrom. Cray's dream was to build a number cruncher capable of 150 to 200 million calculations per second. It would have between 20 and 100 times the capacity of then current general-purpose computers—the equivalent of half a dozen IBM 370/195s.

In the spring of 1976 the first CRAY-1 rolled out of the firm's production plant in Chippewa Falls and directly into the basement of NSA. A second was quietly delivered to NSA's secret think tank, the Communications Research Division of the Institute for Defense Analysis at Princeton University.

The CRAY had a random access semiconductor memory capable of transferring up to 320 million words per second, or the equivalent of about 2,500 300-page books; NSA could not have been disappointed. And when it was hooked up to the computer's specialized input-output subsystem, the machine could accommodate up to forty-eight disk storage units, which could hold a total of almost 30 billion words, each no farther away than 80 millionths of a second.

In a field where time is measured in nanoseconds—billionths of a second—seven years is an eternity. Thus it was with tremendous excitement that in June 1983 the agency made space in its basement for a new arrival from Chippewa Falls, the CRAY X-MP. Serial number 102 stamped on its side, the machine was the first X-MP to be delivered to a customer; NSA thus had the most powerful computer in the world at the time. The six-ton brain, which contained forty-five miles of wiring and required a fifty-ton refrigeration unit to keep it cool, was revolutionary. Rather than achieving its gains in speed simply by using a faster processor, the X-MP used two processors, working in parallel. Two separate jobs could be run at the same time, or one job could run on both processors. This capability made the X-MP five times faster than even the most advanced CRAY-1, the CRAY-1S/1000.

To NSA, parallel processing was the wave of the future. Among the projects the agency was closely involved with was the Butterfly processor, which linked 148 microprocessors. Developed by the Defense Advanced Research Projects Agency's (DARPA's) Strategic Computing Program, Butterfly could have been scaled up to combine 256 or 512 or even 1,000 linked processors. Future testing included plans to link about 1 million processors.

The X-MP arrived just in time. That same year NSA secretly put into operation an enormous worldwide computer network codenamed Platform. The system tied together, into a single cyber-web, listening posts belonging to NSA, GCHQ, and other Sigint agencies around the world, with NSA as the central brain.

Two years later, in 1985, NSA's basement complex became even more crowded with the long-awaited arrival of the CRAY-2. With its bright red Naugahyde base and transparent, blue-tinted towers of bubbling liquid coolant, Seymour Cray's latest masterpiece looked more like bordello furniture than a super number cruncher in a codebreaking factory. Nicknamed Bubbles, the $17.6 million computer was almost human, with cool, bubbling Fluorinert, also used as an artificial blood plasma, running through its system. The liquid was necessary to keep the enormous heat generated by electrons flowing through the tightly packed circuit boards from causing a meltdown.

The unit of speed used in assessing supercomputers is the "flop," "floating point operations per second." Whereas it may take the average person several minutes to calculate with a pencil the correct answer to a single multiplication problem, such as 0.0572 x 8762639.8765, supercomputers are measured by how many times per second they can solve such problems. If it takes one second to come up with the answer, including where to place the "floating" decimal point, then the computer is said to operate at one flop per second. Bubbles, on the other hand, was able to perform at an astonishing 1.2 gigaflops, or 1.2 billion mathematical calculations a second. This made it up to twelve times faster than its predecessor and 40,000 to 50,000 times faster than a personal computer of that time.

By 1988 workers were laying wires and arranging power for still another new product from the backwoods of Wisconsin, the CRAY Y-MP. So dense were the chips on the new machine that engineers were now able to squeeze eight processors into a space originally designed for only one. Working together, and under ideal conditions, the processors were capable of performing between 2 billion and 4 billion operations a second.

In the mid to late 1980s, the pace of supercomputer development was so fast that NSA barely had enough time to boot up each new megamachine before a newer one was wheeled into its basement "flop house."

The race to build the fastest supercomputer began to resemble a mainframe Grand Prix. Sleek, shiny, and ever more powerful new machines were continuously zooming to the starting line while engineers worked on ever more powerful and speedy designs. Nobody wanted to be left in the dust. In September 1987, Steve Chen, the Chinese-born computer superstar who lead the Cray Research design team on the X-MP and Y-MP projects, left Cray after his machines became too expensive and risky. He was quickly hired by IBM. "Five years from now," boasted an IBM executive, "we should be at 100 billion gigaflops. A problem that takes three months to do now, we want to do in a day."

Off in the shadows, the Sandia National Laboratory, in Albuquerque, was tweaking a chunky little blue box. Three feet on a side and known as the Ncube, or hypercube, the computer was "massively" parallel, with 1,024 processors, each as powerful as a traditional minicomputer. In a test, Sandia asked the computer to calculate the stresses inside a building beam supported only at one end. A powerful minicomputer working twenty-four hours a day would have taken twenty years to arrive at an answer, but the lightning-fast Ncube accomplished it in a week.

At ETA, a subsidiary of Control Data Corporation, a dark, bubble-topped box known as the ETA 10 was unveiled. An eight-processor powerhouse, it used computer chips that were smaller and denser than those used by Cray Research. Liquid nitrogen carried away the excess heat. And by using only one circuit board, the engineers were able to reduce the space that electrons have to travel during calculations. The end result was a $30 million black box designed to operate at a peak rate of 10 billion calculations per second, 30 times faster than previous supercomputers.

Not to be outdone, Los Alamos National Laboratories, by stringing together an array of supercomputers and associated networks, was able to perform more computing work in a twenty-four-hour period than had been done by all of humanity before the year 1962. And that estimate was considered conservative by other researchers, who suggested that a date in the late 1970s might be more accurate.

The speed of electrons, however, was not NSA's most immediate problem; the agency was also worried about the speed of the Japanese. Japan was the only other nation aggressively pursuing supercomputer development. In the summer of 1988, a gathering of leading computer science experts, among them NSA's director of supercomputer research, met to assess Japan's progress in supercomputers. If they felt confident when they walked into the meeting, they were more than a little nervous when they left. Starting only six years earlier, Japan had already matched or surpassed the United States in a field the United States invented and had been advancing for twenty years.

The main problem for the American supercomputer industry was dependence on Japanese computer companies—their arch-competitors in a cutthroat business—for critical parts, such as computer chips, for their machines. This was a result of the gradual abandonment of semiconductor manufacturing in the United States during the mid to late 1980s. In 1986, for example, NSA was virtually dependent on a Japanese company, Kyocera, for critical components that went into 171 of its 196 different computer chips, according to the minutes of a Department of Defense study group. When, without warning, Kyocera stopped making a component known as a ceramic package, used in a key chip, NSA began to shudder.

In a worst-case scenario, Japanese computer manufacturers could slow down or cut off the supply of essential components to their American supercomputer competitors—and NSA. This fear led the panel to conclude that within a few years, "U.S. firms would be most fortunate if they found themselves only a generation or so behind."

As a result of such worries, NSA, with the help of National Semiconductor, built its own $85 million microelectronics production and laboratory plant, known as the Special Processing Laboratory. Located in Crypto City, the ultra-modern, windowless, 60,000-square-foot building first began producing chips in 1991. Today it employs several hundred people. The building contains 20,000 square feet of "class 10" clean rooms—rooms whose air is 10,000 times cleaner than normal air. The water must also be ultra-pure because the particles in the water can destroy a transistor.

Building its own plant also solved another problem for NSA: the need for supersecrecy in producing highly customized parts for use in the agency's unique codebreaking machines. These components, "applications specific integrated circuits" (ASICs), are often the "brain" of a codebreaking system, thus making outside procurement "a nightmare," said one NSAer. With the ability to squeeze 1 million or more transistors on a single piece of silicon, designers can now build entire algorithms on a chip—a complete crypto system on a piece of material many times smaller than a dime. For such a chip to fall into the wrong hands would be disastrous.

So NSA added another new feature: a secret self-destruct mechanism. Developed by Lawrence Livermore and Sandia National Laboratories, NSA's chips are shielded by special self-destructing coatings. "If a hostile agent tries to take off the lid," said one knowledgeable source, "the coating literally rips out the top [circuit] layer."

Six months after the 1988 computer science panel meeting, fear over Japan's rapid push into the supercomputer industry once again surfaced. On December 6, 1988, Japan's Fujitsu—a key supplier of critical chips to Cray—announced a major new advance: a blisteringly fast computer with a theoretical top speed of 4 billion operations per second. This equaled and perhaps beat Cray's top-of-the-line machine, the Y-MP, which had been on the market for less than a year. The problem for NSA was that the Japanese company could easily sell the superfast computer to other nations, which might then use it to develop encryption systems far too fast for NSA's codebreaking computers to conquer.

But while Japanese companies were catching up and maybe even passing their American competitors in speed, the U.S. supercomputer industry was far ahead in both software development and the use of parallel processing. As fast as the Fujitsu computer was, it had only two processors. Cray and ETA had both developed machines with eight processors—eight brains, in a sense—which could simultaneously attack separate parts of a problem.

To Seymour Cray, sixteen brains were better than eight, and for several years he had been trying to prove it by building a sixteen-processor CRAY-3. It was an expensive and time-consuming endeavor—too much so, it turned out, for Cray Research, the company he had founded but no longer owned. In May 1989, the two split. Seymour Cray took 200 employees and $100 million and moved to Colorado Springs to found Cray Computer, Inc., as a wholly owned subsidiary of Cray Research. Eventually, it was planned, Cray Computer would become independent.

Like a race-car driver with his foot stuck to the accelerator, Cray continued to push for more and more speed; he hoped to break sixteen billion operations a second. The secret would be to make the hundreds of thousands of chips that would constitute the soul of the new computer not out of conventional silicon but out of a radical new material: gallium arsenide. Although it was more difficult and costly to work with, electrons could travel up to ten times as fast through the new compound as through silicon.

But as "the Hermit of Chippewa Falls," as Cray was affectionately known, quietly pushed ahead in his new laboratory in Colorado Springs, the world around him began shifting and turning. The Cold War had ended and weapons designers were no longer shopping for supercomputers. The fat Reagan years of Star Wars were giving way to the Clinton era of cutbacks and deficit reduction. And industry was turning away from the diamond-encrusted CRAYs, made of a small number of superpowerful processors, and toward less pricey massively parallel computers made up of thousands of inexpensive microprocessors. The enormously expensive, hand-built Formula One racers were being forced off the track by cheap stock cars packed with store-bought superchargers and sixteen-barrel carburetors.

At ETA Systems, which had pushed the supercomputer speed envelope with its ETA 10, 800 employees showed up for work on a spring Monday in 1989 to find the doors locked shut. The company had developed a super debt of $400 million.

Four years later, Steve Chen folded up his new company, Supercomputer Systems, when IBM finally cut off funding for his SS-1. Partly funded by NSA, Chen had spent half a decade attempting to build a computer a hundred times faster than anything on earth. But in the end, the innovations were overtaken by excessive costs and endless missed deadlines. A few months after the company's doors closed, one of its former engineers driving past a farm spotted a strange but familiar column of metal. A closer look confirmed his worst fears: it was the outer frame for the SS-1, and it had been sold for scrap.

In 1991, Thinking Machines Corporation delivered to NSA its first massively parallel computer—the Connection Machine CM-5, which the agency named Frostberg. Used until 1997, the futuristic black cube with long panels of blinking red lights looked like something left over from a *Star Wars* set. Just two years after the $25 million machine was installed, NSA doubled its size by adding 256 additional processor units. This allowed Frostberg to take a job and break it into 512 pieces and work on each piece simultaneously, at 65.5 billion operations a second. Equally impressive was the Frostberg's memory, capable of storing up to 500 billion words.

By the time the CRAY-3 at last made its debut in 1993—clocking in at roughly 4 billion operations a second—there were no takers. Nearly out of money, the company spent a year looking for customers and finally landed a deal with its old partner, NSA. In August of 1994, the agency awarded Cray $4.2 million to build a highly specialized version of the CRAY-3 for signal processing and pattern recognition—in other words, eavesdropping and codebreaking. Named the CRAY-3/Super Scalable System, the machine would become the brain of what has been dubbed "the world's ultimate spying machine." It would link two supercomputer processors with a massively parallel array of chips containing more than half a million inexpensive processors designed by NSA's Supercomputer Research Center.

But while hoping for Cray to succeed, NSA scientists were also working in-house on new ideas. One was a processor called Splash 2, which, when attached to a general-purpose computing platform, was able to accelerate the machine's performance to super-Cray levels at only a fraction of the Cray cost.

As Seymour Cray struggled to complete his CRAY-3, he was also in a race with his old parent company, Cray Research, which was building a successor to its Y-MP called the C-90. The company was also near completion on a powerhouse known as the T-90, which would operate at up to 60 billion operations per second. Meanwhile, Seymour Cray hoped to leapfrog his competitors once again with his CRAY-4, due out in 1996.

By the fall of 1994, work on the CRAY-4 was going surprisingly well. Cray Computer in Colorado Springs was predicting a completion date in early 1995 with a machine with twice the power of the CRAY-3 at one-fifth the cost. There was even talk of a CRAY-5 and CRAY-6 before the planned retirement of Seymour Cray. Which was why the yellow tape came as such a shock. When employees came to work on the morning of March 24, 1995, they were first confused to see the yellow police tape sealing the doors. But when they saw the white flag that had been run up the flagpole, they did not need a supercomputer to conclude that the end had finally arrived. The man with the unlimited ideas that reached to the stars had tumbled to the bottom of his finite bank account.

Ever optimistic, Seymour Cray pulled together a few of his most loyal followers, scraped together some money from their own bank accounts, and formed SRC (Seymour Roger Cray) Computers. Cray felt almost liberated at this chance to "start from a clean sheet of paper." It was also, he believed, a chance to finally break the speed barrier by building the first teraflop supercomputer, capable of a trillion mathematical operations a second—12,000 times more than his CRAY-1.

But the enemy had landed. In the spring of 1996, even the U.S. government had turned its back on all the Cray companies and awarded a $35 million contract to the Japanese computer giant NEC for its 128-processor SX-4 supercomputer. The SX-4 would go to the National Center for Atmospheric Research. The agency was worried because meteorological centers in Australia, Canada, England, and elsewhere were installing systems that by January 1998 would be capable of between 20 and 80 billion operations a second. And Cray Research, the agency concluded, was just not producing computers fast enough. "Simply put," said William Buzbee, head of the weather center, "Cray Research lost this procurement because their offer had unacceptable technical risk."

Others, too, knew that despite the never-say-die bravado and the endless promises of illions of flops, the luster was at last disappearing from Cray's blinding star. "The rules changed when it became clear that Cray Computer Corp. wasn't going to make it," said John Mashey, director of systems technology at Silicon Graphics. "It's like watching your favorite quarterback, who won the Super Bowl many times. But it's not 1976 anymore—his knees are gone and those three-hundred-pound defensive tackles are fierce. While he keeps getting up, it's agonizing to watch and you really wish he could have quit on a high."

A few months later, while returning from a brief trip to a software store, Cray was seriously injured when his black Grand Cherokee was struck by another car and rolled over three times. Two weeks later, on October 5, 1996, the shy maverick who hand-built the fastest machines on earth, with the meticulous care and fine craftsmanship of a Swiss watchmaker, died, never having regained consciousness. His ashes were scattered among the cragged peaks and somber valleys of the Colorado mountains. They had served as his inspiration, and as silent comforters, during his last years. "In the days before PCs brought megaflops to the masses," said one computer expert, "Cray was the computer industry's closest equivalent to a rock star."

Sadly, only months before Cray's death, the daring company he had given birth to in Chippewa Falls, Wisconsin, decades earlier, also died. Following the worst financial year of its life, in which it was forced to cut nearly a quarter of its employees, and facing an uncertain future, Cray Research called it quits. It was acquired by Silicon Graphics, Incorporated—later known simply as SGI—a Mountain View, California, manufacturer of high-performance workstations, the sort of machines that became Cray's greatest competitor. "Cray represents the last of the 1980s pure plays in the supercomputer market," one market analyst said wistfully. "There are no other major players left standing from the supercomputer battles of the 1980s and 1990s."

In fact, there was one. The shakeout and the death of Seymour Cray left a single independent to fight the army of "killer micros," the massively parallel microprocessors that turned the budget-draining, high-performance supercomputer into an endangered species. The large, rumpled man with the Don Quixote dream was Burton Smith, whose company, Tera Computer, stunned many in the field by building a machine that in 1997 set a world speed record for sorting integers. Burton's idea was to increase speed by decreasing the waiting time it took for processors to be sent new data on which to work. This, Burton believed, would overcome the Achilles' heel of powerful computing—the gap between a computer's short-term theoretical "peak" speed and its long-term "sustained" speed.

Smith no doubt had his eye on NSA as a key future customer for his machines, which would cost as much as $40 million. He spent three years working for NSA's Supercomputer Research Center before leaving in 1988 to found Tera. Much of his early money, in fact, came from NSA's partner, DARPA.

Encouraged by Smith's research, a "senior intelligence official" approached Sid Karin, the director of the San Diego Supercomputer Center, and asked him to help support Tera. "We don't have a lot of innovative architects like Burton Smith and Seymour Cray," the intelligence official told Karlin, "and they need to be nurtured and supported." So, in 1998, Smith installed his first system in the San Diego center.

Nevertheless, Smith still has his skeptics. One well-known computer designer fondly refers to the Tera system as "Burton's folly." And even Smith acknowledges the long odds: "Most people think we're out of our mind." Still, noted one observer, "Burton Smith is the last man standing."

As the supercomputer business began crashing, worries increased at NSA. For decades the agency had quietly underwritten a large portion of the industry; the massive number crunchers were the engines that powered its codebreaking machines. Now agency officials watched SGI, following its takeover of Cray, like spectators at a slow-motion automobile accident. Within a year and a half of the acquisition the company was in turmoil. SGI posted a loss of over $50 million, a major layoff was announced, and the longtime chief executive officer resigned. Noting that only three years earlier the company had produced the graphics that made the motion picture *Jurassic Park* possible, one reporter quipped, "The question was whether the company was in danger of going the way of the dinosaur."

By 1999, SGI looked like a boxer struggling to rise before the final count. Its stock had plunged more than 20 percent, another chief executive officer had called it quits, and the firm said it would cut as many as 3,000 jobs and spin off its Cray supercomputer division. NSA was worried: it had contracted with the company to build its newest supercomputer, the CRAY SV2.* The decision was made to open the drawer of the cash register. "The United States is committed to maintaining and building on its long-held position as the global leader in supercomputing," said NSA's chief scientist, George Cotter. "These powerful computers are absolutely essential to U.S. national security interests. To that end, the U.S. government is committing significant support to SGI's CRAY SV2 program."

Cotter also noted the critical need for NSA to continue similar joint supercomputer projects. "The government support reflects a continuing need for government-industry cooperative development of critical technologies for high-end computing," he said. "The SV2 will include technology jointly developed with the U.S. government. This will considerably extend the combination of custom-designed high-end processors with the high-speed memory access that current Cray supercomputers offer." The new system was expected to dramatically extend the capability of NSA's supercomputers with exceptional memory bandwidth, interconnections, and vector-processing capabilities. Its peak speed was estimated to be in the tens of teraflops, faster than any supercomputer in existence.

In 2000 the supercomputer business came full circle. Like two

*Despite the capabilities of massively parallel computers, supercomputers are still useful for attacking specific codebreaking problems.

broke gamblers at a racetrack putting their change together for one last bet, Burton Smith's Tera Computer acquired Seymour Cray's former Cray Research from SGI. Thus was reborn Cray, Inc., once again an independent company. It was good news for NSA. One report said the agency was involved in the deal "because it wants at least one U.S. company to build state-of-the-art supercomputers with capabilities beyond the needs of most business customers." Work would continue on NSA's SV2, with delivery scheduled for 2002.

At the same time, Cray began work on a new Department of Defense contract, one to upgrade a CRAY T3E-1200 supercomputer. With the addition of 816 processors to its existing 272 processors, the new machine will be the largest Cray system ever built, with 1,088 processors and a record speed of 1.3 teraflops—1.3 trillion calculations per second. Four years after Seymour Cray died, a machine bearing his name would at last break the tera barrier.

But despite the encouraging signs, the supercomputer shakeout had convinced many at NSA of the need to move away from the insecurity of the outside world and to return to the black computer laboratories of Crypto City.

The massive brain transplant began in February 1997, as the first supercomputer began its slow trip from the basement of OPS 1. Its destination was the top floor of the Tordella Supercomputer Facility, hidden away in a wooded corner of Crypto City. More than a year later, the final supercomputer was carefully nudged into place and connected by a spinal cord of secure fiber optic nerves to the main body of the agency, a mile away. Once the operation was completed, NSA possessed the most powerful electronic brain on earth.

Surrounded by thick woods and protected by guard posts, double fences, and concrete barriers, the Tordella Supercomputer Facility, is located on Crypto City's Ream Road, a street named after NSA's fourth deputy director. The nearly windowless outside walls of the 183,000-square-foot facility are decorated with attractive, light-colored enameled metal panels. The life-support equipment is housed on the first floor—an 8,000-ton chilled water plant, mechanical and electrical support facilities, and 29-megavolt-amperes of electrical power, enough to supply half of Annapolis.

The top floor's five rooms contain, among other things, the Computer Operations Command Center and approximately 150,000 magnetic tapes moved there from storage in "silo-farms" back in the main part of Crypto City. Supercomputers, such as the CRAY Y-MP EL and the Silicon Graphics Power Challenge, occupy the rest of the floor. Also installed in 1999 was the new IBM RS/6000 SP. This is a faster version of the system that powered the company's supercomputer "Deep Blue," which won a grueling six-game chess match against virtuoso Garry Kasparov in 1997. The extra power and speed come from IBM's new Power3 microprocessor, which is capable of crunching through 2 billion instructions per second—more than double the power of the Power2 Super Chip. The computer is the centerpiece for a system IBM called Deep Computing. One of its primary uses is "data mining," searching through enormous quantities of data, such as intercepted communications or complex cipher systems, and coming up with the answer. The RS/6000 SP, said IBM executive David Turek, is "supercomputing at your fingertips."

Moving the tremendous amounts of information into and out of the supercomputers, like the ultimate jukebox, is the massive dodecagonal Automated Cartridge System. As big as a small room, and weighing more than four tons, this high-speed storage device can hold 6,000 cartridges containing a total of 300 terabytes of information—the equivalent of more than 150 billion pages of text. According to NSA, this is the equivalent of one and a half million years of the *Wall Street Journal;* it is also enough pieces of paper to circle the globe 3,000 times, or to fill a wall of books stacked eleven deep and running from New York City to Los Angeles.

The robotic arm has two cameras and a "hand"; the cameras find the bar code of the requested cartridge, and the hand moves it to the retrieval area, where the needed cartridge can be extracted. The arm can move cartridges in and out of the computers at the rate of 450 an hour.

Such a system is necessary when one considers NSA's information storage capabilities. To store the massive amounts of data flowing in from its worldwide listening posts, NSA a few years ago turned to E-Systems, long a key contractor on secret projects for the agency. The solution was to link several computers the size of telephone booths. When completed the system was capable of storing 5 trillion pages of text—a stack of paper 150 miles high. Included was a new retrieval system that permitted the access of any piece of information almost instantly.

As the supercomputer industry began crumbling around it, NSA turned inward, creating a top secret facility for developing its own classified computers. Known as the Supercomputer Research Center (SRC), it was built in 1984 in order to leapfrog over the rest of the world in computer power, as Project Lightning had thirty years earlier. Only this time, the work would be done in total secrecy. According to Lieutenant General Lincoln D. Faurer, the NSA's director at the time, a principal goal of the SRC was to build a new generation of computers that would be 10,000 times faster than the current generation.

Over the years millions of dollars would go into research on subjects such as specialized parallel processing algorithms, which would give computers the superspeed needed to break increasingly powerful foreign encryption systems. At the same time, SRC would develop ways to push American cryptographic systems beyond the reach of hostile codebreakers. Little, if any, of the research done by the SRC would ever see the light of day outside of Crypto City, so NSA would be far ahead in the race for the fastest and most powerful computers on earth.

Constructed at a cost of $12 million on a twenty-acre site at the University of Maryland's Science and Technology Center in Bowie, the SRC is actually operated by the Communications Research Division (CRD), part of the Institute for Defense Analysis. For more than four decades the CRD has run NSA's own highly secret think tank. Originally known as the NSA Research Institute, it was first approved by President Eisenhower in 1958. Its purpose was to carry out long-range, theoretical, and advanced research in mathematical and statistical problems related to NSA's codebreaking and eavesdropping missions. The institute also conducted a special summer program that brought together members of the academic community and introduced them to members of the cryptologic community.

At one point, in 1965, the institute developed a unique piece of codebreaking machinery that proved enormously successful. "That one piece of equipment," said a secret 1965 NSA report, "by itself, has been judged to be well worth the total cost of the Institute thus far."

Among the early directors of the institute was Dr. J. Barkley Rosser, a professor of mathematics at the University of Wisconsin, noted for his work in symbolic logic and number theory. Dr. A. Adrian Albert, dean of the division of physical sciences at the University of Chicago and an expert in linear algebra and number theory, followed him in 1961.

Originally, the NSA Research Insitute was located behind a high wall on the campus of Princeton University. But as a result of the antiwar protests of the 1960s, NSA, fearing for the continued secrecy and security of the institute, moved it to a boxy, three-story brick building virtually hidden in an isolated wooded area off campus. Windowless except for the third floor, the mysterious building has no signs to indicate the name or nature of the occupant. Eventually, to further hide its connection to NSA, the Research Institute's name was changed to the Communications and Computing Center. Specializing in such esoteric codebreaking and eavesdropping disciplines as cryptomathematics, cryptocomputing, speech research, and special signals processing techniques, the IDA-C3I, as it is sometimes known, received $34 million in funding in 1994 and employed a technical staff of 149.

In addition to the Supercomputer Research Center, NSA also has a Laboratory for Physical Sciences (LPS), which is part of the agency's Directorate of Technology. Like the NSA Research Institute, LPS was born in the 1950s, when the NSA's Scientific Advisory Board recommended that the agency establish a "window on the world of academia and academic research in the physical sciences." As a result, the agency collaborated with the University of Maryland to create the LPS, with quarters built adjacent to the school's College Park campus.

In 1992 the LPS moved into a new, nondescript 63,500-square-foot building on Greenmead Drive in College Park. Leased from the university for $480,000 a year, the facility, near a Moose lodge, draws little attention and does not appear in the campus telephone directory. "We don't know what they do there," said the administrator of the veterinary center next door.

The lab was built at a cost of $10.9 million; its ultra-advanced technology is designed to fast-forward NSA's ability to eavesdrop. Using magnetic microscopy, scientists are able to study the minute tracks on magnetic tape and greatly increase data density, thus enabling intercept operators to pack ever more conversations into their recorders. Increasing computer speed is also critical. To achieve this acceleration, the LPS contains a state-of-the-art molecular beam epitaxy (MBE) facility to develop miniature lasers, optical amplifiers, and other components made out of gallium arsenide.

But speed equals heat. Thus the LPS is also pushing the limits on such technologies as the development of synthetic diamonds, which are many times more efficient for heat conduction than copper and far less expensive than real diamonds. For example, an integrated circuit mounted on ordinary ceramic will turn a very warm 87 degrees centigrade when its surroundings are at room temperature. One mounted on synthetic diamonds, however, will reach only 54 degrees centigrade, allowing NSA's codebreaking machines to be relatively cool as well as fast.

Speed not only equals heat, it also equals massive demand for data storage. Increasing use of space-eating multimedia files compounds the problem, as does the need to make the information available to an ever larger group of customers. One solution was Project Oceanarium, which for the first time automated the storage of NSA's masses of multimedia Sigint reports.

At the same time, Oceanarium modernized the way in which reports were retrieved and distributed. Where once each spy agency jealously guarded its individual intelligence files behind thick fortresses, today the buzz phrase is "sharable databases." Through Oceanarium, NSA's dark secrets can now be retrieved not only over its own internal intranet, Webworld, but throughout the intelligence community via highly classified programs such as Intelink.

Because the breadth and depth of NSA's data storage sea is finite, scientists are turning to newer ways to narrow the rivers of information emptying into it. Among the most promising are microscopic magnets, only one molecule in size. Scientists at Xerox believe that such a magnet, made of a special combination of manganese, oxygen, carbon, and hydrogen, may be able to pack data thousands or even millions of times more densely than today's systems of memory storage. Using these molecule-sized magnets, experts believe, it may someday be possible to store hundreds of gigabytes of data—millions of typed pages—on an area no larger than the head of a pin.

By 2001, NSA's tape and disk storage capacity approached a density of ten gigabytes per square inch—the equivalent of more than half a million typed, double-spaced pages. But the closer data are packed, the harder they are to erase and the more chance that telltale secrets will remain behind on reused media. Therefore, another key area of research at NSA's LPS is exploring the microscopic properties of data storage and erasure to find more effective ways to rid used tapes and hard drives of all their old secrets. According to computer expert Simson Garfinkel, tiny pieces of a hard drive can still contain sizable amounts of information. For instance, a 1/16-inch-square piece of a six-gigabyte hard drive can hold 750,000 bytes—enough to fill a 300-page book. "A spy could remove a hard disk, grind it up, and smuggle out the data in little pieces like pocket lint," said Garfinkel. To solve the problem, NSA developed a drive-controlled disk sanitization device, which attaches to the head disk assembly and can completely eradicate the sensitive information used on disks and drives.

Inside NSA's Supercomputer Research Center, the secret race for the fastest computer seems almost unworldly. In 1994 and 1995 NSA scientists participated in a series of meetings devoted to exploring the feasibility of a great leap forward in computer technology. The goal was to advance from billions, past trillions, to more than a quadrillion operations a second—pentaflop speed—within two decades.

Among the ideas developed by NSA for achieving speeds of over a quadrillion (10^{15}) mathematical operations a second was the placement of processors in the middle of memory chips. Processor-in-memory chips, or PIMs, have the advantage of reducing the time it normally takes for electronic signals to travel from the processors to the separate memory chips. These PIM chips are now among the products manufactured by the agency's Special Processing Lab.

By 2001, the SRC had long since broken the teraflop barrier and was approaching petaflop speeds—at which point time is measured in femtoseconds, the shortest events known to science. With such extraordinary speed, a machine would be capable of pounding a stream of intercepted, enciphered text with a quadrillion—a million billion—possible solutions in the time it takes to wink. Original estimates by scientists were that the outside world would reach that point sometime around 2010, but IBM intends to cut the wait in half with a mega-supercomputer dubbed Blue Gene.

Over five years, between 2000 and 2005, the company plans to build the fastest computer on earth—500 times faster than anything currently in existence. "It will suck down every spare watt of electricity and throw off so much heat that a gas turbine the size of a jet engine is required to cool it off," said one report. According to the company, the computer would be about forty times more powerful than the aggregate power of the forty fastest supercomputers in the world today—or 2 million times more powerful than the fastest desktop in existence.

The ultimate goal of Blue Gene is to solve a puzzle of a different sort from those at NSA—although NSA may also secretly be a customer. Blue Gene's singular objective is to try and model the way a human protein folds into a particular shape. Because proteins are the molecular workhorses of the human body, it is essential to discover their molecular properties. In a sense, Blue Gene is like NSA's old RAMs, which were designed to attack one specific encryption system.

When completed, Blue Gene will consist of sixty-four computing towers standing six feet high and covering an area forty feet by forty feet. Inside will be a mind-boggling one *million* processors. The target speed is a petaflop.

When NSA crosses the petaflop threshold, if it hasn't already, it is unlikely that the rest of the world will know. By 2005 the SRC, with years of secret, highly specialized development accumulated, will likely be working with computers operating at exaflop speeds—a quintillion operations a second—and pushing for zettaflop and even yottaflop machines, capable of a septillion (10^{24}) operations every time a second hand jumps. Beyond yottaflop, numbers have not yet been named. "It is the greatest play box in the world," marveled one agency veteran of the NSA's technology capability. "They've got one of everything."

Operating in the exaflop-and-above world will be almost unimaginable. The key will be miniaturization, an area in which NSA has been pushing the theoretical envelope. By the mid-1990s, NSA's Special Processing Laboratory had reduced the size of a transistor so much that seventy of them would fit on the cross section of a human hair. NSA is also attempting to develop a new generation of computer chips by bombarding light-sensitive material with ions to etch out microscopic electronic circuit designs. Using ion beams instead of traditional light in the process provides the potential for building far smaller, more complex, more efficient chips.

In the late 1990s NSA reached a breakthrough when it was able to shrink a supercomputer to the size of a home refrigerator-freezer combination. Eventually the machine was pared down to the size of a small suitcase, yet its speed was increased by 10 percent. In 1999, a joint NSA and DARPA program demonstrated that portions of a supercomputer could be engineered to fit into a cube six inches on a side—small enough to fit into a coat pocket. The circuitry was made of diamond-based multichip modules and cooled by aerosol spray to remove the 2,500 watts of heat from the system.

But to reach exaflop speed, computer parts—or even computers themselves—may have to be shrunk to the size of atoms, or even of subatomic particles. At the SRC, scientists looking for new and faster ways to break into encryption systems have turned to quantum computing. This involves studying interactions in the microscopic world of atomic structures and looking for ways to harness individual atoms to perform a variety of different tasks, thereby speeding up computer operations to an unthinkable scale.

NSA has had a strong interest in quantum computing as far back as 1994, when Peter Shor, a mathematician at Bell Laboratories, which has long had a close and secret relationship with the agency, discovered the codebreaking advantages of the new science. Since then, NSA has spent about $4 million a year to fund research at various universities, and put additional money into studies at government laboratories.

Operated at top speed, a quantum computer could be used to uncover pairs of enormously large prime numbers, which are the "passwords" for many encryption systems. The largest number that ordinary supercomputers have been able to factor is about 140 digits long. But according to another Bell Labs scientist, Lov K. Grover, using quantum computing, 140-digit-long numbers could be factored a billion times faster than is currently possible. "On paper, at least," said Glover, "the prospects are stunning: . . . a search engine that could examine every nook and cranny of the Internet in half an hour; a 'brute-force' decoder that could unscramble a DES [Data Encryption Standard—the encryption standard used by banks and most businesses] transmission in five minutes."

A quantum computer could also be used to speed through unfathomable numbers of intercepted communications—a "scan" in NSA-speak—searching for a single keyword, a phrase, or even, with luck, a "bust." Long the secret leading to many of NSA's past codebreaking successes, a bust is an abnormality—sometimes very subtle—in a target's cryptographic system. For example, it may be an error in a Russian encryption program, or a faulty piece of hardware, or a sloppy transmission procedure. Once such a hairline crack is discovered, NSA codebreakers, using a massive amount of computer power in what is known as a brute force attack, can sometimes chisel away enough of the system to expose a golden vein of secret communications.

A breakthrough into quantum computing came in April 1998, when researchers at MIT, IBM, the University of California at Berkeley, and the University of Oxford in England announced they had succeeded in building the first working quantum computers. The processor consisted of a witches' brew of hydrogen and chlorine atoms in chloroform. Digital switches were shrunk down to the smallest unit of information, known as a quantum bit, or qubit. Where once a traditional computer bit would have to be either, for example, 0 or 1, a qubit could be both simultaneously. Instead of just black or white, a qubit could become all the colors of the rainbow.

According to John Markoff, who has long followed the issue for the *New York Times,* another milestone came in July 1999. That was when researchers at Hewlett-Packard and the University of California at Los Angeles announced that they had succeeded in creating rudimentary electronic logic gates—one of the basic components of computing—only a single molecule thick. Four months later, scientists at Hewlett-Packard reported they had crossed another key threshold by creating rows of ultramicroscopic conductive wires less than a dozen atoms across.

Translated into practical terms, a quantum computer could thus perform many calculations simultaneously, resulting in a hyperincrease in speed. Now, instead of a supercomputer attempting to open a complex cipher system—or lock—by trying a quadrillion different keys one after another, a quantum computer will be able to try all quadrillion keys simultaneously. Physicists speculated that such machines may one day prove thousands or even millions of times faster than the most powerful supercomputer available today.

The discovery was greeted with excitement by the codebreakers in Crypto City. "It looked for a long time like a solution without a problem," said NSA's Keith Miller. At Los Alamos, where NSA is secretly funding research into the new science, quantum team leader Richard J. Hughes added: "This is an important step. What's intriguing is that they've now demonstrated the simplest possible algorithm on a quantum computer."

Also heavily involved in molecular-scale electronics, known as moletronics, is DARPA, long NSA's partner in pushing computing past the threshold. Scientists working on one DARPA program recently speculated that it may soon be possible to fashion tiny switches, or transistors, from tiny clusters of molecules only a single layer deep. Such an advance, they believe, may lead to computers that would be 100 billion times as fast as today's fastest PCs. According to James Tour, a professor of chemistry at Rice University who is working on molecular-scale research, "A single molecular computer could conceivably have more transistors than all of the transistors in all of the computers in the world today."

On the other side of the city, however, the code*makers* welcomed the news with considerable apprehension. They were worried about the potential threat to NSA's powerful cipher systems if a foreign nation discovered a way to harness the power and speed of quantum computing before the United States had developed defenses against it. By 1999, for example, Japan's NEC had made considerable progress with the development of a solid-state device that could function as a qubit. "We have made a big step by showing the possibility of integrating quantum gates using solid-state devices," said NEC's Jun'ichi Sone. "It takes one trillion years to factorize a two-hundred-digit number with present supercomputers," he said. "But it would take only one hour or less with a quantum computer."

As intriguing as quantum computing is, perhaps the most interesting idea on how to reach exa-speed and beyond came out of the series of "great leap forward" meetings in which the NSA took part in the mid-1990s. The computer of the future—already with a circulatory system of cool, bubbling Fluorinert, an artificial blood plasma—may be constructed partly out of mechanical parts and partly out of living parts.

"I don't think we can really build a machine that fills room after room after room and costs an equivalent number of dollars," said Seymour Cray, one of those at the meetings. "We have to make something roughly the size of our present machines but with a thousand times the components." One answer to scaling down to the nanometer, according to Cray, was to fabricate computing devices out of biological entities. At the same time, other biological processes could be used to manufacture nonbiological devices—for example, bacteria could be bioengineered to build transistors.

By 2001, researchers at MIT were actively attempting to marry the digital with the biological by altering the common *E. coli* bacterium to function as an electronic circuit. Such a melding would produce a computer part with the unique ability to continually reproduce itself. Through such a process, enormous numbers of nearly identical processors could be "grown." "We would like to make processors by the wheelbarrow-load," said MIT computer scientist Harold Abelson. Abelson and his colleagues are hoping to someday map circuitry onto biological material, in a process they call amorphous computing, thus turning living cells into digital logic circuits. However, since the cells could compute only while alive, millions or billions of the tiny biocomponents would have to be packed into the smallest spaces possible.

Bell Labs, part of Lucent Technologies, is also perusing the idea of a "living" computer by creating molecular-size "motors" out of DNA—motors so small that 30 trillion could fit into a single drop of water. According to Bell Labs physicist Bernard Yurke, it might eventually be possible to bind electronic components to DNA. Then, by linking the

DNA strands together, a computer could be created with incredible speed and storage capacities.

Eventually NSA may secretly achieve the ultimate in quickness, compatibility, and efficiency—a computer with petaflop and higher speeds shrunk into a container about a liter in size, and powered by only about ten watts of power: the human brain.

APPENDIX A

DIRECTORS AND DEPUTY DIRECTORS OF THE AFSA AND NSA

Armed Forces Security Agency

Director

Rear Admiral Earl E. Stone, USN
15 July 1949–25 July 1951

Major General Ralph J. Canine, USA
15 July 1951–4 November 1952

Vice Director

The following served concurrently and had specific areas of responsibility in addition to representing their respective services.

Colonel S. P. Collins, USA

Captain Joseph N. Wenger, USN

Colonel Roy H. Lynn, USAF

National Security Agency

Director

Major General Ralph Canine, USA (Acting)
4 November 1952–21 November 1952

Lieutenant General Ralph Canine, USA
21 November 1952–23 November 1956

Lieutenant General John A. Samford, USAF
24 November 1956–23 November 1960

Vice Admiral Laurence H. Frost, USN
24 November 1960–30 June 1962

Lieutenant General Gordon A. Blake, USAF
1 July 1962–31 May 1965

Lieutenant General Marshall S. Carter, USA
1 June 1965–31 July 1969

Vice Admiral Noel Gayler, USN
1 August 1969–31 July 1972

Lieutenant General Samuel C. Phillips, USAF
1 August 1972–14 August 1973

Lieutenant General Lew Allen, Jr., USAF
15 August 1973–4 July 1977

Vice Admiral Bobby R. Inman, USN
5 July 1977–31 March 1981

Lieutenant General Lincoln D. Faurer, USAF
1 April 1981–27 March 1985

Lieutenant General William E. Odom, USA
5 May 1985–31 July 1988

Vice Admiral William O. Studeman, USN
1 August 1988–8 April 1992

Vice Admiral J. M. McConnell, USN
22 May 1992–22 February 1996

Lieutenant General Kenneth A. Minihan, USAF
23 February 1996–15 March 1999

Lieutenant General Michael V. Hayden, USAF
25 March 1999–

Deputy Director

Rear Admiral Joseph N. Wenger, USN*
2 December 1952–28 July 1953

Brigadier General John B. Ackerman, USAF*
26 October 1953–4 June 1956

Major General John A. Samford, USAF*
4 June 1956–24 November 1956

Joseph H. Ream
2 February 1957–18 September 1957

Dr. Howard T. Engstrom
18 October 1957–1 August 1958

Dr. Louis W. Tordella
1 August 1958–21 April 1974

Benson K. Buffham
22 April 1974–30 April 1978

Robert E. Drake
1 May 1978–30 March 1980

Ann Z. Caracristi
1 April 1980–30 July 1982

Robert E. Rich
31 July 1982–3 July 1986

Charles R. Lord
9 July 1986–13 March 1988

Gerald R. Young
14 March 1988–28 July 1990

Robert L. Prestel
29 July 1990–1 February 1994

William P. Crowell
2 February 1994–12 September 1997

Barbara A. McNamara
8 November 1997–30 June 2000

William B. Black, Jr.
22 September 2000

*Title was actually vice director.

APPENDIX B

NSA LINGUISTIC CAPABILITY

NSA has provided training for linguists in at least ninety-five languages, including:

Afrikaans
Albanian
Algerian
Amharic
Arabic
Armenian
Azerbaijani
Basque
Belarussian
Bengali
Berber
Bulgarian
Burmese
Cambodian
Chinese, all dialects
Czech
Danish
Dari
Dutch
Egyptian
Estonian
Finnish
French
Georgian
German
Greek
Haitian Creole (Kreyol)
Hebrew
Hindi
Hungarian
Icelandic
Ilocano
Indonesian
Iraqi
Italian
Japanese
Jordanian
Kazakh
Kirghiz
Korean
Kurdish
Kuwaiti
Kyrgyz
Lao
Latvian
Levantine
Libyan
Lingala
Lithuanian
Macedonian
Malaysian
Moldovan
Mongolian
Moroccan
Nepali
Norwegian
Papiamento
Pashto
Persian-Farsi
Polish
Portuguese, all dialects
Punjabi
Pushto
Quechua
Romanian
Russian
Saudi
Serbo-Croatian

Sinhalese
Slovak
Slovene (Slovenian)
Somali
Sotho
Spanish
Sudanese
Swahili
Swedish
Syrian
Tagalog
Tajik
Tamil
Thai
Tibetan
Tigrinya
Turkish
Turkmen
Tunisian
Ukrainian
Urdu
Uzbek
Vietnamese (all dialects)
Visayan-Cebuano
Xhosa
Yemeni
Yoruba
Zulu

Also, all dialects of Arabic, including Libyan, Algerian, Moroccan, Tunisian, Egyptian, Levantine, Syrian, Jordanian, Sudanese, Saudi, Kuwaiti, Iraqi, Yemeni, and Modern Standard.

APPENDIX C

CRYPTOLOGIC OCCUPATIONS AT NSA

EXPERT SIGINT LINGUIST
SENIOR LANGUAGE ANALYST
LANGUAGE ANALYST
LANGUAGE INTERN
These occupations are involved with the translation into English of technical documents and the content analysis of materials of special significance or priority.

EXPERT VOICE LINGUIST
SENIOR VOICE LANGUAGE ANALYST
VOICE LANGUAGE ANALYST
Convert foreign language voice intercept into written English. This may involve gisting (reproducing the essence of an intercepted conversation) and content analysis of voice intercepts to determine significance and priority.

EXPERT CRYPTOLOGIC LINGUIST
SENIOR CRYPTOLOGIC LANGUAGE ANALYST
CRYPTOLOGIC LANGUAGE ANALYST
The application of linguistic principles, theories, and practices to the analysis and solution of a wide variety of cryptologic problems concerning foreign written and voice communications. Analysts advise on the construction, grammar, and syntax of language, and vocabulary development. Other work may involve translation, transcribing, gisting, and scanning.

EXPERT RESEARCH LINGUIST
SENIOR LANGUAGE RESEARCH ANALYST
LANGUAGE RESEARCH ANALYST
The planning and development of glossaries, course materials, dictionaries, and reference works. These occupations also involve computer studies of the characteristics of target languages.

CRYPTANALYTIC EXPERT
SENIOR CRYPTANALYST
CRYPTANALYST—GENERAL
CRYPTANALYST—MACHINE
CRYPTANALYST—MANUAL
CRYPTANALYTIC SUPPORT TECHNICIAN
CRYPTANALYSIS INTERN
The application of analytic techniques, methods, and procedures for the analysis or solution of complex cipher problems.

TRAFFIC ANALYTIC EXPERT
SENIOR TRAFFIC ANALYST
TRAFFIC ANALYST
TRAFFIC ANALYST INTERN
The analysis of telecommunications patterns for intelligence and cryptanalytic purposes.

SIGNALS ANALYSIS EXPERT
SENIOR SIGNALS ANALYST
SIGNALS ANALYST
SIGNALS ANALYSIS INTERN
The analysis and evaluation of foreign signals to derive and compile strategic, technical, and scientific intelligence. Also

the exploitation of raw electronic signals and processed signal components to derive valuable intelligence information on the identity, function, characteristics, and capabilities of the signal and radiating equipment.

COLLECTION EXPERT
SENIOR COLLECTION MANAGER
COLLECTION MANAGER
Development and evaluation of programs, policies, requirements, and instructions involved in signals intelligence collection.

SENIOR COLLECTION OPERATIONS CONTROLLER
COLLECTION OPERATIONS CONTROLLER
Managing, administering, directing, advising on, or performing work involved with the production of signals intelligence.

MORSE COLLECTOR
All positions with duties involved in the study or interception of radio emanations transmitted in international Morse or similar codes. The intercept operator may search for, identify, collect, record, and/or transcribe the signals.

MULTIMODE COLLECTOR
Duties involving the identification, reporting, and processing of foreign electromagnetic emissions.

SIGNALS CONVERSION EXPERT
SENIOR SIGNALS CONVERSION SPECIALIST
SIGNALS CONVERSION SPECIALIST
Advise on, supervise, or perform work involving the transformation of signals into a format or media amenable to their identification for further analysis.

CRYPTOLOGIC ENGINEER
ENGINEERING INTERN
Positions at the supergrade level that require the highest degree of technical knowledge and skill in order to plan, develop, direct, advise on, and implement engineering programs that deal with NSA's key cryptologic missions.

CRYPTOLOGIC COMPUTER SCIENTIST
COMPUTER SCIENTIST
COMPUTER ANALYST
Study and analyze cryptanalytic problems to evaluate whether and how solutions might be obtained using computer technology.

SENIOR FREQUENCY MANAGEMENT SPECIALIST
FREQUENCY MANAGEMENT SPECIALIST
Perform a variety of duties associated with radio frequency engineering and management, radio-wave propagation, and electromagnetic compatibility. The work requires the ability to study and advise on technical and general operational aspects of telecommunications systems with a view toward supporting NSA projects.

EXPERT CRYPTOLOGIC MATHEMATICIAN
SENIOR CRYPTOLOGIC MATHEMATICIAN
CRYPTOLOGIC MATHEMATICIAN
CRYPTANALYTIC MATHEMATICIAN INTERN
Perform work involving the development and application of mathematical methods for the investigation and numerical and analytical solution of cryptologic problems in various subject-matter fields where the exactitude of the relationships,

the rigor and economy of mathematical operation, and the logical necessity of results are the controlling consideration.

SENIOR OPERATIONS RESEARCH ANALYST
OPERATIONS RESEARCH ANALYST
OPERATIONS RESEARCH INTERN
Design, develop, and adapt mathematical, statistical, econometric, as well as other scientific methods and techniques to analyze cryptologic problems. Performance of this responsibility requires the ability to construct quantitative models that will provide insight into the probable effects of alternative solutions to the problems. The primary purpose of operations research studies and evaluations is to provide a decision maker with sound, scientific, and quantitative bases by which to sharpen intuition and judgment in making his decisions.

CRYPTOLOGIC SCIENTIST
Positions at the supergrade level that require the highest degree of technical knowledge and skill in order to plan, develop, direct, advise on, and implement one or more complex and important physical science (physics or chemistry) programs to accomplish NSA's cryptologic mission.

CRYPTOLOGIC EDUCATION AND TRAINING EXPERT
Advise on, administer, and perform professional work involving research, conceiving and planning comprehensive training programs for use at the National Cryptologic School and elsewhere.

SENIOR INVESTIGATOR
INVESTIGATOR
Positions involved with investigating candidates for employment or access, reinvestigations of employees and other affiliated personnel, and counterintelligence activities and the investigations of other matters under the jurisdiction of the director, NSA.

SENIOR POLYGRAPH EXAMINER
POLYGRAPH EXAMINER
Administration and supervision of polygraph examinations as part of counterintelligence and personnel security investigations.

TECHNICAL SECURITY OFFICER
TECHNICAL SECURITY SPECIALIST
Performs technical security research and surveys.

SENIOR CRYPTOLOGIC MATERIAL CONTROLLER
CRYPTOLOGIC MATERIAL CONTROLLER
Involved with the planning, development, and operation of systems that assure accountability of cryptologic equipment and other materials, such as magnetic tapes. This also includes the forecasting of cryptologic material requirements and trends.

CRYPTOMATERIAL CHECKER
Operation of inspection and quality control systems for the prepublication editing, proofreading, and checking of cryptographic materials.

INFOSEC EXPERT
Perform research into programs designed to safeguard U.S. and other designated telecommunications from unauthorized disclosure or exploitation.

INFOSEC OPERATIONS OFFICER
INFOSEC OPERATIONS ANALYST
Develop Infosec systems for U.S. and

other designated communications. Review established information security programs for communications insecurities. Analyze foreign intelligence systems and practices, technological advances, trends, and developments in order to develop and interpret data on the cryptologic accomplishments and potential of foreign countries.

INFOSEC SYSTEMS OFFICER
INFOSEC SYSTEMS ANALYST
INFOSEC INTERN

Determine vulnerabilities of communications systems and devise or develop the methodology for minimizing those vulnerabilities.

NOTES

ABBREVIATIONS USED IN THE NOTES

HSTL: Harry S. Truman Presidential Library
DDEL: Dwight David Eisenhower Presidential Library
JFKL: John Fitzgerald Kennedy Presidential Library
LBJL: Lyndon B. Johnson Presidential Library
NSAN: National Security Agency Newsletter
NSA: Unless otherwise noted, all NSA items came from the National Security Agency.
JCS: Joint Chiefs of Staff
FRUS: U.S. Department of State, Foreign Relations of the U.S. Series
ARRB: Assassinations Records Review Board
TICOM: Army Security Agency, Top Secret/Cream report, "European Axis Signal Intelligence in World War II as Revealed by 'TICOM' Investigations and by Other Prisoner of War Interrogations and Captured Material, Principally German" (May 1, 1946). Nine volumes.
Lemnitzer's Private Summary: Long-hidden, handwritten fifty-two-page private account of the Bay of Pigs affair by General Lyman L. Lemnitzer (undated). Kept in Lemnitzer's private papers at his family home in Pennsylvania.

CHAPTER 1: Memory

Page

1 The Munitions Building was located at the corner of Nineteenth Street and Constitution Avenue in Washington.

1 Friedman walk to the vault: Frank B. Rowlett, *The Story of Magic: Memoirs of an American Cryptologic Pioneer* (Laguna Hills, CA: Aegean Park Press, 1998), p. 34.

2 "Welcome, gentlemen": ibid., p. 35.

2 Rowlett's clothes: ibid., p. 34.

2 Sinkov and Kullback background: James Bamford, *The Puzzle Palace: A Report on NSA, America's Most Secret Agency* (Boston: Houghton Mifflin, 1982), p. 30.
2 more than 10,000 messages: ibid., p. 16.
3 the Chamber's demise: ibid., pp. 16–17.
3 given its cautious approval: Rowlett, op. cit., pp. 37–38.
3 State Department . . . never to know: ibid.
3 vault twenty-five feet square: ibid., p. 34.
4 "The NSA Christmas party was a big secret": NSA, Top Secret/Umbra, Oral history of Robert L. Prestel (December 21, 1993), p. 14.
4 "For a long time we didn't tell anybody": Laura Sullivan, "Secret Spy Agency Puts On Human Face," *Baltimore Sun* (March 21, 2000).
5 "They picked him up": ibid.
5 NSA leased the entire building: ibid.
5 "I do this with some trepidation": Address by Vice Admiral William O. Studeman to the Baltimore/Washington Corridor Chamber (June 29, 1990).

CHAPTER 2: Sweat

Page

7 "the United States will be": Office of Strategic Services, secret memorandum, William O. Donovan to President Truman, with attached report, "Problems and Objectives of United States Policy" (May 5, 1945), pp. 1, 2 (HSTL, Rose Conway File, OSS Memoranda for the President, Box 15).
8 TICOM: Army Security Agency, Top Secret/Cream report, "European Axis Signal Intelligence in World War II as Revealed by 'TICOM' Investigations and by Other Prisoner of War Interrogations and Captured Material, Principally German," (May 1, 1946). Nine volumes. (Hereafter referred to as TICOM.)
8 Colonel George A. Bicher: TICOM, vol. 1, p. 2.
8 Marshall message to Eisenhower: War Department message, Marshall to Eisenhower (August 7, 1944), contained in TICOM, vol. 8, p. 55.
9 "the plan contemplated": ibid., p. 3.
9 "a. To learn the extent . . . war against Japan": ibid.
10 "was no longer feasible": TICOM, vol. 8, p. 52.
10 "take over and exploit": TICOM, vol. 1, p. 3.
10 suburban location was chosen: Gordon Welchman, *The Hut Six Story: Breaking the Enigma Codes* (New York: McGraw-Hill, 1982), p. 9.
10 "was brilliantly conceived": TICOM, vol. 2, p. 1.
10 "Allied Comint agencies had been exploiting": NSA, Robert J. Hanyok, "Defining the Limits of Hell: Allied Communications Intelligence and the Holocaust During the Second World War, 1939–1945" (1999). This paper was presented at the Cryptologic History Symposium at NSA on October 27, 1999.
11 "One day we got this frantic call": NSA, Secret/Comint Channels Only, oral history of Paul E. Neff (January 26, 1983).
12 "Apparently they had": ibid., p. 45.

12 At thirty-eight: Background information about Whitaker is drawn from an interview with Dr. Paul K. Whitaker (January 1999); diary of Paul K. Whitaker, copy in author's collection.

13 Selmer S. Norland: Information about his background is drawn from Thomas Parrish, *The Ultra Americans: The U.S. Role in Breaking the Nazi Codes* (Briarcliff Manor, NY: Stein & Day, 1986), p. 102.

13 Arthur Levenson: Background information comes from ibid., pp. 86–87.

13 British policy had forbidden: Signal Security Service, secret report by William F. Friedman, "Report on E Operations of the GC & CS at Bletchley Park" (August 12, 1943), p. 9.

14 "I eventually got my commission": NSA, Secret/Comint Channels Only, Oral History of Dr. Howard Campaigne (June 29, 1983), pp. 2–3.

14 Swordfish: NSA, "The Docent Book" (January 1996). Among the variations of the "Fish" were machines nicknamed by American codebreakers "Tunny" and "Sturgeon." The Tunny (better known in English as the tuna) was the Schlusselzusatz 40 (SZ40). It was manufactured by the German firm Lorenz and was used by the German army for upper-echelon communications. The Sturgeon, actually a Siemens T-52, was developed at the request of the German navy, with the first units manufactured in 1932. The German air force began using it in 1942. Unlike the Enigma, the Sturgeon did not use wired rotors. The rotors have a series of cogs that open and close on electrical contacts.

Unless otherwise noted, all details of the hunt for the Fish machine are from Paul K. Whitaker's personal diary (unpaginated), a copy of which is in the author's possession.

14 "The impressions were": Whitaker diary.

14 "The roads were lined": ibid.

15 "How are things down there?": ibid.

16 "They were working": ibid.

17 Dustbin: TICOM, Top Secret/Ultra report, "Narrative and Report of the Proceedings of TICOM Team 6, 11 April–6 July 1945" (September 5, 1945).

17 Among those clandestinely brought: ibid.

17 "It is almost certain": TICOM, vol. 3, p. 8.

17 "We found that the Germans": NSA, Secret/Comint Channels Only, Oral History of Dr. Howard Campaigne (June 29, 1983), pp. 2–3.

18 "European cryptanalysts were unable": TICOM, vol. 1, p. 6. Other systems solved by Germany included between 10 and 30 percent of intercepted U.S. Army M-209 messages. Except where keys were captured, it was usually read too late to be of tactical value. Almost 100 percent of messages sent by the U.S. Army in Slidex, Codex, bomber code, assault code, aircraft movement code, map coordinate codes, and cipher device M-94 where employed, were read regularly (TICOM, vol. 1, p. 5).

18 SIGABA: NSA, "The Docent Book" (January 1996). The Army SIGABA was designated M134C and the Navy SIGABA was the CSP 888.

18 It was finally taken out of service: ibid.

18 "practically 100% readable": TICOM, vol. 1, Appendix: "Results of European Axis Cryptanalysis as Learned from TICOM Sources" (88 pages, unpaginated).

19 "cryptanalytic attack had been": ibid. See also Army Security Agency, Top Secret/Ultra report, "The Achievements of the Signal Security Agency in World War II" (February 20, 1946), p. 31.

19 more than 1 million decrypted messages: NSA, Top Secret/Umbra, "On Watch" (September 1986), p. 11.

19 "Overnight, the targets that occupied": ibid., p. 13.

19 Gone were the army intercept stations: Prior to the war, intercept stations were located at Fort Hancock, New Jersey; the Presidio, San Francisco, California; Fort Sam Houston, Texas; Corozal, Panama Canal Zone; Fort Shafter, Territory of Hawaii; Fort McKinley, Philippine Islands; and Fort Hunt, Virginia. During the war additional intercept stations were added at Indian Creek Station, Miami Beach, Florida; Asmara, Eritrea; Amchitka, Aleutian Islands; Fairbanks, Alaska; New Delhi, India; Bellmore, New York; Tarzana, California; and Guam (Army Security Agency, Top Secret/Ultra report, "The Achievements of the Signal Security Agency in World War II" (February 20, 1946), pp. 11–12).

19 Vint Hill Farms Station: In 1999 the station was taken over by the Federal Aviation Administration as the new home of a consolidated radar operations center for the Washington-Baltimore area's four major airports—Dulles, Reagan National, Baltimore-Washington, and Andrews Air Force Base. The system is known as TRACON (Terminal Radar Approach Control).

20 At war's end: By V-J Day 7,848 people were working at Arlington Hall (Army Security Agency, "The Achievements of the Signal Security Agency in World War II" (February 20, 1946), p. 3. (National Archives and Records Administration, RG 457, Box 107, SRH-349.)

20 "They intercepted printers at Vint Hill": NSA, Top Secret/Comint Channels Only, Oral History of Colonel Russell H. Horton (March 24, 1982), p. 64.

20 "For a few months in early 1942": NSA/CIA, Cecil James Phillips, "What Made Venona Possible?" in "Venona: Soviet Espionage and the American Response, 1939–1957" (1996), p. xv.

21 Phillips estimated that between 1942 and 1948: David Martin, "The Code War," *Washington Post Magazine* (May 10, 1998), p. 16.

21 Long black limousines: The description of the UN's founding conference draws on Linda Melvern, *The Ultimate Crime: Who Betrayed the UN and Why?* (London: Allison & Busby, 1995), p. 23.

22 the French delegation: Details on breaking French codes and ciphers come from TICOM, vol. 1, Appendix: "Results of European Axis Cryptanalysis as Learned from TICOM Sources."

22 "Our inclusion among the sponsoring": War Department, Top Secret/Ultra report, "Magic" Diplomatic Summary (May 2, 1945), p. 8.

22 "Pressure of work": Signal Security Agency, Top Secret report, Rowlett to Commanding Officer, SSA, "Semimonthly Branch Activity Report, 1–15 June 1945."

23 "Russia's prejudice": War Department, Top Secret/Ultra report, "Magic" Diplomatic Summary (April 30, 1945), pp. 7–12.
23 Spanish decrypts: ibid.
23 Czechoslovakian message: ibid.
23 "a situation that compared": NSA, David A. Hatch with Robert Louis Benson, "The Korean War: The Sigint Background" (June 2000), p. 4.
23 "a remarkably complete picture": ibid.
23 "perhaps the most significant": ibid., p. 5.
23 Black Friday: ibid., p. 4.
24 a gregarious Russian linguist: Details concerning William Weisband are drawn from NSA/CIA, "Venona: Soviet Espionage and the American Response, 1939–1957" (1996), p. xxviii.
24 "three-headed monster": NSA, Top Secret/Codeword, Oral History of Herbert J. Conley (March 5, 1984), pp. 58, 59.
24 "He couldn't control": ibid.
24 Korea barely registered: Unless otherwise noted, details on Sigint in Korea are from NSA, David A. Hatch with Robert Louis Benson, "The Korean War: The Sigint Background" (June 2000), p. 4.
25 "AFSA had no Korean linguists": NSA, Top Secret/Umbra/Handle via Talent and Keyhole Comint Control Systems Jointly, Dr. Thomas R. Johnson, *American Cryptology During the Cold War* (1995), p. 36.
25 Buried in stacks of intercepted Soviet traffic: ibid., pp. 39–40.
25 Joseph Darrigo, a U.S. Army captain: ibid., p. 40.
25 "AFSA (along with everyone else) was looking": ibid., p. 54.
25 arriving ten to twelve hours after intercept: NSA, Jill Frahm, "So Power Can Be Brought into Play: Sigint and the Pusan Perimeter" (2000), p. 6; see also NSA, Patrick D. Weadon, "Sigint and Comsec Help Save the Day at Pusan," pp. 1–2.
26 Father Harold Henry had spent a number of years: NSA, "Korea," pp. 42–43.
26 "When we got into the . . . Perimeter": Donald Knox, *The Korean War: An Oral History* (New York: Harcourt Brace Jovanovich, 1985), p. 77.
26 provided him with such vital information as the exact locations: NSA, "So Power Can Be Brought into Play: Sigint and the Pusan Perimeter," p. 10.
26 "ground-return intercept": NSA, "The Korean War: The Sigint Background," p. 12.
27 "One of our problems in Korea": NSA, Top Secret/Comint Channels Only, Oral History of Paul Odonovich (August 5, 1983), p. 33.
27 low-level voice intercept (LLVI): NSA, "Korea," pp. 47–48.
27 A team set up in Nanjing . . . "poor hearability": NSA, Top Secret/Umbra, "Comint and the PRC Intervention in the Korean War," *Cryptologic Quarterly* (Summer 1996), p. 4.
27 the British had been secretly listening: ibid., p. 6.
28 "clear and convincing evidence": NSA, "Korea," p. 44.

28 Sigint reports noted that some 70,000 Chinese troops: NSA, "Comint and the PRC Intervention in the Korean War," p. 11.

28 "Very little": ibid., p. 15.

28 twenty troop trains were heading: ibid., p. 14.

28 "We are already at war here": NSA, "Korea," p. 44.

28 intercepts during the first three weeks: NSA, "Comint and the PRC Intervention in the Korean War," p. 18.

29 AFSA reports demonstrated clearly: ibid., p. 17.

29 "No one who received Comint product": ibid., p. 1.

29 "During the Second World War, MacArthur had disregarded": ibid., p. 21.

29 NSA later attributed this caution: NSA, "Korea," p. 55.

30 "The . . . last three major": ibid., p. 36.

30 "It has become apparent": NSA, "The Korean War: The Sigint Background" (June 2000), p. 15.

30 A year later NSA director Ralph Canine: NSA, "So Power Can Be Brought into Play: Sigint and the Pusan Perimeter," p. 15.

30 "gravely concerned": CIA, Top Secret/Codeword memorandum, "Proposed Survey of Communications Intelligence Activities" (December 10, 1951) (HSTL, President's Secretary's File, Intelligence, Box 250).

30 Truman ordered the investigation: National Security Council, Top Secret/Codeword memorandum, "Proposed Survey of Intelligence Activities" (December 13, 1951) (HSTL, President's Secretary's File, Intelligence, Box 250).

31 put it together again: For the Brownell Report, see Committee Appointed to Survey Communications Intelligence Activities of the Government, Top Secret/Comint Channels Only, "Report to the Secretary of State and the Secretary of Defense" (June 13, 1952) (National Archives, Record Group 457, Special Research History 123).

31 "step backward": ibid.

31 meeting with the president: White House, President's Appointment Schedule for Friday, October 24, 1952 (HSTL, Files of Mathew J. Connelly). Secretary of State Dean Acheson was giving a speech on Korea at the UN General Assembly at the time of the meeting (HSTL, Secretary of State Dean Acheson Appointment Book, Box 46).

31 leaving a voting booth: White House, President's Appointment Schedule for Tuesday, November 4, 1952 (HSTL, Files of Mathew J. Connelly).

31 "The 'smart money' ": NSA, Tom Johnson, "The Plan to Save NSA," in "In Memoriam: Dr. Louis W. Tordella" (undated), p. 6. In fact, only four days before NSA opened its doors, the FBI's J. Edgar Hoover sent a snippy letter to the National Security Council complaining about the new agency: "I am concerned about the authority granted to the Director of the National Security Agency" (FBI, Personal and Confidential letter, Hoover to James S. Lay, Jr., Executive Secretary of the NSC [October 31, 1952]) (DDEL, Ann Whitman File, NSC Series, Box 194).

CHAPTER 3: Nerves

Page

33 "With all the electrical gear": Bruce Bailey, "From the Crow's Nest," *Air & Space* (September 1994), p. 33.

34 "an ugly, overweight": ibid.

35 Nicknamed Project Homerun: Details of the project are drawn from R. Cargill Hall, "The Truth About Overflights," *MHQ: The Quarterly Journal of Military History*, vol. 9, no. 3 (Spring 1997), pp. 36–39.

37 "The stringent security measures imposed": CIA, Secret Noforn report, "The CIA and the U-2 Program, 1954–1974" (1992), p. 2.

38 "The weather was gorgeous": Paul Lashmar, *Spy Flights of the Cold War* (Gloucestershire, England: Sutton Publishing Ltd., 1996), p. 84.

38 "The guns won't work": ibid., p. 85.

39 "the first major test": NSA, Top Secret/Umbra/Noforn report, "The Suez Crisis: A Brief Comint History" (1988) (Special Series, Crisis Collection, vol. 2), p. 1.

39 his long experience with pack mules: "Ralph J. Canine," *The Phoenician* (Fall 1992), p. 12.

39 "People were scared of him": NSA, Secret Comint Channels Only, "Oral History of Colonel Frank L. Herrelko" (November 8, 1982), pp. 31, 42.

40 agreed to by Israeli prime minister David Ben-Gurion, defense minister Shimon Peres, and armed forces chief of staff Moshe Dayan: Donald Neff, *Warriors at Suez* (Brattleboro, Vt.: Amana Books, 1998), pp. 342–44.

40 intercepts from Spain and Syria: White House, Top Secret/Eyes Only memorandum for the record (August 6, 1956), p. 3.

40 "communications between Paris and Tel Aviv": NSA, Top Secret/Umbra/Noforn report, "The Suez Crisis: A Brief Comint History" (1988) (Special Series Crisis Collection, vol. 2), p. 19.

41 To make matters worse: NSA, Top Secret/Umbra/Talent/Keyhole/Noforn report, "American Cryptology During the Cold War, 1945–1989. Book 1: The Struggle for Centralization 1945–1989" (1995), p. 236.

41 "1956 was a bad time": ibid.

41 "about as crude and brutal": Department of State, memorandum of telephone call to the president (October 30, 1956) (DDEL, Papers of John Foster Dulles, Telephone Calls, Box 11).

41 "It was the gravest": Department of State, memorandum of telephone call from Allen Dulles (October 30, 1956) (DDEL, Papers of John Foster Dulles, Box 5).

41 "It would be a complete mistake": White House Top Secret memorandum, Discussion at the 302nd Meeting of the National Security Council (November 1, 1956), pp. 6–13. (DDEL, Ann Whitman File, NSC Series, Box 8).

41 Harold Stassen objected: ibid.

41 "One thing at least was clear": ibid.

41 "As for crisis response": NSA, Top Secret Umbra/Talent/Keyhole/ Noforn report, "American Cryptology During the Cold War, 1945–1989. Book 1: The Struggle for Centralization 1945–1989" (1995), p. 239.

42 consultants from McKinsey and Company: ibid.

42 "modified geographical concept": NSA, Top Secret/Umbra/Talent/Keyhole/Noforn report, "American Cryptology During the Cold War, 1945–1989. Book 1: The Struggle for Centralization 1945–1989" (1995), p. 239.

42 Internal organization: See James Bamford, *The Puzzle Palace: A Report on America's Most Secret Agency* (Boston: Houghton Mifflin, 1982), pp. 90–91.

42 "Canine . . . stands out": NSA, Secret/Comint Channels Only, Oral History of Dr. Howard Campaigne (June 29, 1983), p. 125.

43 Details of Powers's wait on the airstrip come from Francis Gary Powers with Curt Gentry, *Operation Overflight: The U-2 Spy Pilot Tells His Story for the First Time* (New York: Holt, Rinehart & Winston, 1970), p. 76.

43 "He would sometimes cut out": Richard M. Bissell, Jr., Oral History (November 9, 1976), p. 11 (DDEL).

44 "the System-V unit worked well": CIA, Top Secret/Codeword mission folder 4019 (December 22, 1956) (contained in CIA/U2P, p. 126).

44 "We usually flew from Turkey": Powers with Gentry, *Operation Overflight*, pp. 46–47.

44 "The equipment we carried on such occasions": ibid.

45 Powers locked his canopy: His preparations for the U-2 flight are described in Powers with Gentry, *Operation Overflight*, p. 78.

45 "Minister of Defense Marshal Malinovsky reporting": Strobe Talbott, ed., *Khrushchev Remembers* (Boston: Little, Brown, 1974), pp. 443, 444.

45 "Shoot down the plane": ibid.

45 "We were sick and tired": ibid.

45 A missile launch was considered: CIA, Colonel Alexander Orlov, "A 'Hot' Front in the Cold War," *Studies in Intelligence* (Winter 1998–1999), web pages.

45 "An uncomfortable situation": ibid.

46 "Shame!": ibid.

46 "If I could become a missile": ibid.

46 "I was sure": Powers with Gentry, *Operation Overflight*, p. 80.

46 "In view of the improving": CIA, Top Secret/Talent report, "Annex to the report of DCI Ad hoc Panel on Status of the Soviet ICBM Program," August 25, 1959 (DDEL, Office of Staff Secretary, Intelligence, Box 15).

47 "Evidence indicates": White House, Top Secret memorandum, "Discussion at the 442nd Meeting of the National Security Council, April 28, 1960" (April 28, 1960), p. 8. (DDEL, Ann Whitman File, National Security Council series, Box 12).

47 "Destroy target": Orlov, "A 'Hot' Front," web pages.

47 "My God, I've had it now!": Powers with Gentry, *Operation Overflight*, p. 82.

47 "Instinctively I grasped the throttle": ibid.

48 "I reached for the destruct switches": ibid., p. 83. Powers was killed on August 1, 1977, at the age of forty-seven, in the crash of a helicopter he was flying for a Los Angeles television station. He was buried with honors in Arlington National Cemetery. A decade later the U.S. Air Force awarded him posthumously the Distinguished Flying Cross.

48 "The plane was still spinning": ibid., p. 84.

48 "It was a pleasant": ibid.

49 "He's turning left!": Jack Anderson, "U.S. Heard Russians Chasing U-2," *Washington Post,* May 12, 1960.

50 "the hideout": White House, Top Secret memorandum, "Notes for Use in Talking to the Secretary of State about the U-2 and the NSC" (June 14, 1960) (DDEL, White House Office, Box 18).

51 "Following cover plan": Top Secret memorandum (No addressee; May 2, 1960) (DDEL, White House, Office of Staff Secretary, Box 15).

52 the president huddled: This and other details of the events following the U-2 shootdown are from White House, Top Secret/Limited Distribution, "Chronological Account of Handling of U-2 Incident" (June 14, 1960) (DDEL, White House Office, Box 18).

52 "we had an understanding": Colonel William D. Johnson and Lieutenant Colonel James C. Ferguson, Andrew J. Goodpaster Oral History (January 9, 1976), p. 45 (U.S. Army Center for Military History).

52 Walter Bonney was forced: Michael R. Beschloss, *Mayday: Eisenhower, Khrushchev and the U-2 Affair* (New York: Harper & Row, 1986), pp. 51–52; David Wise and Thomas B. Ross, *The U-2 Affair* (New York: Random House, 1962), p. 83.

53 "Almost instantly": Richard Strout, "T.R.B.," *New Republic,* May 16, 1960.

53 "While the President": Department of State, telephone calls, May 9, 1960 (DDEL, Papers of Christian A. Herter, Telephone Calls, Box 10).

53 "I would like to resign": Ann Whitman diary, May 9, 1960 (DDEL).

53 Dulles, Eisenhower said: The account in this paragraph is from Department of State, telephone calls, May 9, 1960 (DDEL, Papers of Christian A. Herter, Telephone Calls, Box 10).

54 "Our reconnaissance was discovered": White House, Top Secret memorandum, "Discussion at the 444th Meeting of the National Security Council, May 9, 1960" (May 13, 1960), p. 2 (DDEL, Ann Whitman File, National Security Council series, Box 12).

54 "extensive aerial surveillance": Department of State, Press Announcement, May 9, 1960 (DDEL).

54 "Call off": The quotations in this paragraph come from Department of State, memorandum of telephone conversation with General Goodpaster, June 1, 1960 (DDEL, Christian A. Herter Papers, Telephone Calls, Box 10).

54 "It was as though": Talbott, ed., *Khrushchev Remembers,* p. 451.

55 "We couldn't possibly": ibid., p. 452.

56 "It appeared": White House, Top Secret memorandum, Gordon Gray meeting with the president, May 24, 1960 (DDEL, Office of the Special Assistant for National Security Affairs, Box 4).

56 "The President": This and the preceding description of a typical NSC meeting draw on Robert Cutler, *No Time for Rest* (Boston: Little, Brown, 1965), p. 302.

56 The description of the NSC meeting draws on photos from DDEL.

56 "to play up the U-2 incident": White House, Top Secret memorandum, "Discussion at the 445th Meeting of the National Security Council, May 24, 1960," p. 3 (DDEL, Ann Whitman File, National Security Council Series, Box 12).

57 "It was clear": ibid., p. 5.
57 "Administration officials": ibid., p. 5.
57 "Some investigators": ibid., p. 17.
57 "No information": ibid., p. 8.
57 "What's more . . . that's under oath": Thomas Gates Oral History, Columbia University Oral History Project.
57 "The investigation, once started": White House, Top Secret memorandum, "Discussion at the 445th Meeting of the National Security Council, May 24, 1960," p. 8 (DDEL, Ann Whitman File, National Security Council Series, Box 12).
58 "Accordingly . . . the investigation": ibid., p. 8.
58 "Mr. Dulles": ibid.
58 "The speech": ibid., p. 9.
58 "Congress could be told": ibid., p. 5.
58 "The impression": ibid.
59 "We handed Khrushchev": David Wise and Thomas B. Ross, *The U-2 Affair* (New York: Random House, 1962), p. 172.
60 "trace the chain": Michael R. Beschloss, *Mayday: Eisenhower, Khrushchev and the U-2 Affair* (New York: Harper & Row, 1986), p. 313.
60 "What the CIA": ibid.
60 "heartily approved of the inquiry": White House, memorandum of Congressional breakfast meeting, May 26, 1960 (DDEL, Ann Whitman File, Eisenhower diaries).
60 "just gobbledy-gook": Beschloss, *Mayday*, p. 314.
61 Dillon's boss went much further: U.S. Congress, Senate Committee on Foreign Relations, *Events Incident to the Summit Conference: Hearings Before the Committee on Foreign Relations,* 86th Cong., 2d sess., May 27, 31, June 1, 2, 1960, p. 103.
61 "They were all sworn": Beschloss, *Mayday*, p. 314.
61 "You now stand": Thomas Powers, *The Man Who Kept the Secrets: Richard Helms and the CIA* (New York: Alfred A. Knopf, 1979), pp. 304–305.
62 "very disturbed": Department of State, memorandum of telephone conversation, June 1, 1960 (DDEL, Christian A. Herter Papers, Telephone Calls, Box 10).
62 "At the present time": White House, Clark Clifford memorandum for the record, January 24, 1961 (FRUS, Vol. X, #22).
63 "In the long run": Department of Defense, Robert S. McNamara memorandum to President Kennedy, January 24, 1961 (FRUS, Vol. X, #22).
63 The only answer: Lemnitzer's private summary, p. 6.

CHAPTER 4: Fists

Page

64 By daybreak: Details of the preparation for the Inauguration are drawn from Department of Defense, General Order No. 1, Inaugural Parade (January 20,

1961), pp. 1–84; JCS, Memorandum for General Lemnitzer, "Summary of Inaugural Activities, 20 January 1961" (January 17, 1961) (Lemnitzer Papers, National Defense University).

65 Quarters 1: What was then Quarters 1 is today Quarters 6.

65 "The presence of a benign and popular General of the Army": Donald Janson and Bernard Eismann, *The Far Right* (New York: McGraw-Hill, 1963), p. 6.

66 Warren should be hanged: ibid., p. 138.

66 One of those was Major General Edwin A. Walker... *The Overseas Weekly*, charged that Walker: "President Kennedy and the Ultra Right Extremists," web site http://www.geocities.com/CapitolHill/4035/disunity.htm.

67 "It seems in this Administration": Drew Pearson, "Another Admiral's Speech Censored," *San Francisco Chronicle*, February 21, 1961.

67 "Studious, handsome, thoughtful-looking": Bill Henry, "Doughboy Will Have His Day," *Los Angeles Times*, August 19, 1960.

67 "The most important military job": "Who Envies Gen. Lemnitzer?" *Los Angeles Times*, October 2, 1960.

67 "He thoroughly enjoyed himself": personal letter, Lemnitzer to Lois and Henry Simpson, January 14, 1961 (Lemnitzer Papers, National Defense University).

67 "bordered on reverence": L. James Binder, *Lemnitzer: A Soldier for His Time* (Washington, D.C.: Brassey's, 1997), p. 239.

68 he ordered his Joint Chiefs Chairman: ibid., p. 242.

68 find a way to secretly torpedo: ibid., p. 252.

68 "I have been involved in some very rugged": personal letter, Lemnitzer to Ernest Lemnitzer, March 3, 1960 (Lemnitzer Papers, National Defense University).

69 "The *Certain* Trumpet": Binder, *Lemnitzer*, p. 236.

69 "Here was a president with no military experience": General Lyman L. Lemnitzer Oral History (March 3, 1982) (LBJL).

69 "Nearly all of these people were ardent": Admiral Arleigh A. Burke Oral History (November 1972–January 1973) (U.S. Naval Institute, Annapolis).

70 "I would offer the suggestion": Letter, Lemnitzer to Victor Henderson Ashe II, August 22, 1961 (Lemnitzer Papers, National Defense University).

70 Lemnitzer and the Chiefs knew: JCS, Top Secret report, "Evaluation of Possible Military Courses of Action in Cuba," January 16, 1961 (FRUS Vol. X, #19).

71 passed the Secret Service booth: Frank M. Matthews, "Private Citizen Ike at His Farm," *Pittsburgh Post-Gazette*, January 21, 1961.

72 "This is the first known": NSA, Secret/Kimbo intercept, February 1, 1961.

72 "What is required is a basic expansion of plans": White House, Top Secret memorandum of conference with the president, January 25, 1961 (JFKL, National Security Files, Chester V. Clifton Series, JCS Conferences with the President, Vol. I, drafted on January 27 by Goodpaster) (FRUS 1961–1963, Vol. X, #26).

72 "I'm not going to risk": Michael R. Beschloss, *The Crisis Years: Kennedy and Khrushchev, 1960–1963* (New York: HarperCollins, 1991), p. 114.

73 "We can confidently assert": CIA, Top Secret report, "Inspector General's Survey of the Cuban Operation," October 1961, p. 60.

73 "the Agency was driving forward": ibid., p. 50.

73 elaborate instructions: Drew Pearson, "Merry-Go-Round," *San Francisco Chronicle*, February 21, 1961.

73 eight-page biography: Lemnitzer biography, prepared as part of his testimony before the House of Representatives, Committee on Science and Astronautics, March 23, 1961.

73 "*Planners are a funny lot*": Lemnitzer Papers, National Defense University.

74 "In view of the rapid buildup": Lemnitzer's private summary, p. 8.

74 "Evaluation of the current plan": ibid., pp. 10–11.

74 twenty-minute discussion: ibid., p. 36.

75 insisted that the choice of Zapata for a landing site: ibid., pp. 22–23.

76 "The [NSA] effort was very small": NSA, Secret/Comint Channels Only, Oral History of Harold L. Parish (October 12, 1982).

77 "possibly arrived at a Cuban port": NSA, Secret/Sabre intercept, April 10, 1961.

77 U-2s were crisscrossing: CIA, Secret/Noforn report, "The CIA and the U-2 Program, 1954–1974" (1992), p. 198.

77 NSA voice-intercept operators: CIA, Top Secret report, "An Analysis of the Cuban Operation by the Deputy Director (Plans)," January 18, 1962, Section V, "The Assessment of the Adequacy of the Plan," p. 3.

77 "Arms urgent": This and the other quotations in this paragraph come from CIA, Top Secret report, "Inspector General's Survey of the Cuban Operation," October 1961, p. 109.

77 "It wasn't much that was done": NSA, Secret/Comint Channels Only, Oral History of Harold L. Parish (October 12, 1982), p. 29.

78 "We are out of ammo": CIA, Top Secret report, "Inspector General's Survey of the Cuban Operation" (October 1961), pp. 32–33.

78 "In water. Out of ammo": ibid.

78 scores of their comrades: A total of 114 brigade members were killed and 1,189 were wounded.

78 "Am destroying all equipment"; convoy heading for the beach reversed course: CIA, Top Secret report, "Inspector General's Survey of the Cuban Operation" (October 1961), pp. 32–33.

79 "those employees on it": CIA, Secret, Richard Bissell memorandum for the record, November 5, 1961 (FRUS, Vol. X, #272).

79 "The traditional civilian control of the military": Janson and Eismann, *The Far Right*, p. 184. On April 10, 1963, Lee Harvey Oswald, who seven months later would assassinate President Kennedy, attempted to assassinate Walker as he sat at his desk in his Dallas home. Using the same rifle with which he killed Kennedy, Oswald shot at Walker through a window but

missed by inches. Walker died in relative obscurity in Dallas on October 31, 1993.

79 "extreme right-wing, witch-hunting": ibid., p. 194.

80 Foreign Relations Committee . . . warned: David Burnham, United Press International wire report, July 20, 1961.

80 "thesis of the nature of the Communist threat": ibid.

80 "an example of the ultimate danger": ibid.

80 "Concern had grown that a belligerent": Janson and Eismann, *The Far Right*, p. 197.

81 "I had considered sending this information": Letter, Personal/Confidential/Eyes Only, Lemnitzer to Norstad, February 28, 1961 (Lemnitzer Papers, National Defense University).

81 "You and Charlie are probably wondering what": ibid.

81 "civilian hierarchy was crippled": Walter S. Poole, JCS, General Lyman L. Lemnitzer Oral History (February 12, 1976) (U.S. Army Center of Military History, Washington, D.C.).

82 "The Bay of Pigs fiasco broke the dike": Janson and Eismann, *The Far Right*, pp. 6–7.

83 "could think of manufacturing something": White House, Top Secret, memorandum of meeting with the president, on January 3, 1961 (January 9, 1961).

83 Lansdale was ordered: Department of State, Top Secret/Sensitive memorandum, "The Cuba Project," March 2, 1962 (FRUS, Vol. X, #309).

83 "World opinion": Joint Chiefs of Staff, Top Secret/Special Handling/Noforn report, "Report by the Department of Defense and Joint Chiefs of Staff Representative on the Caribbean Survey Group to the Joint Chiefs of Staff on Cuba Project," March 9, 1962 (ARRB).

84 "the objective is": Joint Chiefs of Staff, Top Secret/Special Handling memorandum, Craig to Lansdale, February 2, 1962 (ARRB).

84 "a series of well coordinated": ibid.

84 "We could blow up a U.S. ship": JCS, Top Secret/Special Handling/Noforn, Note by the Secretaries to the Joint Chiefs of Staff on Northwoods, Annex to Appendix to Enclosure A, "Pretexts to Justify U.S. Military Intervention in Cuba" (March 12, 1962), p. 8 (ARRB).

84 "We could develop a Communist Cuban terror campaign": ibid., pp. 8–9.

85 "Exploding a few plastic bombs": ibid., pp. 9–10.

85 "create an incident which will": The plan is in ibid., pp. 9–11.

86 "It is recommended": JCS, Top Secret/Special Handling/Noforn memorandum, Lemnitzer to McNamara, March 13, 1962 (ARRB).

86 At 2:30 on the afternoon of . . . March 13: Lemnitzer's official diary for March 13, 1962 (Lemnitzer Papers, National Defense University).

87 Kennedy told Lemnitzer: Department of State, Secret memorandum, written by U. Alexis Johnson and dated March 16; attached to "Guidelines for Operation Mongoose" (March 14, 1962) (FRUS, Vol. X, #314). Ironically, President

Gerald Ford in 1975 appointed Lemnitzer to a blue-ribbon panel to investigate domestic activities of the CIA.

87 "The Joint Chiefs of Staff believe that the Cuban problem must be solved": JCS, Top Secret/Special Handling/Noforn memorandum, Lemnitzer to McNamara, April 10, 1962, pp. 1–2 (ARRB).

87 "The Joint Chiefs of Staff believe that the United States": ibid.

87 "[T]he Joint Chiefs of Staff recommend": ibid.

87 "I am the senior military officer": Binder, Lemnitzer, p. 279.

88 Lemnitzer ordered Gray to destroy all his notes: ibid., p. 273.

89 "A contrived 'Cuban' attack on an OAS": Office of the Secretary of Defense, Top Secret/Sensitive policy paper, "War Between Cuba and Another LA State" (1963), p. 1 (ARRB).

89 "Any of the contrived situations described above": ibid., p. 3.

89 "The only area remaining for consideration": ibid.

89 "a possible scenario": Department of Defense, Top Secret/Sensitive memorandum, Assistant Secretary of Defense for International Security Affairs Paul Nitze to Bundy, May 10, 1963 (JFKL, National Security Files, Meetings and Memoranda Series, Standing Group Meeting) (FRUS, Vol. XI, #337).

90 "If the U.S. did institute": ibid.

90 About a month later: Department of State, Top Secret/Eyes Only, Acting Secretary of State George Ball to the president, June 25, 1963 (JFKL, National Security Files, Countries Series, Cuba) (FRUS, Vol. XI, #352).

CHAPTER 5: Eyes

Page

93 ADVA and GENS were combined; new organizational structure: James Bamford, *The Puzzle Palace: A Report on NSA, America's Most Secret Agency* (Boston: Houghton Mifflin, 1982), pp. 90–91.

93 U.S. intelligence budget reached $2 billion: White House, Top Secret/Eyes Only memorandum, "Discussion at the 473rd Meeting of the National Security Council, January 5, 1961," p. 3.

93 $1.4 billion: ibid., p. 2.

93 proclaimed that NSA was a ship: "An Old Timer Is One Who . . . ," NSA, *Cryptolog* (November 1982), p. 17.

93 Soviets had used a fleet: Joint Chiefs of Staff, Joint Reconnaissance Center, Top Secret, *The Pueblo Incident* (January 24, 1968), p. 3.

93 "The Soviets had a vast intelligence program": interview with Oleg Kalugin, CBS News transcript (undated), p. 35.

94 President Eisenhower authorized: U.S. Navy, Confidential memorandum, CNO to Secretary of the Navy, April 26, 1960 (Naval Operational Archives, U.S.S. *Oxford* File).

94 "Oxford" was chosen: U.S. Navy, memorandum, C.O., U.S.S. *Oxford*, to CNO, February 5, 1962 (Naval Operational Archives, U.S.S. *Oxford* File).

94 "Signaling another first in communications": ibid.

94 first operational cruise: U.S. Navy, memorandum, C.O., U.S.S. *Oxford*, to CNO, January 25, 1963 (Naval Operational Archives, U.S.S. *Oxford* File).

94 the moon-bounce antenna: For details, see NSA, Top Secret/Umbra/Noforn, "In The Shadow of War" (June 1969), p. 108.

95 another four-month surveillance mission: U.S. Navy, memorandum, C.O., U.S.S. *Oxford*, to CNO, January 25, 1963 (Naval Operational Archives, U.S.S. *Oxford* File).

95 "in response to highest priority": U.S. Navy, Top Secret/Dinar, "Memorandum for the Secretary of the Navy," July 16, 1962.

95 "at least four, and possibly five": NSA, Secret/Kimbo intercept, "Unusual Number of Soviet Passenger Ships En Route Cuba," July 24, 1962, p. 1.

95 fifty-seven Soviet merchant ships: NSA, Top Secret/Dinar report, "Status of Soviet Merchant Shipping to Cuba," August 23, 1962, p. 1.

95 "In addition to the shipping increase": Oral History of Admiral Robert Lee Dennison (August 1975), p. 407 (U.S. Naval Institute, Annapolis).

96 "It is therefore believed": NSA, Secret/Sabre report, "New Soviet Cargo Ship En Route Cuba with Possible Military Cargo," June 5, 1962, p. 1.

96 first telltale sounds: NSA, Secret intercept, "First ELINT Evidence of Scan Odd Radar in Cuban Area" (June 6, 1962), p. 1.

96 "Comint sources reveal Russian": NSA, Secret/Kimbo intercept, "Reflection of Soviet Bloc Pilots/Technicians in Cuban Air Force Training (1 May–4 August '62)," August 24, 1962, p. 1.

96 "I thought Frost was one of the": NSA, Secret/Comint Channels Only, Oral History of Dr. Howard Campaigne (June 29, 1983), p. 126.

96 "I saw him chew out Frank Raven": Farley quoted in ibid.

96 "I hadn't been north of Minneapolis": NSA, Top Secret/Comint Channels Only, Oral History of Lieutenant General Gordon A. Blake (April 19, 1984), p. 5.

97 "So all of a sudden": ibid., pp. 17–19.

97 "Jack Frost was under some nebulous": ibid., pp. 57–58.

99 "I left that one to Lou": ibid., p. 71.

99 "NSA has been directed": NSA, Top Secret/Comint Channels Only message, DIRNSA to CNO (July 19, 1962).

99 "From the ship we could look up": NSA, Secret/Sensitive, Oral History of Harold L. Parish (October 12, 1982), p. 20.

100 an Elint operator on the *Oxford:* NSA, Secret intercept, "Whiff Radar in Cuba" (August 17, 1962).

100 "We were called down and told": NSA, Secret/Comint Channels Only, Oral History of Harold L. Parish (October 12, 1982), p. 3.

100 told one high-level group: CIA, "Chronology of John McCone's Suspicions on the Military Build-up in Cuba Prior to Kennedy's October 22 Speech," August 17, 1962.

100 "It was for most of us our initial": ibid., pp. 36–37.

101 "We would recess for a few hours": NSA, Top Secret/Comint Channels Only, Oral History of Lieutenant General Gordon A. Blake (April 19, 1984), p. 52.

101 "One collection facility . . . against x-hundred emitters": NSA, Secret/Comint Channels Only, Oral History of Harold L. Parish (October 12, 1982), pp. 87–89.

101 "Concentrated efforts have been made": NSA, Secret/Kimbo intercept, "Reflection of Soviet Bloc Pilots/Technicians in Cuban Air Force Training," August 24, 1962.

101 nighttime jet gunnery exercises: NSA, Secret/Kimbo intercept, "Night Aerial Gunnery Exercises by Cuban Jet Aircraft," August 28, 1962.

101 NSA issued a dramatic report: NSA, Top Secret/Dinar report, "Further Information on Soviet/Cuban Trade," August 31, 1962.

102 "Sigint evidence of Cuban acquisition": NSA, Top Secret/Dinar/Noforn/Limited Distribution, Funnel Handling, September 11, 1962.

102 "This [equipment] is now operating": White House, Top Secret/Sensitive memorandum, Carl Kaysen, Deputy Special Assistant to the President for National Security Affairs, to President Kennedy, September 1, 1962 (FRUS, Vol. X, #405).

102 "I feel that our first priority": NSA, Top Secret/Comint Channels Only, DIRNSA to Klocko, October 10, 1962.

102 "shipborne collection platform"; "NSA is therefore commencing": NSA, Top Secret message, DIRNSA to JCS, September 17, 1962.

103 "It was very difficult": NSA, Top Secret/Comint Channels Only, Oral History of Lieutenant General Gordon A. Blake (April 19, 1984), pp. 58–59.

103 326th ASA Company: The Army Security Agency's detachment at Homestead eventually became permanent. In August 1967 the field station's activities were consolidated with similar Air Force and Navy operations in a newly constructed operations building on Card Sound Road, about fifteen miles south of Homestead Air Base. The operations building was known as Site Alpha. U.S. Army Intelligence and Security Command, "INSCOM and Its Heritage: An Organizational History of the Command and its Units" (1985), pp. 98–100.

103 "What had been sort of a lazy tempo": Owen Englander, "A Closer Look at the Early Days of NSG at Key West," *NCVA Cryptolog* (Winter 1997), pp. 3, 5.

104 World War I bunker: ibid. The original listening post was set up in Key West in July 1961. In 1981 the Naval Security Group Detachment, Key West, moved to the Naval Air Base at Truman Annex, where it occupied a 40,000-square-foot building that once housed the Navy Sonar School. It employed over 250 officers, enlisted and civilian personnel. The station was closed in 1996. See Commander Thomas P. Herlihy and CTR1 Gerard A. Bradman, "NSGA Key West, Florida," *NCVA Cryptolog* (Spring 1996), p. 7.

104 "Collection at thirteen miles was pretty good": This and other remarks are drawn from the author's interview with John Arnold, July 2000.

106 "Spoon Rest": NSA, Secret intercept, "New Radar Deployment in Cuba," September 19, 1962.

107 "By smoothly varying the length": Details of Palladium are drawn from Gene Poteat, "Elint and Stealth," *The Intelligencer* (December 1999), pp. 12–13. *The Intelligencer* is published by the Association of Former Intelligence Officers.

108 At the meeting: CIA, memorandum for the executive director (prepared on February 28, 1963) (FRUS, Vol. X, #421).

108 Cuban air defense system: NSA, Secret/Kimbo intercept (DTG: 1649), October 10, 1962.

109 "Communications security has been": NSA, Secret/Sabre intercept, "Cuban Air Force VHF Communications Procedure," May 17, 1962, p. 2.

109 Instead, NSA depended mostly on: NSA also depended to some extent on "traffic analysis"—examination of the "externals" of encrypted messages. These externals could give indications of the cargo's importance because of the frequency or precedence of the messages sent. Unable to read encrypted messages sent to the Soviet cargo ships *Khabarovsk* and *Mikhail Uritskij,* for example, NSA nevertheless could conclude that they were on important missions because of the "high precedence" of the messages sent to it. Such intelligence, NSA noted, "may indicate these two ships are engaged in other than routine activities." NSA, Secret/Kimbo intercept, "Unusual Number of Soviet Passenger Ships En Route Cuba," July 24, 1962, p. 2.

109 "electronic intelligence led to the photographic intelligence": Department of the Navy, John Keppler, *A Bumpy Road: The United States Navy and Cuba 1959–1963* (Summer 1991), p. 37 (The Naval Historical Center, Naval Operational Archives).

109 "They would send vessels out": NSA, Secret/Comint Channels Only, Oral History of Harold L. Parish (October 12, 1982), p. 21.

109 "We were all listening for Russian communications": interview with Aubrey Brown (January 2000).

109 "Jesus Christ": interview with Max Buscher, May 2000.

110 McCone brought up: ibid.

110 "You kind of know": Aubrey Brown interview.

110 "The codebreakers were having a tough time": Buscher interview.

111 "We had constructed": NSA, Secret/Comint Channels Only, Oral History of Harold L. Parish (October 12, 1982), p. 5.

111 plotting board: information from former NSA official Vera Ruth Filby, NSA Symposium (October 27, 1999).

112 "One of our T Branchers": Buscher interview.

112 McCone discussed the *Terek:* White House, Top Secret, Minutes of the 507th Meeting of the National Security Council (October 22, 1962) (JFKL, National Security Files, Meetings and Memoranda Series, NSC Meetings) (FRUS, Vol. XI, #41); CIA, Top Secret/Eyes Only, "DCI Notes for DCI Briefing," October 22, 1962 (CIA, Cuban Missile Crisis, 1962, pp. 271–73).

112 At 1:00 P.M. the Strategic Air Command: JCS, Top Secret report, "Chronology of the JCS Decisions Concerning the Cuban Crisis," January 4, 1963, pp. 2, 28 (Lemnitzer Papers, National Defense University).

113 Kennedy addressed: text of President Kennedy's radio/television address to the nation, October 22, 1962 (JFKL).

113 "I had the first watch": NSA, Secret/Comint Channels Only, Oral History of Harold L. Parish (October 12, 1982), p. 64.

113 "I was thinking": interview with Keith Taylor, May 2000.

113 "After the president's announcement": Brown interview.

114 listening post intercepted: NSA, Secret/Sabre intercept (DTG: 0516Z), October 23, 1962.

114 *Kura:* NSA, Secret/Sabre intercept (DTG: 0636Z), October 23, 1962.

114 *Nikolaevsk:* NSA, Secret/Sabre intercept (DTG: 1326Z), October 23, 1962.

114 more than half spoke Russian: NSA, Secret/Kimbo intercept (DTG: 2115Z), October 23, 1962.

115 "A Flash precedence message": Pete Azzole, "Afterthoughts," *NCVA Cryptolog* (Summer 1993), p. 13.

115 A Pentagon official told him: CIA, Top Secret/Eyes Only, Memorandum for the Files, "John McCone meeting with the President," October 23, 1962 (FRUS, Vol. XI, #51).

115 Details on the *Urgench:* NSA, Secret/Sabre intercept (DTG: 1638Z), October 24, 1962.

115 Harry Eisenbeiss: Dino A. Brugioni, *Eyeball to Eyeball* (New York: Random House, 1991), p. 391.

116 "has altered course and is probably": NSA, Secret/Sabre intercept (DTG: 1917Z), October 24, 1962.

116 "HFDF . . . fix on the Soviet cargo ship": NSA, Secret/Sabre intercept (DTG: 1533Z), October 24, 1962.

116 passed the note to McCone: White House, Top Secret/Sensitive, Third Meeting of the Executive Committee of the NSC, October 24, 1962 (JFKL, National Security Files, Meetings and Memorandum Series, Executive Committee, Vol. I).

116 "Mr. President, we have a preliminary report": Robert F. Kennedy, *Thirteen Days* (New York: Norton, 1969), p. 71.

116 "no ships . . . be stopped": ibid., pp. 71–72.

116 "Have you got the word": Department of State, Memorandum of Telephone Conversation, Bundy to Ball, October 24, 1962 (FRUS, Vol. XI, #58).

116 "desperate signals": U.S. Mission to the UN, Confidential/Limited Distribution memorandum, Schlesinger to Stevenson, October 25, 1962 (JFKL, National Security Files, Countries Series, Cuba, General).

117 "In view of these signals": ibid.

117 "Although no additional missiles": JCS, Top Secret report, "Chronology of the JCS Decisions Concerning the Cuban Crisis," January 4, 1963, p. 36 (Lemnitzer Papers, National Defense University).

118 "DF line bearings indicate": NSA, Secret/Sabre intercept (DTG: 0645Z), October 27, 1962.

118 "One mission aborted for mechanical": White House, Top Secret/Sensitive, "Summary Record of the Eighth Meeting of the Executive Committee of the NSC," October 27, 1962 (JFKL, National Security Files, Meetings and Memoranda Series, Executive Committee, Vol. I, Meetings 6–10).

118 "If our planes are fired on": ibid.

118 "The wreckage of the U-2 was on the ground": ibid.

119 "Any time the Cubans scrambled": NSA, Secret/Comint Channels Only, Oral History of Harold L. Parish (October 12, 1982), pp. 40–41.

119 "You'd debrief in the airplane": ibid.

119 "The plan was to lure": Bruce Bailey, "The RB-47 & RB-135 in Vietnam," web posting at <http://www.55srwa.org/55_vietnam.html> (May 1, 2000).

120 "In the last two hours": Department of Justice, Top Secret memorandum, Robert Kennedy to Rusk, October 30, 1962 (JFKL, President's Office Files, Cuba Missile Crisis, Khrushchev Correspondence) (FRUS, Vol. XI, #96).

120 "I said that he had better understand": ibid.

120 "I said a letter had just been transmitted": ibid.

121 "Any steps toward easing tensions": ibid.

121 " 'Because of the plane' ": Dobrynin's cable to the Soviet Foreign Ministry, October 27, 1962.

121 "The most important thing": ibid.

122 "then we should take out the SAM sites": White House, Top Secret/Sensitive, "Summary Record of the Ninth Meeting of the Executive Committee of the National Security Council," October 27, 1962 (JFKL, National Security Files, Meetings and Memoranda Series, Executive Committee, Vol. I, Meetings 6–10) (FRUS, Vol. XI, #97).

122 "unless irrefutable evidence of the dismantling": JCS, Top Secret report, "Chronology of the JCS Decisions Concerning the Cuban Crisis," January 4, 1963, p. 39 (Lemnitzer Papers, National Defense University).

122 "When I reported in": NSA, Secret/Comint Channels Only, Oral History of Harold L. Parish (October 12, 1982), pp. 6–8.

122 "The Soviet government": message from Chairman Khrushchev to President Kennedy, October 28, 1962 (JFKL, National Security Files, Countries Series, USSR, Khrushchev Correspondence) (FRUS, Vol. XI, #102).

122 "I remember during the period": NSA, Secret/Comint Channels Only, Oral History of Harold L. Parish (October 12, 1982), p. 60.

123 "All the communications that we had": NSA, Secret/Comint Channels Only, Oral History of Harold L. Parish (October 12, 1982), p. 6.

123 "After the offensive weapons were removed": ibid, pp. 15–16.

123 "very, very bad things": ibid., pp. 17–18.

123 "During the crisis": ibid., p. 22.

123 "There were times": Robert D. Farley, quoted in ibid.

124 "We had photographs of missile launchers": Robert McNamara, interviewed on CNN *Worldview,* June 18, 1998.

124 Lourdes: According to the CIA, the exact location of the listening post is 22 59 15N and 84 27 50W.

125 vast area of twenty-eight square miles: President Ronald Reagan, quoted in "President's Speech on Military Spending and a New Defense," *New York Times,* March 24, 1983.

125 "the general dissatisfaction of the President": CIA, Secret/Eyes Only, Helms Memorandum for the Record, October 16, 1962 (FRUS, Vol. XI, #19).

125 "I stated that we were prepared": ibid.

125 "We suggested to them": NSA, Secret/Comint Channels Only, Oral History of Harold L. Parish (October 12, 1982), pp. 38–39.

126 "The tubes would burn out": ibid.

126 "NSA will continue an intensive program": CIA, Top Secret memorandum, McCone to Bundy (December 15, 1962) (JFKL, National Security Files, Meetings and Memoranda Series, NSAM 208) (FRUS, Vol. XI, #248).

126 "Duty station for the *Muller*": Bill Baer, "USNS Joseph E. Muller, TAG–171," web site http://www.asa.npoint.net/baer01.htm (January 3, 2000).

127 "We only had": ibid.

127 "Since they used microwave": Mike Sannes, "USNS *Muller* and the ASA," at web site http://www.asa.npoint.net/sannes01.htm (January 3, 2000).

127 "Often they sent": ibid.

127 "It would be a good idea to assassinate": NSA, Secret/Kimbo intercept (DTG: 1551Z), January 16, 1963.

128 "Mr. McCone cabled me this morning": CIA, Secret letter, Carter to Bundy, May 2, 1963 (JFKL, National Security Files, Countries Series, Cuba, Intelligence Material) (FRUS, Vol. XI, #332).

129 "Lechuga hinted that Castro": Department of State, Secret memorandum, Attwood to Gordon Chase of the NSC, November 8, 1963 (LBJL, National Security File, Country File, Cuba, Contact with Cuban Leaders) (FRUS, Vol. XI, #374).

129 Major René Vallejo: ibid.

129 "Castro would go along": Department of State, Top Secret/Eyes Only memorandum, Attwood to Gordon Chase of the NSC (November 22, 1963) (LBJL, National Security File, Country File, Cuba, Contact with Cuban Leaders) (FRUS, Vol. XI, #379).

130 "At the President's instruction": White House, Secret/Sensitive, Bundy Memorandum for the Record, November 12, 1963 (LBJL, National Security File, Country File, Cuba, Contact with Cuban Leaders) (FRUS, Vol. XI, #377).

130 "Vallejo's manner": Department of State, Top Secret/Eyes Only memorandum, Attwood to Gordon Chase of the NSC, November 22, 1963 (LBJL, National Security File, Country File, Cuba, Contact with Cuban Leaders) (FRUS, Vol. XI, #379).

130 "I believe that the approaching": NSA, Top Secret/Dinar, *Report on Cuba's Internal Problems with Rebels* (November 22, 1963) (ARRB).

131 NSA Sigint Command Center: Details are in NSA, Top Secret/Dinar, "Record of Events Log," November 22, 1963 (ARRB).

131 Don Gardiner: Details of what the Foreign Intelligence Advisory Board, Taylor, and McNamara were doing at the time of the assassination are in William Manchester, *The Death of a President* (New York: Harper & Row, 1967), pp. 140–44, 190.

132 "When this monstrously terrible thing happened": CIA, Carter to Judy Eithelberg, November 30, 1963 (Carter papers, George C. Marshall Research Library, Lexington, VA).

132 "President Kennedy is dead": ibid.

132 "Thousands upon thousands of miles away": George Morton, "Kami Seya—1963," *NCVA Cryptolog* (Fall 1992), p. 9.

132 *Valdez:* Ron Briggs, quoted at web site <http://www.geocities.com/swabbyctr1/MemoriesPage2. html>.

132 NSA continued: For NSA activities immediately after the assassination, see NSA, Top Secret/Comint Channels Only, Eugene F. Yeates Memorandum for the Record, June 15, 1978 (ARRB).

132 "A state of alert is ordered": NSA, Top Secret/Dinar/Noforn, "SIGINT Daily Summary Number Twenty," November 23, 1963 (ARRB). See also NSA, Top Secret/Dinar, Watch Report 0600 22 November–0600 23 November 1963 (ARRB).

133 "military units are being relocated": NSA, Top Secret/Dinar intercept, "Cuba's Reaction to Kennedy's Murder," November 27, 1963 (ARRB).

133 Mexico, Venezuela, and Colombia: NSA, Top Secret/Dinar intercept, "Latin American Countries Place Military Units on Alert," November 22, 1963 (ARRB).

133 "I got the immediate impression": NSA, Top Secret/Dinar intercept, "Comment on Castro's Reaction to Death of Kennedy," November 27, 1963 (ARRB).

133 "The assassination of Kennedy": NSA, Top Secret/Dinar intercept, "Cuban Statement on Visa for Oswald," November 25, 1963 (ARRB).

133 "were unanimous in believing": NSA, Top Secret/Dinar intercept, "Cuban Authorities State Views Concerning Death of Kennedy," November 27, 1963 (ARRB).

133 "In diplomatic circles": NSA, Top Secret/Dinar intercept, "Robert Kennedy Viewed as Leading Contender to Succeed His Brother in 1964," November 22, 1963 (ARRB).

134 Egyptian diplomats: NSA, Top Secret/Dinar intercept, "Egyptian Reaction to President Kennedy's Murder," November 23, 1963 (ARRB).

134 Dutch intercepts: NSA, Top Secret/Dinar intercept, "Information Requested about Foreign Representatives' Attendance at Kennedy Funeral," November 26, 1963 (ARRB).

134 "will considerably weaken": NSA, Top Secret/Dinar intercept, "Kennedy's Death Felt to Weaken Foreign Policy," November 23, 1963 (ARRB).

134 "After signing the register": NSA, Top Secret/Dinar intercept, "American Ambassador Believes Russia and Cuba Involved in Kennedy's Death," November 25, 1963 (ARRB).

134 "Behind the mysterious crime": NSA, Top Secret/Dinar/Minimum Distribution intercept, "President Kennedy's Assassination a Zionist Conspiracy," November 25, 1963 (ARRB).

134 Italian ambassador to Syria: NSA, Top Secret/Dinar intercept, "Syrians Claim Zionists Responsible for Death of President Kennedy," November 29, 1963 (ARRB).

134 "Certain ill-intentioned persons": NSA, Secret/Sabre intercept, "Reaction to Kennedy's Assassination," November 25, 1963 (ARRB).

134 "were deeply touched": NSA, Top Secret/Dinar intercept, "Hungarian Reaction to News of Assassination of President Kennedy," November 25, 1963 (ARRB).

135 "alarming . . . anti-Communist hysteria": NSA, Top Secret/Dinar intercept, "Reactions to Kennedy's Death," November 27, 1963 (ARRB).

135 "In spite of the antagonism": NSA, Secret/Sabre intercept, "Official Cuban Statement on Death of President Kennedy," November 23, 1963 (ARRB).

135 "The manner of perforating": NSA, Secret/Comint Channels Only, Meredith K. Gardner Memorandum for the Record, June 15, 1964 (ARRB).

135 "the names appearing in Lee's and Marina's address books": ibid.

135 "The appearance of the term 'micro dots' ": ibid.

136 "I have eliminated two items": NSA, Secret/Comint Channels Only memorandum, Rowlett to Tordella, June 16, 1964 (ARRB).

136 "I do not believe a statement": ibid.

136 "The ball is in our court": White House, Top Secret/Eyes Only/Sensitive memorandum, Chase to Bundy, December 2, 1963 (LBJL, National Security File, Country File, Cuba, Contact with Cuban Leaders) (FRUS, Vol. XI, #382).

137 "I assume you will want to brief the President": White House, Top Secret/Eyes Only memorandum, Chase to Bundy, November 25, 1963 (LBJL, National Security File, Country File, Cuba, Contact with Cuban Leaders) (FRUS, Vol. XI, #378).

137 "Lechuga . . . and the Cubans in general": White House, Top Secret/Eyes Only memorandum, Chase to Bundy, December 11, 1963 (LBJL, National Security File, Country File, Cuba, Contact with Cuban Leaders) (FRUS, Vol. XI, #387).

137 "He asked": CIA, "Memorandum of DCI Meeting with President Johnson," November 28, 1963 (FRUS, Vol. XI, #381).

137 Johnson later approved: White House, Top Secret/Sensitive, "Chase Memorandum of Meeting with the President," December 19, 1963 (LBJL, National Security File, Country File, Cuba, Meetings) (FRUS, Vol. XI, #388).

138 "Until the tragic death of President Kennedy": NSA, Top Secret/Dinar intercept, "Castro Interview on Relations with U.S.," January 3, 1964 (ARRB).

CHAPTER 6: Ears

Page

139 Nate Gerson: Nate Gerson, "Collaboration in Sigint: Canada–U.S.," *La Physique au Canada* (November–December 1998), pp. 359–62.

140 "Study your globe": William M. Leary and Leonard A. LeSchack, *Project Coldfeet: Secret Mission to a Soviet Ice Station* (Annapolis, Md.: Naval Institute Press, 1996), p. 18.

140 "vicious winds"; Drifting Station Alpha: Details on Station Alpha, and the quotations from Smith, come from ibid., pp. 38–42.

141 Nate Gerson concluded: Gerson, "Collaboration in Sigint," pp. 359–62.

142 Canada's most important listening post: "Northernmost Weather Station Called Major Link for Espionage," *Toronto Globe and Mail,* January 12, 1974.

144 "It was the most desolate": Leary and LeSchack, *Project Coldfeet*, p. 128.
145 "Instantly upon loss of sight of the buildings": ibid., p. 144.
146 Its budget had risen: Richard Fryklund, "Two House Groups Set to Probe NSA Secrets," *Evening Star* (Washington, D.C.), September 14, 1960.
147 broken the cipher systems: "Text of Statements Read in Moscow by Former U.S. Security Agency Employees," *New York Times*, September 7, 1960; Osgood Caruthers, "Two Code Clerks Defect to Soviet: Score U.S. 'Spying,' " *The New York Times*, September 7, 1960.
147 Mike Stockmeier: His account is in his article "Before Elmendorf," *NCVA Cryptolog* (Winter 1992), p. 23.
148 *Cold and icy blue*: Edward Bryant Bates, "Station X Adak Aleutian Islands, 1943–1945," *NCVA Cryptolog* (January 1994), p. 24.
148 "I have been told": Karl Beeman, "Thesis on the Advantages of Living in Adak, Or, There Are None!" Reprinted in *NCVA Cryptolog* (Special Edition, 1991), p. 34.
149 committing suicide: Edward Bryant Bates, "What! Adak Again?" *NCVA Cryptolog* (Special Edition, 1991), pp. 33–34.
149 Melody: Gene Poteat, "Elint and Stealth," *The Intelligencer* (December 1999), pp. 10–13. *The Intelligencer* is published by the Association of Former Intelligence Officers.
150 a giant sixty-foot satellite dish: ibid.
150 Field Station, Berlin: U.S. Army Intelligence and Security Command, "INSCOM and Its Heritage: An Organizational History of the Command and Its Units" (1985), pp. 95–97.
151 "It was acting as a great big antenna": John Diamond, "Ex-Spies' Memories Full of Past Intrigue," *Chicago Tribune* (September 13, 1999).
151 Bremerhaven: U.S. Naval Security Group Activity, Bremerhaven, "Command Histories," 1968–1973. The facility was established in 1950 and disestablished on December 31, 1972. Most of the intercept operators were then transferred to listening posts at Edzell, Scotland, and Augsburg, West Germany.
151 "You're trying to pull": interview with Aubrey Brown, January 2000.
152 "One would have had to experience": Jeff Tracy, "The Merry Men of Todendorf," *NCVA Cryptolog* (Winter 1992), p. 22. The facility was first activated in the late 1950s and decommissioned in the late 1970s.
152 "a target-rich environment": e-mail from Richard E. Kerr, Jr., January 26, 2000.
152 "At night": F. Harrison Wallace, Jr., "The History of Eckstein Border Site 1958–1993." Web posting at <http://members.tripod.com/adm/popup/roadmap.shtml?946895392450> (January 2, 2000).
152 "There was no running water on the mountain": ibid.
153 "The finest hour for Eckstein": ibid.
153 Creek Rose, Creek Stone, and Creek Flea: The details in this paragraph are drawn from U.S. Air Force, Secret, Headquarters, 7499th Support Group, "Command History, January 1, 1967, to June 30, 1967" (U.S. Air Force Historical Research Center, Maxwell AFB, Alabama).

154 "provided precise measurements": ibid.

154 able to detect East German missile equipment being moved: ibid.

154 "We couldn't listen": Interview with former Karamürsel intercept operator.

155 "Our mission": Jack Wood, Internet posting at <http://www.delphi.com/karamursel/messages/?msg=50.1&ctx=1> (July 21, 1999).

155 "Malfunction!!!": "Was Gagarin's Flight a Near Disaster?" *Space Views Update,* March 16, 1996.

155 a place called Kamiseya: See generally "Kami Seya Special," *NCVA Cryptolog* (Fall 1997).

156 Misawa Air Base: U.S. Army Intelligence and Security Command, "INSCOM and Its Heritage: An Organizational History of the Command and Its Units" (1985), pp. 105–106.

157 "Security was hermetic on that post": For information about Torii Station, I have drawn on an e-mail from David Parks, February 8, 2000.

157 "It was reflected in the stuff we copied every day": interview with former intercept operator at Okinawa.

159 "Along the way, our ground stations would listen in": Robert Wheatley, Internet posting, <http://38.158.99.147/Part3_Page.htm> (April 29, 2000).

160 "locate intercept stations": NSA, Dr. Howard Campaigne Oral History, p. 66.

160 rugged, windswept desert of Eritrea: U.S. Army, *A History of Kagnew Station and American Forces in Eritrea* (undated).

161 "The Operations Center . . . went on strike": Arthur Adolphsen, "Kagnew Recollections," Internet posting, <http://www.fgi.net/~kagnew/stories/14.html> (July 19, 1999).

162 "The priority tasks from the NSA": This and other details on Aden come from Jock Kane, "GCHQ: The Negative Asset," pp. 162–72. This manuscript was seized by the British government under the Official Secrets Act in 1984, and the book was never published. The author obtained a copy of the manuscript before the seizure.

162 Ascension Island: Andrew Marshall, "Remote Island Home of Spies and Turtles Opens Its Doors to Tourists," *The Independent* (London), February 5, 1998.

162 "I looked and looked": Phillip Yasson, "Midway Island 1960," *NCVA Cryptolog* (Winter 2000), pp. 10, 15.

164 "There was a château": This and the early background of Diego Garcia are taken from Simon Winchester, *The Sun Never Sets: Travels to the Remaining Outposts of the British Empire* (New York: Prentice Hall, 1985), pp. 27–58.

164 "They were to be given no protection": ibid.

165 "A Soviet trawler maintained station": This and other details of Jibstay are drawn from Monty Rich, "NSGA Diego Garcia: The Prelude," *NCVA Cryptolog* (Spring 2000), p. 1.

165 "All we had was seahuts": Gregor McAdam quoted in Internet posting at http://www.zianet.com/tedmorris/dg/warstories.html on August 11, 1999.

165 Classic Wizard: U.S. Naval Communications Station Diego Garcia, "Command Histories, 1973–1977." The Naval Security Group was officially activated on May 1, 1974, and the Classic Wizard facility was completed on April 20, 1976.

165 White Cloud: Other ground stations for the White Cloud satellite system were built at Adak, Alaska; Blossom Point, Maryland; Guam; Edzell, Scotland; and Winter Harbor, Maine. Winter Harbor also served as the training facility for the program.

166 "On those few occasions": Stephen J. Forsberg quoted in http://www.zianet.com/tedmorris/dg/warstories.html on August 11, 1999.

166 a small private sailboat: Winchester, *The Sun Never Sets,* pp. 53–58.

166 By 1989 the Naval Security Group: James Yandle, "Naval Security Station Visit," *NCVA Cryptolog* (Fall 1989), pp. 5, 7.

166 presence on Cyprus: Brendan O'Malley and Ian Craig, *The Cyprus Conspiracy* (London: I. B. Tauris & Co., 1999), pp. 79–84.

167 at Akrotiri: Mike Theodoulou, "News of the World," *Times* (London), January 16, 1999.

167 Mission of the USS *Halfbeak;* Cassidy comments: Interview with George Cassidy, August 2000.

173 Details on the *Kursk* and the USS *Memphis:* Steven Lee Myers and Christopher Drew, "U.S. Spy Sub Said to Record Torpedo Blast Aboard Kursk," *New York Times* (August 29, 2000), p. 1.

174 30,000 five-figure groups: Andy Thomas, "British Signals Intelligence after the Second World War," *Intelligence and National Security* (October 1988), p. 104.

174 Earl Richardson: William C. Grayson, *Chicksands: A Millennium of History* (Crofton, Md.: Shefford Press, 1999), p. 221. Chicksands was closed in 1995 and is now the home of the Defence Intelligence and Security Center, a defense agency responsible for providing training throughout the spectrum of the military intelligence and security community.

174 "Much of the caution was perverse": ibid.

176 "We would go into bays": This and the following quotations come from the author's interview with George A. Cassidy, January 2000.

176 "the weather conditions were so bad": Interview with Aubrey Brown, January 2000.

177 the CIA dumped some $12 million: Philip Agee, *Inside the Company* (New York: Stonehill, 1975), p. 321.

177 "put the guys": Brown interview.

178 "Every time we got it": Interview with George A. Cassidy, January 2000.

178 "I was called to Washington in the mid-fifties": Oral History of Captain Phil H. Bucklew, USN (Ret.) (March 1982) (U.S. Naval Institute, Annapolis).

178 "I was probably the father of it at NSA": interview with Frank Raven, July 23, 1981.

179 "They complained very bitterly": ibid.

179 "The *Valdez* was my dream ship": ibid.

180 "The bigger ships": interview with Lieutenant General Marshall S. Carter, July 17–18, 1980.

180 "Revelation of some sensitive": NSA, Top Secret/Umbra report, "A Review of the Technical Research Ship Program 1961–1969" (undated), pp. 126–27.

181 Every day at 8:00 A.M., 2:30 P.M.: William Galvez, *Che in Africa* (Hoboken, N.J.: Ocean Press, 1999), p. 224.

181 "It seems excessive": ibid.

182 "Those of us aboard *Liberty*": Details of the *Liberty*'s Congo cruise come from Robert Casale, "Drama on the Congo," *U.S. Naval Cryptologic Veterans Association* (Paducah, Ky.: Turner Publishing Co., 1996), p. 77.

CHAPTER 7: Blood

Page

185 "Now, frankly": interview with Frank Raven, July 23, 1981.

186 "We . . . had a choice": *New York Times,* August 21, 1982.

187 a contingency plan: Details on the selection of the *Liberty* for the Middle East mission come from NSA, Top Secret/Umbra, "Attack on a Sigint Collector, the USS *Liberty*" (1981), pp. 5–13.

188 MAKE IMMEDIATE PREPARATIONS: James M. Ennes, Jr., *Assault on the Liberty* (New York: Random House, 1979), p. 19.

188 "It was a message from the Joint Chiefs": ibid., p. 15.

188 "I mean, my God": Raven interview, August 11, 1981.

189 Bryce Lockwood: interview with Bryce Lockwood, February 2000.

190 "who was communicating": Raven interview, August 11, 1981.

190 "You can sit in Crete and watch": ibid.

191 "We have an FBIS report": Details on Rostow come from Hugh Sidey, "The Presidency: Over the Hot Line—the Middle East," *Life,* June 16, 1967.

192 "Early this morning": Department of State, Secret Flash message from Barbour, U.S. Embassy, Tel Aviv, to Secretary of State and White House, June 5, 1967 (LBJL).

193 the hot line was activated: Department of Defense, press release, August 30, 1963; A. Golikov, "Direct Line, Moscow–White House," *Ogonyok* (Russian magazine), August 25, 1963, p. 1; Robert Cahn, " 'Hot Line'—Never a Busy Signal," *Christian Science Monitor,* June 10, 1965.

193 "Premier Kosygin is on the hot line": Robert S. McNamara, *In Retrospect: The Tragedy and Lessons of Vietnam* (New York: Vintage Books, 1995), pp. 278–279.

194 Johnson told Kosygin that the United States did not intend: "Hot Line Diplomacy," *Time,* June 16, 1967.

195 "We were in disbelief and mystified": Unless otherwise noted, all details about the flight of the EC-121 Willy Victor come from e-mail, Marvin E. Nowicki to author, March 4, 2000. Nowicki was the chief Hebrew/Russian linguist aboard the EC-121.

197 Some twenty Soviet warships: NSA, Top Secret/Umbra, "Attack on a Sigint Collector, the USS *Liberty*" (1981), p. 19.

197 Then he asked if any consideration was being given: NSA, Secret/Spoke/Limited Distribution, "USS *Liberty:* Chronology of Events" (undated), p. 3.

197 "For God's sake": Raven interview, August 11, 1981.

198 the message never reached her: For details on the message delays, I rely on NSA, Top Secret/Umbra report, "Attack on a Sigint Collector, the USS *Liberty*" (1981), pp. 21–23.

199 "Uniform of the Day": USS *Liberty*, Plan of the Day for June 8, 1967.

199 John Scott noticed: U.S. Navy, Court of Inquiry transcript, Testimony of Ensign John Scott (June 10, 1967), p. 59.

199 "Fabulous morning": Ennes, *Assault on the Liberty*, p. 49.

199 the naval observer: Israeli Defense Force, Confidential, Court of Inquiry Report, Decision of Examining Judge, Lieutenant Colonel Yishaya Yerushalmi (July 21, 1967).

199 "What we could see": "Attack on the *Liberty*," Thames Television (London), 1987.

200 "How would it affect our mission": Ennes, *Assault on the Liberty*, pp. 43–44.

200 reconnaissance was repeated at approximately thirty-minute intervals: NSA, Top Secret/Umbra, "Attack on a Sigint Collector, the USS *Liberty*" (1981), p. 25.

200 "It had a big Star of David on it": interview with Richard L. Weaver, February 2000.

200 the minaret at El Arish could be seen: NSA, Top Secret/Umbra, "Attack on a Sigint Collector, the USS *Liberty*" (1981), p. 25.

200 Commander McGonagle . . . radar: U.S. Navy, Court of Inquiry transcript, testimony of Commander McGonagle (June 10, 1967), p. 31.

201 One Israeli general: Robert J. Donovan and the staff of the *Los Angeles Times*, *Israel's Fight for Survival* (New York: New American Library, 1967), p. 71.

201 A convoy: My account of the Israeli attack on the UN convoy is drawn from the *Toronto Globe and Mail*, June 16, 1967.

202 "I saw a line of prisoners": The account of the massacre comes from Youssef M. Ibrahim, "Egypt Says Israelis Killed P.O.W.'s in '67 War," *New York Times*, September 21, 1995; "Israeli Killing of POWs in '67: Alleged Deaths of Hundreds Said Known to Leaders," *Newsday* (August 17, 1995).

202 Gabi Bron saw: quoted by Serge Schmemann, "After a General Tells of Killing P.O.W.'s in 1956, Israelis Argue over Ethics of War," *New York Times*, August 21, 1995.

202 Aryeh Yitzhaki, who worked: His account appears in "Israel Reportedly Killed POWs in '67," *Washington Post* (August 17, 1995); "Israeli Killing of POWs in '67: Alleged Deaths of Hundreds Said Known to Leaders," *Newsday* (August 17, 1995).

202 One of his men: Barton Gellman, "Debate Tainting Image of Purity Wrenches Israel," *Washington Post* (August 19, 1995).

202 "I had my Karl Gustav": Schmemann, "After a General Tells of Killing P.O.W.'s in 1956, Israelis Argue over Ethics of War."

202 "If I were to be put on trial": Katherine M. Metres, "As Evidence Mounts, Toll of Israeli Prisoner of War Massacres Grows," *Washington Report on Middle East Affairs* (February/March 1996), pp. 17, 104–105.

202 Sharon . . . refused to say: Gellman, "Debate Tainting Image of Purity Wrenches Israel," *Washington Post* (August 19, 1995).

203 "indirectly responsible": Andrew and Leslie Cockburn, *Dangerous Liaison: The Inside Story of the U.S.-Israeli Covert Relationship* (New York: HarperCollins, 1991), p. 333; see also "The Commission of Inquiry into Events at the Refugee Camps in Beirut" (Kahan Commission), Final Report, published as *The Beirut Massacre* (Princeton, N.J.: Karz-Cohl, 1983).

203 he [Sharon] set off the bloodiest upheaval: Deborah Sontag, "Violence Spreads to Israeli Towns; Arab Toll at 28," *New York Times* (October 2, 2000).

203 "Israel doesn't need this": Gellman, "Debate Tainting Image of Purity Wrenches Israel."

203 "The whole army leadership"; "Israeli Killing of POWs in '67: Alleged Death of Hundreds Said Known to Leaders," *Newsday* (August 17, 1995).

203 not releasing a report he had prepared: Naomi Segal, "Historian Alleges POW Deaths in 1956, 1967," Jewish Telegraph Agency (August 17, 1995).

203 lies about who started the war: By at least June 7, Israel was still lying about who started the war. Israeli Defense Minister Moshe Dayan continued to contend, "Arabs attacked Israel" (Department of State, Secret/Limited Official Use, Chronology of US-Israeli Consultations on the Middle East, May 17–June 10, 1967 [June 15, 1967]).

203 "any instrument which sought to penetrate": Dr. Richard K. Smith, "The Violation of the *Liberty*," *United States Naval Institute Proceedings* (June 1978), pp. 63–70.

203 $10.2 million: NSA, Top Secret/Umbra, "Attack on a Sigint Collector, the USS *Liberty*" (1981), p. 64.

204 At 10:39 A.M., the minaret at El Arish: U.S. Navy, Court of Inquiry transcript, Testimony of Commander McGonagle (June 10, 1967), p. 32.

204 "I reported this detection": "Attack on the *Liberty*," Thames Television.

204 "an electromagnetic audio-surveillance ship": Israeli Defense Force, Confidential, Court of Inquiry Report, Decision of the Examining Judge, Lieutenant Colonel Yishaya Yerushalmi (July 21, 1967).

206 "Between five in the morning": Oral History of James M. Ennes, Jr. (November 12, 1998). (Unless otherwise indicated, the oral histories of the *Liberty* crewmembers were conducted by former Naval Security Group member Richard G. Schmucker.)

206 range of such guns: See U.S. Navy, Top Secret/Limited Distribution/Noforn, "Findings of Fact, Opinions and Recommendations of a Court of Inquiry Convened by Order of Commander in Chief, United States Pacific Fleet, to Inquire into the Circumstances Relating to the Seizure of USS *Pueblo* (AGER-2) by North Korean Naval Forces" (April 9, 1969), p. 12.

207 "He longed for the sea": Ennes, *Assault on the Liberty*, p. 11.

208 "I was told to be on the lookout": Oral History of Charles L. Rowley (February 11, 1999).

209 "Process and reporting": Lockwood interview.

209 "You'd better call": U.S. Navy, Court of Inquiry transcript, Testimony of Lt. (jg) Lloyd C. Painter (June 10, 1967), p. 54.

209 "All of a sudden I heard": Weaver interview.

210 "And then it happened again": e-mail, Stan White to author (March 7, 2000).

210 "I immediately knew what it was": interview with Bryce Lockwood (February 2000).

210 "absolutely no markings": Oral History of Lt. (jg) Lloyd C. Painter (November 21, 1998).

210 "I was trying to contact these two kids": U.S. Navy, Court of Inquiry transcript, Testimony of Lt. (jg) Lloyd C. Painter (June 10, 1967), p. 55.

210 grabbed for the engine order annunciator: U.S. Navy, Court of Inquiry transcript, Testimony of Commander McGonagle (June 10, 1967), p. 35.

210 "Oil is spilling": transcript of cockpit conversations, "Attack on the *Liberty*," Thames Television (London), 1987.

210 "They shot the camera": Rowley oral history.

211 "Any station, this is Rockstar": Ennes, *Assault on the Liberty*, p. 74.

211 "Great, wonderful, she's burning": "Attack on the *Liberty*," Thames Television.

211 "Hey, Sarge": Lockwood interview.

211 "We had a room where we did voice": ibid.

211 "It was as though they knew": *U.S. Naval Cryptologic Veterans Association* (Paducah, Ky.: Turner Publishing Co., 1996), p. 79.

211 "It appears to me that every tuning section": oral history of David E. Lewis (November 10, 1998).

212 "Schematic, this is Rockstar" ... "you son-of-a-bitch": Ennes, *Assault on the Liberty*, p. 78.

212 "He's hit her a lot": "Attack on the *Liberty*," Thames TV.

212 "Menachem, is he screwing her?" "Attack on the *Liberty*," Thames TV.

213 "I said, 'Fred, you've got to stay' ": Weaver interview.

214 "Horrible sight!": White e-mail to author.

214 "I was running as fast as I could": U.S. Navy, Court of Inquiry transcript, Testimony of Lt. (jg) Lloyd C. Painter (June 10, 1967), p. 55.

214 A later analysis would show: NSA, Top Secret/Umbra, "Attack on a Sigint Collector, the USS *Liberty*" (1981), p. 28.

214 "He's going down low with napalm": "Attack on the *Liberty*," Thames TV.

214 "It would be a *mitzvah*": A. Jay Cristol, quoted in "Seminar on Intelligence, Command and Control," Harvard University, Program on Information Resources Policy.

215 "The captain's hurt": U.S. Navy, Court of Inquiry transcript, Testimony of Lt. (jg) Lloyd C. Painter (June 10, 1967), p. 55.

215 "Pay attention": "Attack on the *Liberty*," Thames TV.

215 A later analysis said it would take: oral history of George H. Golden (November 12, 1998). One report indicates that several shots were fired at the torpedo boats from the starboard gun mount on the *Liberty*. However, by then all gun mounts had been completely destroyed. "The starboard gun mount was destroyed and the machine gun was inoperable. I know this for a fact because I

pulled one of my shipmates out of that gun mount blown to bits and that gun mount was unusable. We never fired a shot at the Israelis." Oral history of Phillip F. Tourney (November 9, 1998).

215 Commander McGonagle ordered the signalman: U.S. Navy, Court of Inquiry transcript, Testimony of Commander McGonagle (June 10, 1967), pp. 37–38.

216 "Stand by for torpedo": NSA, Top Secret/Umbra, "Attack on a Sigint Collector," p. 28.

216 "Dear Eileen": Lockwood interview.

216 "There was just a": ibid.

217 "They told me that they saw the torpedo": Raven interview.

217 "I did just as I was told": oral history of Donald W. Pageler, by Joyce E. Terrill (June 1987).

217 "We knelt down and braced ourselves": White e-mail to author.

217 "I could feel a lot of warmth": Weaver interview.

218 "We were laying there": ibid.

219 "Do you require assistance?": U.S. Navy, Court of Inquiry transcript, Testimony of Commander McGonagle (June 10, 1967), p. 39.

219 the torpedo boats continued: oral history of Robert Schnell (November 21, 1998).

219 "They must have known": Weaver oral history.

219 "I watched with horror": Letter, Painter to Richard Schmucker (May 8, 2000). See also oral history of Lloyd Painter (November 21, 1998).

219 "When 'prepare to abandon ship' was announced": *U.S. Naval Cryptologic Veterans Association*, p. 80.

219 "If you don't go down with the ship": Pageler oral history.

219 "As soon as the lifeboats hit the water": oral history of Phillip F. Tourney (November 9, 1998).

220 "They made circles": oral history of Larry Thorn (November 11, 1998).

220 "Our biggest fear": Tourney oral history.

220 "We heard Israeli traffic": Rowley oral history.

220 "told me that he wanted to scuttle the ship": George H. Golden Oral History, November 12, 1998.

222 "Sending aircraft": COMSIXTHFLT message (1305Z, June 8, 1967).

222 "Request examine all communications": NSA, Top Secret/Comint Channels. Only message from DIRNSA (June 8, 1967).

222 Eleven minutes after: A later study determined that while NSA's special Criticomm network, over which CRITICs were sent, operated relatively well, the Pentagon's Flash system met its mark only 22 percent of the time.

222 "The *Liberty* has been torpedoed": NSA, Top Secret/Umbra, "Attack on a Sigint Collector," p. 32.

222 McNamara called Carter at NSA: NSA, Secret/Spoke/Limited Distribution, "USS *Liberty:* Chronology of Events" (undated), p. 13.

223 "After considerations of personnel safety": NSA, Top Secret/Umbra, Tordella memorandum for the record (June 8, 1967).

223 "Captain Vineyard had mentioned": ibid.

223 "a distinct possibility": NSA, Top Secret/Umbra, "Attack on a Sigint Collector, the USS *Liberty*" (1981), p. 57.

223 "If it appeared the ship was going to sink": NSA, Secret/Spoke/Limited Distribution, "USS *Liberty:* Chronology of Events" (undated), p. 15.

223 "She was a communications research ship": NSA, Top Secret/Umbra, "Attack on a Sigint Collector, the USS *Liberty*" (1981), p. 48.

224 "destroy or drive off": ibid., p. 31.

224 "Flash, flash, flash": Ennes, *Assault on the Liberty*, p. 47.

224 Johnson feared that the attack: letter, Christian to James M. Ennes, Jr. (January 5, 1978).

224 Ernest C. Castle: Later, about 6:30 P.M. *Liberty* time, before sunset, Castle made a feeble attempt to fly to the *Liberty* aboard an Israeli helicopter. Out of uniform, without any megaphone or any other means of communicating, he dropped an orange on the deck with his business card tied to it. "Have you casualties?" he had written on the back. A later NSA report remarked, "The bodies of three crew members had not yet been removed from the forecastle and must have been observed by those in the helicopter." (NSA, Top Secret/Umbra, "Attack on a Sigint Collector, the USS *Liberty*" [1981], p. 34.)

Commander McGonagle testified before the court of inquiry: "There were numerous blood streams the full length from the 01 level on the forecastle to the main deck, at machine gun mount 51, where one body was still lying. I do recall that now. With his head nearly completely shot away. As I recall now, there was also another body in the vicinity of mount 51" (U.S. Navy, Court of Inquiry transcript, Testimony of Commander McGonagle [June 10, 1967], p. 51).

224 NSA claims that it first learned: NSA, "Attack on a Sigint Collector," p. 57; also, NSA, Top Secret/Umbra, Tordella memorandum for the record (June 8, 1967).

225 Details of Rakfeldt and the hot line: interview of Harry O. Rakfeldt (February 2000).

225 "We have just learned": NSA, Top Secret/Umbra, "Attack on a Sigint Collector, the USS *Liberty*" (1981), p. 32.

225 "Embassy Tel Aviv": Department of State, Secret/EXDIS, Chronology of US-Israeli Consultations on the Middle East, May 17–June 10, 1967 (June 15, 1967).

226 "President Johnson came on with a comment": oral history of David E. Lewis (November 10, 1998).

227 "Do whatever is feasible": NSA, Top Secret/Umbra, "Attack on a Sigint Collector, the USS *Liberty*" (1981), p. 44.

228 "If you ever repeat this to anyone else ever again": Weaver oral history.

228 "I took a crew": White e-mail to author.

228 "Below it was this guy's arm": Pageler oral history.

228 sold for scrap: details of *Liberty*'s end are drawn from NSA, Top Secret/Umbra, "Attack on a Sigint Collector, the USS *Liberty*" (1981), p. 64.

228 $20,000 to each of the wounded crewmen: Richard K. Smith, "The Violation of the *Liberty*," *United States Naval Proceedings* (June 1978), p. 70.

228 Ten months earlier: Department of State, Press Release (May 13, 1969).

229 the U.S. government asked: Bernard Gwertzman, "Israeli Payment to Close the Book on '67 Attack on U.S. Navy Vessel," *New York Times* (December 19, 1980).

229 Motor Torpedo Boat 203 display: photo and caption in A. Jay Cristol, "The *Liberty* Incident," a Ph.D. dissertation submitted to the University of Miami in 1997, p. 331.

230 "I must have gone to the White House": memorandum, Moorer to AMEU (June 8, 1997).

230 "The government is pretty jumpy about Israel": Ennes, *Assault on the Liberty,* p. 194.

231 no U.S. naval vessel since World War II had suffered a higher percentage: Paul N. McCloskey, Jr., "The U.S.S. *Liberty* 1967–1989," *NCVA Cryptolog* (Fall 1989), p. 1.

231 "Throughout the contact": Israeli Defense Force, Confidential, Court of Inquiry Report, Decision of Examining Judge, Lieutenant Colonel Yishaya Yerushalmi (July 21, 1967).

231 a small task force led by Walter Deeley: NSA, Top Secret/Umbra, "Attack on a Sigint Collector, the USS *Liberty*" (1981), p. 58.

232 "There is no way that they didn't know": Quoted in Cristol, "The *Liberty* Incident," pp. 161–162, n. 49.

232 "There was no other answer": interview with Lieutenant General Marshall S. Carter (July 17–18, 1980).

232 "Mr. Mahon probed several times": NSA, Top Secret/Umbra, Dr. Louis Tordella memorandum for the record (June 20, 1967).

233 "A nice whitewash": NSA, Top Secret/Umbra, "Attack on a Sigint Collector, the USS *Liberty*" (1981), p. 41.

233 "Nobody believes that explanation": interview with retired Major General John Morrison (July 2000).

233 many in NSA's G Group: NSA, Top Secret/Umbra, "Attack on a Sigint Collector, the USS *Liberty*" (1981), p. 63.

233 "The Israelis got by": Letter, Tourney to Senator John McCain (May 11, 2000).

233 "After many years I finally believe": oral history of William L. McGonagle (November 16, 1998).

233 McGonagle died: Michael E. Ruane, "An Ambushed Crew Salutes Its Captain," *Washington Post* (April 10, 1999).

233 "Frankly, there was considerable skepticism": letter, Christian to James M. Ennes, Jr. (January 5, 1978).

234 "Exculpation of Israeli nationals": NSA, Top Secret/Umbra, "Attack on a Sigint Collector, the USS *Liberty*" (1981), p. 61.

234 "Though the pilots testified to the contrary": ibid., p. 41.

234 "The fact that two separate torpedo boat commanders": ibid.

235 "A persistent question relating to the *Liberty*": ibid., pp. 63–64.

235 "I believed the attack": NSA, Top Secret/Umbra, Dr. Louis Tordella memorandum for the record, June 20, 1967.

235 "It was not an official policy": From "Israel Reportedly Killed POWs in '67," *Washington Post* (August 17, 1995).

235 "To speculate on the motives of an attack group": Lieutenant Commander Walter L. Jacobsen, JAGC, USN, "A Juridical Examination of the Israeli Attack on the U.S.S. *Liberty*," *Naval Law Review* (Winter 1986), pp. 1–52. The quoted text appears on p. 51.

237 "I have to conclude that it was Israel's intent to sink the *Liberty*": Memorandum, Moorer to AMEU (June 8, 1997).

237 a CIA report: CIA, FOIA release of documents and television transcript (January 28, 1985).

237 "The Israelis have been very successful": CIA, Secret/Noforn/Nocontract/Orcon, "Israel: Foreign Intelligence and Security Services" (March 1979), p. 32.

238 "The principal targets of the Israeli intelligence": ibid., p. 9.

238 "Congress to this day": Memorandum, Moorer to AMEU (June 8, 1997).

238 "I saw Abed lurch out": Details of the killing were reported by William A. Orme, Jr., "BBC Says Unprovoked Israeli Fire Killed an Employee in Lebanon," *New York Times* (June 22, 2000).

CHAPTER 8: Spine

Page

240 "The Navy was very interested in having a trawler program": NSA, Top Secret/Umbra, oral history of Eugene Sheck (December 16, 1982), p. 2.

241 "We talked once": Oral History of Admiral David Lamar McDonald, USN (Ret.) (November 1976) (U.S. Naval Institute, Annapolis, Maryland).

242 "We were operating": Sam Tooma, "USS *Banner* Anecdotes," USS *Pueblo* web site <http://www.usspueblo.org/v2f/incident/incidentframe.html> (April 15, 2000).

242 The most serious incident took place: Joint Chiefs of Staff, Joint Reconnaissance Center, Top Secret, "The Pueblo Index: Experience of Harassment" (January 24, 1968), pp. 1–2.

243 "There were some touchy situations": Oral History of Vice Admiral Edwin B. Hooper, USN (Ret.) (1978) (U.S. Naval Institute, Annapolis, Maryland). Hooper was commander, Service Force, Pacific Fleet, based in Hawaii.

243 "The *Liberty*[-size] ships were owned by NSA": interview with Stephen R. Harris (February 2000).

244 "The location of the first mission hadn't been decided upon": Trevor Armbrister, *A Matter of Accountability: The True Story of the Pueblo Affair* (New York: Coward-McCann, 1970), p. 154; NSA, Top Secret/Umbra, Oral History of Eugene Sheck, December 16, 1982.

244 "would do one patrol in response": Sheck oral history.

245 "I want to sell you top secrets": Pete Early, *Family of Spies: Inside the John Walker Spy Ring* (New York: Bantam, 1988), p. 63.

245 Starting in May: This account of increasing North Korean activity draws on

CIA, Secret, "North Korean Intentions and Capabilities with Respect to South Korea" (September 21, 1967), p. 1.

246 "We were about": Details of the attack on the RB-47 are from George V. Back, "North Korean Attack on RB-47," web posting at <http://www.55srwa.org/55_back.html> (May 1, 2000).

248 "This young fellow": Sheck oral history.

248 "The following information is provided to aid": U.S. House of Representatives, Committee on Armed Services, Special Subcommittee on the U.S.S. *Pueblo,* Inquiry into the U.S.S. *Pueblo* and EC-121 Plane Incidents, Hearings, 91st Cong., 1st Sess. (1989).

249 "This was the first voyage": ibid.

249 "NSA has a pretty strong voice": Sheck oral history.

250 On January 2, 1968: Unless otherwise noted, all details of the voyage of the USS *Pueblo,* as well as the prior approval process, come from U.S. Navy, Top Secret/Limited Distribution/Noforn, "Findings of Fact, Opinions and Recommendations of a Court of Inquiry Convened by Order of Commander in Chief, United States Pacific Fleet, to Inquire into the Circumstances Relating to the Seizure of USS *Pueblo* (AGER-2) by North Korean Naval Forces" (April 9, 1969). Details on General Steakley and Captain Gladding: Trevor Armbrister, *A Matter of Accountability: The True Story of the Pueblo Affair* (New York: Coward-McCann, 1970), pp. 192–199.

251 "Determine the nature and extent of naval activity": U.S. House of Representatives, Committee on Armed Services, Special Subcommittee on the U.S.S. *Pueblo,* Inquiry into the U.S.S. *Pueblo* and EC-121 Plane Incidents, Hearings, 91st Cong., 1st Sess. (1989), pp. 762–767.

251 "I was very upset when we found out": Harris interview.

252 "*Out of Japan*": E. M. Kisler, "Bucher's Bastards," written in North Korea in September 1968.

253 "It . . . infiltrated scores of armed boats": FBIS Transcript, Pyongyang KCNA International Service in English (November 27, 1967).

253 "Drawn into the spy ring": FBIS Transcript, Pyongyang KCNA International Service in English (November 10, 1967).

253 "As our side has declared time and again": FBIS Transcript, Pyongyang KCNA International Service in English (December 1, 1967).

253 quoted in a Japanese newspaper: *New York Times,* January 27, 1968.

253 "The U.S. imperialist aggressor troops": FBIS Transcript, Pyongyang KCNA International Service in English (January 11, 1968).

254 "Although the seas were calm": Stu Russell's remarks are quoted from Stu Russell, "Cold and Getting Colder," U.S.S. *Pueblo* web site, <http://www.usspueblo.org/v2f/incident/incidentframe.html> (April 15, 2000).

255 "We had a crew meeting and we were told": interview with member of ship's crew.

255 "In the New Year, the U.S. imperialist aggressors": FBIS Transcript, Pyongyang KCNA International Service in English (January 10, 1968).

257 "We were close enough to see the crew": Russell, "Cold and Getting Colder."

258 "Subchaser No. 35": Secret, "Chronology of Events Concerning the Seizure of the USS *Pueblo*" (NSA, undated), pp. 1–4.

258 "A guy comes steaming back": Sheck oral history, p. 30.

260 SC-35 then instructed all North Korean vessels: Secret, "Chronology of Events Concerning the Seizure of the USS *Pueblo*" (NSA, undated), pp. 1–4.

261 "The Koreans requested from the United States": interview with former U.S. Air Force F-4 pilot Bruce Charles (February 2000).

262 "in excess of that necessary or desired": Department of Defense, Secret memorandum, "What Reaction Forces Were Available and What Were Our Reaction Options?" (January 24, 1968).

262 That left Okinawa: For the F-105s on Okinawa, see Thomas C. Utts, "After North Korea Seized USS *Pueblo* on the Eve of Tet, It Looked Like the Communists Had Opened a Two-Front War," *Vietnam* magazine (date illegible on author's copy).

262 Bucher's actions during the attack: See, generally, Lloyd M. Bucher with Mark Rascovich, *Bucher: My Story* (New York: Doubleday, 1970).

263 "For ten days": Henry Millington, quoted in Sheck oral history.

263 "That happened around two o'clock": ibid.

267 "Each time the mike was keyed": Russell, "Cold and Getting Colder."

268 "That's guys' lives": "Betrayal: The Story of the USS *Pueblo*," History Channel (1997).

268 "They were on their own": Sheck oral history.

269 "We were, it seemed": Russell, "Arrival in Wonsan," USS *Pueblo* web site, <http://www.usspueblo.org/v2f/incident/incidentframe.html> (April 15, 2000).

269 "General Carter read it, and then he got up": Sheck oral history.

270 Within hours of the incident: Details of McNamara's war council come from Department of Defense, Top Secret, Memorandum for the Secretary of Defense (January 25, 1968).

271 "We had F-4s lined up wingtip to wingtip": oral history of Gen. Charles H. Bonesteel, III, Volume 1 (1973), p. 348 (U.S. Army Military History Institute, Carlisle Barracks, Pennsylvania). Bonesteel was commanding general, 8th U.S. Army; commander-in-chief, United Nations Command; and commander, U.S. Forces Korea.

271 "They wanted to provoke": This and the subsequent quotations from Gene Sheck are from Sheck oral history.

273 "My first pass started off near Vladivostok": This and details on the A-12 come from Paul F. Crickmore, *Lockheed SR-71: The Secret Missions Exposed* (London: Osprey Aerospace, 1993), pp. 31–33.

273 "Our mission was to support the captain": Rakfeldt's comments and details concerning the USS *Volador* come from Harry O. Rakfeldt, letter to author (April 17, 2000).

275 "The KGB did not plan to capture": interview with Oleg Kalugin, unpublished CBS News transcript (undated), p. 9.

276 "The Soviets had been allowed to inspect": ibid., pp. 12–13.

276 "The ciphers and codes are considered": ibid., pp. 8–9.

276 "perhaps the best operative" . . . "read your cables!": Pete Early, "Interview with the Spy Master," *Washington Post Magazine*, April 23, 1995.

277 Jerry Whitworth: Early, *Family of Spies*, p. 137.

277 "Using the keylists provided by John Walker": interview with Oleg Kalugin, unpublished CBS News transcript (undated), pp. 13–14.

277 In some instances, classified information was passed on: The Court of Inquiry reported that one crew member "cooperated with the North Koreans during detention in that he amplified classified information which the North Koreans had captured and provided additional information which was not otherwise available." Other crew members, said the Court, "may also have disclosed significant classified information to a lesser degree, but the actual degree of such disclosure, over and above what was already available to the North Koreans, could not be determined from the evidence." U.S. Navy, Top Secret/Limited Distribution/Noforn, "Findings of Fact, Opinions and Recommendations of a Court of Inquiry Convened by Order of Commander in Chief, United States Pacific Fleet, to Inquire into the Circumstances Relating to the Seizure of USS Pueblo (AGER-2) by North Korean Naval Forces" (April 9, 1969), p. 94.

278 "Americans were shocked": William J. Taylor, Jr., "Remembering Seizure of the Pueblo," *Washington Times* (December 27, 1994).

278 "When a fourth-rate": "Betrayal," History Channel (1998).

278 "I will sign the document": *New York Times* (December 23, 1968), p. 3.

278 "A determination": U.S. Navy, Top Secret/Limited Distribution/Noforn, "Findings of Fact, Opinions and Recommendations of a Court of Inquiry Convened by Order of Commander in Chief, United States Pacific Fleet, to Inquire into the Circumstances Relating to the Seizure of USS *Pueblo* (AGER-2) by North Korean Naval Forces" (April 9, 1969), p. 84.

279 "He should have persisted": ibid., p. 88.

279 "failed completely in the execution": ibid., p. 89.

279 "With few exceptions": ibid.

280 "You're surrounded": Sheck oral history.

280 Naval Security Group officers at Pacific Fleet Headquarters: The court of inquiry recommended that Captain Everett B. Gladding, Director, Naval Security Group Pacific, be given a letter of reprimand for allegedly "failing to ensure the readiness of *Pueblo*'s research detachment" and "[failing] to provide intelligence support to *Pueblo* during the mission." But Gladding's boss, Admiral Hyland, the Commander-in-Chief, Pacific Fleet, vetoed the recommendation.

280 "Folks out there said": Sheck oral history.

280 "They had total incapacity": Bonesteel oral history.

281 "They have suffered": U.S. Navy, press release (May 6, 1969).

281 "The *Pueblo* incident": interview with Oleg Kalugin, unpublished CBS News transcript (undated), pp. 32–33, 24–25.

281 moved to a pier: AP World News (October 26, 1999).

281 Led by a former NSA contractor; "The sooner, the better": "North Korea Moves *Pueblo*," *The Lonely Bull* (newsletter of the crew of the *Pueblo*) (November 1999), p. 1.

CHAPTER 9: Adrenaline

Page

284 "I believe that the enemy will attempt": Military Assistance Command, Vietnam (MACV), Secret message, Westmoreland to General Earle Wheeler, January 22, 1968. (LBJL, National Security File, Country File, Vietnam, Box 68–69.)

285 "Japanese reports back to Tokyo": NSA, Top Secret/Umbra, "On Watch" (September 1986), pp. 33–41.

286 "Thus began the Indochina War": ibid.

286 "true autonomous self-government": Stanley Karnow, *Vietnam: A History*, rev. ed. (New York: Penguin, 1997), p. 148.

286 "would mean extremely adverse reactions": CIA, Secret memorandum, "Intelligence Memorandum No. 231: Consequences of Communist Control of French Indochina" (October 7, 1949), pp. 1–3. (HSTL, President's Secretary's File, Intelligence File, Box 250.)

286 aid, weapons, and U.S. forces: On August 2, 1950, the first ten U.S. officers arrived in Saigon. Sixty others soon followed, and before Truman left office in January 1953, 200 more would be sent in to help the French fight off Vietnamese opponents.

286 witless CIA officer: Sedgwick Tourison, *Secret Army Secret War: Washington's Tragic Spy Operation in North Vietnam* (Annapolis, Md.: Naval Institute Press, 1995), p. 7.

287 The operation began on March 13, 1954: CIA, William M. Leary, "Supporting the 'Secret War': CIA Air Operations in Laos, 1955–1974," *Studies in Intelligence* (Winter 1999–2000).

287 "I recall very dramatically": interview with David W. Gaddy (May 2000).

287 "couldn't find any hard evidence": NSA, Top Secret/Umbra, "On Watch" (September 1986), p. 39.

288 "the current situation in South Vietnam": Director of Central Intelligence Directive 6/3, quoted in NSA, Top Secret/Umbra/Noforn, "In the Shadow of War" (June 1969), pp. 30–31.

288 400th ASA Special Operations Unit (Provisional): In September 1961 its name was changed to the 82nd Special Operations Unit. By mid-1966 the organization had grown considerably; it was thereafter named the 509th ASA Group.

289 "Cryptography must be secret, swift, and accurate"; "During the decades past": NSA, *Essential Matters: A History of the Cryptographic Branch of the People's Army of Viet-Nam, 1945–1975* (translated and edited by David W. Gaddy, NSA, 1994), pp. xiii–xiv.

289 "destroyed the entire set of [cryptographic] materials": ibid, p. 106.

290 "As a civilian from NSA": NSA, Top Secret/Umbra, "Deployment of the First ASA Unit to Vietnam" (undated), p. 80.

290 James T. Davis: For this account, I have relied on Army Intelligence and Security Command, "Biographical Data on Specialist Four James T. Davis" (undated).

292 "Many of us who knew about the 34A operations": Robert S. McNamara with Brian VanDeMark, *In Retrospect: The Tragedy and Lessons of Vietnam* (New York: Vintage Books, 1996), p. 130.

292 "By midsummer of 1964 the curtain was going up": NSA, Top Secret/Umbra, "On Watch" (September 1986), p. 41.

293 DeSoto patrols: ibid., p. 43.

293 another DeSoto mission was scheduled: Unless otherwise noted, details of the Gulf of Tonkin incident come from Edwin E. Morse's excellent study, *Tonkin Gulf and the Escalation of the Vietnam War* (Chapel Hill: University of North Carolina Press, 1996); and NSA, Top Secret/Umbra, "On Watch" (September 1986), Chapter 6, "The Gulf of Tonkin Incident, the DeSoto Patrols and OPLAN 34A," pp. 43–50.

297 "It seems likely that": Department of State, Top Secret memorandum, Forrestal to Secretary of State (August 3, 1964) (Department of State, *FRUS* 1964–1968, vol. 1, p. 599).

299 "Everybody was demanding the Sigint": Morse, *Tonkin Gulf*, pp. 197, 199.

300 "I must address the suggestion": U.S. Senate, Foreign Relations Committee, "The Gulf of Tonkin: The 1964 Incidents," Hearings (February 20, 1968), p. 19.

300 Operation Northwoods: JCS, Top Secret/SpecialHandling/Noforn, Note by the Secretaries to the Joint Chiefs of Staff on Northwoods, Annex to Appendix to Enclosure A, "Pretexts to Justify U.S. Military Intervention in Cuba" (March 12, 1962), p. 8. Details of the operation are covered in more detail in chapter 4, "Fists."

300 to send the Sigint ship *Banner:* See chapter 8, "Spine."

301 "At the time there's no question": Michael Charlton and Anthony Moncrieff, *Many Reasons Why: The American Involvement in Vietnam* (New York: Hill & Wang, 1989), p. 108.

301 number of cryptologic personnel: 1,322 were from ASA; 246 from the Air Force; and 179 from NSA and the Navy. NSA, Top Secret/Umbra/Noforn, "In the Shadow of War" (June 1969), p. 118.

302 "U.S. personnel with the ability to read Vietnamese": ibid., p. 55.

302 "We found that we had adequate": interview with a former senior NSA B02 Group official.

303 "And of course there was always": interview with another former senior NSA B Group official.

303 "There was no blotter large enough": NSA, Top Secret/Umbra/Noforn, "Working Against the Tide," part one (June 1970), p. 14.

303 "Through interrogation of these men": NSA, Secret/Noforn, "Deadly Transmissions" (December 1970), p. 4.

304 "The inescapable conclusion from the captured documents": ibid., p. 5.

304 "The enemy might disappear from a location": Lieutenant General Charles R. Myer, "Viet Cong Sigint and U.S. Army Comsec in Vietnam," *Cryptologia* (April 1989), pp. 144–45.

305 "Even as late as the spring of 1969": NSA, Top Secret/Umbra/Noforn, "Working Against the Tide," part one (June 1970), p. 14.

305 "It was . . . likely that they could gain": ibid., p. 3.

305 "some tortuous evolutions": Myer, "Viet Cong Sigint and U.S. Army Comsec in Vietnam," p. 147.

306 "Signal security, particularly in voice": ibid., p. 150.

306 During 1967, Comsec monitors eavesdropped on: NSA, Top Secret/Umbra/Noforn, "Working Against the Tide," part one (June 1970), p. 35.

306 "it was shot at the whole way": ibid., p. 19.

306 "capstone of the enemy's Sigint operations": ibid., p. 9.

307 estimated to be around $15 million: ibid.

307 "All of our primary operational communications": ibid., p. 16.

307 "Walker is not responsible for your failures": Pete Early, "Interview with the Spy Master," *Washington Post Magazine* (April 23, 1995).

307 "We certainly provided": interview with Oleg Kalugin, unpublished CBS News transcript (undated), pp. 15–16.

310 "compromising cipher-signal anomalies": Details on the *Izmeritel* and Guam: NSA, Top Secret/Umbra/Noforn, "Working Against the Tide," part two (June 1970), p. 202.

310 "The communications were in plain language": ibid.

311 "Comsec monitors and analysts had an advisory": NSA, Top Secret/Umbra/Noforn, "Working Against the Tide," part one (June 1970), p. 16.

311 "35 kilometers north of here tomorrow;" "On landing, the assault force": ibid., p. 35.

312 "a veritable flood": ibid., p. 38.

312 "Most U.S. commanders in Vietnam": ibid., p. 50.

313 orders were transmitted to the ship on May 26: USS *Oxford*, "Command History" (January 6, 1966), Enclosure 1.

313 "In Africa we were looking at some of the local links": interview with George A. Cassidy (January 2000).

314 "They tried to keep the *Oxford* movements very highly classified": interview with John De Chene (February 5, 2000).

315 "I was on the back of a flat pickup truck": interview with Ray Bronco (February 17, 2000).

315 "There was always a rivalry between our sister ship": e-mail from Richard E. Kerr, Jr., to author (January 26, 2000).

316 "a world of their own": Bronco interview.

318 "The operators hung a long wire out the back": This and other details of the RU-6A Beaver and the RU-8D Seminole aircraft are drawn from NSA, "Army Security Agency Aerial Reconnaissance: Mission and Sacrifice" (undated), pp. 2–6; NSA, "National Vigilance Park RU-8 Aircraft Dedication Ceremony" (May 12, 1998).

318 "Whoever controlled the shipping channel": This and Richard McCarthy's other comments come from his e-mail to author (February 25, 2000). Mc-

Carthy served in Vietnam from December 1965 to August 1967 and was awarded aircrew wings and the air medal with twenty-seven oak-leaf clusters.

319 "Naturally, that particular flight element": Major General Doyle Larson, "Direct Intelligence Combat Support in Vietnam: Project Teaball," *American Intelligence Journal* (Spring/Summer 1994), pp. 56–58.

320 "MiG-21s would streak out": This and Bruce Bailey's other remarks are from "The RB-47 & RC-135 in Vietnam," his web posting at 55th Strategic Reconnaissance Wing Association web site <http://www.55srwa.org/55_vietnam.html> (May 1, 2000).

321 "They were designed to intercept": Details on the drones are from Bruce Bailey, "Drones in Southeast Asia," web posting at 55th Strategic Reconnaissance Wing Association web site <http://www.55srwa.org/55_bruce.html> (May 1, 2000).

322 the planes were soon assigned exclusively to Sigint: The CIA conducted a photo mission over North Vietnam on August 15, 1961. Between 1962 and 1964, CIA U-2s staged a total of thirty-six photographic missions over North and South Vietnam. By April 1964, however, photographic requirements were changing from strategic reconnaissance to tactical support as the Vietcong became more active. As a result of the increasing level of combat in Indochina, the U.S. Intelligence Board gave responsibility for aerial reconnaissance of the areas where fighting was taking place to the Strategic Air Command. Following the Gulf of Tonkin Resolution, the Air Force assumed responsibility for all of Indochina (CIA, "The CIA and the U-2 Program, 1954–1974" [1998], pp. 222–31).

322 "All I had to do was throw a switch": Ben R. Rich and Leo Janos, *Skunk Works* (Boston: Little, Brown & Company, 1994), p. 185.

322 "The pilot did not operate the receivers": Bailey's comments and details of the U-2 come from Bruce Bailey, "The View from the Top," web posting at 55th Strategic Reconnaissance Wing Association web site <http://www.55srwa.org/55_bruce.html> (May 1, 2000).

323 "Throttles to Max A/B"; details on March 21, 1968, SR-71 flight: Paul F. Crickmore, *Lockheed SR-71: The Secret Missions Exposed* (London: Osprey Aerospace, 1993), pp. 1–8.

324 "The SR-71 was excellent for 'stimulating' ": Richard H. Graham, *SR-71 Revealed: The Inside Story* (Osceola, Wisc.: Motorbooks International, 1996), pp. 83–84.

325 "As a member of the Army Security Agency": This and David L. Parks's other remarks are from his e-mail to author (February 15, 2000).

326 the 199th Light Infantry Brigade: This was composed of a headquarters company and three battalions (three thousand men, more or less) of infantry troops.

330 "If SD and SSD are included": CIA report, Harold P. Ford, "CIA and the Vietnam Policymakers: Three Episodes 1962–1968" (1998), p. 85.

331 "MACV used mainly Confidential-level documents": ibid., p. 93.

331 "frustratingly unproductive": ibid.

332 "I was frequently and sometimes tendentiously interrupted": ibid.

332 NSA began reporting that two North Vietnamese Army divisions: U.S. District Court, Southern District of New York, *General William C. Westmoreland* v. *CBS, Inc., et al.* (82 Civ. 7913), Stipulation of Facts, p. 2; hereinafter, *Westmoreland v. CBS.*

332 "also told MACV headquarters personnel": William E. Rowe, "Defending Long Binh," *Vietnam* (February 1995), pp. 47–52.

332 NSA issued the first in a series: *Westmoreland v. CBS,* exhibit 518, "Treatment of Indications in Finished Intelligence: NSA."

333 "A 'we are winning' consensus pretty much": CIA report, Harold P. Ford, "CIA and the Vietnam Policymakers: Three Episodes 1962–1968" (1998), p. 108.

333 "It would seem to us that there is a relationship": James J. Wirtz, *The Tet Offensive: Intelligence Failure in War* (Ithaca, N.Y.: Cornell University Press, 1991), p. 213.

333 the *Oxford* sailed to Bangkok: USS *Oxford,* Confidential, 1968 "Command History" (March 19, 1969), p. 2.

333 "Coordinated Vietnamese Communist Offensive Evidenced": *Westmoreland v. CBS,* exhibit 64, p. 26.

333 "Evening missions were usually very quiet": McCarthy e-mail to author (February 25, 2000).

334 Westmoreland finally saw: The following account is from CIA, Harold P. Ford, "CIA and the Vietnam Policymakers: Three Episodes 1962–1968" (1998), p. 115.

334 "At twelve midnight": e-mail from David L. Parks to author (February 18, 2000).

334 "They had been hiding in tunnels and foxholes": Rowe, "Defending Long Binh."

335 "They've hit the embassy and palace": NSA, account by Gary Bright, NSA Cryptologic Museum.

336 the *Oxford*'s crew: USS *Oxford,* Confidential, 1968 "Command History" (March 19, 1969), p. 2.

336 "The National Security Agency stood alone": CIA, Harold P. Ford, "CIA and the Vietnam Policymakers: Three Episodes 1962–1968" (1998), pp. 116, 141.

337 "The National Security Agency extends its heartiest": NSA, telegram, Carter to Truman (May 8, 1968) (Carter Papers, George C. Marshall Library, Box 40, Folder 36).

337 Lyndon Johnson was being compared in the press to General George Custer: Art Buchwald, *Washington Post* (February 6, 1968).

337 "Nothing had been done to attend to their wounds": e-mail from David L. Parks to author (February 12, 2000).

339 "My opinion of 1969 on *Oxford*": Kerr e-mail to author (January 26, 2000).

339 95,000 people: testimony of Secretary of Defense James Schlesinger, U.S. House of Representatives, Committee on Appropriations, Subcommittee on Department of Defense, Department of Defense Appropriations for 1975, Part 1, 93rd Cong., 2nd Sess., p. 598.

339 In Southeast Asia alone: NSA, audiotape in the agency's Cryptologic Museum.

339 "monstrous": interview with Lieutenant General Marshall S. Carter (July 17–18, 1980).

340 "you couldn't tell whether": ibid.

340 "termite level": letter, Carter to William D. Pawley (May 19, 1997), Carter Papers, George C. Marshall Library, Lexington, Ky., Box 39, Folder 3.

340 "I am not winning": Letter, Carter to McCone (January 13, 1969), Carter Papers, George C. Marshall Library, Lexington, Ky., Box 37, Folder 8.

340 the sixth NSA director: NSA, "Vice Admiral Noel Gayler, USN, Becomes Agency's New Director," *NSAN* (August 1969), p. 2; Navy biography.

341 "At the end of World War II": Department of the Army, Major Commanders' Annual Report to Headquarters of the Army, Command Presentation, United States Army Security Agency (October 7, 1971), p. 19.

341 "declaration of war": interview with Richard P. Floyd, former chief, Procurement Support Division, Office of Procurement, NSA (January 19, 1981).

341 "The strategy paper": ibid.

342 "He wasn't a ballplayer": ibid.

342 Lieutenant General Samuel C. Phillips: NSA, "General Samuel Phillips Receives Thomas D. White Space Trophy," *NSAN* (September 1972), pp. 4–5.

342 "It came on thirty seconds after the missile's launch": interview with John Arnold (July 2000).

343 "They dumped": ibid.

343 Guardrail: The system is scheduled to be replaced by forty-five new intelligence, surveillance, and reconnaissance planes by 2006 under a new program codenamed Common Sensor. *Defense News On-Line* (March 1, 1999).

343 "From A-4 you could see the middle": interview with a former intercept operator (February 2000).

344 Earlier in March: Col. G. H. Turley, USMC, *The Easter Offensive: The Last American Advisors, Vietnam 1972* (Annapolis, Md.: Naval Institute Press, 1985), p. 43.

345 "Shortly after daylight the NVA": ibid., pp. 49–50.

345 refused to believe: ibid., p. viii.

346 "The hut would burn for a couple of days": information from a former A-4 intercept operator.

346 Samuel Phillips left NSA: Phillips died of cancer at his home in Palos Verdes Estates in California at the age of sixty-eight on January 31, 1990.

346 Lew Allen, Jr.: NSA, "Lieutenant General Lew Allen, Jr., USAF, Named Director," *NSAN* (August 1973), p. 2; Air Force biography.

347 "Have just received word to evacuate": NSA, Secret/Comint Channels Only message (1310Z April 28, 1975).

347 "I took the last fixed-wing aircraft": NSA, videotape interview with Ralph Adams. Decades later, Adams would rise to become executive director of NSA, the agency's number three position.

348 "THEY CANNOT GET": NSA, Secret/Comout/Fastcast message (1211Z April 29, 1975).

348 "I saw the ambassador briefly": Frank Snepp, *Decent Interval: An Insider's Account of Saigon's Indecent End Told by the CIA's Chief Strategy Analyst in Vietnam* (New York: Vintage, 1978), p. 553.

348 "Goddamnit, Graham!": ibid., p. 489.

349 "NO AMBASSADOR": NSA, Secret Comout/Fastcast message (1213Z April 29, 1975).

349 "THE AMBASSADOR WILL NOT": NSA, Secret Comout/Fastcast message (1628Z April 29, 1975).

349 "A PRESIDENTIAL MSG": NSA, Secret Comout/Fastcast message (1907Z April 30, 1975).

350 "LADY ACE 09 . . . IS NOT": NSA, Secret Comout/Fastcast message (2043Z April 30, 1975).

350 "LADY ACE 09 IS ON THE ROOF": NSA, Secret Comout/Fastcast message (2051Z April 30, 1975).

350 "THERE HAS BEEN AN SA-7 LAUNCH": NSA, Secret Comout/Fastcast message (2052Z April 30, 1975).

350 "President Ford has directed": Snepp, *Decent Interval*, p. 559.

350 "LADY ACE 09 IS TIGER TIGER TIGER": NSA, Secret Comout/Fastcast message (2058Z April 30, 1975).

351 "THERE ARE 200 AMERICANS LEFT": NSA, Secret Comout/Fastcast message (2109Z April 30, 1975).

351 "NUMEROUS FIRE FIGHTS" . . . "OUT REPEAT OUT": NSA, Secret Comout/Fastcast message (2142Z–2318Z April 30, 1975).

352 "Delicate political moves": This and the following are quoted from NSA, Gary Bright, "Don Vi' 600" (undated), pp. 1–5.

CHAPTER 10: Fat

Page

354 "I have been around long enough": "Ann Caracristi Accepts," *Colloquy* (Twentieth Anniversary Issue, 1999), p. 24.

354 Within days: Details of Caracristi's background are from NSA, Secret/Comint Channels Only, oral history of Ann Caracristi (July 16, 1982); "Ann Caracristi," 1999 Annual Awards Testimonial Dinner Program, Security Affairs Support Association (May 27, 1999), p. 5.

355 "NSA opened its doors": NSA, Tom Johnson, "The Plan to Save NSA" (undated), p. 6.

355 One CIA official called: ibid.

356 "Monetary considerations": Commission on Organization of the Executive Branch of the Government, Top Secret/Comint Channels Only/U.S. Eyes Only report, Task Force on Intelligence Activities (Hoover Commission) (May 1955), Appendix, p. 3.

356 "to bring the best": ibid.

356 "potentially our best": The President's Board of Consultants on Foreign Intelligence Activities, Top Secret letter, Killian to the president (De-

cember 20, 1956), p. 7 (DDEL, Ann Whitman File, Administrative Series, Box 13).

356 "that the Director": Office of Defense Mobilization, memorandum (July 6, 1955), "Hoover Commission Report" (DDEL, Office of Staff Secretary, Box 13).

356 above $500 million: The President's Board of Consultants on Foreign Intelligence Activities, Top Secret letter, Killian to the president (December 20, 1956), p. 7 (DDEL, Ann Whitman File, Administrative Series, Box 13).

356 more than half; Killian said; "Intelligence is approaching a $1-billion-a-year operation": White House, Top Secret memorandum, "Memorandum of Conference with the President, January 17, 1957," p. 1 (DDEL, Ann Whitman File, Box 21).

356 "Because of our having been": ibid.

356 "was numb at the rate": White House, Top Secret/Eyes Only memorandum, "Discussions at the Special Meeting in the President's Office, January 17, 1957," p. 4 (DDEL, White House Office, Box 7).

356 "It would be extremely valuable": ibid.

357 "In our judgment": The President's Board of Consultants on Foreign Intelligence Activities, Top Secret letter, Killian to the president (December 20, 1956), p. 8 (DDEL, Ann Whitman File, Administrative Series, Box 13).

357 "An essential step": ibid.

357 Baker . . . was appointed: CIA, Top Secret memorandum, Dulles to National Security Council (April 25, 1957) (DDEL, Office of Staff Secretary, Box 7). The Baker Committee was officially known as the President's Ad Hoc Task Force for Application of Communications Analysis for National Security and International Security.

357 Baker recommended that NSA have complete dominance: These recommendations were translated into a new Top Secret charter for NSA, the National Security Council Intelligence Directive (NSCID) No. 6, dated September 15, 1958. This replaced NSA's original charter, NSCID No. 9, dated July 1, 1948: NSC, Top Secret/Comint Channels Only, Special Limited Distribution, "National Security Council Intelligence Directive No. 6: Communications Intelligence and Electronics Intelligence" (September 15, 1958), pp. 1–11 (DDEL, Post-Presidential Papers, Box 2).

358 "I finally did produce a report": interview with Richard M. Bissell, Jr. (November 30, 1984).

358 "I could never tell how close": interview with a former director of Central Intelligence.

359 "When they went bust": interview with a former NSA official.

360 "One good intercept is worth $5 million": This quotation and Gerson's remarks are drawn from N. C. Gerson, "Sigint in Space," *La Physique au Canada* (November–December 1998), pp. 353–58.

360 "This has great promise for monitoring": White House, Top Secret, Memorandum of Conference with the President (February 10, 1959) (DDEL, White House Office, Office of Staff Secretary, Intelligence, Box 15).

361 Users are warned: *Material Safety Data Sheet* (October 1990).

363 the West Virginia State legislature: State of West Virginia, Radio Astronomy Zoning Act, House Bill No. 2 (August 9, 1956).

363 30,000 tons of steel: U.S. House of Representatives, Committee on Appropriations, Military Construction Appropriations, Hearings for 1962, Part 1, 87th Cong., 1st Sess., pp. 242–45. It should be noted that records of the sanitized hearings contain no references to the intelligence mission of Sugar Grove.

363 "almost beyond": The description of the calculations' complexity is in U.S. House of Representatives, Committee on Appropriations, Military Construction Appropriations, Hearings for 1961, Part 1, 86th Cong., 1st Sess., pp. 568–71.

364 At a Howard Johnson's: Philip J. Klass and Joseph C. Anselmo, "NRO Lifts Veil on First Sigint Mission," *Aviation Week & Space Technology* (June 22, 1998).

364 "The wife and two children were asleep": Mayo's account is from an NSA audio interview with Reid Mayo, NSA Cryptologic Museum.

365 "Piggy-back Satellites Hailed": Charles Corddry, "Piggy-back Satellites Hailed as Big Space Gain for U.S.," *Washington Post* (June 23, 1960).

365 Details of the GRAB satellite are from Naval Research Laboratory, "GRAB: Galactic Radiation and Background" (1998), pp. 1–10.

366 "With Eisenhower's concern": Ivan Amato, *All Things Considered,* National Public Radio (June 18, 1998).

368 "The satellites would pick up the signals": interview with former NSA official.

369 "They were huge umbrellas": ibid.

371 "They came back with very, very poor quality": Arnold's comments and details of Operation Ivy Bells and the USS *Halibut* are from my interview with John Arnold (July 2000).

374 It had been a long ride: for Inman's early life, see Robert Sam Anson, "Requiem for the Smartest Spy," *Esquire,* April 1994, pp. 84–86.

375 Inman and James Guerin: See Alan Friedman, *Spider's Web: The Secret History of How the White House Illegally Armed Iraq* (New York: Bantam Books, 1993), pp. 56–67; Elaine Sciolino, "Change at the Pentagon: Man in the News—Bobby Ray Inman, An Operator for the Pentagon," *New York Times* (December 17, 1993).

375 "I was an analyst for thirty-three months": Harvard University, Center for Information Policy Research, Program on Information Resources Policy, "Seminar on Command, Control, Communications, and Intelligence" (1980), p. 141.

376 "The idea of going back to be director"; Inman's Comments: NSA, Top Secret/Talent/Keyhole/Umbra, Admiral Bobby Ray Inman oral history (June 18, 1997), p. 1.

377 "Few could understand this": Thomas E. Ricks and Michael K. Frisby, "Herd Instinct: How Inman Could Go from Superstar to 'Bizarre' in Such a Short Time," *Wall Street Journal,* January 21, 1994.

378 "You have my vote": Barton Gellman, "Critical Spotlight Stings Behind-the-Scenes Man," *Washington Post,* January 19, 1994.

378 "simply one of the smartest": quoted in ibid.

378 "a superstar": ibid.

378 "Inman's reviews": Howard Kurtz, "Inman Statements Surprise Some Former Confidants in Media," *Washington Post,* January 21, 1994.

378 "I have over the years": Gellman, "Critical Spotlight."

378 "He certainly knew how to play the game": Kurtz, "Inman Statements."

378 "the single biggest leaker": ibid.

379 "Inman was in control of unequaled information": Suzanne Garment, "Of Secrecy and Paranoia: What Is Inman's Real Story?" *Los Angeles Times,* January 23, 1994.

379 "There were certain rules": Robert Sam Anson, "The Smartest Spy," *Omni* (n.d.), pp. 248, 250.

379 Edward J. Derwinski: Linda Greenhouse, "A Nominee's Withdrawal; Inman and The New York Times: An Examination of the Accusations of Bias," *New York Times,* January 19, 1994. See also Robert Boettcher with Gordon L. Friedman, *Gifts of Deceit: Sun Myung Moon, Tongsun Park, and the Korean Scandal* (New York: Holt, Rinehart & Winston, 1980), pp. 263–66. The *New York Times* article on Derwinski can be found in the paper's October 27, 1977, issue.

379 he believed he had a secret agreement: Anson, "Requiem for the Smartest Spy."

379 Sulzberger apparently had a different opinion: Greenhouse, "A Nominee's Withdrawal."

379 "The truth is there was nothing": ibid.

379 Woodward occasionally proposed a story: Kurtz, "Inman Statements."

380 "My name is really Bobby Ray, much as I hate it": NSA, Top Secret/Talent/Keyhole/Umbra, Admiral Bobby Ray Inman oral history (June 18, 1997).

380 he would wake up: Gellman, "Critical Spotlight."

380 "not deceptive": ibid.

380 "deliberately [sought them out]": "Bowing Out with a Bang," *Time,* January 31, 1994.

380 "wound tighter than a hummingbird": Tony Kornheiser, "You Got Thin Skin, Inman," *Washington Post,* January 23, 1994.

380 Captain Queeg: "Bowing Out with a Bang."

380 now saw plots: ibid.

380 "was very direct that if I didn't": Anson, "Requiem for the Smartest Spy."

380 Safire wrote: This episode is described in ibid.

381 "I try to do it": Harvard University Center for Information Policy Research, Program on Information Resources Policy, "Seminar on Command, Control, Communications, and Intelligence" (Cambridge, Mass.: Harvard University Press, 1980), Inman lecture, p. 152.

382 "a brittle golden boy": Anson, "Requiem for the Smartest Spy."

382 James Guerin: See Alan Friedman, *Spider's Web: The Secret History of How The White House Illegally Armed Iraq* (New York: Bantam Books, 1993), pp. 56–67.

382 "the largest . . . ever perpetrated": Elaine Sciolino, "Change at the Pentagon: Man in the News—Bobby Ray Inman: An Operator for the Pentagon," *New York Times,* December 17, 1993.

382 Inman wrote a letter: ibid.

383 "I said, 'Sure' "; Inman's comments: NSA, Top Secret/Talent/Keyhole/Umbra, Admiral Bobby Ray Inman oral history.

384 "deliberate withholding": George Lardner, Jr., "Agency Is Reluctant to Share Information," *Washington Post* (March 19, 1990), p. A4.

386 George Stephanopoulos was worried: For this account, see George Stephanopoulos, *All Too Human: A Political Education* (Boston: Little, Brown, 1999), pp. 233–37.

387 "Leaks are not the answer": address by Lieutenant General Lincoln D. Faurer before the Phoenix Society on May 22, 1982; quoted in *Phoenician* (Fall 1982), pp. 2–7.

388 Faurer was allegedly: "Pentagon Said to Be Forcing Retirement of NSA Head over Budget Cuts," Associated Press (February 1, 1985).

388 "The health of the Agency": address by Lieutenant General Lincoln D. Faurer, quoted in *Phoenician* (Fall 1982), pp. 2–7.

389 "created a big fuss": Faurer's departure is recounted in Robert C. Toth, "Head of NSA Is Dismissed for Opposing Budget Cuts," *Los Angeles Times,* April 19, 1985, p. 1; see also *CBS Evening News* (January 31, 1985).

389 Faurer's premature departure: Following his departure from NSA, Faurer became president and CEO of Corporation for Open Systems. Funded by a consortium of more than sixty computer and communications industry leaders, this research and development corporation was aimed at accelerating a worldwide "open systems" environment. In 1991 Faurer formed LDF, Inc. (for Lincoln D. Faurer), which provides consulting services concerning command, control, communications, computing, and intelligence. In 1998 he was named to the board of directors of TSI TelSys, Inc., which designs and manufactures high-performance protocol processing systems for the remote-sensing satellite ground station market (News release, TSI TelSys, Corp., November 2, 1998).

389 The Joint Chiefs of Staff recommended: Toth, "Head of NSA Is Dismissed for Opposing Budget Cuts."

390 claiming that intelligence leaks: Bill Gertz, "NSA Director Stresses Harm of Intelligence Leaks in Press," *Washington Times,* October 12, 1988.

390 "There's leaking from Congress": "Electronic Spy Chief Says Leaks Increasingly Hurt U.S. Intelligence," *Boston Globe,* September 3, 1987.

390 "irrefutable" proof: Address by President Ronald Reagan on April 14, 1986: "On March 25th, more than a week before the attack, orders were sent from Tripoli to the Libyan People's Bureau in East Berlin to conduct a terrorist at-

tack against Americans, to cause maximum and indiscriminate casualties. Libya's agents then planted the bomb. On April 4th, the People's Bureau alerted Tripoli that the attack would be carried out the following morning. The next day they reported back to Tripoli on the great success of their mission. Our evidence is direct, it is precise, it is irrefutable. We have solid evidence about other attacks Qaddafi has planned against United States installations and diplomats and even American tourists."

390 "Libya, sure. Just deadly losses.": Norman Black, "Gen. Odom Blames Leaks for 'Deadly' Intelligence Loss," *Washington Times,* September 3, 1987.

391 Details and quotations concerning Wobensmith case: Stephen Engelberg, "A Career in Ruins in Wake of Iran-Contra Affair," *New York Times,* June 3, 1988.

392 nominated by the agency for a Federal Career Service Award: "Claxton, Wobensmith Are Federal Career Award Finalists," *NSAN* (June 1981), p. 7.

392 shown the door: Bill Gertz, "Superseded General Expected to Resign," *Washington Times,* February 21, 1988.

393 Joint Chiefs of Staff unanimously recommended: Stephen Engelberg, "Head of National Security Agency Plans to Retire," *New York Times,* February 23, 1988. See also *Aviation Week and Space Technology* (February 29, 1988), p. 34.

393 "It was made clear to him": "Superseded General Expected to Resign," *Washington Times,* February 21, 1988.

393 "I've had a hell of an impact": Engelberg, *New York Times,* February 23, 1988; *Aviation Week and Space Technology* (February 29, 1988).

393 "I think it was just fortuitous": These quotations are drawn from NSA, Top Secret/Umbra/Talent/Keyhole/Plus, oral history of Admiral William O. Studeman (October 18, 1991), pp. 1–12.

393 "It was clear this agency did not want to spend": ibid.

394 UKUSA Communications Intelligence Agreement: In 1948 the United States and Canada entered into a similar bilateral agreement called the CANUSA Agreement.

394 Communications Security Establishment: See Government of Canada, "50 Years of Service: Agenda for CSE's 50th Anniversary Year Celebration" (1996).

Control of Canadian Sigint is vested in the Interdepartmental Committee on Security and Intelligence, under the general direction of the Cabinet Committee on Security and Intelligence. The ICSI maintains general policy control over all aspects of the collection, processing, and dissemination of Sigint; it exercises this control through the Intelligence Advisory Committee for national Sigint, and through the Canadian Forces for tactical Comint and Elint (Government of Canada, Intelligence Advisory Committee, Sigint Memorandum No. 1).

The directors of the CBNRC and the CSE were Ed Drake (1946–1971), Kevin O'Neill (1971–1980), Peter Hunt (1980–1989), and A. Stewart Woolner (1989–present). Woolner was previously the CSE's chief of communications security.

396 Among the CSE's listening posts: Bill Robinson, "Intelligence, Eavesdropping and Privacy: Who Watches the Listeners?" In Craig McKie, ed., *The System: Crime and Punishment in Canadian Society: A Reader* (Toronto: Thompson Educational Publishers).

397 "They spied on the Mexican trade representative": UPI dispatch, November 14, 1995.

397 "Knowledge is power": Nomi Morris, "Inside Canada's Most Secret Agency," *Maclean's*, September 2, 1996, pp. 32–34.

398 "It made us look ridiculous": This and Tovey's subsequent comments are from Barrie Penrose, Simon Freeman, Donald Macintyre, "Secret War," *Sunday Times* (London), February 5, 1984.

398 "Some sixty percent of the GCHQ radio operators": Jock Kane, "GCHQ: The Negative Asset" (unpublished manuscript), p. 61. This manuscript was seized by the British government under the Official Secrets Act in 1984, and the book was never published. The author obtained a copy of the manuscript before the seizure.

399 "I was able to spell out": Donald Macintyre, Barrie Penrose, Simon Freeman, "Peace Moves in Spy Centre Union Row," *Sunday Times* (London), n.d.

399 "The massive response to the strike call": Kane, "GCHQ," p. 114.

400 "the Government listens": Colin Hughes, "Solidarity Criticizes GCHQ Union Ban," *The Independent*, October 12, 1988.

400 "Dependence is total": Duncan Campbell, "The Parliamentary Bypass Operation," *New Statesman* (January 23, 1987), pp. 8–12.

400 NSA broke the Argentine code: "America's Falklands War," *The Economist*, March 3, 1984, p. 25.

400 "We can ask the Americans to do things": Mark Urban, "The Magnum Force," *Electronic Telegraph*, September 1, 1996.

400 codenamed Zircon: Campbell, "Bypass Operation," describes this project.

400 "macho politics": Campbell, "Bypass Operation."

401 "The UK simply isn't able": Mark Urban, "American Satellite Spied on Britain," *Electronic Telegraph*, September 1, 1996.

401 Major paid his first visit: Allan Smith, "Major Visits GCHQ," (U.K.) Press Association Newsfile (November 25, 1994).

401 the Queen herself: Peter Archer, "Prince Meets Spycatchers," (U.K.) Press Association Newsfile (March 7, 1995).

401 6,228 people at its headquarters: Stephen Bates, "HMSO Reveals Britain Employs 10,766 Spies at Home and Abroad," *The Guardian*, March 25, 1994, p. 11.

401 space-age complex: "GCHQ Opts for Benhall," *Gloucestershire Echo*, May 7, 1999, pp. 1–2; Maurice Chittenden and Simon Trump, "GCHQ Ties Up Millions in 'Doughnut,' " *Sunday Times* (London), August 13, 2000.

402 "We must go back to our roots with GCHQ": James Bamford, "Loud and Clear: The Most Secret of Secret Agencies Operates Under Outdated Laws," *Washington Post* (November 14, 1999).

402 Australian intelligence documents: Joint Intelligence Organisation, Fourth Annual Report, 1974, Canberra (November 1974), Part 2, pp. 4–5. (cited in Jeffrey

T. Richelson and Desmond Ball, *The Ties That Bind: Intelligence Cooperation Between the UKUSA Countries* (Sydney: Allen & Unwin, 1985), p. 42.

403 the newest and smallest member: Nicky Hager, *Secret Power: New Zealand's Role in the International Spy Network* (Nelson, New Zealand: Craig Potton, 1996), pp. 93–94.

404 Platform: James Bamford, *The Puzzle Palace: A Report on NSA, America's Most Secret Agency* (Boston: Houghton Mifflin, 1982), p. 102.

404 "We link the world's telecommunications": "What is INTELSAT?" INTELSAT home page, <http://www.intelsat.com/> (May 18, 2000).

405 "We grew so fast in the '80's we got buried": NSA, Top Secret/Umbra, oral history of Robert L. Prestel (December 21, 1993), p. 14.

CHAPTER 11: Muscle

Page

406 Details on INTELSAT 707: Jet Propulsion Laboratory, Mission and Spacecraft Library, INTELSAT 7, 7A.

407 "I know that I have leaned": letter, Hooper to Carter (July 27, 1969) (Lieutenant General Marshall S. Carter Papers, George C. Marshall Research Library, Lexington, Virginia).

407 "He says, 'Well, look, you can turn' ": interview with Lieutenant General Marshall S. Carter (July 17–18, 1980).

408 "satellite communications processing and reporting": U.S. Air Force, *Air Intelligence Agency Almanac* (1997).

408 "collection, identification, exploitation"; FORNSAT (Foreign Satellite Collection): Chief Warrant Officer 3 Katherine I. O'Neal and Warrant Officer 1 Keith J. Merryman, "Signals Collection/Identification Analyst (98K) Training," *Military Intelligence* (July–September 1998), pp. 20–22.

408 "98Ks will 'break' ": ibid.

409 India's nuclear weapons establishment, for example, uses this method: Seymour M. Hersh, "The Intelligence Gap," *The New Yorker*, December 6, 1999, p. 58.

409 Australia's station at Geraldton: Frank Cranston, "Australia's Plans for New Listening Post," *Jane's Defence Weekly* (April 4, 1987), p. 582.

410 Osama bin Laden: interview with intelligence official.

410 "With regard to encryption": interview with former government official.

411 "U.S. intelligence operates what is probably": Admiral William O. Studeman, Remarks at the Symposium "National Security and National Competitiveness: Open Source Solutions" (December 1, 1992).

411 C-802 missile: Unless otherwise noted, all quotations and information concerning the C-802 missile come from documents at the National Security News Service.

411 "mighty attack capability": House of Representatives, Committee on International Relations, Report, Urging the Executive Branch to Take Action Regarding the Acquisition by Iran of C-802 Cruise Missiles, 105th Cong., 1st Sess. (October 6, 1997), p. 4.

412 "clear and present danger": U.S. Senate, Committee on Governmental Affairs, Subcommittee on International Security, Proliferation, and Federal Services, Hearings (April 10, 1997), p. 24.

412 phone call from Tehran: NSA, Secret/Spoke message (July 11, 1997) (National Security News Service documents).

413 "When you're buying arms": This and the details on Monzer al-Kassar are from Roy Rowan, "Pan Am 103: Why Did They Die?" *Time,* April 27, 1992, p. 24.

413 "The meeting had gone very well": NSA, Secret/Spoke message (August 12, 1997) (National Security News Service documents).

413 GCHQ dutifully intercepted the list: NSA, Secret/Spoke message (September 23, 1997) (National Security News Service documents).

413 Chinese officials told . . . U.S. intelligence reports: DIA, Secret/Spoke/Noforn/Orcon/Specat report (November 13, 1997) (National Security News Service documents).

414 a letter of credit: NSA, Secret/Spoke/US/UK/CAN/AUS Eyes Only message (November 7, 1997) (National Security News Service documents).

415 "It is our understanding": Department of State, Secret/Release France memorandum (undated) (National Security News Service documents).

415 "mask involvement in Iranian anti-ship cruise missile": NSA, Secret/Spoke/AUS/CAN/UK/US Eyes Only message (December 12, 1997) (National Security News Service documents).

416 Jafari marched over: NSA, Secret/Spoke message (December 12, 1997) (National Security News Service documents).

416 While Jafari listened: ibid.

416 "policymakers": ibid.

416 "The future looked bleak": ibid.

417 "the current situation had already": ibid.

417 In February 1998 he learned: NSA, Secret/Spoke message (February 20, 1998) (National Security News Service documents).

417 "The complaints lodged by Tehran": Department of State, Secret/Spoke/Noforn report (February 10, 1998) (National Security News Service documents).

417 "According to IDF DMI, Iran signed a contract": DIA, Secret/Noforn message (March 17, 1998) (National Security News Service documents).

418 "Ninety percent": interview with former government official.

418 "Recent intelligence reports suggest": DIA, Secret/Spoke report (April 29, 1998) (National Security News Service documents).

418 "technologically self-sufficient": John Mintz, "Tracking Arms: A Study in Smoke," *Washington Post,* April 3, 1999.

418 "Within Gamma they had double G": interview with former government official.

418 "FRD": NSA, Top Secret/Dinar intercept, "Castro Interview on with U.S." (January 3, 1964) (ARRB).

419 "ILC": Department of Justice, Top Secret/Umbra/Comint Channels Only, "Report on Inquiry into CIA Related Electronic Surveillance Activities" (June 30, 1976), p. 28.

419 "I looked for": interview with former government official.
419 "They had pictures": ibid.
420 "In order to bring": ibid.
420 "The Agency": ibid.
420 "We'd never go in": ibid.
421 Once GCHQ intercepted: ibid.
421 French export inspectors: Mintz, "Tracking Arms."
421 "It doesn't mean": ibid.
422 "very different": ibid.
422 "Celebrating fifty years of successful partnership": NSA, BRUSA–UKUSA 1946–1996 plaque.
423 "There are a substantial number of legal problems": Author's audiotape of Studeman's address to the Baltimore/Washington Corridor Chamber of Commerce (June 29, 1990).
424 "The real issue for us": ibid.
424 "What we use the intelligence instrument for": Tony Capaccio, "Spy Agency Is Against Industrial Espionage for U.S. Firms," *Defense Week* (March 20, 1995), p. 1.
424 "We will be definitely": Author's audiotape of Studeman's address to the Baltimore/Washington Corridor Chamber of Commerce (June 29, 1990).
425 "If we had any certain evidence": Capaccio, "Spy Agency Is Against Industrial Espionage."
425 "Yes, my continental European friends": R. James Woolsey, "Why We Spy on Our Allies," *Wall Street Journal*, March 17, 2000.
426 "has directed me to come here": Carol Vinzant, "Kantor Arrives in Geneva for Japan Car Talks," Reuters (June 25, 1995).
426 an NSA team: For NSA involvement in the Geneva talks, see David E. Sanger and Tim Weiner, "Emerging Role for the CIA: Economic Spy," *New York Times*, October 15, 1995.
426 frequently bypassed: ibid.
426 "would be a breach of duty": Writ between Her Majesty's Attorney General and Jock Kane, High Court of Justice, Queen's Bench Division, #1984 A, No. 1116 (March 28, 1984), p. 5.
427 "Much of the targeting": Jock Kane, "GCHQ: The Negative Asset" (unpublished manuscript), p. 79.
427 capable of storing 5 *trillion* pages: John Mintz, "The Secret's Out: Covert E-Systems Inc. Covets Commercial Sales," *Washington Post*, October 24, 1994.
427 Nasser Ahmed: See "A Blow for Secret Evidence," *Washington Post* editorial, August 6, 1999.
428 another federal judge ruled: Lorraine Adams and David A. Vise, "Classified Evidence Ruled Out in Deportation," *Washington Post*, October 21, 1999.
429 names on its watch lists: Bob Woodward, "Messages of Activists Intercepted," *Washington Post*, October 13, 1975.
429 "MINARET information specifically includes": U.S. Senate, Select Committee to Study Government Operations with Respect to Intelligence Activities, The

National Security Agency and Fourth Amendment Rights, Hearings, Vol. 5, 94th Cong., 1st Sess. (1976), p. 150.

429 "I tried to object": interview with Frank Raven.

430 "Based on my review of the information": U.S. Senate, Select Committee on Intelligence, Book III, Supplementary Detailed Staff Reports on Intelligence and the Rights of Americans, Final Report (April 23, 1976), p. 937, n. 45.

430 "The president chewed": ibid.

430 "nothing less than a heaven-sent": ibid., p. 965.

430 "NSA Contribution to Domestic Intelligence" and "to program for coverage": U.S. Senate, Select Committee to Study Government Operations with Respect to Intelligence Activities, The National Security Agency and Fourth Amendment Rights, Hearings, Vol. 5, 94th Cong., 1st Sess. (1976), pp. 156–57.

430 "went through the ceiling": U.S. Senate, Select Committee on Intelligence, Book III, Supplementary Detailed Staff Reports on Intelligence and the Rights of Americans, Final Report (April 23, 1976), p. 956.

430 no one challenged Hoover: ibid., p. 933.

431 "Well, what the hell is this?": This conversation may be found in *Transcripts of Newly Released White House Tapes* (February 25, 1999), Richard Nixon Library.

434 L. Britt Snider: His remarks are quoted from CIA, L. Britt Snider, "Unlucky Shamrock: Recollections of the Church Committee's Investigation of NSA," *Studies in Intelligence* (Winter 1999–2000).

435 a story appeared in the *New York Times:* Nicholas Horrock, "National Security Agency Reported Eavesdropping on Most Private Cables," *New York Times,* August 8, 1975.

436 "During the 1950s, paper tape had been the medium": CIA, Snider, "Unlucky Shamrock."

438 "The companies had a duty": ibid.

441 "I want to make it clear": interview with senior intelligence official (July 2000).

441 886 eavesdropping warrants: Letter from Attorney General Janet Reno to House Speaker J. Dennis Hastert (April 27, 2000).

441 "The networks have collapsed": interview with senior NSA official.

442 "whom we may target": NSA, Secret/Comint Channels Only, USSID 18 Guide (April 15, 1998), p. 2.

442 United States Signals Intelligence Directive 18: NSA, Secret/Comint Channels Only, USSID 18 (May 26, 1976), pp. 1–15 plus Annexes. The directive is regularly revised over the years, including on July 27, 1993.

442 "These concerns are legitimate": NSA, Confidential/Comint Channels Only, "USSID 18 and Its Relevance to the Production of Foreign Intelligence" (June 1, 1999), p. 6.

442 "such as a hijacking or a terrorist attack": NSA, Secret/Comint Channels Only, "U.S. Identities in Sigint" (March 1994), p. 4. See also NSA, Top Secret/

Comint Channels Only memorandum from Office of General Counsel (Operations) (July 25, 1997), p. 7.

443 "When specific, actionable threat": NSA, Secret/Comint Channels Only, USSID 18 Guide (April 15, 1998), pp. 3–4.

443 "we bump into violations": U.S. House of Representatives, House Permanent Select Committee on Intelligence, Hearings, Testimony of Lieutenant General Michael Hayden (April 12, 2000).

443 "As a general rule": NSA, Confidential/Comint Channels Only memorandum from W9R3 to W Group Reporting Elements (September 30, 1997), p. 1–2.

443 "Please remember": ibid.

444 "You have reason to believe": NSA, Secret/Comint Channels Only, "USSID 18 Questions and Answers" (November 11, 1996), p. 4.

444 referred to by *title:* Interestingly, the use of titles for senior officials of the judicial and legislative branches does need special approval. And only the CIA director can approve the inclusion of the names of members of Congress in Sigint reports. See NSA, Secret/Comint Channels Only memorandum from P052 (February 5, 1993).

444 "The NSA Office of the General Counsel . . . has advised": NSA, Confidential/Comint Channels Only memorandum from P052 (January 4, 1993).

444 names of United Nations officials: NSA, Secret/Comint Channels Only, USSID 18 Guide (April 15, 1998), p. 6.

445 What was her status?: NSA, Confidential/Comint Channels Only, "Status of First Lady as Government Official" (June 29, 1993).

445 "Mrs. Clinton may be identified": NSA, Confidential/Comint Channels Only, "Reporting Guidance on References to the First Lady" (July 8, 1993).

445 "The current U.S. Administration has cautiously": NSA, Secret/Comint Channels Only memorandum from P052 (December 15, 1994).

446 "The direct involvement of the Central Intelligence Agency": "Legislator: CIA Operative Ordered Guatemala Killings," *Minneapolis Star Tribune,* March 23, 1995.

446 "any information concerning events": NSA, Secret/Comint Channels Only memorandum from Chief, Special Product Control Branch (March 31, 1995).

447 "The political parties of the U.S. are": NSA, Confidential/Comint Channels Only memorandum from Chief, P0521 (June 6, 1996).

447 "USSID 18 procedures for Search and Development": NSA, Top Secret/Comint Channels Only memorandum from the Office of General Counsel (Operations) (July 25, 1997), pp. 1–9.

448 details on the briefing memorandum: ibid.

448 "raw traffic storage systems": NSA, Secret/Comint Channels Only, USSID 18 Guide (April 15, 1998), p. 6.

448 "Do your research before": NSA, Top Secret/Comint Channels Only memorandum from the Office of General Counsel (Operations) (July 25, 1997), pp. 1–9.

448 "Americans were never listed": interview with knowledgeable source.

449 "If the [Sigint] report goes out": interview with a senior intelligence official involved in Sigint (July 2000).

449 "communications identified as domestic": NSA, Secret/Comint Channels Only, USSID 18, Appendix 1, "Standard Minimization Procedures for NSA Surveillance," Section 5 (a) (Domestic Communications/Dissemination). See also NSA, Secret/Comint Channels Only memorandum (re: "Collection, Processing, Retention, and Dissemination of 'Domestic' Communications under the Foreign Intelligence Surveillance Act") from Office of General Counsel (Operations) (February 25, 1998), pp. 1–4.

449 "significant foreign intelligence": NSA, Secret/Comint Channels Only, USSID 18 Guide (April 15, 1998), p. 5.

449 one party to which is a U.S. official: ibid.

450 "The primary purpose of the collection activity": NSA, Secret/Spoke, "Guidelines for . . . Narcotics-Related Sigint Collection" (undated), pp. 1–3.

450 "If the Sigint business": interview with senior intelligence official.

450 "When I was at the National Security Agency": Stewart A. Baker, "Should Spies Be Cops?" *Foreign Policy* (Winter 1994).

451 " 'Trust us' is the NSA's implicit message": David Ignatius, "Where We Can't Snoop," *Washington Post*, April 17, 2000.

452 "It was the whole net": interview with Lieutenant General Michael V. Hayden (February 2, 2000).

452 "What do I tell the workforce?": ibid.

452 Details on Universe and Normalizer: Vice Admiral John M. McConnell, Director, NSA, "Intelligence Processing," *Government Executive* (December 1994), p. 24.

453 "As each day passes": NSA, DIRNSA's Desk, *NSAN* (August 1998), p. 3.

453 "In some cases": NSA, Kathy Baskerville, "Y2K Oversight Office Tackles Millennium Problem," *NSAN* (August 1998), pp. 8–9.

453 "Solving the Y2K problem": NSA, DIRNSA's Desk, *NSAN* (August 1998), p. 3.

453 stickers were placed: NSA, Action Line, *NSAN* (November 1998), p. 11.

454 "We covered the whole thing": Maurice Chittenden and Simon Trump, "GCHQ Ties Up Millions in 'Doughnut,' " *Sunday Times* (London), August 13, 2000.

454 12 to 15 percent of capacity: interview with a senior NSA official.

454 "The network outage was a wake-up call": Lieutenant General Michael V. Hayden, address to the Kennedy Political Union of American University (February 17, 2000).

454 "I'll state right up front": NSA, DIRNSA's Desk, *NSAN* (May 1999), p. 3.

455 Born on March 17, 1945: Hayden's background is described in Department of the Air Force, Biography of Major General Michael V. Hayden (September 1998), pp. 1–2.

455 "Other than the affront to truthfulness": interview with Lieutenant General Michael V. Hayden (February 2, 2000).

456 "The term 'warlordism' ": interview with an NSA official (January 2000).

456 "I don't know how anything gets done": ibid.

456 "The budget is one of his biggest problems": ibid.

456 "As an agency, we now face our greatest": NSA, DIRNSA's Desk, *NSAN* (February 2000), p. 3.

457 "The NSA used to have the best computers": Bob Drogin, "NSA Blackout Reveals Downside of Secrecy," *Los Angeles Times,* March 13, 2000.

457 "Most of what they were expert in": ibid.

457 "Believe me": ibid.

457 "This should have come as a surprise to no one": U.S. House of Representatives, Permanent Select Committee on Intelligence, Report, Intelligence Authorization Act for Fiscal Year 2001, 106th Cong., 2nd Sess. (May 16, 2000).

457 "Signals intelligence is in a crisis": John I. Millis, address to the Central Intelligence Retirees Association (CIRA) (October 5, 1998), transcript printed in *CIRA Newsletter* (Winter 1998/1999).

458 "Increasingly": Vice Admiral J. M. McConnell, USN, "New World, New Challenges: NSA into the 21st Century," *American Intelligence Journal* (Spring–Summer 1994), p. 8.

458 "We've got to do both": interview with Lieutenant General Michael V. Hayden (February 2, 2000).

458 "Forty years ago": Barbara McNamara, address before the American Bar Association, Standing Committee on National Security Law, Washington, D.C. (May 18, 2000).

459 304 million people with Internet access: Vernon Loeb, "This Just In," *Washington Post,* June 20, 2000.

459 about 1,500 "immediate" requests for intelligence: information from senior NSA official.

459 "Well, what are all these communications": interview with senior intelligence official involved in Sigint (July 2000).

460 "So far": Barbara McNamara, address before the American Bar Association.

460 "Technology has now become": Bob Brewin, Daniel Verton, and William Matthews, "NSA Playing IT Catch-Up," *Federal Computer Week* (December 6, 1999).

460 only 2 percent of AT&T's voice and data: information provided by a senior NSA official (September 2000).

461 it fought against export: Michael S. Lelyveld, "Fiber-Optic Curbs on Ex-USSR Tied to Missile Fear," *Journal of Commerce* (March 24, 1992); Michael S. Lelyveld, "Spy Concerns Help Shape U.S. Export Policy, Experts Say," *Journal of Commerce* (March 24, 1992).

461 "The ability to get bits down a fiber": Jeff Hecht, "Wavelength Division Multiplexing," *Technology Review* (MIT) (March 1, 1999).

461 details on WDM and Project Oxygen: ibid.

461 "producing hundreds of kilometers": Chappell Brown, "System Design: Nonlinear Material, Low Costs Build Fiber Infrastructure," *Electronic Engineering Times* (January 11, 1999), p. 59.

462 Lucent Technologies unveiled: "Lucent Technologies Delivers Record-Breaking Optical Networking Capacity," M2 Press Wire (January 27, 1998).

462 the Netherlands' KPN Telecom B.V.: Brown, "System Design."

462 For two decades William O. Baker served: Security Affairs Support Association, Annual Awards Testimonial Dinner (May 27, 1999), p. 7.

462 David P. Kokalis: GAO Review of Federal Advisory Committees, *1997 Annual Report.*

462 NSA has also joined: "Breakthrough Technology Added to Government Research Network," *Business Wire* (July 19, 1999).

463 "We're going to drown in fiber": Hecht, "Wavelength Division Multiplexing."

463 increases in volume at 20 percent a year: Paul Korzeniowski, "Telepath: Record Growth Spurs Demand for Dense WDM—Infrastructure Bandwidth Gears Up for Next Wave," *Communications Week* (June 2, 1997).

463 "Today you have no idea": Tabassum Zakaria, "Top Secret U.S. Spy Agency Shapes Up for a New World," Reuters (December 13, 1999).

463 "The mere fact of digitizing": interview with former NSA official.

463 "Crypto policy is the wave of the past": Richard Lardner, "New National Security Agency Director Sure to Face Major Challenges," *Inside the Pentagon* (November 5, 1998).

463 "No matter what we do": John I. Millis address to the Central Intelligence Retirees Association (October 5, 1998).

464 "only 10 percent of communications": information from a senior NSA official (September 2000).

464 "Difficulties posed by new technologies": David Ensor, "Biggest U.S. Spy Agency Choking on Too Much Information," CNN web posting (November 25, 1999).

464 "Hard of Hearing": Gregory Vistica and Evan Thomas, "Hard of Hearing," *Newsweek,* December 13, 1999, p. 78.

464 "One criticism is that we're omniscient": Bryan Bender, "U.S. National Security Agency Faces Data Deluge, Says Chief," *Jane's Defence Weekly* (March 22, 2000).

464 "The projections that we made": NSA, videotape, "A Conversation Between the Deputy Director for Services and the NSA Technical Work Force" (September 30, 1999).

465 "postal service": "Computing's Next Superpower," *Fortune,* May 12, 1997.

465 "If you can see": NSA, videotape, "A Conversation Between the Deputy Director for Services and the NSA Technical Work Force" (September 30, 1999).

465 "surveillance, mine warfare": Drogin, "NSA Blackout Reveals Downside of Secrecy."

465 "the massive volume of stuff": interview with Lieutenant General Michael V. Hayden (February 2, 2000).

466 "We spend more money": John I. Millis address to the Central Intelligence Retirees Association (October 5, 1998).

466 Integrated Overhead Signals Intelligence Architecture–2: U.S. Senate, Armed Services Committee, U.S. National Security Space Programs and Issues, Testimony of NRO Director Keith R. Hall (March 11, 1998).

466 "the magnitude of the job": Jeremy Singer, "Sophisticated Fiber Optics Also Problematic for NSA," *Defense News* (June 12, 2000), p. 1.

466 "NSA now faces new": U.S. House of Representatives, Permanent Select Committee on Intelligence, Report, Intelligence Authorization Act for Fiscal Year 2001, 106th Cong., 2nd Sess. (May 16, 2000).

467 "There was an attitude": NSA, videotape, "Address by Timothy Sample at the Cryptologic History Symposium" (October 27, 1999).

469 "Not Congress": interview with Lieutenant General Michael V. Hayden (February 2, 2000).

469 "I think in the history of the agency": interview with NSA official.

470 "Our agency must undergo change": NSA, DIRNSA's Desk, *NSAN* (January 2000), p. 3.

470 "There has been much discussion about this change": ibid.

470 "responsible anarchists": Bob Brewin, Daniel Verton, William Matthews, "NSA Playing IT Catch-Up," *Federal Computer Week*, December 6, 1999, p. 1.

470 "Absent profound change at NSA"; details from the New Enterprise Team: NSA, "New Enterprise Team (NETeam) Recommendations: The Director's Work Plan for Change" (October 1, 1999).

471 "slowness"; details from the outside team: NSA, "External Team Report: A Management Review for the Director, NSA" (October 22, 1999).

472 "In a broad sense": interview with Lieutenant General Michael V. Hayden (February 2, 2000).

472 "Even the best game plan": NSA, DIRNSA's Desk, *NSAN* (January 2000), p. 3.

472 So Hayden threw out the unwieldy: ibid.

472 he chose Beverly Wright: NSA, "Director of National Security Agency Welcomes Ms. Beverly Wright, Chief Financial Manager," *NSAN* (February 2000), p. 2.

473 Black background: Interview with an NSA official. At SAIC, Black served as assistant vice president and director of information operations in its Columbia, Maryland, office.

474 "The CIA is good at stealing": Jeff Stein, "Spy Business Leaves Little Room for Intelligence," *Newsday* (December 7, 1995), p. 48.

474 "Perhaps the most compelling": CIA, Gates quoted in John H. Hedley, "The Intelligence Community: Is It Broken? How to Fix It?" *Studies in Intelligence* (1996), p. 18.

474 no more than ten or fifteen: Walter Pincus, "CIA Chief Cited Loss of Agency's Capabilities," *Washington Post*, May 25, 1998.

474 "a sorry blend": Edward G. Shirley, "Can't Anybody Here Play This Game?" *The Atlantic Monthly*, February 1998.

474 "Not a single Iran-desk chief": ibid.

475 "had few competent Arabic-speaking officers": Letters to the Editor, *The Atlantic Monthly*, May 1998.

475 "The CIA's spy service": Melvin A. Goodman, "Starting Over at the CIA," *IntellectualCapital.com* (Internet magazine), June 17, 1998.

475 "It is fair to say that the cupboard is nearly bare": Walter Pincus, "CIA's Espionage Capability Found Lacking," *Washington Post*, May 10, 1998.

475 "huge increase": John Diamond, "Bill Pumps Money into Intelligence," Associated Press (October 8, 1998).

475 "windfall": Walter Pincus, "Much of Intelligence Funding Will Go to Satellites," *Washington Post*, October 23, 1998.

475 "much smaller": CIA, Gates quoted in Hedley, "The Intelligence Community," p. 16.

475 "We don't really have a Director": ibid., p. 17.

476 only 15 percent: Vernon Loeb, "Inside Information," Washingtonpost.com (December 27, 1999).

476 "It is very difficult to exercise": John I. Millis address to the Central Intelligence Retirees Association (October 5, 1998).

476 Camp Perry: interview with a senior CIA official (October 22, 1999).

476 "At the end of the day": Vernon Loeb, "Drug Plant Attack on Target, Says CIA Chief," *Washington Post*, October 21, 1999, p. A27.

477 Special Collection Service: Unless otherwise noted, this information comes from interviews with senior CIA officials.

477 "As it happened": NSA, Secret/Comint Channels Only, oral history of Dr. Abraham Sinkov (May 1979), p. 119.

478 "1. *IDENTIFICATION":* (ARRB).

479 "Yesterday's code clerk": interview with senior CIA official.

479 Springfield Road: Federation of American Scientists, Intelligence Resource Program, at FAS web site http://www.fas.org/irp/facility/cssg.htm (June 21, 2000).

479 live room: Tom Bowman and Scott Shane, "Espionage from the Front Lines," *Baltimore Sun* (special series, December 3–5, 1995).

479 "Sometimes that's a very small antenna": "Spy Machines," *Nova* (PBS, 1987).

480 "in motion" . . . "at rest": interviews with senior intelligence officials.

480 first transatlantic intercept station: See James Bamford, *The Puzzle Palace: A Report on NSA, America's Most Secret Agency* (Boston: Houghton Mifflin, 1982), pp. 155–56.

CHAPTER 12: Heart

Page

481 fifty buildings: NSA, Dana Roscoe, "NSA Hosts Special Partnership Breakfast," *NSAN* (January 2000), p. 4.

481 more than $500 million: *Baltimore/Washington Corridor Chambergram* (March 1989), p. 1.

481 1.5 million square feet: Vice Admiral William Studeman, Address to the Baltimore/Washington Corridor Chamber of Commerce (June 29, 1990).

481 $152.8 million more: NSA, "Everything You Ever Wanted to Know About NSA but Were Afraid to Ask," *NSAN* (July 1994), p. 9.

481 "Were we a corporate company": NSA, videotape, "A Conversation Between Deputy Director for Support Services Terry Thompson and the NSA Technical Work Force" (September 30, 1999).

481 NSA's overall budget: These figures were the result of a slip accidentally included in Part Three of the Senate defense appropriations subcommittee's fiscal 1994 hearing volumes.

482 approximately 38,000 people: This figure is an extrapolation from a chart, "Relative Personnel and Funding Sizes of Major Intelligence Agencies," contained in the report "Preparing for the 21st Century: An Appraisal of U.S. Intelligence" (March 1, 1996), p. 132. The report was prepared by the Commission on the Roles and Capabilities of the U.S. Intelligence Community.

482 secret city's own cops: Until 1986 the city was protected by the General Services Administration's Federal Protective Service. That year the GSA delegated protection authority to the director of NSA.

482 3,850 miles each month: NSA, T. C. Carrington and Debra L. Z. Potts, "Protective Services—More Than Meets the Eye," *NSAN* (September 1999), pp. 8–10.

482 Emergency Response: NSA, Andrew Plitt, "Emergency! Emergency!" *NSAN* (September 1991), pp. 8–9.

482 Emergency Reaction Team: NSA, "Here Come the Men in Black," *NSAN* (June 1999), p. 4.

482 Executive Protection Unit: Carrington and Potts, "Protective Services—More Than Meets the Eye."

482 $4 million screening center: Tanya Jones, "NSA, Fort Meade Await Federal Building Funds," *Baltimore Sun,* July 24, 1997.

483 Explosive Detection Canine Unit: NSA, "NSA's Anti-Terrorism Security Measures," *NSAN* (February 1999), p. 4.

483 monthly electric bill: NSA, "The National Security Agency: Facts & Figures" (1999). NSA pays more than $21 million a year to the Baltimore Gas and Electric Company.

483 243,000 pounds: Some of the statistics in this paragraph are from Vice Admiral William Studeman's Address to the Baltimore/Washington Corridor Chamber of Commerce (June 29, 1990).

483 fire department: NSA, "Fire Prevention Week, *NSAN* (January 2000), p. 11.

483 blood donor program: NSA, "Work/Life Services" (1999). Also NSA, Dana Roscoe, "NSA Hosts Special Partnership Breakfast." Laura Sullivan, "Secret Spy Agency Puts on Human Face," *Baltimore Sun,* March 21, 2000.

484 *Pathfinder* and *Touki Bouki:* NSA, *NSAN* (June 1997), p. 12.

484 *My Village at Sunset:* NSA, "CLA Film Festival," *NSAN* (May 1999), p. 5.

484 Wolof: NSA's keen interest in Wolof likely stems in part from Mauritania's support of Saddam Hussein in Desert Storm. In particular, Saddam sent his wife and other relatives to Mauritania for protection.

484 *Wend Kuuni:* NSA, "September Film Festival," *NSAN* (September 1999), p. 12.

484 *Harvest: 3000 Years:* NSA, "March CLA 1998 Film Series 'Africa-Asia Month,' " *NSAN* (March 1998), p. 12.

484 *A Mongolian Tale:* NSA, "May CLA Film Festival 2000," *NSAN* (May 2000), p. 11.

484 more than 105 films in 48 foreign languages: NSA, "CLA Film Library Acquisitions," *NSAN* (August 1999), p. 12.

484 its own ticket agency: *Baltimore/Washington Corridor Chambergram* (March 1989), p. 1.

484 twentieth largest in the country: Vice Admiral William Studeman, Address to the Baltimore/Washington Corridor Chamber of Commerce (June 29, 1990).

484 Children's World: NSA, "Child Care: NSA, the New National Priorities," *NSAN* (July 1998), pp. 8–10.

485 "a lot of junk food addicts": NSA, Sherry Copeland, "A Look 'Inside' NSA's Drugstore," *NSAN* (December 1999), pp. 4–5.

485 Arundel Yacht Club: NSA, Club Notes, *NSAN* (May 2000), p. 16.

485 More than 3,200 employees: NSA, "NSA's Civilian Welfare Fund," *NSAN* (December 1998), p. 10.

485 Family Historians Genealogy Club: NSA, "Family Historians Genealogy Club," *NSAN* (February 1999), p. 7.

485 *Sex Hormones vs. GS Ratings*: NSA, *NSAN* (August 1996), p. 12.

485 Gay, Lesbian, or Bisexual Employees (GLOBE): NSA, Club Notes, *NSAN* (February 2000), p. 12.

486 "All American Festival": NSA, " 'Agency All-American Festival' Schedule of Events," *NSAN* (June 2000), pp. 10–11.

486 "For many years": ibid.

486 eleven cafeterias: NSA, *NSAN* (June 1998), p. 11.

486 on December 13: NSA, *NSAN* (February 1994), p. 3.

487 food sales totaled: NSA, *NSAN* (November 1994) p. 4.

487 SHAPE: NSA, *NSAN* (August 1993), p. 10; NSA, "SHAPE—Your New Year's Resolution Solution," *NSAN* (January 1998), p. 12; NSA, *NSAN* (December 1998), p. 5; NSA, "Work/Life Services" (1999).

487 Learned Organizations: NSA Crypto-Linguistic Association brochure (February 1973).

488 "Accumulated along every hallway": NSA, Action Line, "Trapped Down Under," *NSAN* (April 1995), p. 12.

488 burned-out car: NSA, Action Line, "Let's Talk Trash," *NSAN* (August 1999), p. 12.

488 "If I use the south tunnel": NSA, Action Line, "Dark Tunnels and Deserted Stairwells," *NSAN* (April 1994), p. 11.

488 the real building: NSA, "On a Clear Day You Can See the Washington Monument?" *NSAN* (April 1984), pp. 4–5.

488 shielding technique is used throughout much of the city: Barton Reppert, Associated Press, " 'Electromagnetic Envelope' for NSA," *Washington Post*, March 30, 1984.

490 "NSOC": personal observation.

490 Operation Silkworth: "Silkworth Security Guidelines," in *United States of America ex rel. Margaret A. Newsham and Martin Overbeek Bloem v. Lockheed Missiles and Space, Inc.*, U.S. District Court, Northern District of California, Civil Act. No. C88–20009.

490 red badge: interview with former NSA official.

490 "clearance status not indicated": ibid.

490 "After you leave an NSA installation": NSA, For Official Use Only, "NSA Employee Handbook."

490 Visitor Control Center: personal observations.

490 "sinister talons": NSA, "The National Security Agency Insignia."

490 Aperiodic Inspection Team: NSA, "Protective Services Celebrates 10th Anniversary," *NSAN* (October 1996), pp. 8–9.

491 "Furby Alert": Vernon Loeb, "A Toy Story of Hairy Espionage," *Washington Post*, January 13, 1999.

491 "No Classified Talk!": Personal observations.

491 14,000 security posters: NSA, Action Line, *NSAN* (January 1991), p. 11.

492 On the very day: ibid.

492 "a not-too-subtle": ibid.

492 "must find them surreal": NSA, Action Line, *NSAN* (June 1991) p. 11.

492 "If Cal's identified": Tony Capaccio, "Ripken in a Matter of National Security," *USA Today*, June 6, 1996.

493 "Members of the SSOC": NSA, "Protesters at NSA on the 4th of July," *The Communicator* (August 27, 1996).

494 "an unequivocal success": ibid.

494 "Very efficient": ibid.

494 National Cryptologic Memorial Wall: NSA, Picture This, *NSAN* (July 1996), p. 7; NSA, "NSA/CSS Memorial Day Observance," *NSAN* (July 1997), p. 12.

494 "I drive myself": Interview with Lieutenant General Michael V. Hayden (February 2, 2000).

495 his corner office: personal observations during several visits in 2000.

496 "When I've talked": Hayden interview (February 2, 2000).

498 "in consonance": NSA, For Official Use Only, NSA/CSS Regulation No. 10-11, "Release of Unclassified NSA/CSS Information," Annex B (June 16, 1987), p. B-2.

498 his own "ambassadors": ibid., p. B-3.

499 United States Signals Intelligence Directives: Until 1957 it was known as the Manual of U.S. Sigint Operations (MUSSO). NSA, Top Secret/Codeword, Oral History of Herbert L. Conley (March 5, 1984), p. 87.

499 "pursuing an area": This and the information about Taylor's background come from NSA, "The Newest SALT Members," *The Communicator* (April 9, 1996).

499 "Operations encompasses all the activities": NSA, Linda Lewis, "DO and DT Focus Days," *NSAN* (January 2000), p. 2.

500 Tiiu Kera: U.S. Air Force, biography of Major General Tiiu Kera (March 1999).

501 "leadership and management of a newly formed organization": "DOD Distinguished Civilian Service Awards Presented," *Regulatory Intelligence Data* (November 4, 1999).

501 NSOC: personal observation during visit in April 2000.

501 USS *Cole*: interview with senior NSA official.

502 Worldwide Video Teleconferencing Center: NSA, "Across the World—By Video Teleconferencing," *NSAN* (September 1998), pp. 4–5.

502 the organization's seal: NSA, "Celebrating a Quarter Century," *NSAN* (July 1989), p. 7.

502 "You didn't want NORAD": interview with Lieutenant General Daniel O. Graham (December 1984).

503 "initial analysis and reporting": NSA, "DEFSMAC Dedication," "Director's Talking Points" (April 7, 1998).

503 more than doubled: "DEFSMAC: A Quiet Hero in Anti-Proliferation Fight," *Intelligence Newsletter* (November 26, 1998).

503 "It has all the inputs from all the assets": Harvard University, Center for Information Policy Research, Program on Information Resources Policy, Seminar on Command, Control, Communications and Intelligence (Cambridge, Mass.: Harvard University Press, 1980), Raymond T. Tate lecture, p. 30.

503 "DEFSMAC not only detects": interview with former NSA official.

503 "the . . . premier": NSA, Chary Izquierdo, welcoming remarks at DEFSMAC Dedication Ceremony (April 7, 1998).

503 Topol-M single-warhead: David Hoffman, "Russian Rocket Explodes in Test," *Washington Post*, October 24, 1998. See also Sid Balman, Jr., "U.S. Sees More Iranian Tests," UPI (July 23, 1998).

504 DEFSMAC officials would immediately have sent: NSA, Chary Izquierdo, welcoming remarks at DEFSMAC Dedication Ceremony (April 7, 1998).

504 DIA Alert Center: This is a twenty-four-hour-a-day indications and warning center, responsible for providing time-sensitive intelligence to the secretary of defense, the Joint Chiefs of Staff, and others.

504 National Telemetry Processing Center: For the information in this paragraph, I have drawn on NSA, telemetry display, NSA Cryptologic Museum.

505 mobile medical center: NSA, "OHESS Is Going Mobile . . . Again!" *NSAN* (August 1999), pp. 4–5.

505 Oilstock: NSA, "The Docent Book" (January 1996), p. 26.

505 Main Library: NSA, Ann Bubeck, "NSA/CSS Libraries—'Putting Knowledge to Work,' " *NSAN* (April 1997), pp. 4–5.

505 "an astounding record of successful operations": "DOD Distinguished Civilian Service Awards Presented," *Regulatory Intelligence Data* (November 4, 1999).

506 "With today's rapidly evolving": NSA telemetry display, NSA Cryptologic Museum.

506 "Consider that hundreds or thousands of channels": NSA, "Career Opportunities in Signals Analysis" (2000).

506 "Demodulating and unraveling the internal structure": ibid.

506 "*extremely sensitive*": NSA, security handout, "NSA Security 'Seal' of Approval" (July 1987).

506 "completely by a black cloth": ibid.

507 "The Malfunctioning Santallite": NSA, "CWF Holiday Door Decorating Contest," *NSAN* (February 2000), p. 16.

507 "Using biometrics for identifying and authenticating": Gerald Lazar, "Agencies Scan Biometrics for Potential Applications," *Federal Computer Week* (January 20, 1997).

507 In 1999, NSA installed: Charlotte Adams, "Software Bundles Biometric Solutions," *Federal Computer Week* (May 10, 1999).

507 High Security Portal: NSA, "Eye Scans and Key Access Machines," *NSAN* (June 1993), p. 5.

508 Automated Key Access Machine: ibid.

508 secure phones: For details on the STU-I, STU-II, and STU-III, see NSA, "The Docent Book" (January 1996), p. 24.

509 Details on the STE: interview with Michael J. Jacobs (September 23, 2000).

509 it will remain fully secure: ibid.

509 NSA's ACCESS menu: NSA, "ACCESS the NSA/CSS Connection," *NSAN* (April 1997), p. 12.

509 Operators average 250,000 assisted calls: NSA, Kathy Gleason, "Telephone Switching Services (J532)," *NSAN* (June 2000), p. 6.

510 "because it was the only bidder": Bob Berwin, "Intercepts," *Federal Computer Week* (May 11, 1998).

510 Channel 50: NSA, "Multimedia Expo '93," *NSAN* (March 1993), p. 4.

510 Television Center: NSA, "On the Air in 5-4-3-2-1 . . . ," *NSAN* (June 1999), p. 6.

510 "If you enjoy": NSA, "Attention Talk Show Junkies!" *NSAN* (August 1994), p. 10.

510 On March 25: NSA, "Talk NSA 'On Location,' " *NSAN* (March 1998), p. 12.

510 "Ask short, straightforward questions": NSA, "How to . . . , for Future Day's Worldwide Virtual Event," *The Communicator* (October 8, 1996).

510 6,000 people . . . 36,711 lines of text: NSA, *The Communicator* (November 6, 1996).

511 "long before CNN": George Lardner, Jr., "On This Network, All the News Is Top Secret," *Washington Post*, March 3, 1992.

511 "If Warren Christopher": William F. Powers, "Cloak and Dagger Internet Lets Spies Whisper in Binary Code," *Washington Post*, December 8, 1994.

511 "a major breakthrough": ibid.

512 "Essentially": ibid.

512 "pizza truck" and "a brilliant use of cyberspace": press release, Computer Sciences Corporation, 1998.

512 "Collaboration with our counterparts": Fredrick Thomas Martin, *Top Secret Intranet* (Upper Saddle River, N.J.: Prentice Hall, 1999), p. 34.

513 Wer'zit!?: ibid., p. 164.

513 WebChat: ibid., p. 186.

513 have caused concern: ibid., p. 189.

514 four separate networks: ibid., pp. 53–55.

514 "Intelink-P": press release, Computer Sciences Corporation, 1998.

514 single largest data repository: Martin, *Top Secret Intranet*, p. 55.

514 expanding worldwide: ibid., p. 56.

514 Advanced Technology Demonstration Network: Don Clark, "What's Ahead: New Technologies Promise a Quantum Leap in Performance," *Wall Street Journal*, November 14, 1994.

515 Fastlane: Charlotte Adams, "Reorg Stresses Schedules, Customers," *Federal Computer Week* (July 4, 1994), p. 24.

515 "a *feast* of the world's most": Martin, *Top Secret Intranet*, p. 270.

515 SIGSUM: ibid.

515 Beamrider: ibid., pp. 272–74.

515 the *National SIGINT File:* ibid., pp. 276–79.

516 "Is the National Security Agency": U.S. House of Representatives, Committee on Appropriations, "Military Construction Appropriations," Hearings for 1974, 93rd Cong., 1st Sess., p. 466.

516 "That means": General Accounting Office, Report to the Congress by the Comptroller General of the United States, "Oversight of the Government's Security Classification Program—Some Improvements Still Needed," LCD-81-13, December 16, 1980, p. 14.

518 "Try to imagine": NSA, "Latest Findings in the Automatic Waste Collection System," *NSAN* (April 1983), pp. 4–5.

518 In 1998, the agency took in: NSA, Karen Gray, "Reduce + Reuse + Recycle = Good Business," *NSAN* (December 1998), pp. 4–5.

519 "The Paper Chase": NSA, "The Paper Chase," *NSAN* (September 1999), p. 5.

519 438 tons of metal: NSA, "NSA Does It All and Does It Well!" *The Communicator* (October 8, 1996).

519 degausser operators: NSA, "New Data on Electromagnetic Field Exposure," *NSAN* (February 1999), p. 5.

519 more than 129 million documents: GPO, "Report of the Commission on Protecting and Reducing Government Secrecy" (1997), p. 74.

519 "The sheer number of records": NSA, "E.O. 12958—A Classification Update," *The Communicator*, vol. 6, no. 1 (1996).

520 11 million "permanent records": NSA, "Archives and Records Center Gets New Look," *NSAN* (March 1991), p. 5.

520 "The German was a past master": Tim Weiner, "Pentagon Spy Agency Bares Some Dusty Secret Papers," *New York Times*, April 5, 1996.

520 Automated Declassification System": NSA, *The Communicator* (Summer 1998).

520 "Sometimes I think we just collect": CIA, John H. Hedley, "The Intelligence Community: Is It Broken? How to Fix It?" *Studies in Intelligence* (1996), pp. 17–18.

521 CYPRIS microprocessor: NSA, "The CYPRIS Microprocessor," *NSA Technical Fact Sheet* (1999).

521 At one time NSA accounted for 50 percent: NSA, *Focus Your Intelligence* (2000).

521 electron-beam maskmaking: ibid.

522 "The problem of providing power": NSA, "The Microencapsulated Betacell," *NSA Technical Fact Sheet* (1999).

522 Robert E. Stevens: SASA, SASA Spring 1997 program, "National Cryptologic Strategy for the 21st Century."

522 computer wafers to half a micron: NSA, "Wafer and Die Thinning Technology," *NSA Technical Fact Sheet* (1999).

522 $2 billion market: "Sigint Is Hot Market," *NCVA Cryptolog* (Winter 2000), p. 16.

522 more than 13,000 contracts: Roscoe, "NSA Hosts Special Partnership Breakfast."

523 J. Michael McConnell: "Roster," *Federal Computer Week* (April 15, 1996).

523 William P. Crowell: SASA, SASA Spring 1997 program, "National Cryptologic Strategy for the 21st Century."

523 Charles R. Lord: "In Memoriam," *NCVA Cryptolog* (Spring 1993), p. 16. Lord died of a cerebral hemorrhage on February 8, 1993.

523 bridge between: SASA was established in April 1979 to "enhance the relationships and understanding among those in government, industry and academe . . ." (SASA, SASA Fall 1998 program, "The Emerging Challenge.")

523 2001 budget authorization: Subsequent quotations are drawn from U.S. House of Representatives, Permanent Select Committee on Intelligence, Report, Intelligence Authorization Act for Fiscal Year 2001, 106th Cong., 2nd Sess. (May 16, 2000).

524 "The explosive growth of the global network": NSA, DIRNSA's Desk, *NSAN* (July 2000), p. 3.

524 "The magnitude of their education": Interview with Lieutenant General Marshall S. Carter (July 17, 1980).

525 Military Elint Signal Analysis Program: NSA, Picture This, *NSAN* (September 1992), p. 5.

525 NSA Graduate Studies Center: NSA, "JMIC Graduate Center Dedicated," *NSAN* (April 1997), p. 11; NSA, Michael L. Barksdale, "The Part-time Master of Science of Strategic Intelligence Program," *NSAN* (December 1999), p. 2.

525 master of science in strategic intelligence: NSA, Mary C. Parker, "A Master's Degree: Yours for the Taking," *NSAN* (November 1996), pp. 8–9.

525 largest computerized training: NSA, "NSA Testing Center," *NSAN* (May 1993), p. 7.

525 Senior Technical Development Program: NSA, "STDP Class of 1998 Graduates," *NSAN* (September 1998), p. 5.

525 "best of the best": ibid.

525 Roadhouse Café: NSA, " 'Roadhouse' Rhonda," *NSAN* (October 1996), p. 10.

525 $5 million for additional courses: Roscoe, "NSA Hosts Special Partnership Breakfast."

525 "have the potential": NSA, NSA/CSS Office of Contracting, Research Grant, 7/30/84.

526 "His brilliant achievements": NSA, "Frank Rowlett Retires," *NSAN* (Special Edition) (January 1966), p. 1.

526 "This building": NSA, Tom Johnson, "OPS 3 Building Dedicated to Cryptologic Pioneer," *NSAN* (March 1999), p. 10.

527 "Despite NSA's size and success": NSA, Confidential/Comint Channels Only, "Beyond Codes and Ciphers: The Expanded Meaning of Cryptology in the Late Twentieth Century," *Cryptologic Quarterly* (Winter 1990), pp. 27, 34.

527 "labyrinth of letters": Jorge Luis Borges, "The Library of Babel," quoted in Emir Rodriguez Monegal, *Jorge Luis Borges: A Literary Biography* (New York: E.P. Dutton, 1978), p. 26.

CHAPTER 13: Soul

Page

528 with between fourteen and eighteen years of experience: Richard Lardner, "The Secret's Out," *Government Executive* (August 1998), p. 26.

528 59 percent of the workers are male: NSA, DIRNSA's Desk, *NSAN* (March 1998), p. 3.

528 Sixty-three percent: NSA, "Deputy Director for Support Services," *NSAN* (April 1993), p. 7.

528 13 percent . . . 27 percent . . . 3.3 percent: NSA, "A Quick True or False Quiz," *NSAN* (May 1993), p. 3.

528 four generals and admirals: General Accounting Office report (June 16, 1997), Appendix III.

528 the top 10 percent . . . $9.4 million in air travel . . . $65 million in state income taxes: NSA, "Everything You Ever Wanted to Know About NSA But Weren't Allowed to Ask," *NSAN* (July 1994), p. 9.

528 largest collection of mathematicians: NSA, *Focus Your Intelligence* (2000).

529 "She's known as the 'tire lady' ": interview with former intelligence official.

529 "There is no dress code at all": Cort Kirkwood, "Our Friendly Neighborhood Colony of Spies," *Baltimore Magazine*, reprinted in *NCVA Cryptolog* (Winter 1994), pp. 1, 9.

529 Brent Morris: NSA, "From Magic to Math and Back Again," *NSAN* (July 1993), p. 7.

529 Eileen Buckholtz: NSA, Read-All-About-It, *NSAN* (January 1991), p. 16.

529 Frederick Bulinski: NSA, Read-All-About-It, *NSAN* (November 1992), p. 24.

529 "The results show that the personality": NSA, Gary L. Grantham, *Who Is NSA* (April 1985), p. 1 (National War College).

530 "This contrasts markedly": ibid., p. 8.

530 "You can always tell an NSA extrovert": Warren P. Strobel, "Incredible 3-Day NSA Computer Failure—Sound of Silence," *U.S. News & World Report*, February 6, 2000.

530 "The great predominance of introverts": NSA, Grantham, *Who Is NSA*, p. 9.

530 "The predominance of thinking types": ibid., p. 11.

531 "The overwhelming preference among NSA managers": ibid.

531 "From my perspective": NSA, "Everything You Ever Wanted to Know About NSA but Weren't Allowed to Ask."

531 "Perhaps one of the first security practices": NSA, *NSA Handbook* (undated), pp. 1–2.

532 "We in NSA comprise": NSA, "Editorial Comment: Why Work for NSA?" *NSA Technical Journal* (undated), pp. i–ii.

532 "Your challenge": NSA, recruitment brochure, "If Math Is Your Area of Expertise, We'd Like to Introduce You to Ours" (undated; circa 1998).

532 "The challenge is": Bob Drogin, "Help Wanted: U.S. Intelligence Agencies Make No Secret of Need for Workers," *Minneapolis Star Tribune*, November 16, 1999.

532 "We're looking": ibid.

532 Undergraduate Training Program: NSA, "NSA Salutes 'Father of the Undergraduate Training Program (UTP),' " *NSAN* (February 1999), p. 2.

533 "It is appalling": NSA, Action Line, *NSAN* (September 1997).

533 Co-operative Education Program: NSA, "1997 Co-op Graduation," *NSAN* (September 1997), p. 12.

533 "Our recruiting strategy has historically been built": NSA, videotape, "A Conversation Between Deputy Director for Services Terry Thompson and the NSA Technical Workforce" (September 30, 1999).

533 initiated a streamlined hiring process: NSA, Cynthia Scourtis, "Hiring for the Future," *NSAN* (November 1998), p. 2.

533 e-mail address: Résumés can also be mailed to NSA, P.O. Box 8787, Gaithersburg, MD 20898, or faxed to (301) 947-2086.

534 "they undoubtedly represent": NSA, Confidential/Comint Channels Only, "Beyond Codes and Ciphers: The Expanding Meaning of Cryptology in the Late Twentieth Century," *Cryptologic Quarterly* (Winter 1990), p. 31, n. 5.

534 One math major: Internet posting by <proff@iq.org>, "An Interview with the NSA" (February 11, 1999).

535 SSBI: General Accounting Office, "Background Investigations: Impediments to Consolidating Investigation and Adjudicative Function" (1995).

In 1992 the NSA spent about $154,000 on SSBIs. This, however, did not include the costs associated with SSBIs conducted on military personnel assigned to the NSA, which were paid for by the individual military services. General Accounting Office, *Classified Information: Costs of Protection Are Integrated with Other Security Costs* (October 1993), pp. 11–12.

535 Rob Fuggetta: This account appears in Paul Mandelbaum, "Your Boss Is Spying on You," *Baltimore Magazine* (May 1985), pp. 79, 127.

535 NSA officials are fighting a new proposal: "Background Investigations Procedures Change," *Los Angeles Times,* April 6, 1998; "Pentagon Security Investigation Backlog," *AFIO Weekly Intelligence Notes* (June 11, 1999).

536 900,000 investigations: Walter Pincus, "900,000 People Awaiting Pentagon Security Clearances," *Washington Post,* April 22, 2000.

536 94 percent: GAO, National and International Affairs Division, Report B-283901, "DOD Personnel—Inadequate Personnel Security Investigations Pose National Security Risks" (October 27, 1999), p. 8.

536 arrested on October 28 and charged with espionage: Department of Defense, Rear Admiral Craig Quigley news conference (November 30, 1999).

536 allegedly confessing to mailing a computer disk and details on NSA's undersea cable-tapping operations: *CBS Evening News* (November 29, 1999).

536 "respiration, electro-dermal responses": NSA, NSA/CSS Regulation No. 122-3, "Polygraph Examination and Examiners," Annex D (April 6, 1984), p. 2.

537 "Polygraph! The word alone": NSA, "To Tell the Truth," *NSAN* (October 1994), pp. 8–9.

537 a study at NSA: U.S. House of Representatives, Committee on Education and Labor, Subcommittee on Employment Opportunities, Polygraphs in the Workplace: The Use of "Lie Detectors" in Hiring and Firing, 95th Cong., 1st Sess. (1986), pp. 147–70.

537 From July 1983 to June 1984: U.S. House of Representatives, Committee on Armed Services, Investigations Subcommittee, Hearing on H.R. 4681 Relating to the Administration of Polygraph Examinations and Prepublication Review Requirements by Federal Agencies, 98th Cong., 2nd Sess. (1984), p. 111.

538 "The worst experience of my life": Kirkwood, "Our Friendly Neighborhood Colony of Spies."

538 "termination of employment": NSA memorandum, "Personnel Security Procedures" (September 27, 1982).

538 four leaks a year: Testimony of the chief of NSA's Operations Directorate Intelligence Staff [name deleted], U.S. House of Representatives, Committee on the Judiciary, Subcommittee on Civil and Constitutional Rights, Presidential Directive on the Use of Polygraphs and Prepublication Review, Hearings, 98th Cong., 1st and 2nd Sess. (1983–1984), p. 150.

538 topics covered during NSA's counterintelligence polygraph examination: NSA, For Official Use Only, NSA/CSS Regulation No. 122-06, Personnel Security Programs for Continued Access (July 29, 1991), p. 4.

539 "the work force at NSA": U.S. House of Representatives, Committee on Armed Services, Investigations Subcommittee, Hearing on H.R. 4681 Relating to the Administration of Polygraph Examinations and Prepublication Review Requirements by Federal Agencies, 98th Cong., 2nd Sess. (1984), pp. 46–47.

539 Under the aperiodic exam program: ibid.

539 According to the chief of the Polygraph Division: ibid.

540 an analysis of 20,511 applicants between 1974 and 1979: U.S. House of Representatives, Committee on Education and Labor, Subcommittee on Employment Opportunities, Polygraphs in the Workplace: The Use of "Lie Detectors" in Hiring and Firing, 95th Cong., 1st Sess. (1986), pp. 147–70.

541 Polygraph Assisted Scoring System: NSA, "Computerized Soft Decision Making from Multiple Sensor Inputs," *NSA Technology Fact Sheet* (1999).

542 "In the near future": NSA, "To Tell the Truth."

542 Asked whether: U.S. House of Representatives, Committee on the Judiciary, Subcommittee on Civil and Constitutional Rights, Presidential Directive on the Use of Polygraphs and Prepublication Review, 89th Cong., 1st and 2nd Sess. (1983–1984), p. 59.

542 Senate Select Committee: Walter Pincus, "Senators Question Polygraph Use," *Washington Post*, July 24, 1999.

542 "In our situation": ibid.

543 "The Soviets seem to have": White House, Top Secret memorandum, "Discussion at the 463rd Meeting of the National Security Council, October 13, 1960" (DDEL, Ann Whitman File, NSC Series, Box 13).

543 Anderson was also concerned: ibid.

544 GLOBE: NSA, Club Notes, *NSAN* (October 1999), p. 12; NSA, Club Notes, *NSAN* (December 1999), p. 12.

544 "Clearly during the Iran-Iraq war": Studeman's comments were made in an address before the Association of Former Intelligence Officers (February 4, 1991), reprinted in *NCVA Cryptolog* (Fall Extra, 1991), pp. 2, 11.

545 "While standing amongst the weeds": Rodney R. Ingram, "Marietta, Washington, Forty Years Later," *NCVA Cryptolog* (March 1994), p. 2.

546 deactivation ceremonies at Edzell: "Final Flag Lowered at RAF Edzell, Scotland," *Dundee* (Scotland) *Courier & Advertiser* (October 1, 1997), p. 1.

546 Kamiseya ordered closed: Jay R. Browne, "Kami Seya—The Last Years," *NCVA Cryptolog* (Fall 1997), p. 43.

546 Eckstein: F. Harrison Wallace, Jr., "The History of Eckstein Border Site 1958–1993." Web posting at http://asa.npoint.net/eckstin.htm (October 2, 2000).

547 "Most of the [intercepted information]": Nicky Hager, *Secret Power: New Zealand's Role in the International Spy Network* (Nelson, New Zealand: Craig Potton, 1996), pp. 85–88. The Unit was located next to the DSD headquarters building on the grounds of the Australian Department of Defence's Victoria Barracks on St. Kilda Road, Melbourne.

547 Hong Kong: Glenn Schloss, "U.K. Spy Site Razed to Keep Its Secrets," *South China Morning Post*, November 30, 1997, p. 4.

547 Planted in the walls: "British 'Bugs' Listen In on Generals," *Intelligence Newsletter* (April 23, 1998).

547 "If we can stay at 4,500": Bill Goodwin, "Overmanned and Expensive to Run?" *Electronic Times* (November 30, 1995).

548 "Who remembers what we did": Robert R. Payne, "I Was Never There, But I Remember Skaggs Island . . . ," *NCVA Cryptolog* (Special Issue 1996), pp. 3–4.

548 "Technology has progressed": Jay R. Browne, "Introduction," *NSGA Cryptolog* (Fall 1997), p. 2.

549 a retired Navy cryptologist wrote: Commander Mike Loescher, *United States Naval Institute Proceedings* (February 2000).

549 "There will continue to be a Naval Security Group": As of 1999, the Naval Security Group operated the following stations. Naval Security Group Detachments: Barbers Point, Hawaii; Brunswick, Maine; Digby, U.K.; London, U.K.; Monterey, California; Pensacola, Florida; South Korea; Yakima, Washington. Naval Security Group Activities: Bad Aibling, Germany; Bahrain; Denver, Colorado; Fort Meade, Maryland; Fort Gordon, Georgia; Groton, Connecticut; Guantánamo Bay, Cuba; Kunia, Hawaii; Medina, Texas; Menwith Hill, U.K.; Misawa, Japan; Naples, Italy; Norfolk, Virginia; Northwest, Virginia; Pearl Harbor, Hawaii; Rota, Spain; Sabana Seca, Puerto Rico; San Diego, California; Sugar Grove, West Virginia; Whidbey Island, Washington; Yokosuka, Japan. Naval Security Group Communications Detachment: Washington, D.C., Naval Security Group Support Detachment Four, Edzell, U.K. Naval Security Group Departments: NAVCOMTELSTA Guam; NAVCOMTELSTA Diego Garcia; NAVCOMTEL Area Master Station, Pacific, Wahiawa, Hawaii. See "Security Group Listing," *NCVA Cryptolog* (Spring 1999), p. 10.

549 "people [were] stacked almost three deep": Thomas Hasler, "Security Agency Expanding Facilities," [Baltimore] *Evening Sun*, June 18, 1982.

549 NSA building projects: Thomas Hasler, "The Secret's Out: Hush-hush NSA Is Expanding," [Baltimore] *Evening Sun*, April 23, 1983.

549 what it had been in 1980: CIA, Robert Gates, quoted in John H. Hedley, "The Intelligence Community: Is It Broken? How to Fix It?" *Studies in Intelligence* (1996), p. 14.

549 number of spy satellites: ibid.

549 "NSA's relative piece": Studeman's comments are from NSA, memorandum, Admiral W. O. Studeman to All Employees (April 8, 1992), pp. 1–2.

549 cut its staff by 17½ percent: NSA, "NSA Transition Book for the Department of Defense" (transition from Bush to Clinton administrations) (December 9, 1992), p. 13.

549 24 percent by 2001: "U.S. Spy Agencies Bloated, Panel Finds," *Los Angeles Times*, March 2, 1996.

549 Brown said that at least: ibid.

549 "We found that the growth of the Agency": Department of Defense, Inspector General, Intelligence Review Directorate, Policy and Oversight Report, "Final Report on the Verification Inspection of the National Security Agency" (February 13, 1996), p. 11.

550 "NSA personnel will be deeply affected": NSA, "NSA Plans for the Future," *NSAN* (January 1993), p. 4.

550 A White House study: Commission on the Roles and Capabilities of the United States Intelligence Community, "Preparing for the 21st Century: An Appraisal of U.S. Intelligence" (March 1, 1996), p. 96.

550 "Employees should": NSA, "NSA Plans for the Future."

551 "While our neighbors and family members": NSA, Action Line, *NSAN* (December 1992), p. 11.

551 a bond had been broken: NSA, "Rep. Steny Hoyer Visits NSA," *The Communicator* (September 3, 1996).

551 "I had visions": NSA, Secret/Comint Channels Only, Oral History of Dr. Howard Campaigne (June 29, 1983), pp. 130–31.

551 Soft Landing: NSA, Karen Anderson Cianci, "NSA's Soft Landing Program," *NSAN* (April 1997), p. 7. See also "Soft Landing for Ex-Spies," *Intelligence Newsletter* (September 3, 1998); *Defense Information and Electronics Report* (August 21, 1998).

551 Barbara Prettyman retired: NSA, "Update on Soft Landing," *NSAN* (November 1998), p. 4.

552 "Four Navy chiefs and one NSA civilian": NSA, "The Magic of CSGs," *The Communicator* (March 4, 1996).

552 "I have three": Loch K. Johnson, *Secret Agencies: U.S. Intelligence in a Hostile World* (New Haven, Conn.: Yale University Press), p. 21.

553 "There now exists a world full of 'Navajo Code Talkers' ": Vice Admiral J. M. McConnell, USN, "New World, New Challenges: NSA Into the 21st Century," *American Intelligence Journal* (Spring/Summer 1994), p. 8.

553 fully 58 percent . . . 13 percent: CIA, former CIA director Robert Gates, quoted in Hedley, "The Intelligence Community, p. 11.

553 asked fifteen colleges: Mark Mayfield, "Feds Recruit Students to Study Russian," *USA Today*, September 13, 1983, p. 3A.

553 a shortage of Berber translators led to a critical delay: Frank Greve, "Linguist Might Have Averted Fatal Disco Terrorist Bombing," Knight-Ridder News Service (November 28, 1986).

553 "steadily deteriorating language training": ibid.

554 "a group of approximately 125 linguists": Al Kamen, "Join the Army and See Sarajevo," *Washington Post*, May 4, 1993, p. 19.

554 "When Haiti blew up": NSA videotape, "A Conversation between Deputy Director for Services Terry Thompson and the NSA Technical Work Force" (September 30, 1999).

554 the tedium of the job: Kirkwood, "Our Friendly Neighborhood Colony of Spies."

554 Florida A&M University: "Language Program with Spy Ties," *Intelligence Newsletter* (December 16, 1992).

555 "NSA is faced with the growing problem": NSA, "Multi-Lingual Document Image Analysis," *NSA Technical Fact Sheet* (1995).

555 The machine was eventually able: Colin Campbell, " 'Intelligent' Computer Reads Many Typefaces," *New York Times*, August 19, 1984, p. 22.

555 SYSTRAN: SYSTRAN Software, Inc., fact sheet (undated), pp. 2, 9.

555 NSA has also developed a technique: NSA, "Information Sorting and Retrieval by Language or Topic," *Technology Fact Sheet* (1999).

556 Semantic Forests: Suelette Dreyfus, "Spies in the 'Forests,' " *The Independent* (November 22, 1999).

556 Berger-Liaw Neural Network: University of Southern California Press Release #0999025 (September 30, 1999).

557 "It's a good-size problem": Interview with Lieutenant General Michael V. Hayden (February 2, 2000).

557 "Group Three languages": ibid.

557 "We need to hire a lot more people": NSA videotape, "A Conversation between Deputy Director for Services Terry Thompson and the NSA Technical Work Force" (September 30, 1999).

558 In a series of lectures at NSA: NSA, National Cryptologic School, *The Friedman Lectures on Cryptology* (1965).

558 "The philosophy here": Neal Thompson, "Call for Mathematicians No Secret," *Baltimore Sun*, January 10, 1998.

558 "the agency succumbed": NSA, Confidential/Comint Channels Only, "Beyond Codes and Ciphers: The Expanded Meaning of Cryptology in the Late Twentieth Century," *Cryptologic Quarterly* (Winter 1990), pp. 27–29.

558 "irrelevant to (and unintelligible to)": ibid.

559 "The Cold War": Thompson, "Call for Mathematicians."

559 "Over a three-year period": ibid.

559 42 percent fewer graduates: interview with Michael J. Jacobs (September 23, 2000).

559 "I have been here at NSA": This and the following quotations are drawn from U.S. Department of Defense, Office of the Inspector General, "Review of Hiring and Promotion Practices at the National Security Agency" (1994), pp. 56–57.

560 "The philosophy": ibid., p. 20.

560 Southwestern Recruiting Office: ibid., p. 17.

560 in 1993 women made up: U.S. House of Representatives, Permanent Select Committee on Intelligence, Hearing, Central Intelligence Agency, Defense Intelligence Agency and National Security Agency: Minority Hire, Retentions and Promotions, 103rd Cong., 1st Sess. (1994), p. 2.

561 "we have probably": ibid., pp. 27–33.

561 encouraging his recruiters to make: U.S. House of Representatives, Permanent Select Committee on Intelligence, Hiring, Promotion, Retention and Overall Representation of Minorities, Women and Disabled Persons Within the Intelligence Community, 103rd Cong., 2nd Sess. (1995), pp. 61–63.

561 fewer than 200: NSA, "Director Appears on TALK NSA," *The Communicator* (June 19, 1996). There was a projection of 500 hires for 1996.

561 "So far I haven't gone to court": U.S. House of Representatives, Permanent Select Committee on Intelligence, Hiring, Promotion, Retention and Overall Representation of Minorities, Women and Disabled Persons Within the Intelligence Community, 103rd Cong., 2nd Sess. (1995), p. 124.

561 presentation by storyteller Penny Gamble Williams: NSA, Jennifer Pelletier, "The Native American/Alaskan Employment Program," *NSAN* (November 1999), pp. 8–9.

562 6917 Electronic Security Group: NSA, From the Director's Desk, *The Communicator* (March 12, 1996).

562 one of his chief assignments: R. Jeffrey Smith, "Military Men Named to Top Intelligence Posts," *Washington Post*, January 25, 1996, p. 9.

562 "They would use the phrase": NSA, Top Secret/Comint Channels Only, Oral History of Lieutenant General Kenneth A. Minihan (March 8, 1999), pp. 1–26.

562 "It . . . really surprised me": ibid.

563 "He was a 'geek' ": Fredrick Thomas Martin, *Top Secret Intranet* (Upper Saddle River, N.J.: Prentice Hall, 1999), pp. 271–72.

563 "The DDIR [deputy director] is part of the seducing": NSA, Top Secret/Comint Channels Only, Oral History of Lieutenant General Kenneth A. Minihan (March 8, 1999), pp. 1–26.

563 "I was very disruptive": ibid.

563 "My first two or three weeks": ibid.

564 "You could hear the groans": ibid.

564 "Ann knew": NSA, Top Secret/Talent/Keyhole/Umbra, Oral History of Admiral Bobby Ray Inman (June 18, 1997).

564 "I am honored to have been sworn in before you today": NSA, "Day of Celebration," *NSAN* (January 1998), p. 4.

564 race and gender issues: In 1998 Asian Pacific Americans (APAs) comprised only 1.3 percent of the NSA workforce, compared to 3.9 percent of the federal workforce. Between 1990 and 1996 NSA hired 89 APAs. See NSA, "Come Celebrate Asian Pacific American Heritage Month," *NSAN* (May 1998), p. 8.

565 By 1997: The material in this and the following paragraphs draws on Scott Wilson, "NSA's Quest for Diversity Called Threat," *Baltimore Sun*, July 6, 1997.

565 the government later settled with him [Sonntag]: James C. Ho, "A Year of Bill Lan Lee," op-ed article in *Washington Times*, December 24, 1998.

565 Mary Ann Sheehy: NSA, Office of the Inspector General, Report CO-94-0317 (April 18, 1996); interview with Mary Ann Sheehy.

At NSA, "Personnel Employment Information" is defined in NSA/CSS PMM 30-2, chapter 303, paragraphs 1–4 and 2–2(b), as "information contained in an employee's Official Personnel Folder and limited to

1. Name and present or forwarding address
2. Present and past position titles, grades, tenure, and salaries
3. Civil service status, if applicable
4. Date and reason for separation, if applicable, and
5. Comments provided by management constituting a letter of reference."

566 "I am quite concerned about this": NSA letter from Dr. Michael J. Wigglesworth, clinical psychologist, to Mary McGowan (October 5, 1994).

567 "no evidence of improper or illegal activity": NSA, letter from Reginald J. Bowman, Senior Assistant Inspector General for Investigations to Mary Ann Sheehy (April 18, 1996).

567 "NSA believes it is above the law": Letter, Mary Ann Sheehy to Attorney General Janet Reno (May 17, 1999).

567 "While we sympathize": letter from Department of Justice, Criminal Division, to Mary Ann Sheehy (November 26, 1999).

567 The U.S. Attorney's Office responded: letter from United States Attorney, District of Maryland, Northern Division, to Mary Ann Sheehy (April 13, 2000).

567 The U.S. Attorney's Office eventually dismissed her complaint: letter from United States Attorney, District of Maryland, Northern Division, to Mary Ann Sheehy (April 26, 2000).

567 "You should look for another job": interview with Mary Ann Sheehy (September 22, 2000).

567 "all parts of the Agency together with ideas": NSA, Lieutenant General Kenneth A. Minihan, From the Director's Desk, *NSAN* (January 1998), p. 3.

567 "I think it's magnificient": NSA, Top Secret/Comint Channels Only, Oral History of Lieutenant General Kenneth A. Minihan (March 8, 1999), p. 8.

568 "No one will work harder": NSA, Lieutenant General Kenneth A. Minihan, From the Director's Desk, *NSAN* (April 1996), p. 3.

568 "Out-of-the-box thinking": NSA, From the Director's Desk, *The Communicator* (March 12, 1996).

568 Skunk Works: NSA, "Skunk Works," *The Communicator* (April 16, 1996).

568 "Now is the time for Team NSA": NSA, Lieutenant General Kenneth A. Minihan, From the Director's Desk, *NSAN* (January 1997), p. 3.

568 "Where are my hip boots?": NSA, Action Line, *NSAN* (March 1997), p. 11.

569 "We now have people talking about both sides": Terry L. Thompson in "Terry L. Thompson, Deputy Director for Support Services," *NSAN* (September 1997), p. 4.

569 "very large changes": Walter Pincus, "Panel Ties NSA Funds to Changes at Agency," *Washington Post*, May 7, 1998.

570 "The NSA FY 1997 financial statements": "Black Money Hole," *Federal Computer Week* (August 31, 1998).

570 "cannot track allocations": Pincus, "Panel Ties NSA Funds to Changes."

570 In a plan approved in late April: U.S. Department of Defense News Release, "DOD Announces Reorganization of C3I Office" (May 13, 1998). See also Richard Lardner, "The Secret's Out," p. 27.

570 seriously mismanaging: NSA, "The Agency's CIO," *NSAN* (July 1998), p. 2.

571 "Just as control of industrial technology": NSA, Lieutenant General Kenneth A. Minihan, From the Director's Desk, *NSAN* (November 1997), p. 3.

571 "Information will give us the power to pick all the locks": Major General Kenneth A. Minihan, USAF, "The Challenge for Intelligence," *American Intelligence Journal* (Spring/Summer 1995), p. 38.

571 "Information dominance for America": NSA, Top Secret/Comint Channels Only, Oral History of Lieutenant General Kenneth A. Minihan (March 8, 1999), pp. 6–7.

571 "Though new technologies provide": NSA, DIRNSA's Desk, *NSAN* (July 1998), p. 3.

571 "Information warfare poses a strategic risk": NSA, Lieutenant General Kenneth A. Minihan, From the Director's Desk, *NSAN* (May 1996), p. 3.

572 "The committee believes": Vernon Loeb, "A Key Panel Asks: Why Only One Spy Probe?" *Washington Post,* July 7, 1999.

572 "Looking back": Richard Lardner, "New National Security Agency Director Sure to Face Major Challenges," *Inside the Pentagon* (November 5, 1998).

572 "It's the hardest job I've ever had": NSA, Top Secret/Comint Channels Only, Oral History of Lieutenant General Kenneth A. Minihan (March 8, 1999), p. 24.

572 "I think it will be catastrophic": ibid., p. 17.

572 Minihan walked between: NSA, "Agency Events Celebrate Distinguished Career of Lt. Gen. Minihan," *NSAN* (May 1999), p. 2.

572 chilly air of retirement: Minihan became president and chief operating officer of TeleHub Communications Corporation, a provider of voice, video, and data to ATM networks worldwide. "TeleHub Communications, Inc., Secures 'Million Dollar' Men," *Canadian Corporate News* (July 7, 1999).

573 near the kitchen is a plaque: Personal observation.

573 outside contractors: NSA, Dana Roscoe, "NSA Hosts Special Partnership Breakfast," *NSAN* (January 2000), p. 4.

573 Groundbreaker: Vernon Loeb, "NSA to Turn Over Non-Spy Technology to Private Industry," *Washington Post,* June 7, 2000.

573 "more than 3,000": NSA, Dana Roscoe, "NSA Hosts Special Partnership Breakfast."

574 "information technology infrastructure": Loeb, "NSA to Turn Over Non-Spy Technology."

574 "They're buying all those new toys": Neal Thompson, "Putting NSA Under Scrutiny," *Baltimore Sun,* October 18, 1998.

574 "the intelligence failure": ibid.

574 "There is a significant amount of concern": NSA, videotape, "A Conversation Between Deputy Director for Services Terry Thompson and the NSA Technical Work Force" (September 30, 1999).

575 Employee Assistance Service: NSA, "NSA's Helping Hand," *NSAN* (January 1999), p. 5.

575 "It's a real worry": Richard Lardner, "The Secret's Out," p. 24.

575 "Our hiring program skims": NSA, videotape, "A Conversation Between Deputy Director for Services Terry Thompson and the NSA Technical Work Force" (September 30, 1999).

576 "While average starting salaries": U.S. Department of Commerce, "America's New Deficit: The Shortage of Information Technology Workers" (1997).

576 "the unique nature of our work": Arik Hesseldahl, "Uncle Sam Wants Spooks," *Wired News* (October 26, 1998).

576 "This is simply insufficient": Commission on the Roles and Capabilities of the United States Intelligence Community, report, "Preparing for the 21st Century: An Appraisal of U.S. Intelligence" (March 1, 1996), pp. 96–97.

576 "Our budget has declined": NSA, videotape, "A Conversation Between Deputy Director for Services Terry Thompson and the NSA Technical Work Force" (September 30, 1999).

577 "The nose is pointing down": "Federal Bytes," *Federal Computer Week* (February 3, 1997).

CHAPTER 14: Brain

Page

578 "I had five and a half acres": interview with Lieutenant General Marshall S. Carter (July 17, 1980).

578 "It's double that today": interview with an NSA official.

580 SSA's cryptanalytic: Army Security Agency, Top Secret/Ultra report, "The Achievement of the Signal Security Agency in World War II" (February 20, 1945), p. 16.

581 "The author believes": NSA, J. T. Pendergrass, "Cryptanalytic Use of High-Speed Digital Computing Machines" (1946), pp. 1–2.

581 "We had the biggest collection": NSA, Secret/Comint Channels Only, Oral History of Dr. Howard Campaigne (June 29, 1983), pp. 75, 89.

582 "A copy of this report hit my desk": Sam Snyder, "Sam and Ray and Abner," *The Phoenician* (a publication of the Phoenix Society, the association of NSA retirees) (Winter 1995–1996), pp. 13–14.

582 "We chose the name": ibid.

582 "From then on": NSA, Tom Johnson, "The Plan to Save NSA" (undated NSA brochure issued upon the death of Dr. Louis Tordella), pp. 7–8.

583 PACE 10: NSA, "The Docent Book" (January 1996), p. 25.

583 "Dammit, I want you fellows": NSA, "Influence of U.S. Cryptologic Organizations on the Digital Computer Industry" (May 1977), pp. 1–28.

583 "After the ideas of Harvest": NSA, Secret/Comint Channels Only, Oral History of Dr. Howard Campaigne (June 29, 1983), p. 62.

583 "We were always surprised": ibid., pp. 73–74, 76.

584 "In the late sixties": ibid., pp. 74, 88, 95.

584 to less than 4 percent: NSA, Top Secret/Comint Channels Only, Oral History of Lieutenant General Kenneth A. Minihan (March 8, 1999), p. 3.

584 "What the research-and-development people": NSA, Secret/Comint Channels Only, Oral History of Dr. Howard Campaigne (June 29, 1983), pp. 83–84.

585 "There is no such thing": ibid., p. 104.

585 "All those committee chairs were very friendly in those days": NSA, Arthur Levenson quoted in "Louis Tordella: As Colleagues Remember Him," *Cryptolog* (Spring 1996), p. 13.

585 "We didn't have any in those days": Cecil Corry quoted in ibid.

585 "We had in the past": NSA, Secret/Comint Channels Only, Oral History of Dr. Howard Campaigne (June 29, 1983), p. 73.

586 "As the computers became": NSA, Top Secret/Comint Channels Only, Oral History of Dr. Solomon Kullback (August 26, 1982), p. 136.

586 "The idea . . . was to have": NSA, Secret/Comint Channels Only, Oral History of Dr. Howard Campaigne (June 29, 1983), p. 62.

586 "He didn't interfere with us": ibid., p. 85.

586 "IBM regarded it as": ibid., p. 62.

587 "It was clear to us": ibid., p. 64.

587 "You save enough": NSA, Top Secret/Comint Channels Only, Oral History of Dr. Solomon Kullback (August 26 1982), p. 129.

588 not only: Details of Harvest are from NSA, "HARVEST: NSA's Ultra High-Speed Computer," *Cryptologic Milestones* (November 1968), pp. 1–4.

588 "there was little purpose": White House, Top Secret/Eyes Only memorandum, "Discussion at the 378th Meeting of the National Security Council, August 27, 1958" (August 28, 1958), p. 2. (DDEL, Ann Whitman Files, NSC, Box 10). See also CIA, Top Secret/Eider memorandum, Huntington D. Sheldon to Andrew J. Goodpaster (January 19, 1959) (DDEL, Office of Staff Secretary, Intelligence, Box 15).

588 CRITICOMM: NSA, "The SIGINT Communications System," *Cryptologic Milestones* (September 1965), pp. 1–4; Tom Johnson, "The Plan to Save NSA."

589 Rye: NSA, "Remote-Access Computer Systems," *Cryptologic Milestones* (August 1965), pp. 1–4.

589 "It's beautiful, but it doesn't work": NSA, Top Secret/Comint Channels Only, Oral History of Dr. Solomon Kullback (August 26, 1982) (comment by Robert D. Farley, pp. 133–34).

589 "The Soviet Union could achieve": White House, Top Secret/Noforn, "Report of the Computer Panel of the President's Science Advisory Committee" (September 11, 1959), p. 3.

590 "expensive love seat": interview with an NSA official.

590 "is to supercomputers": Phillip Elmer-DeWitt, "Fast and Smart," *Time,* March 28, 1988, pp. 54–57.

591 "I work when I'm at home": ibid., p. 57.

591 Engineering Research Associates: See Erwin Tomash and Arnold A. Cohen, "The Birth of an ERA: Engineering Research Associates, Inc., 1946–1955," *Annals of the History of Computing,* vol. 1, no. 2 (October 1979), pp. 83–96.

592 Butterfly processor . . . about 1 million: "New Computer," *Aviation Week* (April 15, 1985), p. 13.

592 Details on the CRAY-2: Philip Elmer-DeWitt, "A Sleek, Superpowered Machine," *Time,* June 17, 1985, p. 53.

593 "we should be at 100 billion gigaflops": IBM vice president Irving Wladawsky-Berger quoted in Elmer-Dewitt, "Fast and Smart," p. 58.

593 Ncube: "Faster Than a Speeding Chip," *Newsweek,* March 28, 1988, p. 63.

594 ETA 10: "Filter Center," *Aviation Week* (July 13, 1987), p. 147; "Fast Computer in a Small Package," *Insight* (July 18, 1988), p. 54.

594 all of humanity: William B. Scott, "Los Alamos Carries Research Beyond All Physical Boundaries," *Aviation Week* (July 25, 1988), p. 36.

594 minutes of a Department of Defense study group: Keith Bradsher, "Industries Seek Protection as Vital to U.S. Security," *New York Times,* January 19, 1993.

595 "U.S. firms would be most fortunate": David E. Sanger, "A High Tech Lead in Danger," *New York Times,* December 18, 1988.

595 National Semiconductor: "Electronic Intelligence," *Aviation Week* (April 19, 1989), p. 86.

595 20,000 square feet: NSA, "Microelectronics Completes the Circuit," *NSAN* (November 1989), p. 8.

595 "If a hostile agent": William D. Marbach, "Developments to Watch," *Business Week* (April 3, 1989), p. 110.

596 CRAY-3: John Markoff, "A Computer Star's New Advance," *New York Times,* February 17, 1994.

597 ETA Systems: Charles J. Murray, *The Supermen* (New York: John Wiley & Sons, 1997), p. 196.

597 the outer frame for the SS-1: ibid., p. 211.

597 Details on Frostberg: NSA, NSA Museum.

597 the agency awarded: William M. Bulkeley, "Technology: Cray Computer Gets U.S. Pact," *Wall Street Journal,* August 18, 1994.

597 "the world's ultimate": John Markoff, "A Spy Agency Gives Contract to Cray Computer," *New York Times,* August 18, 1994.

598 Splash 2: NSA, "A New Direction in High Performance Computing," *NSA Technical Fact Sheet* (1993).

598 "start from a clean sheet of paper": Murray, *The Supermen,* p. 219.

599 meterological centers in Australia, Canada, England: John Markoff, "Cray Said to Have Lost Sale Because Offer Was Inferior," *New York Times,* August 28, 1997.

599 "Simply put, Cray Research lost": ibid.

After the contract was awarded to NEC, Cray Research accused the Japanese company of "dumping" its computer in the United States. Political pressure was also exercised in favor of Cray, and in 1997 the U.S. International Trade Commission ruled unanimously against NEC, saying, in essence, that the Japanese were selling four machines for the price of one.

599 "The rules changed when it became clear": Alexander Wolfe and Loring Wirbel, "Quirky Cray Hailed for Vision, Tenacity," *Electronic Engineering Times* (October 14, 1996), p. 1.

599 "In the days before": ibid.

600 "There are no other major players left standing": Steve Alexander, "SGI Will Buy Cray Research: Supercomputer Firm Has Price Tag of $736 Million," *Minneapolis Star Tribune,* February 27, 1996.

600 "We don't have a lot of innovative architects": John Markoff, "A Maverick Builds a New Supercomputer in a PC World," *New York Times,* February 9, 1998.

600 "Burton's folly": ibid.

600 "Most people": ibid.

600 "Burton Smith is the last": ibid.

601 "The question was": Jaikumar Vijayan, "SGI Results Worse Than Expected; McCracken Out, Layoffs Planned," *Computerworld* (November 3, 1997), p. 3.

601 Its stock had plunged: "Silicon Graphics Will Spin Off Cray, Cut Up to 3,000 Jobs in Restructuring," *Minneapolis Star Tribune,* August 11, 1999.

601 "The United States is committed": "U.S. Government to Support SGI Vector Supercomputer," *Mainframe Computing* (November 1, 1999).

602 Tera Computer acquired Cray Research from SGI: "Tera Computer Company to Acquire Supercomputer Pioneer Cray from SGI," *Business Wire* (March 2, 2000).

602 One report said: Steve Alexander, "Struggling Firm Buys Struggling Cray Research," *Minneapolis Star Tribune,* March 3, 2000.

602 upgrade a CRAY T3E-1200 supercomputer: "Cray Inc. Lands $18.5 Million U.S. Army Contract for One of World's Most Powerful Supercomputers," *Business Wire* (May 10, 2000).

602 Tordella Supercomputer Facility: NSA, Dedication brochure (October 29, 1996), p. 4; NSA, Tom Johnson and Jerome Taylor, "Tordella Supercomputer Facility Transition Begins," *NSAN* (January 1997), p. 4.

603 RS/6000 SP: Daniel Verton, "IBM Upgrades SP Server," *Federal Computer Week* (February 8, 1999).

603 Automated Cartridge System: NSA, "The Docent Book," p. 26.

603 robotic arm: ibid.

604 5 trillion pages of text: John Mintz, "The Secret's Out: Covert E-Systems Inc. Covets Commercial Sales," *Washington Post,* October 24, 1994.

604 Supercomputer Research Center: NSA, "Questions and Answers with Regard to the Supercomputer Research Center," pp. 1–5.

604 According to Lieutenant General Lincoln D. Faurer: Rudolph A. Pyatt, Jr., "R&D Center Set for P.G.," *Washington Post,* November 28, 1984.

604 10,000 times faster: ibid.

604 $12 million on a twenty-acre site: "Cray Inc. Lands $18.5 Million U.S. Army Contract."

604 part of the Institute: For further details, see James Bamford, *The Puzzle Palace: A Report on America's Most Secret Agency* (Boston: Houghton Mifflin, 1982), pp. 342–43.

605 "That one piece of equipment": NSA, "NSA Research Institute," *Cryptologic Milestones* (March 1965), p. 2.

605 IDA-C3I: General Accounting Office, "Federally Funded R&D Centers: Information on the Size and Scope of DOD-Sponsored Centers" (April 1996), p. 24.

605 Laboratory for Physical Sciences: NSA, Lois G. Brown, "The Laboratory for Physical Sciences," *NSAN* (November 1996), p. 6.

606 "We don't know": Jayson T. Blair, "Spy Agency Toils Quietly on Campus," *Washington Post,* July 10, 1997.

606 magnetic microscopy: NSA, "Applications of Magnetic Microscopy to Magnetic Recording," *NSA Technical Fact Sheet* (1999).

606 synthetic diamonds: NSA, "NSA Pioneers New Diamond-Based Technology," *NSAN* (November 1999), p. 4.

606 Project Oceanarium: Fredrick Thomas Martin, *Top Secret Intranet* (Upper Saddle River, N.J.: Prentice Hall, 1999), p. 275.

606 microscopic magnets: John Markoff, "Tiny Magnets May Bring Computing Breakthrough," *New York Times,* January 27, 1997.

607 "A spy could remove": Charles C. Mann, "The Mole in the Machine," *New York Times Magazine* (July 25, 1999).

607 drive-controlled disk sanitization device: NSA, "Drive Controlled Disk Sanitization," *NSA Technology Fact Sheet* (1999).

608 femtoseconds: a femtosecond is one millionth of a nanosecond.

608 Blue Gene: Justin Gillis, "IBM to Put Genetics on Fast Track," *Washington Post,* June 3, 2000; Steve Lohr, "IBM Plans Supercomputer That Works at Speed of Life," *New York Times,* December 6, 1999.

608 "It will suck down": Gillis, "IBM to Put Genetics on Fast Track."

608 "It is the greatest play box": Richard Lardner, "The Secret's Out," *Government Executive* (August 1998), p. 24.

609 seventy of them would fit: The SPL reduced the feature size (the smallest dimension of any feature of an ASIC, typically the transistor gate length) of an ASIC to 0.5 micron.

609 size of a small suitcase: NSA, "NSA Pioneers New Diamond-Based Technology."

609 fit into a cube six inches on a side: ibid.

609 about $4 million a year: Tom Siegfried, "Computers Poised for a Quantum Leap," *Dallas Morning News,* March 16, 1998.

610 "On paper, at least": Lov K. Grover, "Quantum Computing," *The Sciences* (July/August 1999).

610 "bust": NSA, Top Secret/Umbra, *Cryptolog* (March 1982).

610 A breakthrough into quantum computing: John Markoff, "Quantum Computing Is Becoming More Than Just a Good Idea," *New York Times,* April 28, 1998.

610 rudimentary electronic logic gates: John Markoff, "Computer Scientists Are Poised for Revolution on a Tiny Scale," *New York Times,* November 1, 1999.

611 wires less than a dozen atoms across: ibid.

611 "It looked for a long time like a solution": Siegfried, "Computers Poised for a Quantum Leap."

611 "What's intriguing is that": Markoff, "Quantum Computing Is Becoming More Than Just a Good Idea."

611 moletronics: C. P. Collier, E. W. Wong, M. Belohradsk, "Electronically Configurable Molecular-Based Logic Gates," *Science* (July 16, 1999), pp. 391–94; John Markoff, "Chip Designers Search for Life After Silicon," *New York Times,* July 19, 1999.

611 "A single molecular computer": John Markoff, "Tiniest Circuits Hold Prospect of Explosive Computer Speeds," *New York Times,* July 16, 1999.

611 "We have made a big step": Yoshiko Hara, "Computers Make a Quantum Leap," *EE Times* (July 6, 1999).

612 "great leap forward" meetings: Ivars Peterson, "Pentacrunchers," *Science News* (April 15, 1995), p. 23.

612 "I don't think": ibid.

612 *E. coli:* ibid.

612 "We would like to make processors": Markoff, "Chip Designers Search for Life After Silicon."

612 "motors" out of DNA: Andrew Pollack, "Researchers Harness DNA for Tiny Motors That Could Widen Use of Genetic Code," *New York Times,* August 10, 2000.

612 according to Bell Labs physicist Bernard Yurke: ibid.

INDEX